The Anthropology of Politics

Blackwell Anthologies in Social and Cultural Anthropology
Series Editor: Parker Shipton, Boston University

Series Advisory Editorial Board:
Fredrik Barth, University of Oslo and Boston University
Stephen Gudeman, University of Minnesota
Jane Guyer, Northwestern University
Caroline Humphrey, University of Cambridge
Tim Ingold, University of Aberdeen
Emily Martin, Princeton University
John Middleton, Yale Emeritus
Sally Falk Moore, Harvard Emerita
Marshall Sahlins, University of Chicago Emeritus
Joan Vincent, Columbia University and Barnard College Emerita

Drawing from some of the most significant scholarly work of the nineteenth and twentieth centuries, the *Blackwell Anthologies in Social and Cultural Anthropology* series offers a comprehensive and unique perspective on the ever-changing field of anthropology. It represents both a collection of classic readers and an exciting challenge to the norms that have shaped this discipline over the past century.

Each edited volume is devoted to a traditional subdiscipline of the field such as the anthropology of religion, linguistic anthropology, or medical anthropology; and provides a foundation in the canonical readings of the selected area. Aware that such subdisciplinary definitions are still widely recognized and useful – but increasingly problematic – these volumes are crafted to include a rare and invaluable perspective on social and cultural anthropology at the onset of the twenty-first century. Each text provides a selection of classic readings together with contemporary works that underscore the artificiality of subdisciplinary definitions and point students, researchers, and general readers in the new directions in which anthropology is moving.

1   Linguistic Anthropology: A Reader, *edited by Alessandro Duranti*
2   A Reader in the Anthropology of Religion, *edited by Michael Lambek*
3   The Anthropology of Politics: A Reader in Ethnography, Theory, and Critique, *edited by Joan Vincent*

The Anthropology of Politics

A Reader in Ethnography, Theory, and Critique

Edited by

Joan Vincent

Blackwell
Publishing

© 2002 by Blackwell Publishing Ltd
except for editorial material and organization © 2002 by Joan Vincent

BLACKWELL PUBLISHING
350 Main Street Malden, MA 02148-5020, USA
9600 Garsington Road, Oxford OX4 2DQ, UK
550 Swanston Street, Carlton, Victoria 3053, Australia

First published 2002 by Blackwell Publishing Ltd

14   2014

Library of Congress Cataloging-in-Publication Data

The anthropology of politics : a reader in ethnography, theory, and critique / edited by
Joan Vincent.
     p.   cm.—(Blackwell anthologies in social and cultural anthropology ; 3)
   Includes bibliographical references and index.
   ISBN: 978-0-631-22439-6 (alk. paper); ISBN: 978-0-631-22440-2 (pb. : alk. paper)
   1. Political anthropology.   I. Vincent, Joan.   II. Series.

GN492 .A593 2002
306.2—dc21
                                                                  2001043232

A catalogue record for this title is available from the British Library.

Set in 10 on 12 pt Sabon
by Kolam Information Services Pvt. Ltd, Pondicherry, India
Printed and bound in Singapore
by C.O.S. Printers Pte Ltd

The publisher's policy is to use permanent paper from mills that operate a sustainable
forestry policy, and which has been manufactured from pulp processed using
acid-free and elementary chlorine-free practices. Furthermore, the publisher ensures
that the text paper and cover board used have met acceptable environmental
accreditation standards.

For further information on
Blackwell Publishing, visit our website:
www.blackwellpublishing.com

Contents

Acknowledgments

For permission to reproduce copyright material, grateful acknowledgment is made to the copyright holders for the following works. If any copyright holder has been inadvertently overlooked, the publishers will be pleased to make the necessary arrangements at the first opportunity.

Ferguson, A. Of Civil Liberty [1767]. In F. Oz-Salzberger (ed.) *An Essay on the History of Civil Society*, Cambridge: Cambridge University Press, 1995.

Smith, A. An Inquiry into the Nature and Causes of The Wealth of Nations [1776], ed. E. Cannan. Chicago: University of Chicago Press, 1976.

Kant, I. Perpetual Peace: A Philosophical Sketch [1795]. In H. Reiss (ed.) *Kant: Political Writings*, Cambridge: Cambridge University Press, 1970.

Kant, I. Idea for a Universal History with a Cosmopolitan Purpose [1784]. In H. Reiss (ed.) *Kant: Political Writings*, Cambridge: Cambridge University Press, 1970.

Kant, I. Preface [1797]. In M. J. Gregor (ed.) *Immanuel Kant: Anthropology from a Pragmatic Point of View*, The Hague: Martinus Nijhoff, 1974.

Maine, H. S. The Effects of Observation of India on Modern European Thought (Rede Lecture). In *Village-Communities in the East and West* [1887], 5th edn. London: John Murray.

Morgan, L. H. *Ancient Society; or, Researches in the Lines of Human Progress from Savagery through Barbarism to Civilization* [1877], edited and with an introduction by Eleanor Leacock. New York: World Publishing, 1974.

Marx, K. Economic and Philosophic Manuscripts of 1844. *Karl Marx: Early Writings*, ed. T. B. Bottomore. New York: McGraw Hill, 1964.

Marx, K., and F. Engels. *The Communist Manifesto* [1847], ed. Samuel H. Beer. Arlington Heights: AHM Publishing Corporation, 1955.

Mooney, J. Introduction. In *The Ghost-Dance Religion and the Sioux Outbreak of 1890* [1896], ed. A. F. C. Wallace. Chicago: University of Chicago Press, 1965.

Evans-Pritchard, E. E. *The Nuer: A Description of the Modes of Livelihood and Political Institutions of a Nilotic People*. Oxford: Clarendon Press, 1940, courtesy of International African Institute, London.

Hutchinson, S. E. Nuer Ethnicity Militarized. *Anthropology Today* 16(3). Blackwell Publishers, 2000.

Gluckman, M. *Analysis of a Social Situation in Modern Zululand* [1940]. Manchester: Manchester University Press, 1958.

Frankenberg, R. *Custom and Conflict in British Society*. Manchester: Manchester University Press, 1982.

Asad, T. Market Model, Class Structure and Consent: A Reconsideration of Swat Political Organization. *Man* (NS) 7 (1972).

Leach, E. R. *Pul Eliya: A Study of Land Tenure and Kinship*, Cambridge: Cambridge University Press, 1961.

Bailey, F. G. *Stratagems and Spoils: A Social Anthropology of Politics* [1965]. Oxford: Blackwell Publishers, 1969.

Turner, V. W. *Dramas, Fields and Metaphors: Symbolic Action in Human Society*. Ithaca: Cornell University Press, 1974.

Swartz, M. J., V. W. Turner and A. Tuden (eds.) *Political Anthropology*. Chicago: Aldine Press, 1966.

Gough, K. New Proposals for Anthropologists. *Current Anthropology* 9(5) (1968). Chicago: University of Chicago Press, 1968.

Wolf, E. R. Introduction. In R. Aya and N. Miller (eds.) *National Liberation*. San Francisco: The New Press, 1971.

Asad, T. From the History of Colonial Anthropology to the Anthropology of Western Hegemony. In G. Stocking (ed.) *Colonial Situations: Essays on the Contextualization of Ethnographic Knowledge*, vol. 7 in *History of Anthropology*. Madison: University of Wisconsin Press, 1991.

Fox, R. G. East of Said. In M. Sprinker (ed.) *Edward Said: A Critical Reader*. Oxford: Blackwell Publishers, 1992.

Stoler, A. Perceptions of Protest: Defining the Dangerous in Colonial Sumatra. *American Ethnologist* 12(4) (1985). Reprinted by permission of the American Anthropological Association.

Taussig, M. Culture of Terror – Space of Death: Roger Casement's Putumayo Report and the Exploration of Culture. *Comparative Studies in Society and History* 26 (1984). © Society for the Comparative Study of Society and History, published by Cambridge University Press.

Roseberry, W. Images of the Peasant in the Consciousness of the Venezuelan Proletariat. In *Anthropologies and Histories: Essays in Culture, History, and*

Political Economy. New Brunswick, NJ: Rutgers University Press, 1985. Copyright Greenword Press.

Comaroff, J. and J. L. *Of Revelation and Revolution*, vol. 1: *Christianity, Colonialism, and Consciousness in South Africa.* Chicago: University of Chicago Press, 1991. Copyright © University of Chicago Press.

Gal, S. Between Speech and Silence: The Problematics of Research on Language and Gender. In M. di Leonardo (ed.) *Gender at the Crossroads of Knowledge: Feminist Anthropology in the Postmodern Era.* Berkeley: University of California Press, 1991. Copyright © 1991 The Regents of the University of California.

Wolf, E. Facing Power – Old Insights, New Questions, *American Anthropologist* 92 (1990). Reprinted by permission of the American Anthropological Association.

Nash, J. Ethnographic Aspects of the World Capitalist System. *Annual Review of Anthropology* 10: (1981).

Anderson, B. The New World Disorder. *New Left Review* 193 (1992).

Appadurai, A. Grassroots Globalization and the Research Imagination. *Public Culture* 12(1) (2000).

Friedman, J. Transnationalization, Socio-political Disorder, and Ethnification as Expressions of Declining Global Hegemony. *International Political Science Review* 19(3) (1998). Reprinted by permission of Sage Publications Ltd.

Reyna, S. P., and R. E. Downs (eds.) *Deadly Developments: Capitalism, States and War.* Amsterdam: Gordon and Breach, 1997.

Nugent, D. *Modernity at the Edge of Empire: State, Individual and Nation in the Northern Peruvian Andes, 1885–1935.* Stanford: Stanford University Press, 1997.

Tsing, A. L. *In the Realm of the Diamond Queen.* Princeton: Princeton University Press, 1993. Copyright © 1993 by Princeton University Press. Reprinted by permission of Princeton University Press.

Ong, A. Flexible Citizenship among Chinese Cosmopolitans. In P. Cheach and B. Robbins (eds.) *Cosmopolitics: Thinking and Feeling Beyond the Nation.* Minneapolis: University of Minnesota Press, 1998.

Glick Schiller, N., and G. Fouron. Long-distance Nationalism Defined. In *Georges Woke Up Laughing: Long-distance Nationalism and the Search for Home.* Durham, NC: Duke University Press, forthcoming.

Verdery, K. Theorizing Socialism: A Prologue to the "Transition." *American Ethnologist* 18(1) (1991). Reprinted by permission of the American Anthropological Association.

Humphrey, C. *Marx Went Away – But Karl Stayed Behind.* Ann Arbor: University of Michigan Press, 1998.

Ferguson, J. *The Anti-politics Machine: "Development," Depoliticization and Bureaucratic Power in Lesotho.* Cambridge: Cambridge University Press, 1990.

Edelman, M. *Peasants Against Globalization: Rural Social Movements in Costa Rica*. Stanford: Stanford University Press, 1999.

Farmer, P. On Suffering and Structural Violence: A View from Below. In A. Kleinman, V. Das, and M. Lock (eds.) "Issues on Social Suffering," reprinted by permission of *Daedalus, Journal of American Academy of Arts and Sciences* 125(1) (Winter 1996).

Gledhill, J. *Power and its Disguises: Anthropological Perspectives on Politics*. London: Pluto Press, 2000.

Spivak, G. C. *Thinking Academic Freedom in Gendered Post-coloniality*. Cape Town: University of Cape Town Printing Department, 1992. Copyright G. C. Spivak.

Introduction

Joan Vincent

Anthropology's definition of politics and its political content has almost invariably been so broad that politics may be found everywhere, underlying almost all the discipline's concerns. At one time colleagues in political science criticized anthropologists for viewing politics simply as a matter of power and inequality (Easton 1959). Today, political anthropologists consider sensitivity to the pervasiveness of power and the political a prime strength.

Looking for articles to include in this Reader, I was very aware that a collection built around theory or intellectual history alone would fail to represent the dynamic processes through which political anthropology has defined itself, its relation to politics in the "outside" world, and the manner in which its accumulation of knowledge has taken place. What gives political anthropology its vitality is the complex play of field research with ethnography, ethnography with theory, and theory with critique.

The Reader's four parts, as narrative, are organized in approximate chronological order with field research, ethnography, theory, and critique represented in each part. Each part has an introduction, which focuses on themes or issues addressed in its chapters. These place the readings within the context of their times and suggest links with other chapters in the Reader, thus enabling the reader to see how similar problems and issues are addressed at different times in the history of the subfield. The introductions to parts also alert the reader to moments of change in subject matter or approach. Suggestions for Further Reading provide resources to further supplement theory with ethnography, and to locate alternative arguments in critique.

The rest of this introductory chapter has two simple objectives. The first is to provide an overview of the paths taken by anthropologists of politics and the second is to introduce a, perhaps surprising, finding that emerges only when one considers the readings as a whole. This is the subterranean presence of the ideas and values of the eighteenth-century European Age of Enlightenment in the anthropology of politics. A short conclusion characterizes some driving political changes that occurred with the outbreak of the Cold War in 1946 and questions whether the theoretical approaches adopted within political anthropology are adequate to ana-lyze and understand those changes. Appreciative of what has been achieved by the anthropologists whose work is represented in the Reader, it ends on an optimistic note.

The Anthropology of Politics: An Overview

Political anthropology was a late subfield specialization within social and cultural anthropology. Between 1940 and the late 1960s a generation of political anthro-pologists was exceptionally cohesive, establishing a canon and setting out a program for the subfield. But apart from that short period, anthropology's conception of politics has been inclusive enough for political aspects and content to be identifiable in nearly every branch of the discipline throughout its long professional history. For political anthropology a suitable starting point may be found in Lewis Henry Morgan's study of the league of the Iroquois (Morgan 1851). This was described by the first director of the United States government's Bureau of American Ethnol-ogy as "the first scientific account of an Indian tribe given to the world" (Powell 1880: 115). "In the beginning," as the English philosopher John Locke put it, "all the world was America."

The objective world fashions political anthropology as much as anthropology constructs and reconstructs the world in which its practitioners find themselves (Vincent 1990). In its broadest outline, the anthropology of politics can be narrated in terms of an intellectual history framed initially by British cultural hegemony over an anglophone imperial world and then by United States cultural hegemony over a world system dominated by Cold War concerns. A critical turning point in the subdiscipline came with the decline of empire and American defeat in the war in Vietnam.

Three phases may be recognized in anthropology's relationship with politics. In the first formative era (1851–1939) anthropologists studied the political almost incidentally to other interests. This phase is not represented in the Reader. In the second phase (1940 to about 1972) political anthropology developed a body of systematically structured knowledge and a self-conscious discourse.

This phase is represented in the Reader in Part II, "Classics and Classics Re-visited." The first six chapters take the reader back to the political ethnography of E. E. Evans-Pritchard among the Nuer peoples of the southern Sudan, the South African ethnography of Max Gluckman, the Swat ethnography of Norwegian anthropologist, Fredrik Barth, and an ethnographic case study from a village in Ceylon (now Sri Lanka) of Edmund Leach. These are "revisited" in these pages by Sharon Hutchinson, an American anthropologist working in war-torn Sudan among the Nuer from the 1980s to the present; by Ronald Frankenberg, who discusses the lasting value of Gluckman's "situational analysis" of the opening of a bridge in Zululand; and Talal Asad's critical re-evaluation of Barth's work, which suggests an alternative theoretical model that better accounts for the political organization Barth describes. It is suggested that the reader might accept Edmund Leach's invitation to reanalyze the intricate fieldwork data he presents.

The second section of Part II contains five new approaches, or calls for new approaches, that began to emerge in the 1960s. These range from Action Theory, through Symbolic Theory to Systems Theory, and then explode, as it were, with two challenges to anthropology to break away from "business as usual" (i.e. developing the canon) in order to confront the issues of the objective world of national liberation movements, imperialism and colonialism, communism, and growing global inequalities. This opens a third phase in political anthropology, when all disciplinary specialization came under severe challenge.

As new paradigms challenged the earlier dominating, coercive systems of knowledge, political anthropology was first decentered and then deconstructed. The political turn taken by contingent disciplines such as geography, social history, literary criticism, and, above all, feminism, revitalized anthropology's concern with power and powerlessness. This is reflected in the readings in Part III (most of which come from the 1970s and 1980s), which I have called "Imperial Times, Colonial Places." The political issues addressed in these chapters, I suggest, provided a launchpad for an anthropology of politics that may contribute to a better understanding of the "phantasmagoric representations" of modernity in what has been termed "the Second Coming of capitalism" (Reyna 1999; Comaroff and Comaroff 2000).

The Enlightenment and its Challenges

> Without a plan . . . the citizen of the world remains very limited in his anthropology.
> (Immanuel Kant)

This section sets out on an exploration of "the real" Enlightenment (to echo those of our Eastern European friends who are replacing the study of socialist ideologies with that of actually existing societies). It is, in part, a response to the fact that the ideas and values of the seventeenth- and eighteenth-century European Enlightenment are alive, if not well, at the beginning of the twenty-first. Increasingly, Enlightenment concepts such as "civil society" and "cosmopolitan" are being tested for their usefulness and questioned for their Eurocentrism.

The reader will find that over one quarter of the chapters in Part II, just over one half in Part III, and three-quarters in Part IV address the Enlightenment in one way or another. Thus, to take but a few examples, one moves from Kathleen Gough's Enlightenment visions of "the science of Man" and Eric Wolf's socialists and libertarians whose "root is man" in Part II; through Fox's European utopians, Unitarians, simplifiers, and sexual libertarians, and Taussig's *muchachos* of Putumayo who "traded their identity as savages for a new social status as civilized Indians and guards," to the Comaroffs' narrative of a "postenlightenment process of colonization in which Europe set out to grasp and subdue the forces of savagery, otherness and unreason" in Part III. And all this and more before embarking on Part IV, where the post-Enlightenment world of modernity (Friedman), the Enlightenment principles of equality, citizenship, individual rights and protection, sanctity of private property, popular sovereignty, progress and common good (Nugent), the emergence of modernity (Reyna), stereotypes of unilinear evolution to modern and postmodern (Tsing), enlightened cosmopolitans (Ong), civil society (Verdery), unexpected consequences (Ferguson), and the invisible hand of Adam Smith (Edelman) precede what I like to think of as the "sting in the tail." This takes the form of Spivak's suggestion in the last chapter that we do not "turn our backs on the Enlightenment but rather . . . learn how to revise and recycle it through lessons learned from below."

The influence of the eighteenth-century western European Enlightenment has been so profound and so widespread that it has become imperceptible. Ever since ethnologists began to study politics, they have adopted a vocabulary born of the ideas and debates of Enlightenment writers. Consider, for example, the terms community, contract, civil society, cosmopolitan, *habitus*, manifold, property – just to dip into Howard Caygill's provocative *Kant Dictionary* (1995) – as well as innocent-sounding terms like "common sense." All have been absorbed into the analytical tool kit of twenty-first-century political anthropology. That several of these terms are commonly attributed to more recent thinkers, such as Gramsci or Bourdieu, suggests how imperceptible, indeed, have been Enlightenment thought and values.

The Enlightenment, we now know, was an entity constructed only in the late nineteenth century (Pocock 1987). The label itself was clearly derived from the writings of the German philosopher Immanuel Kant (1724–1804) who pronounced (perhaps with self-protective political intent) that his own era – the Germany of Frederick the Great – was an age of enlightenment that sought to use reason to solve the manifold problems of humanity. It is no coincidence, surely, that the construction of *the* Enlightenment occurred at a time when European academics were setting out to institutionalize the sciences of man in discrete university disciplines. Enlightenment ideas provided genealogical legitimacy for an ethnology problematically straddling the humanities and sciences (Stocking 1996; Wolf 1964).

Shadowy counter-enlightenments have always existed alongside *the* Enlightenment and these also manifested themselves in political anthropology. The historian Jack Hexter, provides our metaphor when he writes of "The Sown and the Waste", in a medieval village community (1972). Although called "waste", the commons that lay around the medieval village were not really wasteland at all. Commons were grazing areas worked, unlike the well-cultivated plots, by labor-extensive methods. The anthropology of politics contains within itself just such a relationship. There coexist "cultivated patches of systematically structured knowledge" and, beyond the sown, "not desert, not mere ignorance and confusion," but "waste" rich in knowledge of a qualitatively different kind.[1]

The Enlightenment's systematically structured knowledge was the ideological scaffolding of industrial capitalism that Jean and John Comaroff (1991: 60) have captured so succinctly, even as they call for something more:

> Much has been made, quite correctly, of the rise of utilitarian individualism: in particular, its celebration of the virtues of the disciplined, self-made man; of private property and status as signs of personal success, poverty as a fitting sanction for human failure; of enlightened self-interest and the free market, with its "invisible hand," as the mechanism for arriving at the greatest public good; of reason and method, science and technology, as the proper means for achieving an ever more educated and elevated, civilized and cultivated mankind.

The something more they wish to hear is the voice of those who challenge the pursuit of pure reason and enlightened self-interest, advocating a return to a world of the spirit and the imagination. This is a voice broadcast in art and literature in the eighteenth century (Butler 1981; Herzfeld 1997) but one harder to retrieve from the archives of non-conformist religious sects and working-class friendly societies (Erdman 1991; Thompson 1993.) In parochial terms, political anthropologists might hear this as a call for anthropological political economy *plus* symbolism, imagery, and social poetics, as in Victor Turner's "Passages, Margins, and Poverty" (chapter 8). Rapprochment was happily achieved in the 1980s, as several of the chapters in Part III attest. Systematically structured knowledge – science and reason, progressive evolution, the commercial paradigm of the Enlightenment – tends towards homogeneity and exclusivity and to become hegemonic. Witness its presence in the Reader. Subaltern knowledge tends to remain multiplex and fractured, "passing" under many labels, shadow paradigms in the grey literature of a counter-Enlightenment (Beiser 1992; Hulme and Jordanova 1990). The reader must ask to what extent this grey literature is represented in these pages. The eighteenth-century counter-enlightenments were lodged in the "systematic disbelief"[2] of mystical and fundamentalist religion and in working-class protest movements. Hence its place in the political interpretations of nineteenth-century Irish American ethnographer James Mooney; he wrote a path-breaking account of a political rebellion among the Sioux Indians and of their infamous massacre by the United States military on the battlefield of Wounded Knee (Mooney 1896, 1965).[3] But where is this voice in today's world? The ideas of Immanuel Kant, Adam Ferguson, and Adam Smith are the building blocks of a standing monument to the Enlightenment belief in reason and rationality, but the "systematic disbelief" of, say, the Italian philosopher Giambattista Vico, whom Edmund Leach admired, or the poet-engraver William Blake, much cited by Victor Turner, Edward Said, and Edward Thompson, is but the shattered ruin of an alternative vision.

Addressing a session of the American Anthropological Association on the subject of "Representations of the Colonized" organized by William Roseberry and Talal Asad in 1987, the literary critic Edward Said preached to the converted (Asad 1973, 1987, 1992, 1993, and chapter 12 in this volume). He reminded his listeners that "there is no discipline, no structure of knowledge, no institutions or epistemology that can or has ever stood free of the various sociocultural, historical and political formations that give epochs their peculiar individuality" (Said 2000: 299). More recently Clifford Geertz credited historians Quentin Skinner and John Pocock with having got round to writing history as "a story of the engagement of intellectuals with the political situations that lie around and about them, rather than as an immaculate procession of doctrines moved along by the logic of ideas" (Geertz 2000: 218). Observations such as these marginalize political anthropology's long-standing appreciation and use of the work of intellectual historians.[4] Let us, therefore, turn directly to the invisible complicities of power and knowledge in the age of Enlightenment and revisit case-specific political ethnography (some of which appears in the Reader) that has contributed to this explanation.

Enlightenment scholars were men of three worlds.[5] First, they inhabited a small bourgeois world. Many were university professors, some of them (like Immanuel Kant) living and dying in the place where they were born. They were blessed with a rapidly changing social environment in the cities of eighteenth-century Europe where clubs and societies furthered their intellectual transactions. With the growth of political awareness among widening sectors of society, periodicals and learned journals multiplied as did a "reading public." Many of their works were translated promptly and received wide circulation (Oz-Salzburger 1995a, 1995b). Benedict Anderson's *Imagined Communities: Reflections on the Origin and Spread of Nationalism* (1983) has set out clearly what is involved in the imaginative construction of such a world. At its core he found a specific form of capitalism that he called "print capitalism" The invention of printing was as revolutionary a form of communications technology then as Pan-Am, email and the world wide web were in the twentieth century.

A second world of the Enlightenment intellectual was one of aggressive nationalism. Kant's self-ascribed Age of Reason and Criticism was also an Age of Militarization and Revolution. Relations between the nation states of which the Enlightenment scholars were citizens tended to take the form of either war or trade, with war either interrupting established trade patterns or furthering new ones. The eighteenth century is not an era that most anthropologists of state formation have entered upon, and it is necessary to turn to historians for enlightenment as Stephen Reyna does in his essay on "deadly developments" (1999, chapter 24 in this volume). Reyna describes how the capitalist nation states of Atlantic Europe developed as "killing machines" through reciprocity between military regimes and merchants. They established, in short, military-capitalist complexes that profited from state expansion (1999: 57–8). In this transnational European milieu, a social movement of intellectuals addressed the nature of political society, the extent to which differences between nations reflected temporal and geographical variation, types of government, patterns of progress and decline, and the tension between "private" and "public" man (Oz-Salzberger 1995b). Their questions remain salient for political anthropology today but their answers, given the times that produced them, smack of what one philosopher has called hypocrisy and another hubris. No wonder, then, that Asad urges anthropology to "take the cultural hegemony of the West as its object of inquiry" (1993: 24).

The third world in which the Enlightenment movement flourished – and on which it fed – was that of imperial expansion. The process by which European Atlantic states and market interests acquired footholds in the Americas and the Orient in the eighteenth century has been reconstructed for a later period (Stoler, chapter 14) largely using European archival sources. The experience of the indigenes in contact with the West tends to elude us despite family memories that have been passed down over the generations – the Prices' Surinam perspective not withstanding (Stedman 1988). Enlightenment scholars were highly concerned with the making of a civilized humanity worldwide but less concerned with the change that their western European brand of "civilization" was introducing. Some of these changes are recorded in Eric Wolf's magisterial *Europe and the People Without History* (1982: chs. 2–8). June Nash reviews the adequacy of post-Enlightenment analysis of *the* modern world systems analysis in chapter 20. Her attention to colonized and neo-colonized "passive peripheries" of indigenous peoples recalls the agenda set forth in 1967/8 by Kathleen Gough (chapter 10), her critique of market models of political organization that of Talal Asad (chapter 5).

But there is an underside that up until now has only been hinted at: the making of a transnational laboring class. In the new transatlantic economy of the seventeenth and eighteenth centuries, this was made up of seamen, slaves, indentured Irishmen, Native Americans, and pirates from Europe, Africa, the Caribbean and North America brought together through the circular transmission of human labor. European merchants, manufacturers, planters, and government officials organized workers from Africa, the Americas, and Europe to produce and transport commodities such as gold bullion, furs, fish, tobacco, sugar, and manufacturers. To their masters this first modern industrial proletariat was a many-headed monster, a symbol of continuously self-replenishing disorder and resistance, which constantly threatened state formation, empire, and capitalism. Insurrections fringed the North Atlantic, launching the Age of Revolution first in Jamaica and America and then in Haiti, France, Ireland, and England.

In arriving at this hidden history of "the revolutionary Atlantic" in their book *The Many-Headed Hydra*, historians Peter Linebaugh and Marcus Rediker trace lineal descent from Adam Smith, "the first theorist of capitalism" and Karl Marx, "its profoundest critic" (Linebaugh and Rediker 2000: 327). But they head their concluding chapter "Tyger! Tyger!," signifying that they have moved beyond Enlightenment to counter-Enlightenment themes. Now, "Tyger! Tyger!" is one of the most popular of William Blake's poems and, to make their message quite clear, they reproduce several of Blake's engravings that evoke the terror of John Gabriel Stedman's *Narrative of a Five Years Expedition against the Revolted Negroes of Surinam* (1988). Michael Taussig's classic "Culture of Terror – Space of Death" (chapter 15) grimly documents the oppressive conditions of plantation labor in Africa and Latin America a century later.

But political anthropology's interconnectedness with this new historical thesis is even closer. A reproduction of Blake's engraved image of "Europe Supported by Africa and America" (Linebaugh and Rediker 2000: 350), showing a naked, long-tressed white-skinned woman (Europe) supported by the two naked dark-skinned female figures of (Africa) and (America), furthers the connection. Europe drapes a plaited rope across her two "supporters." It is no coincidence that anthropologist Sidney Mintz used that self-same engraving as frontispiece in his *Sweetness and Power: The Place of Sugar in Modern History* (1985). After reading Eric Wolf's threnody of anthropology's failure to produce a satisfactory ethnography of global capitalism (chapter 19) we might consider this a step along a fourth path not yet pursued quite far enough in anthropology's analysis of global politics.

But Mintz went a fair way along that fourth path. Over twenty years earlier he had criticized in characteristically ethnographic voice the "so-called world system" of Immanuel Wallerstein. He had identified the Caribbean plantation system as the first site of industrial capital, dependent on the slave trade, and with a distinctive culture of labor (Mintz 1977). In an earlier publication (1974), he had moved anthropology away from both the Enlightenment market model of Adam Smith and the post-Enlightenment mode of production model of Karl Marx. Hinted at but never quite formulated, his focus on trans-Atlantic movements of laboring men and women might have provided political anthropology with the counter-Enlightenment global model it lacks.

But it is not the colonial implications that I wish to stress but the value of the trans-oceanic dimensions of Linebaugh and Rediker's historical research. It opens up promising directions for a grounded analysis of politics at several levels of a global politics (See Ong, chapter 27). A further step beyond *post*-Enlightenment systems analysis entails an exploration of a specifically different brand of men-in-movement – the dispossessed – in the making of the modern world. This is an analysis to which the Peruvian ethnography of Gavin Smith (1989) alerted us. He also provides the text from Marx that appears in Part I.

> Political economy...does not recognize the unoccupied worker...in so far as he happens to be outside this labour-relationship. The cheat-thief, swindler, beggar, and

unemployed man; the starving, wretched and criminal working-man – these are figures who do not exist for political economy but only for other eyes, those of the doctor, the judge, the grave-digger and the bum-bailiff, etc; such figures are spectres outside the domain of political economy.[6]

In a twentieth-first century disordered world of near-permanent refugee and resettlement camps and prisons and asylums of militarized regimes, those dispossessed of land, livelihood, civil rights, and human dignity have been recalled, as by Paul Farmer in his essay "On Suffering and Structural Violence: A View from Below" on Haiti (chapter 33), not in the language of post-Enlightenment thought, but in that of Bertholt Brecht, Human Rights Watch, and liberation theology.

Conclusion

Around the time that Boas was completing his first bout of field research in the Pacific Northwest at the turn of the nineteenth century, American "dollar imperialism" began to expand at the expense of Europe's more overt political empires. It is barely recalled today that after the Spanish-American war – America's "coming out party" – she rapidly acquired an overseas empire that included the Philippines, Guam, a portion of Samoa, Hawaii, Alaska, Puerto Rico, the Virgin Islands, the Canal Zone, Guantanamo Bay, the Corn Islands, and miscellaneous small islands in the Pacific. When it was suggested in 1902 that American anthropology should "follow American interests overseas," a pathway was opened up for Roy Franklin Barton's long-term field research (1905–12) among Ifugao in the Philippine islands that changed hands at the end of the Spanish-American War. In the 1930s Robert Redfield described himself as "following capital" to Mexico and in the 1940s David Schneider's scientific research began in the trust territories of Micronesia under the auspices of the US Navy (Bashkow 1991). Not a lot changed in the metropole's enlightened approach to imperialism: in the 1920s the government sent boatloads of schoolteachers to open up the Philippines; in the 1940s they sent forty-two scientists to Micronesia, most of them anthropologists (Bashkow 1991).[7]

With the Cold War developing in 1946 after World War II, the United States perceived its security interests to have changed, and intervention in what then became known as the Third World of non-aligned nations changed with it (Part IV). The Cold War arose over the fate of Central Europe, but it was fought out in "proxy wars" in Asia, Africa, and Central and South America. In retrospect, Charles W. M. Hart, an Australian teaching at Wisconsin in 1953 appears extraordinarily perceptive. "As the old style colonial governors move out," he wrote, "the commissars from Moscow and the promoters from New York move in" (1953: 207). The turn of events in North Korea, Indonesia, and Latin America fuelled his observation.

This was two generations ago. To come almost up to date, Keith Hart in his "Reflections on a Visit to New York" (2000), writes of American expansion in the 1990s following the collapse of the Soviet Union. He invokes a new American imperialism based on the communications revolution, its restructuring industries at home and abroad, and new financial instruments (such as derivatives) to address uncertainty in a high speed global marketplace. To understand globalization, he suggests, begin in New York. "Three dozen corporations have an annual turnover of $30–50 billion, more than the GDP of all but eight countries: and the majority of them are American" (2000: 2). But can that be all there is to understanding globalization?

The question arises whether the theoretical approaches currently adopted in the anthropology of politics are adequate for analyzing and understanding the world around us today (Anderson, chapter 21; Friedman, chapter 23). Consider the concepts itemized by Jonathan Friedman in characterizing the tectonic movement of declining cultural hegemonies. They include: the transhistorical; neo-traditionalism; modernity, modernism, postmodernism; developmentalism; alterity; ethnicity, ethnification, multiethnification; individualization; nation state, national identity, transnationalization; as well as modern world system, cosmopolitanism, and globalization (chapter 23). Most of these might be applied retroactively, as it were, to the North Atlantic in the eighteenth century.

The foundational metaphor of the Enlightenment is system. But, as Mary Poovey has pointed out, what is systemic discounts individual experience for more general gains. These gains may be those of the philosopher (or ethnologist) whose production of general systematic knowledge sets him apart from the common man. They may be those of the policy-maker for whom a systems model "submits that policies should support – and could be defended as supporting – the general and long-range effects that experts recognized rather than what individuals experienced as their immediate interests" (Poovey 1998: 234). Poovey limits her discussion to the science of wealth and society as it shifts from conjectural history to political economy in the making of the modern fact. Her point is well taken in view of political anthropology's historical engagement with national policy-making. In the 1870s, researchers at the Bureau of American Ethnology provided systems models of the political organization of Native Americans that contributed to the latter's pacification. A century later European and American anthropologists contributed systemic analyses to international development projects in Africa and central America. Gayatri Spivak, in the talk from which chapter 35 is extracted, "Thinking Academic Freedom in Gendered Post-Coloniality," is devastating in her account of the *speed* with which Bangladesh "fell into the clutches of transnational global economy" intent on unrestricted "development." Such development obliged the newly postcolonial state "to veer away from any possibility of redistributive functions" (1992: 21). Thus we are reminded in our discourse on the frailty of the state or the widening gap between rich and poor throughout the globe, that the precise *timing* of a colonial or postcolonial intervention is crucial to the outcome and so to our analysis of a whole range of political realities. Ultimately, Spivak, the self-ascribed native informant (Spivak 1999) legitimates ethnographic inquiry that is both "local" and historical.

For the most part, however, the anthropology of politics has remained firmly in the grip of systems thinking. Before we proceed any further towards the political anthropology of the twenty-first century we need to step back and recall the making of an anthropology of politics long before political anthropology was recognized as a subfield specialization (see Vincent 1990).

Part IV of the Reader opens with chapters by Benedict Anderson, Arjun Appadurai, and Jonathan Friedman that are staged, as it were, as a debate on whether there is really anything new in the postmodernity of late capitalism. Looking back at the readings on "Imperial Times, Colonial Places" (Part III) may suggest that a scaffolding has already been put in place. If it has, political anthropology has the tools to tackle New World Disorder, its description (ethnography), analysis (theory) and critique (Anderson, chapter 21). What is not clear is whether political anthropology in the twenty-first century (and beyond) will refine the Enlightenment ideas and values with which it has grown up; whether it will question and reject them on the grounds of their eurocentrism and offer in their place cultural and historical alternative hegemonies; or whether it will create a different (certainly trans-disciplinary) understanding in which the shadowy world of Enlightenment and counter-Enlightenment and post-Enlightenment and counter-post-Enlightenment confront each other at every step.

Marshall Sahlins suggested that what seemed like enlightenment to the philosophers of the eighteenth century has turned out to be nothing more than "the parochial self-consciousness of European expansion and the *mission civilisatrice*" (1999: ii). But whether the Enlightenment was nothing more than a packaging of European folklore is a problem that the anthropology of politics is currently grappling with as it confronts the unfolding of the New Millennium (see Part IV). Amidst terror of new world disorder, failing nation states, the moral dilemmas of human rights abuses on a world scale, global poverty and pandemic disease, Enlightenment discourse takes on new life as it comes under intellectual scrutiny once again.

Kant's "Anthropology from a Pragmatic Point of View" introduced both a humanistic anthropology and a knowledge of man as a citizen of the world, which the social sciences later displaced. This theme surfaces again and again in the pages that follow: a humanist strain within anthropology that is captured in the image of Franz Boas, one of its founding fathers in the United States, seated in his igloo in Baffinland reading Kant. "Where is today's Boas to lend the authority of academic anthropology to this old political struggle against division of the common human interest?", asks Keith Hart (2000: 2). This is an old political struggle, we may note. It began as a generational struggle when Kant's student, Johann Gottfried Herder (1744–1803), first introduced "culture" in its modern pluralizing sense, thus carving up Kant's ideational human universe.

Systems of thought are, in William Blake's unforgettable phrase, "mind forg'd manacles." Appropriately enough, Edward Said reminds us of this at the end of his analysis of "Orientalism," a ground-breaking literary ethnography of The Enlightenment in operation. Thus in this Reader, Richard Fox (chapter 13) and Aihwa Ong (chapter 27) suggest that Edward Said's representation of orientalism (1978) is a European construction of knowledge that is, in part, derived from Enlightenment ideas and values. They seek to show the extent to which "orientals" involved themselves in the making of "orientalism."

As ever, William Blake provides the envoy:

> I must Create a System, or be enslav'd by another Mans
> I will not Reason and Compare: my business is to Create.

One thing is certain: the world of political anthropology is wide enough for both foxes and hedgehogs: for those who seek to construct systems and for those who delve into particulars. As the Greek philosopher Archilocus observed, "The fox knows many things, but the hedgehog knows one big thing." Both foxes and hedgehogs are well represented in this Reader.

(July 2001)

NOTES

1   The politics of progress where the rights of the common people are threatened by "improvement" is a counter-Enlightenment theme common to both history and anthropology. It has, perhaps, been most succinctly expressed in popular verse:

> The law locks up the man or woman
> Who steals the goose from off the common
> But lets the greater villain loose
> Who steals the common from the goose.

For a recent political ethnography in this vein, see Darby 2000. The struggle continues, of course, in the name of development (chapters 31 and 32).

2   "Systematic disbelief" is a phrase Collingwood (1965) uses to characterize the vision of Giambattista Vico (Herzfeld 1997).

3   A reconstruction of this aspect of Mooney's political ethnography is beyond the scope of this brief Introduction. It rests on papers in the Mooney archive and the "recovery" of ten chapters in his original report to the government on the Sioux outbreak of 1890 (Mooney 1896). These were omitted from the text edited by Anthony Wallace (Mooney 1965.) The quotation from Mooney at the end of Part I provides an Introduction in the Wallace edition. In the Report it is page 657 and is headed by lines from the Irish poet, George Moore:

> There are hours long departed which memory brings
> Like blossoms of Eden to twine round the heart.

Mooney calls the narrative that accompanies it "Paradise Lost."

4   For the use of the very historians Geertz names, see Eric Wolf's *Anthropology* (1964) and Joan Vincent's *Anthropology and Politics* (1990).

5   My characterization draws on Oz-Salzberger 1995b, which narrates the relations among Scottish and German Enlightenment scholars. A focus on Adam Ferguson and Immanuel Kant is particularly valuable inasmuch as their ideas were foundational in British and American anthropology respectively.

6   This is an extract from Karl Marx (1844), in T. Bottomore (ed.) *Karl Marx: Early Writings*, New York: McGraw Hill, p. 85.

7   I attempt to trace the effect of these acquisitions on the development of American political anthropology in Vincent 1990. Clearly that story is too complex to engage us here but its now subterranean existence may be suggested by a reminder that Rudyard Kipling's poetic call "Take up the White Man's burden . . ." was written to commemorate American, not as is often assumed British, imperialism.

REFERENCES

Anderson, B. (1983) *Imagined Communities: Reflections on the Origin and Spread of Nationalism*. London: Verso. Revised and expanded edn. (1991). London and New York: Verso.

Asad, T. (1973) *Anthropology and the Colonial Encounter*. London: Ithaca Press.

——. (1992) Conscripts of Western Civilization? In C. Gailey (ed.) *Dialectical Anthropology: Essays in Honor of Stanley Diamond*. Miami: University Presses of Florida.

——. (1993) Introduction. *Genealogies of Religion: Discipline and Reasons of Power in Christianity and Islam*. Baltimore: Johns Hopkins University Press.

Bashkow, I. (1991) The Dynamics of Rapport in a Colonial Situation: David Schneider's Fieldwork on the Islands of Yap. In G. Stocking (ed.) *Colonial Situations: Essays on the Contextualization of Ethnographic Knowledge*. Madison: University of Wisconsin Press, pp. 170–242.

Beiser, C. (1992) *Enlightenment, Revolution, Romanticism*. Cambridge, Mass.: Harvard University Press.

Berlin, I. (1980) *Against the Current: Essays in the History of Ideas*. New York: Viking Press.

Butler, M. (1981) *Romantics, Rebels, and Reactionaries: English Literature and its Background 1760–1830*. Oxford: Oxford University Press.

Caygill, H. (1995) *A Kant Dictionary*. Oxford: Blackwell Publishers.

Collingwood, R. (1965) *Essays in the Philosophy of History*. Austin: University of Texas Press.

Comaroff, J. and Comaroff, J. L. (1991) *Of Revelation and Revolution: Christianity, Colonialism, and Consciousness in South Africa*. Chicago: University of Chicago Press.

—— and ——. (2000) Millennial Capitalism: First Thoughts on a Second Coming. *Public Culture* 12(2): 291–343.

Darby, W. (2000) *Landscape and Identity: Geographies of Nation and Class in England*. Oxford: Berg.

Easton, D. (1959) Political Anthropology. In B. Siegel (ed.) *Biennial Review of Anthropology 1959*, pp. 210–62.

Erdman, D. (1991) *Blake, Prophet Against Empire*, 3rd edn. New York: Dover.

Geertz, C. (2000) *Available Light: Anthropological Reflections on Philosophical Topics*. Princeton: Princeton University Press.

Hart, C. (1953) Colonial Peoples in Transition. In F. Daniels and T. M. Smith (eds.) *The Challenge of our Times*. Madison: University of Wisconsin Press.

Hart, K. (2000) Reflections on a Visit to New York. *Anthropology Today* 16(4): 1–3.

Herzfeld, M. (1997) *Cultural Intimacy: Social Poetics in the Nation State*. New York: Routledge.

Hexter, J. (1972) The Sown and the Waste, or the Second Record. In *The History Primer*. London: Allen and Urwin.

Hulme, P. and Jordanova, L. (1990) (eds.) *Enlightenment and its Shadows*. New York: Routledge.

Leach, E. (1954) *Political Systems of Highland Burma: A Study of Kachin Social Structure*. London: Bell and Sons.

Linebaugh, P. and Rediker, M. (2000) *The Many-headed Hydra: Sailors, Slaves, Commoners, and the Hidden History of the Revolutionary Atlantic*. Boston: Beacon Press.

Mintz, S. (1974) The Rural Proletariat and the Problem of Rural Proletarian Consciousness. *Journal of Peasant Studies* 1: 291–325.

——. (1977) The So-called World System: Local Initiative and Local Response. *Dialectical Anthropology* 2: 5–16.

——. (1985) *Sweetness and Power: The Place of Sugar in Modern History*. New York: Viking.

Mooney, J. (1896) The Ghost-dance and the Sioux Outbreak of 1890. *Fourteenth Annual Report of the Bureau of Ethnology*, Part 2. Washington, DC: Government Printing Office.

——. (1965) *The Ghost-Dance Religion and the Sioux Outbreak of 1890*. ed. A. Wallace. Chicago: University of Chicago Press.

Morgan, L. (1851) *League of the Ho-de-no-sau-nee, or Iroquois*. Rochester, NY: Sage and Broa.

——. (1877) *Ancient Society: or, Researches in the Lines of Human Progress from Savagery through Barbarism to Civilization*. New York: World Publishing.

Oz-Salzberger, F. (1995a) Introduction. In *An Essay on the History of Civil Society*. Cambridge: Cambridge University Press.

——. (1995b) *Translating the Enlightenment: Scottish Civic Discourse in Eighteenth Century Germany*. Oxford: Clarendon Press.

Pocock, J. (1987) Enlightenment and the Revolution: The Case of North America. In *Seventh International Congress on the Enlightenment: Introductory Papers*. Oxford: The Voltaire Foundation.

Poovey, M. (1998) *A History of the Modern Fact: Problems of Knowledge in the Sciences of Wealth and Society*. Chicago: University of Chicago Press.

Powell, J. (1880) Sketch of Lewis H. Morgan, president of the American Association for the Advancement of Science. *Popular Science Monthly* 18: 114–21.

Price, R. and Price, S. (1992) *Stedman's Surinam: Life in an Eighteenth-century Slave Society*. Baltimore: Johns Hopkins University Press.

Reyna, S. (1997) The Force of Two Logics: Predatory and Capital Accumulation in the Making of the Great Leviathan, 1415–1763. In S. Reyna and R. Downs (eds.) *Deadly Developments: Capitalism, States and War*. Amsterdam: Gordon and Breach.

Sahlins, M. (1999) "What is Anthropological Enlightenment? Some Lessons of the Twentieth Century." *Annual Review of Anthropology* 28: i–xxiii.

Said, E. (1978) *Orientalism*. New York: Pantheon Books. 2nd edn., with Afterword (1984) New York: Vintage Books.

——. (2000) *Reflections on Exile and Other Essays*. Cambridge, Mass.: Harvard University Press.

Smith, G. (1989) *Livelihood and Resistance: Peasants and the Politics of Land in Peru*. Berkeley: University of California Press.

Spivak, G. (1992) *Thinking Academic Freedom in Gendered Post-coloniality*. Cape Town: University of Cape Town Publishing Office.

——. (1999) *A Critique of Postcolonial Reason: Toward a History of the Vanishing Present*. Cambridge, Mass.: Harvard University Press.

Stedman, J. (1988) *Narrative of a Five Years Expedition against the Revolted Negroes of Surinam* [1790]. Edited and with an introduction and notes by Richard Price and Sally Price. Baltimore: Johns Hopkins University Press.

Stocking, G. (1996) *Volksgeist as Method and Ethic: Essays on Boasian Ethnography and the German Anthropological Tradition*, vol. 8 of *History of Anthropology*. Madison: University of Wisconsin Press.

Thompson, E. P. (1993) *Witness Against the Beast: William Blake and the Moral Law*. Cambridge: Cambridge University Press.

Vincent, J. (1990) *Anthropology of Politics: Visions, Traditions and Trends*. Tucson: University of Arizona Press.

Wolf, E. (1964) *Anthropology*. Englewood Cliffs, NJ: Prentice-Hall.

——. (1982) *Europe and the People Without History*. Berkeley: University of California Press.

Part I

Prelude: The Enlightenment and its Challenges

Introduction

Moral phil / political econ.

"The Enlightenment" is best thought of as a social movement that emerged among eighteenth- and early nineteenth-century intellectuals in western Europe. This Prelude to the *Anthropology of Politics* focuses first on Adam Ferguson, Adam Smith, and Immanuel Kant as representatives of the Scottish and German Enlightenments, since their ideas contributed most to the shaping of British and American political anthropology. The Enlightenment movement was built in part on an exchange of theory formulated to address two sets of interrelated problems. First, questions of moral philosophy such as the relationship between a state (governance) and its citizens (civil society); the relationship between the individual and society; notions of community (*Gemeinschaft*) and society (*Gesellschaft*); relations among national, international, and cosmopolitan law; and of cosmopolitics and universal peace. And second, questions of political economy such as the relation of the division of labor to the development of civilization; the nature of the market and the place of individual self-interest within it; and the principle of private property and its relation to progressive evolutionism or "modernization." Adam Smith figured prominently in the first discourse, Kant in the second, and Ferguson bridged both, contributing seminal insights both to the division of labor debate and to that on civil society. Following their thought, we appreciate the critical role their work plays in political anthropology's thinking and rethinking individualism, the development of capitalism, modernity, and what is now called "globalization."

The almost excessive ideological emphasis that Enlightenment scholars placed on *reason* in the global affairs of mankind alerts us to the problematic political and economic conditions in the world around them that appeared to rest on neither reason nor recognition of the unity of mankind. Among them were slavery and the slave trade, wars of religion between European nations and struggles between them for territorial possessions in the Americas and the Orient, an ever-widening gap between the rich and the poor in the civilized western European world, and an even wider gap between the civilization of the western Atlantic nation states and the savagery and barbarism of those its citizens encountered in the world beyond their shores.

For a theoretical understanding of the changes that accompanied the emergence of the nation state in Europe and the growth first of trans-Atlantic market economies and then of industrial capitalism, anthropology has turned to post-Enlightenment writers and, specifically (as the "Prelude" reflects) to Henry Sumner Maine, Lewis Henry Morgan, Karl Marx and Friedrich Engels. In their writings we encounter a *critique* of many of the ideas of Enlightenment moral philosophy and the classical political economy that developed alongside it.

This "Prelude" offers a selection of extracts from eighteenth- and nineteenth-century classics in European philosophical thought. It begins with the Scottish moral philosopher Adam Ferguson's balanced notion of "civil society" (as contrasted to "political society") and its relation to war, law, and justice. A relationship among law, property, and "desire for lucre" (i.e. financial profit) underlies, he suggests, social and economic inequalities and the abuse of power. These are concerns that appear fleetingly, but persistently, throughout modern theorizing on the anthropology of politics, but particularly in relation to imperialism, colonialism and postcolonialism, and western global hegemony.

The economic underpinning of Ferguson's model of relations among nations was provided by Adam Smith. Here an extract has been selected from his vast classic *The Wealth of Nations* (1776). He suggests the dangerous imperfections of the global marketplace as it breeds unemployment and social disorder within the national economy. Smith's study encapsulated a move away from a humanitarian moral philosophy to a classical political economy that became hegemonic – and was challenged – throughout the nineteenth century.

While the Scottish philosophers provided many of the seminal understandings of political and civil society for political anthropology's founding fathers in Britain in the 1940s (see Part II), it was the German philosopher, Immanuel Kant, who most influenced the anthropology of politics that developed in the United States around the same time. Here three extracts from Kant's writings introduce the concept of "cosmopolitan" (hence "cosmopolitics") and issues of peace and international law and order. Note that Ferguson (a Scot) and Kant (a German) were alike in regarding social relations as inherently antagonistic and "civil society" as essentially problematic.

Kant's *Anthropology from a Pragmatic Point of View* (1797) is a methodological piece written after his retirement from university teaching as if in response to a comment on his ideas: "All very well, but how do we do this philosophy of yours?" The existence of this book has rarely been acknowledged – or, perhaps, even read – by anthropologists. Yet it now appears extraordinarily prescient as a charter for the modern and postmodern discipline of anthropology. It suggests the value of what today we would call "eye-witnessing" and fieldwork, as well as cognate disciplines such as history and literature. Reading even plays and novels are, as Kant puts it, "auxiliary means in building up anthropology." A trend in this direction began when political anthropologists began to place more emphasis on culture and process while retaining a sense of political systems and structures (see Part III).

Extracts from the nineteenth-century writers, Maine, Morgan, Marx and Engels, developed and refined the ideas of the Scottish moral philosophers and jointly composed, in effect, a nineteenth-century post-Enlightenment. All were men of action, Marx and Engels on the frontiers of industrial capitalism and Maine and Morgan on the frontiers of imperialism. As a jurist, Maine had first-hand experience of imperial administration in India before becoming Professor of Jurisprudence at Oxford in 1869. Morgan was a lawyer and amateur ethnographer of the league of the Iroquois in upper New York state in the mid-nineteenth century. Marx and Engels, German political radicals exiled in England, were their contemporaries. Maine's contribution singled out here, was threefold: first, his delineation of the Comparative Method; second, the essentially anthropological notion that the West could learn from the East; and third, his understanding that general sociological concepts such as "corporations" and "village-communities" (elsewhere he calls them "village-republics") are best applied globally and transhistorically. In contrast, the extract from Morgan projects an evolutionary rather than an historical notion of society. "The Property Career of Mankind" climaxes his large and ambitious evolutionary study of human progress from savagery through barbarism to civilization in *Ancient Society* (1877). Optimistically, Morgan views trends towards democratic government, equality, and universal education as indicators of progress towards his ideal of liberty, equality, and fraternity.

Not surprisingly, Morgan's attention to property in industrializing, capitalist, society attracted the attention of both Marx and Engels. The major contribution of Marx and Engels to post-Enlightenment thought lay in their systematic critique of classical political economy. "Spectres Outside the Domain of Political Economy" prefigures the analytical recognition of what we now call an underclass. Their writing on the world market links the ideas of Ferguson, Smith, and Kant while, at the same time, adding a class dimension. Thus the expanding free market is seen as dispersing the bourgeoisie (the capitalist middle class) "over the whole surface of the globe." In the world around them, they see the cosmopolitan free-market economy destroying long-established national industries. Written in the 1840s, an age of revolutionary fervor in Europe, this argument marks an early expression of today's political concern over globalization and "the new world disorder" (see Part IV).

Finally, an extract from the work of James Mooney has been selected as a stand-in for the muted voice of the counter-Enlightenment. Writing in the 1890s on the eve of a new millennium, he calls for recognition of the power of memory and remembrance among conquered peoples (having in mind, no doubt, not only the Native Americans among whom he worked, but his own Irish forebears). Thus was Enlightenment rationality challenged by the irrationality of sentiment.

Mooney's counter-Enlightenment discourse stands for a subterranean, alternative anthropology of politics that, at a certain moment in time, was relegated to the past; it was excluded from the construction of the new academic subfield of political anthropology that took the discipline by storm in the 1940s (see Part II). Those British anthropologists who established the new subfield embraced Enlightenment discourse wholeheartedly, adopting its scientific vocabulary of structure and system, society and polity, social order and progress. Those who followed them implicitly adopted the marketplace model of the enlightened self-interested individual with which the name of Adam Smith will always be associated. In the war of words against nonscientific alternatives, the new political anthropology ruled war outside of its definition of a polity. This reflected its structural-functional concern with social order but, in omitting warfare from its research agendas, it missed not only one of the key elements in the eighteenth century's search for enlightenment but one of the key dynamics of the political situation in which it carried out its field research.

SUGGESTIONS FOR FURTHER READING

G. W. Stocking opens *Victorian Anthropology* (Madison: University of Wisconsin Press, 1987) with a look back at the Age of Enlightenment, focusing particularly on French and Scottish writers, primitivism, and ideas of progress towards civilization. He traces the romantic tendencies in American cultural studies to the writings of Kant's student, Johann Gottfried Herder. For an account of progressive evolutionism, see R. L. Meek, *Social Science and the Ignoble Savage* (Cambridge: Cambridge University Press, 1976).

On Enlightenment and post-Enlightenment ideas in American anthropology, see several works by Eric Wolf, including *Anthropology*, passim (New York: Norton, 1964, reprinted 1974); *Europe and the People Without History* (Berkeley: University of California Press, 1982), and, above all, his "Contested Concepts," in *Envisioning Power: Ideologies of Dominance and Crisis* (1999), pp. 21–67 (Berkeley: University of California Press, 1999). For a commentary on texts of Kant, Hegel, and Marx, see a critique of "metropolitan postcolonialism" as voiced by the "native informant" in G. C. Spivak, *A Critique of Pure Reason: Toward a History of the Vanishing Present*, pp. 1–111 (Cambridge, Mass.: Harvard University Press, 1999). For the underpinnings of an Anglo-Indian political ideology in Maine's writings on the Indian village community that came to symbolize the world man had lost, see C. Dewey, "Images of the Village Community: A Study in Anglo-Indian Ideology," *Modern Asian Studies* 6(3) (1972): 291–328.

For the use Marx made of the writings of Morgan and Maine see L. Krader, *The Ethnological Notebooks of Karl Marx* (Assen: Van Gorcum, 1972). A complementary work by Krader, *Dialectic of Civil Society* (Assen: Van Gorcum, 1976), traces the notion of "civil society" from the sixteenth century (through Hobbes, Locke, Vico, Mandeville, Rousseau, and Ferguson) to Tocqueville, Marx and Morgan in the nineteenth century.

M. Sahlins, "What is Anthropological Enlightenment? Some Lessons of the Twentieth Century," *Annual Review of Anthropology* 28 (1999): i–xxiii asks what ethnography has done to problematize the eighteenth-century Kantian understanding of the universal human condition and the civilizing mission of those who pinned their faith on "progress." Sahlins views anthropology's inherited Enlightenment ideas as dogmas of native western folklore passing as universal understanding of the human condition. S. Reyna, *Deadly Developments: Capitalism, States and War* (Amsterdam: Gordon and Breach, 1999), sets us on one path towards addressing Sahlins's question.

Civil Society

If war, either for depredation or defence, were the principal object of nations, every tribe would, from its earliest state, aim at the condition of a Tartar horde; and in all its successes would hasten to the grandeur of a Tartar empire. The military leader would supersede the civil magistrate; and preparations to fly with all their possessions, or to pursue all their forces, would, in every society, make the sum of their public arrangements. . . . It is in conducting the affairs of civil society, that mankind find the exercise of their best talents, as well as the object of their best affections. It is in being grafted on the advantages of civil society, that the art of war is brought to perfection; that the resources of armies, and the complicated springs to be touched in their conduct, are best understood. . . . there is no peace in the absence of justice. It may subsist with divisions, disputes, and contrary opinions; but not with the commission of wrongs. The injurious and the injured, are, as implied in the very meaning of the terms, in a state of hostility. . . .

Law is the treaty to which members of the same community have agreed, and under which the magistrate and the subject continue to enjoy their rights, and to maintain the peace of society. The desire of lucre is the great motive to injuries: law therefore has a principal reference to property. . . . Many of the establishments which serve to defend the weak from oppression, contribute, by securing the possession of property, to favour its unequal division, and to increase the ascendant of those from whom the abuses of power may be feared.

Mankind come under this description the moment they are seized with their passions for riches and power. But their description in every instance is mixed: in the best there is an alloy of evil; in the worst a mixture of good. Without any establishments to preserve their manners, besides penal laws, and the restraints of the police, they derive, from instinctive feelings, a love of integrity and candour, and, from the very contagion of society itself, an esteem for what is honourable and praise-worthy. They derive from their union, and joint opposition to foreign enemies, a zeal for their own community, and courage to maintain its rights.

Adam Ferguson (1767)

Free-market Policies

The case in which . . . it is proper to restore the free importation of foreign goods, after it has been for some time interrupted, is, when particular manufactures, by means of high duties or prohibitions upon all foreign goods which can come into competition with them, have been so far extended as to employ a great multitude of hands. Humanity may in this case require that the freedom of trade should be restored only by slow gradations. . . . Were those high duties and prohibitions taken

From Adam Ferguson, "Of Civil Liberty" [1767], in F. Oz-Salzberger (ed.) *An Essay on the History of Civil Society* (Cambridge: Cambridge University Press, 1995), pp. 148–51, 155–6.

From Adam Smith, *An Inquiry into the Nature and Causes of the Wealth of Nations* [1776], ed. E. Cannan (Chicago: University of Chicago Press, 1976), p. 491.

away all at once, cheaper foreign goods...might be poured so fast into the home market, as to deprive all at once many thousands of our people of their ordinary employment and means of subsistence. The disorder which this would occasion might no doubt be very considerable.

Adam Smith (1776)

Perpetual Peace

The peoples of the earth have entered in varying degrees into a universal community, and it is developed to the point where a violation of law in *one* part of the world is felt *everywhere*. The idea of a cosmopolitan law is therefore not fantastic and overstrained; it is a necessary complement to the unwritten code of political and international law, transforming it into a universal law of humanity.

Immanuel Kant (1795)

Universal History with Cosmopolitan Purpose

The means which nature employs to accomplish the development of all faculties is the antagonism of men in society, since this antagonism becomes, in the end, the cause of a lawful order of this society.... The latest problem for mankind...is the achievement of a civil society which administers law generally...This problem is the most difficult and at the same time the one which mankind solves last.... The problem of a perfect civic constitution depends upon the problem of a lawful external relationship of the states and cannot be solved without the latter.

Immanuel Kant (1784)

Anthropology from a Pragmatic Point of View

A systematic treatise comprising our knowledge of man (anthropology) can adopt either a physiological or a pragmatic point of view. Physiological knowledge of man investigates what nature makes of him: pragmatic, what man as a free agent makes, or can or should make, of himself....

This kind of knowledge, regarded as knowledge of the world that must come after our schooling, is not properly called pragmatic when it is an extensive knowledge of things in the world – for example, the animals, plants and minerals of various lands and climates – but only when it is knowledge of man as a citizen of the world.

Besides, the two expressions: to know one's way about in the world are rather far removed in meaning, since in the first case we only understand the play we have

From Immanuel Kant, "Perpetual Peace: A Philosophical Sketch" [1795], in *Kant: Political Writings*, ed. H. Reiss (Cambridge: Cambridge University Press, 1970), pp. 107–8.

From Immanuel Kant, "Idea for a Universal History with a Cosmopolitan Purpose" [1784], in *Kant: Political Writings*, ed. H. Reiss (Cambridge: Cambridge University Press, 1970), pp. 120–2.

From Immanuel Kant, "Preface," in *Immanuel Kant: Anthropology from a Pragmatic Point of View* [1797], ed. M. J. Gregor (The Hague: Martinus Nijhoff, 1974), pp. 3–5.

witnessed, while in the second we have participated in it. But the anthropologist is in a very unfavorable position for judging the so-called great world, or high society; for its members are too close to one another and too far removed from other people. One of the ways of extending the range of anthropology is traveling, or at least reading travelogues. But if we want to know what we should look for abroad in order to extend it, we must first have acquired knowledge of men at home, by associating with our fellow townsmen and countrymen. Without a plan of this kind...the citizen of the world remains very limited in his anthropology...

Finally, world history, biography, and even plays and novels are auxiliary means in building up anthropology, though they are not among its sources...

If an anthropology written from a pragmatic point of view is systematically formulated and yet popular...it has this advantage for the reading public: that it gives an exhaustive account of the headings under which we can bring the human qualities we observe, and each heading provides an occasion and invitation for the reader to add his own remarks on the subject...In this way the devotees of anthropology find its labors naturally divided among them, while the unity of its plan gradually unites these labors into a whole – an arrangement that promotes and accelerates the development of this generally useful science.

Immanuel Kant (1797)

The Effects of the Observation of India on European Thought

If such a science as I have endeavoured to shadow forth in this Lecture is ever created, if the Comparative Method applied to laws, institutions, customs, ideas, and social forces should ever give results resembling those given by Comparative Philology and Comparative Mythology, it is impossible that the consequences should be insignificant. No knowledge, new and true, can be added to the mental stock of mankind without effects penetrating deeply and ramifying widely. It is conceivable that, as one result, we of Western Europe might come to understand ourselves better....

I refrain from more than a mere reference to one set of effects which observation of India might have on European thought, those which might be conceived as produced by the spectacle of that most extraordinary experiment, the British government of India, the virtually despotic government of a dependency by a free people.... Observation of the British Indian political system might throw a flood of new light on...the history of the Romans under the Empire.... British India teaches us that part of the destroying process is inevitable; for instance the mere establishment of a Court of Justice...in Gaul would alter and transform all the customary rights of the Gallic Celts by arming them with a sanction. On the other hand, certain institutions of a primitive people, their corporations and village-communities, will be preserved by the suzerain state governing them, on account of the facilities which they afford to civil and fiscal administration. Both the good and the evil of the Roman Empire are probably reproduced in British India.

Henry Sumner Maine (1887)

From H. S. Maine, Rede Lecture, in *Village-Communities in the East and West* [1887], 5th edn. (London: John Murray), pp. 230–2, 236.

The Property Career of Mankind

Since the advent of civilization, the outgrowth of property has been so immense, its forms so diversified, its uses so expanding and its management so intelligent in the interests of its owners, that it has become, on the part of the people, an unmanageable power. The human mind stands bewildered in the presence of its own creation. The time will come, nevertheless, when human intelligence will rise to the mastery over property, and define the relations of the state to the property it protects, as well as the obligations and the limits of the rights of its owners. The interests of society are paramount to individual interests, and the two must be brought into just and harmonious relations. A mere property career is not the final destiny of mankind, if progress is to be the law of the future as it has been of the past. The time which has passed away since civilization began is but a fragment of the ages yet to come. The dissolution of society bids fair to become the termination of a career of which property is the end and aim; because such a career contains the elements of self-destruction. Democracy in government, brotherhood in society, equality in rights and privileges, and universal education, foreshadow the next higher plane of society to which experience, intelligence and knowledge are steadily tending. It will be a revival, in a higher form, of the liberty, equality and fraternity of the ancient gentes.

Lewis Henry Morgan (1877)

Spectres outside the Domain of Political Economy

Political economy, therefore, does not recognize the unoccupied worker, the workman, in so far as he happens to be outside this labour-relationship. The cheat-thief, swindler, beggar, and unemployed man; the starving, wretched and criminal working-man – these are figures who do not exist for political economy but only for other eyes, those of the doctor, the judge, the grave-digger and bum-bailiff, etc.; such figures are spectres outside the domain of political economy.

Karl Marx (1844)

The World Market

The need of a constantly expanding market for its product chases the bourgeoisie over the whole surface of the globe. It must nestle everywhere, settle everywhere, establish connections everywhere.

The bourgeoisie has through its exploitation of the world market given a cosmopolitan character to production and consumption in every country. To the great

From L. H. Morgan, *Ancient Society, or Researches in the Lines of Human Progress from Savagery through Barbarism to Civilization* [1877], ed. Eleanor Leacock (New York: World Publishing, 1974), pp. 561–2.

From K. Marx, Economic and Philosophic Manuscripts of 1844, in *Karl Marx: Early Writings*, ed. T. B. Bottomore (New York: McGraw Hill, 1964), p. 85.

From K. Marx and F. Engels, *The Communist Manifesto* [1847], ed. Samuel Beer (Arlington heights: AHM Publishing Corporation, 1955), p. 13.

chagrin of reactionaries, it has drawn from under the feet of industry the national ground on which it stood. All old established national industries have been destroyed or are daily being destroyed. They are dislodged by new industries, whose introduction becomes a life or death question for all civilized nations, by industries that no longer work up indigenous raw material, but raw material drawn from the remotest zones; industries whose products are consumed, not only at home, but in every quarter of the globe. In place of the old wants, satisfied by the production of the country, we find new wants, requiring for their satisfaction the products of distant lands and climes. In place of the old local and national seclusion and self-sufficiency, we have intercourse in every direction, universal inter-dependence of nations.

Karl Marx and Friedrich Engels (1847)

The Dream of a Redeemer

The wise men tell us that the world is growing happier – that we live longer than did our fathers, have more of comfort and less of toil, fewer wars and discords, and higher hopes and aspirations. So say the wise men; but deep in our own hearts we know they are wrong. For were we not, too, born in Arcadia, and have we not – each one of us – in that May of life when the world was young, started out lightly and airily along the path that led through the green meadows to the blue mountains on the distant horizon, beyond which lay the great world we were to conquer? And though others dropped behind, have we not gone on through morning brightness and noonday heat, with eyes always steadily forward, until the fresh grass began to be parched and withered, and the way grew hard and stony, and the blue mountains resolved into gray rocks and thorny cliffs? And when at last we reached the toilsome summits, we found the glory that had lured us onward was only the sunset glow that fades into darkness while we look, and leaves us at the very goal to sink down, tired in body and sick at heart, with strength and courage gone, to close our eyes and dream again, not of the fame and fortune that were to be ours, but only of the old-time happiness that we have left so far behind. [Nostalgia]

As with men, so it is with nations. The lost paradise is the world's dreamland of youth. What tribe or people has not had its golden age, before Pandora's box was loosed, when women were nymphs and dryads and men were gods and heroes? And when the race lies crushed and groaning beneath an alien yoke, how natural is the dream of a redeemer, an Arthur, who shall return from exile or awake from some long sleep to drive out the usurper and win back for his people what they have lost. The hope becomes a faith and the faith becomes the creed of priests and prophets, until the hero is a god and the dream a religion, looking to some great miracle of nature for its culmination and accomplishment. The doctrines of the Hindu avatar, the Hebrew Messiah, the Christian millennium, and the Hesunanin of the Indian Ghost dance are essentially the same, and have their origin in a hope and longing common to all humanity.

James Mooney (1896)

From J. Mooney, "Introduction," in *The Ghost Dance Religion and the Sioux Outbreak of 1890* [1896], ed. A. F. C. Wallace (Chicago: Chicago University Press, 1965), p. 1.

Part II

Classics and Classics Revisited

Introduction

Characteristic of a classic is that it lives on: as ancestral legacy, valuable methodological tool, as testimony to an iconic field site. These eleven chapters reflect the establishment of political anthropology as a specialized subfield within social anthropology between 1940 and 1972 and the dissent it generated. It is hard to remember now that its founding fathers were all young men in their thirties: E. E. Evans-Pritchard (1902–73), Meyer Fortes (1906–83), Edmund Leach (1910–89), Max Gluckman (1911–75).

All carried out fieldwork in Africa apart from Edmund Leach, who worked in Asia and the Middle East.

The year 1940 saw the publication of *The Nuer*, Evans-Pritchard's ethnography of a southern Sudanese people among whom he carried out field research in 1933 (see chapter 1). It also saw the publication of *African Political Systems* (*APS*), edited by Meyer Fortes and E. E. Evans-Pritchard, with a preface by A. R. Radcliffe-Brown (1881–1955), the doyen of British structural-functionalism. Together the two volumes innovated the recognition and study of what were called acephalous (literally, "without a head") political systems. The structural-functional approach involved synchronic analysis of societies as isolated wholes. Each society was conceptualized organically as a set of systems (social, political, economic, etc.) related to each other. Institutions, positions, and roles were studied in a search for equilibrium and social order.

Evans-Pritchard's account of Nuer social order quickly became generalized into models of "acephalous polities" and "segmentary lineage theory" and gave rise to a plethora of taxonomies of "primitive" political systems in the 1950s and 1960s. From the moment of its publication, Evans-Pritchard's canonical work on the Nuer inspired consideration of alternative explanations of his data by anthropologists and historians.

A further characteristic of a classic is that it is revisited by later generations of scholars. In what follows, this takes three forms. First, a researcher may go to the actual field site of the classic ethnography, as Sharon Hutchinson does (see chapter 2). A second form of revisiting involves a reappraisal and reapplication of the field methods used in the classic ethnography, as in the case of Ronald Frankenberg (see chapter 4). Revisiting takes a third form when the analytic argument of a classic ethnography is at one and the same time re-presented through extensive use of lengthy quotations from the classic and rebutted from an alternative theoretical perspective. This is what Talal Asad does when he "reconsiders" Fredrik Barth's classic ethnography of political leadership among the Swat Pathans (see chapter 5).

Sharon Hutchinson first visited Evans-Pritchard's field site among the Nuer of the southern Sudan in the early 1980s and she has returned many times since. After the outbreak of civil war in 1983, she continued to carry out extensive research in the Nuer villages, at times within the war zone, and in refugee camps. Her article, "Nuer Ethnicity Militarized" (chapter 2), reflects on a change that has taken place in the construction of Nuer identity in the course of the fighting. Her fluent command of the Nuer language and her gendered eye-witness perspective on the violence that has come to characterize postcolonial African and global politics contrast sharply with Evans-Pritchard's own precarious eleven-month research situation in the 1930s. Evans-Pritchard had found the Nuer, recently defeated by the British in 1929, to be a profoundly egalitarian people with acephalous political organization based on kinship and residence, linked by feuding and alliances.

Half a century later, in an ethnography that holds the promise of becoming a classic in its own right, *Nuer Dilemmas: Coping with Money, War, and the State* (1996), Hutchinson describes the Nuer as "a highly politicized people, deeply conscious of the vast, untapped oil wealth of their lands and of their tenuous integration into the national-state structure of Sudan" (p. 27). At this point the reader might wish to turn momentarily to chapter 24 for an analysis of other deadly wars, states, and capitalism elsewhere in contemporary Africa.

Our second revisit involves the continuous reapplication of the method introduced in a classic monograph. Again the year is 1940 which, besides the structural-functional approach of the Nuer ethnography, saw a different mode of analysis coming from another direction entirely with Max Gluckman's *Analysis of a Social Situation in Zululand*, an essay popularly known as "The Bridge" (see chapter 3). This alternative perspective on African politics offered analysis of contemporary political activity at a moment in time rather than the reconstruction of timeless political structures. As Gluckman himself observed in a working-class metaphor, it is more important to study the shift than the strike. Conflict and change in southern Africa were in the nature of things: it was order that had to be explained. Several case studies adopting the method – variously called situational analysis, event analysis, and the extended case method – have appeared every decade since, but here we focus on commentaries that urge its use in contemporary conflict settings in Britain (see chapter 4), in Latin America and for grounding ethnography of post-modern globalism. (See the works given in "Suggestions for further reading" by W. Roseberry and M. Burawoy respectively on the latter two contexts.)

Our third revisit (chapter 5) provides a model of how an ethnographic critique should be written. Talal Asad "reconsiders" the Norwegian Fredrik Barth's classic ethnography of a small kingdom in northwest Pakistan: *Political Leadership among the Swat Pathans* (1959). His goal is to suggest that class analysis provides a more valid explanation of Swat political organization than the "intellectual tradition in contemporary anthropology" to which Barth subscribes. The argument is divided into five parts, the last of which is omitted here. First Asad summarizes Barth's analysis of Swat as an acephalous political system comprised of the sum of all the choices of individuals giving their allegiance to others, *using Barth's own words*. He then points out the actual assumption in Barth's model of a Hobbesian sovereign class, i.e. landlords – again on the basis of his reading of Barth's own words. At this point Asad comes up against Barth's lack of concern with ideology, a lack that rendered him unable to explain what gave landlords their authority (i.e. legitimacy). Asad can, however, demonstrate their power to dominate and exploit the landless. This puts Swat into quite a different category for political anthropology: not a market-type, individualistic, contractual model of political structure, but the collective exploitation of a peasantry by a dominant landowning class. Asad is even able to show, *using Barth's own words*, that small intermediary landowners are being progressively eliminated.

A good ethnography empowers the reader, and in *Pul Eliya: A Village in Ceylon* (1961) Edmund Leach does just that. He was always a little out of step with his structural-functional colleagues. After a classic and better-known monograph, *Political Systems of Highland Burma* (1954) – reputed to be based on lost fieldnotes – he undertook fresh research in Ceylon (now Sri Lanka) in 1954. This led Leach to a critique of the now familiar structural-functional kinship paradigm through an extended analysis of kinship politics in struggles over land rights in the peasant village of Pul Eliya.

In *Pul Eliya* Leach focused on the natural and man-made material context of social and political behavior, and on economic self-interest. He supported his argument by detailed case studies based on intensive field observation and patient questioning, represented here by his analysis of "The Troubles of Ranhamy Ge Punchirala" (see chapter 6). Leach is not at all apologetic for the extensive ethnographic detail on which his argument rests: "The extra detail goes in at the cost of readability, but I cannot avoid that. The result is not bedside reading, but there is plenty to exercise the acrostic-making talent of the industrious undergraduate." A further invitation may be extended: the reader is invited to take up and reconsider Leach's ethnography of Pul Eliya in much the same way as Asad reconsidered Barth's ethnography of Swat.

The early classic systems-oriented political anthropology initiated with Fortes and Evans-Pritchard's *African Political Systems* in the 1940s blazed a trail for successive generations of their students. Then, in the course of its routinization, as with any paradigm, new questions were raised ansd had to be assimilated. Two of the most innovative challenges came from Max Gluckman's students, F. G. Bailey, and Victor Turner, at Manchester University. Recognition of the weaknesses in methodological individualism and the transactional approach to politics (such as those of Leach and Barth) led to refinements and more restricted claims for their usefulness. Drawing on an ethnographic trilogy that he had written, grounded in case studies of political interaction at the level of village, region, and state in the newly independent Republic of India, F. G. Bailey here seeks to delineate a general model of pragmatic human behavior in formal political settings. This is largely based on his application of game theory in economics to his own field experience of actor-driven politics (see chapter 7).

The use of character-full field notes as an integral feature of ethnography was brought to perfection by Victor Turner, a student and colleague of Gluckman in

Zambia. In his first monograph, *Schism and Continuity in an African Society* (1957), Turner presented his argument about witchcraft accusations and healing ritual processes in a Zambian village through the analysis of several social dramas. For example:

Social Drama I (compiled from informants): The Bewitching of Kahali Chandenda by his nephew Sandombu.

Social Drama VII (my own observations): Two Headmen Dispute over a Head Payment.

Note his methodological precision in recording sources. The social dramas are accompanied by diagrams, maps, settlement charts, and genealogies so that the reader can follow the action throughout the narrative series of political disputes. Subsequently Turner builds on the political processual analysis of his early ethnography to create a new and highly influential paradigm in political anthropology. This is illustrated here first by an extract on poverty, passage from one political status to another, and marginalization, which elaborates the concept of social fields or "fields of force" (in chapter 8), and then in a systems analysis of politics (in chapter 9) co-edited with two American scholars, Marc Swartz and Arthur Tuden in 1966.

And then, a series of crises in the objective world brought the gradualism of accumulated political anthropological knowledge to a halt. In 1968, widespread unrest in city streets and on university campuses in Europe and the Americas over United States involvement in the Vietnam War made political anthropology's "business as usual" appear petty and irrelevant. It fuelled dissent already expressed in the American academy over the dominance of quantitatively-driven, ahistorical, middle-range theory in the social sciences – the very approach that was held in such high esteem in the subfield of political anthropology. This is the political arena in which Kathleen Gough (chapter 10) and Eric Wolf (chapter 11) called for radical change in the agenda of political anthropology. The challenge to the classical structural-functional paradigm and its replacement by political analysis of western imperialism and colonialism opens Part III.

SUGGESTIONS FOR FURTHER READING

For a discussion of the part played by structural-functionalism in the establishment of political anthropology as a subfield and, particularly, the ethnocentrism of Radcliffe-Brown's introduction to *APS*: John Gledhill, *Power and its Disguises: Anthropological Perspectives on Politics*, chapter 1 (London: Pluto Press, 2000).

For a general overview of the impact of Nuer ethnography and *APS* and figures showing the taxonomies of political systems that emerged, see J. Vincent, "Politics in the Comparative Mode" *Anthropology and Politics: Visions, Traditions and Trends*, pp. 255–83 (Tucson: University of Arizona Press, 1990).

For a rebuttal of the Eurocentric perception that the modern centralized polity is radically different from acephalous and supposedly kin-based societies such as the Nuer, see M. Herzfeld, *Cultural Intimacy: Social Poetics in the Nation-State* (New York: Routledge, 1997). Evans-Pritchard presents an informant's model of the political structure and, although the patrilineal segments at the village level are a reality, the patrilines represented by the largest blocs in his diagram are largely fictitious. The distinction he makes in chapter 1 between political structure and political system allows for the inclusion of other political elements (such as the leopard-skin chief and prophets) within the latter.

In a prologue, S. Hutchinson, in *Nuer Dilemmas: Coping with War, Money and the State* (Berkeley: University of California Press, 1996), describes the book as being "a processual, actor-oriented account of the ways global historical factors of ever-increasing scale and complexity are subtly registered within regionally specific social and cultural fields." Its intellectual influences ranged from the Zambian project of the 1950s, through the work of Talal Asad, Pierre Bourdieu, Michel Foucault, and Jean and John Comaroff (see Part III) to the global concerns of today (see Part IV). It reflects not only significant links between historical developments and contemporary anthropological practice, but the continuing value of reading the classics throughout the complex interplay of theory and practice across the generations.

On the development of Gluckman's methods and insights, see S. F. Moore, "Uncertainties in Situations, Indeterminacies in Culture," in S. F. Moore and B. Myerhoff (eds.) *Symbols and Politics in Communal Ideology* (Manchester: Manchester University Press, 1975). Two further commentaries on "The Bridge" are: W. Roseberry, "Social Fields and Social Encounters," in G. M. Joseph, C. C. Legrand, and R. D. Salvatore (eds.) *Close Encounters of Empire: Writing the Cultural History of U.S. – Latin American Relations* (Durham: Duke University Press, 1998) and M. Burawoy, *Global Ethnography: Forces, Connections, and Imaginations in a Postmodern World* (Berkeley: University of California Press, 2000). An Indonesian case study using the method is C. Jayawardena, "Analysis of a Social Situation in Acheh Besar: An Exploration of Micro-history," *Social Analysis* 22 (1987): 30–46.

On Turner's methodological innovations and how they overcame contradictions between structure-oriented and actor-oriented political perspectives, see B. Kapferer, "Preface," in V. W. Turner, *Schism and Continuity in an African Society: A Study of Ndembu Village Life* (Oxford: Berg, 2000). Turner set out his own agenda for a new humanist political anthropology in "Process, System, and Symbol: A New Anthropological Synthesis," *Daedalus* 106(3) (1977): 61–80. On Action Theory, see J. Vincent, "Political Anthropology: Manipulative Strategies," *Annual Review of Anthropology* 7 (1978): 175–94. See also J. Vincent, *Anthropology and Politics: Visions, Traditions and Trends*, pp. 225–387 (Tucson: University of Arizona Press, 1990). Critiques of actor-oriented political anthropology include: S. Silverman, "Bailey's Politics," *Journal of Peasant Studies* 2 (1974): 111–20.

For the wider political arena in which both Gough and Wolf operated see R. J. Barnet, *Intervention and Revolution: The United States in the Third World* (New York: World Publishing Company, 1968). On academic dissent and popular protest: K. Gough, "World Revolution and the Science of Man," in L T. Roszak (ed.) *The Dissenting Academy* (New York: Random House, 1967).

1

Nuer Politics: Structure and System

E. E. Evans-Pritchard

The political structure of the Nuer can only be understood in relation to their neighbours, with whom they form a single political system. Contiguous Dinka and Nuer tribes are segments within a common structure as much as are segments of the same Nuer tribe. Their social relationship is one of hostility and its expression is in warfare.

The Dinka people are the immemorial enemies of the Nuer. They are alike in their oecologies, cultures, and social systems, so that individuals belonging to the one people are easily assimilated to the other; and when the balanced opposition between a Nuer political segment and a Dinka political segment changes into a relationship in which the Nuer segment becomes entirely dominant, fusion and not a class structure results.

As far as history and tradition go back, and in the vistas of myth beyond their farthest reach, there has been enmity between the two peoples. Almost always the Nuer have been the aggressors, and raiding of the Dinka is conceived by them to be a normal state of affairs and a duty, for they have a myth, like that of Esau and Jacob, which explains it and justifies it. Nuer and Dinka are represented in this myth as two sons of God who promised his old cow to Dinka and its young calf to Nuer. Dinka came by night to God's byre and, imitating the voice of Nuer, obtained the calf. When God found that he had been tricked he was angry and charged Nuer to avenge the injury by raiding Dinka's cattle to the end of time. This story, familiar to every Nuer, is not only a reflection of the political relations between the two peoples but is also a commentary on their characters. Nuer raid for cattle and seize them openly and by force of arms. Dinka steal them or take them by treachery. All Nuer regard them – and rightly so – as thieves, and even the Dinka seem to admit the reproach, if we attribute correct significance to the statement made to Mr. K. C. P. Struvé in 1907 by the Dinka keeper of the shrine of Deng dit at Luang Deng. After recounting the

From *The Nuer: A Description of the Modes of Livelihood and Political Institutions of a Nilotic People* (Oxford: Clarendon Press, 1940, courtesy of International African Institute, London), pp. 125–6, 130–2, 139, 142–4, 147–8, 181.

myth of the cow and calf, he added, 'And to this day the Dinka has always lived by robbery, and the Nuer by war.'

Fighting, like cattle husbandry, is one of the chief activities and dominant interests of all Nuer men, and raiding Dinka for cattle is one of their principal pastimes.... Boys look forward to the day when they will be able to accompany their elders on these raids against the Dinka, and as soon as youths have been initiated into manhood they begin to plan an attack to enrich themselves and to establish their reputation as warriors. Every Nuer tribe raided Dinka at least every two or three years, and some part of Dinkaland must have been raided annually. Nuer have a proper contempt for Dinka and are derisive of their fighting qualities, saying that they show as little skill as courage....

We have remarked that Nuer feel Dinka to be nearer to themselves than other foreigners, and in this connexion we draw attention to the fact that Nuer show greater hostility towards, and more persistently attack, the Dinka, who are in every respect most akin to themselves, than any other foreign people. This is undoubtedly due, in some degree, to the ease with which they can pillage the vast Dinka herds. It may also, in part, be attributed to the fact that of all neighbouring areas Dinkaland alone opposes no serious oecological handicaps to a pastoral people. But it may be suggested further that the kind of warfare that exists between Nuer and Dinka, taking into consideration also the assimilation of captives and the intermittent social relations between the two peoples between raids, would seem to require recognition of cultural affinity and of like values. War between Dinka and Nuer is not merely a clash of interests, but is also a structural relationship between the two peoples, and such a relationship requires a certain acknowledgement on both sides that each to some extent partakes of the feelings and habits of the other. We are led by this reflection to note that political relations are profoundly influenced by the degree of cultural differentiation that exists between the Nuer and their neighbours. The nearer people are to the Nuer in mode of livelihood, language, and customs, the more intimately the Nuer regard them, the more easily they enter into relations of hostility with them, and the more easily they fuse with them. Cultural differentiation is strongly influenced by oecological divergences, particularly by the degree to which neighbouring peoples are pastoral, which depends on their soils, water-supplies, insect life, and so forth. But it is also to a considerable extent independent of oecological circumstances, being autonomous and historical. The cultural similarity of Dinka and Nuer may be held largely to determine their structural relations; as, also, the relations between the Nuer and other peoples are largely determined by their increasing cultural dissimilarity. The cultural cleavage is least between Nuer and Dinka; it widens between Nuer and the Shilluk-speaking peoples; and is broadest between the Nuer and such folk as the Koma, Burun, and Bongo-Mittu peoples.

Nuer make war against a people who have a culture like their own rather than among themselves or against peoples with cultures very different from their own. The relations between social structure and culture are obscure, but it may well be that had the Nuer not been able to expand at the expense of the Dinka, and to raid them, they would have been more antagonistic to people of their own breed and the structural changes which would have resulted would have led to greater cultural heterogeneity in Nuerland than at present exists. This may be an idle speculation, but we can at least say that the vicinity of a people like themselves who possess rich herds that can be plundered may be supposed to have had the effect of directing the aggressive impulses of Nuer away from their fellow-countrymen. The predatory tendencies, which Nuer share with other nomads, find an easy outlet against the Dinka, and this may account not only for the few wars between Nuer tribes but also, in consequence, be one of the explanations of the remarkable size of many Nuer tribes, for they could not maintain what unity they have were their sections raiding one another with the persistence with which they attack the Dinka. . . .

The Political System

Nuer tribes are split into segments. The largest segments we call primary tribal sections and these are further segmented into secondary tribal sections which are further segmented into tertiary tribal sections. . . . A tertiary tribal section comprises a number of village communities which are composed of kinship and domestic groups.

Thus, the Lou tribe, as shown in the diagram below, is segmented into the Gun and Mor primary sections. The Gun primary section is segmented into the Rumjok and Gaatbal secondary sections. The Gaatbal secondary section is further segmented into the Leng and Nyarkwac tertiary sections. . . .

Lou Tribe

Mor primary section   Gun primary section

Gaaliek secondary section	Rumjok secondary section	
Jimac secondary section	Leng tertiary section	Gaatbal secondary section
Jaajoah secondary section	Nyarkwac tertiary section	

The smaller the tribal segment the more compact its territory, the more contiguous its members, the more varied and more intimate their general social ties, and the stronger therefore its sentiment of unity. As we shall see, a tribal segment is crystallized around a lineage of the dominant clan of the tribe and the smaller the segment the closer the genealogical relationship between members of this clan fragment. Also the smaller the segment the more the age-set system determines behaviour and produces corporate action within it. Political cohesion thus not only varies with variations of political distance but is also a function of structural distance of other kinds.

Each segment is itself segmented and there is opposition between its parts. The members of any segment unite for war against adjacent segments of the same order and unite with these adjacent segments against larger sections. Nuer themselves state this structural principle clearly in the expression of their political values. Thus they say that if the Leng tertiary section of the Lou tribe fights the Nyarkwac tertiary section – and, in fact, there has been a long feud between them – the villages which compose each section will combine to fight; but if there is a quarrel between the Nyarkwac tertiary section and the Rumjok secondary section, as has occurred recently over water rights at Fading, Leng and Nyarkwac will unite against their common enemy Rumjok which, in its turn, forms a coalition of the various segments into which it is divided. If there is a fight between the Mor and the Gun primary sections, Rumjok and Gaatbal will unite against the combined Mor sections: Gaaliek, Jimac, and Jaajoah. If there is fighting against the Gaajok or the Gaawar the primary sections, Gun and Mor, will, at any rate in theory, combine and a united Lou tribe will take the field, since both sections belong to the same political group and since their dominant lineages belong to the same clan. Certainly they used to unite in raids on the Dinka. . . .

This principle of segmentation and the opposition between segments is the same in every section of a tribe and extends beyond the tribe to relations between tribes, especially among the smaller Western Nuer tribes, which coalesce more easily and frequently in raiding the Dinka and in fighting one another than the larger tribes to the east of the Nile. . . . It can be stated in hypothetical terms by the Nuer themselves and can best be represented in this way. In the diagram below, when Z^1 fights Z^2 no other section is involved. When Z^1 fights Y^1, Z^1 and Z^2 unite as Y^2. When Y^1 fights X^1, Y^1 and Y^2 unite, and so do X^1 and X^2. When X^1 fights A, X^1, X^2, Y^1, and Y^2 all unite as B. When A raids the Dinka A and B may unite. . . .

A		X	B	Y
		X^1		Y^1
		X^2		Z^1 / Z^2 — Y^2

We may use the diagram above to emphasize the principle of contradiction in political structure. A member of Z^2 tertiary section of tribe B sees himself as a member of Z^2 in relation to Z^1, and all other members of Z^2 see themselves as members of that group in relation to Z^1 and are so regarded by members of Z^1. But he regards himself as a member of Y^2 and not of Z^2 in relation to Y^1 and is so regarded by members of Y^1. Likewise he regards himself as a member of Y and not of Y^2 in relation to X, and as a member of the tribe B, and not of its primary section Y, in relation to tribe A. Any segment sees itself as an independent unit in relation to another segment of the same section, but sees both segments as a unity in relation to another section; and a section which from the point of view of its members comprises opposed segments is seen by members of other sections as an unsegmented unit. Thus there is, as we have pointed out earlier, always contradiction in the definition of a political group, for it is a group only in relation to other groups. A tribal segment is a political group in relation to other segments of the same kind and they jointly form a tribe only in relation to other Nuer tribes and adjacent foreign tribes which form part of the same political system, and without these relations very little meaning can be attached to the concepts of tribal segment and tribe. We make here the same point as we made in discussing the word *cieng* [residence]: that political values are relative and that the political system is an equilibrium between opposed tendencies towards fission and fusion, between the tendency of all groups to segment, and the tendency of all groups to combine with segments of the same order. The tendency towards fusion is inherent in the segmentary character of Nuer political structure, for although any group tends to split into opposed parts these parts must tend to fuse in relation to other groups, since they form part of a segmentary system. Hence fission and fusion in political groups are two aspects of the same segmentary principle, and the Nuer tribe and its divisions are to be understood as an equilibrium between these two contradictory, yet complementary, tendencies. Physical environment, mode of livelihood, poor communications, a simple technology, and sparse food-supply – all, in fact, that we call their oecology – to some extent explain the demographic features of Nuer political segmentation, but the tendency towards segmentation must be defined as a fundamental principle of their social structure....

The lack of governmental organs among the Nuer, the absence of legal institutions, of developed leadership, and, generally, of organized political life is remarkable. Their state is an acephalous kinship state and it is only by a study of the kinship system that it can be well understood how order is maintained and social relations over wide areas are established and kept up. The ordered anarchy in which they live accords well with their character, for it is impossible to live among Nuer and conceive of rulers ruling over them.

The Nuer is a product of hard and egalitarian upbringing, is deeply democratic, and is easily roused to violence. His turbulent spirit finds any restraint irksome and no man recognizes a superior. Wealth makes no difference. A man with many cattle is envied, but not treated differently from a man with few cattle. Birth makes no difference. A man may not be a member of the dominant clan of his tribe, he may even be of Dinka descent, but were another to allude to the fact he would run a grave risk of being clubbed.

2

Nuer Ethnicity Militarized

Sharon Elaine Hutchinson

"nationalism as
an self drive n
conservation"

Ever since leadership struggles within the Sudan People's Liberation Army (SPLA) split the movement into two warring factions in 1991, rural Nuer (*Nei ti naath*) and Dinka (*Jieng*) communities in the South have been grappling with an expanding regional subculture of ethnicized violence. These two groups have supplied the bulk of the guerrilla forces that have been fighting since 1983 to overthrow a northern-dominated, national state government in Khartoum increasingly guided by Islamist political agendas and ideals. Since 1991, however, these people's homelands have also provided the major battlefield for escalating military confrontations among South Sudanese themselves (Human Rights Watch 1999; Johnson 1998; Jok and Hutchinson 1999; Nyaba 1997). These struggles have coalesced around two main figures: Dr John Garang, a Dinka and long-standing Commander-in-Chief of the SPLA, and Dr Riek Machar, a Nuer, who formed the break-away 'SPLA-Nasir' faction following his botched coup attempt against Garang in August 1991. Initially, the 'two doctors' divided over the question of whether or not the SPLA should abandon its declared aim of creating a 'united, democratic, secular Sudan' in favour of 'self-determination' or 'political independence' for the South. It was not long, however, before questions of 'nationalism' gave way to a more basic drive for self-preservation. Both Garang and Machar eventually reached for the 'ethnic' card. What followed were years of increasingly anarchic south-on-south violence that have since destroyed hundreds of Dinka and Nuer communities throughout the Western Upper Nile, Bahr-el-Ghazal and Jonglei Provinces. This tragic turn of events has made prospects for peace in Sudan more elusive than ever.

After months of intense south-on-south fighting in late 1991, mostly targeting the civilian population along ethnic lines, this military situation began to stalemate in late 1992. Garang's, predominantly Dinka, 'SPLA-Mainstream' (or 'SPLA-Torit') forces controlled most of the Bahr-el-Ghazal and Equatoria, while Machar's, pre-dominantly Nuer, 'SPLA-Nasir' forces held most of the countryside in the Upper Nile. Outbreaks of inter-ethnic violence, however, continued unabated though 1999.

From *Anthropology Today* 16(3) (2000) (Blackwell Publishers, 1999), pp. 6–13.

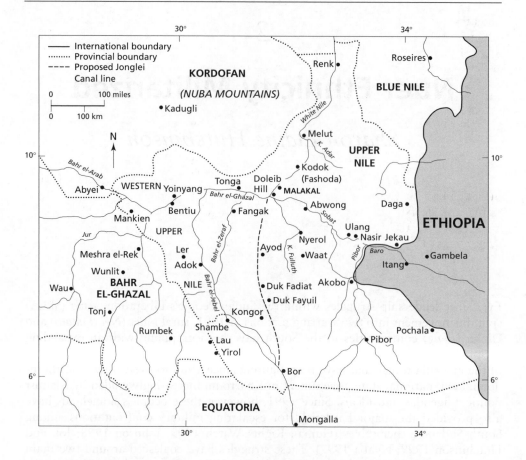

While individual southern military commanders struggled to establish their own fields of military and economic dominance, the Sudanese Army concentrated its attacks on Garang's positions in the northern Bahr-al-Ghazal and Eastern Equatoria with devastating consequences for the civilian population.

The central government in Khartoum, of course, rejoiced over the collapse of SPLA unity and proceeded to fan the flames of conflict between rival southern military leaders. These efforts formed part of a broader governmental strategy aimed both at developing a proxy war against John Garang and the SPLA and at reasserting control over the vast oil wealth of the south – and especially, the abundant deposits located in Nuer and Dinka regions of the Western Upper Nile Province. As early as 1986, the Sudanese Army began supplying northern Baggara 'Arab' groups with AK-47 rifles and bullets and encouraging them to raid Nuer and Dinka civilians located deep within the Western Upper Nile and the Northern Bahr-al-Ghazal. These government-sponsored militias were trained in counter-insurgency methods to attack the subsistence base and lives of southern civilians who might offer support to SPLA guerrillas. It was thus during these Baggara militia attacks that Nuer and Dinka women and children were consciously targeted not only for enslavement but for direct military attack. And yet, despite the tremendous losses of life and multiple displacements of Nuer and Dinka civilians as a direct result of

Baggara raiding between 1986 and 1991, the Government of Sudan failed to gain sufficient military control over southern oil deposits to permit commercial exploit-ation until after the explosion of south-on-south violence sparked off by the 1991 splitting of the SPLA.

As the military stalemate between rival SPLA factions dragged on, Machar's faction grew steadily weaker, owing to internal power struggles and recurrent defections to the sides of both Garang and the Sudanese government. The growing instability of Machar's command was reflected in, among other things, a series of political 'make-overs' in which 'SPLA-Nasir' was transformed into 'SPLA-United' in 1993 and then, into the Southern Sudan Independence Movement/Army (SSIM/A) in 1994. Finding himself without access to the international frontier, and thus without means of resupplying his troops in the Upper Nile, Machar was drawn deeper and deeper into the government's net. What apparently began as early as 1992 as a secret alliance with the Sudanese Army aimed at securing additional arms for his fight against Garang was eventually transformed into a full-fledged 'Peace Agreement' with the National Islamic Front (NIF) government in 1997. The infamous 'April 1997 Peace Agreement' committed Machar (and other southern signatures) to grafting his remaining SSIM/A forces onto the national army as the 'Southern Sudan Defense Forces' (SSDF) for the purpose of coordinating future assaults on Garang and the 'SPLA-Mainstream'. The agreement also committed Machar to accepting 'Islam and custom' as the overarching principles to which all national legislation must conform. In exchange for what many South Sudanese viewed as little more than unconditional surrender to the National Islamic Front government, Machar was offered a weakly worded, governmental promise that South Sudanese 'rights of self-determination' would be recognized through a south-ern-wide referendum to be held after an 'interim period' of four – or more – years. This agreement, however, brought anything but peace to Nuer regions nominally under Machar's control. By mid-1998, ordinary Nuer villagers had become alarmed at the increasingly transparent intentions of the central government to exploit the unbounded 'interim period' specified in the 'April 1997 Peace Agreement' for the strategic deployment of northern troops in formerly 'liberated' Nuer regions and, more disturbingly, for the rapid extraction of previously untapped southern oil deposits in the Western Upper Nile. Both governmental objectives were being pursued by instigating political rivalries and armed confrontations among allied Nuer and Dinka SSDF commanders (see Human Rights Watch 1999 and 2000).

As I write these lines, the immediate life circumstances for most rural Nuer and Dinka civilians in the South continued to spiral downwards through early 2000, as a deeply fragmented and increasingly predatory southern military elite confronts the possibility of permanently losing control over the estimated 1.2 billion barrels of proven oil reserves in the Western Upper Nile to a consortium of international companies, spear-headed by that Canadian giant, Talisman (Human Rights Watch 1999). Aided by an estimated 20,000 imported Chinese labourers, the Sudanese government completed construction of a 1,110-km oil pipeline in December 1998. The pipeline, which has an initial carrying capacity of 150,000 bbl/d to be expanded to 250,000 bbl/d by 2001, began pumping southern crude from 'Unity field' in the Western Upper Nile Province to newly constructed oil refineries and export termin-als in the North during September 1999. More ominous still, the Government of

Sudan has already began channelling the anticipated profits from this 1.6 billion dollar oil development scheme into the domestic construction of sophisticated weapons factories in order to bolster its 18-year-long assault on South Sudanese civilian populations and other politically marginalized groups in Sudan (see Human Rights Watch 1999 and 2000).

Whatever currents of optimism flow through the hearts of Nuer and Dinka civilian populations at present issue primarily from recent steps taken by leading Dinka and Nuer chiefs to end the vicious cycle of south-on-south violence sparked off by the 1991 splitting of the SPLA. Breaking free of the seven-year-long stranglehold on inter-ethnic communication imposed by the paranoia of rival southern military groups, scores of prominent Dinka and Nuer chiefs gathered together, first, in Lokichokkio, Kenya, in June 1998 and, later again, in Wunlit, Bahr-el-Ghazal, during February-March 1999 in order to negotiate a mutually binding, grassroots peace agreement aimed at ending, as one chief put it: 'this nasty little war that the educated [southern military elite] makes us fight!' With financial and logistical supported garnered by the New Sudan Council of Churches from a wide variety of international humanitarian and religious institutions, these peace workshops (both of which I attended) succeeded in greatly reducing tensions between Nuer and Dinka communities running along the turbulent Western Upper Nile/ Eastern Bahr-el-Ghazal divide. They also pressured opposed southern military leaders into investigating and restraining the cattle-raiding activities of some of their most abusive field commanders. Nevertheless, it remains to be seen whether or not this civilian drive for regional peace and reconciliation will triumph over intensifying government efforts to foment further mistrust and violence among southern military leaders and warlords in order to regain control over the vast oil wealth of the South. Beginning in April 1998, the central government began moving northern troops into the Western Upper Nile and proceeded to undermine Machar's military command by funding the military exploits of a rogue Nuer warlord by the name of Paulino Matiep Nhial. Beginning in June 1998 and continuing through the time of writing, Commander Paulino Matiep Nhial has taken the lead in driving Nuer civilian populations out of southern regions of the Western Upper Nile with the aim of clearing a path for extending the oil pipeline from the provincial capital, Bentiu, to Adok, a Nuer community lying on the White Nile approximately 120 kilometres further south (see Human Rights Watch 2000 for details). If nothing else, the government's lunge for southern oil deposits had motivated renewed contact and cooperation between SPLA and SSDF field commanders on the ground by 1999, despite the continuing unwillingness or inability of John Garang and Riek Machar to compromise their personal ambitions for the greater good and unity of the South. In November 1999, there was a major realignment of Nuer forces during which nearly all abandoned the government's side and formed an anti-government force, the Upper Nile Provisional Military Command Council (UNPMCC), which operates independently of Garang's SPLA. Of the estimated 70,500 Nuer civilians displaced from the Western Upper Nile between June 1998 and December 1999 as a result of continuing conflicts between the government and various southern factions over the oil fields, many eventually sought refuge among the Bahr al Ghazal Dinka, who received them well owing to the renewed spirit of cooperation and non-violence generated by the success of the 1999 Wunlit Peace Conference.

As of the time of writing, the '1997 Peace Agreement' is a dead issue. Alleging repeated government violations of both the terms and spirit of that agreement, Machar resigned from the Sudanese government in February 2000 and eventually returned via Nairobi to the Western Upper Nile, where he is struggling to salvage his former political prominence *vis-à-vis* an increasingly powerful UNPMCC.

My concern in this paper is with the rapid polarization and militarization of Nuer/ Dinka ethnic identities during the 1991–1999 period. Specifically, I want to discuss some of the historical conditions that led to the abrupt, post-1991, abandonment of ethical restraints on Nuer/Dinka violence previously respected by both sets of combatants. In the process, I want to show how growing numbers of Nuer men and women began to reject what I call a 'performative' concept of ethnicity in favour of a more 'primordialist' concept rooted in procreative metaphors of shared blood. This war-time shift of perspective, I argue, contributed not only to a dramatic escalation in the viciousness of Nuer/Dinka warfare after the SPLA split but, more uniquely, to a reformulation of the relationship between gender and ethnicity in Nuer eyes.

The Shifting Ethics of Nuer/Dinka Warfare

Before this war and, indeed, up until the collapse of SPLA unity in 1991, Nuer and Dinka fighters did not intentionally kill women, children or elderly persons during violent confrontations among themselves. The purposeful slaying of a child, woman or elderly person was universally perceived not only as cowardly and reprehensible but, more importantly, as a direct affront against God as the ultimate guardian of human morality. Such acts were expected to provoke manifestations of divine anger in the form of severe illness, sudden death and/or other misfortunes visited on either the slayer or some member of his immediate family. Acts of homicide within each ethnic group, more over, were governed by a complex set of cultural ethics and spiritual taboos aimed at ensuring the immediate identification and purification of the slayer and at the payment of bloodwealth cattle compensation to the family of the deceased. Regional codes of warfare ethics also precluded the burning of houses and the destruction of crops during Nuer/Dinka inter-community confrontations. Cattle, of course, were fair game. And it was not uncommon for past generations of raiders to carry off young women and children to be absorbed as full members of their families.

The gradual unravelling of these ethical restraints on intra- and inter-ethnic warfare during the course of this war represents the gravest threat to the future viability of rural Nuer and Dinka communities in the South today. While the main reason for this escalation in the killing of Nuer and Dinka women and children stems from the broader military objectives of the central government aimed at reasserting control over southern oil deposits, it also marks a major turning point in the relationship between southern military leaders and their civilian constituencies. Although often portrayed in pro-government propaganda tracts as the release of 'ancient tribal hatreds' which have been supposedly simmering for years, the causes of this surge in Nuer/Dinka violence were more fluid and complex. First of all, processes of 'identity' creation – whether defined in terms of 'ethnic', 'regional', 'racial', 'religious' or 'national' affiliations (to name only those most pertinent to

Sudan's unresolved civil war) – are always historically contingent and socially contested. As Liisa Malkki (1992: 37) expressed this idea: 'Identity is always mobile and processual, partly self-construction, partly categorization by others, partly a condition, a status, a label, a weapon, a shield, a fund of memories...a creolized aggregate.' Second, Nuer and Dinka communities have never been organized into neatly circumscribed 'tribes'. Rather, members of both groups have held overlapping and sometimes competing identities and loyalties to a wide spectrum of named social units, including patrilineal clusters, regional court systems, town groupings, temporary confederacies, and large, flexible networks of cross-cutting kinship ties. Both groups have also intermarried heavily for generations and continue to recognize their common ancestry through a variety of oral traditions and shared cultural practices. During the early nineteenth century, breakaway Nuer groups began migrating out of their original homelands on the west bank of the White Nile eastwards into Dinka and Anyuak occupied lands. By the end of that century, these Nuer groups had reached the Ethiopian frontier, effectively tripling their original land base and assimilating tens of thousands of Dinka residents, captives and immigrants in their wake. As one contemporary Nuer man laughingly summed up the results of this long-standing assimilation trend: 'There are no [real] Nuer. We are all Dinka!'

In complex historical situations such as these, the crucial questions to ask are: In whose image and whose interest have these ethnic labels been most recently forged? And when and why did these two groups' politicized sense of their own identity become threaded through with pressures for their menfolk to take up arms? And when and why did this militarization process begin to pit the 'ethnic soldiers' of each group against one another's entire populations? Discussing processes of militarization more generally, Cynthia Enloe has argued that: '[m]ilitarization occurs because some people's fears are allowed to be heard...while other people's fears are trivialized and silenced' (1995: 26). Following her lead, it will be important to understand the complex and paradoxical ways that women have been implicated in the polarization and militarization of Nuer and Dinka ethnic identities during this war.

Evolving Nuer Concepts of Ethnicity

One key to understanding the tragic developments begins with an appreciation of contemporary differences in Nuer and Dinka understandings of the socio-physical bases of their ethnic identities. For reasons that no doubt date back to the early nineteenth century, Nuer today regard themselves as more 'hospitable' to the assimilation of 'ethnic' outsiders than their Dinka neighbors. Throughout their famous nineteenth century expansion eastwards across the White Nile into Dinka and Anyuak-occupied lands (Evans-Pritchard 1940; Gough 1971; Kelly 1985), individual Nuer men competed with one another for positions of political leadership and independence by gathering around themselves as many co-resident Dinka clients and supporters as possible. The 'enduring loyalty' of these clusters of co-resident Dinka was secured, primarily, through the generous provision of Nuer cattle and Nuer wives. What underwrote the dramatic expansion of Nuer communities during the nineteenth century, in other words, was the rapidity and completeness with which they made ethnic outsiders feel like insiders.

Accordingly, what made someone 'Nuer' in their eyes was primarily how that person behaved. Language skills, a love of cattle, co-residence, community participation and moral conformity were all central in ways that biological parentage was not. In other words, past and present generations of Nuer tended to view ethnic unities and distinctions in more 'performative' terms.

Contemporary Dinka, in contrast, tended to stress the overwhelming importance of 'human blood lines' in determining who was and who was not a 'Dinka'. The 'primordialist' thrust of contemporary Dinka concepts of their ethnic affinity makes eminent 'sense' when viewed in light of their nineteenth-century experiences. Many Dinka men and women came under heavy pressure during that period to jettison their *Jieng* identity and to become *Naath*. And thus, one way Dinka groups could defend themselves against the sticky grasp of their Nuer neighbors was to reaffirm the fundamental insolubility of their ethnic identity through an elaboration of blood-based metaphors of procreative descent. Whereas it remained common practice during the 1980s, for example, for descendants of immigrant Dinka to be accepted as 'Nuer' government chiefs, the reverse scenario rarely, if ever, occurred. This was because most Dinka considered *Jieng* to be born, not made. Although some Dinka communities – particularly those inhabiting the Bahr-al-Ghazal – appear to have been more assimilative than others, the 1991 splitting of the SPLA resulted in a decade of division that played right into the hands of oversimplified government propaganda campaigns aimed at reifying 'tribal' differences between Nuer and Dinka and at muting more fluid and flexible ethnic identifications between these two groups.

Contemporary Nuer, in contrast, tended to treat their ethnic identity more like an 'honorific title' which is conferred together with the social approval of other community members. And thus, just as Nuer believed that anyone could potentially become 'a real person' or 'a true human being' (*raam mi raan*) by conforming to certain behavioural norms so, too, a person could be stripped of this status for major transgressions of those same norms. I recall a case during the early 1980s, for instance, in which a Nuer man, who had been born and raised by Nuer parents, scandalized the extended community by making an especially shocking rape attempt. Most people's immediate gut reaction was: 'No Nuer would do such a thing! That man must be a Dinka!'

What appears to be happening since the 1991 SPLA split, however, is a gradual sealing off of this formerly permeable inter-ethnic divide, a trend that has had especially disastrous consequences for the most vulnerable segments of society. Whereas during previous periods of inter-ethnic turmoil younger women and children were more likely to be kidnapped than slain by Nuer and Dinka fighters, the reverse was true during the 1991–9 period. Militarized segments on both sides of this ethnic divide attempted to justify their intensifying viciousness as 'retaliation' for abominations earlier experienced. However, there is more behind the conscious targeting of unarmed women and children for elimination than a rhetoric of revenge. People's concepts of ethnicity themselves have been mutating in ways that bode ill for the future. Nuer fighters, in particular, appear to have adopted a more 'primordialist', if not 'racialist', way of thinking about their ethnic 'essence' in recent years. And it is precisely this kind of thinking that can so easily be twisted into military justifications for the intentional killing of unarmed women and children residing among these ethnic groups.

Guns and the Military

Nevertheless, it is important to realize that local ethical codes of intra- and of inter-ethnic warfare began unravelling long before the 1991 splitting of the SPLA. Throughout the first eight years of this war, southern military leaders consciously sought to undercut the significance of ethnic differences among their new recruits. This was done not only to arrest the possibility of ethnic conflicts within their ranks and to engender greater feeling of southern unity and nationalism but, also, to ensure an effective chain of command. Since South Sudanese were forcibly drafted by the national army as well as by the SPLA, members of the same ethnic group were often forced to confront one another on the battlefield. Consequently, it was necessary for SPLA regional commanders to make sure that their troops unhesitatively carried out their orders, even when those orders required them to kill members of their own ethnic groups. This in turn necessitated the dismantling – or, at least, situational suspension – of earlier restraints on intra-ethnic violence, which were also a fundamental element of the ethical codes of warfare respected by both Nuer and Dinka at the start of this war.

During the late 1980s, for example, Riek Machar, who was at that time reigning SPLA Zonal Commander of the Western Upper Nile, endeavored to convince Nuer civilians as well as rank-and-file recruits that acts of inter-Nuer homicide carried out in the context of a 'government war' were devoid of the social and spiritual risks associated with acts of intra-ethnic homicide generated by more localized fighting and feuding. There was no need, he argued, for a slayer to purify himself of the 'embittered' blood of the slain. Nor was there any possibility of the family of the slain seeking bloodwealth cattle compensation from the slayer's family. In essence, the SPLA leadership was arguing that the overarching political context of the present war should take precedence over the personal identities and social inter-relations of the combatants in people's assessments of the social and spiritual ramifications of intra-ethnic homicide (see Hutchinson 1998 for a fuller discussion of these issues).

Furthermore, as guns burned deeper and deeper into regional patterns of warfare, many Nuer began to wonder whether the spiritual and social consequences of intra-ethnic gun slayings were the same as those realized with spears. Whereas the power of a spear, they reasoned, issues directly from the bones and sinews of a person who hurls it, that of a gun is eerily internal to it. And thus, additional elements of 'social distance' and 'attenuated responsibility' were added to the psychological arsenal of SPLA recruits. Unlike individually-crafted spears, more over, the source of a bullet lodged deep in someone's body was far more difficult to trace. Often a fighter would not know whether or not he has killed someone. And thus, acts of intra- and inter-ethnic homicide became increasingly 'depersonalized' and 'secularized' in Nuer eyes (see Hutchinson 1996 and 1998 for details).

The traumatic shift from spears to guns as the dominant weapon of Nuer and Dinka warfare during the early years of this war was aggravated by recourse to novel military tactics, such as surprise, night-time attacks, the burning of houses and the intentional destruction of local food supplies. Nevertheless, it was not until after the collapse of SPLA unity in 1991 that the killing of unarmed women and children became 'standard practice' between Nuer and Dinka combatants. God, it seems, was no longer watching.

From Mobile Assets to Military Targets

In many ways, women and girls were less firmly rooted than were men in the ethnic identities of Nuer and Dinka at the start of this war. This was because women and girls could potentially confer any ethnic identity on their children, depending upon who married them. Both groups are exogamic in the sense that women and girls may only be married by men who are, by definition, 'strangers' or 'outsiders'. Both groups also share a strong bias toward patrilineality since children generally take on the lineage affiliations and ethnic identities of their fathers rather than of their mother's people. Third and finally, wives in both groups tend to take up residence in their husband's homes after marriage. For all of these reasons, most Dinka and Nuer before the war took the attitude that 'A woman has no [fixed] "cattle camp".' She could be married by several men during her life-time and bear heirs for all of them. Similarly, people stated that: 'A girl belongs to everyone' – meaning she is a potential marriage partner for all unrelated men.

Women's more ambiguous position at the crossroads of ethnic unities and distinctions afforded them a certain degree of protection and mobility at the start of this war. They were the points through which adversarial relations between men could be potentially defused and transformed into relations of affinity through marriage. And for this reason, women and children were perceived by both groups as illegitimate targets during periods of inter- and intra-ethnic violence. There was, in fact, an elaborate ethical code among Nuer that treated women and girls as 'points of safe refuge' for fleeing or wounded men. Before the widespread dissemination of guns by the SPLA, Nuer women often accompanied their husbands, brothers and sons into battle in order to protect them and carry away the wounded. A woman could protect a man who had fallen in battle by throwing herself over him confident that the advancing warriors from the other side, whether Nuer or Dinka, would not dislodge her in order to 'finish off' the man beneath her. Similarly, any Nuer or Dinka warrior who retreated to someone's cattle byre or house was not pursued by his opponents. These rules were firm and respected, since any breech of them would have caused the original conflict to spin rapidly out of control. Consequently, Nuer and Dinka men alike regarded the slaying of a women, child or elderly person during major inter-ethnic confrontations as, by definition, 'accidental'.

The gendered division of tasks in both groups was one in which only men bore arms. Women and children, in contrast, were treated more as mobile assets and, as such, were sometimes kidnapped during major inter-ethnic confrontations. However, they were not intentionally slain. But following the widespread introduction of guns and of novel fighting techniques targeting entire cattle camps and civilian villages by the SPLA, unarmed Nuer and Dinka women and children were thrown willy-nilly onto the front lines. The SPLA did not promote the taking of war captives. Their limited food supplies and mobility requirements militated against this. And thus, in an area of recurrent starvation caused by the intentional destruction of the 'enemy's' support base among local civilian populations, women and children were gradually recast by rival southern military factions as legitimate targets of ethnic annihilation.

As Garang and Machar squared off, their troops, sometimes under orders and sometimes on their own initiative, began to slit the throats or otherwise slaughter women and children encountered during their cattle camp raids. And the spiral of Nuer/Dinka 'vengeance' attacks soon spun out of control.

More important for my purposes, the purposeful killing of women and children necessitated a major reformulation of the presumed socio-physical roots of ethnic affiliations, particularly for Nuer combatants. The rationale for killing a Dinka child entailed an assumption, whether implicit or explicit, that the child would mature into a 'Dinka'. That child's ethnic identity, in other words, was presumed to be fixed at birth. The idea that such a Dinka child could potentially become a 'Nuer' or vice versa was thus lost in the fury of 'revenge attacks'.

Like military movements worldwide, the SPLA had also sought to inculcate in its recruit an ideology of 'hyper-masculinity', equated with demonstrations of aggressiveness, competitiveness and the censure of emotional expression. The training of new military recruits glorified the raw 'masculine' power of guns. Recruits were told that they only thing that had separated the South from the political reins of power in the past was a lack of guns. Backed by the power of the gun, anything was possible – a theme clearly reflected in the 'graduation song' allegedly taught to all SPLA trainees prior to the 1991 split upon the conferral of their first rifles:

> Even your father, give him a bullet!
> Even your mother, give her a bullet!
> Your gun is your food, your gun is your wife.

Similarly, the SPLA's emphasis on male-to-male bonding was such that relationships with women and the family were increasingly de-emphasized and displaced. For example, I heard several reports of a disturbing incident that occurred during the mid-1990s in which a beautiful young girl, who had been carried off by ex-SPLA soldiers loyal to the Dinka warlord, Kerubino Kuanyin Bol, became the source of a heated argument. Three different soldiers all wanted to claim her as their consort. After summoning the three men and the girl and hearing their respective arguments, the Commander allegedly settled the dispute once and for all. Pulling out his revolver he reportedly shot the girl between the eyes and declared that no woman would be permitted to cause dissension in his ranks. The three soldiers allegedly shrugged off the incident. But the logic of the Commander was clear: the girl's life meant nothing in the context of troop solidarity and discipline.

A growing sense of 'entitlement' to the domestic and sexual services of related and unrelated women also pervaded this hyper-masculinized and militarized world view. Just as Dinka and Nuer men saw themselves as responsible for maintaining 'the war front', so, too, women, they reasoned, should be active in keeping up 'the reproductive front'. Pressures for women to disregard the 'weaning taboo' (which prohibits their having sexual relations during lactation) steadily mounted, as husbands and lovers on short, unpredictable military leaves returned home determined to conceive another child. Similarly, women are feeling pressured by husbands and in-laws to reduce the 'fallow period' between pregnancies by weaning their infants earlier. Whereas before this war infants were usually suckled for 18 months or more, many Dinka and Nuer men now argue that a period of nine months is enough. And because most Nuer and Dinka women do not feel free to refuse their husbands or lovers sexual access on demand for fear of a beating, they are increasingly forced to make choices that no woman should have to make. 'How can I take the risk of another pregnancy and childbirth when I can't even feed the children I already have?' 'Should I attempt to abort, knowing how many other women have died or become infertile in the process?' 'How would my husband and his family react if they discovered I aborted "their" child?' 'Who will care for my children, if I die?' 'Will God punish me for these thoughts?' Dr Jok Madut Jok portrayed the agony of these reproductive dilemmas among contemporary Dinka women of the Bahr-al-Ghazal in his publication (Jok 1999) – a portrayal that rings true to my own experience of similar trends among Nuer women of the Western Upper Nile. These are not communities that have accumulated generations of knowledge or experience in medicinally or physically provoking abortions. It is thus not surprising that the frequency of maternal deaths attributed to 'excessive bleeding' has been rising in both regions during the course of this war.

To these feminine hardships must be added the ever-present dangers of rape and of the forceful commandeering of scarce household resources by gun-toting men. Nearly every Nuer and Dinka woman has experienced threatening demands by armed men for the immediate provision of cooked or stored food, porterage services and/or sexual access. Satisfying these unpredictable and, often, recurrent demands severely limited the energies and resources these women were able to devote to their children.

Nevertheless, women were more than passive victims of these militarizing trends. Many Nuer and Dinka women actively reinforced this 'militarized mentality' by encouraging their brothers, husbands and sons to join the military or to participate as civilians in collective cattle raids and 'vengeance attacks' on neighboring ethnic groups. For example, during a 1996 field trip to the Western Upper Nile, I learned of a bitter debate ranging between two rival women, named Rebecca Nyanciew and Elizabeth Nyawana Lam. These women were, respectively, the elected heads of the Women's Union for the Bul and Leek Nuer. The issue these two women squared off on was whether or not Nuer military forces should resort to the killing of Dinka women and children during their cattle raids. Rebecca was allegedly an outspoken advocate of 'an eye for an eye'. Dinka soldiers had killed Nuer children so Nuer soldiers should do the same. Elizabeth vehemently objected. No woman with breasts and a womb for bearing children, she argued, should support the killing of women and children under any circumstances, regardless of whatever atrocities Dinka soldiers had committed in the past.

This debate, which radiated outwards through local military units and the wider civilian population, took a dramatic turn during the following year. Rebecca was arrested, beaten and jailed for her alleged role in 'fanning' (*kuothe*) the flames of intra-ethnic violence between Bul and Leek Nuer communities during the mid-1990s (discussed below). Elizabeth was pivotal in this outcome. Rebecca, who reportedly lost a pregnancy as a result of the beating, was later 'pardoned', released and brought to Khartoum under orders from Commander Machar.

Women were also capable of banding together to restrain eruptions of inter-community violence, especially those in which local military units were not directly involved. For example, there was a series of mixed spear/gun battles that erupted between the Bul and Leek Nuer in late 1995 which were successfully quelled by Elizabeth Nyawana Lam, in her capacity as the elected head of the Leek Nuer Women's Union. Elizabeth Nyawana had already earned a reputation for extraordinary courage by that time for having been trained and having actively served in the

SPLA fights against 'the Arabs' during the early years of this war. She was also a well-known peace-maker. She successfully ended this particular confrontation by ordering all the Bul and Leek Nuer women who ran to the battle scene together with their menfolk to return home immediately. Before the outbreak of the current civil war, it was standard practice, as I explained, for western Nuer women to accompany the brothers, husbands and sons to the battlefield, where they took responsibility for retrieving spears and, more importantly, for protecting and carrying away the wounded. Without the assurance of these feminine protections for the dead and wounded, Nuer fighters on both sides of the battle line decided to withdraw as well.

Although these feminine support systems have been increasingly undermined by the widespread dissemination of guns, Nuer women, at least, have retained considerable influence over patterns of inter-community violence through their well-recognized abilities 'to shame' their husbands, brothers and sons into either participating or not in specific military campaigns. As one young Nuer woman explained:

> Men say that 'women are women' but men do a lot of listening to us! Women are good at persuasion; we can convince men in a quiet way. Men pretend not to be listening but it [the woman's message] is already recorded!

Understanding the complex and paradoxical ways women have been implicated in these regional processes of militarization opens up novel possibilities for 'rolling back' these same processes. That, at least, is my hope. Perhaps it would be possible to convince individual southern field commanders that observing former ethical restraints on the killing of women and children, even if pursued unilaterally, would be politically and military advantageous in the long run. For example, there was a series of major clashes during 1997 and 1998 between the Murle and Lou Nuer. At one point, a group of Murle raiders slit the throats of several Nuer children they came across. Although Murle raiders often kidnapped small numbers of Nuer children in the past, the intentional killing of women and children had never before occurred during confrontations between these two ethnic groups. Incensed by this blatant transgression of established fighting norms, Lou Nuer organized a counter raid. Although Lou Nuer raiders openly discussed the possibility of killing Murle women and children, they decided not to respond in kind. After successfully driving off the defenders of their Murle target, the Lou Nuer men grabbed sticks and beat the Murle women and youth who had been left behind. The women were reportedly told that 'next time' they would be killed unless their menfolk stopped killing Nuer women and children during their cattle raids. This strategy proved remarkably effective. Under pressure from these women, the Murle initiated peace negotiations with the Lou Nuer and, shortly thereafter, returned nearly two dozen Nuer children carried off in earlier cattle raids.

Conclusions

As local codes of inter- and intra-ethnic warfare have twisted and collapsed beneath the weight of AK-47 rifles and the heavy blows of rival southern military leaders, ordinary Nuer and Dinka men and women have been forced to reassess the social bases of their personal and collective security. And of the many thorny issues requiring rethinking, one of the most fundamental and far-reaching concerns the nature, significance and scope of their ethnic affiliations. On the one hand, this war has witnessed the violent rise of 'ethno-nationalist' ideologies on previously un-imaginable scales within both ethnic groups. On the other hand, whatever sense of ethnic unity these groups have fostered in the context of continuing political rivalries between John Garang and Riek Machar has been repeatedly shattered from within. Breakaway warlords intent on carving out their own domains of military dominance have fractured and destroyed countless local communities.

While the former fluidity of Nuer and Dinka ethnic identities can be traced back to the early 1800s and beyond, contemporary Nuer men and women, in particular, appear to be moving away from a 'performative' concept of their ethnic oneness to a more closed and fixed 'primordialist' concept based on procreative metaphors of shared human blood. This perspectival drift has contributed, I have argued, not only to a deepening of the Nuer/Dinka divide but, more tragically, to a reformulation of women's and children's former status as immune from intentional attacks.

Women's more fluid and ambiguous position at the margins of ethnic unities and distinctions has thus been turned against them during the course of this war. What was formerly a source of both social protection and individual mobility for women became a dual liability. From a perspective internal to Nuer social networks, Nuer women continue to be regarded as less fully 'persons', less complete 'human beings' than are their militarily active menfolk. If anything, women's status as independent agents in men's eyes has declined in the context of militarized glorifications of the raw 'masculine' power of guns. The irony is that, despite the 'hyper-masculinized' military subculture, Nuer men – like their Dinka counterparts – have become less and less capable of fulfilling their most important social role as the protectors of their immediate families, homesteads and herds. This failure has provoked what might be called a 'crisis of masculinity' – a crisis that manifests itself in rising rates of domestic violence and sexual abuse against women. As the primary agents of cultural and individual continuity, women have come under heavy pressure to conceive and procreate, even in situations that threaten their physical well-being and their nurturing responsibilities toward their children. And thus, women's involvement in the civil war effort and, in particular, their roles in keeping up 'the procreative front' has often been brutally turned against them.

With respect to Nuer/Dinka violence, women's position on the margins of ethnic difference has been over shadowed by an externally imposed perception of eth-nic rigidity. In the eyes of both Nuer and Dinka assailants, unarmed women and children belonging to the opposite ethnic group have been progressively redefined from mobile assets to targets of ethnic annihilation. The vast majority of civil war victims have been defenseless women and children – an historical trend that, tragic-ally, mirrors late twentieth-century patterns of militarized violence throughout the world. This article has underscored the importance of a 'primordialist' turn in Nuer notions of ethnicity – propelled in large part by northern military strategies of 'divide and rule' – as pivotal in the emergence of this globalized trend in South Sudan. Let us hope that the atmosphere of inter-ethnic trust created by the 1999 Wunlit Peace Conference will continue to reawaken Nuer and Dinka men and women to the historical fluidity and contemporary permeability of their ethnic identities for the greater good of the South.

REFERENCES

Enloe, C. (1995) Feminism, Nationalism and Militarism: Wariness without Paralysis? In
C. R. Sutton (ed.) *Feminism, Nationalism and Militarism*, pp. 13–34. Washington, DC:
Association of Feminist Anthropology and the American Anthropological Association.

Evans-Pritchard, E. E. (1940) *The Nuer: A Description of the Modes of Living and Political
Institutions of a Nilotic People*. Oxford: Clarendon Press.

Gough, K. (1971) Nuer Kinship: A Re-examination. In T. O. Beidelman (ed.) *The Translation
of Culture: Essays to E. E. Evans–Pritchard*, pp. 79–121. London: Tavistock Publications.

Human Rights Watch. (1999) *Famine in the Sudan, 1998: The Human Rights Causes*. New
York: Human Rights Watch.

Human Rights Watch. (2000) *Sudan, Oil and Human Rights*. New York: Human Rights
Watch.

Hutchinson, S. (1996) *Nuer Dilemmas: Coping with Money, War and the State*. Berkeley:
University of California Press.

——. (1998) Death, Memory and the Politics of Legitimation: Nuer Experiences of the
Continuing Second Civil War. In R. Werbner (ed.) *Memory and the Postcolony: African
Anthropology and the Critique of Power*, pp. 58–71. London: Zed Books.

Johnson, D. (1998) The Sudan People's Liberation Army and the Problem of Factionalism. In
C. Clapham (ed.) *African Guerrillas*, pp. 53–72. Oxford: James Currey.

Jok, J. M. (1998) *Militarization, Gender and Reproductive Health in South Sudan*. New York:
Edwin Mellen Press.

——. (1999) Militarism, Gender, and Reproductive Suffering: The Case of Abortion in
Western Dinka. *Africa* 69: 194–212.

Jok, J. M., and S. Hutchinson. (1999) Sudan's Prolonged Second Civil War and the Militarization of Nuer and Dinka Ethnic Identities. *African Studies Review* 42(2): 125–45.

Kelly, R. (1985) *The Nuer Conquest: The Structure and Development of an Expansionist
System*. Ann Arbor: University of Michigan Press.

Malkki, L. (1992) National Geographic: The Rooting of Peoples and the Territorialization of
National Identity among Scholars and Refugees. *Cultural Anthropology* 7(1): 24–44.

Nyaba, P. A. (1997) *The Politics of Liberation in South Sudan: An Insider's View*. Kampala:
Fountain Publishers.

3

"The Bridge": Analysis of a Social Situation in Zululand

Max Gluckman

...As a starting point for my analysis I describe a series of events as I recorded them on a single day. Social situations are a large part of the raw material of the anthropologist. They are the events he observes and from them and their inter-relationships in a particular society he abstracts the social structure, relationships, institutions, etc., of that society. By them, and by new situations, he must check the validity of his generalizations. As my approach to the sociological problems of modern Africa has not previously been made in the study of what is called 'cul-ture-contact', I am presenting this detailed material by which it can be criticized. I have deliberately chosen these particular events from my note-books because they illustrate admirably the points I am at present trying to make, but I might equally well have selected many other events or cited day-to-day occurrences in modern Zululand life. I describe the events as I recorded them, instead of importing the form of the situation as I knew it from the whole structure of modern Zululand into my description, so that the force of my argument may be better appreciated.

The Social Situations

In 1938 I was living in the homestead of Chief's Deputy Matolana Ndwandwe, thirteen miles from the European magistracy and village of Nongoma and two miles from Mapopoma store. On January 7th I awoke at sunrise and, with Matolana and my servant Richard Ntombela, who lives in a homestead about half-a-mile away, prepared to leave for Nongoma, to attend the opening of a bridge in the neighbour-ing district of Mahlabatini in the morning, and a magisterial district meeting at Nongoma magistracy in the afternoon. Richard, a Christian living with three pagan brothers, came dressed in his best European clothes. He is 'son' to Matolana, for his father's mother was Matolana's father's sister, and he prepared Matolana's attire for

From *Analysis of a Social Situation in Modern Zululand* [1940] (Manchester: Manchester University Press, 1958), pp. 2–8.

state occasions – khaki uniform jacket, riding breeches, boots and leather gaiters. When we were about to leave the homestead we were delayed by the arrival of a Government Zulu policeman, in uniform and pushing his bicycle, with a handcuffed prisoner, a stranger in our district who was accused of sheep-stealing elsewhere. The policeman and prisoner greeted Matolana and me, and we gave the policeman, who is a member of a collateral branch of the Zulu Royal family, the salutes due to a prince (*umtwana*). He then reported to Matolana how he, assisted by one of Matolana's private policemen, had arrested the prisoner. Matolana upbraided the prisoner, saying he would have no *izigebengu* (scoundrels) in his district; then he turned to the policeman and criticized Government which expected him and his private police to assist it in arresting dangerous people, but paid them nothing for this work and would not compensate their dependants if they were killed. He then pointed out that he, who worked many hours administering the law for Government, had no salary; he had a good mind to stop doing this work and go back to the mines where he used to earn ten pounds a month as a 'boss-boy'.

The policeman went on with his prisoner. We drove in my car to Nongoma, stopping on the way to pick up an old man who is the head of his own small Christian sect with a church building in his homestead; he regards himself as supreme in his church but his congregation, which is not recognized by Government, is referred to by the people as part of the Zionists, a large separatist Native church. He was going to Nongoma to attend the afternoon meeting as a representative from Mapopoma district, a role he always fills partly because of his age, partly because he is the head of one of the local kinship-groups. Anyone may attend and speak at these meetings, but there are representatives recognized as such by the small districts. At the hotel in Nongoma we separated, the three Zulu to breakfast in the kitchen at my expense, and I to a bath, and then breakfast. I sat at a table with L. W. Rossiter, Government Veterinary Officer (*infra* G.V.O.) for the five districts of Northern Zululand. We discussed the condition of roads and local Native cattle sales. He also was going to the opening of the bridge as, like myself, he had a personal interest in it since it was built under the direction of J. Lentzner of the Native Affairs Department Engineering Staff, a close friend and old schoolfellow of both of us. The G.V.O. suggested that Matolana, Richard and I should travel to the bridge in his car; he was taking only one of his Native staff with him. He already, through me, had friendly relations with both Matolana and Richard. I went to the kitchen to tell them we were going with the G.V.O. and stayed a while talking with them and the Zulu hotel servants. When we came out and met the G.V.O., they exchanged greetings and polite questions about one another's health, and Matolana had a number of complaints (for which he is noted among officials) about the cattle dipping. Most of the complaints were technically unjustified. The G.V.O. and I sat in the front of the car, the three Zulu at the back.

The significance of a ceremonial opening of the bridge was that it was the first bridge built in Zululand by the Native Affairs Department under the new schemes of Native development. It was opened by H. C. Lugg, Chief Native Commissioner for Zululand and Natal (*infra* C.N.C.). It is built across the Black Umfolosi River at Malungwana Drift, in Mahlabatini magisterial district, on a branch road to Ceza Swedish Mission Hospital, a few miles upstream from where the main Durban-Nongoma road crosses the river on a concrete causeway. The Black Umfolosi rises rapidly in heavy rains (sometimes twenty feet) and becomes impassable; the main purpose of the bridge which is a low level (five foot) bridge is to enable the Mahlabatini magistrate to communicate with part of his district which lies across the river, during slight rises of the river. It also makes possible access to the Ceza Hospital which is famous among Zulu for its skill in midwifery; women often go up to seventy miles to be confined there.

We drove along discussing, in Zulu, the various places we passed. I noted of our conversation only that the G.V.O. asked Matolana what the Zulu law of punishment for adultery is, as one of his Zulu staff was being prosecuted by the police for living with another man's wife, though he had not known she was married. Where the road forks to Ceza, the Mahlabatini magistrate had posted a Zulu in full warrior's dress to direct visitors. On the branch road we passed the car of Chief Mshiyeni, Regent of the Zulu Royal House, who was driving from his home in Nongoma district to the bridge. The Zulu in the car gave him the royal salute and we greeted him. His chauffeur was driving the car and he was attended by an armed and uniformed *aide-de-camp* and another courtier.

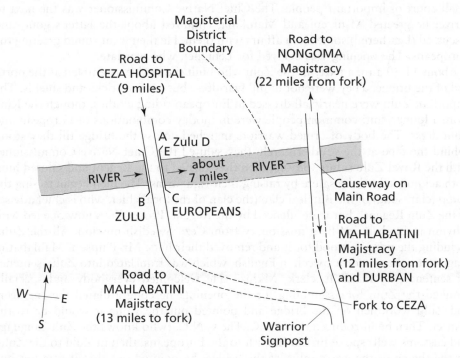

The bridge lies in a drift, between fairly steep banks. When we arrived, a large number of Zulu was assembled on both banks (at A and B in sketch map); on the southern bank, on one side of the road (at C) was a shelter where stood most of the Europeans. They had been invited by the local magistrate, and included the Mahlabatini office staff; the magistrate, assistant magistrate and court messenger from Nongoma; the district surgeon; missionaries and hospital staff; traders and recruiting agents; police and technical officials; and several Europeans interested in the district, among them C. Adams, who is auctioneer at the cattle-sales in Nongoma and Hlabisa districts. Many were accompanied by their wives. The Chief Native

Commissioner and Lentzner arrived later, and also a representative of the Natal Provincial Roads Department. The Zulu present included local chiefs and headmen and their representatives; the men who had built the bridge; Government police; the Native Clerk of Mahlabatini magistracy, Gilbert Mkhize; and Zulu from the surrounding area. Altogether there were about twenty-four Europeans and about four hundred Zulu there.

Arches of branches had been erected at each end of the bridge and across the one at the southern end a tape was to be stretched which the Chief Native Commissioner would break with his car. At this arch stood a warrior in war-dress, on guard. The G.V.O. spoke to him, for he is a local *induna*, about affairs at the local dip, and then introduced me to him, so that I could tell him about my work and request his assistance. The G.V.O. and I were caught up in conversation with various Europeans while our Zulu joined the general body of Zulu. Matolana was welcomed with the respect due to an important adviser of the Regent. When the Regent arrived, he was given the royal salute and joined his subjects, quickly collecting about himself a small court of important people. The Chief Native Commissioner was the next to arrive: he greeted Mshiyeni and Matolana, enquired about the latter's gout, and discussed (I gathered) some Zulu affairs with them. He then went round greeting the Europeans. The opening was delayed for Lentzner, who was late.

About 11.30 a.m. a party of the Zulu who built the bridge assembled at the north end of the bridge. They were not in full war-dress but carried sticks and shields. The important Zulu were nearly all dressed in European riding clothes, though the King wore a lounge suit; common people were in motley combinations of European and Zulu dress. The body of armed warriors marched across the bridge till they stood behind the tape at the southern arch: they saluted the Chief Native Commissioner with the Royal Zulu salute, *Bayete*, then they turned to the Regent and saluted him. Both acknowledged the salute by raising their right arms. The men began to sing the *ihubo* (clan-song) of the Butelezi clan (the clan of the local chief, who is chief adviser of the Zulu Regent), but were silenced by the Regent. Proceedings now opened with a hymn in English, led by a missionary from Ceza Swedish mission. All the Zulu, including the pagans, stood for it and removed their hats. Mr. Phipson, Mahlabatini magistrate, then made a speech in English, which was translated into Zulu, sentence by sentence, by his Zulu clerk, Mkhize. He welcomed everybody and specially thanked the Zulu for assembling for the opening; he congratulated the engineers and Zulu workmen on the bridge and pointed out the value it would be to the district. Then he introduced the C.N.C. The C.N.C. (who knows the Zulu language and customs well) spoke first in English to the Europeans, then in Zulu to the Zulu, on the theme of the great value of the bridge; he pointed out that it was but one example of all that Government was doing to develop the Zulu tribal reserves. The representative of the Provincial Roads Department spoke shortly and said that his Department had never believed a low-level bridge would stand up to the Umfolosi floods, though they had been pressed to build one; he congratulated the Native Affairs engineers on this bridge which, though built at little cost, had already stood under five feet of flood water; and he added that the Provincial Department was going to build a high-level bridge on the main road. Adams, an old Zululander, was the next speaker, in English and in Zulu, but he said little of interest. The final speech was by the Regent Mshiyeni, in Zulu, translated sentence by sentence into English by Mkhize. Mshiyeni thanked the Government for the work it was doing in Zululand.

He said the bridge would enable them to cross the river in floodtime and would make it possible for their wives to go freely to the Ceza Hospital to have their children. He appealed to the Government, however, not to forget the main road where the river had often held him up and to build a bridge there. He announced that the Government was giving a beast to the people and that the C.N.C. had said that they must pour the gall over the feet of the bridge according to Zulu custom for good luck and safety for their children when crossing the bridge. The Zulu laughed and clapped this. The Regent ended and was given the royal salute by the Zulu who, following the Europeans' lead, had clapped the other speeches. The C.N.C. entered his car and, led by warriors singing the Butelezi *ihubo*, drove across the bridge; he was followed by the cars of a number of other Europeans and of the Regent, in haphazard order. The Regent called on the Zulu for three cheers (hurrahs, Zulu *hule*). The cars turned on the further bank, and, still led by the warriors, returned: on the way they were stopped by the European magisterial clerk who wanted to photograph them. All Zulu present sang the Butelezi *ihubo*.

The Europeans went into the shelter and had tea and cake. A woman missionary took some outside to the Regent. In the shelter the Europeans were discussing current Zululand and general affairs; I did not follow this as I went to the northern bank where the Zulu were assembling. The local Zulu had presented the Regent with three beasts and these, as well as the Government beast, were shot on the northern bank by him and his *aide-de-camp* amid great excitement. The Regent ordered Matolana to select men to skin and cut up the cattle for distribution. The Regent withdrew to a nearby copse (D on the sketch) to talk with his people and drink Zulu beer of which large quantities were brought for him. He sent four pots, carried by girls, to the C.N.C. who drank from one pot and kept it; he told the carriers to drink from the others and then give them to the people. This is proper according to Zulu etiquette.

The C.N.C. and nearly all the Europeans went away. Most of the Zulu had assembled on the northern bank. There they were divided, roughly, into three groups. At the copse (sketch map, D) was the Regent with his own and local *indunas*, sitting together, while further off were the common people. They were drinking beer and talking while they waited for meat. Just above the river bank at A (sketch map) were groups of men rapidly cutting up three beasts under Matolana's supervision; they were making a great noise, chattering and shouting. The G.V.O., Lentzner and the district European Agricultural Officer were watching them. Behind them, further up the bank, the Swedish missionary had collected a number of Christians who were lined up singing hymns under his direction. In their ranks I noticed a few pagans. Lentzner got two warriors to pose on either side of him for a photograph on his bridge. Singing, chattering, talking and cooking continued till we left; I passed from group to group except for the hymn-singers, but most of the time I talked with Matolana and Matole, the Butelezi chief, whom I met that day for the first time. Matolana had to stay to attend on the Regent and we arranged that the latter should bring him to the Nongoma meeting. We left with Richard and the veterinary office-boy. The gathering at the bridge was to last all day.

We lunched, again apart from the Zulu, in Nongoma, and we went separately to the magistracy for the meeting. About 200–300 Zulu were present, chiefs, *indunas* and commoners. The start of the meeting was delayed some time as Mshiyeni had not yet arrived, but finally the magistrate started it without him. After a general discussion of district affairs (cattle sales, locusts, breeding from good bulls), the members of two of the tribes in the district were sent out of the meeting. . . . one tribe was told to remain as the magistrate wanted to discuss with them faction fights which were occurring between two of their tribal sections: the Amateni chief and his chief *induna* were told they could remain . . . but the magistrate did not want the common people of other tribes to hear him reprimand the Mandlakazi. This he did in a long speech, reproaching them for spoiling the homestead of Zibebu (*umzi kaZibebu*, i.e. the tribe of the great prince, Zibebu), and for putting themselves in a position where they had to sell their cattle to pay court fines instead of to feed, clothe and educate their wives and children. While he was speaking Mshiyeni, attended by Matolana, came in, and all the Mandlakazi rose to salute him, interrupting the magistrate's speech. Mshiyeni apologized for being late, then sat down with the other chiefs. When the magistrate had spoken at some length in this strain he asked the Mandlakazi chief to speak, which the latter did. He upbraided his *indunas* and the princes of the quarrelling tribal sections, and then sat down. Various *indunas* spoke justifying themselves and blaming the others; one, a man who according to other Zulu is currying favour with the magistrate for political promotion, spent his speech praising the wisdom and kindliness of the magistrate. A prince of the Mandlakazi house, who is a member of one of the fighting sections and who is also a Government policeman, complained that the other section was being assisted in the fights by members of the Usuthu tribe who live in Matolana's ward near them. Finally Mshiyeni spoke. He cross-examined the Mandlakazi *indunas* fiercely, and told them that it was their duty to see who started the fights and arrest these, and not allow the blame to be borne by everybody who fought. He exhorted the Mandlakazi not to ruin the 'homestead of Zibebu' and said that if the *indunas* could not watch over the country better they should be deposed. He denied the charge that his people were participating in the fights. The magistrate endorsed all the Regent had said and dismissed the meeting.

4

"The Bridge" Revisited

Ronald Frankenberg

... The best way to explore some of Gluckman's other views and their interrelation-ships is through *Analysis of a Social Situation in Modern Zululand*, hereinafter referred to as The Bridge. Here we shall find expounded for the first time what Gluckman later called the extended case method approach, later again renamed by Van Velsen situational analysis. (Gluckman is careful to note its antecedents in his Oxford friends and colleagues Fortes and Evans-Pritchard.) We shall see in it the analysis of paradox; a concern with social process (as against the more usual soci-ology of individual attribute); the development of the ideas of contradiction and what Gluckman calls cleavage (comparable to the antagonistic contradiction of some Marxists, and to Mao's principal contradiction); and the intertwining of co-operation and conflict. The whole is achieved in an analogous manner to Marx's *18th Brumaire* and Goffman's *Encounters*, by theoretically informed, detailed direct observation.

The events described are those of a single day and mainly happen at two places, one of which is the Bridge. The analysis begins with a notebook ethnographic description of the journey to, and the events surrounding, the ceremonial opening of the first bridge to be built in Zululand by the Native Affairs Department of the South African government. It describes, for example, who was in Gluckman's car, how they were seated, how they were directed on their way by a 'Zulu in full warrior's dress', how they passed the car of the Zulu Regent and eventually arrived at the Bridge itself. It then describes who was present at the Bridge, what they said and to whom, what they did afterwards and when and to where they, in due course, dispersed. Finally it describes the departure of Gluckman and a group of officials to a meeting at the Magistracy at Nongoma some thirty miles away.

Thus Gluckman describes at the outset 'several events which were linked by my presence as an observer, but which occurred in different parts of Northern Zululand and involved different groups of people'. (1940: 8–9). These are seen as a social situation because they are studied as part of the field of sociology:

From *Custom and Conflict in British Society* (Manchester: Manchester University Press, 1982), pp. 4–11.

social situation is thus the behaviour on some occasions of members of a community as such, analysed and compared with their behaviour on other occasions, so that the analysis reveals the underlying system of relationships between the social structure of the community, the parts of the social structure, the physical environment, and the physiological life of the community's members.

In a later footnote response to criticism by Phyllis Kaberry, Gluckman explains the use of the word community:

> I did not intend to convey that Zulu and white formed an harmonious well-integrated lot of people, but a lot of people co-operating and disputing within the limits of an established system of relations and cultures. (1958: 35, n.1)

... The whole discussion of a social situation may seem so obvious as not to have been worth stating even in 1940 if one were not aware of the persistent view that sociology is about social things rather than social relations (an aspect of Durkheim from which Gluckman later firmly dissociates himself). . . .

In such a social situation, Gluckman argues, *contra* Malinowski, Zulu and whites are systematically interrelated into a single system, which the situation creates and reinforces, and which can in turn be studied, analysed and understood through the situation. However much the interests of Zulu and whites, rulers and ruled, managers and managed, are opposed, they have to be seen as part of a single field of social relations. The meeting was organised by the magistrate; those he summoned came from farthest away and were mostly white. With one or two exceptions, the only Zulu present were local. This reflects the differing scale of European and Zulu life. The Christian Regent was accompanied by his wife; the whites brought their wives. The handful of Zulu women were there by hazard. This reflects the family structure and the nature of participation of women in the two parts of the society. At the meeting whites and Zulu met formally at particular moments but were formally separate.

> However, socially enforced and accepted separation can be a form of association, indeed co-operation, even where carried to the extreme of avoidance, as witness the silent trade in West Africa in ancient times. This separation implies more than distinction which is axiomatically present in all social relationships. Black and White are two categories which must not mix, like castes in India, or the categories of men and women in many communities. (1940: 12)

Gluckman continues to point out that these are exclusive groups – whites cannot become blacks, or blacks whites (unlike sons and fathers) and that the relationship is asymmetrical – the Europeans are at all times and at all places dominant, overtly or covertly. When the separation is (legitimately) broken down, temporarily or permanently, it is at their choice and on their terms. Whites, or course, define what is legitimate and have the power so to do. One such legitimate intermixture is that which 'allows' Zulus to work for whites. The white enclosure at the Bridge included some Zulus – as domestic servants to serve tea. One of the whites present was the labour recruiter for the Rand gold mines. Some of the wages Zulu received they were permitted to pay in taxes. 'The economic integration of Zululand into the South African industrial and agricultural system dominates the social structure' (1940:

14–15). It takes Zulu away from Zululand and the power of their chiefs, and integrates them with other migrant labourers in the towns. To the authority figures – Government Official, Zulu Chief, White Employer, Family Head – are added Shift Boss, and ones of a new kind, Separatist Church and Trade Union Leader. Gluckman has no doubt that the government's claimed function of 'developing' tribal lands is subordinated to its function of ensuring an adequate flow of labour to the mines. Nor has he any illusions about the consent of the governed or the ineffectiveness of opposition from chiefs, separatist Churches and trade unions.

> Therefore the opposition occasionally breaks out in riot and assaults on police and officials, which are forcibly repressed. These events provoke violent reaction from the white group and without apparent basis but in line with modern witchcraft-thought the immediate accusation without enquiry is that they are due to Communist propaganda.
>
> The political and economic ascendancy of European over Zulu, as capitalists and skilled workers on the one hand, and unskilled peasants and labourers on the other, may be paralleled in some respects in other countries. In all these countries the structure can be analysed in similar terms of differentiation and co-operation between economic and political groups. (1940: 17)

He shows the way in which structural unity and division is repeated in and reinforced by cultural cleavage in terms of language, daily life and religion. In the same way as he shows the Bridge provides a setting for the playing out of structural social relations at a reserve-wide and nation-wide level, so he suggests the family as the key setting for understanding the progress of social change. Here personal, ideological, structural, religious and political conflicts are all centred, fought out and sometimes resolved. This argument has (at least for me) taken on a new political, as well as sociological, significance as a result of feminist influence on social science. When I first read this essay at Cambridge in 1949 my reaction was to welcome an anthropology capable of encompassing Marx and Freud and to seek immediately to meet its author and, later, postgraduate training in Manchester.

Gluckman's conclusion to the descriptive analysis of the Bridge emphasises the concept of equilibrium to which he was often to return. He claims to have shown through it, and by implicit and explicit comparison with other situations in Zululand, that here exists an equilibrium defined as 'the interdependent relations between different parts of the social structure of a community at a particular period'. He asserts both its temporary nature and 'the superior force of the White group' as 'the final social factor' in its maintenance (1940: 25). He argues, following Fortes and Evans-Pritchard, that

> The shifting membership of groups in different situations is the functioning of the structure, for an individual's membership of a particular group in a particular situation is determined by the motives and values influencing him in that situation. Individuals can thus live coherent lives by situational selection from a medley of contradictory values, ill assorted beliefs and varied interests and techniques. (1940: 26)

But he also recognises that contradictions become conflicts, and that Zulu see themselves more and more as Africans as against whites, and have this perception qualitatively and quantitatively confirmed by the situations in which they are involved.

It is these conflicts within the Zululand structure which will lead to its future developments, and by clearly defining them in my analysis of the temporary equilibrium, I hope
to relate my cross-section study to my study of change. Therefore, I suggest that in order
to study social change in South Africa the sociologist must analyse the equilibrium of
the African-White community at different times and show how successive equilibria are
related to one another.

The second part of the Bridge is devoted to an analysis of Zulu history which has
now become a bone of contention to professional historians – who argue not only
its content but also whether it is to be regarded as a primary or a secondary source.
In a surprisingly short space of time Gluckman has become seen not only as an
analytical spectator but as an actor on the stage of history, one of the white Africans,
whose sayings and doings are in turn to be historically situated and analysed (Brown
1979).

From our point of view, we are concerned only with his methodology. The
placement of the descriptive history in the text is itself significant, since it follows
the analysis of the ceremony which defines its relevance (cf. Thompson 1977: 16). It
is here that Gluckman introduces his theme of rebellions in contrast to revolutions,
for he argues that there was a political balance between ruler and subject based on a
lack of class – as I have argued elsewhere, I do not accept this part of the argument,
which seems to me based on a confusion between relations of consumption and of
production all too common in sociology and social anthropology (Frankenberg
1978). Nevertheless the distinction rebellion/revolution is a useful one in many
contexts, although Gluckman himself repudiated the extreme functionalism of his
early view that civil wars were necessary to sustain repetitive social systems (1963:
23). In the Zulu polity threats to the king came only through his kin, who alone
could replace him.

> Through all these periods of Zulu history, in the equilibrium of the ruler – subject
> relationship, the force or organization behind the ruler was balanced against division in
> the ranks of the ruled. Intriguers for power sought popular support and the people
> turned to those men who were near in power to their rulers, to escape from intolerable
> oppression. The political balance persisted so long as the ruler observed the norms of
> rule and the values accepted by the subject. When he transgressed these rules, his
> subjects knew of no other political system, nor could they establish another under the
> social conditions then prevailing. They could be rebels, not revolutionaries. The King's
> danger came from rivals who could be installed in his place, with similar powers in a
> similar organisation; he was deposed, but his office remained unaffected, as is shown in
> the ability of his successor immediately to undertake religious functions, to symbolize
> the values of the society, and to express them in ceremonial. (1963: 32–3)

This situation was perpetuated, in Gluckman's view, because although the king
could command wealth he 'could not himself consume this wealth nor change it
into capital under the rudimentary mode of production which persisted unchanged'
(1940: 34). This may be (and has been) seen as an unduly static view, but in this
passage Gluckman appears clear as to where 'determination in the last instance' lies.

Thus he sees Zulu history before the arrival of the whites as a set of equilibria of
like nature, which succeeded each other interrupted by periods of upheaval that
changed the personnel but not the structure of positions and the culture they

generated and which legitimated and reinforced them. This in the third part of the Bridge is seen as the basis of *repetitive* society. The coming of the whites changed all this through power of conquest; through the seduction of law, a magistrate wrote triumphantly in 1892 when the first Zulu dispute was submitted to him for solution (1940: 39); through the social control of medicine, especially during epidemics (p. 40); and above all through money and tax.

> The small groups of Whites in Zululand derive their control over the Africans from their technical superiority, but it was money, rather than the Maximum gun or telephone, which established social cohesion, by creating common, if dissimilar, interests in a single economic and political system, though it is one with many irreconcilable conflicts. (1940: 42)

> Africans and Whites were divided into two sharply dichotomized groups, almost castes, with fixed standards of living, modes of work, degrees of citizenship, endogenous barriers and social ostracism, but which were held together in the cohesion of a common economic system. (p. 43)

Finally, in the modern system, co-operation continues but opposition develops which at the same time revives old customs [43] but also now looks forward rather than backwards in time. The greatest conflict (which he later calls the dominant cleavage), determines the lines of development of society. Thus what seems rational attempts to control overstocking by white veterinary officers, to the Zulu are attempts to prevent them becoming rich in cattle. The potentially unifying force of Christianity is the basis for expressing opposition to the whites through separatist Churches and so on.

The coming of the whites and by implication the articulation of Zululand into the capitalist system by forcing Zulu out to work alongside other Africans, and the taking of their land, end the repetitive system; unresolvable conflicts of inequality are introduced into the equilibrium and change the pattern.

> The lines of change, and the form of the new pattern, are determined by the original pattern. The inequality at first produces changes which are not widespread; the tempo of change, since every change heightens the disturbance, accelerates, and the ultimate alteration of pattern is violent and rapid. (1940: 47)

Even then, in what has become a revolutionary situation, some patterns of stability remain, and here Gluckman unconsciously echoes Simmel and foreshadows Coser.

> All social relationships have two aspects, one of fission, in which divergent interests tend to rupture the relationship, the other of fusion, by which the common ties in a system of social cohesion reconcile these divergent interests. Fission and Fusion are not only present in the histories of individual groups and relationships: they are inherent in the nature of the social structure. Thus every social group was defined by its not being some other social group, usually formed on the same pattern, and by its acting as a group only in a situation when it stood opposed to the other. Therefore it depended for its strength on the latent conflict between them. (1940: 47)

While the bridge ceremony could be analysed in terms of contemporaneous social relations independently of researching the history, real or supposed, of each group or the biography of each individual participant, once the equilibrium it revealed was described, it was worth comparing this with earlier states of equilibrium and showing how the contradictions within each worked to produce a state from which a new equilibrium emerged. . . .

Such a roundabout methodology was needed, he argued, because of what we have since learned to call overdetermination. . . .

> In the field of reality effects and causes are not only interdependent, but every causal event in its turn becomes an effect and every event is produced by many causes and produces many effects (1940: 50) . . .

To understand the total situation, therefore, Gluckman taught us to look at partial situations, chosen for their typicality, for it was these we were capable of handling, and it was these social relations in action, rather than artefactual *things*, that made up the culture of a community (1940: 56).

REFERENCES

Brown, R. (1979) Passages in the Life of a White Anthropologist: Max Gluckman in Northern Rhodesia, *Journal of African History* 20: 525–41.

Frankenberg, R. (1978) Economic Anthropology or Political Economy: The Barotse Formation. In J. Clammer, *The New Economic Anthropology*. London: Macmillan.

Gluckman, M. (1940) *Analysis of a Social Situation in Modern Zululand*, Manchester: Manchester University Press. Reprinted 1958.

——. (1963) *Order and Rebellion in Tribal Africa: Collected Essays with an Autobiographical Introduction*. London: Cohen and West.

Thompson, E. P. (1977) *Whigs and Hunters: The Origin of the Black Act*. Harmondsworth: Penguin Books.

5

Market Model, Class Structure and Consent: A Reconsideration of Swat Political Organization

Talal Asad

This article is one of several reconsiderations of outstanding monographs in which I have tried to explore kinds of assumption about consent found in political anthropology, and to examine the theoretical roots and consequences of such assumptions. In choosing Professor Barth's book *Political Leadership among the Swat Pathans* I have taken a study that is and deserves to be a modern classic. I should stress that in offering the following critique I do not intend to make a gratuitous show of academic ingenuity at the expense of what remains a superb analysis. My concern is rather to criticise a dominant intellectual tradition in contemporary political anthropology. But since this article is polemical in intent, I am concerned that it should not be thought that I may have misrepresented Barth's analysis. For this reason I have made use of extensive and lengthy quotations from his book, as well as from a number of articles on Swat which he wrote at about the same time.

The remainder of this article falls into five parts. In the first, I reconstruct, more or less in Barth's own words, what I call the pure model of Swat political organisation. In the second part I draw attention to certain logical similarities between this model and that of Hobbes, whose theory constitutes one of the main formative influences in the development of Western political thought (both as inspiration and as irritant). Discussion of the similarities will enable us to complete Barth's model, which I shall then criticise in the third and fourth sections. In the concluding pages I offer some general observations arising from the reconsideration.

When Fredrik Barth carried out his fieldwork, Swat was a centralised state, of some half a million souls, under the authority of a princely Ruler who had been recognised as autonomous first by the Government of British India, and then by the Government of Pakistan. The book, published in 1959, concentrates on the acephalous political system of Swat prior to the foundation of Swat state in 1917, a system

From *Man* NS 7(1) (1972), pp. 74–89.

which, in its essentials, was still largely intact at the time the fieldwork was conducted in 1954. A final, short chapter summarises the historical events which led to the establishment of Swat state, and describes the minor modifications this event has brought about in the original system (1959a).

The Theoretical Problem

In the Introduction to his book, Barth explains that: 'In Swat, persons find their place in the political order through a series of choices, many of which are temporary or revocable' (1959a: 2); that individuals distinguish 'between private and group advantage, and when faced with a choice they tend to consider the former rather than the latter' (p. 2) and that 'This is most clearly demonstrated by the way in which members of any group may secede and attach themselves to another when this is to their advantage' (p. 2).

Since it follows from this that 'the political system in Swat [is] the sum of all the choices of individuals giving their allegiance to others' (p. 2), Barth adopts a theoretical approach which derives from 'writers such as Weber. . . who analyses the bases of legitimacy, and de Jouvenel . . . who sees political activity in a means-to-end framework as directed towards rallying supporters for desired purposes. In such a framework, allegiance is regarded not as something which is given to groups, but as something which is bartered between individuals against a return in other advantages. The system of authority and the alignment of persons in groups is thus in a sense built by the leaders through a systematic series of exchanges. This corresponds closely to the Pathan idea of relations between super- and sub-ordinates as reciprocal but differentiating contracts' (p. 2). And so the central problem of the book can be stated as being 'to explore the kinds of relationship that are established between persons in Swat, the way in which these may be systematically manipulated to build up positions of authority, and the variety of politically corporate groups which result' (p. 2).

'While *the existing [political] organization is the result of a multitude of choices*, certain structural features of the society', which Barth refers to as 'frameworks', 'serve to define and restrict the alternatives which are offered to each actor' (p. 3).

These structural features include the territorial subdivisions of Swat, and the subdivision of its population into groupings of caste and lineage (which articulates the land tenure system). In addition, there are other, less formal, frameworks which also constitute limiting conditions with reference to which individual choices are made – namely, local neighbourhoods and networks of kinship and affinity. Barth is insistent that 'no position in the above frameworks, or local webs of relationships, necessarily implies allegiance to a particular political office-holder, or dominance over any specific other person. *All relationships implying dominance are dyadic relationships of a contractual or voluntary nature*. The primary elements from which the system of authority is constructed are such dyadic relations' (p. 3).

The Frameworks Defining Individual Choice

Territorially, Swat is divided into thirteen major regions, each subdivided progressively into named local areas, villages and wards. Wards are composed of houses and each house is occupied by a household 'maintaining itself as an independent economic unit' (1959a: 15–16). Houses are generally owned by members of the Pakhtun caste, as is virtually all the agricultural land. But Pakhtuns form a minority of the total population of Swat, varying in proportion between a fifth and a tenth from one major region to another. The total population is divided into roughly ten major castes which are defined by Barth for the purposes of his study as 'patrilineal, hereditary, ranked occupational groups, conceptually endogamous' (p. 16). All Pakhtuns are landowners, but some non-Pakhtuns also own land. Non-Pakhtuns follow a variety of occupations, but most are directly engaged in agricultural work. The two highest castes are Pakhtuns are Saints – the latter being persons who claim sacred descent. (It seems there is some ambiguity at this point in the caste hierarchy, for 'Politically powerful Pakhtuns can denigrate the sacred status of Saints and claim rank equality with them; Saints on the other hand are adamant in their claim that all Saints *ipso facto* rank higher than all Pahktuns' (1960: 140).)

If Saints have saintly genealogies legitimating their high caste position, Pakhtuns have Pakhtun genealogies which validate *their* superior position. For Pakhtuns as members of the Yusufzai tribe legitimate their rights to land in Swat by traditions of conquest. These genealogies define a series of segmentary patrilineal groups which correspond to the territorial subdivisions. But this correspondence is direct only in the case of the major region and the sub-tribe. All lower-order lineage segments have rights to shares in land, not to specific plots of land, for a periodic re-allotment takes place once every ten years or so. (At least this was the situation until the 1920s when the founder of Swat state declared the existing allotments to be final.) Lineage membership entitles one to attend the tribal assemblies at which administrative issues are discussed and disputes aired.

Caste position, which is acquired by patrilineal descent, in general defines not only one's rank but also one's occupation. In Swat there are many hereditary occupations, represented by craftsmen such as carpenters and blacksmiths, and by other specialists such as agriculturists and muleteers. Since Swat's is essentially a non-monetary economy, the co-ordination of agricultural work is achieved through the formation of voluntary multi-caste productive teams.

> Within such teams each specialist contributes with the skills and equipment or resources appropriate to his status, and receives in return a fraction of the resultant product... The landowner is the pivot on which the organization is based. The team is formed through a series of dyadic contracts between the landlord and each separate specialist; there are no contracts between the different specialists, although in fact they directly coordinate their work. Similarly, remuneration for services flows from the landlord and not from the persons to whom the actual services were rendered. (1960: 120–1)

Thus '*Every man is free to choose to which particular groups – whether they be for political, economic, recreational or other purposes – he wishes to belong*. Caste membership merely limits the range of positions to which a man can aspire' (1959a: 22). This applies not only to caste, but also to the other frameworks in terms of which individual choice is made in Swat, including the Pakhtun descent groups. Barth emphasises in this context the Pakhtun descent groups 'do *not* formally form corporate groups for the purpose of political action... Their main importance is in relation to the land re-allotment system, and to the public assemblies for negotiating settlements within local communities' (p. 30).

The major frameworks constitute in effect a set of definitions of the rules (including advantages and handicaps) which rational Swati decision-makers must observe when pursuing their political objectives. The political objectives themselves may be summed up as (a) the attraction or giving of support through voluntary transactions in which economic rewards and military security can be exchanged for economic skills and military manpower, and (b) the confrontation of rivals in a continuous attempt to maximise one's advantages and minimise one's vulnerability by undermining their support.

The Creation of a Following

A village – or the basic unit of government, a ward of a village – is thus inhabited by a diverse group of persons. Each ward is usually led by a single chief, who must be a Yusufzai landowner and is confirmed in his position by all landowners of the ward. Such a chief has a variety of relationships with different categories of his subjects: his fellow landowners who are his lineage equals and potential rivals; his own tenants and dependants; the tenants and dependants of other landowners; 'holy' men, and the tenants, dependants and religious followers of the 'holy' men. Relations with persons outside the ward are equally complex.

The political activities of the chief, designed to maintain or enhance his position, centre in the very important Pakhtun instruction of the men's house. In each ward there is at least one men's house, dominated by a chief; and the political, economic and recreational life of the men of the ward revolves around this common centre. Allegiance to the chief is expressed by the mere act of visiting his men's house. This allegiance is reinforced and deepened by the acceptance of hospitality from the chief. The chief is continually giving food, and occasionally other valuables, and thus creating debts and dependence on the part of the persons who sit in his men's house (1959a: 11).

Politically corporate groups are created by the action of leaders. Any such group consists of all the persons whom a leader is able to mobilise in the event of a conflict. Its limits are undefined except in relation to the leader, and its solidarity derives from the latter's authority. This authority may be attained in various ways. Persons may be committed by previous arrangements to support a given leader. Their services may be bought by gifts and promises. Their support may be won by the leader's prestige and moral or ethical fitness. Or, finally, their support may be compelled by force.

Previous commitments of followers are mainly those arising from house tenancy or occupational contracts. In these relationships the leader is in a position to exercise control by threatening to withdraw benefits, and the follower, on the other hand, can obtain advantages through his leader's success. The ability to give gifts depends on superior wealth and so ultimately on the control of land. Direct force is of limited use in winning supporters, since it pre-supposes a strong following... (pp. 72–3).

In general it may be said of virtually all a leader's potential following, as it can be said of his house tenants, that *'their political loyalty... is for sale to the highest bidder – in terms of rewards and security* (p. 52).

In most parts of Swat there is no necessary connexion between the different relationships that imply political submission...The position of a leader is thus never secure; his following may swell or shrink almost without warning (p. 73).

Followers seek those leaders who offer them the greatest advantages and the most security. With this aim they align themselves behind a rising leader who is successfully expanding his property and field of influence. In contrast, the followers of leaders who are on the defensive suffer constant annoyance from the members of the expanding groups. Under this pressure they tend to abandon their old leaders and seek protection and security elsewhere. Leaders are thus forced to engage in a competitive struggle. *A position of authority can be maintained only through a constant successful struggle for the control of sources of authority* (p. 73).

The Bases of Authority and the Need for Aggrandisement

The main sources of authority available to chiefs are ownership of land, the provision of hospitality and a reputation for honour:
1. Pathans greatly admire a man who possesses

a reputation for willingness to defend his honour and interests, for violence and impetuousness, for bravery and valour...Thus feuds in defence of honour become demonstrations of the relative abilities and powers of opponents; he who wins in such feuds and defends his honour thereby demonstrates his capacity as a powerful chief and competent leader. Little wonder that people admire him and that followers flock to his men's house; his reputation serves as protection to his followers as well as to himself. Little wonder, also, that *leaders are driven to adopt this pattern* in their relations with their rivals (1959a: 85).

2. However, honour is also acquired and maintained through lavish hospitality and gift-giving.

The importance for chiefs of the bonds created by hospitality is best seen by their actions when under political pressure, or when their income falls short of its usual level. In such circumstances the hospitality offered in the men's house is intensified rather than reduced; and if a sale of real property can be negotiated without too much publicity, the amount realized will be expended so as to maintain this higher level (p. 80).

3. But in the final analysis the capacity to distribute wealth lavishly, as well as the ability to sustain one's honour and defend one's interests most effectively depends on the control of land.

The competition between chiefs is thus largely for the control of land, and the acquisition of land is an important move in a political ascent (p. 74).
    Conflicts over land have the advantage, from the chief's point of view, that they automatically involve the self-interest of many of his non-Pakhtun followers. If his title is threatened, their rights are threatened too, if his property is expanded, their profits are expanded as well. Conflicts over land mobilize all the tenants of the land-owners concerned in groups based on common interest; they divide co-villagers and identify followers more closely with their leaders. They enable the landowner to cement the

unity of his own following by leading them in activities where their common interest is clear (p. 77).

Thus in Swat *'The authority of a chief depends...on the mandate he is able, at any given time, to wrest from each of his followers individually'* (p. 90).

The Containment of Conflict

Although the circumstances and reasons behind the Pakhtun leader's drive to increase his authority and compete with others for land are apparent, both drives are controlled by similar rational checks: thus 'there is an upper limit to every chief's aggressiveness, since he must always keep the number of his enemies lower than the total force of his following' (1959a: 76). Also, in a manipulative, contractual system 'a leader is freer to calculate the optimum size of his own following and maintain only such supporters as he sees fit. He may slough off dependants at any time by dissolving his contractual ties with them; or again, when the need for more men arises, he may seek supporters wherever he chooses' (pp. 88–9).

In this system of competition between Pakhtun landowners, Saints act as intermediaries, and it is in their capacity as successful intermediaries that they acquire political influence and authority. Thus in the conflict between Pakhtun chiefs balance is restored directly, as a result of rational calculation on the part of each opponent, or indirectly, through the mediation of a politically successful Saint who applies the appropriate criteria of reasonableness and fair play.

The Dynamic Equilibrium between Political Blocs

The contracts, alliances and competitive struggles that individual landowners engage in lead inevitably to the emergence of larger formations or political blocs. This constitutes the real political organisation of Swat. Indeed, in a sense this organisation is nothing more than the working out of the same kind of individual, contractual maximising behaviour at a higher level.

> *The striking feature of the political organization of Swat is the emphasis on free choice and contract which is fundamental to the organization on lower levels, and also characterizes the wider political alignments.* Thus the political organization does not derive directly from any one of the frameworks of organization previously described; it is a distinctive framework of its own, based on a series of explicitly political contracts or alliances. (1959a: 104)

Within each locality a given set of alliances is opposed to another set thus forming rival political blocs, and 'the blocs of neighbouring regions pair off, so that a pervasive two-party system emerges, extending through the length and breadth of the Yusufzai area" (p. 106). The blocs have no permanent existence, but find expression in and through the activity of individual political leaders, most of whom "*are compelled by the pressure of circumstances to attempt to enlarge the unit under their control so as to provide followers with the spoils'*. (p. 124)

Barth makes it clear that individual motive and choice in the aggregate are what constitute the wider political structure. For not only do these motives and interests produce the basic two bloc system; over time they also contribute to the maintenance of a dynamic equilibrium between the two blocs.

> As the majority bloc grows increasingly powerful, political rivalries will develop within it. This rivalry is encouraged by its opponents, and finally one of the subsidiary leaders of the stronger group is enticed to go over to the other side and become its leader. In this way they gain the military superiority, and the tables are turned. (p. 112)

There is another condition which also militates against the indefinite growth of the majority bloc. For:

> In terms of the simple self-interest of the persons on the winning coalition, absconders from the losing coalition will not be welcomed, since such a movement would imply a proportional decrease in the total distributable loot available to the winning side . . . On the basis of this model one would expect the dominant bloc in Pathan politics to be hesitant about accepting absconders and to remain moderately evenly matched in numbers with the weaker bloc, as is indeed the case. (1959b: 16)

At the individual level a similar logic prevails: 'To increase the area of land under his control at any appreciable rate, a political leader must use violence or the threat of it.' This inevitably involves killings, and:

> Such killings call for blood revenge, so that the extension of a man's estate inevitably creates a steadily mounting number of persons dedicated to wreak vengeance on him . . . Thus the more rapidly a man increases his estate and thereby the centralized group under his control, the greater the chance that his career will be cut short. (1959a: 125)

But even if this does not happen, other leaders

> are both jealous and afraid of one who is too successful. Their remedy is to support some rival for his position. Once he has been reduced, support may be withdrawn from his rival too, and balance in the acephalous bloc system thus be restored . . . (p. 126)

This balance constitutes the political system because it secures social order, and the securing of social order is the central feature of every political organisation.

Is Swat an Acephalous Society?

What I have done so far is to provide an outline of what Barth sees as the functioning political organisation of Swat. I have in effect tried to reconstruct more or less in Barth's own words the model by which he seeks to explain the way in which the political system of Swat maintains itself and helps to create social order. The model consists of a number of closely interconnected theoretical elements: (1) rules (legal, moral and prudential); (2) individual motivations (specific purposes and general strategies); (3) the formation of fluid interest groups through multiple dyadic transactions (as in a free market place); (4) the systematic compulsion to expand one's control of resources in order to survive (as in a self-regulating capitalist system); (5) a dynamic equilibrium underlying the concrete manifestations of political strength and weakness. It is primarily to this explanatory model that I shall refer when I criticise Barth's analysis of the political system of Swat.

It should be clear from the outline in the previous section that Barth's full account is formed round a coherent and persuasive logical structure. And yet there is something missing, an assumption not made explicit, which renders the argument really coherent. But paradoxically, when we make this assumption explicit, far from being strengthened, the model is revealed in a different light altogether.

Let me first make explicit a question to which a brief answer has already been suggested in the reconstruction of Barth's argument: what is it that makes the Swat system function as a *system*? More concretely: why do men take such pains to acquire a following, build up their authority, and engage in continuous and vigorous political struggle? Barth's answer, in effect, was this: for the same reasons that men attach themselves to leaders, accept positions of obedience, and consent to be represented in the authority of their chiefs – i.e. because of individual cupidity, aggressiveness or insecurity.

The similarity of this view of Swat Pathans with the Hobbesian vision of human nature and political society is striking and significant:

> So that in the first place, I put for a general inclination of all mankind, a perpetual and restless desire of Power after power, that ceaseth only in Death. And the cause of this, is not alwayes that a man hopes for a more intensive delight, than he has already attained to; or that he cannot be content with a moderate power: but because he cannot assure the power and means to live well, which he hath present, without the acquisition of more...
>
>   Competition of Riches, Honour, Command or other power, enclineth to Contention, Enmity and War: Because the way of one Competitor, to the attaining of his desire, is to kill, subdue, supplant, or repell the other. (Hobbes 1962: 49–50)
>
> So that in the nature of man, we find three principal causes of quarrell. First, Competition; Secondly, Diffidence; Thirdly, Glory.
>
>   The first, maketh man invade for Gain; the second for Safety; and the third, for Reputation. The first use Violence, to make themselves Masters of other men's persons, wives, children and cattell; the second, to defend them; the third, for trifles, as a word, a smile, a different opinion, and any other signs of undervalue, either direct in their Persons or by reflexion in their Kindred, their Friends, their Nation, their Provession, or their Name. (ibid. p. 64)

Since according to Hobbes this is the essential condition of human nature, order, security and justice can only be achieved if men are unconditionally subordinated to an absolute sovereign. For it is the function of the sovereign (the wielder of dominant power and authority) to determine and apply the rules whereby men might live in relative peace among themselves, and in relative security from external threat, and in so doing to deny his subjects the opportunity of making any significant political choice.

And this too is precisely the assumption that underlies Barth's analysis of Swat.

On the face of it Barth's thesis appears to be directly opposed to this, for after all is he not concerned to argue that order, security and justice, in so far as these are found in Swat, are achieved precisely in the absence of an absolute sovereign? Surely, the principle of voluntary and temporary contractual relations between supporters (whether economic specialists or junior political allies) permeates the system at every level, and in the final analysis it is the unceasing struggle between Pakhtun leaders that secures the balance as a guarantee of order? But the disparity between Hobbes's argument and that of Barth is apparent, not real.

A simple connexion might be made between Barth's picture of Swat and Hobbes's model by noticing that each landlord-chief and his following forms an island of authority. As Barth writes: 'The organization of villagers under chiefs in Swat is thus not an all-embracing system. Each chief establishes, as it were, a central island of authority, in the form of a men's house group, in a politically amorphous sea of villages' (1959a: 91). Perhaps this is not very different from Hobbes's observation 'that a great Family if it be not part of some Common-wealth, is of it self, as to the Rights of Sovereignty, a little Monarchy; whether that Family consist of man and his children; or of a man and his servants; or of a man, and his children, and servants together: wherein the Father or Master is the Sovereign' (Hobbes 1962: 107).

A superficial parallel may be there, but clearly Barth's islands of authority are more unstable, have indeterminate boundaries, and display a far more fluid membership than Hobbes would allow by definition to his little monarchies. This definition is not an arbitrary one, for Hobbes is concerned to argue that the essential condition for order, security and justice, is the presence of an absolute sovereign. It will be observed in this connexion that neither the Pakhtun chief's island of authority, nor the larger political bloc of allies, possesses a sovereign in Hobbes's sense. Does this mean, then, that in Barth's analysis of Swat political organisation we have a refutation of Hobbes's thesis? Or does it rather mean that the analysis does not allow us to identify the Hobbesian sovereign in Barth's model clearly?

It is popularly supposed that Hobbes equated absolute sovereignty with the absolute and arbitrary rule of a single man, but this is not so. In fact he classified ordered political societies, or commonwealths, into three types:

> When the Representative is One man, then is the Commonwealth a MONARCHY: when an Assembly of All that will come together, then it is a DEMOCRACY, or Popular Commonwealth: when an Assembly of a Part onely, then it is called an ARISTOCRACY. (Hobbes 1962: 97)

> The difference between these three kindes of Commonwealth, consisteth not in the difference of Power; but the difference of Convenience, or Aptitude to produce the Peace, and Security of the people; for which end they were instituted. (ibid., p. 98)

Hobbes argued that by these criteria monarchy was clearly the most preferable. But although he made it clear that an entire class could constitute a sovereign, he made no attempt to explore the implications of class interest and class rule for his model of political order. Nevertheless, it should be noted that for Hobbes political order entailed a rule-dominated society, and a rule-dominated society necessarily implied the presence of a sovereign who was instituted on a basis of consent. And it should be noted further that this formula applies equally to a society conceptualised in terms of a market model as it does to one conceptualised in terms of patriarchal authority.

If Swat political organisation is to be viewed as a consensual rule-structured activity, the question arises: who defines and applies the rules of the game? Who articulates and upholds the handicaps and advantages which are summed up in the major frameworks within which Swat's political competition takes place? Barth's answer is quite clear: it is the Pakhtun landowners who carry out these functions. Pakhtuns man the councils which come together to resolve in debate major disputes, in which the relevance of customary norms and Islamic law is presumably made manifest. Pakhtuns have a single genealogical charter by which they validate their collective right to land and their collective right to rule. They may not possess a corporate executive organisation, and their administrative authority may be vested equally in individual chiefs. But collectively, in relation to the rest of society, they occupy the position of a ruling authority, a sovereign class, with distinctive interests, privileges and powers. *It is the cumulative consequence of political decisions for these distinctive interests, privileges and powers that constitutes the primary criterion for defining the historical presence of such a class.* By itself, neither the range of influences impinging on political decisions, nor the boundary of the arena in which such decisions are made, is of crucial significance in this context.

The implicit assumption in Barth's model, then, is the presence of a sovereign landowning class. This means that the system does not regulate itself as it were after the consent of all participants has been obtained. It is regulated by a dominant class of landowners who exploit the landless. Once the agrarian class structure is recognised as the basic political fact, the political strength and weakness of persons appears more clearly as linked to developing economic, demographic and ideological factors. It becomes no longer possible to represent the political system as essentially made up of opposing blocs in dynamic equilibrium, a system which is simply the result of a multitude of choices. This conclusion, together with evidence about village and kinship loyalties among Swatis in general, must render inadequate the market-type, individualistic, contractual model as the basic analytic framework for understanding the total political structure of Swat.

Individual Consent and Dyadic Links versus Collective Exploitation and Class Structure

Barth does, in a sense, make explicit the class character of Swat. For example when he describes the traditional share system with its periodic re-allotment of land and its consequent re-positioning of Yusufzai landowners, he observes that 'the land tenure system thus emphasized the division between landowning Yusufzai conquerors and their subjects, the former being a dominant, cosmopolitan "gentry", the latter a parochial subordinate population serving a succession of different lords' (1959a: 10). Furthermore, throughout the book reference is made to the basic distinction between landowners and non-landowners, or between Pakhtuns and non-Pakhtuns, and some information is provided about the concrete character of this relationship.

But the inclusion of these important facts does not in itself mean that Barth accepts the fundamental political significance of class. On the contrary, as we have seen, the political system of Swat is analysed in terms of dyadic relations, voluntary contract, and individual choice.

In this analysis the basic class structure of Swat is refracted through the categories of *caste* and *lineage*. As applied by Barth, caste serves to articulate the system of prestige ranking, by which individuals can be evaluated and assigned to the appropriate rank position (an evaluation that may or may not be accepted by individuals so assigned). Caste also serves to co-ordinate agricultural production in a non-monetary economy, for by segregating economic roles, it permits separate economic specialists to be brought together into a productive team by the individual, contracting, landowner. In neither case does caste focus on the basic structural relationship between opposed classes. Similarly, the patrilineal descent system serves to define the pattern of territorial segmentation on the one hand, and the lines of tension and solidarity between patrilineal kin on the other. Far from helping to maintain the overall unity of the ruling class, we are told that 'Unilineal descent...places each Pakhtun...in a unique position in a segmentary system' (p. 22).

According to Barth, '*Most statuses and rights are usually defined by contractual agreements between persons; that is to say, they are achieved*' (p. 23). The categories of caste and lineage define, as it were, the rules of the game within which individual players achieve their positions. In these circumstances each man's aim may be seen as the adoption of the strategy that will serve his own interests best. And so the Pakhtun landowner comes to be conceptualised by Barth as someone driven by the *individual motive* to maximise, someone who makes contracts with other single persons driven by similar motives, rather than someone whose opportunities and disabilities are structured by his *class position* in a non-capitalist, agrarian society.

At a crucial point in the development of his analysis Barth argues as follows:

> Different Pakhtuns in a local area are competing partners in a privileged position; together they control a resource in the form of a limited area, the gross productivity of which, as a result of the highly developed irrigation system, is practically a constant. A Pakhtun's profits may theoretically be increased in either of two ways. All the Pakhtuns of an area may combine to exploit the non-landowners by demanding the maximum share of gross income for themselves; or an individual may extend his control over a larger proportion of the land, thus increasing his own profits at the expense of other landowners. The second of these courses is that generally adopted, as is apparent from the kinds of bonds between persons described above. *By adopting this strategy a landowner can build up common interests with a body of followers vis-à-vis rival landlords.* Bonds with fellow landowners, on the other hand, are largely undeveloped.
>
> The strategy of severe exploitation by a combination of landowners is in fact not practicable. The non-landowners are already living barely above subsistence level, and would be below it were not a part of the taxes they pay returned to them in the form of the chief's hospitality in the men's houses. Furthermore, landowners are greatly outnumbered by non-landowners, and could not maintain themselves as a group if the latter were united against them. It is by becoming the leader of the non-landowners, not by turning them against himself, that a Pakhtun landowner maintains his position. (p. 68)

Clearly these are not mutually exclusive alternatives, for up to a point both courses may be followed. Strictly speaking it is not possible to evaluate the first alternative accurately because the relevant economic data are not available (e.g. rate of population increase, demand for different categories of land on the part of farmers, accessibility of sources of livelihood outside Swat, flow of earnings from trade and migrant labour, etc.). Until we have this kind of information it is difficult to show that profits can be continually increased by all the Pakhtuns of an area combining to demand the maximum share of gross income from non-landowners (I shall later argue that the alleged *need* to increase profits in Swat is an assumption without much foundation). But even if we admit that (in a relatively static, agrarian economy) they could not increase their profits in this way, it does not follow that 'The strategy of severe exploitation by a combination of landowners is in fact not practicable.' On the contrary, it is practicable and it is practised. And the point I want to stress is that what this fact represents is not so much an optional strategy followed by individuals in the aggregate, but a class structure.

Most of the land in Swat valley (and the best land too) is owned by the Yusufzai minority. Landlords collect from three-quarters to four-fifths of the gross crop in rent from their tenants. Further, only landowning Pakhtuns are members of the *jirga*, the tribal council, and a Pakhtun who loses all his land loses this membership. Since the *jirga* systematically excludes all non-landowners, it does represent a kind of political expression of class unity. It is an assembly of Pakhtuns as against non-Pakhtuns, deliberating as theoretical equals on the ground that they all have common interests which derive from the ownership of land. Hence there is, argu-ably, a combination of landowners which helps to maintain for them a maximum share of gross income (maximum as understood in a traditional economy) though it may not be directed at a continuous increase of that share. This is not inconsistent with the attempt by some individual landowners to increase their control over land (and hence their profits) at the expense of other owners. But the system does not compel landowners to do so in order to survive. However, in order to understand the full significance of this fact we must first return to Barth's model to look more closely at the way the specifically political relationship between Pakhtun chiefs and their non-Pakhtun followers is represented.

Barth recognizes that there are fundamental differences between the life-situation of Pakhtun landowners and of landless non-Pakhtuns: 'To the sedentary villagers, whether tenants, craftsmen or others, the Pakhtun represents an unnecessary impos-ition. They have their own web of kinship ties, their local associations for life crises; between them they have all the skills and man-power necessary to maintain the economic system; they have built and must keep their own houses, they know the fields and the irrigation system better than the Pakhtuns' (pp. 68–9). But the distinction is presented in terms of the individuating features of caste (kinship links, rank position, and occupational roles) rather than in terms of the collective and asymmetric relations between classes (differential group access to power and sources of livelihood). And since this is how the formal distinction is presented, the Pakhtun landlord appears to be unnecessary to the system. And since he is unnecessary, his position is viewed as acutely problematic, and represented as being resolved by an individual strategy in which he can barter economic gain for political authority through a series of dyadic contracts.

> The problem that faces the Pakhtun . . . is how to make himself indispensable to the villagers, how to tie as many of them as possible to himself. The answer is found in the Pakhtun's claim to ownership of all land, and in an organization based on this assump-tion, using the different kinds of contracts described in the previous chapters.

Within such a framework of ideas, let us adopt, for the moment, the point of view of non-landowners. Each separate villager clearly sees himself as exercising a choice. Either he may make every possible contract with one leader and so to speak, join his 'island'. Or he may establish no contract with any leader, and thus remain entirely outside the different fields of authority. Both alternatives have readily apparent advantages and disadvantages. In the former the villager makes himself subject to the whims of a leader, but profits materially and obtains protection. In the latter, he remains free of external control at the price of considerable material discomfort, and must also manage without any protection against aggression. (p. 69)

The relevant data suggest a very different picture: in a society where a small group of landowners owns most of the land, where all subsistence is ultimately based on agriculture, where there is high population density, under-employment and land scarcity, where most non-landowners live barely above subsistence level, the land-lord's dominant position is not problematic. The Pakhtun maintains his position by virtue of his control of scarce land, not by cajoling the landless into accepting his authority. Of course 'control' is dependent not only on certain objective circum-stances (relative access to physical force, ratio of owners to non-owners, etc.) but also on subjective perceptions (e.g. that Pakhtuns are perceived in some sense as 'owners' of the land). Nevertheless he acquires his political authority by virtue of his membership in a politically dominant class, not by persuading freely consenting individuals to become his political followers. The fact that the landless greatly outnumber the landowners is not a source of weakness but of strength in the latter's position. The landlords do not need to worry about how to make themselves indispensable to the landless: it is the latter who must worry about making them-selves acceptable to the landlords.

Authority and Dominant Power in Swat

I have been arguing, as against Barth, that horizontal cleavages into asymmetric classes are more important than vertical ones into homologous blocs. The tenant's class interests are always opposed to those of his landlord. This is not to say that vertical bonds between landlord and tenant are of no social consequence in Swat, but only that such bonds derive their special character from the horizontal class divisions – i.e. they are bonds of solidarity between members of exploiting and exploited classes, between those who are able to exercise significant political choice and those who are not. And as such they are quite different from the contractual relations which partly define a pure market system, in which individual buyer meets individual seller as jural equal in the unceasing pursuit of profit. For at any given moment the concrete position of the non-landowner is determined not only by the collective subordination of his class to the class of landowners, but also by the conscious ties of communal loyalty with members of his own class as well as of the ruling class. Barth himself tells us that 'The village is the most important unit of territorial reference for a Swat Pathan, and its occupants are the main focus of his loyalties' (1959a: 13). And elsewhere, reference is made to 'a strong explicit value: that one should show neighbourliness and a positive interest in the life of all members of one's local community' (p. 32). It must be emphasised that although such facts help to undermine the picture of Swat as a competitive, individualist, contractual society, they do not imply the absence of class structure and class interest. In other words, they cast doubt equally on the assertion that people's 'political loyalty is for sale to the highest bidder', and on the assumption that 'all relationships implying dominance are dyadic relationships of a contractual or voluntary nature'.

Class interest relates primarily not to individual motive or identification, but to collective position in a developing system of social reproduction and political domination. The subtle interaction between individual motive, communal loyalty and class position, through which social and political life finds expression, brings us into the realm of ideological analysis which cannot be attempted for Swat on the basis of the material given. Yet it is only when such an analysis is carried out that we can begin to answer the important question: What is it that gives members of the Pakhtun ruling class their *authority* in the eyes of their subjects?

Barth does not clearly distinguish authority from power, two concepts which, though intimately connected, are very different. For authority refers to the subordination of human consciousness to a legitimate rule (and contingently to those who determine the rule) while power refers to the relation between an agent and an object as means (that is to the opposition between exploiter and exploited).

The need for distinguishing between the two may be illustrated briefly: it would appear that, for Pakhtun chiefs, not only are power and authority combined but that in some way they tend to re-inforce each other. For Saints, on the other hand, the opposite seems to be the case. 'Truly "Saintly" behaviour implies moderation, piety, indifference to physical pleasure, and withdrawal from the petty and sordid aspects of common life' (p. 101). Where this is the source of a Saint's authority, the more saintly a man is, the smaller is his scope for exercising political power; and conversely, the more actively he exercises political power, or accumulates land and other possessions, the less saintly he becomes. Thus, if Saints in Swat are persons who are expected by most people to live a saintly life, there will presumably be a tension between their access to political power and their claim to saintly authority. But if Saints are simply big landlords claiming descent from a holy ancestor, their saintliness is equivalent to a form of social ranking, and their class position identical with that of exploitative Pakhtun landowners.

Yet although Barth does not distinguish between power and authority, he does implicitly raise the question I have just asked when he refers to the numerical preponderance and economic competence of the non-Pakhtuns. How is it, he enquires in effect, that the Pakhtun landowners can maintain their dominant position? Unfortunately the context of the whole discussion (which is about strategies of exploitation) prevents him from realising that the question has a significance for authority as well as for power.

In the domain of exploitative relations, the numerical preponderance of non-Pakhtun peasants helps to explain the fact of objective power possessed by the landowners. In the domain of authority relations, the numerical preponderance and the linked poverty of the peasants serves to define part of the problem of Pakhtun domination, a problem which must be answered in terms both of peasant modes of consciousness, and of the objective conditions of landlord power (economic and military).

It may be argued that information on non-Pakhtun peasant modes of conscious-ness is already to be found in the book's discussion of caste and lineage. But if this is so then it is evident that the book fails to make the essential distinction between the anthropological frame of reference and the indigenous ideology. The two cannot be identical if the misconceptions, distortions and contradictions contained in that ideology are not to be directly reproduced in the analysis. Thus, if the concepts of caste and lineage are to be understood as parts of Swati ideology, they must be related *critically* to the structural positions of different Swati social groups, so that it can be shown how their modes of consciousness contribute to the authoritative domination of the landowners and the exploited condition of the landless. All one can say, in the absence of the relevant ideological information, is that there is no a priori reason to assume that non-Pakhtun modes of consciousness are identical or even congruent with those of their Pakhtun or Saint landlords, since the acceptance of common authority does not exclude the presence of different modes of perceiving, evaluating and constructing the social world. And yet it is only when this kind of ideological analysis is available that we can get an adequate understanding of the historical circumstances within which class domination has taken shape in Swat.

Is the Distribution of Power in Equilibrium?

Although it is not possible to attempt an adequate analysis of Swat class structure, the fundamental political importance of class alignment can be indicated briefly yet further.

Throughout the book reference is made to landowners and non-landowners, but no systematic use is made of the distinction between *landlords* and *owner-farmers*. Of all Pakhtun landowners a very small proportion holds most of the land. So that the majority of landowners in Swat are smallholders, and the remainder possess very large estates. In other words very few Pakhtuns are in a position to make the traditional economic contracts with agricultural tenants and labourers.

The economic evidence shows that for all practical purposes the tenant has no choice whether to take up a tenancy or not, and that the taking up of a particular tenancy involves the subordination of the tenant to his landlord. In this case the leader-follower relationship simply represents the deployment of tenants, agricul-tural labourers and other insecure economic dependants in situations of open conflict. Very different is the leader-follower relationship where the latter is a Pakhtun smallholder. It is surely only in relation to this kind of follower that it might be said 'the position of a leader is never secure'. But since the numerical value of this category of following is in any case very small (Pakhtuns as a whole are greatly outnumbered by non-Pakhtuns), the leader's security is not seriously threatened by the choices of his Pakhtun peasant followers.

In any case, wealthy landlords can and do stand on their own because they control a large force of dependants. Groups of small landowners cannot wield a critical leverage as junior allies, or constitute a significant threat as members of an opposing bloc.

In terms of formal alignment, sentiment, rank, the Pakhtun smallholder belongs with the landlord. But in terms of his meagre economic resources and precarious structural position he is closer to the tenant. Hence his anomalous class position. Yet from the point of view of Swat society as a whole, the class structure seems stark and simple: on the one side a small group of dominant, wealthy landlords possessing an overwhelming proportion of the total land, on the other an overwhelming proportion of the total population owning no land. 'In the idiom of Swat Pashto, the world is divided into two kinds of people: *mōṛ saṛī*, "satisfied men", and *wúge saṛī*, "hungry men". The "satisfied men" have enough food in their storehouses to feed the families of scores of "hungry men" throughout the year' (1959a: 79). Where do the independent Pakhtun smallholders fit into this simple scheme? If the class structure is viewed in terms of (the peasant's?) ideology, they may be seen as *mōṛ saṛī*. If the class structure is represented empirically as the arrangement of social strata at a frozen instant of time, they belong with neither, but appear as one stratum among many. If the class structure is conceptualised theoretically as an unfolding process in which the life-chances of individuals are determined by the practical and ideological relationship of groups to the means of reproduction, they belong with the 'hungry men'.

> In fact the evidence indicates that in the present century the sloughing-off process [whereby Pakhtuns who lose all their land forfeit their Pakhtun status] has more than offset the natural growth of the Pakhtun population and that land has been progressively concentrated in fewer lines and fewer hands. (p. 112)

In other words the see-saw pattern that Barth postulates for the overall political system obscures the fact that small landowners are progressively eliminated. The class structure, based on the ownership of land, is revealed in the historical process of polarisation. The possibility of successfully shifting one's political alliances is only feasible for relatively powerful, ambitious landlords apparently competing among themselves, but in effect doing so at the expense of the smallholder. Indeed small landowners cannot retain their independence in the long run whatever alliances they make. And the reason for their insecurity has probably to do as much with the economic non-viability of their land holdings as with the insatiable greed of big landlords.

Since the rates of land fragmentation must be more critical for Pakhtun smallholders than for the big landlords, and the scale of agricultural debt greater among them than among the latter, there is in fact no need to attribute their insecurity to an anarchic condition of warring chiefs, or to the insatiable greed of landlords. (The book itself does not contain any information about agricultural debt, but there is published evidence of its prevalence during the early 'fifties in districts immediately neighbouring Swat.) Or to put it another way: it is difficult to see why in a non-market agrarian society, where a small class of landlords possesses disproportionate wealth, overwhelming power, and unquestioned authority, its individual members can be said to be under the *pressing need* to increase their property, even at the cost of bitter mutual hostility, in an elusive search for security.

But perhaps the answer is that there is no such pressing need. For as Barth himself notes towards the end of his article 'Segmentary Opposition and the Theory of Games':

> The interest of the chiefs in limiting the opposition between the blocs is proverbial, and has been noted by British political agents, who contrast the attitudes of young warrior 'hot-heads' with the more reasonable attitudes of chiefs and headmen. Popularly, this

interest in maintaining relative peace is related to a great variety of causes; its mere recognition is sufficient for the present argument. (1959b: 19)

Covetous, unscrupulous and even violent though some Pakhtuns may be, these facts do not add up to make of Swat an acquisitive, individualist, market-type society. On the contrary, it is likely that with the passage of time, as land became increasingly controlled by fewer families, the conditions for relatively stable class domination were enhanced, and that it was this process in turn that facilitated the successful emergence of a princely agrarian state in Swat, eventually supported and further stabilised by the Imperial Government of British India....

NOTE

I am grateful to Fredrik Barth for his detailed comments on an early draft of this article.

REFERENCES

Barth, Fredrik. (1959a) *Political Leadership among the Swat Pathans*. London: Athlone Press.
——. (1959b) Segmentary Opposition and the Theory of Games: A Study of Pathan Organization. *Journal of the Royal Anthropological Institute* 89: 5–21.
——. (1960) The System of Social Stratification in Swat, North Pakistan. In *Aspects of Caste in South India, Ceylon and North-west Pakistan*, ed. E. R. Leach. Cambridge: Cambridge University Press.
Hobbes, Thomas. (1962) *Leviathan* (Everyman edition). Introduction by A. D. Lindsay. London: J. M. Dent & Sons.

6

The Troubles of Ranhamy Ge Punchirala (X:4)

E. R. Leach

When I first arrived in Pul Eliya the villagers had no precedent for coping with an Englishman who planned a prolonged stay. The problem of where I should live evoked agitated discussion. Clearly no one wanted me to live inside the main village area. A sly suggestion from Naidurala (Dx:Y) that perhaps the Village Headman (A2:7) would let me live in his garden was quickly voted down on the grounds that the site was too damp.[1] But the opposite extreme, that I had best be kept right outside in the jungle, was too inhospitable; the site was dry and private, but I might be attacked by elephants! The compromise which put me in the derelict village dispensary...suited everyone.

I soon discovered that my immediate neighbours were the only other complete outsiders resident in the community. On the one side there was the schoolmaster, on the other R. Punchirala (X:4). Inevitably I saw a great deal of Punchirala, and his troubles fill many pages of my note-books. His 'case' illustrates so many of the themes which have been running through this book that it seems worth while to give the story at length.

On the face of it the root of the trouble is an issue of caste, and the conventional anthropological approach would be to argue that Punchirala was in difficulty over land and water *because* of his questionable caste and kinship status. And this is precisely how the villagers themselves tried to explain the matter. But caste and kinship are phenomena in the field of ideas compared with which such matters as digging irrigation ditches and going to law are objective items of behaviour. In the end it seemed to me that all the complicated arguments about Punchirala's kinship status amounted simply to a way of talking about a quarrel over land and water. Had Punchirala himself been of a less litigious nature, or had his wife been slightly less inclined to insult her neighbours, there would have been no problem. We cannot understand a trouble case of this sort without going into the intricacies of the kinship pattern; but the kinship pattern is not the *cause* of what happens, it merely provides

From *Pul Eliya: A Study of Land Tenure and Kinship* (Cambridge: Cambridge University Press, 1961), pp. 310–19.

a framework of ideas in terms of which actual behaviour may be justified. The model of correct behaviour which is provided by the kinship ideology sets limits to what may be considered reasonable behaviour; but it does not finally determine what men do.

I shall recount the story in two halves, first as an issue of caste, secondly as an issue of land and water, and I shall present both in chronological sequence. In my note-books the material is recorded in quite a different way; the latest events appear first while the caste issues and the land issues are inextricably mixed up. The reader needs to remember not only that it is the end rather than the beginning of the story which is currently important but also that the caste–land dichotomy of my story roughly corresponds to an administrative change.

From one point of view the whole tale is a long story of litigation, but whereas the first part of the case consisted of litigation in the *variga* [sub-caste] court (and was therefore couched in the language of caste and kinship), the later phases of the same case have been brought before the civil administration in the persons of the Government Agent, the D.R.O. and the V.C.O. and have, therefore, been couched in the language of agricultural economics and title to land. Punchirala (X:4), the central figure of the story, was well known to the Anurādhapura District Office (Kachcheri) as one of the most persistent litigants in the whole area; the Pul Eliya villagers' description of him as a man of wrong *variga* was another way of saying the same thing. From both points of view he was a man who did not fit, and an infernal nuisance!

The Caste Issue

Early in this century Pul Eliya had a village priest who came from Nawana in Kurunegala District. He resided in the *Vihāra* [Buddhist temple] compound. In the same compound there lived one Ranhamy (X:1), who worked as a gardener and general servant for the priest and who also came from the Nawana area, as did his wife (X:2). The precise caste status of this man is not clear; the personal names of his kinsmen indicate that he was a Goyigama. He certainly had no connection with the Pul Eliya *variga* and may have belonged to a Goyigama sub-caste which owed traditional service duties to the priesthood...

The priest was a relative of the present Kadawatgama High Priest but was, at that time, unrelated to the people of Pul Eliya. Later a lay cousin of the priest (also called Ranhamy (C:N)) came to live in Pul Eliya and married Walli Etani (C:7), daughter of Kadirathe Gamarāla (D2:C). No one made any fuss. They seem to have gone through the formality of a *variga* court case and a formal marriage ceremony; in the outcome the present Pul Eliya villagers now say that the Kadawatgama High Priest is of their *variga*.

Ranhamy (X:1), the gardener, was a popular character. When the Pul Eliya priest died and the *Vihāra* compound was left empty the Vel Vidāne of the day (Appurala Vidāne (A1:W)) helped him to purchase a *sinakkara* [freehold] house-site on Crown land (house-site 1: compound X); this was in 1921. He was not provided with any agricultural land.

When his eldest son R. Mudalihamy (X:3) grew up, the Temple connection proved useful and the Kadawatgama priest arranged for a *binna* [uxorilocal] marriage in Kadawatgama [village]. This was around 1935. This marriage failed, though only after some years, by which time the issue of Ranhamy's (X:1) *variga* had become so contentious that it seemed politic to go further away. Mudalihamy (X:3), around 1937/8, married *binna* into a well-to-do family in Syambalagaswewa [village]; this marriage was successful and later his youngest brother (X:5) married Mudalihamy's wife's 'sister' (also in *binna*).

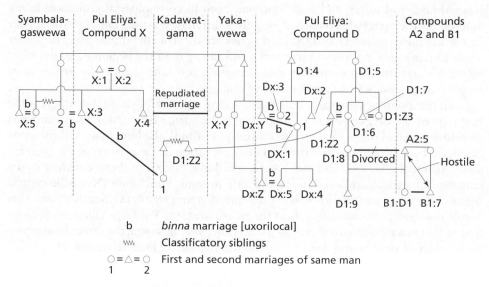

b　　　　*binna* marriage [uxorilocal]

⋙　　　Classificatory siblings

○＝△＝○　First and second marriages of same man
1　　　2

Genealogy illustrating case history material

R. Mudalihamy's second wife's mother had come from Yakawewa [village] and, through this connection, his younger brother Punchirala (X:4) arranged a *binna* marriage with S. Ran Manika (X:Y) of Yakawewa. She was mother's brother's daughter to Mudalihamy's wife. This was around 1938/9.

Punchirala's wife's father's brother's son, M. Naidurala (Dx:Y), then living in Yakawewa, was already working land in Pul Eliya which belonged to his wife (Dx:1). Punchirala's marriage was thus of a different kind from those of his brothers. Neither the Syambalagaswewa nor the Kadawatgama marriages were likely to affect Pul Eliya land rights, but if Punchirala's children were to marry Naidurala's children, as they would be expected to do, since they were affines, *their* children would have the status of Pul Eliya *minissu* [insiders].

The Yakawewa people seem to have had similar objections. However, the marriage had the approval of Punchirala Gamarāla (D2:C), the senior living member of Pul Eliya compound D, and also of the Pul Eliya Vel Vidāne, Mudalihamy Baddarāla (B1:3), who was an officer of the *variga* court. The *variga* court duly met and fined R. Punchirala (X:4); Punchirala paid the fine and became thereby, in his own estimation, a fully qualified member of the Pul Eliya *variga*.

But evidently the court's decision was not generally acceptable for, on the death of Mudalihamy Baddarāla (B1:3) which occurred around 1940, the case was somehow or other reopened. This time the *variga* court disintegrated without being able to produce any agreed ruling and a major row ensued. Naidurala (Dx:Y) and his 'brother-in-law', R. Punchirala (X:4), fled from Yakawewa and in 1941 set up house in Pul Eliya compound Dx. This land, which Naidurala now holds on *badu* [Crown] lease, had previously been held by Punchirala Gamarāla (D2:C) on similar terms. At the same time J. Punchirala (Dx:2), Naidurala's wife's brother, who had until this time been living in Pul Eliya compound D1, found it politic to leave home and go to live with his wife's people in Watarekkewa [village].

At this time Ranhamy (X:1), the gardener, was still alive and still living in compound X, but he evidently kept out of the dispute. At his death his son, R. Punchirala (X:4), moved from compound Dx to compound X.

In 1954 R. Punchirala still laid great stress on the fact that he was Naidurala's *massinā* [cross-cousin], and Naidurala did not deny the relationship. But R. Punchirala was never invited to any family or village gathering (other than a house-building *kayiya* [work-team] in Naidurala's compound). In contrast Naidurala had become so wealthy and influential that, in the Vel Vidāne's estimation, he was the fourth senior individual in the village – the official 'Pangu List' placed Naidurala immediately after the Vel Vidāne (B1:7), the Village Headman (A2:7) and the ex-Vel Vidāne (A2:4).

Meanwhile J. Punchirala (Dx:2) had returned from Watarekkewa and was living in compound Dx with Naidurala; Naidurala's son, N. Punchi Banda (Dx:4), had built himself a house in compound D1.

In 1954 R. Punchirala (X:4) held land totalling 2 acres (plot 118) and his Syambalagaswewa brother R. Mudalihamy (X:3) owned of an acre (plot III), leased *andē* [share-cropping] to R. Punchirala. Neither brother owned any land in the Old Field. In the 'old days', before the days of *sinakkara* and *badu* plots, the kind of ostracism which the Pul Eliya villagers applied would have forced R. Punchirala to leave the village.

Since he had not done so, but had instead fought back with every legal means he could lay hands on, a kind of guerrilla warfare had developed, with the unanimous villagers on one side and the embattled R. Punchirala, relying on government protection, on the other. But the issues involved were not simply those of caste purity. Nor was the Kadawatgama marriage of R. Punchirala's brother quite so irrelevant as I have here implied.

The Land and Water Issue

To understand the territorial context of R. Punchirala's troubles we need to start elsewhere and to remember that the long-term factionalism of the community... has ranged compound D with compound C in opposition to the alliance between compounds A and B. In 1920 luck was running strongly in favour of the A + B group as represented by the Vel Vidāne, Appurala Vidāne (A1:W) and his son-in-law, W. Mudalihamy (B1:3).

This was a period when the possibility of purchasing *sinakkara* fields gave an outstanding advantage to the Vel Vidāne and his close friends. The government authorities were eager to award *sinakkara* grants, so the main problem from the villagers' point of view was that of irrigation. It was no good applying for land until you could be certain of a water supply. Around 1919 Punchirala Gamarāla (D2:C), who had his eye on the land now represented by plots 138–47, had tried his hand at constructing an irrigation channel which would feed this land, but he got his levels wrong, and the water flowed the other way. Next year, when U. Kadirathe (A2:4) tried his hand at the same task, the new trace proved entirely satisfactory and it became plainer than ever that compound A was being favoured by the planetary deities. Observing this, A. Mudalihamy (D1:Z2) took the unprecedented step of marrying off his daughter Ukkuhamy (D1:8) to U. Sirala (A2:5), Kadirathe's younger brother, instead of reserving her for someone in compound C as precedent might have suggested.

In 1921 Kadirathe and his three brothers (U. Sirala (A2:5), U. G. Pinhamy (H:A2), U. Wannihamy (A2:6)) and their new *māmā* [mother's brother], A. Mudalihamy (D1:Z2), formed a partnership and obtained a *sinakkara* grant to the 9-acre block represented by plots 141–7, and the following year they applied in the same way for the $4\frac{3}{4}$-acre block represented by plots 138–40a. Of the total $13\frac{3}{4}$ acres, the allocations were: Kadirathe 5, Sirala $1\frac{1}{2}$, U. G. Pinhamy 4, Mudalihamy 2, Wannihamy $1\frac{1}{4}$. Kadirathe's extra share was because of his skill as irrigation engineer; U. G. Pinhamy got extra because his father-in-law Appurala Vidāne (A2:W) put up part of the capital; Wannihamy got least because he was only a boy of 10. A. Mudalihamy (D1:Z2) provided the capital for Sirala's share and K. Murugathe (A2:3) found the money for Wannihamy.

Meanwhile similar developments were taking place on the other side of the Old Field. In 1922/3 Appurala Vidāne (A2:W) in partnership with K. Velathe (B1:6) and P. Jangurala (D1:4) acquired the *sinakkara* land represented by plots 120–3, 125–7. Here again compound D1, in the person of P. Jangurala, was allied with compounds A and B instead of with compound C.

But Punchirala Gamarāla (D2:C) was still influential. He made life so unpleasant for his D1 group neighbours that when P. Jangurala died in 1924 his 'son', A. Mudalihamy (D1:Z2), purchased a house-site right outside the village and went to live there.

As time went on A. Mudalihamy's relations with his son-in-law Sirala (A2:5) deteriorated but even so, around 1938/9, he married one of his granddaughters to Sirala's sister's son, V. Menikrala (B1:7), thus further consolidating his alliance with the dominant faction in the community.

Now A. Mudalihamy (D1:Z2) had come from Kadawatgama and, in an exchange marriage, his brother-in-law, K. Pinhamy (D1:7) had married Mudalihamy's sister, A. Sitti Etani (D1:Z3). This latter couple, who had originally lived *binna* in Kadawatgama, joined up with A. Mudalihamy (D1:Z2) in Pul Eliya around 1936.

It was about this time that R. Punchirala's eldest brother (X:3) had married *binna* in Kadawatgama. The girl in question was a distant niece ('brother's daughter') to Mudalihamy. This placed him under a potential caste taint in much the same way as M. Naidurala (Dx:Y) later became tainted by his 'sister's' marriage to R. Punchirala (X:4). Moreover, since Naidurala's wife and Mudalihamy's wife were cross-cousins, the whole of Pul Eliya compound D1 had become indirectly tainted by these two wrong *variga* marriages.

At this point, that is around 1938/40, a series of disasters made it evident that compound D1 was altogether out of favour with the planetary deities.

The usual Pul Eliya version was that K. Pinhamy (D1:7) unearthed some temple treasure while assisting his cross-cousin J. Punchirala (Dx:2) to cultivate (illicitly) part of plot 124. He had been chased home by the spirit guardian of the treasure and that night he and his daughter died in agony. A Mudalihamy (D1:Z2) died a few days later. At this time Mudalihamy's *sinakkara* land was all on *andē* to his son-in-law U. Sirala (A2:5), who chose this moment to divorce his wife Ukkuhamy (D1:8) and misappropriate the land. A violent quarrel ensued between Sirala and the members of compound B1, particularly V. Menikrala (B1:7), who had been expecting his wife to inherit a part of Mudalihamy's land.... What followed is obscure.

Ukkuhamy's relatives sued Sirala in the government court, but meanwhile Sirala had adroitly managed to transfer the title of the land to his elder brother U. G. Pinhamy (H:A2), a circumstance which was aided by the fact that the Vel Vidāne Mudalihamy (B1:3) had just died and been succeeded by Sirala's brother, Kadirathe (A2:4). Sirala spent a period in gaol, but afterwards got the land back (or at any rate most of it). The bitter enmity between Sirala and his son-in-law Menikrala (B1:7) dates from this point in the story.

The sudden collapse of the fortunes of compound D1 through death and litigation provided the spark to generate caste and witchcraft animosities. A. Mudalihamy's widow, K. Punchi Etani (D1:6), drove her sister-in-law A. Sitti Etani (D1:Z3) out of the house, saying that she must have been responsible for the deaths of Mudalihamy (D1:Z2) and Pinhamy (D1:7). At the same time the Yakawewa people expelled M. Naidurala (Dx:Y) and R. Punchirala (X:4). The real connection between the two cases is remote, but the common element of caste taint was present in both of them and this served to canalise the animosities of Pul Eliya public opinion.

By a complex process of reasoning the deaths of Mudalihamy Badderāla (B1:3), A. Mudalihamy (D1:Z2), K. Pinhamy (D1:7) and Pinhamy's daughter were all held to have been 'caused by' the wrong *variga* marriages of Ranhamy's sons (X:3 and X:4).

But the caste scandal would soon have been forgiven had not R. Punchirala (X:4) got himself entangled in a major economic feud with the members of compounds B1 and A2.

Here we must go back again. The development of Plot 3D (plots 108–17) under the leadership of Appurala Vidāne (A1:W) has been outlined [already]. Plot 111 and the uncleared strip 'b' were there allocated to Appurala Vidāne's half-brother Kirihamy (W:5). Appurala Vidāne also had a foster-daughter Kiri Etani, who married one P. V. Bandathe (Z(A1)) in Walpola. Kirihamy mortgaged his land to a trader Antoni in Wiralmurippu and then married *binna* in Kadawatgama where he struck up a friendship with R. Mudalihamy (X:3), who was then married there. On his deathbed Kirihamy gave the mortgage deed to Kiri Etani, but at the same time suggested to R. Mudalihamy that, since P. V. Bandathe was blind, he might be able to buy out the rights. R. Mudalihamy in fact purchased the mortgage deed and later redeemed the land, thus becoming a Pul Eliya landowner. This was land which, in the ordinary way of things, should have passed to the direct heirs of Appurala Vidāne, that is to members of Pul Eliya compounds A1 and B1.

By 1954 R. Mudalihamy (X:3) was safely out of the way in Syambalagaswewa, but he still owned the land in plot 3D which was regularly leased *andē* to his brother R. Punchirala (X:4). Thus the quarrel with the heirs of Appurala Vidāne continued unabated.

To make matters worse R. Punchirala (X:4) had become the owner, on *badu* title, of plot 118. Many years ago K. Velathe (B1:6) had sought to purchase this land on *sinakkara* grant and had actually 'asweddumised' it and cultivated it 'illicitly' for

several years. Then the Land Office had ruled that this land lay outside the boundaries of Pul Eliya village and title had reverted to the Crown. But around 1946 the
Land Office had changed their policy about village boundaries and had allocated the
plot *badu* to R. Punchirala (X:4). Velathe's son V. Menikrala (B1:7) had appealed
but lost his case. So R. Punchirala had added to his troubles by earning the enmity of
the Pul Eliya Vel Vidāne.

Although by 1952 R. Punchirala had personal title to plot 118, and *andē* title to
plot 111, his enemies could still make things very difficult for him by cutting off his
water supply.

The obvious way to irrigate plot 118 would be to draw off water from the bottom
corner of plots 116–17, but these belonged to Punchirala's enemies, V. Menikrala
(B1:7) and A. V. Punchi Etani (B1:A1).

After a series of lawsuits on the subject, R. Punchirala constructed an irrigation
ditch δ–γ through the uncleared strip 'b' which belongs to his brother R. Mudalihamy (X:3). He then tried to tap this into the main channel α–β which feeds the
strips of plot 3D. Again he ran into the difficulty that in order to reach the main
channel his feed channel must at some point cross land which was owned or claimed
either by Menikrala (B1:7) or by the descendants of Appurala Vidāne (A1:W).
Punchirala constructed his channel but his opponents blocked it up again. They
were always careful to stick to their strict legal rights. The block was always made
on private land, never on Crown territory.

In 1953 R. Punchirala had got to the point of threatening murder, but he had
somehow or other made his peace with V. Menikrala (B1:7). His enmity with
A. V. Punchi Etani (B1:A1) continued. He had arranged to extend his channel
through to plot 124.

The point of this is that Punchirala's 'brother-in-law' Naidurala had lately been
redeveloping plot 124. This is, strictly speaking, 'encroached Crown land'. It is also,
by reputation, haunted land, and it was through digging here that K. Pinhamy
(D1:7) had met his death. M. Naidurala (Dx:Y) had ingeniously restored a small
tank known as Kana-hiti-yawa which he claimed would supply his encroached field.
In actual fact by a private arrangement with the Vel Vidāne he also drew water from
the main tank.

In 1954, Punchirala's channel δ–γ had been extended north and tapped into
Naidurala's channel from Kana-hiti-yawa. It was quite obvious that Naidurala
found this extremely inconvenient from every point of view, but R. Punchirala was
his *massinā* [cross-cousin]. Naidurala did not assist Punchirala to dig the ditch, but
he did not block it up when it had been dug. Whether this really marked R.
Punchirala's final victory I do not know. If he goes on residing in Pul Eliya he will
permanently remain an outsider until he can behave in a sufficiently politic manner
to marry off one or more of his children to a Pul Eliya resident.

So long as there is no such marriage alliance everyone will continue to point out
that he is not of 'our *variga*'; he is not a recognised relative. But a switch of attitude
could easily take place. In 1954 his eldest son was already 14 years old. If it should
suit everyone's convenience, the caste issue would vanish overnight. I should not be
surprised to learn that by this time R. Punchirala's son has married the daughter of
his 'enemy' V. Menikrala.

If we look at the whole story in its historical perspective as I have presented it here
we see that the initial crisis was really the divorce of S. Jaymanhamy's parents,

U. Sirala (A2:5) and Ukkuhamy (D1:8) and the total disintegration of compound D1 which followed. Yet despite lawsuits, witchcraft accusations and all the rest, S. Jaymanhamy (D1:9) remained Sirala's heir, and in 1954 there was something of a *rapprochement* between father and son. In that year Sirala and Jaymanhamy worked a *vi hena* [highland plot] together, an unprecedented event which evoked much favourable comment in the village.

To the reader it may seem that Sirala's divorce and R. Punchirala's troubles are independent events, but from the village point of view they were, in some rather undefined way, aspects of the same thing. It was not accidental that in the year that U. Sirala began to make peace with Jaymanhamy, M. Naidurala's family should start moving back into compound D1 and R. Punchirala's water problems should at last find a partial solution.

It was on the same day that I had been discussing with B. Ausadahamy (A2:7) this favourable turn of events that Ausadahamy remarked for the first time that S. Jaymanhamy's father-in-law (a resident of Kadawatgama) was after all a distant '*ayiya*' ('elder brother') of R. Punchirala; however, he did not take the further step of admitting his own quite close relationship with R. Punchirala's wife.

The point I want to make is that R. Punchirala's caste troubles were quite 'real' in that they affected the behaviour of his neighbours, but since they corresponded to nothing substantial, they might disappear at any time.

The *variga* ostracism which kept R. Punchirala in the status of outsider was not simply a private game played by the Pul Eliya villagers for their own amusement, but part of an agreed pattern of behaviours.

NOTE

1 The names of the places and people recorded in Pul Eliya are the actual names recorded by Leach in the field. The mention of a name is usually accompanied by a code number, thus: Ranhamy Ge Punchirala (X:4). The letter and figure to the left of the colon indicate where the individual normally resides; the letter and figure to the right, where the individual was born. (Ed.)

7

Stratagems and Spoils

F. G. Bailey

In 1963 I watched on television in America an enquiry by a committee of their Senate into a criminal organization called *cosa nostra* ('our thing' or 'our affair'). A man named Vallachi, once a member of the organization, had been persuaded to 'sing', and for several days a large television audience watched and listened while he spoke in an unassuming, undramatic, friendly, indeed almost homely fashion, about the techniques of crime, about the contests for gang leadership, about violence and about murder.

The 'Vallachi hearings', as they were called, aroused a great deal of local interest. Much of the cross-examination was reported verbatim in the newspapers, especially those parts which enlivened local history by revealing that it was in the nearby town that X had arranged for the murder of Y or that one of the leaders of *cosa nostra* (which the newspapers also called the 'Mafia') had been a locally resident and apparently respectable businessman. The television performances gripped their audience because they showed a contest between Vallachi and his cross-examiners, because they were about life-and-death struggles for power in the criminal world, and because they revealed a degree of organization in that criminal world, which, although revealed many times before, continued both to frighten and to fascinate. The casting too, if one may put it like that, was good: particularly striking were Vallachi's patient and good-humoured explanations to one of his senatorial inquisitors who appeared to be slow-witted. Finally there was always the chance that the *cosa nostra* might silence Vallachi by murdering him: it might even be seen on the television.

At first sight it is the history (and possibility) of violence which fascinates in an affair like this. But interest was in fact sustained not by the stories of murders and massacres but by the revealed orderliness of the criminal world. Of course one quickly understands that large scale rackets have to be run on businesslike principles. But beyond this, even when *cosa nostra* leaders fought and murdered one another to

From *Stratagems and Spoils: A Social Anthropology of Politics* (Oxford: Blackwell Publishers, 1969), pp. vii–viii, 1–7.

gain supremacy, they seemed to do so in predictable ways, even, one might say, according to the rules of their game. Certainly, leaving aside the question of how consciously the gangsters themselves thought in terms of right and wrong conduct within their own world, the manoeuvres in which they engaged were capable of being analysed. Indeed, for a tantalizingly brief moment, there appeared on the television screen charts which showed the process by which one leader replaced another.

Those charts, of which I had no more than a glimpse and have never seen again, started this book. After looking at them for a few seconds, and taking in the pattern of competitive interaction which they pictured, I had the strongest of feelings that I had seen them before. At first I thought they might have been in a newspaper report of an earlier day's hearings; but this was not so. Then I realized that while I had not seen those particular charts before, I was familiar with the pattern of interaction which they described. Not long before I had been arguing about it with some of my colleagues and with students: it was a pattern of contests for leadership described by a Norwegian anthropologist, Fredrik Barth, writing about the Swat Pathans, who live near the north-western frontier of Pakistan. The people of Swat and the criminals of the American *cosa nostra* arranged their violent successions in broadly the same fashion.

So what? What does it matter to any civilized person if they do? What conceivable benefit, intellectual or otherwise, can be got out of knowing a fact like that? The behaviour of murderous ruffians, whether they belong in the backward mountain vastnesses of Asia or in the barbarous enclaves that remain in our civilized societies of the west, may be of use to the world of entertainment, but it has nothing to do with the world of science and learning. Social anthropology, it seems, picks on the exotic and the eccentric and the deviant and the aberrant: it cannot deal with the normal and the usual. The subject is, as one particularly obtuse critic said, merely barbarology; and my implied excitement at discovering the Pathans behaved like the *cosa nostra* gangsters would have confirmed him in this view.

Games, Fights and Politics

To make a beginning, think of politics as a competitive game. Games are orderly. Although the competitors are matched against one another, and may even dislike one another, the fact that they are playing a game means that they agree about how to play and what to play for. They agree that the prize is worth having and they accept some basic rules of conduct. A game is not a game if the outcome of the contest is certain: consequently the players must, within limits, be evenly matched. The weaker player should have, as we say, at least a sporting chance of winning. Furthermore, conduct which would make it impossible to play the game again is forbidden. Although particular opponents may be eliminated (and elimination is, of course, defined by the rules of the game), the total elimination of all opponents would mean that the game could never again be played. In short, rules are an essential part of games: indeed, in a sense a game *is* a set of rules, for it can only be defined by a statement of these rules.

Up to a point, this is true of a political structure: this, too, is a set of rules for regulating competition: beyond that point politics ceases to be a competition and becomes a fight, in which the objective (we cannot call it a prize, as we can in a game) is not to defeat the opposition in an orderly 'sporting' contest, but to destroy one 'game' and establish a different set of rules

But, it may be objected, the comparison between a game and politics is inept because politics is a serious business, while games are, by definition, trivial. Dejected losers are comforted, and puffed-up victors deflated by being told 'It's only a game'; meaning that games are a side-affair which are not to be compared with, nor allowed to interfere with, the serious side of life, with education, with making a living, and so forth. Sometimes people say of politics that it too is only a game: but this is only said in moments of anger or cynicism and the claim has an air of paradox not present when applied to actual games.

On the other hand there is a sense in which politics *are* secondary. When politics interfere with raising families or producing enough to eat, then people say that something has gone wrong with that political structure. This can happen when politics has ceased to be an orderly competition and become a fight: when conflict takes place without the control of an agreed set of rules; when, it seems, few holds are barred because the fight is to decide which set of rules will in future regulate political competition.

Some of my readers may already be thinking that 'real politics' – the politics which matter – are what I have just been calling fights. The day-to-day routine of Westminster, the complex but almost wholly predictable manoeuvres of American pressure politics certainly have an intellectual fascination. Yet, somehow, they seem less important than those occasions when history leaps suddenly in a new direction – the coup of 1967 in Greece, the Congo disorders or the less violent emergence of other new nations, the Russian Revolution and so forth.

But what is the meaning of 'important'? Coups and revolutions are certainly more violent and more dramatic than the Westminster routine. But surely it is impossible to assert, in any absolute sense, that they are more important. Importance is relative to the values of whoever is making the judgement: it is not an attribute of events themselves.

Furthermore, understanding and analysing routine and relatively orderly politics is not an entirely different business from making sense of revolutions. In both, one has to ask questions about leaders and how they attract and hold and reward followers, how they take decisions and how they settle disputes among their followers. In both kinds of conflict there is an idiom of confrontation and encounter. Moreover, even in revolutions, some holds are in fact barred because, for one reason or another, they damage the attacker as well as his victim.

Even in 'real politics' – the politics of coups and revolutions – there are rules of how to get things done. These are not rules in the sense of moral directives mutually agreed between the contestants, but rules which recommend courses of action as being effective. These same 'pragmatic rules' (to be described shortly) exist also in orderly politics...

Let us begin by looking at an example.

How to Play and How to Win

In the autumn of 1935, when Harold Nicolson was about to become a candidate for Parliament, he went to see his cousin.[1]

Having dressed soberly but not unimpressively, I went to see Buck De LaWarr in the Ministry of Agriculture. He was very pleasant and cousinly. I told him I was in a difficulty. I knew nothing whatsoever about the rules of the game. In fact my ignorance of even the elements was as if a man sitting down to play bridge with Mrs Keppel were to exclaim brightly, 'Tell me, Alice, are those clover-shaped cards spades or diamonds?'

In saying this, Nicolson was not undervaluing himself as a politician or as a potential Member of Parliament: he was merely disclaiming any expertise in electioneering. An electoral contest was a kind of game, with rules of fair play, and other kinds of rules about how to win, and of these – he said – he knew nothing.

So they began to teach him.

[Jarvis] began by saying that it was most important that I should stand as 'The National Government Candidate' and not as 'National Labour'. I let Buck answer that point as I am all at sea about these labels. Buck said he agreed. I said, 'But supposing people ask me what party I belong to, what am I to say?' Buck said that I must say that I was a follower of Ramsay MacDonald. The conversation went on in this way with me sitting all good and quiet on the sofa. Then I realised that something must be done. I said it was no use asking me about these things, but that what was important was that I should not get a single vote under false pretences. I would be anything they liked except all things to all men. I would not pretend to be a Tory to catch the Tory vote and so on. I would get muddled if my own position was not quite clear and straight from the start. 'I am very bad,' I said, 'at *prolonged* deception.' Anyhow they agreed and told me not to fuss about MY HONOUR.

Almost the same thing happened when the lesson was continued at Leicester, where he was standing.

I sat there twiddling my hat while I was discussed as if I were not present. They decided that I should stand as British Government candidate. Then I intervened. I said that was all very well. But that in fact I was standing as National Labour. I was quite prepared to call myself a 'National Candidate', but if asked, I should reply that I was a supporter of Ramsay MacDonald. They said that this would lose me votes. I said that if I suppressed the fact, I should be getting votes under false pretences. I would never agree to that. They looked down their noses. Mr. Flaxman said angrily, 'But surely, Mr. Nicolson, you do not suppose that a General Election is a vestry meeting?' I said that I would not stand as a candidate unless I started on an open and honest basis. Mr. Flaxman cast up his hands in horror. Jarvis said, 'Yes, you're right. Quite right.'

The two latter passages describe part of the lesson which Harold Nicolson received in how to win an election. He was being taught the rules of how to win the game, in particular a rule which says, very simply 'Don't link yourself with parties or people whom the electors don't like': or, more specifically in this case, 'Don't call yourself Labour if you hope to get Liberal and Tory votes.' Rules like this are not what we usually mean by 'rules of the game': they are practical instructions about how to win. . . . These are *pragmatic* rules.

It seems, however, that for Harold Nicolson certain other rules were sacred and could not be sacrificed even to win an election. He wanted to be honest: and said so. His advisers . . . clearly thought this sentiment inappropriate: something, no doubt, which would sound well from the platform but did not belong in the Committee Rooms. But, after all, he was a beginner and so they humoured him by saying that he was quite right, but telling him that he should not fuss about HIS HONOUR (his capitals). Rules which express such ultimate and publicly acceptable values are called *normative* rules. Besides, he was learning the language of practical politics quickly enough to add that he was no good at *prolonged* (his italics) deception and would surely trip himself up. In this way he reinforced a rule which he saw as an ultimate value to be publicly pronounced 'One must be honest' with a pragmatic rule: 'It pays to be honest'. . . .

In this way politics has its public face (normative rules) and its private wisdom (pragmatic rules). My interest is largely in the latter kind of rule: that is, not so much in the ideals and ends and standards which people set themselves in public affairs, but rather how they set about winning. *This does not mean that I will be talking only about how individuals advance themselves: it is the tactics which are of interest, and the same tactics, by and large, apply whether it is a principle or an individual which is being advanced.*

The distinction between the two kinds of rule is important and requires elaboration.

Normative rules do not prescribe a particular kind of action, but rather set broad limits to possible actions. They leave some choice about what exactly the player will do. Some normative rules, like those implied in the concept of 'honesty' or 'sportsmanship', are extremely vague, and the most disparate kind of conduct can be condemned or defended in their name. Other rules, like the rule requiring that the referee shall be obeyed, are more precise: but even here there is a leeway for interpretation both because the word 'obedience' is itself vague, and through the notion that referees can exceed their powers and so forfeit the right to obedience.

Normative rules are very general guides to conduct; they are used to judge particular actions ethically right or wrong; and within a particular political structure they can be used to justify *publicly* a course of conduct. Use in this way is probably the readiest test of whether or not a particular rule is to be given normative status. For example, I can think of no part of our own society where a leader can say 'I did this because I enjoy ordering people about and I like to be famous': but he can say 'I did this for the common good.'

The further directives which come into existence to fill the empty spaces left by norms, are the pragmatic rules. These recommend tactics and manoeuvres as likely to be the most efficient: whether the scrum shall pack 3–2–3 or 3–4–1, in what conditions to bring on the slow bowlers, whether to box defensively or aggressively, how to dress when being interviewed by one's sponsor, and so forth. Pragmatic rules are statements not about whether a particular line of conduct is just or unjust, but about whether or not it will be effective. They are normatively neutral. They may operate within the limits set by the rules of the game: or they may not. They range from rules of 'gamesmanship' (how to win without actually cheating) to rules which advise on how to win by cheating without being disqualified (what may be done, for example, on the 'blind' side of the referee in the boxing ring).

Such devices are known to those who sit on committees, and some have been recorded in *Microcosmographia Academica*. When bankrupt of good arguments to defeat a motion, openly accept the principle of the motion but suggest that the wording could be improved. Cornford calls it 'starting a comma', picturing the pack of committeemen in full cry after the hare of punctuation. This at least delays acceptance of the motion if it does not wreck it altogether.[2]

Frankenberg, writing about a village in North Wales, tells of an acrimonious committee meeting, in which one side alleged that a certain matter had been agreed at their previous meeting, while the other claimed that it had not. They called for the minute book, but the secretary said that she had left it at home. When they offered to fetch it, she said that she had not written up the minutes. The secretary was on the side of those who had opposed the motion.[3]

There are hundreds of other examples of how people try to win their way in political competition, displaying a private wisdom which lies behind the public face of politics. Each culture – English politicians, academics, villagers in Wales, villagers in India, villagers anywhere, a Vatican Council, the racketeers of the American cities as revealed in Whyte's book[4] or in the 1963 Senate hearings, when Vallachi took the lid off the *cosa nostra* – each culture has its own set of rules for political manipulation, its own language of political wisdom and political action. Like Harold Nicolson, you have to learn the appropriate language and the rules of the game before you can play effectively. Those stately manoeuvres which C. P. Snow[5] lovingly describes would not be effective among the *cosa nostra*, because the racketeers would literally not understand the signals which were being transmitted.

Nevertheless, one may look for similarities behind the wide variation. Just as different languages may have similar structures, so there may be a common structure behind the different kinds of 'private wisdom'. C. P. Snow's language of manoeuvre and the language of the *cosa nostra* may be structurally similar. Each culture – parliamentary elections, Welsh villages, American racketeers and the rest – has its own idiomatic set of rules which summarize its own political wisdom. Nevertheless, they have something in common, which makes it possible for us to look for the essentials of political manoeuvre, whatever be the culture.

NOTES

1 These extracts are taken from Nicolson 1966. The quotations are on pages 216, 217 and 219 respectively.
2 See Cornford 1953, p. 21.
3 See Frankenberg 1957, p. 140.
4 See Whyte 1943, Part II.
5 See, for example, *The Masters* or *The Corridors of Power*.

REFERENCES

Cornford, F. (1953) *Microcosmographia Academica*. Cambridge: Bowes and Bowes.
Frankenberg, R. (1957) *Village on the Border*. London: Cohen and West.
Nicolson, H. (1966) *Diaries and Letters, 1930–1939*. London: Collins.
Snow, C. P. (1951) *The Masters*. London: Macmillan.
——. (1964) *The Corridors of Power*. London: Macmillan.
Whyte, W. (1943) *Street Corner Society: The Social Structure of an Italian Slum*. Chicago: University of Chicago Press.

8

Passages, Margins, and Poverty: Religious Symbols of Communitas

Victor W. Turner

This chapter is concerned with the study of a modality of social interrelatedness which I have called "communitas" in my book *The Ritual Process*, and which I oppose to the concept of social structure. Communitas is a fact of everyone's experience, yet it has almost never been regarded as a reputable or coherent object of study by social scientists. It is, however, central to religion, literature, drama, and art, and its traces may be found deeply engraven in law, ethics, kinship, and even economics. It becomes visible in tribal rites of passage, in millenarian movements, in monasteries, in the counterculture, and on countless informal occasions. In this chapter I shall try to define more explicitly what I mean by "communitas" and by "structure." Something should be said about the kind of cultural phenomena that started me on this quest for communitas. Three aspects of culture seemed to me to be exceptionally well endowed with ritual symbols and beliefs of non-social-structural type. These may be described, respectively, as liminality, outsiderhood, and structural inferiority.

Liminality is a term borrowed from Arnold van Gennep's formulation of *rites de passage*, "transition rites" – which accompany every change of state or social position, or certain points in age. These are marked by three phases: separation, margin (or *limen* – the Latin for threshold, signifying the great importance of real or symbolic thresholds at this middle period of the rites ...), and reaggregation.

The first phase, separation, comprises symbolic behavior signifying the detachment of the individual or the group from either an earlier fixed point in the social structure or from an established set of cultural conditions (a "state"). During the intervening liminal period, the state of the ritual subject (the "passenger," or "liminar") becomes ambiguous, neither here nor there, betwixt and between all fixed points of classification; he passes through a symbolic domain that has few or none of the attributes of his past or coming state. In the third phase the passage is consummated and the ritual subject, the neophyte or initiand re-enters the social structure, often, but not always at a higher status level. Ritual degradation occurs as well as

From *Dramas, Fields and Metaphors: Symbolic Action in Human Society* (Ithaca: Cornell University Press, 1974), pp. 231–4, 237–8, 241–3, 245–6, 268–70.

elevation. Courts martial and excommunication ceremonies create and represent descents, not elevations. Excommunication rituals were performed in the narthex or porch of a church, not in the nave or main body, from which the excommunicated was being expelled symbolically. But in liminality, the symbolism almost everywhere indicates that the initiand...is structurally if not physically invisible in terms of his culture's standard definitions and classifications. He has been divested of the outward attributes of structural position, set aside from the main arenas of social life in a seclusion lodge or camp, and reduced to an equality with his fellow initiands regardless of their preritual status. I would argue that it is in liminality that communitas emerges, if not as a spontaneous expression of sociability, at least in a cultural and normative form – stressing equality and comradeship as norms rather than generating spontaneous and existential communitas, though of course spontaneous communitas may and does arise in most cases of protracted initiation ritual.

As well as the betwixt- and-between state of liminality there is the state of outsiderhood, referring to the condition of being either permanently and by ascription set outside the structural arrangements of a given social system, or being situationally or temporarily set apart, or voluntarily setting oneself apart from the behavior of status-occupying, role-playing members of that system. Such outsiders would include, in various cultures, shamans, diviners, mediums, priests, those in monastic seclusion, hippies, hoboes, and gypsies. They should be distinguished from "marginals," who are simultaneously members (by ascription, optation, self-definition, or achievement) of two or more groups whose social definitions and cultural norms are distinct from, and often even opposed to, one another (see Stonequist 1937; Znaniecki and Thomas 1918). These would include migrant foreigners, second-generation Americans, persons of mixed ethnic origin, parvenus (upwardly mobile marginals), the déclassés (downwardly mobile marginals), migrants from country to city, and women in a changed, nontraditional role. What is interesting about such marginals is that they often look to their group of origin, the so-called inferior group, for communitas, and to the more prestigious group in which they mainly live and in which they aspire to higher status as their structural reference group. Sometimes they become radical critics of structure from the perspective of communitas, sometimes they tend to deny the affectually warmer and more egalitarian bond of communitas. Usually they are highly conscious and self-conscious people and may produce from their ranks a disproportionately high number of writers, artists, and philosophers....Marginals like liminars are also betwixt and between, but unlike ritual liminars they have no cultural assurance of a final stable resolution of their ambiguity. Ritual liminars are often moving symbolically to a higher status, and their being stripped of status temporarily is a "ritual," an "as-if," or "make-believe" stripping dictated by cultural requirements.

The third major aspect of culture that is of concern to the student of religion and symbolism is "structural inferiority." This again may be an absolute or a relative, a permanent or a transient matter. Especially in caste or class systems of social stratification we have the problem of the lowest status, of the outcast, the unskilled worker, the *harijan*, and the poor. A rich mythology has grown around the poor, as also has the "pastoral" genre of literature (according to W. Empson); and in religion and art, the peasant, the beggar, the *harijan*, Gandhi's "children of God," the despised and rejected in general, have often been assigned the symbolic function of representing humanity, without status qualifications or characteristics. Here the lowest represents the human total, the extreme case most fittingly portrays the whole. In many tribal or preliterate societies, with little in the way of stratification along class lines, structural inferiority often emerges as a value-bearer whenever structural strength is dichotomously opposed to structural weakness. For example, many African societies have been formed by militarily more powerful incomers conquering the indigenous people. The invaders control high political office, such as the kingship, provincial governorships, and headmanships. On the other hand, the indigenous people, through their leaders, frequently are held to have a mystical power over the fertility of the earth and of all upon it. These autochthonous people have religious power, the "power of the weak" as against the jural-political power of the strong, and represent the undivided land itself as against the political system with its internal segmentation and hierarchies of authority. Here the model of an undifferentiated whole whose units are total human beings is posited against that of a differentiated system, whose units are status and roles, and where the social persona is segmentalized into positions in a structure....

...Here I must pause to consider once more the difference between structure and communitas. Implicitly or explicitly, in societies at all levels of complexity, a contrast is posited between the notion of society as a differentiated, segmented system of structural positions (which may or may not be arranged in a hierarchy), and society as a homogeneous, undifferentiated *whole*. The first model approximates to the preliminary picture I have presented of "social structure." Here the units are statuses and roles, not concrete human individuals. The individual is segmentalized into roles which he plays. Here the unit is what Radcliffe-Brown has called the *persona*, the role-mask, not the unique individual. The second model, communitas, often appears culturally in the guise of an Edenic, paradisiacal, utopian, or millennial state of affairs, to the attainment of which religious or political action, personal or collective, should be directed. Society is pictured as a communitas of free and equal comrades – of total persons. "Societas," or "society," as we all experience it, is a process involving both social structure and communitas, separately and united in varying proportions....

...Simpler societies seem to feel that only a person temporarily without status, property, rank, or office is fit to receive the tribal gnosis or occult wisdom which is in effect knowledge of what the tribespeople regard as the deep structure of culture and indeed of the universe. The content of such knowledge, is, of course, dependent on the degree of scientific and technological development, but, so Lévi-Strauss argues, the "savage" mental structure which can be disengaged from the palpable integument of what often seem to us bizarre modes of symbolic representation is identical with our own mental structure. We share with primitive men, he holds, the same mental habits of thinking in terms of binary discriminations or oppositions; like them, too, we have rules, including deep structural rules, governing the combination, segregation, mediation, and transformation of ideas and relations.

Now men who are heavily involved in jural-political, overt, and conscious structure are not free to meditate and speculate on the combinations and oppositions of thought; they are themselves too crucially involved in the combinations and oppositions of social and political structure and stratification. They are in the heat of the battle, in the "arena," competing for office, participating in feuds, factions, and coalitions. This involvement entails such affects as anxiety, aggression, envy, fear, exultation, an emotional flooding which does not encourage either rational or wise reflection. But in ritual liminality they are placed, so to speak, outside the total system and its conflicts; transiently, they become men apart – and it is surprising how often the term "sacred" may be translated as "set apart" or "on one side" in various societies. If getting a living and struggling to get it, in and despite of a social structure, be called "bread" then man does not live "by bread alone."

Life as a series and structure of status incumbencies inhibits the full utilization of human capacities, or as Karl Marx would have said, in a singularly Augustinian fashion, "the powers that slumber within man." I am thinking of Augustine's *rationes seminales*, "seminal reasons," implanted in the created universe at the beginning and left to work themselves out over historical time. Both Augustine and Marx favored organic metaphors for social movement, seen in terms of development and growth. Thus, for Marx, a new social order "grows" in the "womb" of the old and is "delivered" by the "midwife", force....

Communitas is, existentially speaking and in its origins, purely spontaneous and self-generating. The "wind" of existential communitas "bloweth where it listeth." It is essentially opposed to structure, as antimatter is hypothetically opposed to matter. Thus, even when communitas becomes normative its religious expressions become closely hedged about by rules and interdictions – which act like the lead container of a dangerous radioactive isotope. Yet exposure to or immersion in communitas seems to be an indispensable human social requirement. People have a real need, and "need" is not for me "a dirty word," to doff the masks, cloaks, apparel, and insignia of status from time to time even if only to don the liberating masks of liminal masquerade. But they do this freely. And here I would like to point out the bond that exists between communitas, liminality, and lowermost status. It is often believed that the lowest castes and classes in stratified societies exhibit the greatest immediacy and involuntariness of behavior. This may or may not be empirically true, but it is at any rate a persistent belief held perhaps most firmly by the occupants of positions in the middle rungs of structure on whom structural pressures to conformity are greatest, and who secretly envy even while they openly reprobate the behavior of those groups and classes less normatively inhibited, whether highest or lowest on the status ladder. Those who would maximize communitas often begin by minimizing or even eliminating the outward marks of rank as, for example, Tolstoy and Gandhi tried to do in their own persons. In other words, they approximate in dress and behavior the condition of the poor....

There is no doubt that from the perspective of incumbents in positions of command or maintenance in structure, communitas – even when it becomes normative – represents a real danger and, indeed, that for all those, including even political leaders, who spend much of their lives in structural role playing it also represents a temptation. Who does not really want to shuck off that old armor plating? This situation was dramatically exemplified in the early history of the Franciscan order. So many rushed to join St. Francis' following that recruitment to the secular clergy fell off sharply, and the Italian bishops complained that they could not maintain ecclesiastical discipline when their dioceses were overrun by what they considered to be a mendicant rabble. In the last quarter of the thirteenth century Pope Nicholas III decreed that the order modify its rule with regard to the abandonment of all property. In this way a communitarian threat to the jural structure of the church was turned to her advantage, for the doctrine of poverty has left a permanent impress on Catholicism acting as a constant check on the growth of Roman legalism, with its heavy involvement in political and economic structures.

Liminality, then, often draws on poverty for its repertoire of symbols, particularly for its symbols of social relationship. Similarly, as we have seen, the voluntary outsiders of our own society, particularly today's voluntary rural communards, also draw upon the symbolic vocabulary of poverty and indigence. Both the mendicant orders and today's counterculture have affinities with another social phenomenon which has recently aroused great interest among anthropologists and historians. I refer to that range of religious movements, scattered throughout history and of wide geographical provenience, which have variously been described as "enthusiastic," "heretical," "millenarian," "revitalistic," "nativistic," "messianic," and "separatist" – to cite but a few of the terms by which they have been called by theologians, historians, and social scientists. I shall not enter into the problem of providing an adequate taxonomy of such movements, but will content myself with mentioning a few of their recurrent attributes which seem closely similar to those of (1) ritual liminality in tribal societies, (2) religious mendicancy, and (3) the counterculture. In the first place, it is common for members of these movements either to give up what property they have or to hold all their property in common. Instances have been recorded of the destruction of all property by the members of religious movements at the command of their prophetic leaders. The rationale here, I believe, is that in most societies differences in property correspond to major differences of status or else in simpler stateless societies relate to the segmentation of corporate groups. To "liquidate" property... is to erase the lines of structural cleavage that in ordinary life prevent men from entering into communitas....

...Now I would like to bring my argument round full circle and state that from the standpoint of structural man, he who is in communitas is an exile or a stranger, someone who, by his very existence, calls into question the whole normative order. That is why when we consider cultural institutions we have to look in the interstices, niches, intervals, and on the peripheries of the social structure to find even a grudging cultural recognition of this primordial human modality of relationship. On the other hand, in times of drastic and sustained social change, it is communitas which often appears to be central and structure which constitutes the "square" or "straight" periphery. If one may dare to venture a personal evaluation of such matters, one might say that much of the misery of the world has been due to the principled activities of fanatics of both persuasions. On the one hand, one finds a structural and ultimately bureaucratic *übermensch* who would like to array the whole world of lesser men in terms of hierarchy and regimentation in a "New Order," and on the other the puritanical levelers who would abolish all idiosyncratic differences between man and man (even necessary organizational differences for the sake of the food quest), and set up an ethical tyranny that would allow scant scope for compassion and forgiveness. "One Law for the Lion and the Ox is Oppression," said Blake with reference to such ethical tyranny. Yet since both social modalities are indispensable for human social continuity, neither can exist for long without the other. Indeed, if structure is maximized to full rigidity, it invites the nemesis of either violent revolution or uncreative apathy, while if communitas is maximized, it becomes in a short while its own dark shadow, totalitarianism, from the need to suppress and repress in its members all tendencies to develop structural independences and interdependences.

Moreover, communitas, which is in principle boundless and universal, has been in historical practice limited to particular geographical regions and specific aspects of social life. Thus the varied expressions of communitas such as monasteries, convents, socialist bastions, semireligious communities and brotherhoods, nudist colonies, communes in the modern countercultures, initiation camps, have often found it necessary to surround themselves with real as well as symbolic walls – a species of what structural sociologists would call "boundary maintaining mechanisms." When large-scale communites are involved, these tend to take the form of military and police organizations, open and secret. Thus to keep out structure, structure has to be constantly maintained and reinforced. When the great principles regard one another as antagonists, each "becomes what it beholds." What seems to be needed, to quote William Blake again, is to "destroy the negation" and thus "redeem the contraries," that is, to discover what is the right relationship between structure and communitas at a given time and place in history and geography, to give to each its due.

To sum up, a major stumbling block in the development of sociological and anthropological theory has been the almost total identification of the social with the social structural. Even informal relations are considered structural. Many of them are, of course, but not all; these include the most relevant ones, and it is possible to distinguish the deep from the shallow here. This has created enormous difficulties with regard to many problems, such as social change, the sociology of religion, and role theory, to name but a few. It has also led to the view that all that is not social structural is "psychological" – whatever this may mean. It has also led to the positing of a false dichotomy between the individual as subject, and society as object. What seems to be the case is that the social has a free or unbound as well as a bonded or bound dimension, the dimension of communitas in which men confront one another not as role players but as "human totals," integral beings who recognizantly share the same humanity.

Once this has been recognized, it will be possible for the social sciences to examine more fruitfully than hitherto such cultural phenomena as art, religion, literature, philosophy, and even many aspects of law, politics, and economic behavior which have hitherto eluded the structuralist conceptual net. Such domains are rich with reference to communitas. The vain task of trying to find out in what precise way certain symbols found in the ritual, poetry, or iconography of a given society "reflect" or "express" its social or political structure can then be abandoned. Symbols may well reflect not structure, but anti-structure, and not only reflect it but contribute to creating it. Instead, we can regard the same phenomena in terms of the relationship between structure and communitas to be found in such relational situations as passages between structural states, the interstices of structural relations, and in the powers of the weak.

REFERENCES

Stonequist, E. V. (1937) *The Marginal Man*. New York: Scribner.
Znaniecki, F., and W. I. Thomas (1918) *The Polish Peasant in Europe and America*. Boston: Badger.

9

Political Anthropology

Marc J. Swartz, Victor W. Turner, and Arthur Tuden

I

This book [*Political Anthropology*, 1966] is the outgrowth of an experiment. Its editors, curious to explore current trends and styles of analysis in political anthropology, decided to ask a number of distinguished practitioners in this field to contribute papers for presentation at the 1964 Annual General Meeting of the American Anthropological Association. It was decided that the contributors were to be given considerable leeway in their choice and treatment of topics, for our aim was to find out whether "a wind of change" was invading political theory as it had invaded the actual politics of most societies that have been studied by anthropologists.

As the papers came in, it soon became clear that this is indeed the case. Since the last major bench mark in the anthropology of politics, *African Political Systems* (edited by Fortes and Evans-Pritchard, 1940), which has been both stimulus and model for several well-known anthologies, monographs, and articles, there has been a trend – at first almost imperceptible, then gaining momentum in the late 1950s and early 1960s – away from the earlier preoccupation with the taxonomy, structure, and function of political systems to a growing concern with the study of political processes. Professor Firth (1957: 294), with his flair for the detection of new theoretical tendencies, aptly characterized the new mood as one in which anthropologists would forsake "the well-trodden ground of conventional structural analysis for a type of inquiry which is from the outset an examination of 'dynamic phenomena.'"

Indeed, many of the papers we received centered their discussions on dynamic political phenomena and processes. They considered both repetitive and radical political change, the processes of decision-making and conflict resolution, and the agitation and settlement of political issues in a variety of cultural contexts. The papers were pervaded by a "becoming" rather than a "being" vocabulary: they were full of such terms as "conflict," "faction," "struggle," "conflict resolution," "arena,"

From "Introduction," in *Political Anthropology* (Chicago: Aldine Press, 1966), pp. 1–9.

"development," "process," and so forth. It is true that this stress on the processual dimension of politics had been foreshadowed and prepared by a number of important books, some of which had first appeared soon after the publication of *African Political Systems*. Perhaps the most notable of these pioneer studies of political dynamics – although its major emphasis was on law rather than politics – was *The Cheyenne Way* by Llewellyn and Hoebel (1941), which focused attention on conflicts of interests and on the notion that "trouble cases lead us most directly to legal phenomena" (p. 37). The same outlook, applied to political behavior, clearly guides many of the contributors to this present volume. No fewer than five articles are directly concerned with the resolution of conflict and the settlement of disputes.

Few processes of political action run harmonious courses. It is not surprising, therefore, that processual studies tend also to study conflict, as well as its resolution. Several social philosophers have contributed to our vocabulary of concepts for the analysis of conflict; these include Hegel, with his "dialectic," Marx, with his "contradiction" and "struggle," and Simmel with his "conflict." More recently, Coser has done much to familiarize us with a more refined and systematic exposition of Simmel's theoretical standpoint (1956). But within the strictly anthropological tradition, the application of these and related concepts to the data of pre-industrial society is perhaps most fully exemplified by the work of Max Gluckman and the so-called "Manchester School."

These anthropologists, working with "the extended case method," have tended to lay emphasis on the processual aspect of politics in tribal societies, and even in certain sectors of complex societies. In Gluckman's words (1965: 235):

> they are now analyzing the development of social relations themselves, under the conflicting pressures of discrepant principles and values, as the generations change and new persons come to maturity. If we view these relations through a longish period of time, we see how various parties and supporters operate and manipulate mystical beliefs of various kinds to serve their interests. The beliefs are seen in dynamic process within day-to-day social life, and the creation and burgeoning of new groups and relationships.

This formulation, although it depends rather heavily upon the doctrine of the primacy of "interest" and underestimates the capacity of "mystical beliefs" to evoke altruistic responses from members of a social group, is nevertheless a good summary of the main characteristics of this nascent type of analysis. In this book [*Political Anthropology*], the articles by Middleton, Turner, Colson, and Nicholas are markedly influenced by the thinking of the Manchester School. These studies direct attention to conflicts of interests and values and to mechanisms for redressing conflicts and reconciling the parties to them.

The shift in emphasis from static and synchronic analyses of morphological types to dynamic and diachronic studies of societies in change was also evident in Evans-Pritchard's insistence, throughout the 1950s, that modern social anthropologists must consider the histories of the societies they study (1962), in Firth's notion of "organizational change" (gradual and cumulative rather than radical structural change (1959)), and in the Cambridge University work on developmental cycles (Goody 1958). But, in the main, these studies emphasized repetitive change that – at the end of a cycle of institutionally "triggered off" modifications in the pattern and content of social relations – brought about a regular return to the status quo ante. Again it was Gluckman who drew attention to radical change, or change in the social structure, for example, "in the size of a society, the composition or balance of its parts, or the type of organization" (as Ginsberg has defined such change (1956: 10)). Gluckman's fieldwork in the plural society of Zululand led him to reject the then dominant model of a social system as a set of functionally inter connected components, moving by graduated stages through culturally defined equilibria – or, at most, changing so slowly that no disruption of equilibrium or integration could occur.

From the viewpoint of the sociology of knowledge, it is no accident that this alteration of analytical focus from structure to process has developed during a period in which the formerly colonial territories of Asia, Africa, and the Pacific have been undergoing far-reaching political changes that have culminated in independence. Anthropologists who directed or undertook fieldwork during the 1950s and early 1960s found that they could not ignore or neglect the processes of change or resistance to change, whose concrete expressions were all around them. Many of these anthropologists worked in plural societies, characterized by ethnic diversity, sharp economic inequalities between ethnic groups, religious differences, political and legal heterogeneity – in short, major asymmetries of sociocultural scale and complexity between their ethnic constituents.

Such societies, studied by Furnivall (1948), Mitchell (1954), Gluckman (1954, 1965), Wilson (1945), Kuper (1947), Epstein (1958), and Smith (1960), have been conceptualized not so much as tightly integrated systems, modeled on either organic or mechanical analogues, but as social fields with many dimensions, with parts that may be loosely integrated, or virtually independent from one another, and that have to be studied over time if the factors underlying the changes in their social relationships are to be identified and analyzed. Probably because of the magnitude of the new tasks confronting them, anthropologists have so far generally eschewed the attempt to portray and analyze social fields in anything like their full complexity or temporal depth. Rather, they have attempted to isolate single sectors, or subsectors, within a single dimension of such fields, and have then endeavored to say something significant about the processes they have found there. Nevertheless, their work is almost always impregnated by awareness of the wider context and of its major properties – such as plurality, diversity, componential looseness of fit, conflict, variations in degree of consensus (ranging to complete lack of consensus), and the like.

II

The dimension that concerns us . . . is the political dimension, and within it we shall consider those relationships between personalities and groups that make up a "political field." Clearly, such concepts depend on what is meant by "politics." "Politics," however, is almost as difficult to define as it is easy to use as a description of occurrences within societies and their constituent parts. It is easy to sympathize with those who, like Fortes and Evans-Pritchard (1940), avoid defining the term, for the concept has a wide range of useful application and the great variety of data to which it is applied makes operational specification difficult.

Still, we can hardly call this volume *Political Anthropology*, and bombard the reader with political concepts and theoretical constructs, if we do not provide a rather concise idea of what it is that we are talking about.

Several qualities that lead us to consider a process as political are readily noted and widely accepted as characteristic. First, a political process is public rather than private. An activity that affects a neighborhood, a whole community, a whole society, or a group of societies is unquestionably a public activity; whether it is *also* a political activity depends upon other characteristics – in addition to its being public. A religious ceremony may affect entire communities, societies, and even groups of societies, but we may not wish to call it a "political activity" (although – and now we begin to see some of the sorrow that is the lot of the would-be definer of this concept – under some circumstances and/or in certain respects we might want to call a religious ceremony "political").

The second generally accepted quality of politics is that it concerns goals. Combining the first characteristic with this second one, we can go a bit further and say that politics always involves public goals. Although individual, private goals will always be importantly involved . . . the emphasis will be upon goals desired for the group as a whole. These goals will include the achievement of a new relationship *vis-à-vis* some other group or groups: winning independence, fighting a war or making peace, gaining higher prestige than previously held, changing the relative standing of castes or classes within a group, etc.; a change in the relationship to the environment for all or most members of the group, such as building an irrigation project or clearing land for the whole village, etc.; and the allocation of offices, titles, and other scarce resources for which there is a group-wide competition.

From what has already been said about political goals, it will be clear that consciousness of a desired end is present, but this consciousness need be neither complete nor universal. Some of the members of a group may have little or no idea of what is being sought; only the leaders may have a clear idea of the end that is being pursued. The "goal" may be only a wish to escape a vaguely conceived dissatisfaction or to achieve a new state or objective that is not clearly formulated. Leaders may present their publics with goals that are, in a sense, only artifices for furthering a more distant or hidden end. Thus a trade union leader may call a strike over wages and working conditions, and the union members may believe these are the ultimate goals. The leader, however, may be using the strike to improve his position *vis-à-vis* other leaders and/or government officials. It is true that politics always concerns goals, but it is useful to recognize that "goal" is not a univocal concept and that all we are requiring here is that there be a striving for something for which there is competition. This competition, however, must be of a particular kind, and, to explain this, it is necessary to look briefly at what is meant by its being "group-wide."

In our society, money is competed for on a group-wide basis, but we would not say that this competition is necessarily political in character. What is meant here is that political allocations are those that require the consent of an entire group in order to be effectively made. Thus while every individual or unit in a society may be competing with every other individual or unit for an economic good, such as money, the results of these competitions do not require group-wide consent in order to be effective. However, competition for titles in, say, a West African society cannot be said to be settled unless the whole group consents to the allocation of the titles that results from the competition. Thus for allocation to be political in nature it must concern scarce goods, the possession of which depends upon a group's consenting to the allocation.

Another important end that is characteristic of politics is achieving settlements that are of public rather than only private concern. Settlements, to be public, must concern a group as a whole, in a rather direct and immediate way. Settling a quarrel between two friends – or between a man and wife – will be considered a public settlement if its accomplishment (or failure) affects, say, the immediate threat of a schism that would divide the whole group or realign the factions that exist within the group. Clearly, some settlements will be public and some will be private, and others will be hard to identify immediately. In this last (probably large) category, we can extract ourselves from vagueness by adhering to the "by-their-fruits-ye-shall-know-them" doctrine, considering all settlements as possibly political until the consequences of each case can be established by detailed investigation. If we find that a settlement or failure of settlement has implications for a group as a whole, we will call it "political" even though at its outset it did not appear to have group-wide consequences.

It is important to dwell a moment on "failure of settlement" and its implications for what is meant by "politics." Political activity is sometimes devoted to the prevention of settlements and to the subversion of the institutional framework by which settlements are reached. In this sort of situation we would not fail to note that a group, the "rebels," seeks a public goal – namely, the realignment of the resources and members of a larger group with which they were associated – and that this group carries out political activity as we have so far defined it.

The significance of this activity for the definition being presented is twofold. First, it must be made clear that politics does not consist entirely of activities that ultimately, or necessarily, promote the welfare and continued existence of a group, as constituted and organized at any particular time. Political activity includes all sorts of seeking-after-public-goals, which may be as concerned with the deracination of existing structures, mechanisms, and alignments as with their preservation.

Second, this consideration of disjunctive activity in politics provides an opportunity to clarify what is meant by goals and settlements that have consequences for a group. A "group" need not be a whole society, or even a major segment of a society; a number of individuals may join together in rejection of the goals and aims of the larger group of which they were formerly part. These individuals may constitute a faction . . . or a special interest group that devotes its energies to inducing conflict – rather than to promoting settlements – with the aim of overthrowing the organization of its parent body and or changing the basic aims of that body. Such activities are clearly political, and the fact that the faction or special interest group uses noninstitutional means for seeking its ends (violence, for example) does not alter the political nature of its behavior.

A final major characteristic of "politics" is implicit in what has just been said: it involves some kind of focusing of power – using "power" in its broadest sense. This focusing need not entail the existence of a permanent hierarchy of power, but it will always involve the existence of differential behavior concerning public goals. Conceivably, the differential may be no more than that certain individuals announce group goals that have been jointly decided upon by all members of a group, participating equally – or it may be that a very few members determine a group's goals and that the others merely carry out the decisions. A differential will always be present.

We therefore have three characteristics that should serve to start our division of the universe into what is political and what is not. The adjective "political," as we have so far defined it, will apply to everything that is at once public, goal-oriented, and that involves a differential of power (in the sense of control) among the individuals of the group in question.

This tentative definition does not solve the sort of problem illustrated earlier by the example of the religious ceremony. A religious ceremony could have all the characteristics so far proposed: it could be public (everybody participates and is concerned with it), goal-oriented (it changes a group's relationship to the environment by ending a drought), and it could involve a differential possession of power (ritual experts could tell the others what to do), but we might be reluctant to say that the ceremony is primarily a political activity.

An obvious way out of this difficulty would be to overlook our reluctance and declare the ceremony a political activity on the entirely valid grounds that we can define things however we wish without any fear of our definitions being either true or false. But a more satisfying solution is available, which comes from our being able to look at an activity from different points of view. If we look at the religious ceremony from the point of view of the processes by which the group goals are determined and implemented (how it was decided that a ceremony was to be held, how the time and place were determined, how the things to be used in the ceremony were obtained, etc.) and by which power is differentially acquired (which ritual experts are successful in telling the "laity" what to do, how these experts marshal support for their power and undermine that of their rivals, etc.), we are studying politics. If, however, we look at the ritual from the perspective, say, of the way it relates the group to the supernatural and the way this relationship affects the relations among the constituent parts of the group, we are studying religion – or at least we are studying something other than politics.

The study of politics, then, is the study of the *processes* involved in determining and implementing public goals and in the differential achievement and use of power by the members of the group concerned with those goals.

In the remainder of this introduction a good deal will be said about the nature of political processes, so that (for the present) it is enough to point out that these processes are the key elements in politics. From the perspective of politics, processes such as marshaling support, undermining rivals, attaining goals, and achieving settlements are the prime foci of interest. The groups within which these processes occur are important because they constitute the "field" of political activity, but this activity moves across group boundaries without necessarily encountering hindrances, which is another way of saying the political field can expand and contract.

The important point here is that since politics is the study of certain kinds of processes, it is essential to center our attention on these processes rather than on the groups or fields within which they occur. This means, for example, that a political study follows the development of conflicts for power (or for acquiring support for proposed goals) into whatever groups the processes lead – rather than examining such groups as lineages, villages, or countries to determine what processes they might contain. To focus upon groups would be to credit them with a wholeness and a completeness that is not justified, for the understanding of what is happening in a village struggle for leadership may require an examination of the roots of the struggle in the national context.

To put this another way, political anthropology no longer exclusively studies – in structural-functionalist terms – political institutions of cyclical, repetitive societies. Its unit of space is no longer the isolated "society"; it tends to be the political "field." Its unit of time is no longer "structural time"; it is historical time. The combined unit is a spatial-temporal continuum.

A political field does not operate like clockwork, with all the pieces meshed together with finely tooled precision. It is, rather, a field of tension, full of intelligent and determined antagonists, sole and corporate, who are motivated by ambition, altruism, self-interest, and by desire for the public good, and who in successive situations are bound to one another through self-interest, or idealism – and separated or opposed through the same motives. At every point in this process we have to consider each unit in terms of its independent objectives, and we also have to consider the entire situation in which their *inter*dependent actions occur. This independence and this interdependence are emphatically not those of the parts of a machine or an animal. The institutionalization of political relationships may sometimes impose upon the observer the delusory appearance of mechanical or organic phenomena, but they are mere analogies that blind us to some of the most important qualities of political behavior. To understand such behavior, we have to know how the political "units" think, feel, and will in relation to their understanding of the issues that they generate or confront. As Parsons and Emmet have shown us (Parsons 1937; Emmet 1958), the factor of purposiveness is analytically crucial to the concept of political action.

III

Mention of Talcott Parsons reminds us of the impressive contribution that social philosophers and sociologists – Parsons himself, and Durkheim, Weber, Bierstedt, and Bales – and political scientists – such as Lasswell, Kaplan, Easton, M. Levy, and Banfield – to name only a few – have made to the study of political processes. Although anthropologists have tended to be extremely suspicious of the theories of political philosophers, as displayed in many ways – from the strictures in *African Political Systems* (Fortes and Evans-Pritchard 1940) to the less draconic pronouncements in current publications, we consider that the time is now ripe for dialogue, if not for marriage, between anthropology and other disciplines concerned with comparative politics.

From the sociologists and political scientists we hope to obtain a tool kit of concepts that, with some modification, will prove useful to anthropologists when they examine political behavior in real societies – but that will not unduly restrict assumptions about the nature of this behavior. Ideally, concepts for analyzing politics would be as applicable in societies that do not have centralized and/or permanent decision-making units as in societies that have such units; in societies where change is rapid and drastic, and in those where it is slow and gradual; in societies where the great bulk of the population has many important values, motivations, and relationships in common, and in societies where the population has little in common. In short, the purpose here is to present concepts of general applicability, which also allow recognition of the diversity of political systems.

REFERENCES

Coser, L. (1956) *The Functions of Social Conflict*. New York: Free Press of Glencoe.

Emmet, D. M. (1958) *Function, Purpose and Powers*. London: Macmillan.

Epstein, A. L. (1958) *Politics in an Urban African Community*. Manchester: Manchester University Press.

Evans-Pritchard, E. E. (1962) *Essays in Social Anthropology*. London: Faber & Faber.

Firth, R. (1957) Introduction to Factions in Indian and Overseas Indian Societies. *British Journal of Sociology* 8: 291–295.

——. (1959) *Social Change in Tikopia*. London: Allen & Unwin.

Fortes, M. and Evans-Pritchard, E. E. (eds.) (1940) *African Political Systems*. Oxford: Oxford University Press for the International African Institute.

Furnivall, J. S. (1948) *Colonial Policy and Practice*. Cambridge: Cambridge University Press.

Ginsberg, M. (1956) Factors in Social Change. In *Transactions of the Third World Congress of Sociology* I, pp. 10–19. London: International Sociological Association.

Gluckman, M. (1954) Political Institutions. In *Institutions of Primitive Society*, pp. 66–81. Oxford: Basil Blackwell.

——. (1965) *Politics, Law and Ritual in Tribal Society*. Chicago: Aldine.

Goody, J. (ed.) (1958) *The Development Cycle in Domestic Groups*. Cambridge: Cambridge University Press.

Kuper, H. (1947) *An African Aristocracy: Rank among the Swazi*. Oxford University Press for the International African Institute.

Llewellyn, K. N. and Hoebel, E. A. (1941) *The Cheyenne Way*. Norman: University of Oklahoma Press.

Mitchell, J. C. (1954) *African Urbanization in Ndola and Luanshya*, Rhodes-Livingstone Communication No. 6. Livingstone, Northern Rhodesia: Rhodes–Livingstone Institute.

Parsons, T. (1937) *Structure of Social Action*. New York: McGraw-Hill.

Smith, M. G. (1960) *Government in Zazzau*. Oxford University Press for the International African Institute.

Wilson, G. and M. (1945) *Analysis of Social Change*. Cambridge: Cambridge University Press.

10

New Proposals for Anthropologists

Kathleen Gough

This paper was first prepared for an audience of anthropologists in the United States of America, where I have taught and researched for the past twelve years.[1] Some of the questions that it raises apply, although perhaps less acutely, to social and cultural anthropologists from the other industrial nations of Western Europe, North America, Australia, and New Zealand. The international circumstances to which I refer no doubt also create problems for anthropologists born and resident in a number of the Latin American, Asian, and African countries where much anthropological research is carried out. I should be especially glad if this paper stimulates some among the latter anthropologists to comment on how these circumstances are viewed by them and how they affect their work.

Recently a number of anthropologists, and of students, have complained that cultural and social anthropology are failing to tackle significant problems of the modern world. As I have thought this for some time, I should like to make a tentative statement about where I think we stand today, and to follow it with some proposals. This being a new departure, I must ask to be excused if I am both obvious and argumentative.

Anthropology is a child of Western imperialism. It has roots in the humanist visions of the Enlightenment, but as a university discipline and a modern science, it came into its own in the last decades of the nineteenth and the early twentieth centuries. This was the period in which the Western nations were making their final push to bring practically the whole pre-industrial non-Western world under their political and economic control.

Until World War II most of our fieldwork was carried out in societies that had been conquered by our own governments. We tended to accept the imperialist framework as given, perhaps partly because we were influenced by the dominant ideas of our time, and partly because at that time there was little anyone could do to dismantle the empires. In spite of some belief in value-free social science, anthropologists in those days seem to have commonly played roles characteristic of white

From *Current Anthropology* 9(5) (Chicago: University of Chicago Press, 1968), pp. 403–7.

liberals, sometimes of white liberal reformers, in other spheres of our society. Anthropologists were of higher social status than their informants; they were usually of the dominant race, and they were protected by imperial law; yet, living closely with native peoples, they tended to take their part and to try to protect them against the worst forms of imperialist exploitation. Customary relations developed between the anthropologists and the government or the various private agencies who funded and protected them. Other types of customary relationships grew up between anthropologists and the people whose institutions they studied. Applied anthropology came into being as a kind of social work and community development effort for non-white peoples, whose future was seen in terms of gradual education and of amelioration of conditions many of which had actually been imposed by their Western conquerors in the first place.

Since World War II, a new situation has come about. There are today some 2,352,000,000 people in underdeveloped nations.[2] About 773,000,000, or a third of them, have already, through revolution, passed out of the sphere of Western imperialism into the new socialist states of China, Mongolia, North Korea, North Vietnam, and Cuba. However arduous and conflictful their conditions, they are now beyond the domination of the capitalist powers and are off on tracks of their own. Because of the Cold War (and, in the case of Vietnam, the hot war), American anthropologists are unable to study these societies directly and have made few comparisons of their political economies or community structures with those of underdeveloped nations with capitalist or with "mixed" economies. When American studies of socialist societies are made, the built-in assumption that "communism," especially revolutionary communism, is bad and unviable commonly produces distortions of both theory and fact.[3] Granting the difficulties of obtaining reliable information, I believe that more objective studies could be made if greater attention were paid to the work of the few Western social scientists who have lived in these countries, for example, Lattimore 1962; Robinson and Adler 1958; Robinson 1964; Myrdal 1965; and Crook and Crook 1959, 1966. In addition to primary sources from the socialist nations there are also, of course, the writings of Western journalists and other specialists who have lived or travelled in the new socialist countries since their revolutions. Examples are Dumont 1965, 1967; Gelder and Gelder 1964; Greene 1961, 1964, 1966; Snow 1962; Hinton 1966; Han Suyin 1965, 1966, 1967; Strong 1962, 1964; Burchett 1963, 1965, 1966; Taylor 1966; and many others. Most of these writers are favorable to the newer socialisms, and most tend to be neglected or scoffed at in the United States. Yet American social scientists think nothing of using travellers' reports to eke out their knowledge of non-Western societies of the fifteenth to eighteenth centuries, biased or mission-oriented though some of them may have been. Certainly such studies are not discarded on the grounds that their authors happened to like the societies they visited. There is no reason why anthropologists cannot apply similar criteria of objectivity to modern writers who admire China or other socialist countries today.

There remain about 1,579,000,000 people, or 67 percent of the total, in non-Western nations with capitalist or with "mixed" economies. Of those, 49,000,000, or 2 percent of the total, are still in more or less classical colonial societies such as South Africa, Mozambique, or Angola, ruled by small white elites drawn from the "mother country" or else now severed from it as separate settler populations. About another 511,000,000, or 22 percent of the total, live in what may be regarded as satellite or client states, states which have indigenous governments, but are so constrained by Western military or economic aid and by private investments that they have little autonomy. Most of their governments are opposed to social reforms and would probably collapse if Western aid were withdrawn. The largest of these states, with populations of over 5,000,000, are Colombia, Argentina, Peru, Brazil, Ecuador, Chile, Venezuela, the Philippines, South Vietnam, South Korea, Thailand, Taiwan, Malaysia, the Congo, Nigeria, Iran, Southern Arabia, Cameroon, and Turkey. The list is very tentative, for modern neo-imperialism varies in intensity. Some might include Mexico and Pakistan, bringing the total to 657,000,000, or 28 percent of the under developed world. About 318,000,000, of these people or 14 percent of the total, live in nations beholden to the United States, either in Latin America, the traditional preserve of US capital, or else in a fringe around China, where the United States has established satellite regimes in an effort to stave off the spread of revolutionary socialism. If we include Pakistan and Mexico, US client states amount to about 20 percent of the total.

The remaining 873,000,000, or 37 percent of the total, live in nations that are usually considered in the West to be relatively independent, under governments containing popular nationalist leaders. Most of these leaders conducted nationalist struggles against European colonialism a decade or two ago [in the 1950s or before], and some fought wars of liberation. (By contrast, the governments of most of the client states were either installed by, or arose after, military coups at least partly inspired from the West.) Most of the independent "Third World" nations regard themselves as politically neutral and as in some sense socialist or aspiring to become socialist. Because the appeal of their governments is of a multi-class character, Peter Worsley (1964) calls them "populist." The economies of these nations have both a public sector, with an emphasis on national planning, and a large private sector dominated by foreign capital. The largest of these states, with populations over 5,000,000, are India, Burma, Cambodia, Ceylon, Indonesia, Afghanistan, Nepal, Syria, Iraq, Yemen, the United Arab Republic, Algeria, Morocco, Kenya, Tanzania, Sudan, Ethiopia, Uganda, and Ghana.

During the 1950s, many liberal social scientists and others hoped that these neutral nations would form a strong Third World that could act independently of either the Western industrial or the Communist powers. I suggest that in the 1960s this hope has dimmed, and is now almost extinguished, chiefly because of the expansion of American capital and military power, the refusal of European nations to relinquish their own economic strongholds, and the failure of many new govern-ments to improve the living conditions of their people. In the past 15 years, at least 227,000,000 people in 16 nations, or 10 percent of the underdeveloped world, have, after a longer or shorter period of relative independence, moved into, or moved back into, a client relationship, usually with the United States. These nations are Guate-mala, Honduras, the Dominican Republic, Guyana, Venezuela, Brazil, Argentina, Bolivia, Ecuador, Trinidad and Tobago, South Vietnam, Thailand, Laos, the Congo, Togo, and, Gabon. In most of these countries the shift in orientation followed a military coup. A further 674,000,000 in India, Indonesia, Afghanistan, Ceylon, Kenya, and Ghana, which I have classified as "independent," have recently moved into much closer dependence on the United States, so that their future as independent nations is now uncertain. Together with the US client states and colonial dependencies, this brings to 1,140,000,000, or 48 percent of the total, the number of people whose governments' policies are very heavily influenced by the United States. We must also remember that US capital and military power now exert a strong influence on the colonies and client states of European powers (11 percent of the total), as well as on most of the remaining 8 percent of "neutral" states. In these circumstances, US power can truly be said to be entrenched with more or less firmness throughout the underdeveloped world outside of the socialist states.

Countering this re-imposition of Western power, armed revolutionary movements now exist in at least 20 countries with a total population of 266,000,000. These countries are Guatemala, Peru, Venezuela, Ecuador, Paraguay, Brazil, Honduras, Bolivia, Colombia, Angola, Mozambique, the Congo, Cameroon, Portuguese Guinea, Yemen, Southern Arabia, the Philippines, Thailand, Laos, and South Vietnam. About 501,000,000 people live in seven other countries where unarmed revolutionary movements or parties have considerable support, namely India, Rhodesia, Southwest Africa, South Africa, Nicaragua, the Dominican Republic, and Panama. In more than a third of the underdeveloped world, therefore, socialist revolution against both native elites and Western dominance is a considered possibility, while in another third it has already been accomplished. Even in the remaining relatively stable colonial, client, or neutral states, a majority of the people are getting poorer, and a small minority of rich are getting richer. Populations are increasing, discontent is widespread, and revolutionary struggles are quite possible within a decade or two [by the late 1970s or 1980s]. Whereas in the 1950s it looked to some of us as though much of the non-Western world might gain genuine political and economic independence of the West by peaceful means, this is no longer the case. Western dominance is continuing under new guises, even expanding and hardening. At the same time, revolution now begins to appear as *the* route by which underdeveloped societies may hope to gain freedom from Western controls.

In this revolutionary and proto-revolutionary world, anthropologists are beginning to be in difficulties. From the beginning, we have inhabited a triple environment, involving obligations first to the peoples we studied, second to our colleagues and our science, and third to the powers who employed us in universities or who funded our research. In many cases we seem now to be in danger of being torn apart by the conflicts between the first and third set of obligations, while the second set of loyalties, to our subject as an objective and humane endeavour, are being severely tested and jeopardized. On the one hand, part of the non-Western world is in revolt, especially against the United States government as the strongest and most counter-revolutionary of the Western powers. The war in Vietnam has, of course, exacerbated the non-Western sense of outrage, although the actual governments of most of these nations are so dependent on the United States that they soften their criticisms. On the other hand, anthropologists are becoming increasingly subject to restrictions, unethical temptations, and political controls from the United States government and its subordinate agencies, as Beals's (1967) report on problems of anthropological research and ethics amply shows. The question tends to become: what does an anthropologist do who is dependent on a counter-revolutionary government in an increasingly revolutionary world? To complicate matters, into the arena has stepped a fourth and most vociferous public, namely students, who once imbibed knowledge peaceably, but who are now, because of their own crises, asking awkward questions about ethics, commitments, and goals.

There is little wonder that with all these demands many anthropologists bury themselves in their specialties or, if they *must* go abroad, seek out the remotest, least unstable tribe or village they can find. As Peter Worsley (1966) has recently pointed out, however, in a paper called "The End of Anthropology?" we shall eventually have to choose either to remain, or become, specialists who confine themselves to the cultures of small-scale pre-industrial societies, or else, bringing to bear all our knowledge of cultural evolution and of primitive social institutions, embark fully on the study of modern societies, including modern revolutions. If we take the former path, as our subject matter disappears, we shall become historians and retreat from the substantial work we have already done in contemporary societies. If we take the latter path – which is the one some of us must inevitably follow – we shall have to admit that our subject matter is increasingly the same as that of political scientists, economists, and sociologists. The only way that we can *not* admit this is by confining ourselves to studies of small segments of modern society; but as the scale of these societies widens, such studies are less and less justifiable theoretically or methodologically except within a framework of understanding of what is happening to the larger system. Anthropologists have, moreover, some right to demand of themselves that they do study the larger system as a totality, for they have 50 years of experience of analysing the interconnectedness of political, economic, and religious institutions within smaller-scale systems. While they must necessarily depend for much of their data on the other social sciences, anthropologists do have some historical claim to play a synthesizing role.

Unfortunately, we have I think a serious drawback in our own history which makes it very difficult for us to approach modern society as a single, interdependent world social system. This is that although we have worked for over 100 years in conquered societies, and although for at least 50 of them we have emphasized the interconnectedness of parts of social systems, we have virtually failed to study Western imperialism as a social system, or even adequately to explore the effects of imperialism on the societies we studied. Of late a few pioneer works have appeared which attempt this task, notably Worsley's (1964) book, *The Third World*. Wallerstein's (1966) collection, *Social Change: The Colonial Situation*, draws together useful extracts by social scientists and nationalist leaders over the past 20 years. Wolf's study of Mexico (1959), Steward's and others' of Puerto Rico (1956), Epstein's of politics in the Zambian copper-belt (1958), and a number of others also move in this general direction; but it is remarkable how few anthropologists have studied imperialism, especially its economic system.

It is true, of course, that anthropologists have made numerous studies of modern social change in pre-industrial societies, especially in local communities. They have, however, usually handled them through very general concepts: "culture contact," "acculturation," "social change," "modernization," "urbanization," "Westernization," or "the folk-urban continuum." Force, suffering, and exploitation tend to disappear in these accounts of structural processes, and the units of study are usually so small that it is hard to see the forest for the trees. These approaches, in the main, have produced factual accounts and limited hypotheses about the impact of industrial cultures on pre-industrial ones in local communities, but have done little to aid understanding of the world distribution of power under imperialism or of its total system of economic relationships. Until recently there also has been, of course, a bias in the types of non-Western social units chosen for study, with primitive communities least touched by modern changes being preferred over the mines, cash-crop plantations, white settlements, bureaucracies, urban concentrations, and nationalist movements that have played such prominent roles in colonial societies.

Why have anthropologists not studied world imperialism as a unitary phenomenon? To begin to answer this question would take another article. I will merely suggest some possible lines of enquiry, namely: (1) the very process of specialization within anthropology and between anthropology and related disciplines, especially political science, sociology, and economics; (2) the tradition of individual fieldwork in small-scale societies, which at first produced a rich harvest of ethnography, but later placed constraints on our methods and theories; (3) our unwillingness to offend, by choosing controversial subjects, the governments that funded us; and (4) the bureaucratic, counter-revolutionary setting in which anthropologists have increasingly worked in their universities, which may have contributed to a sense of impotence and to the development of machine-like models.

It may be objected that I have ignored the large volume of post-war American writing in applied anthropology and in economic and political anthropology concerned with development. This work certainly exists, and some of it is fruitful. I would argue, however, that much of it springs from erroneous or doubtful assumptions and theories that are being increasingly challenged by social scientists in the new nations themselves. Among these assumptions are (1) that economic backwardness can be explained in terms of values and psychological characteristics of the native population; (2) that it is desirable to avoid rapid, disruptive changes; (3) that the anthropologist cannot take value-positions that oppose official policies; (4) that causation is always multiple; (5) that the local community is a suitable unit for development programs; (6) that the main process by which development occurs is diffusion from an industrial centre; and (7) that revolution is never the only practicable means toward economic advance.[4] In general, applied and economic anthropology stemming from North America has assumed an international capitalist economy in its framework. The harsh fact seems to be, however, that in most countries of the underdeveloped world where private enterprise pre-dominates, the living conditions of the majority are deteriorating and "take-off" is not occurring. If this is true, it will not be surprising if the intellectuals of these countries reject the metropolitan nations' applied social science and seek remedies elsewhere.

There are of course already a large number of studies, indeed a whole literature, on Western imperialism, most although not all by writers influenced by Marx. In addition to the classic treatments by Hobson (1954), Lenin (1939), and Luxemburg (1951), Moon (1925), Townsend (1940), Williams (1944), Steinberg (1951), Baran (1957), and the anthropologist Mukherjee (1958) have provided outstanding examples of such work. More recent studies include, of course, Baran and Sweezy (1966), Nkrumah (1966), Dumont (1965, 1967), Fanon (1963, 1965), and Frank (1967a). Such books tend in America to be either ignored or reviewed cursorily and then dismissed. They rarely appear in standard anthropological bibliographies. I can only say that this American rejection of Marxist and other "rebel" literature, especially since the McCarthy period, strikes me as tragic. The refusal to take seriously and to defend as intellectually respectable the theories and challenges of these writers has to a considerable extent deadened controversy in our subject, as well as ruining the careers of particular individuals. It is heartening that in recent years the publications of Monthly Review Press, International Publishers, *Studies on the Left*, and other left-wing journals have become a kind of underground literature for many graduate students and younger faculty in the social sciences. Both orthodox social science and these Marxist-influenced studies suffer, however, from the lack of open confrontation and argument between their proponents. There are of course political reasons for this state of affairs, stemming from our dependence on the powers, but it is unfortunate that we have allowed ourselves to become so subservient, to the detriment of our right of free enquiry and free speculation.

I should like to suggest that some anthropologists who are interested in these matters could begin a work of synthesis focusing on some of the contradictions between the assertions and theories of these non-American or Un-American writers and those of orthodox American social scientists, and choosing research problems that would throw light on these contradictions. For example:

(1) We might examine Frank's (1967*c*) argument, from United Nations figures, that per capita food production in non-Communist Asia, Africa, and Latin America has declined in many cases to below pre-war levels since 1960, whereas it has risen above pre-war levels in China and Cuba, in contrast to the common assumption in the United States that capitalist agricultural production in underdeveloped countries is poor, but socialist production, is even poorer.

(2) We might develop a set of research problems around comparisons of the structure and efficiency of socialist and capitalist foreign aid. One might, for example, compare the scope and results of American economic and military aid to the Dominican Republic with those of Russian aid to Cuba. Although Americans cannot go freely to Cuba, it is conceivable that a European and an American, co-ordinating their research problems, might do such comparative work. In countries such as India, the UAR, or Algeria, comparable socialist and capitalist aid projects might be studied within the same locality.

(3) We might undertake comparative studies of types of modern inter-societal political and economic dominance which would help us to define and refine such concepts as imperialism, neo-colonialism, etc. How, for example, does Russian power over one or another of the East European countries compare with that of the United States over certain Latin American or Southeast Asian countries with respect to such variables as military coercion, the disposal of the subordinate society's economic surplus, and the relations between political elites? How does Chinese control over Tibet compare, historically, structurally, and functionally, with Indian control over Kashmir, Hyderabad, or the Naga Hills, and what have been the effects of these controls on the class structures, economic productivity, and local political institutions of these regions?

(4) We might compare revolutionary and proto-revolutionary movements for what they can teach us about social change. In spite of obvious difficulties, it is possible to study some revolutions after they have occurred, or to study revolts in their early stages or after they have been suppressed (for a rare example of such a study, see Barnett and Njama 1966). There *are*, moreover, Westerners who live and travel with revolutionary movements; why are anthropologists seldom or never among them? We need to know, for example, whether there is a common set of circumstances under which left-wing and nationalist revolutions have occurred or have been attempted in recent years in Cuba, Algeria, Indo-China, Malaysia, the Philippines, Indonesia, Kenya, and Zanzibar. Are there any recognizable shifts in ideology or organization between these earlier revolts and the guerrilla movements

now taking shape in Guatemala, Venezuela, Colombia, Angola, Mozambique. Laos, Thailand, Cameroon, Yemen, or Southern Arabia? What are the types of peasantry and urban workers most likely to be involved in these revolutions? Are there typologies of leadership and organization? Why have some revolutions failed and others succeeded? How did it happen, for example, that some 1,000,000 Communists and their families and supporters were killed in 1966 in Indonesia with almost no indigenous resistance, and how does this affect the self-assessment and prospects of, say, the Left Communist Party in India?

I may be accused of asking for Project Camelot, but I am not. I am asking that we should do these studies in *our* way, as we would study a cargo cult or kula ring, without the built-in biases of tainted financing, without the assumption that counter-revolution, and not revolution, is the best answer, and with the ultimate economic and spiritual welfare of our informants and of the international community, rather than the short run military or industrial profits of the Western nations, before us. I would also ask that these studies be attempted by individuals or self-selected teams, rather than as part of the grand artifice of some externally stimulated master plan. Perhaps what I am asking is not possible any more in America. I am concerned that it may not be, that Americans are already too compromised, too constrained by their own imperial government. If that is so, the question really is how anthropologists can get back their freedom of enquiry and of action, and I suggest that, individually and collectively, we should place this first on the list.

NOTES

An earlier version of this historic document of the Vietnam War era was printed and circulated by the Radical Education Project (REP) of Ann Arbor, Michigan, in 1967. It then bore the title "Anthropology and Imperialism." This earlier version was also presented at the Southwestern States Anthropological Association meetings in San Francisco, California, in March, 1967. It was broadcast on KPFA radio and later published in *The Economic and Political Weekly*, Bombay, September 9, 1967. Extracts from the paper appear in another article, "World Revolution and the Science of Man," in *The Dissenting Academy*, edited by Theodore Roszak (New York: Pantheon Books, 1967), pp. 135–58.

1   My husband, David F. Aberle, and I left the United States in 1967 to live and work in Canada. We did so partly because of the general problems to which I refer in this paper. More immediately, we were unwilling to allow the academic grades that we gave our male students in their university classes to be used by draftboards, under the Selective Service system, as a criterion of whether or not they should be conscripted for military service in Vietnam. I mention this as an instance, relevant to the subject of this paper, of ways in which the proper goals of intellectual work have been undermined by current nationalist and military policies.

2   I use the term "underdeveloped" to refer to societies which have, or have recently had, particular features of economic structure produced as a result of several decades or centuries of overt or covert domination by Western industrial capitalist nations. I have included in this category all the nations and the remaining colonies of Latin America, Africa, and Asia, with the exception of Japan. These and later figures are derived from United Nations totals of 1961, as provided in the *World Almanac* of 1967. For some of the more general characteristics of underdeveloped economies see Myrdal 1956, especially chapters 11–13; Baran 1957; and Frank 1966, 1967.

3 There are, of course, notable exceptions to this statement, among them, for example, Schurman 1966.
4 For these and other criticisms, see Bonfil Batalla 1966, Onwuachi and Wolfe 1966, Stavenhagen 1966–7, and Frank 1967.

REFERENCES

Aberle, Kathleen Gough. (1967) "Dissent in anthropology," in *Dissent in Social Science*, ed. Theodore Roszak. New York: Pantheon Press. (Part of this article was presented as "New proposals for anthropologists," before the Southwestern Anthropological Association, Plenary Session: "Anthropology in a World in Crisis," San Francisco, March 24, 1967.)
Baran, Paul A. (1957) *The Political Economy of Growth*. New York: Monthly Review Press.
Baran, Paul A., and Paul M. Sweezy. (1966) *Monopoly Capital*. New York: Monthly Review Press.
Barnett, Donald L., and Karari Njama. (1966) *Mau Mau from Within*. New York: Monthly Review Press.
Beals, Ralph L., and the Executive Board of the American Anthropological Association. (1967) Background information on problems of anthropological research and ethics. *Fellow Newsletter A.A.A.* 8(1): 2–13.
Boneil, Batalla, Guillermo. (1966) Conservative thought in applied anthropology: A critique. *Human Organization* 25: 89–92.
Burchett, Wilfred. (1963) *The Furtive War*. New York: International Publishers.
——. (1965) *Vietnam: Inside Story of a Guerrilla War*. New York: International Publishers.
——. (1966) *Vietnam North*. New York: International Publishers.
Crook, David, and Isabel Crook. (1959) *Revolution in a Chinese Village: Ten Mile Inn*. London: Routledge and Kegan Paul.
——. (1966) *The First Years of Yangyi Commune*. London: Routledge and Kegan Paul.
Dumont, René. (1965) *Lands Alive*. New York: Monthly Review Press.
——. (1967) *False Start in Africa*: New York: Grove Press.
Epstein, A. L. (1958) *Politics in an Urban African Community*. Manchester: Manchester University Press.
Fanon, Franz. (1963) *Le Damnés de la terre* (with a foreword by J.-P. Sartre). Paris: Maspero.
——. (1965a) *Studies in a Dying Colonialism*. New York: Monthly Review Press.
——. (1965b) *Por la revolución africana*. México: Fondo de Cultura económica Colección Popular 70.
Frank, Andre G. (1966) The development of underdevelopment. *Monthly Review* 18(4): 17–31.
——. (1967a) *Capitalism and Underdevelopment in Latin America*. New York: Monthly Review Press.
——. (1967b) Sociology of development and underdevelopment of sociology. *Catalyst*, (Buffalo, NY), pp. 20–73.
——. (1967c) Hunger. *Canadian Dimension*.
Gelder, Stuart, and Roma Gelder. (1964) *The Timely Rain: Travels in New Tibet*. Monthly Review Press.
Greene, Felix. (1961) *China*. New York: Doubleday.
——. (1964) *A Curtain of Ignorance*. New York: Doubleday.
——. (1966) *Vietnam! Vietnam!* Palo Alto: Fulton.
Han Suyin. (1965) *The Crippled Tree*. London: Jonathan Cape.
——. (1966) *A Mortal Flower*. London: Jonathan Cape.
——. (1967) *China in the Year 2001*. London: Watts.

Hinton, William. (1966) *Fanshen*. New York: Monthly Review Press.

Hobson, J. A. (1954) *Imperialism: A Study*, 5th printing. London: Allen and Unwin.

Lattimore, Owen. (1962) *Nomads and Commissars: Mongolia Revisited*. London: Oxford University Press.

Lenin, V. I. (1939) *Imperialism, the Highest Stage of Capitalism*. New York: International Publishers.

Luxemburg, Rosa. (1951) *The Accumulation of Capital*. New Haven: Yale University Press.

Moon, Parker T. (1925) *Imperialism and World Politics*. New York: Macmillan.

Mukherjee, Ramkrishna. (1958) *The Rise and Fall of the East India Company*. Berlin: VEB Deutscher Vorlag der Wissenschaften.

Myrdal, Gunnar. (1956) *An International Economy*. New York: Harper.

——. (1965) *Var Truede Verden*. Oslo: Pax.

Nkrumah, Kwame. (1966) *Neo-colonialism, the Last Stage of Imperialism*. New York: International Publishers.

Onwuachi, P. Chikwe, and Alvin W. Wolfe. (1966) The place of anthropology in the future of Africa. *Human Organization* 25: 93–5.

Robinson, Joan. (1964) *Notes from China*. London: Oxford University Press.

Robinson, Joan, and Solomon Adler. (1958) *China: An Economic Perspective*. London: Fabian International Bureau.

Schurman, Franz. (1966) *Ideology and Organization in Communist China*. Berkeley: University of California Press.

Snow, Edgar. (1962) *The Other Side of the River*. New York: Random House.

Stavenhagen, Rodolfo. (1966–7) Seven erroneous theses about Latin America. *New University Thought* 4(4): 25–37.

Steinberg, Fritz. (1951) *Capitalism and Socialism on Trial*. New York: J. Day.

Steward, Julian H. (1956) *The People of Puerto Rico*. Urbana: University of Illinois Press.

Strong, Anna L. (1962) *Cash and Violence in Laos and Vietnam*. New York: Mainstream.

——. (1964) *The Rise of the Chinese People's Communes – and Six Years After*. Peking: New World Press.

Taylor, Charles. (1966) *Reporter in Red China*. New York: Random House.

Townsend, Mary E. (1940) *European Colonial Expansion since 1871*. New York: J. B. Lippincott.

Wallerstein, Immanuel. (1966) *Social Change: The Colonial Situation*. New York: John Wiley.

Williams, Eric. (1944) *Capitalism and Slavery*. Chapel Hill: University of North Carolina Press.

Wolf, Eric R. (1959) *Sons of the Shaking Earth*. Chicago: University of Chicago Press.

World Almanac. (1967) New York: Newspaper Enterprise Association.

Worsley, Peter. (1964) *The Third World*. Chicago: University of Chicago Press.

——. (1966) The end of anthropology? Paper prepared for the Sociology and Anthropology Working Group of the 6th World Congress of Sociology.

11

National Liberation

Eric R. Wolf

In the midst of present-day upheavals, a new social science is beginning to emerge. This volume [*National Liberation*, 1971] is a contribution to this emergence: its constituent papers seek to ask new questions and to supply new answers. This new social science will necessarily have to be radical – radical not only in that it will touch on subject matter only grudgingly admitted into the precincts of the academic disciplines, radical not only in that it will have to be better social science (incorporating but also transcending what has been done in the past), radical not merely in seeking the clash of social forces beneath the integument of formal institutions, but radical above all, in returning to the "root" – to affirm, with the socialists and libertarians, that the "root is man." It is no accident, therefore, that we once again ask questions about alienation, about human capacities and their loss and transformation in different social systems, or that we seek "the primacy of the human factor" in a world increasingly emptied of human significance.

Once again, too, we need to be radical in posing questions about morality and human values, questions about ends as well as human means, in a world too often rendered inhuman by the unholy alliance of technocratic and bureaucratic elites. Perhaps it is true that historically such radical questions are asked most clearly by members of human groups and categories increasingly pushed to the margins of an ongoing social order. Barrington Moore has said recently that "the wellsprings of human freedom lie not only where Marx saw them, in the aspirations of classes about to take power, but perhaps even more in the dying wail of a class over whom the wave of progress is about to roll."[1] Yet the questions of the victims of yesterday reverberate through the corridors of history: the repressed return, time and time again, to pose problems of might and right, of human freedom and coercion, of relevance and purpose. If there is an "iron law of oligarchy," there is also, as Alvin Gouldner has noted,[2] an "iron law of democracy": men doggedly rebuild the bridges of democracy each time the oligarchical waves have washed them away. Only by returning to the human root of human activity can we discover something

From "Introduction," in R. Aya and N. Miller (eds.) *National Liberation* (San Francisco: The New Press, 1971), pp. 1–13.

of the great wellsprings of protest and creativity that rise again and again to beat against the bastions built to contain them. Protest and revolt, confrontation and revolution – as human facts – are the subject matter of the papers collected in this volume.

These papers surely do not yet make a new social science, but, together with many convergent efforts, they will presently. In his essay on "A Redefinition of the Revolutionary Situation," Manfred Halpern sounds some of the recurrent keynotes of these essays. For him, the origin of revolution is not merely and only social imbalance to be redressed and restored to equilibrium, but "incoherence," the anomic result of the "persistent breaking and reconstructing of fundamental linkages between individuals, groups, and ideas that constitute the unique and essential nature of the modern age." Marx was the chief diagnostician of the incipient forms of this incoherence. First, in primitive accumulation, the expanding capitalist system ransacked the world in its search for capital; later, in ever widening circles, it converted the tribesmen and peasants of the world into millhands, rubber-tappers, sugar-cane cutters, miners, or into scavengers and beachcombers on the slag heaps of civilization. It "created the world" as a social system, as Peter Worsley has said,[3] but it did so by converting human labor and natural resources into "free-floating" factors of production, ready-made for allocation within the capitalist market. Yet labor and resources are not abstract conceptual categories; they are human attributes and the attributes of human groups – and their conversion into commodities also liquidated age-old institutions upon which men had long depended for their safety and identity. Hence the triple crisis of the nonindustrial world in our time which I see as the key to modern peasant rebellion and revolution.

But Halpern goes further than this. Predicting that most of the world in the foreseeable future will strive to live with incoherence, by retreating into "apathy, repression, and normless violence," he also poses the other basic question of a new social science: what are to be the new forms of consciousness, of creativity, of institutionalized power, and of justice upon which we are to erect a new future? "To develop linkages and methods that make for conscious, creative transformation," he says, "remains one of the greatest unfinished tasks of our practical imagination." He poses a question of means as well as of ends; once again we are confronted by the great problem of how we are to shape the future through our means, by issues long thought dead – issues of spontaneity and consciousness, of direction from above and initiative from below, of coercion, and of authentic participation.

These means must be, as the situation requires, economic and political, psychological and ideological, warlike or "morally equivalent to war." They must be capable, moreover, of linking men of vastly different past experiences in common communication and action. Surely men have long dreamed of an end to injustice, of new men activating a new order of days in which a new freedom would override imposed and inauthentic constraints; and men have acted to implement these visions on the parochial level of their immediate understandings. The result has often been, however, an endemic and recurrent millenarianism that imagines a great human transformation – to the expensive neglect of the political and economic means required to assert the revolutionary project against its enemies, not only in the moment of its inception, but also in the course of its growth and transformation.

Finally, it has been the socialist argument that human alienation is prerequisite to the formation of a new consciousness, for only with the realization of the societal roots of alienation can we transcend our present incoherence. What is new in the radical politics of the twentieth century are the twin realizations that technology and organization must be joined with the ideology *and* that leaders and people must act in concert within society as a whole to transcend their common alienation. Otherwise, the result is an abortive prepolitical movement, exemplified by the Vietnamese sects... which joined a universal millenarian vision with a parochial politics that only resulted in the cooptation of the parochial millenarian machines by the larger exploitative state.

Action in concert, however, means participation by all and an end of political alienation through such participation. Participation, in turn, releases that burst of creativity which has everywhere marked the revolutionary upsurge, and which forms the ultimate human justification for a radical politics – not merely to end injustice, but, in ending injustice, to create a new world. Yet, if this vision is to remain more than an article of faith, then there is indeed room for a radical social science that systematically investigates what happens in the course of the constituent events. Only the analysts of revolutionary warfare have so far touched upon some of the relevant mechanisms, and then only in passing. When Eqbal Ahmad and I speak, in the papers before us, of "the profound and intense interaction between leaders and followers" in revolutionary warfare; when we discuss the process by which the rebels construct a new self-made social and political order in the recesses of mountain and jungle; when Mark Selden speaks of the development of the "mass-line" technique of linking leaders and followers, we touch upon the multitude of social processes constituting that "sovereignty of the human factor" on which revolutionaries must rely and which the counterrevolution must suppress if "pacification" is ever to become a reality.

Yet what, precisely, is it about men under given historical circumstances that grants such heroic and indestructible primacy to the human factor? What is it that transforms the silent mass of the downtrodden, who seemingly hear no evil, see no evil, and speak no evil, so they may ensure their survival from patient day to patient day, into the active protagonists of a creative political process. Surely Eqbal Ahmad is right in calling attention to the vital process of delegitimizing the established coercive order to overturn the taboos and restrictions that block the vision of new and creative alternatives. More than that, revolution frees men hitherto in bondage for active participation. It has become difficult to remember, fifty years after the Russian Revolution, the enormous release of energy that accompanied the creation of workers' and peasants' soviets in the midst of the revolutionary upsurge.... C. L. R. James, once again, expresses the capacity of the seemingly incoherent crowd, united by common experience and common grievances, to engage in concerted action; also, he draws attention to the emergence, in the political process of protest and confrontation, of innumerable men of the people, previously known only to their kin and friends, as the true heroes of a revolutionary political effort. All village studies carried on in revolutionary areas document the accelerated social mobility and engagement in creative tasks of men and women who might never have had an opportunity to express their talents under the old regime.[4] Often, indeed, the clusters of revolutionary leaders, urban and rural, seem to become the carriers of a speeded up process of learning and innovation.[5]

In this context we also need a new sociology of the creative unit. We now know something about the processes by which men bring their thoughts and attitudes into consonance with those of their fellow men, and the processes by which they are stimulated to seek new skills and knowledge. We are learning something about how individuals restructure their internal organization in terms of new societal visions. But we have not yet undertaken a comparative sociology of participatory groups. In this field of knowledge, it seems to me, lies the greatest challenge to the inherited dichotomy between "spontaneity" and "consciousness," which counterposed the image of the spontaneously acting masses to that of the cool and calculating rational political party. Some beginnings have been made,[6] but we need to assemble and interpret our accumulated knowledge of smaller scale participatory groups, of community action projects, of T-groups, of cooperatives and work brigades, of the revivalist camp meeting, of university seminars, and problem-solving meetings. The experiences of various innovative radical and revolutionary movements are now sufficiently wide-ranging and sufficiently established in daily practice to provide the source material for such systematic scrutiny.

Moreover, to the extent that such middle-level participatory groups form an essential relay between the people at large and the leadership, such scrutiny is also required for a proper understanding of what happens after the revolution has become a fact. Present attention is riveted most often on the synergetic qualities of revolutionary warfare, which seems to redouble and triple human energy; yet one of the key problems of radical transformation lies in how to institutionalize the creativity produced by the *grande fête* of the revolution. The recurrent problem of revolutions lies in the fact. . . . that "organizations tend, at some point in the process of institutionalization, to become counterrevolutionary." So far, he notes, "there appears to be no single organizational form appropriate to permanent revolution." The Russian Revolution sacrificed spontaneity to bureaucracy and was forced to introduce flexibility into the apparatus by "revolution from above," including repeated ukases for shaking up the entrenched official apparatus. The Cultural Revolution, in Mark Selden's words, "reaffirms the fundamental vision and significant institutional features of the Yenan legacy" – it sacrifices bureaucratic efficiency to the energies generated in participation. Yet, despite the centrality of the problem of bureaucracy, there has been precious little analytic radical thought about the nature of bureaucracy, or the need to explore the vital distinction between bureaucratic and nonbureaucratic modes of institutionalization. Talk of a "cult of personality" or of "bureaucratic degeneration" simply substitutes a devil theory of history and society for analysis; such phrases point the finger at satanic saboteurs, instead of seeking explanations of the phenomenon in the wider context of revolutionary transformation. Only recently the late Isaac Deutscher attempted to furnish the beginnings of a socialist explanation of the phenomenon of bureaucracy, by suggesting that bureaucracy gains in proportion to the exhaustion of social forces in the course of revolution.[7] This suggests that resources, including energy, diminish and disappear in the course of a revolution, and that one of the tasks of bureaucracy is to gather up and organize what remains for the next leap. There is surely a measure of truth in this view, but it does not spell out just how this garnering and concentration of resources may be achieved, and what may be its implications for the future course of revolutionary transformation. The essential function of any bureaucracy surely lies in its operation as a machine for allocation. It may be suggested that processes of allocation always have two functions; one is instrumental, the other is in the nature of ritual. We owe to Marx a very important insight into how money acquires its sacred character in capitalist society, because it serves as the chief allocative mechanism of the system.[8] But noncapitalist societies are not immune to the sacralization of their allocative processes; one of the tasks for radicals in the future will be not only to work out means for the control of bureaucratic positions through recall and rotation, as suggested by socialist analyses of the experience of the Paris Commune, but – even more importantly – to devise means for a participatory revision of the allocating process. While the Cultural Revolution has given increased power to the People's Liberation Army as a guarantor of order, as Pfeffer points out in his valuable contribution, it has striven at the same time to mobilize the Red Guards as relevant actors from below. This may ultimately result in a very different system of setting priorities and working out allocative procedures than has been the case in the Soviet Union, which seems as yet unable to subject its allocative process to any but bureaucratic revision.

Finally, a new social science of the order projected in these pages cannot, by its very nature, avoid the question of who is likely to make a revolution, where, when, and under what circumstances. Marx saw the motor of the impending revolution in the proletariat, subject to a massive alienation of its labor under uniform conditions of work. Yet, as Paul Sweezy was tempted to ask recently,

> If, for whatever reason, the emergence of a revolutionary situation is long delayed, what will be the effect in the meantime of modern industry's revolutionary technology on the composition and capabilities of the proletariat?

And he answered his question by saying that

> The revolutionary technology of modern industry, correctly described and analyzed by Marx, has had the effect of multiplying by many times the productivity of basic production workers. This in turn has resulted in a sharp reduction in their importance in the labor force, in the proliferation of new job categories, and in a gradually rising standard of living for employed workers. In short, the first effects of the introduction of machinery – expansion and homogenization of the labor force and reduction in the costs of production (value) or labor power – have been largely reversed. Once again, as in the period of manufacture, the proletariat is highly differentiated; and once again occupational and status consciousness has tended to submerge class consciousness.[9]

Thus the proletariat of the Western industrial nations disappointed socialist hopes for a revolutionary transformation in the heart of the capitalist system. Instead, the occurrence of the Russian Revolution not in the heartland of capitalism, but in an area in which capitalism and labor alienation were in their infancy, prompted the development of the hypothesis that revolution was most likely to occur in "the weakest links" of the capitalist system, rather than in its stronghold. Still later, the developing revolution in Asia prompted tendencies to substitute the peasantry, caught up in the vicissitudes of the capitalist market, as the decisive revolutionary element. In "Peasant Rebellion and Revolution" [in *National Liberation*] and in *Peasant Wars of the Twentieth Century* (Harper Row, 1969), I attempt to sharpen this point still further by declaring that it is precisely the most traditional kind of peasantry, the stratum of "petty bourgeois" middle peasants, whose relative deprivation (to critically adapt a currently fashionable term) is greatest with the advance of the capitalist market, that is likely to furnish the rural motor of modern rebellion and revolution. This raises a much larger point, only touched on occasionally... pages, but clearly of major importance: if it is not the absolute misery of the masses, but relative deprivation in terms of some previous social, cultural, and psychological standard that drives men to action, under what circumstances can action by the ruling classes reduce that sense of relative misery, and hence reduce the drive to revolution? If we are to know under what conditions revolutions can occur, we must also know something about when they do not occur. Barrington Moore, in his marvelous study of the *Social Origins of Dictatorship and Democracy*, has briefly sketched the outlines of the Japanese and German cases as examples of the successful cooptation of peasants by the industrialists, the landlords, and the state. In Russia, the same alternative was posed by the efforts of Pjotr Stolypin to create a broad stratum of relatively prosperous farmers after the abortive revolution of 1905. And it is a measure of Lenin's astute realization that such cooptation through land reform might in fact succeed that he was moved to write:

> Economic inevitability unquestionably causes and is effecting the most far-reaching upheaval in Russia's agricultural order. The question is only whether this is to be brought about by the landlords led by the tsar and Stolypin, or by the peasant masses led by the proletariat.[10]

In [*National Liberation*] the paper by John McLane on South Vietnamese religious "mafias" addresses itself to the same point, with a demonstration of how many South Vietnamese tenants and landless laborers, under the impact of economic and political alienation, joined cultic movements rather than movements of political rebellion, thereby granting political leverage to religious chieftains to create positions for themselves within the ruling South Vietnamese coalition. The term "mafia" seems appropriate, since in Sicily somewhat similar conditions of landlord absenteeism, coupled with the provision of work opportunities through individual informal contracts by labor bosses and administrators, similarly resulted in the development of "mafias" – hierarchical patron-client sets – at the expense of rebellious peasant movements.[11] This should caution us to analyze revolutions only as "just-so" stories in which every factor links up with every other factor to produce the inevitable culmination of the hoped-for final event. We have long known that revolutions ebb and flow, and we need to understand the conditions prompting one as much as the other. In this, too, we need to return to the "sovereignty of the human factor." It is human not only to storm the barricades, red flag in hand, in one grandiose moment of history, but also to endure through suffering and despondency and through the infinite cares of every day. One is our human lot as much as the other, and when a new social science wishes to ask "Why?" it must surely listen also to the words of those who each day weave the fabric of humanity from the warp and woof of their daily experience.

NOTES

1   Barrington Moore, Jr., *Social Origins of Dictatorship and Democracy* (Boston: Beacon Press, 1966), p. 505.

2 Alvin W. Gouldner, "Metaphysical Pathos and the Theory of Bureaucracy," *American Political Science Review* 49(2) (1955), pp. 496–507.

3 Peter Worsley, *The Third World* (London: Weidenfeld and Nicolson, 1964), p. 14.

4 See, for example, Isabel and David Crook, *Revolution in a Chinese Village* (London: Routledge and Kegan Paul, 1959); William Hinton, *Fanshen* (New York: Monthly Review Press, 1966); Jan Myrdal, *Report from a Chinese Village* (New York: The New American Library, 1966).

5 For a discussion of the role of clusters of individuals within social networks in evolutionary change, see the suggestive pages of Margaret Mead, *Continuities in Cultural Evolution* (New Haven, Conn.: Yale University Press, 1964).

6 See, for example, Amitai Etzioni, *The Active Society* (New York: The Free Press, 1968).

7 Isaac Deutscher, "Roots of Bureaucracy," in Ralph Miliband and John Saville (eds.), *The Socialist Register 1969* (London: Merlin Press, 1969), pp. 9–28.

8 T. B. Bottomore and Maximilien Rubel (eds.), *Karl Marx: Selected Writings in Sociology and Social Philosophy*, trans. T. B. Bottomore (London: Watts, 1956), pp. 171–7.

9 Paul M. Sweezy, "Marx and the Proletariat," *Monthly Review* 19(7) (1967), pp. 35–6, 38.

10 Quoted in Alfred G. Meyer, *Leninism* (New York: Praeger, 1957), p. 132.

11 Anton Blok, "Mafia and Peasant Rebellion as Contrasting Factors in Sicilian Latifundism." *Archives Européennes de Sociologie* 10(1) (1969), pp. 95–116.

Part III

Imperial Times, Colonial Places

Introduction

This section addresses the problem of knowledge and power through three key words: Colonialism, Orientalism and Capitalism. In 1946, after the end of the Second World War, an era of worldwide decolonization began. The two-fifths of the globe that made up the British empire, together with former colonial possessions of other European powers, became independent of their metropoles. India, jewel in the British imperial crown, became independent in 1947. These "new nations" were joined by most of Africa and the rest of the colonized world in the late 1950s and 1960s. Jointly these regions became known as the Third World as distinct from the First World (the West) and the Second World (the USSR). The Cold War had begun.

The articles in Part III show how the break-up of empires after the Second World War shifted anthropology's orientation away from its Enlightenment legacy towards the unequal power encounter between "the West" and the "Third World." The First and Second Worlds settled down to the longest era of peace since the nineteenth century. Meanwhile, proxy wars in Third-World territories were justified by the USA as matters of national security and the defense of the free world, and by the USSR as spreading international Communism and the export of revolution. These "small wars" took the form of post-independence revolutions, military coups, and civil wars.

Midway through the period, economic depression in the United States deepened "debt peonage" throughout much of the Third World. US military intervention intensified in central America as did covert intervention in Africa and southeast Asia.

At home, the academy was flooded with perspectives and paradigms to keep pace with it all. Colonialism and capitalism; anthropologies and histories; Marxisms and feminisms; texts and discourses; peasants and proletarians; domination and resistance feature in these nine chapters. More than ever before, field research became a politically charged experience in increasingly dangerous situations replete with moral and ethical dilemmas.

In 1973 Talal Asad launched a mold-breaking critique of the structural-functionalist social anthropology in *Anthropology and the Colonial Encounter*. This launched colonial studies in anthropology – ironically, during the very era when European colonies were being transformed into independent nation states. And so, strictly speaking, these studies were *post*colonial. Overlooked in the rush towards a new and redeeming colonial encounter, was Asad's observation in his book that anthropology was rooted in "an unequal power encounter... which goes back to the emergence of bourgeois Europe, *an encounter in which colonialism is merely one historical moment*" (emphasis added). Asad's "merely" is significant, and here (chapter 12) in his opening one-sentence paragraph that no one could miss, he begins to lay bare the larger narrative of the world in which anthropology emerged.

Asad's 1973 agenda – the historical power relationship between the West and the Third World – clearly embraced orientalism. Indeed, Edward Said's *Orientalism*, published five years later, shares the anthropological critique of the Euro-centered-ness of scholarship on Third World regions. For Fox the question is: How far can Said's theory of orientalism travel and how far should anthropology travel with him? In his ethnography of Punjabi Sikhs it helped him see that anthropology's concept of culture was part of the stereotyping tradition pushing orientalism along. But, in examining the utopian philosophy of Gandhi, Fox finds the theory lacking because it failed to discuss how Orientals, once orientalized by western domination, actually used orientalism itself against that domination (chapter 13).

Like Fox, Stoler (chapter 14) writes of a colonialism under whose aegis the capitalist world system gained a purchase on non-European territories. Here she clarifies the colonial–capitalism nexus in the Indonesian island of Sumatra, a Dutch colony "invaded" by international corporate planter interests in rubber, palm oil, tea, sisal, and tobacco where she carried out field research in the late 1970s. Here she uses company archives and newspapers to contrast the 1870s, when labor violence was personalized and down-played, with the 1920s when it was viewed as a politically motivated prelude to Communist revolt.

Stoler's work was not alone in drawing attention to "the narrative terrain on which colonial violence, fear and *terror* were bred" in *Capitalism and Confrontation in Sumatra's Plantation Belt, 1870–1979* (1995)). Taussig (chapter 15) urges that anthropology's construction of European conquest and colonization not overlook or underestimate the role of terror. He carried out fieldwork in Putumayo, southwest Colombia, between 1969 and 1984, surrounded by escalating militarization in South America, endemic torture and terror. Here he employs the autobiography of a victim of Argentinean torture and imprisonment, the terror of the rubber boom in the Belgian Congo as described by Roger Casement in a report to the British Foreign Office, and Joseph Conrad's novel *Heart of Darkness*, to frame his own interpret-ation of the operations of a British-Peruvian rubber consortium in Putumayo at the beginning of the twentieth century. Specifically, he seeks an explanation for its terrorizing the Indians into working rubber. The banality of cruelty horrifies him, the ordinariness of the extraordinary. The process whereby a culture of torture was created and sustained rested on the rubber planters' consciousness of danger: their fears of the jungle, of savagery, of cannibalism, of Indian rebellion.

Both Stoler and Taussig focus primarily on the consciousness of the colonizers – something of a new departure in political anthropology. Roseberry is concerned with a more traditional theme: emerging proletarian consciousness among coffee growers in Venezuela (See chapter 16). Drawing on the work of historian E. P. Thompson and political scientist James Scott, he discusses the value and limitations of the concept of "the moral economy" for understanding capitalist transformations, class consciousness, and the active force of the past in the present. But to understand the contradictory images, values, and feelings of the peasants turned proletarian, he turns to the literary critic Raymond Williams. Roseberry summarizes: culture cannot be separated from political economy. A dominant culture (such as that of colonialism or capitalism) is never "a coherent integrated cultural system or structure but rather an inchoate set of lived experiences, feelings and relationships within a political and economic order of domination" (see chapter 16). It is, moreover, constantly being constructed and reconstructed.

The Comaroffs approach the issue of domination through the colonization of consciousness (see chapter 17). They focus on the agency of cultural imperialism, as exercised by evangelical missionaries and the establishment of western cultural hegemony through the impact of the "secular" domain. They argue (in *Ethnography and the Historical Imagination*) that "the seeds of cultural imperialism were most effectively sown along the contours of everyday life."

Susan Gal, a linguist and a feminist, provides an overview of the historical silence and the silencing of women within specific institutional and cultural contexts over time (see chapter 18). Her central argument is the essentially gendered nature of the control of any discourse or representation of reality since it occurs in social interaction, is located in institutions, and is a source of social power. It may be at times, therefore, the occasion for coercion, conflict, or complicity.

Asad called for anthropology to consider seriously the *process* of European global power. Eric Wolf (chapter 19) reminds us of three ambitious bodies of research that foreshadowed many of the issues of global power that concern us at the beginning of the twenty-first century. Paths not quite taken to the end but from which we may, nevertheless, learn a great deal. June Nash (chapter 20) takes up this global story first by revisiting Immanuel Wallerstein's paradigm of a world capitalist system, and then by using ethnographic studies to explore features of particular societies in relation to universal characteristics of the human condition. Finally, she writes of the dangers in the contraction of the global system, initially through imperialism and colonialism, and now through transnational corporations. As she points out, new research organizations like Cultural Survival or Survival International have been created to bring anthropological perspectives to bear on worldwide environmental "developments" such as deforestation, the relocation of indigenous groups, ethnocide, genocide and human rights – subjects to be taken up in Part IV.

SUGGESTIONS FOR FURTHER READING

One attempt to counter the Eurocentric perspective on the Third World (of which both Asad and Said wrote) is Eric Wolf's *Europe and the People Without History* (1982). Appreciative summaries and critiques of this monumental work are to be found in W. Roseberry, "European History and the Construction of Anthropological Subjects," in *Anthropologies and Histories: Essays in Culture, History and Political Economy*, (New Brunswick, NJ: Rutgers University Press, 1985), and T. Asad, "Are there Histories of Peoples Without Europe? A Review Article," in *Comparative Studies in Society and History* 29 (1987). For an important work on peripheral capitalism, see S. Amin, *Unequal Development: An Essay on the Social Formations of Peripheral Capitalism* (New York: Monthly Review Press, 1976) and for the global gendering of capitalism, see M. di Leonardo, *Gender at the Crossroads of Knowledge:*

Feminist Anthropology in the Postmodern Era (Berkeley: University of California Press, 1991).

On Orientalism, Edward Said *Orientalism* (New York: Vintage Books, 1978/1994) might well be read in conjunction with T. Brennan, "The Illusion of a Future: *Orientalism* as Travelling Theory," *Critical Inquiry* 26: (2000): 558–83. F. Cooper and A. Stoler (eds.) *Tensions of Empire: Colonial Cultures in a Bourgeois World* (Berkeley: University of California Press, 1997) is probably the most exhaustive examination of colonialism extant. It has an excellent bibliography. See also T. Asad (ed.) *Anthropology and the Colonial Encounter* (London: Ithaca Press, 1973). M. Taussig, *Shamanism, Colonialism, and the Wild Man: A Study in Terror and Healing* (Chicago: University of Chicago Press, 1987) expands on the argument in chapter 15. A critique of his work by Eric Wolf, Sidney Mintz and Terence Turner, along with his response, appears in *Social Analysis* 12 (1987). J. and J. L. Comaroff, *Ethnography and the Historical Imagination* (Boulder: Westview Press, 1992) is the path-breaking first volume of a trilogy on "culture contact" (to use the old-fashioned term) in southern Africa.

J. Scott, *Weapons of the Weak: Everyday Forms of Peasant Resistance* (New Haven: Yale University Press, 1985) by a fieldworking political scientist, is probably the ethnography most widely read by anthropologists. G. Smith, *Confronting the Present: Towards a Politically Engaged Anthropology* (Oxford: Berg, 1999) uses fieldwork experience in Peru and Western Europe to develop a dialectical theory of hegemonic processes. J. Lears, "The Concept of Cultural Hegemony: Problems and Possibilities," *American Historical Review* 90 (1985): 567–93, is critical to the application of Gramscian analysis.

Several papers in G. Sider, and G. Smith (eds.) *Between History and Histories: The Making of Silences and Commemorations* (Toronto: University of Toronto Press, 1997) continue the discourse on silence and silencing opened by Susan Gal in chapter 18. But see, particularly, L. Lamphere, a study of a union drive at a plant in Albuquerque, "Work and the Production of Silence" (pp. 263–83).

For rich ethnographic analysis based on almost twenty years of field research, see K. Warren, "Interpreting *la Violencia* in Guatemala: Shapes of Kaqchikel Resistance and Silence," in K. Warren (ed.) *The Violence Within: Cultural and Political Opposition in Divided Nations*, (Boulder: Westview Press, 1993), pp. 525–60, and, for linkage with "new social movements" theory discussed in Part IV, see K. Warren, *Indigenous Movements and their Critics: Pan-Maya Activism in Guatemala* (Princeton: Princeton University Press, 1998).

12

From the History of Colonial Anthropology to the Anthropology of Western Hegemony

Talal Asad

I

The story of anthropology and colonialism is part of a larger narrative which has a rich array of characters and situations but a simple plot.

When Europe conquered and ruled the world, its inhabitants went out to engage with innumerable peoples and places. European merchants, soldiers, missionaries, settlers, and administrators – together with men of power who stayed at home, they helped transform their non-European subjects, with varying degrees of violence, in a "modern" direction. And of course, these subjects were not passive. The story recounts how they understood initial encounters with Europeans in indigenous cultural terms, how they resisted, adapted to, cooperated with, or challenged their new masters, and how they attempted to reinvent their disrupted lives. But it also tells of how the conditions of reinvention were increasingly defined by a new scheme of things – new forms of power, work, and knowledge. It tells of European imperial dominance not as a temporary repression of subject populations but as an irrevocable process of transmutation, in which old desires and ways of life were destroyed and new ones took their place – a story of change without historical precedent in its speed, global scope, and pervasiveness.

It was in this world that anthropology emerged and developed as an academic discipline. Concerned at first to help classify non-European humanity in ways that would be consistent with Europe's story of triumph as "progress" (Bowler 1989; Stocking 1987), anthropologists then went out from Europe to the colonies in order to observe and describe the particularity of non-European communities, attending to their "traditional" cultural forms or their subjection to "modern" social change.

From G. Stocking (ed.) *Colonial Situations: Essays on the Contextualization of Ethnographic Knowledge*, vol. 7 in *History of Anthropology* (Madison: University of Wisconsin Press, 1991), pp. 314–24.

There is nothing startling today in the suggestion that anthropological knowledge was part of the expansion of Europe's power, although there is a general consensus that the detailed implications of this bald statement need to be spelled out. The question then arises as to whether we want to fill in the broad picture of anthropology's growth that is already familiar to us or to illuminate through anthropology aspects of the transformation of which this discipline was a small part.

It is possible, at any rate, to deal straight away with some vulgar misconceptions on this subject. The role of anthropologists in maintaining structures of imperial domination has, despite slogans to the contrary, usually been trivial; the knowledge they produced was often too esoteric for government use, and even where it was usable it was marginal in comparison to the vast body of information routinely accumulated by merchants, missionaries, and administrators. Of course, there were professional anthropologists who were nominated (or who offered their services) as experts on the social life of subjugated peoples. But their expertise was never indispensable to the grand process of imperial power. As for the motives of most anthropologists, these, like the motives of individuals engaged in any collective, institutional enterprise, were too complex, variable, and indeterminate to be identified as simple political instrumentalities.

But if the role of anthropology for colonialism was relatively unimportant, the reverse proposition does not hold. The process of European global power has been central to the anthropological task of recording and analyzing the ways of life of subject populations, even when a serious consideration of that power was theoretically excluded. It is not merely that anthropological field work was facilitated by European colonial power (although this well-known point deserves to be thought about in other than moralistic terms); it is that the fact of European power, as discourse and practice, was always part of the reality anthropologists sought to understand, and of the way they sought to understand it.

II

What preexisting discourses and practices did anthropologists enter when they went at particular imperial times to particular colonial places? What concepts of dominant power did they assume, modify, or reject, as they tried to observe and represent the lives of "traditional" populations being transformed in a "modern" direction? ...

Stocking's fascinating essay [in Stocking 1991] traces the unfamiliar story of European colonial interventions and ethnographic concerns that preceded Malinowski in New Guinea, and in response to which he formulated many of his views about the study of culture. It was in this context, we discover, that Malinowski acquired his moral ambivalence regarding the consequences of modern change, and his predisposition to credit colonial authorities with good intentions. Stocking makes it clear that Malinowski either suppressed the presence of colonial powers and interests from his account of Trobriand life or represented them as essentially disintegrative of "tradition." Thus in an early passage that represents the classic functionalist doctrine, Malinowski writes:

> every item of culture ... represents a value, fulfils a social function. ... For tradition is a
> fabric in which all the strands are so clearly woven that the destruction of one unmakes

the whole. And tradition is...a form of collective adaptation of a community to its surroundings. Destroy tradition, and you will deprive the collective organism of its protective shell, and give it over to the slow but inevitable process of dying out. (Stocking 1991: 51)

This Burkean notion of tradition has been subjected to critical scrutiny by anthropologists and historians in recent decades. The point has been made repeatedly that in a world subjected for centuries to the forces of European capitalism and imperialism anthropological assumptions about cultural continuity, autonomy and authenticity must be questioned. Much of what appears ancient, integrated, and in need of preservation against the disruptive impact of modern social change is itself recently invented....

There is clearly much to be learned from such scholarly histories of the particular colonial contexts of anthropological practice. I propose that it is worth pursuing even further the critical inquiry they initiate. For in an important sense the concept of tradition employed in them is still the one espoused by Malinowski, and the disagreement is over which existing social arrangements qualify as "genuine" traditions and which as "invented" ones (Hobsbawm and Ranger 1983). Real tradition – so the assumption goes – is a matter of the unreasoning reproduction of custom, and it is therefore opposed to radical change. However, one may note here that this particular conception extends well beyond the writings of functionalist anthropologists and has its origins in the political response of European conservatives to the threat of the French Revolution.

The eighteenth century in Europe witnessed the development of a bourgeois social and moral order based on the principle of individual private property (Hill 1969; Porter 1982). Especially in England, this meant underwriting de facto class privileges through the systematization of law as precedent. The rhetoric of revolutionary France, with its attack on inherited privilege and prejudice in the name of universal reason and justice, was clearly a threat to conservative England. This was how Edmund Burke, the great spokesman of English class privilege, conceptualized the ideological danger facing that class, and how he theorized his counterattack. What made justice, and coherent social life itself, possible, was "tradition," and "tradition" consisted in a reverence for unbroken continuity, for the prejudices of the past, and it *was* indeed antithetical to the irresponsibility of free reason and the disruption of radical change.[1] Thus for Burke "the past" is not a particular (and changing) *conception* of one's inheritance – including those parts that are argued as being relevant to the present as compared with others that are not. "The past" is a palpable point of authority to which one is either linked by mimetic action or from which one is forever severed.

What are the implications of such a political genealogy for the way anthropologists have addressed change in precolonial, colonial, and postcolonial societies? One implication, I would suggest, has been the difficulty of theorizing the place of non-Western traditions within the contemporary scheme of things, except perhaps when they are depicted as "myths" that help people cope with disorientation or resist oppression. Indeed, such depictions often reinforce the assumption (even where this is not explicitly argued or intended) that traditions in the contemporary world may be regarded as functionally valuable insofar as they "empower the weak," but only because the universal principles of the Enlightenment project have not yet been fully realized.

A prominent example of this is the reaction of Western social scientists and Orientalists to the contemporary growth of Islamic rhetoric and practice in the Middle East. Thus, since the nineteenth century, it has not been common to find Western writers expressing the need to *explain* processes of Europeanization and secularization as opposed, that is, to *describing* them. The reason is that those processes are taken to be natural. The political invocations of Islamic traditions in that region have, on the other hand, been the object of a swelling stream of anxious explanation in recent years. What explains the recurrent political assertiveness of Islamic tradition? Typically, the answers tend to be given in terms of the localized failures of modernization,[2] or in terms of an irrational reluctance to abandon tradition.[3] But while there can be no doubt that Muslim societies have changed radically over the past two centuries, and that this has involved the adoption of Western institutions, values, and practices, it is not at all clear that every form of re-argued Islamic tradition must be seen either as an anomaly or as a spurious claim to historicity. The need to explain such developments as anomalies in the modern world indicates something about the hegemonic discourses of "progress," and about some of the fears underlying them in the contemporary West.

III

In an earlier period, when "progressive" Western scholars were less anxious about developments in the societies they studied, there was also a concern to *explain away* what appeared to be anomalies in the process of modernization experienced by colonized populations. An interesting example from the history of British anthropology is the attempt by members of the Rhodes–Livingstone Institute in central Africa to explain the persistence of "tribalism."

It is sometimes forgotten that functionalist anthropologists were as interested in analyzing "modern" change in colonial Africa as they were in reconstructing "traditional" cultures. The Rhodes–Livingstone Institute, in what is now independent Zambia, was a well-known research center devoted from the late 1930s on to documenting economic, political, and religious changes affecting African populations. In spite of all the social problems involved, the move from a "primitive" life toward "civilization" (Wilson 1945) was conceptualized as a progressive development.

When Max Gluckman succeeded Godfrey Wilson as the Institute's second director, the basic categories for apprehending that transformation were altered from "primitive" and "civilized" to "tribal" and "industrial." These categories were central to the administrative discourses of various colonial interests, including the copper mining company of Northern Rhodesia. (Many of the studies by Institute researchers were carried out in response to specific administrative problems (e.g., Epstein 1953, 1958).) A major preoccupation of the Institute, Gluckman wrote in 1961, was to understand the persistence of "tribalism," especially in the mines and townships which represented the most modern sectors of social life. "Tribalism," unlike "nationalism," was not intrinsic to modern life, and its presence needed explaining. Gluckman and his associates (notably Mitchell and Epstein) insisted that "tribalism" in urban areas was nothing more than a form of reconstructed group identity, something that would later be renamed "ethnicity." Since identities were inevitably determined by the economic conditions of towns as contemporary "social fields" (the phrase is Gluckman's), their compatibility with modernity was assured. Such tribalism was not a relic of the (traditional) past but a function of the (modern) present.

> Tribalism acts, though not as strongly, in British towns: for in these Scots and Welsh and Irish, French, Jews, Lebanese, Africans, have their own associations, and their domestic life is ruled by their own national [sic] customs. But all may unite in political parties and in trade unions or employers' federations. Tribalism in the Central African towns is, in sharper forms, the tribalism of all towns. (Gluckman 1961: 76)

Thus even for functionalist anthropologists of the colonial period the normality of colonized peoples was sometimes affirmed by arguing that their life was essentially the same as that of the metropole, albeit perhaps a little less developed along the universal path to modernity.

It is not only what historical events are felt to need explaining but also the terms in which they are thought to be persuasively accounted for that reveals the force of hegemonic discourses. Kuklick's story of the archeological disputes over the origins of the famous ruins of Zimbabwe, in the former British colony that adopted that name, is a revealing illustration of this point. Kuklick describes in detail how,

> seeking to legitimate their rule, British settlers and African nationalists subscribed to very different accounts of the building of the ruins, basing their construction alternatively in ancient times and the relatively recent past, and identifying the builders – or, at least architects – either as representatives of some non-African civilization or members of the indigenous population. (Stocking 1991: 137–8)

Yet what emerges strikingly from her account is the fact that Rhodesian settlers and Zimbabwean nationalists shared the basic terms of a historical argument. They accepted and used the modern European language of *territorial rights* and its essential preconditions: only long, continuous, *settled* association with a given territory could give its inhabitants exclusive title to it. Indeed, that was precisely the point of difference – according to the classical European law of nations – between a wandering "tribe" and a settled "nation." Thus the influential eighteenth-century *philosophe* Emer de Vattel:

> It is asked whether a Nation may lawfully occupy any part of a vast territory in which are to be found only wandering tribes whose small numbers can not populate the whole country. We have already pointed out, in speaking of the obligation of cultivating the earth, that these tribes can not take to themselves more land than they have need of or can inhabit and cultivate. Their uncertain occupancy of these vast regions can not be held as a real and lawful taking of possession; and when the Nations of Europe, which are too confined at home, come upon lands which the savages have no special need of and are making no present and continuous use of, they may lawfully take possession of them and establish colonies in them. (Curtin 1971: 44–5)

Furthermore, both colonialists and nationalists seem to agree that evidence of a relatively sophisticated urban life in its past indicated some capacity for social progress in a colonized people – *and that proof of such capacity was essential to the credibility of its claim to independence.* Imperial administrators might deny the existence of such capacity in the populations over whom they ruled, or insist that at any rate the capacity was too feeble to justify an immediate transfer of sovereignty, but the point is that this was central to the discourses legitimating independence – for colonizers and colonized alike. As they enter the political arena, archeologists and anthropologists too have found themselves inevitably involved in these hegemonic discourses. Gluckman and his colleagues at the Rhodes–Livingstone Institute were by no means exceptional in this regard.

Feit's excellent contribution [in Stocking 1991] provides another example. He shows that Speck's case for the existence of the principle of private property in Algonquian culture was the product of a local "colonial situation," including government policies and settler claims. What emerges from his account is that the defense of Algonquian interests in the face of predatory white settlers was felt to be credibly made only in terms of Western legal concepts. Whether it was Speck himself who conceived this defense, or the Algonquians whose claims he forwarded, the result was an account fully situated in Western discourses of power.

Feit draws on the recent work of Bishop and Morantz which apparently challenges that discourse. This is a work of revisionist history very much of the kind we need if we are to develop an anthropology of Western imperial hegemony. But in resorting to it we should remember to distinguish between legal facts and social practices that might be relevant to the law, for the former have an institutional force that the latter lack. Western legal discourse participates in processes of power by creating modern realities of a special kind, and it should not be thought of as a form of representation that can be subverted by scholarly argument. The realities are special in part because they define social relationships – for individuals as well as for corporate groups – in terms of legal "rights" and "duties" within the modern state.

When Europeans acquired imperial control over subject societies, they set up law courts to administer justice in a radically new way. Thus a legal historian of colonial Africa has recently described how the judicial system instituted there by the British gave some Africans new weapons to fight for their interests in profoundly changed social circumstances, as judicial individuation accompanied an emerging economic individualism. But more important, "defined legal rights and duties, enforceable through institutions, replaced ongoing relationships containing their own sanctions. The general sharpening of rights and sanctions were [sic] a result of 'disintegration' expressing itself through institutional change. 'Rights' were replacing both physical force and compromise" (Chanock 1985: 44). The mere presence of a government-instituted law court (including so-called customary courts) meant that resort to it required the treatment of vague claims and dissatisfactions in accordance with precise rules – that is, as "rights." The concept of "custom," which previously had the status of persuasive instances, now became grounds for judicial decisions, which possessed an entirely different authority, linked to the coercive character of the modern colonial state.

The writings of influential British anthropologists dealing with African law and custom failed to note this transformation in the direction of modern Western institutions (e.g. Gluckman 1955). Instead, they reproduced the hegemonic discourse of colonial administrators (which also later became the discourse of African nationalists), according to which "customary law" under the British was simply a more evolved form of "custom" in the precolonial era. As Chanock rightly points out, they did not recognize that the *representation* of conventional practice as a form of "customary law" was itself part of the process that *constituted* it as a legal instrument. That this was a colonial legal instrument is made plain in the way its effectiveness was defined – most notably, perhaps, in the rule that a "custom" cannot achieve the force of law if it is "contrary to justice and morality":

> Of all the restrictions upon the application of customary laws during the colonial period, the test of repugnancy "to justice or morality" was potentially the most sweeping: for customary laws could hardly be repugnant to the traditional sense of justice or morality of the community which still accepted them, and it is therefore clear that the justice or morality of the colonial power was to provide the standard to be applied. Of course, customary law evolved, as the sense of justice and morality of the community evolved; old rules might appear repugnant to new standards of justice and morality derived from colonial authority or other Western influences. (Read 1972: 175)

The uncritical reproduction of administrative-legal discourse by anthropologists of the colonial period was not confined to those who studied the functioning of African tribal courts. In much anthropological theory of that time the primary form of *all* social relationships in colonized societies was talked about in quasi-legal terms as "rights" and "duties."[4] The indeterminate, contradictory, and open-ended character of social structures was reduced in this way to the status of a precisely articulated and consistent legal-administrative document.

IV

The essays by Tomas (on Radcliffe-Brown in the Andamans) and Bashkow (on Schneider's intellectual biography) are valuable contributions to our knowledge of the history of colonial anthropology. But I have been arguing that we also need to pursue our historical concerns by anthropologizing the growth of Western imperial power, because unless we extend our questions about the cultural character of that hegemony, we may take too much for granted about the relationship between anthropology and colonialism. A number of scholars have begun to address themselves in interesting ways to this extended enquiry (e.g. Cooper and Stoler 1989). It needs to be stressed, however, that it is not enough for anthropologists to note that that hegemony was not monolithic, or that Western power continually evoked resistance. It is not enough because conventional political history of colonial times and places has always been a record of conflict: between different European interests, between different groups of non-Europeans, as well as between colonizers and colonized. We do not advance matters much conceptually if we simply repeat slogans about conflict and resistance in place of older slogans about repression and domination. An anthropology of Western imperial power must try to understand the radically altered form and terrain of conflict in augurated by it – new political languages, new powers, new social groups, new desires and fears, new subjectivities.

Turner's contribution [in Stocking 1991] is an anthropological account of aspects of precisely that transformation. He documents a profound change in Kayapo perspectives over the three decades of his involvement with them. Faced with white power, there is now not only a new assertiveness about their ritual life and conventional dress, but a new conception of their collective identity. Instead of seeing themselves as the autonomous paradigm of humanity, the Kayapo now present themselves as part of a dominated ethnic group (the Indians) engaged in political struggle with a dominant ethnic group (the whites). Turner notes that "over the past half-dozen years, the Kayapo have staged a series of demonstrations against a variety of threats to their political, social, and territorial integrity and their economic subsistence base" (Stocking 1991: 303), and goes on to describe how Kayapo traditions have become politicized and how his own conception of their culture was altered as a consequence of his involvement in their struggles. This involvement came through his use of audio-visual media. Resorted to at first for narrow documentary purposes, audio-visual media soon assumed a critical role in the Kayapo struggle against encroaching white power. "The Kayapo have passed rapidly from the initial stage of conceiving video as a means of recording events to conceiving it as the event to be recorded, and more broadly, conceiving events and actions as subjects for video" (ibid.: 307).

Turner's account of the changing concept of "culture" – from a closed system of mutually referring symbols and meanings to practices of collective identity that are technologically representable and legally contestable – is a substantial contribution to the anthropology of Western imperial hegemony that I am urging. It also illustrates the importance of some points I have argued above, including the ways in which contest and conflict are increasingly relatable to *legal* forms (even when governing powers seek to deny their legality). But in addition it deals with something that needs to be pursued more systematically: the role of Western technologies in transforming colonial subjects. Just as modern modes of locomotion (railways, motorcars, etc.) have altered concepts of time and space (Schivelbusch 1986), so Turner reminds us that modern modes of representation (e.g. film and video) have helped to reconstitute colonized subjectivities. All these things have certainly been very important for the changes that Western hegemony has brought about. It is necessary, however, to extend the concept of technology to include all institutionalized techniques that depend on and extend varieties of social power.

Right through modern imperial times and places, Western techniques for governing subjects have radically restructured the domain we now call society – a process that has reorganized strategies of power accordingly. This process has been extensively written about (and not only by Foucault and his followers) in the context of modern European history, but far less so in the context of Europe's imperial territories. In fact the difference between the processes of transformation in the two contexts remains to be properly explored. Grasping that difference seems to me to require in part a closer examination of the emerging discourses of "culture" (cf. Asad 1990). Until we understand precisely how the social domain has been restructured (constituted), our accounts of the dynamic connections between power and knowledge during the colonial period will remain limited.

NOTES

1   Thus it is with reference to this historical construction that MacIntyre (1980: 63) writes: "from Burke onwards, [conservatives] have wanted to counterpose tradition and reason

and tradition and revolution. Not reason, but prejudice; not revolution, but inherited precedent; these are Burke's key oppositions. Yet if [my] arguments are correct it is traditions which are the bearers of reason, and traditions at certain periods actually require and need revolutions for their continuance. Burke saw the French Revolution as merely the negative overthrow of all that France had been and many French conservatives have agreed with him, but later thinkers as different as Péguy and Hilaire Belloc were able retrospectively to see the great revolution as reconstituting a more ancient France, so that Jeanne D'Arc and Danton belong within the same single, if immensely complex, tradition."

2 For example: "Contrary to their expectations, however, education (even higher education) fails to provide them with the keys to modernity. It is from these circles that the heavy battalions of the Islamicist movement are drawn. They are the living symbols, and their numbers are massive, of the failure of the independent state's modernization project" (Kepel 1985: 218).

3 Thus the eminent Middle East specialist, Leonard Binder (1988: 293): "From the time of the Napoleonic invasion, from the time of the massacre of the Janissaries, from the time of the Sepoy mutiny, at least, the West has been trying to tell Islam what must be the price of progress in the coin of the tradition which is to be surrendered. And from those times, despite the increasing numbers of responsive Muslims, there remains a substantial number that steadfastly [stubbornly] argue that it is possible to progress without paying such a heavy cultural price." Binder's own closely argued book conveys the same Western message to Islam.

4 Thus Radcliffe-Brown (1950: 11): "An important element in the relations of kin is what will here be called the jural element, meaning by that relationships that can be defined in terms of rights and duties . . . Reference to duties or rights are simply ways of referring to a social relation and the rules of behaviour connected therewith. In speaking of the jural element in social relations we are referring to customary rights and duties. Some of these in some societies are subject to legal sanctions, that is, an infraction can be dealt with by a court of law. But for the most part the sanctions for these customary rules are what may be called moral sanctions sometimes supplemented by religious sanctions."

REFERENCES

Asad, T. (1990) Multiculturalism and British Identity in the Wake of the Rushdie Affair. *Politics & Society* 18(4): 455–80.

Binder, L. (1988) *Islamic Liberalism*. Chicago.

Bowler, P. (1989) *The Invention of Progress*. Oxford.

Chanock, M. (1985) *Law, Custom and Social Order: The Colonial Experience in Malawi and Zambia*. Cambridge.

Cooper, F., and A. L. Stoler (eds.). (1989) Tensions of Empire. *American Ethnologist* 16(4): 609–765.

Curtin, P. D. (1971) *Imperialism: Selected Documents*. London.

Epstein, A. L. (1953) *The Administration of Justice and the Urban African*. London.

——. (1958) *Politics in an Urban African Community*. Manchester.

Gluckman, M. (1955) *The Judicial Process among the Barotse of Northern Rhodesia*. Manchester.

——. (1961) Anthropological Problems Arising from the African Industrial Revolution. In *Social Change in Modern Africa*, ed. A. Southall, pp. 67–82. London.

Hill, C. (1969) *From Reformation to Industrial Revolution*. Harmondsworth.

Hobsbawm, E., and T. Ranger (eds.). (1983) *The Invention of Tradition*. Cambridge.

Kepel, G. (1985) *The Prophet and Pharaoh*. London.

MacIntyre, A. (1980) Epistemological Crises, Dramatic Narrative, and the Philosophy of Science. In *Paradigms and Revolutions*, ed. G. Gutting, pp. 54–74. Notre Dame.

Porter, R. (1982) *English Society in the Eighteenth Century*. Harmondsworth.

Radcliffe-Brown, A. R. (1950) Introduction to *African Systems of Kinship and Marriage*, ed. A. R. Radcliffe-Brown and D. Forde. London.

Read, J. S. (1972) Customary Law under Colonial Rule. In *Indirect Rule and the Search for Justice*, ed. H. F. Morris and J. S. Read, pp. 167–212. Oxford.

Schivelbusch, W. (1986) *The Railway Journey: The Industrialization of Time and Space in the Nineteenth Century*. Berkeley.

Stocking, G. (1987) *Victorian Anthropology*. New York.

——. (ed.) (1991) *Colonial Situations: Essays an the Contextualization of Ethnographic Knowledge*, vol. 7 of *History of Anthropology*. Madison: University of Wisconsin Press.

Wilson, G., and M. Wilson. (1945) *The Analysis of Social Change, Based on Observation in Central Africa*. Cambridge.

13

East of Said

Richard G. Fox

The creation of geographies – the recognition and understanding of symbolic territories – is central to Edward Said's work as I understand it. He writes, for example, about the creation of places of exile, of locations where there is a protracted sense of "not yet" and "not here" and a terrain of "national incompleteness" (Said 1986). In *Orientalism* (1978), he writes of lands defined by domination – the borders of the Orient mapped out by the superiority of the West's power to inscribe them.

Even when writing in the abstract, Said is moved to use geographical imagery, and his sense of intellectual movement is phrased in terms of diffusion. Thus, he mounts the notion of "traveling theories" in one of his essays (*The World, the Text, and the Critic*, 1983), which serves as a vehicle for him to consider theory as it moves from one intellectual locale to another. A theory has a point of origin, then travels a certain distance and meets new circumstances upon arrival, and finally, must undergo alterations in the contact situation.

Said's scholarly diffusionism, his own concern for traveling theories and the need to modify them in new circumstances, gives me purchase for these comments. How far can his theory of Orientalism travel? Can it travel East of Suez – where proverbially Europe stopped and Asia began – to reach as far as South Asia? Or does it founder on subcontinental history and culture? How far should anthropology (for I can only hope to judge my own discipline) travel with him? To what extent does the theory redirect anthropology along new paths in the study of culture? Or, conversely, can anthropology move the theory along in its own way?

Asking these questions, which demand measures of "how far" and "how much," rather than an invariant "yes" or "no" in our judgement of Said's Orientalism is, I believe, in itself a step in the right direction. Said's theory has gathered too many hasty fellow travelers . . . who condemn all South-Asian scholarship as Orientalist – a judgement of our collective understanding that is even more stereotyping, dominating, and pejorative than the Orientalism it deplores. Said's theory, conversely, has

From M. Spinkler (ed.) *Edward Said: A Critical Reader* (Oxford: Blackwell Publishers, 1992), pp. 144–56.

also mobilized an unreflective opposition, who refuse to budge from the idea of a value-free scholarship, which is as mythical as any epic tale from India.

I want to move my further comments along in two different ways. The first is a journey of pilgrimage, paying my respects to Said's theory of Orientalism, and charting how far it has taken me. When I came to write about the Sikhs of northern India a few years ago (*Lions of the Punjab*, 1985), Said's Orientalism brought me to a deeper understanding. I saw how British images of what India was like in general and what the Sikhs were like specifically constituted and compelled Sikh consciousness in the late nineteenth and early twentieth century. I saw how far an unreflective Orientalism carried British policy in India. Believing that some Indian "races" were inherently martial, the British recruited an army of Sikhs, who, the military authorities made sure, not only wore the badges of British regiments, but also the marks of Sikh religious orthodoxy, as British officers understood it. Sikh religious commandments became British military commands, and Sikh identity was therefore commandeered by the colonials. Said's theory traveled well to the Punjab I knew, at least as far as it, or I, went.

Along the way, I started thinking about what Orientalism meant for the standard concept of culture in anthropology. Citing Laroui's criticism of a Kroeberian cultural approach to the Near East, Said (1978) intimated that anthropology's concept of culture was part of the stereotyping tradition pushing Orientalism along – the approach in anthropology to the Other as "always Singular, always Capitalized," to quote Clifford Geertz (1985), who also condemns this approach. I think Said is right. With Said's impetus, the Sikh work tried to move away from the unitary, cohesive, constituting, and coercive model of culture that materialists like me, just as much as interpretive anthropologists, have been carrying around for a good while. Going forward with Said's Orientalism gives anthropology, I believe, a much more profound sense of the fictions of ethnography, of the conventions in the culture concept, of the tropes in our scholarly travels than the recent reflexive or postmodern critique does – because Orientalism shows that our fictions, conventions, and tropes are motored by inequalities in the world, not interlocutions in the field.[1]

My second way of approaching Said's Orientalism is not a pilgrimage; it is more like a raiding trip on the theory where I think it is weakest and most in need of modification to fit different circumstances. The starting-point is: how far did Orientalism, not Said's theory of Orientalism now, but the Orientalist domination he has documented, travel to the Orient that was its object and destination? Said allows in passing that Orientalism reached the Orientals (1978), but he does not go on with this idea. Therefore, I think Said's theory of Orientalism does not travel as far as Orientalism itself did. It remains a history of Orientalism from the West and affirms in the very way it is set out the categories of West and East it ostensibly attacks. It also does not allow the possibility that Orientals, once Orientalized by Western domination, could use Orientalism itself against that domination.

To return to the Sikhs: in the 1920s Sikh reformers believed and practiced the Orientalist stereotypes of the Sikh. Nevertheless, they used these stereotypes to lead a mass movement that eventually turned against British colonialism, although never against the British Orientalist image of the Sikh. They now commandeered British military forms and turned them into vehicles of protest. They inducted the martial and now militant Sikhs into rebellion and marched them along in anti-colonial formations. Said's theory stops before reaching this point: it does not map how far

Orientalism traveled and how much Orientalism came to constitute the consciousness of the Orientals. Said's theory also stops before reaching a still more important point: that Orientalism came to enable resistance against Western domination. Such, it seems to me, was the case in India, and not just for the Sikhs.

My current project (*Gandhian Utopia, Experiments with Culture*, 1989), which concerns what I refer to as Gandhian utopia, provides another case in point. The Gandhian utopian vision was a form of resistance to capitalism, colonialism, and the West. *Hind Swaraj*, the essay from 1909 in which Gandhi passionately condemns Western civilization and equally fervidly defends traditional India, powerfully expresses cultural resistance, as I shall soon show.

Where did Gandhi's cultural resistance come from? Many scholars, including K. M. Panikkar, Louis Dumont, Partha Chatterjee, Ashis Nandy, and Lloyd and Suzanne Rudolph, see Gandhi as expressing an indigenous cultural resistance against the West and its domination. . . .

The origins of Gandhian utopia are complex, as I shall indicate below. This history not only takes us far beyond what is in effect an Orientalist notion that it was indigenous resistance, but also prods us to go beyond Said's theory of Orientalism. Both Orientalism and Said's theory of it invest in Otherness. They depend on an elaboration – an exaggeration, I will now argue – of cultural differences and separate histories that certainly no longer existed by the nineteenth century.

Englishtan vs. Wisdom-land

Writing in the *Illustrated London News* for September 18, 1909, G. K. Chesterton exercised his wit on the Indian nationalist movement. Indian nationalism was neither very nationalist nor very Indian, Chesterton asserted. He went on to give weight to his word-play: the Indians putting forth demands for home rule (they wanted an independent, elected government for British India) belonged to an elite that did not represent Indian opinion. According to Chesterton, they were a small and decultured group that existed in a false, shadowed world – shadowed because they had been somewhat enlightened by British education and civilization, yet they were still partly darkened by India's obscure oriental traditions.

These Indian nationalists therefore did not represent the true India, and what they asked for in the way of nationalism was quite inauthentic. After all, Chesterton argued, how could their nationalism be authentic when all they wished for was their own English-style parliament, and their own English-style elections, and their own English-style liberties. Now if they asked for a truly Indian independence, Chesterton maintained, the British should naturally be required at least to listen to them seriously, but this sham nationalism hardly deserved credence.

Chesterton's fulminations profoundly convinced one reader, who wrote home about them in 1909. This reader came to repudiate the brown Englishmen who ran the nationalist movement – Macaulay's bastards, as an Indian character in Anita Desai's novel *Bye-Bye Blackbird* self-deprecatingly calls them, after the mid-nineteenth-century British official who wanted to produce a class of Indians British in all but their skin color – but he reproved them more gently than Chesterton. He came to repudiate the Parliament the nationalists wanted; he agreed with Chesterton that this was not authentically Indian. And he grew to believe in a people's democracy that started in the little republic of the Indian village and built up in "oceanic circles" – village added to village – to form a national government. He also, because he was thorough to a fault, repudiated modern physicians and Western medicine (except for Dr Kellogg's nut butter), trains, lawyers, printed books, telegraphy, and modern civilization in general.

Mohandas Karamchand Gandhi, not yet the Mahatma, read Chesterton's diatribe while in Britain to plead for the plight of South Africa's Indians. He wrote home excitedly, endorsing Chesterton's condemnation of an Indian nationalism that only aped the West:

> Indians must reflect over these views of Mr Chesterton and consider what they should rightly demand . . . May it not be that we seek to advance our own interests in the name of the Indian people? Or, that we have been endeavoring to destroy what the Indian people have carefully nurtured through thousands of years? I . . . was led by Mr Chesterton's article to all these reflections . . . (*Collected Works* (Gandhi 1958–83) hereafter *CWG*, vol. 9: 426)

On the return voyage to South Africa, Gandhi reflected further and even more passionately embraced an Indian nationalism that claimed authenticity by declaiming against the West. In *Hind Swaraj or Indian Home Rule*, written aboard ship, Gandhi inscribed Chesterton's message as the credo for a different Indian nationalism. He went far beyond Chesterton's sarcasm and superficiality. Condemning *ersatz* Indian imitations of the West, as Chesterton had, Gandhi on the one hand broadened it into a fervid rejection of modern civilization, while on the other, he used it as an acclamation of traditional India – and thereby as an apology for contemporary India's "backwardness." Gandhi first disowned a nationalism that "would make India English. And when it becomes English, it will be called not Hindustan but *Englishtan*. This is not the Swaraj that I want" (Gandhi 1938: 30). True nationalism, for Gandhi, must disavow modern civilization and build on India's traditional strengths:

> The tendency of Indian civilization is to elevate the moral being, that of the Western civilization is to propagate immorality. The latter is godless, the former is based on a belief in God. So understanding and so believing, it behoves every lover of India to cling to the old Indian civilization even as a child clings to the mother's breast. (1938: 63)

India needed no Parliament other than the ancient village *panchayat*; no Western enslaving machinery when the peasant's plow had served well for thousands of years; no all-consuming Western consumerism when India's wise ancients had counseled against luxuries and indulgence (1938: 61–2). British colonialists and Indian nationalists who mimicked them wanted to replace India's traditional strength with modern Western weakness, precisely because they mistook strength for weakness:

> It is a charge against India that her people are so uncivilized, ignorant and stolid that it is not possible to induce them to adopt any changes – What we have tested and found true on the anvil of experience, [however,] we dare not change. Many thrust their advice upon India, and she remains steady. This is her beauty. (1938: 61)

Disowning modern civilization in 1909, Gandhi already perceived his utopian vision in broad outline. What precisely brought him to this condemnation? If long-latent beliefs – from Jainism or Indian culture in general – were important influences, why did Gandhi wait to reject modern civilization and "Englishtan" until 1909, when he was forty years old? Even Hay allows that Gandhi's disenchantment with modern, rather than Western, civilization developed as he prepared a talk on "The East and the West" for a British pacifist society ("Jaina Goals and Discipline," Hay 1978: 125). Gandhi delivered this talk on October 13, 1909 (*CWG*, 9: 478).

Let us look into the immediately previous history to see if it throws light on what led to Gandhi's supposed realization of his Jain imprinting. Gandhi stated right after his talk to the pacificsts (*CWG*, 9: 478) that "the thing was brewing in my mind" and in a letter of October 14, 1909, he maintained that his ideas were not "new but they have only now assumed such a concrete form and taken a violent possession of me" (*CWG*, 9: 481).

Did Gandhi's "not new" condemnation in 1909 in fact go back to a Jain past brewing in his mind over many years? It does not seem so. Gandhi's condemnation of an Indian nationalism premised on modern civilization was rapid. In 1906 he thought he would rather live in London than anywhere else (Hunt 1978: 143), but by 1909 he was of a much different mind. He suggested that it might be necessary to visit London, but "I am definitely of the view that it is altogether undesirable for anyone to ... live here" (*CWG*, 9: 389). What made London deplorable in 1909 was modern civilization: "We have trains running underground; there are telegraph wires already hanging over us, and outside, on the roads, there is the deafening noise of trains. If you now have planes flying in the air, take it that people will be done to death. Looking at this land, I at any rate have grown disillusioned with Western civilization" (*CWG*, 9: 426).

Modern civilization had not just come to London between 1906 and 1909. What, then, had come to Gandhi over this short period that produced his disillusionment? Perhaps one precondition was the strong influence of the vegetarian and Theosophist Edward Maitland during Gandhi's early days in South Africa. Maitland corresponded with Gandhi and sent him books. In 1894, Gandhi advertised himself as an agent for Maitland's Esoteric Christian Union in Natal. This organization stood in opposition to "present-day materialism" (Hay 1970: 278). Sometime after 1906, he re-read Tolstoy's affirmation of nonviolence in *The Kingdom of God Is Within You*, which proved much more affecting the second time ... Still, even as late as 1907, Gandhi continued to believe in the benefits of British rule and Western education (Swan 1985: 143–5).

Then in the spring of 1908, Gandhi translated Ruskin's *Unto This Last*, which he had read for the first time some years earlier. This original reading led him to set up his first experimental community, the Phoenix settlement, in 1904. Gandhi played off Ruskin's condemnation of capitalist political economy to argue that British commercialism and industrialism were unsuitable for India (Hunt 1978: 144). Introducing his translation of Ruskin (Spring 1908), Gandhi allowed that imitating the West in some ways might be necessary, but that "many Western ideas are wrong" (*CWG*, 8: 239–41). In a talk to the Johannesburg YMCA in May 1908, Gandhi distinguished modern technology from Christian progress, declining "to believe that it is a symbol of Christian progress that we have got telephones ... and trains" (Hunt 1978: 144). Although he already regarded Western civilization as destructive, he also viewed India as lethargic. Eastern civilization, Gandhi argued at this late date, "should be quickened with the Western spirit," and he saw mutual advantage to the meeting of the British and Indian "races" in India (CWG, 8: 244, 246).

His growing disbelief in the West was further confirmed and sharpened by what he read in London during 1909.[2] Gandhi absorbed Edward Carpenter's "very illuminating work," *Civilization, Its Causes and Cure*, and its condemnation of modern civilization. Carpenter, who called ancient India "the Wisdom-land" (Carpenter 1910: 355), in recognition of its spiritual superiority to the West, led Gandhi to see clearly and afresh the Indian nationalist problem. Gandhi warned his correspondent Polak in a letter of September 8, 1909 that during a previous trip to Bombay Polak saw "Westernized India and not real India." Gandhi also said that he issued this warning upon reading Carpenter's book (CWG, 9: 396). Shortly thereafter he read Chesterton's article; about a month later he wrote *Hind Swaraj* aboard ship. Chesterton and Carpenter, in different ways, clarified for Gandhi that his resistance should not be to the British people, but to modern civilization, and that a truly Indian nationalism – not the simulacrum of the West that Chesterton rightly ridiculed – had to build on ancient traditions and had to be a *swaraj* of the spirit. They helped Gandhi distinguish his nationalism from the Indian "anarchism" adopted by expatriate groups he also met during his London visit (Gandhi 1972: 211). These other Indian nationalists disowned Gandhi for his loyalty to the British, not understanding his more profound disloyalty to modern civilization . . .

Gandhi's new nationalism is compelled by Chesterton's diatribe against what Gandhi shortly thereafter labels "Englishtan" in India. Gandhi accepts the definition of an authentic Indian nationalism that Chesterton thrusts at him – and so he embraces an Indian nation without parliaments, physicians, lawyers, and trains. Chesterton's view of the authentic path for India is obviously shot through with cultural stereotypes – the notions, for example, that parliaments and elections are inherently foreign to India or that the Westernized Indian is fundamentally decultured and unrepresentative. Butting up against the domination encoded in Chesterton's stereotype, Gandhi can only achieve an authenticated Indian nationalism by rejecting "Englishtan." Chesterton also enables Gandhi, however: by saying what an authentic Indian nationalism cannot be, Chesterton gives Gandhi the space to say what it can be: if not "Englishtan," then a Wisdom-land utopia built on the ancient cultural essentials.

In positing this utopia, Gandhi is again compelled and enabled, in a reverse way, by the critics of modern capitalist civilization, Ruskin and Carpenter. Through their resistance to Western materialism and mechanization, Ruskin and Carpenter enable Gandhi's rejection of modern civilization. Carpenter, however, compels Gandhi's nationalism by stereotyping India as a Wisdom-land of spirituality and anti-materialism. He was of course not the first to give a positive image of India, just as Chesterton was not the first to offer a pejorative view. Whether negative or positive, these stereotypes are equally Orientalist, that is, they are equally products of the cultural domination of India by the West, and they equally compel and enable Gandhi's utopian resistance to that domination. Gandhi is compelled against "Englishtan" by Chesterton, and further enabled in that opposition by Carpenter and Ruskin. By Carpenter, however, Gandhi is compelled into an Indian nationalism based on the traditional Wisdom-land, which Chesterton enables by denouncing

"Englishtan." What actualizes Gandhi's utopian denunciation of the West is not some long-latent Jain influence, although this latter may have entered into it. Gandhi's dream develops early in the twentieth century as he struggles with and "bounces off" the negative *and* positive Orientalist stereotypes of India encoded in existing Western domination.

Gandhian cultural resistance depended on an Orientalist image of India as inherently spiritual, consensual, and corporate. This image had a complex authorship and a contradictory character. Pejorative stereotypes of India, mainly portrayed by European detractors, led to one aspect of it. In this view, India was passive, otherworldly, tradition-ridden or superstitious, caste-dominated, morally degraded, unfree and despotic, and therefore weak, backward, and unchanging. Moral degradation was everywhere: in the hereditary associations dedicated to evil, like that of the Thugs, in the so-called self-immolation of widows (*sati*), in female infanticide, and in Untouchability. There were, furthermore, idolatry, indecent ceremonies, slavery, ritual murder, and many other vile practices that all went to show, as Southey put it, "that of all false religions, Hinduism was the most monstrous in effect" (quoted in Bearce 1961: 104). Politics was no less a sink of inequity, for despotism ruled India; James Mill said in 1812 it proved India's incapacity for self-governance (Bearce 1961: 71). So foul a culture justified a harsh cleansing, which could come, in the opinion of colonial administrators like Macaulay, only by turning India from the Brahmans to the British, from superstition to science, from traditional lore to European logic, from the otherworldly to the utilitarian, and from the backward to the modern. Alexander Duff, William Wilberforce, Charles Grant, and many others contriubuted to this pejorative Orientalist stereotype (. . . Bearce 1961; Kopf 1969: 254–61; Müller 1883; Risley 1915).

Affirmative stereotypes of India created another, although contradictory, aspect of this Orientalist image. These stereotypes butted up against the negative image of India and reversed it. What appeared in pejorative Orientalism as India's ugliness now became India's beauty; her so-called weaknesses turned out to be her strengths. Otherworldliness became spirituality, an Indian cultural essential that promised her a future cultural perfection unattained in the West. Passiveness became at first passive resistance and later nonviolent resistance – the age-old Indian character thus provided a revolutionary technique by which to bring on that future perfection. The supposed penchant of India to accept despotism led Gandhi to reject the state entirely. The backward and parochial village became the self-sufficient, consensual and harmonious center of decentralized democracy. An absent national integration turned into the oceanic circles of a people's democracy. Insufficient Indian individualism became altruistic trusteeship, and inadequate entrepreneurial spirit turned into non-possessiveness. This "affirmative Orientalism" owes much to Europeans like the vegetarian Henry Salt, the Theosophist Annie Besant, the Hindu convert Sister Nivedita, the simplifier Edward Carpenter, and the champion of spiritual nonviolence, Tolstoy, all of whom employed these positive stereotypes against a modernized, aggressive, capitalist, materialistic, and carnivorous Europe for which they bore little love. Indian nationalists, in advance of Gandhi or coterminous with him, also contribute to affirmative Orientalism: Lokmanya Tilak and his portrayal of caste as a means to organize society without class conflict; the reformers of the Arya Samaj and the Brahmo Samaj, who believed India's current progress depended on rediscovering the past, when it had been a Wisdom-land; and Veer Savarkar, who justified a modern nationalism by what he took to be an antique spiritual bond between Hindu and Hindustan, the Fatherland . . .

Gandhian utopia reacts against negative Orientalism by adopting and enhancing this positive image. It therefore ends up with a new Orientalism, that is, a new stereotype, of India, but an affirmative one, leading to an effective resistance. In this transformation, Said's theory seems to be left behind.

To be sure, Said's theory started with Europe, and perhaps it was never meant to travel to the Orient itself. But it also skirts some important European history, for example, the consequences for Europe itself of affirmative Orientalism or what Raymond Schwab called the "condescending veneration" of the Orient. Orientalism did not only serve European domination. Affirmative Orientalism furthered the resistance by Europeans to Western capitalism and modern industrial society. Said's theory, because it bounds West from East, misses this world system of authorship – the ramified intellectual work group composed of European utopians, Unitarians, simplifiers, vegetarians, and sexual libertarians like Ruskin, Tolstoy, Carpenter, Salt, and Kingsford, joined by Indian cultural nationalists like Gandhi, Vivekananda, Krishnavarma, Savarkar, and Aurobindo, and linked through "Indians by persuasion" like Besant and Noble. Their affirmative Orientalism not only configured a utopian future for India but also condemned the dystopian present in the European core. If we are enjoined not to be silent about domination, we cannot use categories like West and East that may silence the dynamics of struggle against cultural domination anywhere in the world system.

Orientalism as a theory does not go far enough in recognizing that resistance to Orientalist domination proceeds from within it. In this respect, it may travel too far toward several Third-World writers who stress the autonomy of cultural resistance – for India, for instance, Ashis Nandy or the so-called subaltern scholars, some of whom argue for a peasant revolutionism or a Gandhism contingent on European domination but quite autonomous from it.

Partha Chatterjee, for example, maintains that Gandhi's was an authentic and effective indigenous resistance. It may have utilized European commentaries, but it was in essence unauthorized by British domination, although it never completely escaped its control (Chatterjee 1986: 42). Unlike Chatterjee, Nandy does not see Gandhi as the nearly perfect representative of deeply-rooted Indian cultural values, but he does believe that Gandhi's dream creatively used them. For Nandy, Gandhi operated outside the shared system of ideas that configured both British imperialists and many other Indian nationalists. The Mahatma was neither simply "a genuine son of the soil" nor a "totally atypical Indian" (Nandy 1980: 83). Nevertheless, Nandy agrees that Gandhi championed and transformed folk values that "had remained untamed by British rule" (Nandy 1983: 100), and he thereby constructed a denial of the West that was also not of the West (ibid: 100–6; Nandy 1980: 130–1, prefigures this approach).

But here again we see a retreat to a notion of East is East and West, West, even after 150 years of British Indian colonialism and 350 years of the capitalist world system's penetration of India. Gandhian utopia occurred not in the first flush of indigenous resistance but only after nearly two centuries of the world system's penetration and domination. By the late nineteenth century, British colonialism, under whose aegis the capitalist world system gained a purchase on India, had introduced fundamental changes at all levels of Indian society and culture (for general descriptions of change under colonialism, see Fox 1967 and 1985; Jones 1976; Rudolph and Rudolph 1967; Sarkar 1983; Seal 1970; Srinivas 1962; Washbrook 1976).

Are there really crannies of indigenous culture that remain proof against the world system long after its uninvited arrival, as Nandy and Chatterjee – and, by extension, Said's theory of Orientalism – maintain? Or must we speak of a world system of cultural domination, in which Orientalism – and cultural resistance to it – emerge from a complex global authorship? Orientalism in India travels far and wide – not only on Indian backs, but also in their minds. So, too, the affirmative Orientalism that led to an effective cultural resistance in India makes its way into the world stream, as Gandhi's spiritual and spirited nonviolence, well-fitted to India's traditions (he thought), comes to rest on a bus seat in Montgomery, Alabama or in a California vineyard.

Traveling theories, like any baggage, get knocked about in transit. I do not mean to mishandle Edward Said's Orientalism, but I do think our ultimate destination lies further along than it has travelled – or perhaps can travel. I suspect Said would rather see it tossed about and then reinforced for further travel than have it artificially brought along with kid-glove treatment. Certainly, Orientalism has proved very sturdy in recognizing Western cultural domination and prodding anthropologists and South Asianists to see our complicity in it. But now we have to travel further on, to see the intimacies between European Orientalism's domination and the Third World's cultural resistance. We have only reached this point, however, because Said's theory has traveled so well and because he has been so remarkable a cicerone.

NOTES

1   My reference is to the textual critiques of ethnography – its treatment as a "fiction" or literary construction, as, for example, in Clifford 1983 and Clifford and Marcus 1986.
2   In 1909, Gandhi read a work that was very influential on him, Tolstoy's plea for nonviolence, *Letter to a Hindu*, but which is not discussed here. I deal with this work in the context of the invention of *satyagraha* in *Gandhian Utopia*, ch. 7 [Fox 1989].

REFERENCES

Bearce, George D. (1961) *British Attitudes Towards India, 1784–1858*. London: Oxford University Press.
Carpenter, Edward. (1910) *From Adam's Peak to Elephanta*. London: Swan Sonnenschein.
———. (1921) *Civilization, Its Causes and Cure* [1889]. New York: Scribner's Sons.
Chatterjee, Partha. (1984) "Gandhi and the Critique of Civil Society," in *Subaltern Studies III*, edited by Ranajit Guha. Delhi: Oxford University Press, pp. 153–95.
———. (1986) *Nationalist Thought and the Colonial World, A Derivative Discourse?* London: Zed Books.
Clifford, James. (1983) *The Predicament of Culture: Twentieth-Century Ethnography, Literature and Art*. Cambridge, Mass.: Harvard University Press.
Clifford, James, and George Marcus. (1986) *Writing Culture: The Poetics and Politics of Ethnography*. Berkeley: University of California Press.
Desai, Anita. (1971) *Bye-Bye Blackbird*. Delhi: Hind Pocket Books.
Duff, Alexander. (1840) *India and India Missions*, 2nd. edn. Edinburgh: John Johnstone.

Dumont, Louis. (1970) *Homo Hierarchicus*, trans. Mark Sainsbury. Chicago: University of Chicago Press.

Fox, Richard G. (1967) "Resiliency and Change in the Indian Caste System: The Umar of U. P." *Journal of Asian Studies* 26: 575–88.

——. (1985) *Lions of the Punjab: Culture in the Making*. Berkeley and Los Angeles: University of California Press.

——. (1989) *Gandhian Utopia, Experiments with Culture*. Boston: Beacon Press.

Gandhi, Mohandas Karamchand. (1938) *Hind Swaraj or Indian Home Rule* [1909]. Ahmedabad: Navajivan Publishing House.

——. (1958–83) *Collected Works of Mahatma Gandhi*, 89 vols. Delhi: Publication Division, Ministry of Information and Broadcasting, Government of India.

——. (1972) *Satyagraha in South Africa* [1928], trans. V. G. Desai. Ahmedabad: Navajivan Publishing House.

Geertz, Clifford. (1985) "Waddling In." *Times Literary Supplement*, June 7, pp. 623–4.

Hay, Stephen N. (1970) *Asian Ideas of East and West, Tagore and His Critics in Japan, China, and India*. Cambridge, Mass.: Harvard University Press.

——. (1978) "Jaina Goals and Discipline in Gandhi's Pursuit of Swaraj," in *Rule, Protest, Identity, Aspects of Modern South Asia*, edited by Peter Robb and David Taylor, London: Curzon Press, pp. 120–31.

Hunt, James D. (1978) *Gandhi in London*. New Delhi: Promilla.

Inden, Ronald. (1986) "Orientalist Constructions of India." *Modern Asian Studies* 20: 401–46.

Jones, Kenneth W. (1976) *Arya Dharm: Hindu Consciousness in 19th-Century Punjab*. Berkeley and Los Angeles: University of California Press.

Kopf, David. (1969) *British Orientalism and the Bengal Renaissance*. Berkeley and Los Angeles: University of California Press.

Müller, Max. (1883) *India: What Can It Teach Us?* New York: Funk and Wagnalls.

Nandy, Ashis. (1980) *At the Edge of Psychology*. Delhi: Oxford University Press.

——. (1983) *The Intimate Enemy, Loss and Recovery of Self Under Colonialism*. Delhi: Oxford University Press.

Panikkar, K. M. (1964) *Hinduism and the West: A Study in Challenge and Response* Chandigarh: Panjab University Publications.

Risley, Sir Herbert Hope. (1915) *The People of India*. London: W. Thacker and Company.

Rudolph, Lloyd I., and Suzanne Hoeber Rudolph. (1967) *The Modernity of Tradition: Political Development in India*. Chicago: University of Chicago Press.

Said, Edward W. (1978) *Orientalism*. New York: Vintage Books.

——. (1983) *The World, the Text, and the Critic*. New York: Vintage Books.

——. (1986) *After the Last Sky*. New York: Pantheon.

Sarkar, Sumit. (1983) *"Popular" Movements and "Middle Class" Leadership in Late Colonial India: Perspectives and Problems of a "History From Below."* Calcutta and New Delhi: K. P. Bagchi.

Schwab, Raymond. (1984) *The Oriental Renaissance, Europe's Rediscovery of India and the East 1680–1880*, trans. Gene Patterson-Black and Victor Reinking. New York: Columbia University Press.

Seal, Anil. (1970) *The Emergence of Indian Nationalism: Competition and Collaboration in the Later Nineteenth Century*. Cambridge: Cambridge University Press.

Secretary of State for India, United Kingdom. (1907) *Report and Minutes of Evidence of the Committee Appointed by the Secretary of State for India to Inquire into the Position of Indian Students in the United Kingdom*. London: Eyre and Spottiswoode.

Srinivas, M. N. (1962) *Caste in Modern India*. Bombay: Asia.

Swan, Maureen. (1985) *Gandhi: The South African Experience*. Johannesburg: Ravan Press.

Washbrook, David. (1976) *The Emergence of Provincial Politics: The Madras Presidency, 1870–1920*. Cambridge: Cambridge University Press.

14

Perceptions of Protest:
Defining the Dangerous in
Colonial Sumatra

Ann Stoler

In 1876 the wife and children of a Dutch planter were murdered on a plantation on Sumatra's East Coast. The crime apparently went unreported in the press, barely entering official discourse, much less the public domain. It was literally an unspeakable event. A half century later in 1929, a Javanese coolie killed the wife of a European estate manager. The murder became an Indies-wide scandal. Hundreds of European women on the East Coast sent telegrams to Queen Wilhelmina demanding protection. The Indonesian- and Dutch-language press in Sumatra gave daily coverage to the coolie's trial, sentencing, and hanging a month later, to speculations on the further spread of "dangerous" and "extremist elements," and to expressions of outrage from the European community in the Indies and abroad. Meanwhile Dutch newspapers in Java speculated on a "Moscow-Deli connection" directly construing the incident as proof of a communist threat. Army troops were sent from Java to "restore order" despite the lack of public demonstrations (much less riot) by either the estate-based Javanese or native urban population.

That these two – on the face of it – "similar" events had such enormously different political import and social consequence is not particularly surprising. After all, in 1876 Sumatra's East Coast was still being pioneered and pacified and one could argue that some degree of violence was endemic to the process. By 1929, however, when a fully developed legal and administrative apparatus was in place, when the infrastructure of power had long been established, when colonial authority and the white enclave that lived off it seemed totally secure, such a murder was a social affront, a sexual violation, an outrage.

Again it is not surprising that acts of individual or collective violence should have their historically specific import, interpretation, and intent. In the late nineteenth century the written rhetoric of colonial authorities presented assaults on whites as

From *American Ethnologist* 12(4) (1985), pp. 642–55, 657–8. Reprinted by permission of the American Anthropological Association.

"private" affairs between individuals, in later years as charged "political" statements of subversive intent. The contrasting interpretations of the murders described above represent two different moments in the colonial venture and two different visions of how a colonial order should and could be maintained.

But what do we learn by knowing that in 1876 and in 1929 two seemingly similar events were interpreted in such different ways? How much does the language in which they are described reflect the perceptions of danger and threat held by the colonial elite? What made an act that could have easily been explained as the product of the innately irrational character of the man-child native generalizable into a political statement? What was it about the second killing that transformed it from what might have been dismissed as an isolated case of a Javanese coolie gone amok into a threat to the collective order, and from there into a charged anti-capitalist, anticolonialist symbol of subversion?

Were the ruling class statements about the event really *about* protest at all? In this paper I argue that often they were not, that attributions of personal, economic, or political motive to the individual and collective actions of the plantation workers only partially reflected the intensity of popular resistance *per se* or even the threat of it, and had as much to do with the changing nature of colonial power, specifically with the balance of power between the European planters and the colonial state.

The rhetoric referred to here is of a somewhat different nature than that usually analyzed by anthropologists; it is not oratory, it is not even spoken. It is written, which itself imbues it with a different sort of power. Some of the sources I draw on (especially company archives and government reports) on the face of it appear relatively straightforward, bureaucratic records of colonial minutiae. But whether in statistical or discursive form, nearly all of them contain a strong rhetorical dimension. They are persuasive and public, designed in part to legitimize (Thompson 1977) colonial control, to justify coercion (Alatas 1977), and to persuade (Burke 1973) a diverse audience of their necessity. As I will argue below, these public pronouncements also suggest how social categories were constructed, how meaning was ordered, and thus how colonial power was structured and maintained. Its authors are often anonymous, the texts unsigned: statements from the Deli Planters' Association, reports of the government labor bureau, bicentennial volumes of estate companies, press releases, newspaper articles from a partisan press. The uniqueness of this rhetorical form resides in its fixity – words may be added, new interpretations made, but those already recorded cannot be changed.

This rhetoric of those in power had multiple audiences, perhaps the least important of whom were its colonial subjects whose lives and labors it discussed. Rather, it informed the perceptions of those in power or in close proximity to it. It appeared in reports to and from the plantation syndicate and managers on individual estates, between estate companies and their stock-holders, between planters and civil servants, between state officials and the Dutch parliament, and between elites within the highly stratified Euro-American colonial society.

Like other written rhetoric, this one justified the rule it described but also possessed a more active voice, advocating action (or inaction) in certain prescribed ways. For instance, court sentences depended largely on whether a plantation worker was classified as "dangerous" and therefore involved in actions that could possibly lead to (or be construed to lead to) "unrest." These written interpretations of events and partisan pronouncements were self-confirming; they became the arsenal for evidence of precedent actions and comprised the corpus of historical (read: "indisputable") fact. I take this written rhetoric then not to *reflect* the social relations of life and labor but as a refracted image of them; as social practice that classified and controlled, that highlighted certain discourses and obscured others, that shaped how danger was defined and what kinds of action should be marshalled against it.

The first part of this paper focuses on the form and content of written rhetoric dealing with labor recruitment and control in the early phase of East Sumatra's expansion, drawing on some of the language that dealt with violence and perceptions of it. Part II looks at a rhetorical shift in the 1920s, at the national idioms within which colloquial events were reinterpreted as estate labor relations became public issues and, therefore, state affairs.

Part I

Colonial Vulnerabilities

Ben Anderson notes that "any reading of Dutch colonial literature astounds one with its obsessive concern with a (supposedly fragile) *orde*" (1966: 98). If any motto captures the spirit of Dutch rule it would surely be the ideal of *rust en orde* (peace and order) and a preoccupation with the sundry ways in which it could be (and was being) undermined. This "obsessive concern" was not really with "peace and order" *per se*, but with social disorder as it related to labor discipline, a concern by no means confined to a Dutch colonial context. Cultures of *capitalism* – and certainly that of *colonial* capitalism in its Dutch, British, and French variants maintained similar visions – a society housing an easily disciplined laboring population in abundance, cheap, socially malleable, and politically inarticulate. Within Dutch colonial rhetoric the issue of "peace and order" – and what threatened it – was the leitmotiv that ran from intelligence reports to fictional accounts. Thus *onrust* (unrest) and *onveiligheid* (insecurity) could result either from certain general conditions (demanding changes in state policy) or from specific events (usually demanding police action and the "restoration of order"). For example, in debates over the abolition of indenture, both sides used the same idioms to describe the pros and cons of that system; namely, that increasing violence, insecurity, and disorder on the estates and outside their borders would follow if indenture was abolished (as argued by the planters) or if it was maintained (as argued by their Dutch liberal and Indonesian opponents). In either case, the threat was the same – as was the language of persuasion.

"Peace and order" *(rust en orde)*, "discipline and order" *(tucht en orde)* were shared, abstract colonial ideals for establishing and maintaining authority. What this would look like on the ground, and how this order was to be secured were the objects of discrepant elite interpretations and much debate. In the specific context of East Sumatra this discourse on disorder was particularly charged around issues concerning the expansion of plantation agriculture.

Planter Profits Versus Public Peace

In the 1860s and 1870s most of the plantation belt was still outside the political and economic control of the Dutch. As part of a general pacification scheme throughout the archipelago, the "*openlegging*" (opening) of Deli was strategically important in bringing the Outer Islands more squarely under Dutch authority. In Aceh to the north, troops had been sent in 1870 to repress an armed resistance to colonial rule. But given the shortage of funds and personnel to carry out pacification on the East Coast, ironically, the strategy for pursuing this *Dutch* hegemony was to make it an international affair. Foreign investors from France, Belgium, Germany, Britain, and the United States were welcomed under an "open door policy" and were given license to procure land and labor and most critically to protect those assets as they saw fit. The Dutch state admittedly wanted a rapid settlement of the Outer Islands but also an orderly one. Yet, even from the start, commercial and colonial objectives were at odds. The planters for their part saw their profits contingent on exercising a degree of coercion potentially capable of producing precisely the volatile situation that the government was intent on averting (Stoler 1985: 15–22).

The colonial state was thus maneuvering a difficult course, allowing the planters sufficient *lebensraum* to encourage investment (as a way of subordinating the indigenous population of the Outer Islands), but within the context of a policy sufficiently constrained so as not to risk popular rebellion. In practice, this meant that state intervention in plantation affairs did not occur in response to incidents of planter violence but only to levels of generalized violence sufficient to "*engendre la revolte*" (Stibbe 1912: 8). The planters, on the other hand, wanted full government protection of the industry (and their investments) without any interference in how they ran it. This, not unexpectedly, produced a strained relationship between the state and the planters, rendering certain subjects rhetorically forbidden while highlighting others.

On agrarian issues, for example, the planters and local Malay rulers were initially given enormous leeway in setting leases. But these transactions increasingly transgressed so many popular indigenous land rights that they threatened the subsistence base of Sumatra's native inhabitants. Only then did the state attempt to set common guidelines for company leases, native use rights, and to quell unfettered land speculation. Yet despite these decades of legal juggling over agrarian policy and rhetorical protection of native agriculture, by 1918, at a period when company holdings were still expanding, much of the plantation belt was filled by uninterrupted estate concessions with contiguous borders. Maintaining this block of physical space against trespassing, squatters, government resettlement plans, and other intrusions motivated much of the industry's strategy for workers' housing and labor control (Stoler 1985: 36–43).

On labor issues the planters initially were also given wide latitude. With a native Batak and Malay population neither sufficiently abundant nor willing to meet the planters' labor demands, the companies turned to the long-established clearing-houses of Penang and Singapore where Chinese immigrants were processed for labor markets around the world (DPv 1882: 4). The planters relied heavily on "coolie brokers" in this recruitment, agents who typically procured their gangs by deception and/or by force.

The high investments in obtaining labor encouraged the estates to adopt strong-arm tactics for keeping workers in place and equally strong efforts on the part of workers to disengage. Contract periods of three years were extended in familiar ways by keeping workers indebted and indentured; they were given large advances that took years to pay off. Debts incurred from gambling, from inflated prices of provisions, from payments for sexual services were used to keep male workers in service beyond the initial tenure of their contracts. In addition, punishments for disobedience were meted out in additional labor service, often extending a worker's tenure by months or years. Given the high cost of recruitment, and the industry's profits contingent on cheap labor, the planters had a large stake in keeping their workers in service and within their borders. Deserters, coolies-turned-farmers, -traders, or -vagabonds were portrayed as a major threat not only to the industry's profits but to the public peace and order. Thus the term "dangerous elements" (*gevaarlike elementen*) was first applied to runaway coolies who, the planters claimed, often joined (or themselves organized) roving bands of vagrants predatory on estate produce and property (Anonymous 1925: 66).

Despite such early "external dangers," land and labor arrangements were (and remained) local matters. Far from the seat of the colonial state in Java, the plantation belt was maintained as a veritable "state within a state." The founder and director of one of the major estate syndicates wrote that "Deli was considered an entirely independent district of the Netherlands Indies, oriented exclusively toward Europe and the Straits Settlements" (Martinus 1929: 46). This was manifested in distinct social, fiscal, racial, and even recreational practice. For instance, the early Deli planters, unlike those in Java, had virtually no contact with Dutch officials, arriving on ships directly from Europe or via the British Straits Settlements. Most of these European recruits never dealt with Dutch authorities nor saw their enterprises as significantly "under" the latter's administration. Deli's nearly autonomous status was also reflected in a monetary system geared again toward the international currencies of Singapore and Penang, not Batavia. Thus, staff and coolies were paid successively in Mexican, Japanese, and Straits dollars, and only in later years in the Dutch guilder. And finally, vacations and medical cures were taken on the Malay peninsula, not the hill stations of Java where corporate heads of other Indies-based enterprises and Dutch civil authorities typically established friendships and financial ties (Martinus 1929: 44–50).

For the most part, the estates were run by a multinational European staff who viewed labor discipline, and punishment for those transgressing it, as internal estate affairs. This assumption of authority by the estates was so extensive that Karl Pelzer called the pioneer planters their own "lawyers, policemen, public prosecutors, judges and diplomats" (Pelzer 1978: 89). This was not entirely by industry design. Throughout the nineteenth century, government officials, and especially police personnel, in Deli were in short supply (Volker 1928: 55). With wealth, experience, and local prestige on their side, the planters were able literally to patronize the overworked district heads and lesser civil servants. An official unwilling to accept this subordination had a thankless task, not only because it entailed surmounting the conditions just outlined, but meant challenging a prevailing colonial image of the hearty, paternal planters. This is apparent from a 1876 letter by Valck, a government district head, containing the following bold (and to my knowledge, earliest) account

questioning the received view of these courageous, albeit crude, pioneering entrepreneurs:

> Although I have very little time I want to share with you what troubles me. I would
> very much like it if his excellence the Governor General knew the real situation
> here. When I was appointed to be the Assistant Resident of Deli I knew very well
> that I would not land in a "bed of roses"; but that I would find such a Augean stable
> [of muck] as I did here, I never could have imagined . . . I've heard people in Singapore
> call the situation here "a disgrace to humanity." It would be a miracle indeed if
> respectable Chinese coolies would be attracted to a place where coolies are thrashed
> to death, or at least so mistreated that the beatings leave permanent scars, where
> manhunts are the order of the day . . . The planters and their subordinates are from all
> countries and of all types, adventurers with no faith in God or law, people about whom
> one could rightly say, "they're hopeless delinquents" as the planter Pieterse has said
> of the Chinese coolies. . . . Be assured my friend there are several [planters] among
> them who would not consider it a heinous crime to do away with a government
> officer who would dare to reveal their crimes . . . If you think that I paint a darker
> picture of the situation, that I exaggerate I repeat that the situation is as bad as it can be
> and this is the result of a policy pursued for years of leniency vis-à-vis the planters.
> (Valck 1876)

Unlike the famous writings of Multatuli on corruption in Java published the preceding year, Valck's letter never received a public airing. Several months after writing it
and only five months after taking up his post, he was transferred back to Java. From
there he sent a report attributing the *onveiligheid* (insecurity) in Deli to the woeful
inadequacy of police and judiciary personnel. The next year he was "honorably
dismissed" and, although still relatively young, placed on the retired list of the
colonial service.

Valck's comments are interesting, not only because they describe a much-hidden
state of affairs, but because they also confirm that one effective way for the planters
to avoid state intervention in estate labor issues was simply to control what the
government knew of them. The colonial administration would certainly not have
opposed prostitution, drugs, gambling, and heavy debt (which along with overt
violence were the mainstays of early techniques of labor control) on ethical grounds
(since government pawnshops and the opium tax were also mainstays of state
revenue). These policies, however, were condemned by the state in Deli, where
they threatened to jeopardize the political peace, foreign investments and, ultimately, the more lucrative source of state revenue provided by the estate companies
and their subsidiary manufacturing, retail, and shipping industries.

How then did the planters portray these labor conditions and the causes of
violence? How did their written rhetoric identify "order" and what would threaten
it? What did the written rhetoric look like during these years? There are several
striking features. For one thing – and this is consistent with the estates trying to
control what was known of their affairs – the material is far more limited than that
available for later periods. In 1884 there were just under 700 Europeans in Deli; 40
years later there were thousands. The first Deli newspaper was not established until
1885 (Said 1976: 33). In contrast, by the 1920s a profusion of local European,
Malay, and Chinese dailies, weeklies, and magazines attended to the social activities
of the European staff, the daily fluctuations in world market prices of estate crops,

the petty thefts of estate property, and the famous trials of natives who murdered estate personnel. It was from the plantation sphere that foreign and native politicians, as well as the press in Deli, frequently drew their examples for contesting or defending the form and fact of colonial rule.

That there were many more newspapers on the East Coast in the 1920s still does not explain the dearth of reports, comments, or *public* statements through the turn of the century on incidents of violence perpetrated against workers and vice versa (which do show up, on the other hand, in internal company reports, classified government documents, and personal letters). Why was it that cases of the brutal beatings of coolies might reach government officials only by rumor and long after the fact (Valck 1876)? As late as 1913 a former planter commented that assaults on Europeans were not talked about in public and few of these stories ever came to the attention of the press (Dixon 1913: 59).

A second feature of this record is how strikingly it differs in *content* from that of a later period. While from the 1870s through the early twentieth century, there is a strong tendency to downplay the severity of physical assaults, by the mid-1920s the planters and their press express a fairly hysterical concern with impending violence. By 1929 a disproportionate amount of copy was devoted to what was in fact an increasing but still relatively small number of assaults on Europeans (given the 300,000 plantation workers who by then were employed on the East Coast). After a bout of theft, assault, and arson on plantation property and personnel in 1876, however, one company representative commented some years later, "there seemed a tendency both of [estate] inspectors and the individual head administrators to make little of it. Thus they reported: 'here all is peaceful and all will remain so'" (Anonymous 1925). This was certainly *not* because individual and collective forms of violence were so rare. On the contrary, mention of these events was frequent, but they were invariably explained in the same way, as acts of violence provoked by some "personal" matter, some "private" affair. For example, an estate officer writes, "once again, the cause of the assaults is not political, but based [only] on personal revenge and rapacity" (ibid.: 15). And a company account summing up the explanations of estate violence in 1870 reads, "People repeatedly were uncertain as to whether an assault should be considered as 'hostile' or indeed *only* as 'rapacious' and 'cut-throat' though in fact people lost goods and lives in both cases" (ibid.: 11; emphasis added). Of more than 30 cases of attacks on estates reported in the early 1870s, most were dismissed as acts of plunder (*roofzucht*) and/or [personal] revenge (*wraakzucht*) sought by mistreated coolies (Schadee 1919: 32). Violence among Chinese coolies was attributed to feuding secret societies, while arson on tobacco estates was blamed on greedy local Malay leaders (1919: 119). We can note three common trends: (1) to minimize the number of assaults, (2) to categorically deny the possible political aspect of violence, and (3) to resolutely assert that the coolies were "in hand."

Other evidence from this period suggests that this written rhetoric was not a reflection of a secure colonial power base but a *site of negotiation* over the nature of it. In deleting some topics and emphasizing others, in assigning certain actions to the private rather than public arenas, the companies and the colonial state were contesting control over the industry and its labor force (see Schadee 1919: 32–3). How the planters talked and wrote about dangers and the way they classified violence determined the jurisdiction of various problems. In minimizing labor resistance, its import, and in downplaying its danger, the planters denied the political basis of violence and its *public* consequence – and therefore blocked the state from legitimate intervention. These remained closed company affairs.

Local government officials and higher authorities in the colonial administration were kept at bay, most likely with the silent endorsement of many civil servants who themselves concealed and controlled information. The admission that the coolies were not "in hand" – that there was *political* unrest not merely "disturbances" – would have called for a costly response by the Dutch parliament and colonial administration. Thus, although some intimate observers, such as the District Officer Valck, recommended (in a private letter) that police duties be taken out of the planters' hands (Valck 1876), in fact the estate industry was relatively successful in keeping the state from "meddling" in what it defined as company affairs. When, for example, in 1875 state officials attempted to arbitrate land transactions, the companies argued that there was more theft and murder under the "paternal eye of the government" than when judicial matters were handled by the companies and local sultans (Anonymous 1925: 71). Accusations of abetting disorder were the most common epithets hurled from both sides.

There were other circumstances that also allowed the planters to remain in de facto control. First, the logistics of monitoring complexes spread over thousands of square miles were obviously formidable. By 1912 there were over 200 plantation complexes, nearly 150,000 workers, and between 35,000 and 50,000 new recruits arriving every year (Stibbe 1912: 23). Even the planters' association, which was probably better staffed at this time than the civil service charged with estate matters, procured most of its information on labor incidents through weekly and monthly mailed reports. For the most part, the state gleaned what it knew of the plantation industry from these very sources. And even the Labor Inspectorate, established in 1908, whose main job was to keep abreast of estate labor issues, was too short of manpower and authority to investigate in any depth the circumstances surrounding coolie assaults and planter brutalities. Estate inspections were thus infrequent and tended to be rehearsed performances.

The relationship between the companies and the state, between local estate managers and local government officials was at once collaborative, contentious, and ambiguous. On the one hand, the planters maintained their control because both their enterprises and the financial leverage to which they had access were politically critical to, but *independent* of, the colonial state. On the other hand, much of the planters' power came from their ability to construe their private interests as synonymous with Dutch public welfare, to make protection of their personal investments essential to colonial economic development, and to make the smooth extraction of surplus value an important component for "peace and order."

Profits and the Planter Ethic

Obviously what the planters feared and what they valued went hand in hand. Their profits derived from the employment of a limited number of Europeans, a large number of Asians, and a location conducive to high-quality commodity production. In Deli this translated typically into a plantation with 1 head administrator, 5 assistants, 20 Asian supervisors, and 800 Chinese and Javanese workers living in a central complex surrounded by thousands of acres of rubber or tobacco, usually bordering on a tropical rain forest. The image of colonial power as somehow unshakable in its expansive dominance ignores its vulnerabilities. Deli's planters in particular exercised far more control than they had the physical power to enforce. They were vastly outnumbered, isolated from one another, and although some were equipped with arms, given the sheer number of coolies involved, these would have been poor defense against laborers seriously intent on challenging white authority.

Brutality was one essential means for maintaining discipline, but in daily practice it played a somewhat lesser role. Acts of submission permeated the social relations of everyday life, most evident in the use of language, and in the distinct social space that marked the rigidly imposed division between European supervisors and their Asian subordinates. Unlike estates on Java where Indo-Europeans made up an important part of the estate supervisors, Deli planters prided themselves on the maintenance of strict racial distinctions. In fact many companies refused to employ Indo-European managers or clerks (Martinus 1929: 47). Deference and distance were considered essential to maintaining white authority. Dominance was codified in people, personified in things. The planters (like colonialists everywhere) wrote incessantly of the dangers of losing prestige in the eyes of their (Asian) subordinates. Young supervisors fresh from Europe were more rigorously schooled in the techniques of command than in those of agriculture.

Having the "natives in hand" was considered a necessity, and those planters with reputations for a well-disciplined staff and work force were accorded high prestige. In a novel from the early part of the century, a new assistant is advised by an experienced colleague:

> And now while we're at it I'll teach you a few things, the ABC's of our relations with the natives.... Every native must get out of his vehicle when encountering a white, a company building, office, shed, or house and not get on again until he is at least 10 meters distance.... You may find this somewhat excessive, but you must not forget that we whites stand alone against the masses, and we can only maintain ourselves by such rigid regulations which must function as a form of discipline and restraint. Do you see what I mean? Because the first necessity of the planter is to have the natives in hand, the rest will take care of itself. (Szkéley-Lulofs 1946: 101)

Bravado was also part of the formula for successful labor control. Thus, in the novel *Tropic Fever* written by a Deli planter soon after World War I, fearlessness both *makes for* discipline and provides proof of it:

> As we set out for our work in the dark [before dawn] we took with us only a big crooked stick, no other weapon. It would have been a disgrace, a thoroughly despicable act of cowardice, to put a revolver in one's pocket. A planter in Deli is not afraid and will not even appear so. (Szkéley 1979: 102)

Similarly, few planters were willing to have it known that anything but a "calm peace" reigned on their estates (Dixon 1913: 59). According to a 1913 handbook for new staff, "All news to contrary was countered as much as possible" (Szkéley 1979: 102).

Ben Anderson (1983), in a study of the origins of nationalism, traces its concurrence with "print capitalism," which permitted "imagined communities" expanding beyond the primordial loyalties that local knowledge would allow. In Sumatra where the sheer physical scale of the plantation belt prevented verbal communications, the printed word had an enormous impact on what people identified as dangerous, and on how they dealt with those fears. Planters dispersed over the further reaches of the East Coast had little chance to come together except on special social occasions, on furlough, or in emergency. Nevertheless, nearly every fiction and nonfiction writer has commented on the strong sense of community imbued in the planters' ranks, on the distinctive features that characterized the "Deliaan," on an imagined community of common interests and common fears. Roger Nieuwenhuys writes,

> But what was Deli? In any case more than a name for the gigantic plantation belt on Sumatra's East Coast. Deli was a concept . . . a society within a society, wholly different from that in Java, Java and Deli were entirely different ideas. (1978: 346–7)

Affirmation of community was expressed in the circulars of the Deli Planters' Association, where progress and the presence of "security" were assured; in the yearly chronicle of the East Sumatra Institute, planters reported clubs being built, tennis courts in the making, and news of other accoutrements of the fortified and healthy white enclave. It is this written rhetoric that had such powerful social force.

Thus, silence on matters of labor violence conformed well with the planter ethic. Again, this is not to suggest that no one spoke or wrote of "unrest"; planters wrote incessantly of the dangers of "coolie rows" and how to avoid them. But they wrote about them in a particular fashion. "Coolie rows" were trivialized as explosive yet petty quarrels among the workers, and as the "natural" responses of men-children unfamiliar with a modern order (Breman 1984: 148–9). During this early period neither collective labor actions nor individual assaults were conceived as political acts of protest or labor resistance. The solution to labor problems was always found in more discipline . . . and expansion of the areas in which it was exercised.

Thus the planters' rhetoric addressed two critical audiences – the state and the planters themselves – with the same idioms. While it instructed new European personnel in the behavior that would secure their personal safety, the rhetoric effectively kept the state at bay by affirming that these personnel matters were not public affairs.

The Colonial Order of Things: 1900–1920

Censorship by the planters was not always effective. At the turn of the century several scathing exposés appeared detailing the slave-like conditions of life and labor on the Deli estates. Van den Brand's *Millions out of Deli* (1902) was the most famous and the most vehemently disclaimed by the companies. A Dutch socialist member of parliament reported widespread prostitution, malnutrition, venereal disease, brutal beatings, and high levels of infant mortality (van Kol 1903). The same year a government-sponsored investigation (the infamous and *long-suppressed* Rhemrev Report, see Breman 1984) gave even more vivid detail confirming the accusations made by other more liberal (and therefore less "reliable") observers. Rhemrev reported sick coolies locked in airless shacks, opened only twice a day when food was left and when patients swept their feces from the floor; men and women were beaten with heavy staves and tied to poles to be thrashed with rattan rods. Women workers who fell sick were nearly starved before they deserted. Others were the victims of sexual sadism (Rhemrev in Breman 1984).

In response, both the government and press were supposedly moved to monitor Deli's affairs more carefully, but in reality the public outrage was overshadowed by the administrative and commercial interest in new prospects for estate expansion. Between the time of the Labor Inspectorate's creation in 1908 and 1920, Deli was to be transformed. The growing U.S. automobile industry created an enormous demand for rubber (with companies such as Goodyear and Uniroyal quick to buy up long-term leases from smaller firms). Given these moves toward expanded production, labor recruitment from Java was increased to tens of thousands each year while those from China fell off. From Europe new managers arrived in proportionate number. Most of Deli's contemporary infrastructure also dates from this period: palatial company offices, fortified banks, while pillared planters' homes, golf courses, vacation bungalows in the Batak highlands, and social clubs – erected to mark the profits, prestige, and power of the companies.

As Deli's labor force grew and company revenues rose, there were more estate "disturbances." But now they were increasingly of a different kind. Although the number of assaults on white personnel remained relatively constant through the mid-1920s, the number of *collective* labor actions increased for the same years. While planters often associated these actions with violence, in fact they were mostly temperate requests for fair treatment or petitions making modest economic demands. The planters nonetheless blamed the Labor Inspectorate for these increasingly frequent labor incidents, arguing that the latter's method of estate inspection undermined white prestige and threatened not only the industry but the colonial order.

The Labor Inspectorate, in turn, blamed the increased number of cases of confrontation on an inadequately trained European and Asian supervisory staff, the result of sloppy recruitment policies. The official and planters' rhetoric was shifting; assaults supposedly could now be prevented by strengthening the moral fiber of the *singkeh* (the European "newcomers"). Altercations were seen as the natural outcome of rapid expansion and the slipshod manner of training new staff. "Disturbances" accordingly could be lessened with better management, better control, and ever more discipline than before. New requirements included participation in local language training and some knowledge of Javanese custom. Since the problem was identified as one of individual attitudes, which caused "tactless," "rash," and "rude" behavior, the solution was sought in "quality control" (Heijting 1925: 56). European greenhorns and Asian overseers who insulted, threatened, or physically abused a worker were chided for "misbehaving," as though such incidents were somehow anomalous to the "normal" tenor of labor relations rather than being part and parcel of it.

Hundreds of pages of colonial record were devoted to "upgrading" the behavior and attitudes of the new assistants and Asian overseers "in the interests of peace and order" (Treub 1929: 17). But European underlings in the corporate hierarchy saw the assaults in a somewhat different light, arguing for better working conditions for themselves and their Asian subordinates. The Union of Deli Assistants, which first voiced these demands in 1909, was seen by company executive boards as a direct threat to the European enclave's "united front." Government officials in Batavia labeled the union a sign of "degeneration" in estate (read: European) labor relations, bordering on *chantage* (extortion) (OvSI 1917: 39). In the planters' chronicle of 1916 recommendations were made to improve the working conditions and wages of white staff in order to attract candidates of "better character" (and to make sure they knew whose side they were on).

New policies were implemented meant to alter the nature of the confrontation between white staff and Asian workers. Still other measures were introduced with the intention of averting the confrontation altogether. Pre-dawn roll calls, a frequent site of conflict, were abolished and coolies were forbidden to carry agricultural tools that could be used as weapons (OvSI 1917: 35). Those Deli planters who refused to put these changes in effect were reprimanded for a "misplaced" bravado. Assistants were instructed not to give orders directly, but through Asian foremen, putting the latter rather than European staff in the line of fire (ibid.: 57).

Implicit in these measures was an explanation of assaults that hinged on danger of loss of respect. Accordingly, the general solution involved strategies for safeguarding the traditional acquiescence to white privilege, person, and property. The theory ran that if one acted with authority one was accorded it. Unstated but central to these lessons was always the threatening notion that with a loss of prestige, the "fragile" colonial order would give way to chaos. The presentation of colonialism as legitimate white rule, rather than class power, was essential then to keeping European underlings, as well as Javanese, in line.

Part II

Reinterpreting the Dangerous: 1920–1929

The decade of the 1920s was the heyday of both colonial capitalism in the Netherlands Indies – and the anticolonial movement. In Deli estate labor relations and the rhetoric that described and classified them were clearly shifting. Most importantly, the conflict of interest that had divided state and corporate priorities on several counts was becoming less pronounced. The differences lessened as state and corporate interests in a "united front" strengthened and merged. For many of the same reasons that the content of rhetoric changed, so did the quantity. Communications improved with increasing information available from the Labor Inspectorate, local newspapers, and a well-staffed planters' association. Infrastructure was also enhanced with rail and telegraph services and a highway that ran nearly the entire length of the plantation belt. But the proliferation of written rhetoric was not technologically determined.

By 1920 anticolonial and organized labor activity had already been on the increase in Java for some years, the strongest voice coming from religious and educational organizations. In Sumatra, nationalist and radical political groups were vocal champions of the estate workers' cause, advocating improved working conditions and the abolition of indenture. This focus on indenture sharply colored the interpretation of estate-based events far before there was any indication of nationalist organizations within the estate borders. While in 1916 a planters' chronicle noted 12 native organizations in the area, all were dismissed as posing "no threat to Dutch authority" (OvSI 1917: 54). In succeeding years they were not written off so lightly. Both company and state officials were becoming increasingly concerned that economic demands were concealing the "real" political motive behind various organizations and labor actions. Based on a legal code that endorsed that interpretation, virtually any protest for a just economic grievance was prosecuted as a political action with criminal intent (U.S. Department of Labor 1951: 134).

In contrast to the earlier accounts minimizing violence and its political import, now we find a written rhetoric that quantifies and catalogues individual assaults, construes a political motive for nearly any act of individual violence or collective demand, and repeatedly asserts that the coolies are in other (read: communist) hands. It could be argued that this dramatic rhetorical shift simply reflected a changing Indies-wide political consciousness. But on several counts, it is clear that this was not the case.

As observed above, throughout the early and mid-1920s the number of assaults on white personnel remained relatively constant, but collective labor actions seemed to have increased for the same period. Still, in nearly every case for which the Labor Inspectorate provides detail, no political issues were mentioned. In content, coolie demands had not changed much over the years. But now local events were processed through national idioms and the written rhetoric afforded a new series of classifications. From 1913 to 1923 the Labor Inspectorate's reports included a section on "treatment of worker," but in 1925 a new heading on "labor conflict" was added. In the planters' chronicle, sections on "political agitation and disturbances of the peace" could now be found, and in 1926 these were changed to "labor conflict and disturbances/unruliness" *(ongeregeldheden)*. By 1928 the Labor Bureau's report devoted an entire chapter to "labor issues," with separate divisions for "coolie assaults," "disturbances," and detailed tables breaking down the "causes" of attacks on head managers, assistants, and foremen. In 1929 these sections were expanded yet again.

In the mid-1920s we read that "communist propaganda" was reported on several estates but with still no mention of associated political protest or collective actions (OvSI 1926). In fact, collective actions were staged, although no evidence for "outside agitation" could be substantiated. Nonetheless, in virtually all company and government reports from this period, despite no evidence connecting them, political agitation and customary workers' complaints were inextricably linked.

In addition, descriptions of the generic "coolie" were modified with old labels used in new ways, and new labels connoting several meanings. As always there were "bad elements" on the estates but now the unmarked term invariably carried political content; "bad elements" *(slechte elementen)*, "undesirable elements," "dangerous elements" *(gevaarlijke elementen)* took on a new sense, becoming interchangeable with "extremist," "communist," and "nationalist" agitators. Native estate office clerks were dismissed for "communist tendencies" and the Labor Inspectorate repeatedly referred to shady estate persons who convinced workers to lodge complaints while the "real" culprits "prefer[red] to keep out of harm's way" (KvA 1926: 63).

One could argue that the rhetoric simply reflected the fact that in 1926 there actually was a short-lived communist uprising on Java. But this would ignore the new ways in which threat was identified and danger entitled. What did this massive amount of time and energy devoted to the "political" nature of labor actions do? First it continued to deflect attention away from investigations of labor conditions *per se*, and placed it on events that were at once both external to the estates and within the anticolonial movement. Accusations of "political agitation" and "political intent" became code words for other evaluations. By identifying labor demands as "political" they were also classified as unfounded, illegitimate, and externally induced. Thus in 1920 when Javanese coolies near Medan supported a railway strike off the estates, the Labor Bureau offered this analysis:

> taking into account the indifference and docility of the Javanese, other reasons than obtaining a financial improvement of their lot would have to be at the root of the strikes. The workers' financial desires are not very great so other factors must come into play. Often workers take part in a strike on the prodding of someone from outside the laboring population who for some reason deems it in *his* interest to incite such an action. (KvA 1920: 36)

Second, "political" motivation connoted something into which workers were conned, and from which they needed paternal protection. The simple fact that large numbers of workers participated in labor actions was rarely grounds for examining the validity of their demands. Workers were after all child-like, vulnerable, and all the more "dangerous" because of their political susceptibility.

Images of susceptibility were not fortuitous; they were part of a discourse in which nationalism and communism were conceived as a contagious disease to which those who were weakest were most susceptible; "extremist agitators" were seen as its carriers, plantation coolies as its victims, and stricter discipline as the antidote. "Extremist" agitators had to be "wiped out" and repression was a legitimate response. The prescription was to isolate and remove the carriers from the population by putting them in jail or in exile, preferably weeding out the "bad elements" with a fingerprint identification system before they arrived. In 1925 the carriers were still limited, but by the late 1920s the number of people who fell within the expanded category of "dangerous elements" had reached epidemic proportions.

By 1926 police agents were being paid high bonuses for every communist captured. In 1928 the two plantation syndicates for rubber and tobacco joined forces with the Indies Intelligence Bureau in a cooperative scheme to monitor the political activities on the estates. Intelligence agents paid by the companies were officially invested with the authority of the regular police, allowing the planters a government guise for their spy network (Said 1977: 159).

And with this, explanations of estate-based labor actions moved from the private to public domain. Thus, the staunchly conservative voice of the planters, the *Deli Courant*, now claimed that estate assaults no longer could be dismissed as matters of personal revenge but were the consequence of a new "consciousness" incited by external sources. *De Planter* (published by the Union of Estate Assistants), which had occasionally ventured the argument that coolie attacks were not always the workers' fault, became more and more convinced that "destructive outside influences" were at play (Said 1977: 160–1). With this perception of extremists crossing surreptitiously back and forth across estate borders, the planters began calling upon the colonial state for aid in controlling the estate population, and for protection from the extra-estate causes of labor strife.

Although the prevailing rhetoric on labor violence had clearly changed, there were still those who clung to their old explanations. One particularly good example appeared in the outspoken nationalist Malay-language paper *Pewarta Deli* in April 1929. *Pewarta Deli* was renowned for its snide headlines, often mimicking the rhetoric from the planters' press. Thus during the trial of a coolie who had assaulted and murdered a European estate assistant, *Pewarta Deli*, exasperated with the explanations offered from the planters' quarters, ran an article entitled, "Was it only because of 'a private affair' that the murder occurred?" The expression "a private affair" was in quotation marks – and, most importantly, left in the original Dutch (Pewarta Deli 1929).

What is striking about this 1926 to 1929 period is that although *communist* activity had not only all but ceased on Java and was at most barely evident on the plantations, the hysteria surrounding the surge in "bad elements" and the "weeding out of dangerous elements" increased dramatically (KvA 1927: 137). *Pewarta Deli* noted that with a high price on every communist head, it was no wonder that police agents were so busy rounding up suspects on meager evidence. A 1926 article offered the following appraisal of an incident in which a barber and shopkeeper were arrested for possessing written material critical of the colonial state,

> what puzzles this writer is whether they were arrested for being communist or for reading something in a newspaper which is said to be communist? If the latter is the case, it is the same as saying a person who talks about a theft can be accused of a robbery. Astounding! (Pewarta Deli 1926)

By 1929 the accusations of rampant communism among the coolies were supplemented by ones rallying against nationalism. But even on those estates labeled hotbeds of communist insurgency, evidence of "outside agitators" who incited collective actions was at best insubstantial. Lists of workers' complaints compiled by the Labor Inspectorate contained a familiar if slightly more refined set of grievances against heavy task work, long working hours, forced "holidays," maltreatment, and high prices in company stores (KvA 1929). Complaints of maltreatment by European managers in particular had increased dramatically; but these were not new complaints, nor were they presented with violence (KvA 1927). What had changed was that workers were making more vocal demands for better working conditions. As one estate official put it,

> A coolie will no longer accept treatment that he considered normal 10 or 20 years ago...there is a changed mentality resulting from a growing consciousness...insofar as [this] insubordination manifests in resistance to the employer, the strongest actions should be taken against it. The police and courts must stand shoulder to shoulder against all which is extreme or excessive, or threatens to have that tendency.... This changed attitude is a primary factor with which the government and the planters must deal... (Treub 1929: 22)

By 1929 not only had the maintenance of plantation profits become thoroughly meshed with the public order, but labor control itself became functionally tied to the rhetoric on both. Whereas the companies had once objected strongly to official meddlings in their affairs, by the late 1920s and certainly by the depression in 1929, the estate industry was virtually demanding government protection.

By claiming that the charges described by the industry's management were unfounded, I am not arguing that worker responses to their conditions of existence were unchanged throughout this period. The companies' increasing reliance on the Dutch colonial state was intimately related to changes in the specific forms of labor protest and in the general tenor of resistance to colonial rule. The legal backbone of the estate system of labor control had been the penal sanction which, while effectively dealing with *individual* transgressions of labor contracts, was anachronistic *vis-à-vis* protest staged on a mass-based collective scale (extending the contracts of coolies who refused to work was not a terribly efficient threat if an entire plantation population struck).

In 1921 an estate official remarked that the penal sanction could punish individual acts of resistance, desertion, and refusal to work, but that it was "ineffective against *collective* forms of resistance, against collective refusals to obey orders," since one could not possibly punish individually all the tens of thousands of workers involved (Vierhout 1921: 22–3). In short, by the 1920s it was clear that the penal sanction was quickly becoming a cumbersome method of labor control, since resistance itself had changed in form and content. Labor actions in the form of strikes and organized collective action demanded legal sanctions of another order, and repression of political action outside the plantation borders.

The companies' response to the 1930s depression reflected this change in labor relations. Like most industries during the depression, workers were fired on a massive scale. At the same time, the industry implemented the abolition of indenture legally established some 20 years earlier. Backed by the government, the foreign companies were released of all formal responsibility for the repatriated workers and their families regardless of whether their contracts had expired. Nearly 50 percent of a work force of 336,000 coolies had their contracts terminated and were fired within 3 years (KvA 1932).

State support for this strategy came in other forms. Most of those workers dismissed were required to return to Java. In addition, a careful selection process ensured that only the most docile, trusted, and hardworking married men and women remained. Dangerous elements were "wiped off" the estate map as tens of thousands of "undesirables" left Deli. In the meantime, government authorities played a larger role in securing plantation peace and order. Malay- and Chinese-language newspapers were banned from the plantation complexes and many estate schools were closed to prevent nationalist newspapers and Taman Siswa schoolteachers (known for their strong nationalist sentiments) from gaining access to the Asian staff or workers. And finally, state protection came in the form of a severely restricted production quota for native rubber smallholders, but not for foreign firms (Allen and Donnithorne 1962: 125–6). None of these moves would have been possible on company initiative alone and without government cooperation.

On the Power of Rhetoric

In this light, the rhetoric on labor issues appears not so much as mere reflection or representation of colonial power relations but as a redefinition of them. This is not to suggest that the use of specific categories (such as personal versus political motive for coolie assaults) was always part of a unified and conscious design to prevent administrative intervention at one time and elicit state protection at others. On the contrary, what I have attempted to describe is a planter ethic, a specific colonial consciousness of power and vulnerability that developed out of the structural positioning of the Deli estates within the Netherlands Indies economy and that actively countered the class differences among its European personnel. The common interests of this "imagined community" were experienced and created through a language that defined the ways in which protest was perceived, as well as the appropriate responses to it.

Clearly there was not *one* colonial discourse but a multiplicity of them, creating a field of force in which there were "shifts and reutilizations of identical formulas for contrary objectives" (Foucault 1980: 100). Language thus served not merely to *reproduce* colonial rule but also to shape it. The state and companies often had different visions of what venture capitalism would bring to Deli. As such, their efforts and their aims were neither parallel nor even necessarily complementary. How they classified persons as dangerous determined how resistance would be dealt with and under whose aegis labor control would fall. In this context silences as well as vocalizations provided a powerful form of persuasion demarcating which capitalist priorities would be considered crucial to social welfare and the public order.

Colonial hegemony by definition was never secure. Its power rested on more than control of material resources; it relied on the colonist's ability to establish and *change* the definitions of danger and the perception of the public good, on his ability to give the impression of an impervious authority despite contests to it. The culture of capitalism defined the homeless as vagabonds, runaways as criminals, squatters as thieves, and recalcitrant workers as a political danger to company profits and private property. It ignored or personalized laborer resistance at one time, while attributing political and organizational foresight to violence in a later period, thereby conjuring up a crisis of control. It defined indenture as a necessity for the public good at the turn of the century and 30 years later rejected it on moral grounds, simultaneously redefining it as a danger to *rust en orde* and celebrating the moral virtues of a "free wage labor market" (cf. Cooper 1980). By explaining assaults as acts of personal revenge or outside agitation the planters deflected attention from the relations of power and production on which colonial violence, fear, and rule were based. In a South African context Sartre wrote that colonial rhetoric had to:

> present everyone with the other-violence of the natives as constantly endangering the colonialists everywhere. That is to say, it struck permanent fear into the colonialists and presented this angry fear as pure courage. (1976: 726)

Both the real and imagined extent of this vulnerability shaped how Europeans and Asians experienced much of the colonial encounter.

REFERENCES

Alatas, Syed Hussein. (1977) *The Myth of the Lazy Native*. London: Frank Cass.

Allen, G. C., and A. C. Donnithorne. (1962) *Western Enterprise in Indonesia and Malaysia: A Study in Economic Development*. London: Allen & Unwin.

Anderson, Benedict. (1966) The Language of Indonesian Politics. *Indonesia* (April), 1: 89–116.

——. (1983) *Imagined Communities*. London: Verso.

Anonymous. (1925) *Deli-Batavia Maatschappij 1875–1925*. Amsterdam: Deli-Batavia Maat.

Brand, J. van den. (1902) *De Millionen uit Deli*. Amsterdam: Hoveker & Wormser.

Breman, Jan. (1984) Arbeidsverhoudingen op de Plantages van Sumatra's Oostkust omstreeks de eeuwwisseling. (manuscript located in Rotterdam)

Burke, Kenneth. (1973) *The Philosophy of Literary Form*. Berkeley: University of California Press.

Cooper, Frederic. (1980) *From Slaves to Squatters: Plantation Labor and Agriculture in Zanzibar and Coastal Kenya, 1890–1925*. New Haven: Yale University Press.

Deli Planters' Committee (DPv). (1882) *The Deli Coolie Question*. Deli.

Dixon, C. J. (1913) *De Assistant in Deli*. Amsterdam: J. H. de Bussy.

Foucault, Michael. (1980) *The History of Sexuality*, Vol. 1: *An Introduction*. New York: Vintage.

Heijting, Herman C. (1925) *De Koelie-Wetgeving voor de Buitengewesten van Neder-landsche-Indie*. The Hague: W. P. Stockum.

Kantoor van Arbeid (KvA). (1920) *Verslag van den dienst der arbeidsinspectie in Neder-landsche-Indie. Over het jaar 1919*. Weltevreden.

——. (1926) *Tiende verslag van de arbeidsinspectie voor de Buitengewesten 1926*. Weltevre-den.

——. (1927) *Twaalfde verslag van de arbeidsinspectie voor de Buitengewesten 1927*. Weltevreden.

——. (1929) *Veertiende verslag van de arbeidsinspectie voor de Buitengewesten 1929*. Wel-tevreden.

——. (1932) *Vijftiende verslag van de arbeidsinspectie 1930, 1931, 1932*. Weltevreden.

Kol, van H. (1903) *Uit onze kolonien*. Leiden: A. W. Sijthoff.

Martinus, J. H. (1929) *Veertig Jaren Ervaring in de Deli-Cultures*. Amsterdam: J. H. de Bussy.

Nieuwenhuys, R. (1978) *Oost-Indische Spiegel*. Amsterdam: Querido.

Oostkust van Sumatra Instituut (OvSI). (1917) *Kroniek 1916*. Amsterdam: J. H. de Bussy.

——. (1926) *Kroniek 1925*. Amsterdam: J. H. de Bussy.

Pelzer, Karl. (1978) *Planter and Peasant: Colonial Policy and the Agrarian Struggle in East Sumatra, 1863–1947*. The Hague: Martinus Nijhoff.

Pewarta Deli. (1926) 7 June. Medan.

——. (1929) 1 April. Medan.

Said, Mohammed. (1976) *Sejarah Pers di Sumatera Utara*. Medan: Waspada.

——. (1977) *Koeli Kontrak Tempoe Doeloe*. Medan: Waspada

Sartre, J.-P. (1976) *Critique of Dialectical Reason*. London: New Left Books.

Schadee, W. H. M. (1919) *Geschiedenis van Sumatra's Oostkust, Mede, No. 2*. Amsterdam: Oostkust van Sumatra Instituut.

Stibbe, D. G. (1912) *Werving van contractkoelies op Java. Verslag der vergadering van de Nederlandsche Afd. der Nederlandsche-Indische Maatschappij van Nijverheid en Land-bouw*. Amsterdam: J. H. de Bussy.

Stoler, Ann. (1985) *Capitalism and Confrontation in Sumatra's Plantation Belt, 1870–1979*. New Haven: Yale University Press.

Szkély, Ladislao. (1979) *Tropic Fever: The Adventures of a Planter in Sumatra*. Kuala Lumpur: Oxford in Asia.

Szkély-Lulofs, Madelon. (1946) *De Andere Wereld*. Amsterdam: Elsevier.

Thompson, E. P. (1977) *Whigs and Hunters: The Origin of the Black Act*. New York: Penguin.

Treub. (1929) Onveligheid op de Indische Culturondernemingen. *Vragen en Tijds* (September).

U.S. Department of Labor. (1951) *Labor Conditions in Indonesia*. Washington, DC: Dept. of Labor.

Valck, F. C. (1876) Letter of October 28, stored in the Collective Westerse Hand Schriften in The Hague.

Vierhout, M. (1921) *Het Arbeidsvraagstuk in verband met de Noodzakelijke Ontwikkeling der Buitengewesten*. Weltevreden: Albracht.

Volker, T. (1928) *Van Oerbosch tot Cultuurgebied*. Medan: Deli Planters Vereeningen.

15

Culture of Terror – Space of Death

Roger Casement's Putumayo Report and the Explanation of Torture

Michael Taussig

This essay is about torture and the culture of terror, which for most of us, including myself, are known only through the words of others. Thus my concern is with the mediation of the culture of terror through narration – and with the problems of writing effectively against terror.

Jacobo Timerman ends his recent book, *Prisoner without a Name, Cell without a Number*, with the imprint of the gaze of hope in the space of death.

> Have any of you looked into the eyes of another person, on the floor of a cell, who knows that he's about to die though no one has told him so? He knows that he's about to die but clings to his biological desire to live, as a single hope, since no one has told him he's to be executed.
>
> I have many such gazes imprinted upon me. . . .
>
> Those gazes which I encountered in the clandestine prisons of Argentina and which I've retained one by one, were the culminating point, the purest moment of my tragedy.
>
> They are here with me today. And although I might wish to do so, I could not and would not know how to share them with you.[1]

The space of death is crucial to the creation of meaning and consciousness, nowhere more so than in societies where torture is endemic and where the culture of terror flourishes. We may think of the space of death as a threshold, yet it is a wide space whose breadth offers positions of advance as well as of extinction. Sometimes a person goes through it and returns to us to tell the tale, like Timerman, who entered it, he says, because he believed the battle against military dictatorship had to be fought.[2]

Timerman fought with words, with his newspaper *La Opinion*, in and against the silence imposed by the arbiters of discourse who beat out a new reality in the prison

From *Comparative Studies in Society and History* 26 (1984), pp. 467–88, 492–7. © Society for the Comparative Study of Society and History, published by Cambridge University Press.

cells where the torturers and the tortured came together. "We victims and victim-izers, we're part of the same humanity, colleagues in the same endeavor to prove the existence of ideologies, feelings, heroic deeds, religions, obsessions. And the rest of humanity, what are they engaged in?"[3]

The construction of colonial reality that occurred in the New World has been and will remain a topic of immense curiosity and study – the New World where the Indian and the African became subject to an initially far smaller number of Chris-tians. Whatever conclusions we draw as to how that hegemony was so speedily effected, we would be most unwise to overlook or under estimate the role of terror. And by this I mean us to think through terror, which as well as being a physiological state is also a social fact and a cultural construction whose baroque dimensions allow it to serve as the mediator *par excellence* of colonial hegemony. The space of death is one of the crucial spaces where Indian, African, and white gave birth to the New World.

...With European conquest and colonization, these spaces of death blend as a common pool of key signifiers or caption points binding the culture of the conqueror with that of the conquered. The space of death is preeminently a space of transform-ation: through the experience of death, life; through fear, loss of self and conformity to a new reality: or through evil, good. Lost in the dark woods, then journeying through the underworld with his guide, Dante achieves paradise only after he has mounted Satan's back. Timerman can be a guide for us, analogous to the ways Putumayo shamans I know are guides to those lost in the space of death....

From Timerman's chronicle and texts like Miguel Angel Asturias's *El señor pre-sidente* it is abundantly clear that cultures of terror are based on and nourished by silence and myth in which the fanatical stress on the mysterious side of the mysteri-ous flourishes by means of rumor and fantasy woven in a dense web of magical realism. It is also clear that the victimizer needs the victim for the purpose of making truth, objectifying the victimizer's fantasies in the discourse of the other. To be sure, the torturer's desire is also prosaic: to acquire information, to act in concert with large-scale economic strategies elaborated by the masters and exigencies of produc-tion. Yet equally if not more important is the need to control massive populations through the cultural elaboration of fear.

That is why silence is imposed, why Timerman, the publisher, was so important, why he knew when to be silent and close off reality in the torture chamber. "Such silence," he tells us,

> begins in the channels of communication. Certain political leaders, institutions, and priests attempt to denounce what is happening, but are unable to establish contact with the population. The silence begins with a strong odor. People sniff the suicides, but it eludes them. Then silence finds another ally: solitude. People fear suicides as they fear madmen. And the person who wants to fight senses his solitude and is frightened.[4]

Hence, there is the need for us to fight that solitude, fear, and silence, to examine these conditions of truth-making and culture-making, to follow Michael Foucault in "seeing historically how effects of truth are produced within discourses which are in themselves neither true nor false."[5] At the same time we not only have to see, we also have to see anew through the creation of counterdiscourses.

If effects of truth are power, then the question is raised not only concerning the power to speak and write, but as to what form shall that counterdiscourse take. This issue of form has lately been of much concern to those involved in writing histories and ethnographies. But faced with the endemicity of torture, terror, and the growth of armies, we in the New World are today assailed with a new urgency. There is the effort to understand terror, in order to make *others* understand. Yet the reality at stake here makes a mockery of understanding and derides rationality, as when the young boy Jacobo Timerman asks his mother, "Why do they hate us?" And she replies, "Because they do not understand." And after his ordeal, the old Timerman writes of the need for a hated object and the simultaneous fear of that object – the almost magical inevitability of hatred. "No," he concludes, "there can be no doubt my mother was the one who was mistaken. It is not the anti-Semites who must be made to understand. It is we Jews."[6]

Hated and feared, objects to be despised, yet also of awe, the reified essence of evil in the very being of their bodies, these figures of the Jew, the black, the Indian, and woman herself, are clearly objects of cultural construction, the leaden keel of evil and of mystery stabilizing the ship and course that is Western history. With the cold war we add the communist. With the time bomb ticking inside the nuclear family, we add the feminists and the gays. The military and the New Right, like the conquerors of old, discover the evil they have imputed to these aliens, and mimic the savagery they have imputed.

What sort of understanding – what sort of speech, writing, and construction of meaning by any mode – can deal with and subvert that?

On one thing Timerman is clear. To counterpose the eroticization and romanticization of violence by the same means or by forms equally mystical is a dead end. Yet to offer one or all of the standard rational explanations of the culture of terror is similarly pointless. For behind the search for profits, the need to control labor, the need to assuage frustration, and so on, lie intricately construed long-standing cultural logics of meaning – structures of feeling – whose basis lies in a symbolic world and not in one of rationalism. Ultimately there are two features; the crudest of empirical facts such as the electrodes and the multilated human body, and the experience of going through torture. In his text Timerman does create a powerful counterdiscourse, precisely because, like torture itself, it moves us through that space of death where reality is up for grabs, to confront the hallucination of the military....

Conrad's way of dealing with the terror of the rubber boom in the Congo was *Heart of Darkness*. There were three realities there....: King Leopold's, made out of intricate disguises and deceptions; Roger Casement's studied realism; and Conrad's, which, to quote Karl, "fell midway between the other two, as he attempted to penetrate the veil and yet was anxious to retain its hallucinatory quality."[7]...

Casement offers a useful and startling contrast to Conrad, all the more vivid because of the ways their paths crossed in the Congo in 1890, because of the features common to their political backgrounds as exiles or quasi-exiles from imperialized European societies, Poland and Ireland, and because of an indefinable if only superficial similarity in their temperaments and love of literature. Yet it was Casement who resorted to militant action on behalf of his native land, organizing gun running from Germany to the rebels at Dublin for Easter Sunday 1916, and was hung for treason, while Conrad resolutely stuck to his task as an artist, bathed in nostalgia and guilt for Poland, lending his name but otherwise refusing to assist Casement in the Congo Reform Society, claiming he was but a "wretched novelist." The key text for our purposes is Conrad's letter to his beloved friend and socialist, the aristocrat don Roberto, otherwise known as R. B. Cunninghame Graham . . . In this letter, dated 26 December 1903, Conrad salutes don Roberto on the excellence of his book on the great Spanish conquistador, Hernando de Soto, and especially for the sympathetic insight into the souls of the *conquistadores* – the glamour, the pathos, and romance of those times – which functions as an anodyne inducing one to forget the modern *conquistadores* such as Leopold and the lack of romance and vision in nineteenth- and early -twentieth-century bourgeois imperialism. Conrad then goes on to inform don Roberto about "a man called Casement" and his plans for a Congo reform society to stop the terror associated with the rubber industry there, the same terror which inspired Conrad's novella. Conrad likens Casement to a *conquistador*, and indulges in a hopelessly romanticized image of him – curtly corrected by Brian Inglis, one of Casement's biographers, seventy years later.[8] . . . Writing to John Quinn, Conrad re-images his first acquaintance with Casement, now pigeonholing him not as in the *Congo Diary* as a man who "thinks, speaks well, [is] most intelligent and very sympathetic," but as a labor recruiter. He goes on to disparage Casement as a romantic opportunist and adds:

> He was a good companion, but already in Africa I judged that he was a man, properly speaking, of no mind at all. I don't mean stupid. I mean he was all emotion. By emotional force (Congo report, Putumayo – etc.) he made his way, and sheer emotionalism has undone him. A creature of sheer temperament – a truly tragic personality: all but the greatness of which he had not a trace. Only vanity. But in the Congo it was not visible yet.[9]

Yet it remains a fact that Casement's reports on the Congo and the Putumayo did much to stop the pervasive brutality there and, in Edmund Morel's opinion, "innoculated the diplomacy of this country [Britain] with a moral toxin" such that "historians will cherish these occasions as the only two in which British diplomacy rose above the commonplace."[10]

In addition to the coincidences of imperialist history, what brings Casement and Conrad together is the problem they jointly create concerning the rhetorical power and political effect of social realism and mythic realism. Between the emotional consul-general who wrote effectively on the side of the colonized as a realist and a rationalist, and the great artist who did not, lie many of the crucial problems concerning the domination of culture and cultures of domination.

The Putumayo Report

At this point it is instructive to analyze briefly Casement's Putumayo report, which was submitted to Sir Edward Grey, head of the British Foreign Service, and published by the House of Commons on 13 July 1913 when Casement was forty-nine years old.

At the outset it should be noted that Casement's attachment to the cause of Irish home rule and his anger at British imperialism made his almost life-long work as a

British consul extremely fraught with contradiction; in addition, he felt his experiences in Africa and South America increased his understanding of the effects of the colonialism in Ireland, which in turn stimulated his ethnographic and political sensibilities regarding conditions south of the equator. He claimed, for example, that it was his knowledge of Irish history which allowed him to understand the Congo atrocities, whereas the Foreign Office could not because the empirical evidence made no sense to them. . . .

The essence of his 136-page Putumayo report, based on seven weeks of travel in 1910 through the rubber-gathering areas of the jungles of the Caraparaná and Igaraparaná affluents of the middle reaches of the Putumayo river, and on some six months in the Amazon basin, lay in its detail of the terror and tortures together with Casement's explanation of causes and his estimate of the toll in human life. Putumayo rubber would be unprofitable were it not for the forced labor of local Indians. . . . For the twelve years from 1900, the Putumayo output of some 4,000 tons of rubber cost thousands of Indians their lives. Deaths from torture, disease, and possibly flight had decreased the population of the area by around 30,000 during that time.

The British government felt obliged to send Casement as its consular representative to the Putumayo because of the public outcry aroused in 1909 by a series of articles in the London magazine, *Truth*; the series depicted the brutality of the rubber company, which since 1907 had been a consortium of Peruvian and British interests in the region. Entitled "The Devil's Paradise: A British Owned Congo," these articles were the work of a young "engineer" and adventurer from the United States named Walter Hardenburg, who had with a companion entered the remote corner of the Amazon basin from the Colombian Andes in 1907 and had been taken prisoner by the Peruvian Rubber Company founded by Julio César Arana in 1903. . . .

Casement's report to the House of Commons is staid and sober, somewhat like a lawyer arguing a case and in marked contrast to his diary covering the same experience. He piles fact on brutal fact, suggests an over-all analysis, and makes his recommendations. His material comes from three sources: what he personally witnessed; testimony of 30 Barbados blacks who, with 166 others, were contracted by the company during 1903–1904 to serve as overseers, and whose statements occupy 85 published foolscap pages; and, interspersed with Casement's direct observations, numerous stories from local residents and company employees.

Early on in the report, in a vivid throwaway line, he evokes the banality of the cruelty. "The employees at all the stations passed the time when not hunting Indians, either lying in their hammocks or in gambling."[11] The unreal atmosphere of ordinariness, of the ordinariness of the extraordinary, can be startling. "At some of the stations the principal flogger was the station cook – two such men were directly named to me, and I ate the food they prepared, while many of their victims carried my baggage from station to station, and showed often terrible scars on their limbs inflicted at the hands of these men."[12]

From the evidence of scarring, Casement found that the "great majority" (perhaps up to 90 percent) of the more than 1,600 Indians he saw had been badly beaten.[13] Some of the worst affected were small boys, and deaths due to flogging were frequent, either under the lash, or more frequently, a few days later when the wounds became maggot infested.[14] Floggings occurred when an Indian brought in insufficient rubber and were most sadistic for those who dared to flee. Flogging was mixed with other tortures such as near drowning, "designed," as Casement points out, "to just stop short of taking life while inspiring the acute mental fear and inflicting much of the physical agony of death."[15] Casement was informed by a man who had himself often flogged Indians that he had seen mothers flogged because their little sons had not brought in enough rubber. While the boy stood terrified and crying at the sight, his mother would be beaten "just a few strokes" to make him a better worker.[16]

Deliberate starvation was resorted to repeatedly, sometimes to frighten, more often to kill. Men and women were kept in the stocks until they died of hunger. One Barbadian related how he had seen Indians in this situation "scraping up the dirt with their fingers and eating it." Another declared he had seen them eating the maggots in their wounds.[17]

The stocks were sometimes placed on the upper verandah or residential part of the main dwelling house of the rubber stations, in direct view of the manager and his employees. Children, men, and women might be confined in them for months, and some of the Barbados men said they had seen women raped while in the stocks.[18]

Much of the surveillance and punishment was carried out by the corps of Indian guards known as the *muchachos*. Members of this armed corps had been trained by the company from an early age, and were used to control *salvajes* other than those to whom they were kin. Casement thought them to be generally every bit as evil as their white masters.[19] When Barbados men were present, they were frequently assigned the task of flogging, but, Casement emphasizes, "no monopoly of flogging was enjoyed by any employee as a right. The chief of the section frequently himself took the lash, which, in turn, might be wielded by every member of the civilized or 'rational staff.'"[20]

"Such men," reports Casement, "had lost all sight or sense of rubber-gathering – they were simply beasts of prey who lived upon the Indians and delighted in shedding their blood." Moreover, the station managers from the areas where Casement got his most precise information were in debt (despite their handsome rates of commission), running their operations at a loss to the company which in some sections ran to many thousands of pounds sterling.[21]

It is necessary at this point to note that although the Indians received the brunt of the terror, whites and blacks were also targets. Whether as competitors for Indian rubber gatherers, like the independent Colombian rubber traders who first conquered the Putumayo and were then dislodged by Arana's company in 1908, or as employees of the company, extremely few escaped the ever-present threat of degradation and torture. Asked by Casement if he did not know it to be wrong to torture Indians, one of the Barbados men replied that he was unable to refuse orders, "that a man might be a man down in Iquitos, but 'you couldn't be a man up there.'"[22] In addition, most of the company's white and black employees were themselves trapped in a debt-peonage system, but one quite different from the one the company used in controlling its Indians.

From the testimony of the Barbados men it is clear that dissension, hatred, and mistrust ran riot among all members of the company – to the degree that one has to consider seriously the hypothesis that only in their group ritualization of torturing Indians could such anomie and mistrust be held in check, thus guaranteeing to the company the solidarity required to sustain it as an effective social unit....

Casement's Analysis

Casement's main line of analysis lies with his argument that it was not rubber but labor that was scarce in the Putumayo, and that this scarcity was the basic cause of the use of terror. Putumayo rubber was of the lowest quality, the remoteness of its source made its transport expensive relative to rubber from other zones, and wages for free labor were very high. Hence, he reasons, the company resorted to the use of forced labor under a debt-peonage system, and used torture to maintain labor discipline.

The problem with this argument, which assumes the purported rationality of business and the capital-logic of commodities (such as labor), is that it encounters certain contradictions and, while not exactly wrong, strikes me as giving insufficient weight to two fundamental considerations. The first consideration concerns the forms of labor and economic organization that local history and Indian society made available, or potentially available, to world capitalism in the jungles of the Putumayo. The second, put crudely, is that terror and torture do not derive only from market pressure (which we can regard here as a trigger) but also from the process of cultural construction of evil as well. "Market pressure" assumes the paradigm of scarcity essential to capitalist economism and capitalist socioeconomic theory. Leaving aside the question of how accurate a depiction of capitalist society results from this paradigm, it is highly dubious that it reveals much of the reality of the Putumayo rubber boom where the problem facing capitalist enterprise was precisely that there were no capitalist social institutions and no market for abstract labor into which capital could be fed and multiplied. Indeed, one could go further to develop an argument which begins with the premise that it was just this lack of commoditized social relationships, in interaction with commodity forces emanating from the world rubber market, that accounts for the production of torture and terror. We can say that the culture of terror was functional to the needs of the labor system, but that tells us little about the most significant contradictions to emerge from Casement's report, namely, that the slaughter of this precious labor was on a scale vast beyond belief, and that, as Casement himself states, not only were the station managers costing the company large sums of money but that "such men had lost all sight or sense of rubber-gathering – they were simply beasts of prey who lived upon the Indians and delighted in shedding their blood." To claim the rationality of business for this is to claim and sustain an illusory rationality, obscuring our understanding of the way business can transform the use of terror from the means into an end in itself.

The consideration of local history and economic organization requires far fuller treatment than can be attempted here. But it should be noted in passing that "scarcity" of labor cannot refer to a scarcity of Indians, of whom there seems to have been an abundance, but rather to the fact that the Indians would not work in the regular and dependable manner necessary to a large-scale capitalist enterprise. Casement downplayed this phenomenon, now often referred to as "the backward sloping supply curve of labor," and did so even though in the Congo he had himself complained that the problem was that the natives would not work;[23] he felt sure that if paid with more goods, the Indians would work to the level required by the company without force. Many people with far longer experience in the Putumayo denied this naïve assertion and pointed out, with logic as impeccable as Casement's, that the scarcity of labor and the ease with which the Indians could live off the forest obliged employers elsewhere in the Putumayo to treat them with consideration.[24] In either case, however, with or without use of coercion, the labor productivity obtained fell far short of what employers desired.

The contradictions mount further on close examination of the debt-peonage system, which Casement regards as slavery. It was a pretext, he says, that the Indian in such a relation was in debt, for the Indian was bound by physical force to work for the company and could not escape.[25] One then must ask why the company persisted in this pretense, especially given the means of coercion at its disposal.

Accounts of advances paid in goods (such as machetes, cloth, shotguns) were supposedly kept for each rubber gatherer; the advances were roughly equal to fivepence per pound weight of rubber, which was fetching three shillings tenpence on the London market in 1910. . . . A station manager told Casement that the Indians never asked the price or value of rubber. Sometimes a single coin was given . . . Yet, it would be naïve to suppose that the Indians lacked interest or understanding of the terms of trade and of what the whites got for rubber in the outside world. "You buy these with the rubber we produce," said an Indian chief as one entranced, looking through Casement's binoculars.[26]

Pretext as it was, the debt which ensured peonage was nonetheless real, and as a pretense its magical realism was as essential to the labor organization of the Putumayo rubber boom as is the "commodity fiction" Karl Polanyi describes for a mature capitalist economy.[27] To analyze the construction of these fictional realities we need now to turn to some of their more obviously mythic features, enclosed as they are in the synergistic relation of savagery and business, cannibalism and capitalism. . . .

Jungle and Savagery

There is a problem that I have only hinted at in all of the accounts of the atrocities of the Putumayo rubber boom. While the immensity of the cruelty is beyond question, most of the evidence comes through stories. The meticulous historian would seize upon this fact as a challenge to winnow out truth from exaggeration or understatement. But the more basic implication, it seems to me, is that *the narratives are in themselves evidence of the process whereby a culture of terror was created and sustained.*

Two interlacing motifs stand out: the horrors of the jungle, and the horrors of savagery. All the facts are bent through the prism formed by these motifs, which . . . mediate effective truth not so much through the dissemination of information as through the appeal of temperaments through sensory impressions. Here the European and colonist image of the primeval jungle with its vines and rubber trees and domination of man's domination stands forth as the colonially apt metaphor of the great space of terror and deep cruelties. (Europe – late nineteenth century, penetrating the ancient forests of the tropics.) . . . .

But of course it is not the jungle but the sentiments men project into it that is decisive in filling their hearts with savagery. And what the jungle can accomplish, so much more can its native inhabitants, the wild Indians, like those tortured into gathering rubber. It must not be overlooked that the colonially constructed image of the wild Indian here at stake was a powerfully ambiguous image, a seesawing, bifocalized, and hazy composite of the animal and the human. In their human or human-like form, the wild Indians could all the better reflect back to the colonists the vast and baroque projections of human wildness that the colonists needed to establish their reality as civilized (not to mention business-like) people. And it was only because the wild Indians were human that they were able to serve as labor – and as subjects of torture. For it is not the victim as animal that gratifies the torturer, but the fact that the victim is human, thus enabling the torturer to become the savage.

How Savage Were the Huitotos?

The savagery of the wild Indians occupied a key role in the propaganda of the rubber company....

[Yet] [t]ime and again Casement tells us that the Huitotos and all Upper Amazon Indians were gentle and docile. He downplays their cannibalism, says that they were thoughtless rather than cruel, and regards their docility as a *natural* and remarkable characteristic. This helps him to explain the ease with which they were conquered and forced to gather rubber.... Yet, on the other hand, such docility makes the violence of the whites even harder to understand.

Many points can be contested in Casement's rendering here, such as his assertion of the degree of chiefly power and the deceptive simplicity he evokes with regard to the issue of toughness and tenderness in a society so foreign to his own. It should also not be forgotten that the story he wanted to tell was one of innocent and gentle child-like Indians brutalized by the rubber company, and this controlling image gives his report considerable rhetorical power. In addition there was his tendency to equate the sufferings of the Irish with those of the Indians and see in both of their preimperialist histories a culture more humane than that of their civilizing overlords. (Conrad never indulged in that kind of transference.) Still another factor blended with the foregoing, and that was the innate tenderness of Casement's character and his ability to draw that quality out of others, as testified by numerous people. It is this aspect of his homosexuality, and not sexual lust, which should be dwelt on here, as shown, for example, in this note in his Putumayo diary:

> ...floggings and putting in guns and floggings with machetes across the back....I bathed in the river, delightful, and Andokes [Indians] came down and caught butterflies for Barnes and I. Then a captain [Indian chief] embraced us laying his head down against our breasts. I never saw so touching a thing, poor soul, he felt we were their friends.[28]

Alfred Simson, an Englishman who travelled the Putumayo and Napo rivers in the 1880s and spent far more time there than Casement, conveys a picture quite different from Casement's.[29] ...

Simson was employed on the first steam launch to ascend the Putumayo...Hence he witnessed the opening of the region to modern commerce, and was in a special position to observe the institutionalization of ideologies concerning race and class. Not only does he present a contrary and more complex estimate of Indian toughness than does Casement: he also provides the clue and ethnographic motif necessary to understand why such contrary images coexist and flourish, how Indian images of wildness come halfway, as it were, to meet and merge with white colonial images of savagery, and, finally, how such imagery functions in the creation of terror. . . .

Simson notes that what he calls the "pure Indians of the forest" are divided, by whites and Spanish-speaking Indians, into two classes; Indians (*Indios*) and heathens (*infieles*). The *Indios* are Quichua-speaking, salt-eating, semi-Christians, while the heathens, also known as *aucas*, speak distinct languages, eat salt rarely, and know nothing of baptism or of the Catholic Church.[30] In passing it should be observed that today, if not in times long past, the term *auca* also connotes cannibals who roam the forest naked, are without marriage rules, and practice incest. . . .

I should add that the highland Indian shaman with whom I work in the Colombian Andes which overlook the Putumayo jungles regards the jungle shamans below as *aucas*, as animal/spirit hybrids possessing great magic. He singles out the Huitotos as a spiritual force with whom he makes a mystical pact in incantations and songs, with or without hallucinogens, to assure the success of his own magical battles with evil.

It is crucial to grasp the dialectic of sentiments involved here by the appelation *auca*, a dialectic enshrouded in magic and composed of both fear and contempt – identical to the mysticism, hatred, and awe projected onto the Zionist socialist Timerman in the torture chambers of the military. In the case of the *aucas*, this projection is inseparable from the imputation of their resistance to sacred imperial authority and the further imputation of magical power possessed by lowland forest dwellers as a class and by their oracles, seers, and healers – their shamans – in particular. Moreover, this indigenous, and what may well be a pre-Colombian, construction blends with the medieval European mythology of the Wild Man brought to the Andes and the Amazon by the Spaniards and Portuguese. Today, in the upper reaches of the Putumayo with which I am acquainted, the mythology of *auca* and Wild Man underlies the resort to Indian shamans by white and black colonists who seek cure from sorcery and hard times, while these very same colonists despise Indians as savages.[31] In the rubber boom, with its desperate need for Indian labor, the same mythology nourished incalculable cruelty and paranoia on the part of the whites. . . .

Narrative Mediation: Epistemic Murk

It seems to me that stories like these were the groundwork indispensable to the formation and flowering of the colonial imagination during the Putumayo rubber boom. "Their imagination was diseased," wrote the Peruvian judge Rómulo Paredes in 1911, referring to the rubber-station managers, "and they saw everywhere attacks by Indians, conspiracies, uprisings, treachery etc.; and in order to save themselves from these fancied perils . . . they killed, and killed without compassion."[32] Far from being trivial daydreams indulged in after work was over, these stories and the imagination they sustained were a potent political force without which the work of conquest and of supervising rubber gathering could not have been accomplished. What is essential to understand is the way in which these stories functioned to create, through magical realism, a culture of terror dominating both whites and Indians.

The importance of this fabulous work extends beyond the epic and grotesque quality of its content. The truly crucial feature lies in creating an uncertain reality out of fiction, a nightmarish reality in which the unstable interplay of truth and illusion becomes a social force of horrendous and phantasmic dimensions. To an important extent all societies live by fictions taken as reality. What distinguishes cultures of terror is that the epistemological, ontological, and otherwise purely philosophical problem of reality-and-illusion, certainty-and-doubt, becomes infinitely more than a "merely" philosophical problem. It becomes a high-powered tool for domination and a principal medium of political practice. And in the Putumayo rubber boom this medium of epistemic and ontological murk was most keenly figured and objectified as the space of death.

In his report, Paredes tells us that the rubber-station managers lived obsessed with death. They saw danger everywhere and thought solely of the fact that they were surrounded by vipers, tigers, and cannibals. It is these ideas of death, he writes, which constantly struck their imaginations, making them terrified and capable of any act. Like children who read the *Arabian Nights*, he goes on to say, they had nightmares of witches, evil spirits, death, treason, and blood. The only way they could live in such a terrifying world, he observes, was by themselves inspiring terror.[33]

Sociological and Mythic Mediation: The *Muchachos*

If it was the telling of tales which mediated inspiration of the terror, then it behooves us to inquire a little into the sociological agency which mediated this mediation, namely, the corps of Indian guards trained by the company and known as the *muchachos*. For in Rómulo Paredes's words, they were "constantly devising executions and continually revealing meetings of Indians 'licking tobacco' – which meant an oath to kill white men – imaginary uprisings which never existed, and other similar crimes."[34]

Mediating as civilized or rational Indians between the savages of the forest and the whites of the rubber camps, the *muchachos* personified all the critical distinctions in the class and caste system of rubber production. Cut off from their own kind, whom they persecuted and betrayed and in whom they inspired envy and hatred, and now classified as civilized yet dependent on whites for food, arms, and goods, the *muchachos* wrought to perfection all that was horrifying in the colonial mythology of savagery – because they occupied the perfect sociological and mythic space to do so. Not only did they create fictions stoking the fires of white paranoia, they embodied the brutality which the whites feared, created, and tried to harness to their own ends. In a very literal sense, the *muchachos* traded their identity as savages for their new social status as civilized Indians and guards. As Paredes notes, they placed at the disposal of the whites "their special instincts, such as sense of direction, scent, their sobriety, and their knowledge of the forest."[35] Just as they bought rubber from the wild Indians of the forest, so the whites also bought the *auca*-like savage instincts of the Indian *muchachos*.

Yet, unlike rubber, these savage instincts were manufactured largely in the imaginations of the Whites. All the *muchachos* had to do in order to receive their rewards was to objectify and through words reflect back to the whites the phantoms that populated colonist culture. Given the centuries of colonial mythology concerning the *auca* and the Wild Man, and given the implosion of this mythology in the contradictory social being of the *muchachos*, the task was an easy one. The *muchachos*' stories were, in fact, stories within a much older story encompassing the *muchachos* as objects of a colonialist discourse rather than as its authors.

The trading system of debt-peonage established by the Putumayo rubber boom was thus more than a trade in white goods for rubber gathered by the Indians. It was also a trade in terrifying mythologies and fictional realities, pivoted on the mediation of the *muchachos*, whose storytelling bartered betrayal of Indian realities for the confirmation of colonial fantasies.

The Colonial Mirror

I began this essay stating that my concern was with the mediation of the culture of terror through narration, and with the problems of writing against terror. In part my concern stemmed from my problems in evaluating and interpreting the "facts" constituted in the various accounts of the Putumayo atrocities. This problem of interpretation grew ever larger, eventually bursting into the realization that that problem is precisely what is central to the culture of terror – not only making effective talking and writing against terror extremely difficult, but, even more to the point, making the terrible reality of the death squads, disappearances, and torture all the more effectively crippling of people's capacity to resist.

While much attention is given to "ideology" in the social sciences, virtually none as far as I know is given to the fact that people delineate their world, including its large as well as its micro-scale politics, in stories and story-like creations and very rarely, if ever, in ideologies (as customarily defined). Surely it is in the coils of rumor, gossip, story, and chit-chat [that] ideology and ideas become emotionally powerful and enter into active social circulation and meaningful existence. So it was with the Putumayo terror, from the accounts of which it seems clear that the colonists and rubber company employees not only feared but also themselves created through narration fearful and confusing images of savagery – images which bound colonial society together through the epistemic murk of the space of death. The systems of torture they devised to secure rubber mirrored the horror of the savagery they so feared, condemned – and fictionalized. Moreover, when we consider the task of creating counterrepresentations and counterdiscourses, we must take stock of the way that most if not all the narratives reproduced by Hardenburg and Casement, referring to and critical of the atrocities, were similarly fictionalized, drawing upon the same historically moulded source that men succumbed to when torturing Indians.

Torture and terror in the Putumayo were motivated by the need for cheap labor. But labor *per se* – labor as a commodity – did not exist in the jungles of the Caraparaná and Igaraparaná affluents of the Putumayo. What existed was not a market for labor but a society and culture of human beings whom the colonists called Indians, irrationals, and savages, with their very specific historical trajectory, form of life, and modes of exchange. In the blundering colonial attempt to dovetail forcibly the capitalist commodity-structure to one or the other of the possibilities for rubber gathering offered by these modes of exchange, torture, as Casement alludes, took on a life of its own: "Just as the appetite comes in the eating so each crime led on to fresh crimes."[36] To this we should add that, step by step, terror and torture became *the* form of life for some fifteen years, an organized culture with its systematized rules, imagery, procedures, and meanings involved in spectacles and rituals that sustained the precarious solidarity of the rubber company employees as well as beating out through the body of the tortured some sort of canonical truth about Civilization and Business.

It was not commodity fetishism but debt fetishism drenched in the fictive reality of the debt-peonage institution, with its enforced "advances" and theatre-like farce of business exchanges, that exercised the decisive force in the creation of terror, transforming torture from the status of a means to that of the mode if not, finally, the very aim of production.

From the reports of both Timerman and Casement it is obvious that torture and institutionalized terror is like a ritual art form, and that far from being spontaneous, *sui generis*, and an abandonment of what are often called "the values of civilization," such rites have a deep history deriving power and meaning from those values. What demands further analysis here is the mimesis between the savagery attributed to the Indians by the colonists and the savagery perpetrated by the colonists in the name of what Julio César Arana called civilization.

This reciprocating yet distorted mimesis has been and continues to be of great importance in the construction of colonial culture – *the colonial mirror* which reflects back onto the colonists the barbarity of their own social relations, but as imputed to the savage or evil figures they wish to colonize. It is highlighted in the Putumayo in the colonist lore as related, for instance, through Joaquin Rocha's lurid tale of Huitoto cannibalism. And what is put into discourse through the artful story telling of the colonists is the same as what they practiced on the bodies of Indians.

Tenaciously embedded in this artful practice is a vast and mystifying Western history and iconography of evil in the imagery of the inferno and the savage – wedded to and inseparable from paradise, utopia, and the good. It is to the subversion of that apocalyptic dialectic that all of us would be advised to bend our counterdiscursive efforts, in a quite different poetics of good-and-evil whose cathartic force lies not with cataclysmic resolution of contradictions but with their disruption.

Post-Enlightenment European culture makes it difficult if not impossible to penetrate the hallucinatory veil of the heart of darkness without either succumbing to its hallucinatory quality or losing that quality. Fascist poetics succeed where liberal rationalism self-destructs. But what might point a way out of this impasse is precisely what is so painfully absent from all the Putumayo accounts, namely, the narrative and narrative mode of the Indians which does de-sensationalize terror so that the histrionic stress on the mysterious side of the mysterious (to adopt Benjamin's formula) is indeed denied by an optic which perceives the everyday as impenetrable, the impenetrable as everyday. At least this is the poetics of the sorcery and shamanism I know about in the upper reaches of the Putumayo, but that is another history for another time, not only of terror but of healing as well.

NOTES

1   Jacobo Timerman, *Prisoner without a Name, Cell without a Number* (New York: Vintage Books, 1982), p. 164.
2   Timerman, *Prisoner*, p. 28.
3   Timerman, *Prisoner*, p. 111.
4   Timerman, *Prisoner*, p. 52.
5   Michel Foucault, "Truth and Power" in *Power/Knowledge*, ed. Colin Gordon (New York: Pantheon, 1980), p. 118.
6   Timerman, *Prisoner*, pp. 62, 66.
7   Frederick R. Karl, *Joseph Conrad: The Three Lives* (New York: Farrar, Straus and Giroux, 1979), p. 286.
8   Brian Inglis, *Roger Casement* (London: Hodder Paperbacks, 1974), p. 32....
9   Karl, *Joseph Conrad*, p. 289 n.
10 Inglis, *Roger Casement*, p. 46.
11 *House of Commons Sessional Papers*, 1913, vol. 68 (hereafter cited as Casement, *Putumayo Report*), p. 17.
12 Ibid., p. 34.
13 Ibid., p. 33, 34.
14 Ibid., p. 37.
15 Ibid., p. 39.
16 Ibid., p. 37.
17 Ibid., p. 39.
18 Ibid., p. 42.
19 Ibid., p. 31. From various estimates it appears that the ratio of armed supervisors to wild Indians gathering rubber was somewhere between 1:16 and 1:50. Of these armed supervisors, the *muchachos* outnumbered the whites by around 2:1. See Howard Wolf and Ralph Wolf, *Rubber: A Story of Glory and Greed* (New York: Covici, Friede, 1936), p. 88.
20 Casement, *Putumayo Report*, p. 33.
21 Ibid., p. 44–45.
22 Ibid., p. 55.
23 Inglis, *Roger Casement*, 29.
24 Rocha, *Memorandum de un viaje* (Bogotá: Editorial El Mercurio, 1905), pp. 123–4, asserts that because the Indians are "naturally loafers" they postpone paying off their advances from the rubber traders, thus compelling the traders to use physical violence.
25 Casement, British Parliamentary Select Committee on Putumayo, *House of Commons Sessional Papers*, 1913, vol. 14, p. 113, #2809.
26 Peter Singleton-Gates and Maurice Girodias. *The Black Diaries* (New York: Grove Press, 1959), p. 261.
27 Karl Polanyi, *The Great Transformation* (Boston: Beacon Press, 1957), p. 72. Cf. Michael Taussig, *The Devil and Commodity Fetishism in South America* (Chapel Hill: University of North Carolina Press, 1980).
28 Petes Singleton-Gates and Maurice Girodias, *The Black Diaries* (New York: Grave Press, 1959), p. 251.
29 Alfred Simson, *Travels in the Wilds of Ecuador and the Exploration of the Putumayo River* (London: Samson Low, 1886), p. 170.
30 Alfred Simson, *Travels* p. 58.
31 Michael Taussig, "Folk Healing and the Structure of Conquest," *Journal of Latin American Lore*, 6(2) (1980): 217–78.
32 Rómulo Paredes, "Confidential Report to the Ministry of Foreign Relations, Peru," September 1911, translated in U.S. Consul Charles C. Eberhardt. *Slavery in Peru* 7

February 1913, report prepared for U.S. House of Representatives, 62d Cong., 3d Sess., 1912, H. Doc. 1366, p. 146.

33 Paredes, "Confidential Report," in Eberhardt, *Slavery in Peru*, p. 158.

34 Ibid., p. 147.

35 Ibid., p. 147.

36 Casement, *Putumayo Report*, p. 44.

16

Images of the Peasant in the Consciousness of the Venezuelan Proletariat

William Roseberry

In an influential and controversial book, James Scott suggested that peasants have a "moral economy" by which they evaluate the destructive effects of capitalist expansion and the increasing exactions of the colonial state. Based on a subsistence ethic, the moral economy demands that those who appropriate peasant surpluses offer guarantees for the continued survival of the peasant household. Although precapitalist orders may be seen as exploitative in a Marxist sense, they may be based on patron–client relations that offer survival guarantees and may not be perceived as exploitative by the peasants who enjoy the guarantees. The intrusion of capitalism or the formation of a colonial state may break the social ties of the old moral economy, erode survival guarantees, appear exploitative to the peasantry, and provoke rebellion (Adas 1980; Popkin 1979; Scott 1976; cf. his 1977).

Scott's analysis of peasant politics in Southeast Asia explicitly draws upon the work of E. P. Thompson and others who have emphasized the moral economy of peasants, artisans, and proletarians in eighteenth- and nineteenth-century England and France. This literature has emphasized the active presence of precapitalist traditions, values, and communities in the early working class – traditions that were transformed with the Industrial Revolution and in terms of which the industrial experience was evaluated, criticized, and resisted (Thompson 1963: 63; 1971; cf. Hobsbawm 1959; Rudé 1964). The literature has served an important corrective function with relation to Marxist and non-Marxist economic history, in which the history of capitalism is often considered the history of the capitalists, the history of those who won. Even more important than its recapturing of the history of those who lost, however, the moral economy literature has created the basis for a new theory of consciousness. It has renewed the notion of tradition, not as the dead weight of the past, but as the active, shaping force of the past in the present.

Although the moral economy literature, particularly that dealing with the European experience, must be regarded as advancing our historical understanding, there

From *Anthropologies and Histories: Essays in Culture, History, and Political Economy* (New Brunswick, NJ: Rutgers University Press, 1985), pp. 55–79. Copyright Greenwood Press.

is an unfortunate tendency to treat the peasant or artisan past in unambiguous, uncritical terms. For example, when Thompson analyzes traditional notions of time in his essay "Time, Work-Discipline, and Industrial Capitalism" (1967), he freely draws on examples from the Nuer and other primitive societies without carefully distinguishing among these societies, the nature of their traditions, values, experiences, and communities, and the traditions of the peasants and artisans who were to experience the Industrial Revolution in England. In *Work, Culture and Society in Industrializing America* (1976), Herbert Gutman lumps together under the single label "preindustrial" a wide variety of peasant and artisan traditions from different parts of Europe and North America and at different historical moments. And James Scott (1976) has a tendency to overstate his case, romanticizing the precapitalist past and ignoring the forces of disorder and exploitation that preceded capitalism and the colonial state.

One must, then, question the distance from modernization theory traveled by these theorists. Although they adopt a much more critical stance toward the capitalist transformation than do the classical theorists of modernization, they have remarkably similar starting points for their historical trajectories – a relatively homogeneous, undifferentiated traditional order. More important for our purposes, this weakness has unfortunate consequences for their understanding of consciousness. Although they are correct to point to the active force of the past in the present, their uncritical approaches to the past leave them in poor positions to understand the contradictory images, values, and feelings presented to the emerging proletarian.

In *The Country and the City*, Raymond Williams notes the difficulty in dating the disappearance of an idyllic rural past. For whatever century, it always seems to have recently disappeared or to be in the process of disappearing. In a passage that has special relevance to the moral economy literature, he observes:

> Take first the idealisation of a "natural" or "moral" economy on which so many have relied, as a contrast to the thrusting ruthlessness of the new capitalism. There was very little that was moral or natural about it. In the simplest technical sense, that it was a "natural" subsistence agriculture, as yet unaffected by the drives of a market economy, it is already doubtful and subject to many exceptions; though part of this emphasis can be readily accepted. But the social order within which this agriculture was practiced was as hard and as brutal as anything later experienced. Even if we exclude the wars and brigandage to which it was commonly subject, the uncountable thousands who grew crops and reared beasts only to be looted and burned and led away with tied wrists, this economy, even at peace, was an order of exploitation of a most thoroughgoing kind: a property in men as well as in land; a reduction of most men to working animals, tied by forced tribute, forced labour, or "bought and sold like beasts"; "protected" by law and custom only as animals and streams are protected, to yield more labour, more food, more blood; an economy directed, in all its working relations, to a physical and economic domination of a significantly total kind. (1973: 37–8)

But, some might argue, the "moral economy" need not have existed in the past; it may be *perceived* in the past from the perspective of a disordered present. The images of a moral economy may be a *meaningful* image even if "what actually happened" was less idyllic. But as Williams suggests, the perceptions of the past will depend upon the relative positions of the perceivers; different idealizations and evaluations will emerge depending on distinct experiences of a "physical and economic domination of a significantly total kind."

In a commentary on Frank R. Leavis and Denys Thompson's *Culture and Environment* (1977), Williams turned this point about the past toward an evaluation of consciousness in the present:

> What is true, I would argue, is that a number of new kinds of unsatisfying work have come into existence; a number of new kinds of cheap entertainment, and a number of new kinds of social division. Against these must be set a number of new kinds of satisfying work; certain new kinds of social organization. Between all these and other factors, the balance has to be more finely drawn than the myth allows. (1960: 279)

In pointing to these passages, I do not mean to suggest, just as Williams does not mean to suggest, that the industrial capitalist order represented, on balance, progress for humankind and advances for working people. My point has to do with our approach to consciousness. Too often moral economy theorists, while pointing out the importance of the past in the present, analyze a relatively unambiguous transition from an ordered past to a disordered present. We instead need to view a movement from a disordered past to a disordered present. With such a starting point we can assess the contradictions inherent in the development of working-class consciousness and appreciate that the past provides experiences that may make the transition seem positive as well as experiences that may make it seem negative. Only then can we see the moral economy as a source for protest and accommodation, despair and hope.

With this in mind, I turn to the social history of a segment of the Venezuelan peasantry. Unlike peasantries with which anthropologists are more commonly familiar, the peasantry I examine has relatively shallow historical roots. It formed in the nineteenth century with the emergence of a coffee economy and underwent a proletarianization process in the twentieth century with the rise of Venezuela's petroleum economy. This short historical existence, intimately related to the cyclical development of the world market, corresponds to another basic point of *The Country and the City*: that both country and city (and I would add peasant and proletarian) are ever-changing qualities and, as qualities, are to be understood in the context of capitalist history (Williams 1973: 302 *et passim*).

Before turning to specifics, I offer some introductory comments. First, I do not pretend to analyze the Venezuelan peasantry as a whole. The Venezuelan peasantry never existed as an identifiable whole but only in its regionally differentiated parts. I concentrate on the coffee-producing peasantry of the Andes, which exhibits a number of unique features. My own personal knowledge of the Andean peasantry is dependent on field research in a smaller, specialized region – the Boconó District of Trujillo State (Roseberry 1983). Second, despite such limitation, I do not give a detailed account of the peasantry's history. Such detail can be found elsewhere. Here I simply summarize those aspects of its history that are necessary for cultural analysis. Third, my analysis of peasant and proletarian consciousness is not based upon my presentation of ideas, opinions, or conceptions that were expressed to me by individuals; nor is it based upon the behavior of peasants and proletarians in elections, unions, or related political events and movements. This is, rather, an attempt to outline the cultural possibilities presented to Venezuelan peasants and proletarians in their social history – the constitutive elements of political consciousness.

I examine these cultural possibilities with four symbolic sets that, in deference to a fashion in cultural analysis, are presented as opposed pairs: coffee and petroleum, backwardness and development, country and city, and dictatorship and democracy. This is hardly an esoteric group of images, but the meanings attached to them are constitutive elements of political consciousness. In discussing each set, I first trace the political and economic history that produces and connects the images. I then concentrate on the images themselves and discuss how they are presented to Venezuelans, without distinguishing among different class perceptions. In the process, I attempt to outline the raw materials available for cultural analysis.

Coffee and Petroleum

The Andean peasantry emerged in the nineteenth century with the growth of a coffee economy. At independence, the Andes were not central to Venezuela's economy, which was based on lowland plantation production of cacao for export. Cacao-producing areas were devastated by the War of Independence, and coffee soon displaced cacao as Venezuela's principal export. Such a shift did not immediately involve major political, economic, or demographic upheavals. Plantation owners in the central and coastal lowlands could expand their holdings into surrounding highlands, planting coffee and displacing the garden plots (*conucos*) of their dependent tenants and slaves. Only in the late nineteenth century did the Andes – which had been relatively depopulated and which produced primarily for regional markets during the colonial period – emerge as an important coffee-producing region. By the end of the century, Maracaibo, which served the Andes, was a major port, the Andes produced more than half of Venezuela's exports, and Andeans captured national power in Caracas (Carvallo and Hernandez 1979; Lombardi and Hanson 1970; Rangel 1968; 1969; Roseberry 1983).

Because the Andes were not densely populated during the colonial period, the formation of the coffee economy could not proceed without an intense migration process. Peasants and merchants from other parts of Venezuela (especially the cattle-producing *llanos* to the south, in decline throughout the nineteenth century), as well as migrants from southern Europe, settled on vacant national lands or in the new towns and cities in the temperate zone where coffee was planted. The migrants entered some areas that were virtually unpopulated and other areas that had a long colonial history. The interaction of migrant and resident, coffee economy and colonial economy, is important for understanding regional differentiation in the Andes and the nineteenth-century political battles between liberals and conservatives. Such detail is not crucial for the present analysis, however. More important is an emphasis on the relatively small scale of production throughout most of the temperate coffee-producing zone. Regional differentiation must be stressed here as well, but with the dissolution of colonial forms of landed property, a property-owning peasantry was created. These property-owning peasants, along with those who owned no property but occupied national lands, became the principal coffee producers. For the most part, they entered into direct relations with merchants who loaned them the funds necessary to start a coffee farm and to maintain themselves until the first harvest, and who thus established a claim to most of the product of the coffee farms. The Andean peasantry was therefore unique in many respects. Unlike other parts of Venezuela, where large farms and dependent tenants predominated, a relatively independent peasantry was established in the Andes. Unlike other regions, where landlords were politically and economically dominant, merchants controlled the coffee-producing Andes. This is not to say that landlords were nonexistent; it is to say that the merchant–peasant relationship defined the Andean economy (Rangel 1968, 1969; Roseberry 1980, 1983).

The bright historical possibilities that faced pioneers who had established their own farms and passed them on to their children began to dim in the twentieth century. The coffee economy reached its spatial limits around the turn of the century. Indebtedness became a problem, especially during periodic world market depressions, for example, in the market's virtual closure during the World War I and especially during the 1930s crisis. The depression could be seen as one of a series of cyclical crises in the coffee economy. Two aspects of the Venezuelan situation made the 1930s unique, however. First, the fact that the effective spatial limits to coffee production had been reached meant that the favored response to crisis – increased production through spatial expansion – was available only by expanding on to less productive land. Second, by the 1930s coffee had been displaced by petroleum as the dominant Venezuelan export. Economic displacement was accompanied by political displacement, even while Andeans continued to hold formal positions of state power. Farmers and merchants facing foreclosure, poverty, and in some cases starvation abandoned the coffee economy. Nearby petroleum camps in the Maracaibo basin attracted some Andean migrants, but most of them went to cities such as Caracas and Maracaibo to participate in the commercial and governmental expansion accompanying Venezuela's transformation. This is not to say that the coffee economy disappeared. Indeed, land area planted with coffee increased in the Andes during the decades following the crisis, even as productivity and total production declined, indicating expansion on to less and less favorable land. Except for growing urban centers in the Andes that participated in Venezuela's commercial and governmental expansion, however, most Andean districts either lost population from one census to the next or maintained extremely low levels of population growth. Sons and daughters left the area, aggravating the situation for those coffee farmers who remained.

The nature of the petroleum transformation is discussed in the next section. Here I concentrate on the coffee economy, the peasantry that characterized it, and the images it presented for a moral economy. First, the relative independence of the Andean coffee-producing peasantry must be stressed. Yet it is remarkable to note the disappearance of this peasantry from the political consciousness of contemporary Venezuela. In both the offical versions of Venezuelan history and alternative left-wing versions, the rural landscape has been reduced to a relatively undifferentiated opposition between landlords and dependent tenants, with a peonage relationship defining the social existence of the peasantry. There is some debate about the relative importance of *latifundia* in the Andes, in part due to a tendency to ignore regional differentiation and to aggregate state-level statistics. Nevertheless, one would think that the coffee-farming peasant of the nineteenth century would serve as one basis for the construction of a moral economy pointing to an ordered past.

A number of factors operate against this alternative historical memory, but I mention only those directly related to the coffee economy and the peasantry. The most important is the process of development of the coffee economy. The expansion and hopes of the late nineteenth century gave way to relative stasis in the early twentieth century and finally to the crisis and collapse of the 1930s. During a price crisis in the early twentieth century, a local Andean newspaper struck a note of despair:

> With rare exceptions, what is the capital which has been formed among coffee producers, even when prices were as high as thirty-six or forty pesos for one hundred kilos? None. And when the market presented low prices, our fields were inexplicably and painfully neglected. Many of our *hacendados* had to abandon their farms to go look for another way to survive; others stay on their *haciendas* in a languid, heavy life, with no strength to move themselves. (*El Renacimiento*, Boconó, Venezuela, 4 March 1904)

The people who experienced the years of collapse were the sons and daughters, grandsons and granddaughters of the nineteenth-century pioneers. During the years of crisis, their debt obligations were leading to foreclosures. Their consciousness and memories would not be of independence but of abject dependence.

This leads us to the crucial characteristic of the Andean peasantry that separates it from those peasantries analyzed in the moral economy literature. The moral economists consider peasantries that seem to have deep historical roots. Capitalist development or colonialism intrudes upon that peasantry and disrupts its traditions and forms of organization. There is no sense, however, in which the Andean peasantry was precapitalist. Rather, it emerged in the nineteenth century as the region was incorporated into the world market. It was not oriented toward subsistence but toward commodity production. From the beginning, its fate was tied to the cyclical development of the world market. Because of internal differentiation within the peasantry, some producers could prosper, take advantage of periods of high prices, establish debt relations with poorer farmers, and create a protective cushion to absorb the shock of periods of low prices. Their less fortunate fellows could get by during periods of high prices but suffered at other times. Given their relations with merchants – relations that were essential if the family was to grow coffee – their establishment as a peasantry was simultaneously the establishment of a relationship with a form of capital. While one might legitimately argue about whether that relationship was capitalist or *non*capitalist, there is little historical sense in labeling it *pre*capitalist. The coffee economy presented some raw material for a moral economy that could point to an ordered past, but it also presented raw material for a consciousness that could point to a disordered past.

Backwardness and Development

Were it not for petroleum, Venezuela would have fit the stereotypic model of an underdeveloped country – exporting one or two agricultural raw materials and importing manufactured products. At one level, petroleum extraction and export simply replaced an agricultural raw material by a mineral one without affecting the basic import-export model. Indeed, Venezuela became more dependent on a single product than had ever been the case with coffee or cacao. A number of things were, however, different about petroleum. In the first place, it brought in far greater returns than were possible with agricultural products. During the decade in which petroleum replaced coffee as the principal export, the portion of total export value to which coffee contributed dropped to a minuscule level *before* actual production declined. Second, unlike agricultural and most other mineral products, petroleum was less subject to cyclical fluctuations in demand and price on the world market, at least during these long decades of expansion. Finally, it was a resource on which the developed world was so dependent that producing countries could occasionally exercise some pressure and control in the international market, as demonstrated by the success of the Organization of Petroleum Exporting Countries in the 1970s. In short, more things became possible with petroleum than would have been possible with coffee.

While petroleum extraction made an escape from typical forms of underdevelopment possible, it would be a mistake to automatically link coffee to backwardness and petroleum to development. The petroleum economy simultaneously symbolizes Venezuela's backwardness and its development. The coffee economy was never under foreign control. Import-export houses in port cities were owned by resident foreigners – Germans and English – and their Venezuelan-born children, but local production rested in Venezuela hands. Even when a foreigner controlled some aspect of production or marketing, the foreigner was not a corporation; the Venezuelan patrimony had not been sold. In contrast, the granting of concessions to Anglo-Dutch Shell or the Standard Oil Corporation introduced a wholly new chapter in Venezuela's underdevelopment. The early laws governing the concessions were written by representatives of the companies themselves and called for a modest royalty to be paid to the Venezuelan government, but the vast majority of the oil wealth was extracted by foreign companies to feed foreign capital accumulation. In short, the rise of the petroleum economy meant the insertion of Venezuela within the imperialist system.

A kind of development nevertheless occurred in Venezuela. In the previous section, I referred to the "commercial and governmental expansion" of Venezuela's economy. We must now give some content to that phrase. Venezuela's oil wealth has been distributed primarily by the state. Even in the early years, when foreign companies paid modest royalties to the state, the sums generated allowed for an enormous expansion of the governmental apparatus. As production and the percentage of royalties owed to the state increased over the decades, this apparatus grew even larger. To serve the members of the growing bureaucracy and their families, merchants of consumer goods proliferated. One remarkable result of the petroleum transformation, then, was the growth of an urban middle class, dependent on incomes from government or commerce. Venezuela's industrial structure, however, was weak. It was only with efforts starting in the 1940s to "sow the petroleum" that the growing state began to turn its resources toward stimulating diversified production. Industrial investment and development were promoted by import-substitution policies starting in 1959. The state began in 1974 to encourage basic industry (e.g., petrochemicals) in public and mixed public and private enterprises. But even with these recent attempts to stimulate industrial development, Venezuela has become an urban, essentially nonindustrial country.

This is reflected in statistics on the distribution of gross domestic product (GDP) and population among primary (agriculture, mining), secondary (manufacture, construction, utilities), and tertiary (commerce, transportation, service) sectors. Distribution of GDP among sectors has been relatively stable because of the importance of petroleum earnings in the primary sector. From 1950 to 1969, nevertheless, there was significant slippage in the primary sector (down from 38 percent to 28 percent of GDP), a minor proportional increase in the secondary sector (up from 17 percent to 20 percent), and a larger proportional increase in the tertiary sector (from 45 percent to 52 percent) (Venezuela, Banco Central 1971). If we divide the economically active population among these same sectors, however, a more dramatic change appears. In 1950, 46 percent were working in the primary sector; by 1971, only 22 percent were. The secondary sector has remained relatively stable (rising from 17 percent to 20 percent), and the percentage of the population working in the tertiary sector increased from 34 percent to 42 percent. The major increase was in a group that confounded the census takers and that will be discussed later. The residual "others" increased from 3 percent to 16 percent. The decline in the percentage of people engaged in the primary sector can be explained by the decline in the agricultural sector, which dropped from 43 percent to 20.3 percent of the economically active population (Venezuela, Ministerio de Fomento 1971).

The statistics tell us that a dramatic change has occurred in the structure of the Venezuelan population; one aspect of that change is discussed in the next section. Statistics also indicate the skewed structure of Venezuela's economy – the overwhelming weight of petroleum in the primary sector and of government services and commerce in the tertiary sector. They can only hint, however, at the quality of life that allows Darcy Ribeiro to write of "the 'Puerto-Ricanization' of Venezuela" 1972: 288). He refers in part to the historical importance of the petroleum companies and in part to the increased importance of multinationals in Venezuelan industry and commerce since 1959. He refers as well to a cultural transformation that – especially in urban areas such as Caracas and Maracaibo – affects language, dress, social relations, art, cinema, and other cultural manifestations.

The sketch of economic evolution in this century and of macrolevel statistics also does not indicate the struggles that have been waged around the petroleum sector. Efforts to "sow the petroleum" in the 1940s, increased royalties assessed by the state, import substitution and industrialization in the 1960s and 1970s and, finally, the nationalization of the petroleum companies in 1976 are associated with a series of political movements that are best assessed in our discussion of dictatorship and democracy. These struggles give social content to images of backwardness and development. Venezuela has been defined as a petroleum economy for most of this century. In the selling of Venezuela's patrimony, in the dominance of multinationals, in the cultural influence of New York, Miami, or Paris, the petroleum sector stands for Venezuela's backwardness. In the early labor struggles in the petroleum camps, in the attempts to redefine the relationship between the state and the corporations, in the nationalization of iron and petroleum, in the attempt to promote industrial development, and in the attempt to create and maintain democracy, the petroleum sector is made to stand for the possibility of Venezuela's development. With petroleum embodying both development and backwardness, coffee and the agricultural past occupy an ambiguous position. They are relegated to a relatively ahistorical tradition, largely devoid of social content and the positive and negative valuations that are placed on petroleum. This allows for rather contradictory attitudes toward the countryside.

Country and City

There is perhaps no more visible marker of Venezuela's transformation than urbanization. In 1936, 35 percent of all Venezuelans lived in urban areas; by 1971, the figure was 77 percent. Much of the urban concentration has been in Caracas, but the phenomenon is not limited to the capital. Even the Andean states, once predominantly rural and one of many sources of migrants for Caracas and other urban centers, have become primarily urban. Although the Andean states have been major sources of migrants, they are not the only sources. Migrants to the city come from various regions and a variety of rural experiences. One factor in the urbanization process has been the stagnation of the rural sector, of which the coffee economy is only the most visible example. Another factor concerns the transformation of Venezuela's political economy and the expansion of government services and commerce mentioned earlier.

People who move from rural areas to the city may move into these growing spheres. This is less true for peasants and their sons and daughters than it is for the sons and daughters of the middle class from towns and cities in the interior. Such opportunities are not, however, entirely closed to the peasant. The first urban experience for such a person may be living with a relative in a provincial center while attending secondary school. This can open doors in the educational establishment or for low-level positions elsewhere in the bureaucracy, as a person with a high school degree and modest political connections can become a grade school teacher. For a young daughter, the first urban experience may, however, be living in a provincial center or in Caracas with a family that has hired her as a domestic servant. Or the move for a young man may involve a series of stays with relatives and searches for work during the agricultural dead season. He may eventually stay in the city. The work he finds, if he finds it, probably will not be in industry. It may be in commerce; it may be in petty trades servicing the growing urban population of unemployed; it may be a series of short jobs in construction, commerce, and petty trades. This last group makes up the "other" category that so confuses the census takers. A growing literature on these migrants in other parts of Latin America tells us that their "marginality" is a myth (e.g. Lomnitz 1977; Perlman 1976). This is particularly clear as we pay more attention to the petty trades that elude macrolevel statistics. Just as we cannot glibly label them "marginal," however, we also cannot subsume them within a "proletariat" in the sense of a working population integrated within an industrial economy. The move from country to city is not, in most cases, a move from peasant to proletarian but from peasant to "other." The industrial sector is too constricted to absorb the working population, and the portion of the population it absorbs is not, again for the most part, right off the farm.

Physical evidence of unemployment and underemployment of migrants can be found in the *ranchos* or slums that climb the hillsides and cling to the walls of riverbeds in towns of modest size and in major cities. The existence of the *ranchos* is not to be understood solely in terms of the economic condition of their residents. Some have a rather long history. With time, the cardboard houses give way to concrete tiles and zinc roofs; with time, water and electrical services, as well as public health and educational facilities, may be introduced. (Or the *rancho* may disappear in a landslide. Or it may be displaced by a government-sponsored housing project that *rancho* dwellers cannot afford to live in.) In addition to offering evidence of unemployment and underemployment, then, the *rancho* is also indicative of disordered urban growth. More migrants arrive than a city can absorb, and they find a place by creating one. City services follow at a slower pace and are constantly stretched beyond their capacity.

Even so, no discussion of a city like Caracas is adequate unless one mentions that it is an exciting place. This is obviously true for those who can afford to enjoy its restaurants and clubs, who can buy the latest New York or Paris fashions, or who can while away an afternoon discussing Marxism at a sidewalk *cafetín* – but these people and their historical memories are not central to our analysis. The city can also be an exciting place for those whose possibilities are more limited. Even if urban employment is limited, there is always a chance one will get a job. That chance may not exist in a stagnating countryside. Moreover, the petty trades can offer some opportunity for modest wealth. The city also offers other opportunities. For example, a young woman may find schooling in a place like Barquisimeto or Caracas a necessary step in liberating herself from her family of orientation without getting married.

This brief discussion has indicated something of the contradictory images presented by notions of country and city. In the section on coffee and petroleum, I indicated that the image of the peasant and countryside emerging from the coffee economy is that of a disordered past, but the migrant moves from a disordered countryside to a disordered city. The city that presents itself as a symbol of modern Venezuela also creates its critical opposite: the pastoral countryside. Coffee, the countryside, and the peasant, which serve as symbols of an agricultural past, are also countersymbols to the present. They evoke a half-remembered prepetroleum, preurban, premodern Venezuela. This symbol is less effective for the recent migrant for whom the backwardness of the countryside is part of his or her lived experience. For someone born in the city, perhaps with parents who grew up in the countryside, or for someone who has lived in the city for a number of years, however, the country may be given a positive valuation. The countryside is able to carry this weight because, as noted previously, petroleum and the city that is a product of the petroleum economy simultaneously symbolize backwardness and development. The countryside, purged of its own history, comes to represent the true Venezuela.

This is evident in Venezuelan popular music. Protest music seldom celebrates the city. When it refers to the city at all, it is to the *ranchos*, the "houses of cardboard." The city is an object of protest along with imperialism, the petroleum economy in general, the state, and similar institutions. The countryside, however, has numerous referents. It too may be the object of protest, as songs call attention to the exploited position of the peasant, in the past and in the present, but it can also serve as a counterpoint to the present with the evocation of the simplicity of peasant life, the positive virtues of agricultural labor, and the daily life and interactions of the rural family. In addition to protest music, the production of folklore as an industrial commodity recalls the rural past as well. Recent folk music may nostalgically recall the "streets of my childhood." More importantly, traditional themes of folk music – love, nature, and the family – are placed in a rural setting and are presented in distinctive regional styles, such as the *tonada* (tone poem) of the llanos and the waltz of the Andes. On record albums or on television programs they celebrate a past when the regions mattered. In one sense, disordered urbanization creates an image of a homogenized countryside stripped of history and regional differentiation. In another sense, especially in popular music, regional affiliations are reasserted as differences in style and temperament.

I do not mean to enter into an extended discussion of popular music in Venezuela, but simply to indicate that the disordered nature of Venezuelan development, including the urban disorder of a city like Caracas, calls up the image of a Venezuelan past without disorder. This image can gain expression because most urbanites have some connections with the countryside where they or their parents grew up. Kinship ties connect them with rural regions, and they return to their or their parents' childhood home for Christmas or Holy Week. Some provincial towns organize reunions in which former residents are asked to return for a day-long celebration. While there, the urban resident can go to a country house for a *paseo* (picnic), where a *sancocho* (soup) is prepared, much rum is drunk, and the ideal of rural order is confirmed.

Dictatorship and Democracy

The final symbolic pair requires that we move in a different direction from that implied by our discussion of country and city. It is an essential direction, however, if we are to tie together the various threads of this discussion. The main lines of twentieth-century Venezuelan political history are fairly well known and can be found in literature widely available in North America. I simply indicate a few key features and draw some conclusions important for our cultural analysis.

Coffee was displaced by petroleum during the dictatorship of Juan Vicente Gómez, who ruled from 1908 to 1935 and who, paradoxically, first came to prominence as a coffee grower in the Andean state of Táchira. He oversaw the transformation that removed coffee from its privileged position in the economy. Despite the fact that Andeans held positions of authority in the army or the administration, the entire period of Andean rule represents a progressive loss of political and economic power by Andeans and the coffee economy. The transformation, and the emergent middle class that accompanied it, created an incipient democratic movement. Its first expression was in student protests at the Central University, the most famous of which occurred in 1928 and was led by men who later founded the social democratic party Acción Democrática (AD), which later became the dominant political party. A series of political parties emerged after Gómez's death, although political power continued until 1945 to rest with Andeans, who granted more democratic freedoms than did Gómez. Acción Democrática came to power in a coup that members continue to refer to as the Revolution of '45. The party then organized the first Venezuelan presidential election based on universal suffrage, from which the novelist Rómulo Gallegos emerged victorious. His administration was overthrown by a military coup in 1948, shortly after a number of progressive measures were passed – among them a series of agrarian reform laws and a law requiring the petroleum companies to pay 50 percent royalties. Pérez Jiménez eventually became the strong man of the junta until massive demonstrations in 1958 forced him to flee and ushered in a democratic period that has lasted until the present.

Acción Democrática has dominated this period, although the two major parties – AD and the Christian Democratic COPEI (Committee for Political Organization and

Independent Elections) – exchanged positions every five years in the general elections from 1968 to 1988. When AD came to power in 1959, many in its top leadership maintained their commitment to democracy, but they had abandoned the radical perspectives of their youth. Rómulo Betancourt and his followers defined their project in nationalist terms. They would exact ever greater royalties from the petroleum companies – from 60 percent to 80 percent during the 1960s – and would assume control of the petroleum sector by a series of steps that would culminate in 1976 with nationalization. They would initiate and participate in the formation of OPEC. They would institute import-substitution policies to stimulate industrialization. Diversification – "sowing the petroleum" – had been a concern of AD since the mid-1940s, but diversification and industrialization did not exclude participation by multinationals. The direction of new foreign investment changed dramatically from petroleum and iron extraction to industry and commerce after 1959. Acción Democrática welcomed foreign investment as part of its attempt to alter the course of Venezuelan development.

A number of participants in Acción Democrática, as well as members of other parties including the Communist party, were disillusioned with AD's project and initiated a guerrilla movement in the countryside during the 1960s. The movement never attracted as much support as guerrilla leaders had hoped. One reason was that the movement romanticized and attempted to organize the peasantry during a decade when it was disappearing. By the end of the 1960s, the economically active population engaged in agriculture was only 20 percent of all Venezuelans. More importantly, however, many peasants were sympathetic to AD. This brings us to a point crucial to understanding Venezuelan culture and politics. The initial strength of AD was in popular organizations of peasants, workers, and others without representation in a backward, dictatorial Venezuela. There were two aspects to this. The party owed its existence and support to such organizations, and peasants and workers were first organized and first acted politically through Acción Democrática. These bases of support were not ignored by AD, even if they were not always well served. One of the first measures passed when AD came to power in 1959 was an agrarian reform law – weak, but nonetheless an apparent reform.

There is in the formation of Acción Democrática and the political history of which it is a part an aspect that too often eludes those on the Left who deride Venezuela's democracy. Three movements were symbolically united in AD: development, democracy, and the organization of working people. Acción Democrática gave particular and partial definitions to development and democracy, but it was able to impose those definitions through its organizations. Images of backwardness and development in the petroleum economy are associated with the images of dictatorship and democracy. The backwardness of the petroleum economy is seen as a legacy of the past, of the dictators who sold the Venezuelan patrimony and who, as it happens, were also associated with the coffee economy. The struggle for development is simultaneously presented as a struggle for democracy.

This symbolic association has exercised enormous power in the political consciousness of Venezuelan peasants, proletarians, and "others," but there are two sorts of weakness in that association that require elaboration – the potential failure of development and the potential failure of democracy. Given the fact that the democratic period has lasted for three decades, both sources of weakness have become apparent and have given greater space to movements of the Left and Right than existed in the early 1960s. The failure of democracy results in part from the fact that the political leaders and spokesmen for AD and other parties often pursue individual aims and individual careers. Parties and factions of parties may pursue their own projects and candidacies by endlessly debating relatively trivial matters in congress. There is a tremendous dissipation of energy in Venezuela's democracy, and during periods of economic crisis, when the country's development seems imperiled, "democracy" can seem a nonessential luxury. The failure by leaders pursuing their own goals to attend to the country's "development" calls "democracy" into question and gives organizational space to the Right.

The failure of development results in part from the fact that multiclass democratic parties like AD are nonetheless pursuing class projects. Acción Democrática's class project is associated with an incipient industrial bourgeoisie. The form of development they advocate closely approximates F. H. Cardoso's notion of associated dependent development – linkage between sectors of local capital, state capital, and multinational capital in the diversification and industrialization of the Venezuelan economy (Cardoso 1973; Cardoso and Faletto 1979). Unlike other examples of this model, the linkage between development and democracy is more than a symbol, and Venezuela has so far escaped the more authoritarian forms of government usually associated with this model. Much of the explanation for this rests with the petroleum sector. As indicated, petroleum wealth has been channeled by the state into the tertiary sector, and part of that expansion has been an expansion of social services, subsidies for agricultural producers, marketing organizations, and housing projects. The democrats therefore are simultaneously able to promote dependent development and to incorporate significant segments of the Venezuelan population into the state through social services. However, as the attempt to promote basic industry has in recent years encountered declining petroleum revenues, the state has diverted funds from social services. The results for the fortunes of the two major parties of this diversion are not clear. A class project may no longer be coterminous with a democratic project. The old linkage between democracy and development is therefore imperiled, giving organizational space to both the Left and Right.

Can we put these shifting and contradictory images of Venezuela's past, present, and future into a coherent picture? To address this question, I turn to the cultural analysis suggested by Raymond Williams in *Marxism and Literature* (1977: 108–27, *et passim*). Unlike much recent anthropology, Williams's notion of culture cannot be separated from political economy.... Williams points to the construction of a "dominant culture" that is not a coherent integrated cultural system or structure but a rather inchoate set of lived experiences, feelings, and relationships within a political and economic order of domination. Because it is not a closed system, it is in a constant process of construction and reconstruction. Although many elements could be considered constitutive of a dominant culture, one that Williams points to is of particular relevance to the moral economy literature: tradition as a *selective tradition* – a version (indeed, the ruling version) of a people's history... Tradition as selective tradition is important when we consider one of Williams's central points about dominant culture – that no order of domination is total. There are always sets of relationships and experiences that are excluded and that may serve as points around which alternative, perhaps oppositional, cultural forms can emerge. With the creation of an alternative culture, a basic element must be an alternative tradition – a reinterpretation and rewriting of history, concentrating on events and relationships excluded from the ruling version and pointing to a different set of historical possibilities.

Williams is clearly suggesting a cultural analysis that goes beyond approaches to culture as symbolic systems or shared values or meanings. He has tied his notion of culture to a historical process and to class structures and relationships. Nevertheless, there is no sense in which dominant and emergent culture are coterminous with particular class positions. The images of Venezuela's tradition that have been discussed in this essay are not class specific. A class culture or class discourse is never given; it must be constructed from the cultural raw material presented by history, from the "tradition" that is used to construct both dominant and emergent forms of culture. It is in this sense that I refer in the title of this essay to the consciousness of a proletariat. I can, by analysis of Venezuela's history, indicate the kinds of images that have been used to create a hegemonic order or dominant culture. I can also indicate the kinds of images that are available for a counterhegemony. In both cases, cultural creation and the formation of consciousness are political processes. An emergent culture must be created by using elements of past and present that have been excluded in the dominant culture or by giving new meanings to elements that have not been excluded.

Thus the first point to be made about the dominant culture in Venezuela is that it is political. The linkage between development and democracy created by Acción Democrática is so profound that it sets the terms for all political debate. The principal opposition party, COPEI, accepts the linkage and contests particular policies. Most socialist parties also accept the linkage but argue that the dominant parties are not *really* democratic or that their form of development is not *really* development. To a certain extent, this linkage and associated aspects of dominant culture are consciously promoted and can be seen as constitutive of a ruling ideology. Professors of history sympathetic to AD write histories of Venezuela showing a movement from degradation to democracy and from backwardness to development. All history is a movement toward the progress enjoyed in the present. There is also a constant manipulation of emotions in the use of television, public rallies, and state occasions. For example, the contradictory images of the peasant and the countryside – images that stress an exploited past or that stress pastoral calm and independence – can be expressed simultaneously and played against each other. Official celebrations of the anniversary of the agrarian reform law romanticize the Venezuelan peasant even as they emphasize the exploitative "past." The dominant culture cannot, however, simply be dismissed as conscious manipulation or ruling-class ideology. When these histories are written, or when the past is unfavourably compared with the present, the ideologues are touching on one aspect of the lived experiences of peasants and proletarians. The move from country to city, from peasant to proletarian or "other," or from backwardness to development can be experienced as progress.

Given the contradictory nature of Venezuela's development, the dominant culture can only touch on one aspect of that experience. It can point to Venezuela's progress; it cannot point to all that is troubling and contradictory in that disordered progress. To what extent does the past provide raw material for an emergent culture, a moral economy of protest? The past is certainly available, most obviously in the everyday comparison of present basic food and grain prices with those in effect of generation, a year, or even a month ago. By examining the symbols of coffee and petroleum, backwardness and development, country and city, I have traced the emergence of an image of an ordered rural past that serves as critical counterpoint to the disordered present. Can this image serve as the basis for an alternative emergent tradition? I think not. It represents not historical memory, but historical nostalgia. It has no connection with the lived experience of most peasants or even most proletarians. It simply calls up an idealized past, and as an ideal it can support the present order or, in the event of the failure of Venezuela's models of development and democracy, a fascist turn. Here it is interesting to note that most socialist historians do not fundamentally differ from AD historians on large segments of Venezuela's past. Both stress the dependence and backwardness of the early petroleum economy. They differ on their interpretations of the present and on some of the labels they give to past and present. They differ, in short, in their valuations of Venezuelan forms of development and democracy.

The construction of an emergent culture that can serve a proletarian consciousness, then, cannot turn to an idealized past but must begin with the lived experience of Venezuelan proletarians. The starting point is the very linkage that proved so powerful for the dominant culture – development and democracy. It must recognize and celebrate those aspects of progress in Venezuela's twentieth century that represent historic gains: the emergence of forms of organization of popular masses, the struggle to gain control over petroleum resources and to turn the wealth created by the petroleum sector toward national development, and the struggle for democracy. Because these achievements have been progressive and because historically they are associated with Acción Democrática, they have served as constitutive elements of the dominant culture, but the contradictions inherent in the dominant parties' approach to development mean that these same achievements can be turned into constitutive elements of an emergent political culture. Development and democracy may still serve as the basis for working-class consciousness, but the terms may be given fuller, more critical, more demanding meanings. Workers may demand forms of organization they control, forms of development that exclude multinationals, forms of democracy that give them greater control over their own destiny.

The moral economists argue that a first-generation proletarian or a peasantry first confronted with capitalist development looks backward for its forms of response at the same time that it looks forward. This is true in Venezuela; a less anthropologically inclined writer might argue that it is universally true. When Venezuelan peasants and proletarians look back, however, their view is not clear. Venezuelan peasants and proletarians are confronted with a disordered past that has given way to a disordered present. Their political and cultural task is to take aspects of the past and of the present that have offered promise and turn them into demands for the future.

REFERENCES

Adas, M. (1980) "Moral Economy" or "Contest State?" Elite Demands and the Origins of Peasant Protest in Southeast Asia. *Journal of Social History* 13: 521–46.

Cardoso, F. (1973) Associated Dependent Development: Theoretical and Practical Implications. In A. Stepan (ed.) *Authoritarian Brazil*, pp. 142–76. New Haven: Yale University Press.

Cardoso, F. and Faletto, E. (1979) *Dependency and Development in Latin America*. Berkeley: University of California Press.

Carvallo, G. and Hernandez, J. (1979) *Agricultura y Sociedad: Tres Ensayos Históricos*. Caracas: CENDES.

Gutman, H. (1976) *Work, Culture, and Society in Industrializing America*. New York: Random House.

Hobsbawm, E. (1959) *Primitive Rebels*. New York: Norton.

Leavis, F. R. and Thompson, D. (1977) *Culture and Environment: The Training of Critical Awareness* [1933]. Westport, CT: Greenwood Press.

Lombardi, J. and Hanson, J. (1970) The First Venezuelan Coffee Cycle, 1830–1855. *Agricultural History* 44: 355–67.

Lomnitz, L. (1977) *Networks and Marginality*. New York: Academic.

Perlman, J. (1976) *The Myth of Marginality*. Berkeley: University of California Press.

Popkin, S. (1979) *The Rational Peasant*. Berkeley: University of California Press.

Rangel, D. (1968) *El Proceso del Capitalismo Contemporaneo en Venezuela*. Caracas: Universidad Central.

——. (1969) *Capital y Desarrollo: La Venezuela Agraria*. Caracas: Universidad Central.

Ribeiro, D. (1972) *The Americas and Civilization*. New York: Dutton.

Roseberry, W. (1980) Capital and Class in Nineteenth Century Bocono, Venezuela. *Antropologica* 54: 139–66.

——. (1983) *Coffee and Capitalism in the Venezuelan Andes*. Austin: University of Texas Press.

Rudé, G. (1964) *The Crowd in History*. New York: Wiley.

Scott, J. (1976) *The Moral Economy of the Peasant*. New Haven: Yale University Press.

——. (1977) Hegemony and the Peasantry. *Politics and Society* 7(3): 267–96.

Thompson, E. P. (1963) *The Making of the English Working Class*, New York: Pantheon.

——. Time, Work-Discipline, and Industrial Capitalism. *Past and Present* 38: 56–97.

——. (1971) The Moral Economy of the English Crowd in the Eighteenth Century. *Past and Present* 50: 76–136.

Venezuela, Banco Central. (1971) La economía Venezolane enlos últionas treinta años. Caracas.

Venezuela, Ministerio de Formento. (1971) X censo de población y vivienda: Resumen general. Caracas.

Williams, R. (1960) *Culture and Society*. New York: Columbia University Press.

——. (1973) *The Country and the City*. New York: Oxford University Press.

——. (1977) *Marxism and Literature*. Oxford: Oxford University Press.

17

Of Revelation and Revolution

Jean and John Comaroff

It is sometimes said that, while the literature on religious transformation in Africa is very large, there are few anthropological analyses of the evangelical encounter itself.... Even the most ambitious attempt to write a historical ethnography of a mission "at the grassroots," Beidelman's *Colonial Evangelism*, has been judged "sadly incomplete" precisely because it fails to bring a systematic – or a novel – anthropological perspective to bear on the subject (Gray 1983: 405).

This critique also reflects the more general neglect of colonialism – indeed, of history itself – by a discipline mainly interested until very recently in "traditional" African society and culture. Social historians, on the other hand, have long concerned themselves with, even been fascinated by, Christian evangelists. And they have not been alone. In the great awakening of modern Africa, when the colonized began to write their own histories and to reflect upon the technologies of European domination, they too gave a good deal of attention to "the" missionary – if only to excoriate him as an agent of imperialism (Ayandele 1966; Majeke 1952; Zulu 1972). The condemnation was extended also to scholarly apologies that portrayed European churchmen as well-intentioned philanthropists (e.g., Brookes 1974; Wilson 1969, 1976) or benign imperialists (e.g., Sillery 1971); such accounts being seen by their critics as modern expressions of the same missionizing culture. While this unjoined debate foreshadowed later theoretical disputes over the relative weight of human agency and structural forces in African social change, both arguments were cast with reference to the same tacit question: "Whose side were the Christians really on?"

As a result, complex historical dynamics were reduced to the crude calculus of interest and intention, and colonialism itself to a caricature... Stated thus, moreover, the question presupposed an answer in a certain key: the contribution of the evangelists to the modern African predicament, for good or ill, was judged in terms

From *Of Revelation and Revolution*, vol. 1: *Christianity, Colonialism, and Consciousness in South Africa* (Chicago: University of Chicago Press, 1991), pp. 7–12, 19–24. Copyright © 1991 by The University of Chicago Press.

of their political role, narrowly conceived. This is well exemplified by the so-called "missionary imperialist" thesis. Dachs (1972: 647f.), for instance, claims that as nineteenth-century Tswana rulers resisted their religious activities, the Christians called increasingly on the "political arm of empire" to erode the chiefship and so make local communities more yielding to their ministrations. As we shall see, this is not wrong. But it is distortingly simplistic.

More recently the study of Christian missions, at least in southern Africa, has been affected by a "historiographic revolution" (Marks 1989: 225). This radical shift has encouraged a greater concern with political economy; that is, with long-term processes of colonial conquest, capitalist expansion, state formation, and proletarianization – and, hence, with the part the evangelists played (1) in reorganizing relations of production in rural communities (Trapido 1980); (2) in abetting the penetration of capital and fostering the rise of peasant agriculture (Bundy 1979; Cochrane 1987); and (3) in encouraging the emergence of classes, the rise of black elites, and the availability of tractable industrial labor (Cuthbertson 1987; Etherington 1978). There has, however, been disagreement over their efficacy. At one extreme Denoon (1973: 63f.) declares that they had no historical impact to speak of, certainly not in South Africa; similarly Horton (1971) holds that, in Africa at large, they were never more than incidental catalysts in global processes of rationalization. Elphick (1981), on the other hand, compares them to revolutionaries: their self-conscious elitism and independence, both political and economic, he says, allowed them to dream of transforming all aspects of African life. But this, too, is a minority viewpoint. Cuthbertson (1987: 27), who seems to misread Elphick's argument on the autonomy of the churchmen, counters that they were not only "ideological captives" of the imperialist cause but also "important agents of Western capitalism" (1987: 23, 28). This rebuttal may itself not draw universal agreement, although the implicit notion that "the" role of "the" mission was unambiguous and homogeneous *is* common enough. Nonetheless, most would now concur with one thing: that, as Strayer (1976: 12) once put it, evangelism in Africa can "hardly be regarded as an independent motor of social change."

The obvious limitation in all this – especially for anthropology – is the preoccupation with political economy at the expense of culture, symbolism, and ideology. "Most recent historiography of early mission Christianity," notes Ranger (1986:32), referring to east, central, and southern Africa, "has greatly overplayed the manifest political and economic factors in its expansion." This is hardly unique to the study of religious transformation, of course. It stems ultimately from oppositions (between matter and mind, the concrete and the concept, and so on) at the ontological roots of our social thought – oppositions which persist despite growing agreement that the primary processes involved in the production of the everyday world are inseparably material and meaningful. The impact of Protestant evangelists as harbingers of industrial capitalism lay in the fact that their civilizing mission was simultaneously symbolic and practical, theological and temporal. The goods and techniques they brought with them to Africa presupposed the messages and meanings they proclaimed in the pulpit, and vice versa. Both were vehicles of a moral economy that celebrated the global spirit of commerce, the commodity, and the imperial marketplace. Indeed, it is in the signifying role of evangelical practice – often very mundane, material practice – that we begin to find an answer to the most basic, most puzzling question about the historical agency of Christian missionaries: how it is that they, like other colonial functionaries, wrought far-reaching political, social, and economic transformations in the absence of concrete resources of much consequence.

The question itself raises a much larger methodological issue; namely, the analytic treatment of historical agency *sui generis*. If, as Giddens (1987: 60ff.) has remarked, the relation of "structure and agency" has become a crucial problem for modern social theory, it has not been resolved in the study of colonialism in southern Africa. It is true that the rhetorical influence of Thompson's (1978; cf. Giddens 1987: 203f.) epic battle to save the humanist subject from structuralist extinction is as plain here as it is elsewhere; thus Marks (1989: 225–6) observes approvingly that the new historiography has shown growing interest in "human agency or 'the changing experience of ordinary people.'" Yet, in practice, this seems almost exclusively to involve a concern with (1) the reaction and resistance of blacks to the faceless forces of colonization and control, or (2) the efforts of the "African working class to 'make itself.'" Thompson (e.g., 1975) might have taken care, in the English case, to demonstrate that it is as important to account for the motivations of rulers as it is to understand those of the ruled. With few exceptions (e.g., Ranger 1987), however, comparable attention has not been paid in southern Africa to the consciousness and intentionality of those identified as "agents" of domination. Quite the reverse: their actions continue to be seen largely as a reflex of political and economic processes. An ironic inversion, surely, of the distortions of an earlier liberal historiography!

But there is more than mere irony at stake here. We are challenged to write a historical anthropology of colonialism in southern Africa that takes account of all the players in the game, the motives that drove them, the awareness that informed them, the constraints that limited them. This demands, more generally, that we unravel the dialectics of culture and consciousness, of convention and invention, in this particular part of the world. One consequence of the varied reactions to structuralism over the past decade or so has been to remind us quite how limited our successes have been in just these respects; or, for that matter, in addressing the nature of intentionality, experience, and the imagination. Agency, as we implied earlier, is not merely structure in the active voice. Although the latter may generate the former, it does not always contain it. Social practice has effects that sometimes remake the world (cf. Giddens 1987: 216); it cannot therefore be dissolved into society or culture. But it is also not an abstract "thing." Human agency is practice invested with subjectivity, meaning, and to a greater or lesser extent power. It is, in short, motivated....

Recent writings at the juncture of history and anthropology (e.g., Cooper and Stoler 1989) have begun to show how important were the divisions within colonizing populations; how they were related to distinctions, at home and abroad, of class, gender, and nation; how, over time, they played across the racial line between ruler and ruled, creating new affinities and alliances that blurred the antinomies of the colonial world.... The Christian missions were from the start caught up in these complexities. Not only did the various denominations have diverse and frequently contradictory designs on Africa – designs that sometimes turned out to have unpredictable consequences;...their activities also brought them into ambivalent relations with other Europeans on the colonial stage. Some found common cause, and cooperated openly, with administrators and settlers. Others ended up locked in battle with secular forces for – what they took to be – the destiny of the continent....

It follows, then, that the study of Christianity in Africa is more than just an exercise in the analysis of religious change. It is part and parcel of the historical anthropology of colonialism and consciousness, culture and power; of an anthropology concerned at once with the colonizer *and* the colonized, with structure *and* agency....

Our story is woven from two contrapuntal narratives. One speaks of a specific Christian mission and its consequences; the second, of a more general postenlightenment process of colonization in which Europe set out to grasp and subdue the forces of savagery, otherness, and unreason. We also tell it in two parts.... [W]e trace the early phases of the evangelical onslaught on the "Bechuanas," opening with an exploration of the social and cultural roots – and the ideological motivations – of the Nonconformist mission...In particular, we examine the images of Africa that were to shape the British sense of their engagement with the heathen at the frontiers of civilization...Such popular imaginings bore little resemblance to the nature of society and culture in the "dark" interior..., a universe fashioned by complex historical dynamics which would in time have their own effect on the evangelical encounter and the process of colonization itself. Especially significant were the initial moments of that encounter...These highly ritualized meetings of Europeans and Africans – endowed alike with their own history, their own culture, their own intentions – set the terms of the "long conversation" to follow. In this exchange of signs and substance, each party was to try to gain some purchase on, some mastery over, the other: the churchmen, to convert the Tswana to Christianity; the Tswana, to divert the potency of the churchmen to themselves...In order to facilitate their work, the Nonconformists attempted to drive a wedge between the realm of the spirit and the temporal affairs of government, both indigenous and imperial...The object was to lay the ground for a new moral economy based on the clear separation of church and state, of sacred authority and secular power – to establish, in short, a state of colonialism in anticipation of the colonial state. Ironically, this effort mired some of the Christians in distinctly secular battles; battles they could not win because of the inherent indeterminacy and impotence of their role in the political arena. It was also to reveal fundamental contradictions between the worldview promised by them and the world wrought by the politics of empire, an earthly dominion in which the mission church was anything but powerful.

It was not only in the fraught space between the realm of the spirit and the politics of the colonial state that contradictions were to surface. They were also to arise at the evangelical workface itself. As the Christians set out to rebuild the Tswana lifeworld, they conjured up one kind of society: a global democracy of material well-being and moral merit, of equality before the law and the Lord. Yet their own actions conduced to something quite different: an empire of inequality, a colonialism of coercion and dispossession.... [O]nce the long conversation had set the terms of the encounter, the Nonconformists sought to remake the Africans both through their everyday activities – dress, agriculture, architecture, and so on – and through "formal" education. The impact of this campaign of reconstruction, and the range of reactions to which it led, was mediated by a process of class formation, a process to which the mission itself contributed a great deal. Thus we shall examine the various ways in which the culture sown by the churchmen took root on the social terrain of the Tswana, some of it to be absorbed silently and seamlessly into a reinvented – or, rather, reified – ethnic "tradition," some to be creatively transformed, some to be redeployed to talk back to the whites. We seek to demonstrate, in other words, how parts of the evangelical message insinuated themselves into the warp and weft of an emerging hegemony, while others gave rise to novel forms of consciousness and action.

It was such novel forms of consciousness that were to spark the earliest reactions – the first, often inchoate and stumbling, expressions of resistance – to the contradictions of the civilizing mission. Later, with the rise of a Christian-educated black bourgeoisie, they would fuel black nationalist politics with both causes of complaint and a rhetoric of protest....

Culture, Hegemony, Ideology

The difficulties of establishing what Gramsci may have meant by hegemony are by now notorious. For reasons to do, perhaps, with the conditions of their production, *The Prison Notebooks* do not help us much. Nowhere in them is there a clear or precise definition (Lears 1985: 568). Nowhere do we find, say, the widely cited characterization offered by Williams (1977: 108f.): that is, of "the hegemonic" as a dominant system of lived meanings and values, relations and practices, which shapes experienced reality.... Only in a few places, in fact, does Gramsci come even close to speaking in such terms – and then not about hegemony *per se*. Moreover, the definition quoted most often in recent commentaries – "the 'spontaneous' consent given by the great masses of the population to the general direction imposed on social life by the dominant fundamental group" (Gramsci 1971: 12) – is actually a description of one of "the subaltern functions of social hegemony and political government" exercised by intellectuals. Not only does it raise more problems than it resolves, but it is a far cry from the concept as it has come to be used in much contemporary theoretical writing.

The very fact that Gramsci's notion of hegemony was so unsystematically stated has made it good to think with; as a relatively empty sign, it has been able to serve diverse analytical purposes and positions.... Among poststructuralists its sustained popularity is due in part to the fact that it appears to offer a ready rapprochement between theory and practice, thought and action, ideology and power. But it is also because, as Hebdige (1988: 206) explains, for Gramsci "nothing is anchored to ... master narratives, to stable (positive) identities, to fixed and certain meanings: all social and semantic relations are contestable, hence mutable." Always uncertain, hegemony is realized through the balancing of competing forces, not the crushing calculus of class domination.... Among post-Marxists, too, Gramsci has become "the Marxist you can take home to mother" (Romano 1983), providing an appealing escape from vulgar materialism and essentialism by speaking of production as a continuous ideological, social, and economic process (Hall 1988: 53f.)....

Nonetheless, given suitable specification, the term remains useful for our analytic purposes, since it may be made to illuminate some of the vital connections between power and culture, ideology and consciousness. This having been said, we have no alternative but to spell out our own usage amidst all the ambiguity. We do so, as we have said, by situating it in a more embracing set of analytic terms – and in a particular historical and ethnographic problem.

Some theorists have tried, directly (Williams 1977: 108f.) or indirectly (e.g., Lears 1985: 572f.), to assert the superiority of the notion of hegemony over culture and/or ideology; as if one might subsume and replace the others. Concealed in this argument is the idea that culture *plus* power *equals* hegemony, an equation that simplifies all three terms. Not that the reasoning behind it is surprising..., the anthropological conception of culture has long been criticized, especially by Marxists, for overstressing the implicit, systemic, and consensual, for treating symbols and meanings as if they were neutral and above history, and for ignoring their empowering, authoritative dimensions. Conversely, Marxist theories of ideology and consciousness have been taken to task, by anthropologists, for neglecting the complex ways in which meaning inhabits consciousness and ideology. Neither ideology nor consciousness, goes the argument, is merely culture in the active voice. They are alike products of a process in which human beings deploy salient signs and relations to make their lives and worlds; signs and relations drawn from a structured, largely implicit repertoire of forms that lie below the surfaces of everyday experience. If culture seems to require power to make it complete, then, ideology and consciousness seem to require a good dose of semantics. Add all this together and the sum of the parts may appear to be "hegemony." But there is a problem with both the arithmetic of authority and the mathematics of meaning. Since it is possible, indeed inevitable, for some symbols and meanings *not* to be hegemonic – and impossible that any hegemony can claim all the signs in the world for its own – culture cannot be subsumed within hegemony, however the terms may be conceived. Meaning may never be innocent, but it is also not merely reducible to the postures of power.

Gramsci clearly realized this himself. Rather than posit "hegemony" as a replacement for "culture" or "ideology," he treated the three as quite distinct. At times, furthermore, "culture" was described in a manner to which many anthropologists would not object: as an order of values, norms, beliefs, and institutions that, being "reflected in . . . language" and being also profoundly historical, express a "common conception of the world" embodied in a "cultural-social unity" (1971: 349). This "common conception" was composed of a stock of shared "dispositions," a "popular 'mentality'," which any hegemony had to capture (pp. 348 f., 26 f.). But there is yet more. Gramsci went on to make an explicit chain of associations in which "common conceptions of the world" were equated with "cultural movements" and, by turn, with "philosophies" (p. 328). Significantly, a few pages before (p. 323), "spontaneous philosophy" – i.e. practical, "everyman" philosophy – was said to be contained in (1) language, itself an order "of determined notions and concepts"; (2) common and good sense; and (3) the "entire system of beliefs, superstitions, ways of seeing things and of acting."

Here, the circle closed, we appear to have Gramsci's image of culture as totality. It is the shared repertoire of practices, symbols, and meanings from which hegemonic forms are cast – and, by extension, resisted. Or, in other words, it is the historically situated field of signifiers, at once material and symbolic, in which occur the dialectics of domination and resistance, the making and breaking of consensus. . . . For now . . . following the *Geist* of Gramsci, let us take culture to be the space of signifying practice, the semantic ground on which human beings seek to construct and represent themselves and others – and, hence, society and history. As this suggests, it is not merely a pot of messages, a repertoire of signs to be flashed across a neutral mental screen. It has form as well as content; is born in action as well as thought; is a product of human creativity as well as mimesis; and, above all, is empowered. But it is not all empowered in the same way, or all of the time.

This is where hegemony and ideology become salient again. They are the two dominant forms in which power enters – or, more accurately, is entailed in – culture. It is through them, therefore, that the relationship between power and culture is finally to be grasped, although a further caveat is necessary: that power itself is Janus-faced. Sometimes it appears as the (relative) capacity of human beings to shape the actions and perceptions of others by exercising control over the production, circulation, and consumption of signs and objects, over the making of both subjectivities and realities. This is power in its *agentive* mode: it refers to the command wielded by human beings in specific historical contexts. But power also presents, or rather hides, itself in the forms of everyday life. Sometimes ascribed to transcendental, suprahistorical forces (gods or ancestors, nature or physics, biological instinct or probability), these forms are not easily questioned. Being "natural" and "ineffable," they seem to be beyond human agency, notwithstanding the fact that the interests they serve may be all too human. This kind of *nonagentive* power proliferates outside the realm of institutional politics, saturating such things as aesthetics and ethics, built form and bodily representation, medical knowledge and mundane usage. What is more, it may not be experienced as power at all, since its effects are rarely wrought by overt compulsion. They are internalized, in their negative guise, as constraints; in their neutral guise, as conventions; and, in their positive guise, as values. Yet the silent power of the sign, the unspoken authority of habit, may be as effective as the most violent coercion in shaping, directing, even dominating social thought and action.

None of this is new, of course: identifying technologies and typologies of power, albeit in very diverse terms, has become a growth industry in modern social theory. ... The point, though, goes back a long way. For Marx, to take one instance, the power of the capitalist was clearly different from the power of the commodity, the contrast corresponding broadly to the way in which ideology is portrayed in *The German Ideology* and *Capital* respectively... In the former it comes across primarily as a set of ideas that reflect the interests of the ruling class, ideas which, inverted through a camera obscura, are impressed upon the (false) consciousness of the proletariat (Marx and Engels 1970: 64f.). It is a function, in other words, of the capacity of the dominant to impose their will and their worldview on others. In *Capital*, by contrast, ideology is not named as such, and it is not said to arise mechanically from the politics of class domination. It is held, instead, to reside unseen in the commodity form itself. For commodity production, the dominant mode of value creation in modern capitalism, makes a whole world of social relations in its own image, a world that appears to be governed by natural laws above and beyond human intervention. Indeed, it is the inversion by which relations between people seem to be determined by relations among objects, and not vice versa, that makes commodity fetishism; and in this ontological moment a historically specific set of inequalities take root in subjective and collective experience, determining the way in which the social order is perceived and acted upon (Giddens 1979: 183; Marx 1967: 71 f.). The contrast between the two images of ideation, in short, goes together with that between the two forms of power. The first is directly supported by, in fact hinges on, the agency of dominant social groups; the second derives, as if naturally, from the very construction of economy and society. As it happens, Marx decided to call the one "ideology." The other, to which he applied no term, lays the ground for a characterization of hegemony.

Until now we also have used both of these terms without specification. Significantly, there is a passage in *The Prison Notebooks* in which Gramsci speaks of "ideology" – in quote marks – in its "highest sense." It is here that he comes closest to defining "hegemony," in the spirit of *Capital*, as Williams and others have characterized it – and as theorists like Bourdieu (1977) have transposed and redeployed it. In his own words, it is "a conception of the world that is implicitly manifest in art, in law, in economic activity and in all manifestations of individual and collective life" (Gramsci 1971: 328). This, however, is not just *any* conception of the world. It is the *dominant* conception, an orthodoxy that has established itself as "historically true" and concretely "universal" (p. 348). Building upon this and upon its conceptual roots, we take hegemony to refer to that order of signs and practices, relations and distinctions, images and epistemologies – drawn from a historically situated cultural field – that come to be taken-for-granted as the natural and received shape of the world and everything that inhabits it. It consists, to paraphrase Bourdieu (1977: 167), of things that go without saying because, being axiomatic, they come without saying; things that, being presumptively shared, are not normally the subject of explication or argument (p. 94). This is why its power has so often been seen to lie in what it silences, what it prevents people from thinking and saying, what it puts beyond the limits of the rational and the credible. In a quite literal sense, hegemony is habit-forming. For these reasons, it is rarely contested directly, save perhaps in the roseate dreams of revolutionaries. For once its internal contradictions are revealed, when what seemed natural comes to be negotiable, when the ineffable is put into words – then hegemony becomes something other than itself. It turns into ideology and counterideology, into the "orthodoxy" and "heterodoxy" of Bourdieu's (1977) formulation. More commonly, however, such struggles remain clashes of symbols, the practical iconoclasm that is produced when tensions within the hegemonic – or between the grains of habit and habitat – chafe for immediate resolution.

Ideology in less than the "highest sense," we suggest, is ideology more conventionally understood. Following Raymond Williams (1977: 109), who seems here to have *The German Ideology* in mind, we use it to describe "an articulated system of meanings, values, and beliefs of a kind that can be abstracted as [the] 'worldview'" of any social grouping. Borne in explicit manifestos and everyday practices, self-conscious texts and spontaneous images, popular styles and political platforms, this worldview may be more or less internally systematic, more or less assertively coherent in its outward forms. But, as long as it exists, it provides an organizing scheme (a master narrative?) for collective symbolic production. Obviously, to invoke Marx and Engels (1970) once again, the regnant ideology of any period or place will be that of the dominant group. And, while the nature and degree of its preeminence may vary a good deal, it is likely to be protected, even enforced, to the full extent of the power of those who claim it for their own.

But other, subordinate populations, at least those with communal identities, also have ideologies. And, inasmuch as they try to assert themselves against a dominant order or group, perhaps even to reverse existing relations of inequality, they too must call actively upon those ideologies. To be sure, if it is joined in the name of a collective identity, any such struggle, whether or not it is seen to be specifically "political," is an ideological struggle; for it necessarily involves an effort to control the cultural terms in which the world is ordered and, within it, power legitimized. Here, then, is the basic difference between hegemony and ideology. Whereas the first consists of constructs and conventions that have come to be shared and naturalized throughout a political community, the second is the expression and ultimately the possession of a particular social group, although it may be widely peddled beyond. The first is nonnegotiable and therefore beyond direct argument; the second is more susceptible to being perceived as a matter of inimical opinion and interest and therefore is open to contestation. Hegemony homogenizes, ideology articulates. Hegemony, at its most effective, is mute; by contrast, says de Certeau (1984: 46), "all the while, ideology babbles on."

REFERENCES

Ayandele, E. (1966) *The Missionary Impact on Modern Nigeria, 1842–1914*. London: Longmans, Green.

Bourdieu, P. (1977) *Outline of a Theory of Practice*. Cambridge: Cambridge University Press.

Brookes, E. (1974) *White Rule in South Africa: 1830–1910*. Pietermaritzburg: University of Natal Press.

Bundy, C. (1979) *The Rise and Fall of the South African Peasantry*. London: Heinemann.

Cochrane, J. (1987) *Servants of Power: The Role of English-Speaking Churches in South Africa, 1903–1930*. Johannesburg: Ravan Press.

Cooper, F. and Stoler, A. (1989) Introduction: Tensions of Empire: Colonial Control and Visions of Rule. *American Ethnologist* 16: 609–21.

Cuthbertson, G. (1987) The English-speaking Churches and Colonialism. In C. Villa-Vicencio (ed.) *Theology and Violence: The South African Debate*. Grand Rapids: W. B. Eerdmans.

Dachs, A. (1972) Missionary Imperialism: The Case of Bechuanaland. *Journal of African History* 13: 647–58.

de Certeau, M. (1984) *The Practice of Everyday Life*. Berkeley: University of California Press.

Denoon, D. (1973) *Southern Africa Since 1800*. New York: Praeger.

Elphick, R. (1981) Africans and the Christian Campaign in Southern Africa. In H. Lamar and L. Thompson (eds.) *The Frontier in History: North America and Southern Africa Compared*. New Haven: Yale University Press.

Etherington, N. (1978) *Preachers, Peasants, and Politics in Southeast Africa, 1835–1880: African Christian Communities in Natal, Pondoland, and Zululand*. London: Royal Historical Society.

Giddens, A. (1979) *Central Problems in Social Theory: Action, Structure, and Contradiction in Social Analysis*. Berkeley: University of California Press.

——. (1987) *Social Theory and Modern Sociology*. Stanford: Stanford University Press.

Gramsci, A. (1971) *Selections from the Prison Notebook*. ed. Q. Hoare and G. Smith. New York: International Publishers.

Gray, R. (1983) An Anthropologist on the Christian Kaguru. Review of *Colonial Evangelism*, by T. O. Beidelman. *Journal of African History* 24: 405–7.

Hall, S. (1988) The Toad in the Garden: Thatcherism among the Theorists. In C. Nelson and L. Grossberg (eds.) *Marxism and the Interpretation of Culture*. Urbana: University of Illinois Press.

Hebdige, D. (1988) *Hiding in the Light: On Images and Things*. London: Routledge.

Horton, R. (1971) African Conversion. *Africa* 41: 85–108.

Lears, J. (1985) The Concept of Cultural Hegemony: Problems and Possibilities. *American Historical Review* 9: 567–93.

Majeke, N. (1952) *The Role of the Missionaries in Conquest*. Johannesburg: Society of Young Africa.

Marks, S. (1989) Cultures of Subordination and Subversion. *Social History* 14: 225–31.

Marx, K. (1967) *Capital: A Critique of Political Economy*, 3 vols. New York: International Publishers.

Marx, K. and Engels, F. (1970) *The German Ideology*, ed. C. Arthur. New York: International Publishers.

Ranger, T. (1986) Religious Movements and Politics in Sub-Saharan Africa. *African Studies Review* 29: 1–69.

——. (1987) Taking Hold of the Land: Holy Places and Pilgrimages in Twentieth Century Zimbabwe. *Past and Present* 117: 158–94.

Romano, C. (1983) But Was He A Marxist? Review of *Approaches to Gramsci*, ed. A. Sassoon. *Village Voice* 29, 29 March 1941.

Sillery, A. (1971) *John Mackenzie of Bechuanaland, 1835–1899: A Study in Humanitarian Imperialism*. Capetown: A. A. Balkema.

Strayer R. (1976) Mission History in Africa: New Perspectives on an Encounter. *The African Studies Review* 19: 1–15.

Thompson, E. P. (1975) *Whigs and Hunters: The Origins of the Black Act*. London: Allen Lane.

——. (1978) *The Poverty of Theory and Other Essays*. New York: Monthly Review Press.

Trapido, S. (1980) "The Friends of the Natives": Merchants, Peasants and the Political and Ideological Structure of Liberalism in the Cape, 1854–1910. In S. Marks and A. Atmore (eds.) *Economy and Society in Pre-Industrial South Africa*. London: Longman.

Williams, R. (1977) *Marxism and Literature*. London: Oxford University Press.

Wilson, M. (1969) Co-operation and Conflict: The Eastern Cape Frontier. In M. Wilson and L. Thompson (eds.) *The Oxford History of South Africa*, vol. 1. London: Oxford University Press.

Wilson, M. (1976) *Missionaries: Conquerors or Servants of God?* Address given at the opening of the South African Missionary Museum. Lovedale: South African Missionary Museum.

Zulu, L. (1972) Nineteenth Century Missionaries: Their Significance for Black South Africa. In M. Motlhabi (ed.) *Essays on Black Theology*. Johannesburg: University Christian Movement.

18

Between Speech and Silence

Susan Gal

Introduction

The historic silence of women in public life, and women's attempts to gain a voice in politics and literature, have been major themes of recent feminist scholarship. It has become clear that gender relations are created not only by a sexual division of labor and a set of symbolic images, but also through contrasting possibilities of expression for men and women. Feminists have explicitly written about scholarship's responsibility to "hear women's words" and have rightly argued the theoretical importance of "rediscover[ing] women's voices" (Smith-Rosenberg 1985: 11, 26).

In these writings, silence is generally deplored, because it is taken to be a result and a symbol of passivity and powerlessness: those who are denied speech cannot make their experience known and thus cannot influence the course of their lives or of history. In a telling contrast, other scholars have emphasized the paradoxical power of silence, especially in certain institutional settings. In religious confession, modern psychotherapy, bureaucratic interviews, and in police interrogation, the relations of coercion are reversed: where self-exposure is required, it is the silent listener who judges, and who thereby exerts power over the one who speaks (Foucault 1978: 61–2)....But silence can also be a strategic defense against the powerful, as when Western Apache men use it to baffle, disconcert, and exclude white outsiders (Basso 1979). And this does not exhaust the meanings of silence. For the English Quakers of the seventeenth century, both men and women, the refusal to speak when others expected them to marked an ideological commitment. It was the opposite of passivity, indeed a form of political protest (Bauman 1983).

The juxtaposition of these different constructions of silence highlights the three issues I would like to raise in this chapter. First, and most generally, the example of silence suggests a close link between gender, the use of speech (or silence), and the

From M. di Leonardo (ed.) *Gender at the Crossroads of Knowledge: Feminist Anthropology in the Postmodern Era* (Berkeley: University of California Press, 1991), pp. 175–8, 189–96, 200–3.

exercise of power. But it also shows that the link is not direct. On the contrary, it appears that silence, like any linguistic form, gains different meanings and has different material effects within specific institutional and cultural contexts. Silence and inarticulateness are not, in themselves, necessarily signs of powerlessness. Indeed, my first goal is to draw on a cultural analysis to show how the links between linguistic practices, power, and gender are themselves culturally constructed.

Yet these cultural constructions are not always stable, nor passively accepted and reproduced by speakers. The examples of silence as subversive defense and even political protest suggest that linguistic forms, even the most apparently quiescent, are strategic actions, created as responses to cultural and institutional contexts (Gumperz 1982). . . . Recent reconceptualizations of gender . . . argue that gender is better seen as a system of culturally constructed relations of power, produced and reproduced in interaction between and among men and women. . . . [I]t is in part through verbal practices in social interaction that the structural relations of gender and dominance are perpetuated and sometimes subverted: in social institutions such as schools, courts, and political assemblies, talk is often used to judge, define, and legitimate speakers. Thus, small interactional skirmishes have striking material consequences. My second goal is to show how verbal interaction, whatever else it accomplishes, is often the site of struggle about gender definitions and power; it concerns who can speak where about what.

Finally, such struggles about gaining a voice, and my earlier example of women's silence in public life, draw attention to a currently widespread and influential metaphor in both feminist and nonfeminist social science. Terms such as "women's language," "voice," or "words" are routinely used not only to designate everyday talk but also, much more broadly, to denote the public expression of a particular perspective on self and social life, the effort to represent one's own experience, rather than accepting the representations of more powerful others. And similarly, "silence" and "mutedness" (E. Ardener 1975) are used not only in their ordinary senses of an inability or reluctance to create utterances in conversational exchange, but as references as well to the failure to produce one's own separate, socially significant discourse. It is in this broader sense that feminist historians have rediscovered women's words. Here, "word" becomes a synecdoche for "consciousness." . . .

As my discussion of the culturally defined links between speech and power will show, some linguistic strategies and genres are more highly valued and carry more authority than others. In a classic case of symbolic domination, even those who do not control these authoritative forms consider them more credible or persuasive (Bourdieu 1977b). Archetypal examples include standard languages and ritual speech. But these respected linguistic practices are not simply forms; they deliver characteristic cultural definitions of social life that, embodied in divisions of labor and the structure of institutions, serve the interests of some groups better than others. Indeed, it is in part through such linguistic practices that speakers within institutions impose on others their group's definition of events, people, and actions. This ability to make others accept and enact one's representation of the world is another aspect of symbolic domination. But such cultural power rarely goes uncontested. Resistance to a dominant cultural order occurs when devalued linguistic strategies and genres are practiced and celebrated despite widespread denigration; it occurs as well when these devalued practices propose or embody alternate models of the social world.

Several influential social theories that differ importantly in other respects have in one way or another articulated this insight. Whether we use Gramsci's term "cultural hegemony," or symbolic domination (Bourdieu 1977a); oppositional, emergent, and residual cultures (Williams 1973); or subjugated knowledges (Foucault 1980), the central notion remains: the control of discourse or of representations of reality occurs in social interaction, located in institutions, and is a source of social power; it may be, therefore, the occasion for coercion, conflict, or complicity. Missing from these theories is a concept of gender as a structure of social relations (separate from class or ethnicity), reproduced but also challenged in everyday practice. These theories neither notice nor explain the subtlety, subversion, and opposition to dominant definitions which feminists have discovered in many women's genres, and sometimes embedded in women's everyday talk. Indeed, even the authority of some (male) linguistic forms and their dominance of social institutions such as medicine or the political process remain mysterious without a theory of gender.

This interaction of gender and discourse has been explored by recent feminist analyses in literature and anthropology; some have suggested that women's "voices" often differ significantly in form as well as content from dominant discourse. The importance of integrating the study of everyday talk with the study of "women's voice" becomes apparent: the attention to the details of linguistic form and context typical of research into everyday talk is indispensable in order to gain access to women's often veiled genres and muted "words." And both kinds of studies must attend not only to words but to the interactional practices and the broader political and economic context of communication in order to understand the process by which women's voices – in both senses – are routinely suppressed or manage to emerge. My final aim is to show that, if we understand women's everyday talk and linguistic genres as forms of resistance, we hear, in any culture, not so much a clear and heretofore neglected "woman's voice," or separate culture, but rather linguistic practices that are more ambiguous, often contradictory, differing among women of different classes and ethnic groups and ranging from accommodation to opposition, subversion, rejection, or autonomous reconstruction of reigning cultural definitions.

Thus, my theme is the link between gender, speech, and power, and the ways this can be conceptualized on the basis of recent empirical research. . . . [Here, I] reinterpret women's strategies and linguistic genres as forms of resistance to symbolic domination. . . .

Genres of Resistance

Despite the long-standing Western emphasis on language as primarily a means of representing an already existing reality, anthropologists have long been aware of the ways in which the metaphors, literary genres, and interactional arrangements readily available in a community actively shape the way speakers define the social world. In short, conventional language and its conventional usage are not neutral media for describing social life. Some formulations about social life, when inscribed in a division of labor or other organizational form, serve one group's interests better than that of others. A hegemonic discourse, in this broad sense, is a form of power, and it is sometimes resisted or contested.

This important and quite general notion of a dynamic between dominant and subordinate discourses or practices has been discussed, in many forms and with many terminologies, by a variety of social theorists. However, feminist scholars have been strongly influenced by a limited version of this insight, explicitly applied to women. E. Ardener (1975) and S. Ardener (1975) argue that women, due to their structural positions, have models of reality that differ from the male-dominated societal model. . . . Being unable to express their structurally generated views in the dominant and masculine discourse, women are neither understood nor heeded, and become inarticulate, "muted," or even silent. . . .

The "muted-group" thesis usefully draws attention to the importance of the symbolic language, the form, of dominant and subordinate discourse. However, as I will demonstrate with a series of examples, the Ardeners' formulation is flawed in several respects. First, it assumes that "mutedness" is a static reflex of women's structural position. In contrast, when viewed in terms of broader theories of gender and symbolic domination, "mutedness" becomes only one of many theoretically possible outcomes of gender relations. A much wider array of women's verbal strategies and genres become visible, some considerably more articulate and more actively oppositional to dominant models than the "mutedness" thesis allows. Second, if domination and resistance are matters of interactional practice as well as structure, as I have been arguing, then we must focus not on "mutedness" as a structural product but on the processes by which women are rendered "mute" or manage to construct dissenting genres and resisting discourses. Finally, as Warren and Bourque suggest: "understanding dominance and muting [as processes] requires a broader analysis of the political, economic and institutional contexts in which reality is negotiated" (1985: 261).

Ethnography itself is such a context, for ethnographic reports are deeply implicated in the process of representing self and others, creating images of social reality through language. Keenly aware of this, feminist critics of anthropology have charged that women in the societies studied were ignored or perceived as inert because androcentric ethnographers dismissed women and their concerns, making them appear passive and silent. Feminists challenged the authority and credibility of these male-biased accounts. But the Ardeners' thesis suggests that the problem is more complex. It claims that women rarely "speak" in social anthropological reports because social science investigators of both sexes demand the kind of articulate models provided by men, not by muted women. And indeed, some women anthropologists have also complained of the inarticulateness of women informants in some contexts. It seems there is a need to reexamine how ethnographies are created. Currently, just such a reexamination is also the project of anthropologists who are similarly challenging the authority of ethnographic writing, but on different grounds. Following postmodernist trends in philosophy, they assert that traditional ethnographies mask the actual practice of fieldwork and writing (Clifford and Marcus 1986). By claiming to accurately represent the facts about an exotic culture, the naive realist conventions of ethnographic writing implicitly deny that ethnographic facts are selected, indeed constructed, in the encounter between the anthropologist and the "other" who is her/his subject. In order to reflect the process of ethnographic knowledge, these critics suggest experimentation with literary forms so that writing may be a "polyvocal" and dialogic production in which the ethnographer lets the people speak and ethnographic facts are shown to be jointly produced by ethnographer and informant.

What has received too little attention in all these critiques is the unavoid[...] power-charged verbal encounter in which anthropologists and native speakers, [...] different interests, goals, and deeply unequal positions, meet and attempt to [...] Keesing (1985) provides a fine example of the ethnographic interview as a linguistic practice. In order to record women's versions of native life (kastom) among the Kwaio, a tenaciously traditional group living in the Solomon Islands of the South Pacific, Keesing had to analyze what he calls the "micropolitics" of talk. In response to Keesing's requests, the men created and told life histories eagerly and artfully, even though the Kwaio lack such a genre as well as a tradition of self-revelation and self-explanation on which the Western literary form of the autobiography is based. In contrast, Keesing recounts that he could not elicit autobiographical narratives from women, not even those who were old, knowledgeable, and influential. They spoke to him in a fragmented, inarticulate and joking way, especially in front of elder men who urged them to cooperate. They appeared distressed with what was requested of them: "mute." A subsequent fieldtrip, eight years later, this time with a woman ethnographer, brought quite different results. In sessions with *both* ethnographers, Kwaio women took control of the encounters, even bringing female friends as audience to the recording sessions. But, unlike the men, who had provided societal rules and personal life narratives, the women rejected the ethnographers' personal questions and instead created moral texts about the virtues of womanhood, inserting personal experiences only to illustrate women's possible paths through life. Through their texts, Kwaio women were reformulating and embellishing a long-standing strategy of Kwaio men: to enlist the (at first) unknowing anthropologist in their efforts to codify and authorize Kwaio custom. By legitimating their own customs in an anthropologized form the Kwaio men were able to use it to resist the demands of state regulations, thereby attempting, through vigorous neo-traditionalism, to maintain their political autonomy in the face of colonial and neo-colonial incursions.

A deeper understanding of Kwaio women's talk requires revisions of all three critiques of anthropological fieldwork. Clearly Kwaio women were not so much structurally mute and inarticulate as responsive to the immediate interactional context, especially relations of gender inequality within their own society and in the ethnographic interview. Pragmatic analyses of the interview as a speech event suggest it is the ethnographer's task to discover the conditions under which informants can talk. Similarly, it is not enough to insist, as the postmodernist critics do, that the ethnographic encounter and the genres that emerge from it are jointly produced. Although important and accurate, this observation by itself ignores the importance of gender and other forms of inequality. It omits the several levels of unequal power and privilege that characterize the ethnographic encounter and which also determine who is able to talk and what it is possible or strategic to say. The women's inarticulateness and subsequent "voice," as much as the men's systematization of their culture, were responses to wider fields of force that assure that some texts or genres are more powerful than others, making a simple co-production of ethnographic texts impossible (Asad 1986; Polier and Roseberry 1988: 15). Finally, feminists would have confidently predicted the changes produced by the presence of a woman anthropologist and would have understood that the genre of autobiography is problematic, not only because it is culturally specific to the West, but also because it has been shaped by Western gender ideology that assumes a male subject.

Yet the case of Kwaio women suggests revisions and expansions for gender theories as well: a female ethnographer may be only part of the answer. In this case, the presence of the male anthropologist was also important, for the women were attuned to his established role as mediator between the Kwaio and the outside world. Thus, attention must be paid to relations of power that connect Kwaio society to a world system in which, as the Kwaio are aware, anthropologists, as wielders of Western discourse, have authority that Kwaio women, perhaps differently than men, can try to channel to their own ends through the ethnographic interview. . . .

Women sometimes produce a cultural commentary of gesture and ritual that may be called inarticulate because it rejects words altogether. An important instance occurred in the Nigerian Women's War of 1929. During the massive protests against proposed taxation of women's property by the colonial government, women reformulated on a large scale a locally practiced custom of obscene dancing, called "sitting on a man," that traditionally occurred at the houses of men who had overstepped social mores upheld by women. Contemporary witnesses of the Women's War report that women's protests included marching nude, lying on the ground kicking their legs in the air, and making obscene gestures. As Ifeka-Moller (1975) explains, these gestures were mysterious and alarming to European observers but, for the women and men involved, they constituted an eloquent protest against the male political control and government taxation that women saw as a violation of their rights. . . .

A more verbally explicit and subversive, yet veiled and ambiguous genre, is the oral lyric poetry (ghinnawas) performed among intimates by the Bedouin of Egypt's Western Desert. In describing these delicate, brief, and artfully improvised performances, Abu-Lughod (1986) stresses that the dominant ideology, the "public language" of the Bedouin, is one of honor, autonomy, self-mastery, personal strength, and sexual modesty. The poems directly violate this code of honor and implicitly criticize it by expressing the feelings of dependency, emotional vulnerability, and romantic longing condemned by the official view. The poetry constitutes what Abu-Lughod calls a "dissident or subversive discourse . . . most closely associated with youths and women, the disadvantaged dependents who least embody the ideals of Bedouin society and have least to gain in the system as structured. . . . Poetry is the discourse of opposition to the system and of defiance of those who represent it" (1986: 251). But the poetry is anything but a spontaneous outpouring of feeling. Indeed, its formal properties and context of performance enhance its ability to subtly carry messages counter to official ideals. It is formulaic, thereby disguising the identities of poet, addressee, and subject. It is fleeting and ambiguous, performed by women and youths among trusted intimates who can decipher it exactly because they already know the reciter well. Yet, this poetry of subversion and defiance is not only tolerated; it is culturally elaborated and admired because of the paradoxical intertwining of official and dissident discourse. The oral poetry reveals a fundamental tension of Bedouin social and political life which, while valuing and demanding autonomy and equality between lineages, demands inequality between the genders and generations within lineages and families. "A discourse of defiance by those slighted in the system, [poetry] is exalted because a refusal to be dominated is key to Bedouin political life, and it is avoided by [male] elders because it threatens to expose the illegitimacy of their authority" (Abu-Lughod 1986: 254). Thus, the verbal genre of women and youths reveals the contradictions of the ruling ideology.

My final example is a poetic genre more verbally explicit, more directly critical of social and political relations, and much less accepted by official ideologies. Though limited to a much smaller segment of the female population, it is equally revealing of contradictions in dominant discourses. Migrant laborers, moving between the mines of South Africa and their native Lesotho, compose a genre of poetric songs called *lifela*, performed competitively by "men of eloquence," often for a fee, usually at social gatherings in border towns. They sing of poverty and forced migration; their songs reinforce a rootedness in the rural village, despite migration, and a longing for traditional gerontocratic and patriarchal social relations. However, there are also some women who sing lifela. But their circumstances, as well as the content of their poetry, are significantly different.

In the current migrant system, women's position is in many ways even worse than men's. Women are forbidden to migrate by the legal system, but left alone in the village they must make decisions without being granted the autonomy to do so. "The South African government, the Lesotho government and male Basotho attitudes have openly conspired to prevent female migration, which threatens the divided-family system on which both the migratory labor system and male domestic power are based" (Coplan 1987: 424). Female poets are among those who have managed to escape these constraints and have migrated illegally. Although for men South Africa is unequivocally a land of wage slavery, for these migrant women it represents relative choice, opportunity and autonomy. Women have borrowed the men's genre but have transformed it, providing a considerably more radical social critique. Rather than identifying with rural life, the women's poetry sharply and explicitly criticizes men, proclaims traditional marriage unworkable, but recognizes as well the physical dangers and insecurity of life as an illegal migrant. The women's opposition is palpable not only in the content of the poetry, but also during the performance of the poems/songs in the tavern: "Male...patrons, stung by the critical barbs of female performers routinely rise to sing spontaneous retorts...[but] are shouted down or even pushed aside by [female poets] determined to hold the floor" (Coplan 1987: 429).

Such attempts to silence the protest songs of migrant women in Lesotho return us to the *process* by which women are either rendered "mute" or are able to construct an alternate discourse, resisting attempts to suppress it. I have attempted one approach to this question, examining women's genres as practices, analyzing ethnographic interviews or Bedouin poetry very much as I did earlier examples of "ways of speaking" such as collaborative "floors" and gossip: focusing on the immediate interactional context of the genre – the participant structure of the interview, the intimacy of Bedouin confidantes, the liminality of border taverns – for clues to the forces that allow it to be performed. More broadly, however, the issue of when and how women's subversion or opposition to hegemonic culture emerges is as much a question about the structure of gender systems and political economy as about linguistic practices, genres, and counter-discourses. Comparative work, such as Warren and Bourque's (1985) study of women's public speaking in two quite differently organized Peruvian communities, or study of the social identities of women who sing lifela, can start to illuminate this issue, as can historical research into changing images of sex and gender (Steedman et al. 1985; Walkowitz 1986). Another research tactic is to compare women of different classes and ethnic groups, using linguistic practices to raise the classic issue of the relationship between consciousness and social position....

These diverse examples of women's genres, drawn from many parts of the world and many kinds of sociopolitical formations, were chosen in part to highlight the observation that women's resistance or criticism is sometimes couched in implicit forms such as ambiguity and irony but is, in other cases, much more directly expressed. Indeed, the examples illustrate a range of linguistic explicitness (gestural; brief and ambiguous; extended and explicit); diverse social contexts (public demonstration, closed meeting, intimate conversation, paid performance); and several levels of subversion or opposition to dominant discourses (from self-defeating complicity, to resistance, to open criticism). Interestingly, it seems that these three parameters do not correlate in any simple way. Strong protest can appear in silent gestures, as in the women's war; or in the explicit public performances of critical poetry. Resistance may be knowing yet silent... verbal yet veiled as in Bedouin poetry, verbal but privately expressed... or explicit and public, as in bilingual Austrian women's use of German (Gal 1978). But in each case, women's linguistic practices made visible a crack, a fault line in the dominant male discourse of gender and power, revealing it to be not monolithic but contradictory and thus vulnerable.

REFERENCES

Abu-Lughod, L. (1986) *Veiled Sentiments*. Berkeley, Los Angeles, London: University of California Press.

Ardener, E. (1975) Belief and the Problem of Women. In S. Ardener (ed.) *Perceiving Women*. London: Malaby.

Ardener, S. (1975) Introduction. In S. Ardener (ed.) *Perceiving Women*. London: Malaby.

Asad, T. (1986) The Concept of Cultural Translation in British Social Anthropology. In J. Clifford and G. Marcus (eds.) *Writing Culture*. Berkeley, Los Angeles, London: University of California Press.

Basso, K. (1979) *Portraits of the Whiteman*. New York: Cambridge University Press.

Bauman, R. (1983) *Let Your Words Be Few*. New York: Cambridge University Press.

Bourdieu, P. (1977a) *Outline of a Theory of Practice*. New York: Cambridge University Press.

——. (1977b) The Economics of Linguistic Exchanges. *Social Science Information* 16(6): 645–68.

Clifford, J., and G. Marcus (eds.). (1986) *Writing Culture*. Berkeley, Los Angeles, London: University of California Press.

Coplan, D. B. (1987) Eloquent Knowledge: Lesotho Migrants' Songs and the Anthropology of Experience. *American Ethnologist* 14(3): 413–33.

Foucault, M. (1978) *The History of Sexuality*, vol. 1. New York: Pantheon.

——. (1980) *Power/Knowledge: Selected Interviews and Other Writings*, ed. Colin Gordon. New York: Pantheon.

Gal, S. (1978) Peasant Men Can't Get Wives: Language and Sex Roles in a Bilingual Community. *Language in Society* 7(1): 1–17.

Gumperz, J. (1982) *Discourse Strategies*. New York: Cambridge University Press.

Ifeka-Moller, C. (1975) Female Militancy and Colonial Revolt: The Women's War of 1929, Eastern Nigeria. In S. Ardener (ed.) *Perceiving Women*. London: Malaby.

Keesing, R. (1985) Kwaio Women Speak: The Micropolitics of Autobiography in a Solomon Island Society. *American Anthropologist* 87(1): 27–39.

Polier, N., and W. Roseberry. (1988) Tristes Tropes: Postmodern Anthropologists Encounter the Other and Discover Themselves. *Economy and Society* 18(2): 245–64.

Smith-Rosenberg, C. (1985) *Disorderly Conduct: Visions of Gender in Victorian America*. New York: Oxford.

Walkowitz, J. (1986) Science, Feminism and Romance: The Men's and Women's Club 1885–1889. *History Workshop Journal* (Spring): 37–59.

Warren, K., and S. Bourque. (1985) Gender, Power and Communication: Responses to Political Muting in the Andes. In S. Bourque and D. R. Divine (eds.) *Women Living Change*. Philadelphia: Temple University Press.

Williams, R. (1973) Base and Superstructure in Marxist Cultural Theory. *New Left Review* 82: 3–16.

19

Facing Power – Old Insights, New Questions

Eric R. Wolf

In this essay I engage the problem of power and the issues that it poses for anthropology. I argue that we actually know a great deal about power, but have been timid in building upon what we know. This has implications for both theory and method, for assessing the insights of the past and for raising new questions.

The very term makes many of us uncomfortable. It is certainly one of the most loaded and polymorphous words in our repertoire. The Romance, Germanic, and Slavic languages, at least, conflate a multitude of meanings in speaking about *pouvoir* or *potere*, *Macht*, or *mogushchestvo*. Such words allow us to speak about power as if it meant the same thing to all of us. At the same time, we often speak of power as if all phenomena involving it were somehow reducible to a common core, some inner essence. This conjures up monstrous images of power, Hobbes's Leviathan or Bertrand de Jouvenel's Minotaur, but it leads away from specifying different kinds of power implicated in different kinds of relationships.

I argue instead that it is useful to think of four different modes of power. One is power as the attribute of the person, as potency or capability, the basic Nietzschean idea of power (Kaufmann 1968). Speaking of power in this sense draws attention to the endowment of persons in the play of power, but tells us little about the form and direction of that play. The second kind of power can be understood as the ability of an *ego* to impose its will on an *alter*, in social action, in interpersonal relations. This draws attention to the sequences of interactions and transactions among people, but it does not address the nature of the arena in which the interactions go forward. That comes into view more sharply when we focus on power in the third mode, as power that controls the settings in which people may show forth their potentialities and interact with others. I first came across this phrasing of power in anthropology when Richard Adams sought to define power not in interpersonal terms, but as the control that one actor or "operating unit" (his term) exercises over energy flows that constitute part of the environment of another actor (Adams 1966, 1975). This

From *American Anthropologist* 92 (1990), pp. 586–96. Reprinted by permission of the American Anthropological Association.

definition calls attention to the instrumentalities of power and is useful for under-standing how "operating units" circumscribe the actions of others within determin-ate settings. I call this third kind of power tactical or organizational power.

But there is still a fourth mode of power, power that not only operates within settings or domains but that also organizes and orchestrates the settings themselves, and that specifies the distribution and direction of energy flows. I think that this is the kind of power that Marx addressed in speaking about the power of capital to harness and allocate labor power, and it forms the background of Michel Foucault's notion of power as the ability "to structure the possible field of action of others" (Foucault 1984: 428). Foucault called this "to govern," in the sixteenth-century sense of governance, an exercise of "action upon action" (1984: 427–8). Foucault himself was primarily interested in this as the power to govern consciousness, but I want to use it as power that structures the political economy. I will refer to this kind of power as structural power. This term rephrases the older notion of "the social relations of production," and is intended to emphasize power to deploy and allocate social labor. These governing relations do not come into view when you think of power primarily in interactional terms. Structural power shapes the social field of action so as to render some kinds of behavior possible, while making others less possible or impossible. As old Georg Friedrich Hegel argued, what occurs in reality has first to be possible.

What capitalist relations of production accomplish, for example, is to make possible the accumulation of capital based on the sale of marketable labor power in a large number of settings around the world. As anthropologists we can follow the flows of capital and labor through ups and downs, advances and retreats, and investigate the ways in which social and cultural arrangements in space and time are drawn into and implicated in the workings of this double whammy. This is not a purely economic relation, but a political one as well: it takes clout to set up, clout to maintain, and clout to defend; and wielding that clout becomes a target for compe-tition or alliance building, resistance or accommodation.

This is the dimension that has been stressed variously in studies of imperialism, dependency, or world-systems. Their questions are why and how some sectors, regions, or nations are able to constrain the options of others, and what coalitions and conflicts occur in the course of this interplay. Some have said that these questions have little relevance to anthropology, in that they don't have enough to say about "real people doing real things," as Sherry Ortner put it (Ortner 1984: 114); but it seems to me that they do touch on a lot of what goes on in the real world, that constrains, inhibits, or promotes what people do, or cannot do, within the scenarios we study. The notion of structural power is useful precisely because it allows us to delineate how the forces of the world impinge upon the people we study, without falling back into an anthropological nativism that postulates supposedly isolated societies and uncontaminated cultures, either in the present or in the past. There is no gain in a false romanticism that pretends that "real people doing real things" inhabit self-enclosed and self-sufficient universes.

I address here primarily the relation between tactical (or organizational) power and structural power. I do this because I believe that these concepts can help us to explain the world we inhabit. I think that it is the task of anthropology – or at least the task of some anthropologists – to attempt explanation, and not merely descrip-tion, descriptive integration, or interpretation. Anthropology can be different things to different people (entertainment, exotic *frisson*, a "show-and-tell" of differences), but it should not, I submit, be content with James Boon's "shifting collage of contraries threatening (promising) to become unglued" (Boon 1982: 237). Writing culture may require literary skill and genre, but a search for explanation requires more: it cannot do without naming and comparing things, and formulating concepts for naming and comparison. I think we must move beyond Geertz's "experience-near" understandings to analytical concepts that allow us to set what we know about X against what we know about Y, in pursuit of explanation. This means that I subscribe to a basically realist position. I think that the world is real, that these realities affect what humans do and that what humans do affects the world, and that we can come to understand the whys and wherefores of this relationship. We need to be professionally suspicious of our categories and models; we should be aware of their historical and cultural contingencies; we can understand a quest for explanation as approximations to truth rather than the truth itself. But I also believe that the search for explanation in anthropology can be cumulative; that knowledge and insights gained in the past can generate new questions, and that new departures can incorporate the accomplishments of the past.

In anthropology we are continuously slaying paradigms, only to see them return to life, as if discovered for the first time. The old-time evolutionism of Morgan and Engels reappeared in ecological guise in the forties and fifties. The Boasian insistence that we must understand the ways "that people actually think about their own culture and institutions" (Goldman 1975: 15) has resurfaced in the anthropology of cognition and symbolism, now often played as a dissonant quartet in the format of deconstructionism. Diffusionism grew exhausted after biting too deeply into the seductive apple of trait-list collecting, but sprang back to life in the studies of acculturation, interaction spheres, and world-systems. Functionalism overreached itself by claiming to depict organic unities, but returned in systems theory as well as in other disguises. Culture-and-personality studies advanced notions of "basic personality structure" and "national character," without paying heed to history, cultural heterogeneity, or the role of hegemony in shaping uniformities; but suspiciously similar characterizations of modern nations and "ethnic groups" continue to appear. The varieties of ecological anthropology and the various Marxisms are being told by both user-friendly and unfriendly folk that what they need is "the concept of culture." We are all familiar, I trust, with Robert Lowie's image of "diffusionism laying the axe to evolutionism." As each successive approach carries the ax to its predecessors, anthropology comes to resemble a project in intellectual deforestation.

I do not think that this is either necessary or desirable. I think that anthropology can be cumulative, that we can use the work of our predecessors to raise new questions.

Three Projects

Some of anthropology's older insights into power can be the basis for new inquiry. I want to briefly review three projects that sought to understand what happens to people in the modern world and in the process raised questions about power, both tactical and structural. These projects yielded substantial bodies of data and theory; they opened up perspectives that reached beyond their scope of inquiry; and all were criticized in their time and subjected to reevaluation thereafter. All three were efforts toward an explanatory anthropology.

The first of these projects is the study of Puerto Rico in 1948–9, directed by Julian Steward; the results are in the collective work, *The People of Puerto Rico* (Steward et al. 1956). The original thrust of the project stemmed from Steward's attack on the assumptions of a unitary national culture and national character which then dominated the field of culture-and-personality. The project aimed instead at exhibiting the heterogeneity of a national society. It was also a rejection of the model in which a single community was made to stand for an entire nation. It depicted Puerto Rico as a structure of varied localities and regions, clamped together by islandwide institutions and the activities of an insular upper class, a system of heterogeneous parts and levels. The project was especially innovative in trying to find out how this complex arrangement developed historically, by tracing out the historical causes and courses of crop production on the island, and then following out the differential implications of that development in four representative communities. It promised to pay attention to the institutions connecting localities, regions, and nation, but actually confined itself to looking at these institutions primarily in terms of their local effects. It did carry out a study of the insular upper class, which was conceived as occupying the apex of linkages to the level of the nation. The project's major shortfall, in terms of its own undertaking, was its failure to take proper account of the rapidly intensifying migration to the nearby US mainland. Too narrow a focus on agricultural ecology prevented it from coming to grips with issues already then becoming manifest on the local level, but prompted and played out upon a much larger stage.

While the Puerto Rico project averted its eyes from the spectacle of migration, another research effort took labor migration to the towns and burgeoning mines of Central Africa as its primary point of reference. This research was carried out under the auspices of the Rhodes–Livingstone Institute, set up in 1937 in what was then Northern Rhodesia and is now Zambia. Its research goal was defined by the first director, Godfrey Wilson, whose own outlook has been characterized as an unconscious effort to combine Marx and Malinowski (Brown 1973: 195). Wilson understood the processes affecting Central Africa as an industrial revolution connected to the workings of the world economy. The massive penetration of the mining industry was seen as causal in generating multiple conflicts on the local and regional scene. Then Max Gluckman, the director from 1942 to 1947, drew up a research plan for the Institute which outlined a number of problem-oriented studies, and enlisted a stellar cast of anthropologists to work on such problems as the intersections of native and colonial governance, the role of witchcraft, the effects of labor migration on domestic economy, and the conflicts generated by the tension-ridden interplay of matrilineal descent and patrilocal residence. Dealing with an area of considerable linguistic and cultural diversity, the researchers were able to compare their findings to identify what was variable and what was common in local responses to general processes. But where the project was at its most innovative was in looking at rural locations, mining centers, and towns not as separate social and cultural entities but as interrelated elements caught up in one social field. It thus moved from Wilson's original concern with detribalization as anomic loss toward a more differentiated scenario of variegated responses to the new behavior settings of village, mine, and urban township. In doing so, it opened perspectives that the Puerto Rico project did not address. Its major failing lay in not taking systematic and critical account of the colonial structure in which these settings were embedded.

The third project I want to mention was directed by Richard Adams between 1963 and 1966, to study the national social structure of Guatemala. It is described in the book *Crucifixion by Power* (Adams 1970). The project took account of the intense growth of agricultural production for the market, and placed what was then known about life in localities within that context. Its specific innovation, however, lies in the fact that it engaged the study of national institutions in ways not broached by the two other projects I have referred to. Adams showed how local, regional, and supranational elites contested each other's power, and how regional elites stabilized their command by forging ties at the level of the nation. At that level, however, their power was subject to competition and interference by groups operating on the transnational and international plane. The study of elites was followed by accounts of the development of various institutions: the military, the renascent Guatemalan Church, the expanding interest organizations of the upper sector, and the legal system and legal profession. Adams then showed how these institutions curtailed agrarian and labor demands in the countryside, and produced individualized patron–client ties between the urban poor and their political sponsors in the capital. What the project did not do was to bring together this rich material into a synthesis that might have provided a theoretical model of the nation for further work.

It seems clear now that the three projects all stood on the threshold of a promising new departure in anthropological inquiry, but failed to cross it. They were adventurous, but not adventurous enough. First, in my view, they anticipated a move toward political economy, while not quite taking that next step. The Puerto Rico project, in its concentration on agriculture, failed to come to grips with the political and economic forces that established that agriculture in the first place, and that were already at work in "Operation Bootstrap" to transform the agricultural island into an industrial service station. We did not understand the ways in which island institutions, supposedly "national" but actually interlocked with mainland economics and politics, were battlegrounds for diverse contending interests. Thus, the project also missed an opportunity to deal with the complex interplay of hegemonic and subaltern cultural stances in the Puerto Rican situation. In fact, no one has done so to date; the task remains for the doing.

The Central Africa project was similarly confined by its own presuppositions. Despite its attention to conflicts and contradictions, it remained a captive of the prevailing functionalism, especially when it interpreted disjunctions as mere phases in the restoration of continuity. There was a tendency to take the colonial system as a given and thus to mute both the historical implications of conquest and the cumulative confrontations between Africans and Europeans. New questions now enable us to address these issues. Colonialism overrode the kin-based and tributary polities it encountered. Their members were turned into peasants in the hinterland and into workers in mine and town; peasantization and proletarianization were concomitant processes, often accompanied by force and violence. New ethnic and class identities replaced older, now decentered ties (Sichone 1989). Yet research has also uncovered a multiplicity of African responses in labor and political organization (Epstein 1958; Ranger 1970), in dance societies (Mitchell 1957; Ranger 1975), in a proliferation of religious movements (Van Binsbergen and Schofeleers 1985; Werbner 1989), in rebellion and resistance (Lan 1985). These studies have reemphasized the role of cultural understandings as integral ingredients of the transformation of labor and power.

Adams's project came very close to a new opening. It embodied an historical perspective, it understood the relations among groups as conflict-ridden processes, and it included the operations of multinational and transnational powers in this dynamic. It did not, however, move toward a political economic model of the entire ensemble – perhaps because Adams's own specific interests lay in developing an evolutionary theory of power. It thus also neglected the complex interplay of cultures in the Guatemalan case. Such a move toward synthesis still awaits the future.

The significance of these three projects lies not only in their own accomplishments but in the new questions they lead us to ask. First, they all call attention to history, but not history as "one damned thing after another," as Leslie White used to say. "History," says Maurice Godelier, "does not explain: it has to be explained" (1977: 6). What attention to history allows you to do is to look at processes unfolding, intertwining, spreading out, and dissipating over time. This means rethinking the units of our inquiries – households, localities, regions, national entities – seeing them not as fixed entities, but as problematic: shaped, reshaped, and changing over time. Attention to processes unfolding over time foregrounds organization – the structuring arrangements of social life – but requires us to see these in process and change. Second, the three projects point us to processes operating on a macro-scale, as well as in micro-settings. Puerto Rico was located first in the Hispanic orbit, then in the orbit of the United States. Central Africa was shaped by worldwide industrialization, as well as by the policies of colonial governance. Guatemala has been crucified by external connections and internal effects at the same time. The point continues an older anthropology which spoke first of "culture areas," then of oikumenes, interaction spheres, interethnic systems, and symbiotic regions, and that can now entertain "world-systems." Macroscopic history and processes of organization thus become important elements of a new approach. Both involve considerations of power – tactical and structural.

Organization

Organization is key, because it sets up relationships among people through allocation and control of resources and rewards. It draws on tactical power to monopolize or share out liens and claims, to channel action into certain pathways while interdicting the flow of action into others. Some things become possible and likely; others are rendered unlikely. At the same time, organization is always at risk. Since power balances always shift and change, its work is never done; it operates against entropy (Balandier 1970). Even the most successful organization never goes unchallenged. The enactment of power always creates friction – disgruntlement, foot-dragging, escapism, sabotage, protest or outright resistance, a panoply of responses well documented with Malaysian materials by James Scott (1985) in *Weapons of the Weak*.

Granted the importance of the subject, one might ask why anthropology seems to have relinquished the study of organization, so that today you can find the topic more often discussed in the manuals of business management than in our publications. We structure and are structured, we transact, we play out metaphors, but the whole question of organization has fallen into abeyance.

Many of us entered anthropology when there were still required courses in something called "social organization." It dealt with principles of categorization like gender, generation, and rank, and with groupings, such as lineages, clans, age sets, and associations. We can now see in retrospect that this labeling was too static, because organization was then grasped primarily as an outcome, a finished product responding to a cultural script, and not visualized in the active voice, as process, frequently a difficult and conflict-ridden process at that. When the main emphasis was on organizational forms and principles, it was all too easy to understand organization in architectural terms, as providing the building blocks for structure, a reliable edifice of regular and recurrent practices and ideas that rendered social life predictable, and could thus be investigated in the field. There was little concern with tactical power in shaping organizations, maintaining them, destabilizing them, or undoing them.

If an idea is judged by its fruitfulness, then the notion of social structure proved to be a very good idea. It yielded interesting work and productive insights. It is now evident that it also led us to reify organizational results into the building blocks of hypostatized social architectures, for example, in the concept of "the unilineal descent group." That idea was useful in leading us to think synoptically about features of group membership, descent, jural-political solidarity, rights and obligations focused on a common estate, injunctions of "prescriptive altruism," and norms of encompassing morality. Yet it is one thing to use a model to think out the implications of organizational processes, and another to expect unilineal descent groups with all these features to materialize in these terms, as dependably shaped bricks in a social-structural edifice.

How do we get from viewing organization as product or outcome to understanding organization as process? For a start, we could do worse than heed Conrad Arensberg's advice (1972: 10–11) to look at "the flow of action," to ask what is going on, why it is going on, who engages in it, with whom, when, and how often. Yet we would now add to this behavior-centered approach a new question: For what and for whom is all this going on, and – indeed – against whom? This question should not be posed merely in interactionist terms. Asking why something is going on and for whom requires a conceptual guess about the forces and effects of the structural power that drives organization and to which organization on all levels must respond. What are the dominant relations through which labor is deployed? What are the organizational implications of kinship alliances, kin coalitions, chiefdoms, or forms of state? Not all organizations or articulations of organization answer to the same functional requisites, or respond to the same underlying dynamic.

Furthermore, it behooves us to think about what is entailed in conceiving organization as a process. This is an underdeveloped area in anthropological thinking. Clearly dyadic contracts, networks of various sizes and shapes, kinship systems, political hierarchies, corporations, and states possess very different organizational potentials. Understanding how all these sets of people and instrumentalities can be aggregated, hooked together, articulated under different kinds of structural power remains a task for the future....

Signification

Finally, I want to address the issue of power in signification. Anthropology has treated signification mainly in terms of encompassing cultural unities, such as patterns, configurations, ethos, eidos, epistemes, paradigms, cultural structures. These unities, in turn, have been conceptualized primarily as the outcomes of processes of logico-aesthetic integration. Even when the frequently incongruous and disjointed characteristics of culture are admitted, the hope has been – and I quote Geertz – that identifying significant symbols, clusters of such symbols, and clusters of clusters would yield statements of "the underlying regularities of human experience implicit in their formation" (Geertz 1973: 408). The appeal is to the efficacy of symbols, to the workings of logics and aesthetics in the movement toward integration or reintegration, as if these cognitive processes were guided by a *telos* all their own.

I call this approach into question on several grounds. First, I draw on the insight of Anthony Wallace, who in the late 1950s contrasted views of culture that emphasize "the replication of uniformity" with those that acknowledge the problem of "the organization of diversity." He argued that

> all societies are, in a radical sense, plural societies.... How do societies ensure that the diverse cognitions of adults and children, males and females, warriors and shamans, slaves and masters articulate to form the equivalence structures that are the substance of social life? (Wallace 1970: 110)

This query of Wallace's continues to echo in many quarters: in a feminist anthropology that questions the assumption that men and women share the same cultural understandings; in ethnography from various areas, where "rubbish-men" in Melanesia and "no-account people" on the Northwest Coast do not seem to abide by the norms and ideals of Big Men and chiefs; in studies of hierarchical systems in which different strata and segments exhibit different and contending models of logico-aesthetic integration (India furnishes a telling case). We have been told that such divergences are ultimately kept in check and on track by cultural logic, pure and simple. This seems to me unconvincing. It is indeed the case that our informants in the field invoke metaphoric polarities of purity and pollution, well-being and malevolence, *yin* and *yang*, life and death. Yet these metaphors are intrinsically polysemic, so abundant in possible signifiers that they can embrace any and all situations. To put them to work in particular scenarios requires that their range be constricted and narrowed down to but a small set of referents. What Lévi-Strauss called "the surplus of signifiers" must be subjected to parsimonious selection before the logic of cultural integration can be actualized. This indexing, as some have called it, is no automatic process, but passes through power and through contentions over power, with all sorts of consequences for signification.

Wallace's insights on the organization of diversity also raise questions about how meaning actually works in social life. He pointed out that participants in social action do not need to understand what meanings lie behind the behavior of their partners in interchange. All they have to know is how to respond appropriately to the cues signaled by others. Issues of meaning need not ever rise into consciousness.

This is often the concern only of certain specialists, whose specific job or interest it is to explore the plenitude of possible meanings: people such as shamans, *tohunga*, or academics. Yet there are also situations in which the mutual signaling of expectations is deranged, where opposite and contradictory interests come to the fore, or where cultural schemata come under challenge. It then becomes apparent that beyond logic and aesthetics, it is power that guarantees – or fails.

Power is implicated in meaning through its role in upholding one version of significance as true, fruitful, or beautiful, against other possibilities that may threaten truth, fruitfulness, or beauty. All cultures, however conceived, carve out significance and try to stabilize it against possible alternatives. In human affairs, things might be different, and often are. Roy Rappaport, in writing on sanctity and ritual (Rappaport 1979), has emphasized the basic arbitrariness of all cultural orders. He argues that they are anchored in postulates that can neither be verified nor falsified, but that must be treated as unquestionable: to make them unquestionable, they are surrounded with sacredness. I would add that there is always the possibility that they might come unstuck. Hence, symbolic work is never done, achieves no final solution. The cultural assertion that the world is shaped in this way and not in some other has to be repeated and enacted, lest it be questioned and denied. The point is well made by Valerio Valeri in his study of *Kingship and Sacrifice* in Hawaii. Ritual, he says, produces sense

> by creating contrasts in the continuum of experience. This implies suppressing certain elements of experience in order to give relevance to others. Thus the creation of conceptual order is also, constitutively, the suppression of aspects of reality. (Valeri 1985: xi)

The Chinese doctrine of "the rectification of names" also speaks to this point of the suppressed alternatives. Stipulating that the world works in one way and not in another requires categories to order and direct experience. According to this doctrine, if meanings multiplied so as to transcend established boundaries, social consensus would become impossible – people would harm each other "like water and fire." Hence, a wise government would have to restore things to their proper definitions, in clear recognition that the maintenance of categories upholds power, and power maintains the order of the world (see Pocock 1971: 42–79).

I have spoken of different modes of structural power, which work through key relations of governance. Each such mode would appear to require characteristic ways of conceptualizing and categorizing people. In social formations that deploy labor through relations glossed as kinship, people are assigned to networks or bodies of kin that are distinguished by criteria of gender, distinct substances or essences of descent, connections with the dead, differential distributions of myths, rituals, and emblems. Tributary formations hierarchize these criteria and set up distinct social strata, each stratum marked by a distinctive inner substance that also defines its positions and privileges in society. Capitalist formations peel the individual out of encompassing ascriptive bodies and install people as separate actors, free to exchange, truck, or barter in the market, as well as in other provinces of life. The three modes of categorizing social actors, moreover, imply quite different relations to "nature" and cosmos. When one mode enters into conflict with another, it also challenges the fundamental categories that empower its dynamics. Power will then be invoked to assault rival categorical claims. Power is thus never external to signification – it inhabits meaning and is its champion in stabilization and defense.

We owe to social anthropology the insight that the arrangements of a society become most visible when they are challenged by crisis. The role of power also becomes most evident in instances where major organizational transformations put signification under challenge. Let me offer some examples. In their study of the Plains Vision Experience, Patricia Albers and Seymour Parker (1971) contrast the individualized visions of the egalitarian foragers of the Plains periphery with the standardized kin-group-controlled visions of the horticultural village dwellers. Still a third kind of vision, oriented toward war and wealth, emerged among the buffalo-hunting nomads who developed in response to the introduction of horse and gun. As horse pastoralism proved increasingly successful, the horticulturalists became riven by conflicts between the personal-private visions of young men involved in buffalo hunting, and the visions controlled by hereditary groups of kin.

The development of the Merina state in Madagascar gives us another example (see, for example, Bloch 1986). As the state became increasingly powerful and centralized around an intensified agriculture and ever more elaborate social hierarchy, the royal center also emerged as the hub of the ideational system. Local rites of circumcision, water sprinkling, offerings to honor superiors, and rituals ministering to group icons and talismans were increasingly synchronized and fused with rituals of state.

The royal rituals of Hawaii furnish a third case. Their development was linked to major transformations that affected Hawaii after 1400, when agriculture and aquaculture were extended and intensified (see, for example, Earle 1978; Kirch 1985; Spriggs 1988). Local communities were reorganized; lineages were deconstructed; commoners lost the right to keep genealogies and to attend temples, and were assigned as quasi-tenants to nonlocal subaltern chiefs. Chiefs and aristocrats were raised up, godlike, into a separate endogamous stratum. Conflicts within the elite brought on endemic warfare and attempts at conquest: both fed the cult of human sacrifice. Innovations in myth and ritual portrayed the eruption of war and violence by the coming of outsiders, "sharks upon the land." Sahlins (1985) has offered the notion of a cultural structure to interpret how Hawaiians understood such changes and re-valued their understandings in the course of change. But reference to a cultural structure alone, or even to a dialectic of a structure of meaning with the world, will not yet explain how given forms of significance relate to transformations of agriculture, settlement, sociopolitical organization, and relations of war and peace. To explain what happened in Hawaii or elsewhere, we must take the further step of understanding the consequences of the exercise of power.

I have put forward the case for an anthropology that is not content merely to translate, interpret, or play with a kaleidoscope of cultural fragments, but that seeks explanations for cultural phenomena. We can build upon past efforts and old insights, but we must also find our way to asking new questions. I understand anthropology as a cumulative undertaking, as well as a collective quest that moves in ever expanding circles, a quest that depends upon the contributions of each of us, and for which we are all responsible.

REFERENCES

Adams, Richard N. (1966) Power and Power Domains. *America Latina* 9: 3–5, 8–11.
——. (1970) *Crucifixion by Power: Essays on Guatemalan Social Structure, 1944–1966.* Austin: University of Texas Press.
——. (1975) *Energy and Structure: A Theory of Social Power.* Austin: University of Texas Press.
Albers, Patricia, and Seymour Parker. (1971) The Plains Vision Experience: A Study of Power and Privilege. *Southwestern Journal of Anthropology* 27: 203–33.
Arensberg, Conrad M. (1972) Culture as Behavior: Structure and Emergence. *Annual Review of Anthropology* 1: 1–26. Palo Alto, CA: Annual Reviews.
Balandier, Georges. (1970) *Political Anthropology.* New York: Random House.
Bloch, M. (1986) *From Blessing to Violence: History and Ideology in the Circumcision Ritual of the Merina of Madagascar.* Cambridge: Cambridge University Press.
Boon, James. (1982) *Other Tribes, Other Scribes: Symbolic Anthropology in the Comparative Study of Cultures, Histories, Religions, and Texts.* Cambridge: Cambridge University Press.
Brown, Richard. (1973) Anthropology and Colonial Rule: Godfrey Wilson and the Rhodes–Livingstone Institute, Northern Rhodesia. In *Anthropology and the Colonial Encounter*, ed. Talal Asad. Pp. 173–97. London: Ithaca Press.
Earle, Timothy K. (1978) Economic and Social Organization of a Complex Chiefdom: The Halelea District, Kauai, Hawaii. *Anthropological Papers*, No. 63. Ann Arbor: Museum of Anthropology, University of Michigan.
Epstein, A. L. (1958) *Politics in an Urban African Community.* Manchester: Manchester University Press.
Foucault, Michel. (1984) The Subject and Power. In *Art after Modernism: Rethinking Representation*, ed. Brian Wallis. Pp. 417–32. Boston/New York: David R. Godine/New Museum of Contemporary Art.
Geertz, Clifford. (1973) *The Interpretation of Cultures.* New York: Basic Books.
Godelier, Maurice. (1977) *Perspectives in Marxist Anthropology.* Cambridge Studies in Social Anthropology, No. 18. Cambridge: Cambridge University Press.
Goldman, Irving. (1975) *The Mouth of Heaven: An Introduction to Kwakiutl Religious Thought.* New York: Wiley Interscience.
Kaufmann, Walter. (1968) *Nietzsche: Philosopher, Psychologist, Antichrist.* Princeton, NJ: Princeton University Press.
Kirch, Patrick V. (1985) *Feathered Gods and Fishhooks: An Introduction to Hawaiian Archaeology and Prehistory.* Honolulu: University of Hawaii Press.
Lan, David. (1985) *Guns and Rain: Guerillas and Spirit Mediums in Zimbabwe.* Berkeley/Los Angeles: University of California Press.
Mitchell, J. Clyde. (1957) *The Kalela Dance: Aspects of Social Relationships among Urban Africans in Northern Rhodesia.* Rhodes–Livingstone Paper No. 27. Manchester: Manchester University Press for Rhodes–Livingstone Institute.
Ortner, Sherry B. (1984) Theory in Anthropology since the Sixties. *Comparative Studies in Society and History* 26: 126–66.
Pocock, John G. A. (1971) *Politics, Language and Time: Essays in Political Thought and History.* New York: Atheneum.
Ranger, Terence O. (1970) *The African Voice in Southern Rhodesia, 1898–1930.* London: Heinemann.
——. (1975) *Dance and Society in Eastern Africa, 1890–1970: The Beni Ngoma.* Berkeley/Los Angeles: University of California Press.
Rappaport, Roy A. (1979) *Ecology, Meaning, and Religion.* Richmond, CA: North Atlantic Books.

Sahlins, Marshall D. (1985) *Islands of History*. Chicago, IL: University of Chicago Press.

Scott, James. (1985) *Weapons of the Weak: Everyday Forms of Peasant Resistance*. New Haven, CT: Yale University Press.

Sichone, Owen B. (1989) The Development of an Urban Working-Class Culture on the Rhodesian Copperbelt. In *Domination and Resistance*, ed. Daniel Miller, Michael Rowlands, and Christopher Tilley. Pp. 290–8. London: Unwin Hyman.

Spriggs, Mathew. (1988) The Hawaiian Transformation of Ancestral Polynesian Society: Conceptualizing Chiefly States. In *State and Society: The Emergence and Development of Social Hierarchy and Political Centralization*, ed. John Gledhill, Barbara Bender, and Mogens Trolle-Larsen. Pp. 57–73. London: Unwin Hyman.

Steward, Julian H., et al. (1956) *The People of Puerto Rico*. Urbana: University of Illinois Press.

Valeri, Valerio. (1985) *Kingship and Sacrifice: Ritual and Society in Ancient Hawaii*. Chicago, IL: University of Chicago Press.

Van Binsbergen, Wim M. J., and Matthew Schofeleers (eds.) (1985) *Theoretical Explorations in African Religion*. London: Kegan Paul International.

Wallace, Anthony F. C. (1970) [1961] *Culture and Personality*. New York: Random House.

Werbner, Richard P. (1989) *Ritual Passage, Sacred Journey: The Form, Process and Organization of Religious Movement*. Washington, DC: Smithsonian Institution Press.

20

Ethnographic Aspects of the World Capitalist System

June Nash

Ever since its origin, anthropology has had a worldwide scope. Indeed, the very stimulus to the field were the advancing frontiers of European trade and colonies (77, 195) [see numbered list of works at end of chapter]. What distinguishes the present interest in the world scope of anthropology is the paradigm of integration of all people and cultures within a world capitalist *system*. This approach, fostered by Wallerstein (179–84), has roots in the political economy of dependent development and unequal exchange (2–5, 45) and in anthropological studies of the Third World (4, 7, 19, 178). This paradigm poses a challenge to established ways of describing as well as analyzing our field material. I shall attempt to review recent studies which assess the conceptual categories for placing ethnographic studies in the world system as well as the ongoing self-criticism and refinement of our traditional approaches in the intensive case studies, cross-cultural analyses, and ethnohistorical studies of colonialism and imperialism. I shall also attempt, and this is a much more difficult task, to assess the contributions anthropologists who have not addressed themselves to the specific paradigm of a world system have made as they developed a language for talking about worldwide customs and institutions. Eric Wolf prophesied this role for anthropology (190, p. 97): "in the process of creating that science of man that will underwrite the new world culture and its new possibilities, anthropology will also change itself, and change itself beyond recognition. Some of the changes are already under way. To make them possible, in a world of necessity, is our obligation."

According to Fred Eggan (44, p. 140), during World War II "the worldwide scope of the war made heavy demands on anthropological knowledge and anthropologists emerged with a new position in social science as well as with new ideas and sometimes new careers." With grants available, students turned from North American Indian studies to studies of Africa, Asia, India, and Latin America. British anthropologists had already spelled out the methodological implications of this shift in focus. In his presidential address to the Royal Anthropological Institute of Great Britain and Ireland in 1940, A. R. Radcliffe-Brown (140) stated:

From *Annual Review of Anthropology* 10 (1981), pp. 393–401, 407–11, 413–23.

Let us suppose that we wish to study and understand what is happening in a British or French colony or dependency in Africa, at the present time. Formerly the region was inhabited by Africans having their own social structure. Now a new and more complex social structure has been brought into existence. The population now includes a certain number of Europeans – government officials, traders, missionaries and, in some instances, settlers. The new political structure is one in which the Europeans have a large measure of control, and they generally play an important part in the new economic structure. The outstanding characteristic of this kind of social structure is that Europeans and Africans constitute different classes, with different languages, different customs and modes of life, and different sets of values and ideas. It is an extreme example of a society compounded of heterogeneous elements. As such it has a certain instability, due to the lack of adjustment of divergent interests. In order to understand the social changes that are taking place in a society of this kind, it seems to me essential to study the whole set of relations amongst the persons involved.

In the intervening decades, anthropologists made considerable advances in contextualizing their field observations in the colonial encounter (48, 71, 77, 119, 134, 163, 189) and postwar independence movements (7, 35, 47, 50, 51, 69, 70, 113, 191) and the impact of industrialization (46, 80, 90, 102, 121, 130, 139, 142). Anthropologists have recorded the transformations as stone axes gave way to steel in New Guinea (150) sleds to skiddoos in the Arctic (137), long bows to rifles in the South American jungles (89), and camels to pickup trucks in Saudi Arabia (31). They have recorded the varied responses of people who have shifted from subsistence crops to cash crops (147) and from intensive subsistence plot cultivation to "green revolution" farming (78, 118). Worsley (196, p. 232) summarized the formation of a Third World Coalition in terms that anticipate Wallerstein's model: "The new societies," he said, "have become what they are under the quite specific conditions of an emergent world-system and this external impact shaped their internal development." The emergent world perspective of the 1960s became a central problem in the 1970s. Syntheses of aboriginal societies such as that of Eleanor Burke Leacock and Nancy Oestrich Lurie (104) on North American Indian societies show their evolution in an historical framework that includes all of the political and economic trends affecting their populations. Two of the past presidents of the American Anthropological Association in the 1970s pointed to the new paradigm in their presidential addresses. As a result of world integration, Colson warned (33, pp. 261–2): "Not only is our basic subject matter suspect, but often enough we are told that we are now superfluous given that the 'primitive' cultures, which some assume we study, are disappearing and everyone is now, or is soon to be, a member of a world society dominated by giant industrial bureaucracies and contending imperialism." While she forecasts as a central problem of the 1980s the "implications of the large-scale organizations within which so many of us now spend our lives" (33, p. 264), Bohannon (14, p. 513) asserts that the most important topic might be the "world problematique" concerning population, pollution, and conservation of resources." Some anthropologists have anticipated these programs for the 1980s by studying the implications of transnational corporations (53, 81, 129, 148, 192, 193). Given this accumulating reservoir of case studies contextualized in global changes, and the growing awareness of the dialectical responses to the global forces that shaped the formation of "tribes" and "primitive" cultures, it is unfair to conclude, as Rollwagon (144, p. 370) does, that the field "has been skewed in the direction of conceptualizing cultural systems *in vacuo*," and that "The significance of much of this research is destroyed because the isolationist tradition in cultural anthropology places more emphasis on the search for ethnographic case studies than upon a search for cause or process in the larger system . . ."

In this attempt to assess ethnographic contributions to a world systems understanding, I shall first present the Wallerstein paradigm and some of the criticisms of it that may help direct anthropological studies. I shall then turn to the related approaches in development and dependency studies. Following this, I shall indicate some of the ethnographic concepts and methods developed in their search for universally valid cross-cultural categories. This will include a reassessment of emic and etic distinctions and the cross-cultural studies. I shall conclude with a brief résumé of recent studies in colonization and development.

The World Systems Paradigm

"A world system," as Wallerstein (182, pp. 347–8) defines it, "is a social system, one that has boundaries, structures, member groups, rules of legitimization and coherence. Its life is made up of the conflicting forces which hold it together by tension, and tear it apart as each group seeks eternally to remold it to its advantage." The basis of this world system is an international division of labor mediated through trade exchanges without the need for a unified political structure. This was, in fact, the strength of the system since it permitted flexibility for the various zones, which he calls core, periphery and semiperiphery depending upon their changing role in the overall economy. These zones contain different class structures, used different modes of labor control, and profited unequally from workings of the system (182, p. 162).

Wallerstein was not the first to perceive the operations of a world system in the sixteenth century. Historians such as Parry (136) and Williams (188) sketched the outline of the system as European powers competed for and consolidated economic advantages in the sixteenth and seventeenth centuries. Dodgshon (40) gives credit to at least six precursors, the most important of whom to social scientists is Andre Gundar Frank, whose work (63–5) is discussed below. Worsley (196, p. 14) stated the dimensions of the system a decade before the publication of Wallerstein's first volume:

> Europe had accomplished a transformation which created the world as a social system. It was a world-order founded on conquest and maintained by force. The New 'World' was no egalitarian 'family of nations'; it was essentially asymmetrical. At the one pole stood industrialized Europe, at the other the disinherited. Paradoxically, the world had been divided in the process of its unification, divided into spheres of influence, and divided into rich and poor.

What made the publication of Wallerstein's book an event was possibly the growing dissatisfaction with the development model and the failure of the world to conform to its proscriptions, as well as the breakthroughs these precursors had made in preparing the ground for the new paradigm.

Wallerstein has succeeded in making history available to social scientists interested in contemporary problems of the world system, just as he has linked historical investigation to the current concerns. Braudel (17), the original inspiration for the world paradigm according to Wallerstein, could trace the strength of the system in the flexibility that permitted the growth of innovative firms incorporated in the overarching structure at the same time that he foresaw its demise as growing centralization threatened the basis for change. Wallerstein's view is equally encompassing. The first volume (182) has been followed by one projected for the period 1640–1815 (184), a third will cover material from 1815 to 1917, and finally 1917 on. It is quite possible that anthropologists will have more difficulty with subsequent volumes that tie more directly into their own analyses. I shall present some of those problems as critics have responded to his first volume.

The problem of unitary vs. multiple modes of production

In contrast to the Marxist view that class opposition occurs at the site of production, Wallerstein's thesis maintains, in Lane's (103) words, that "classes are to be understood by their relation to the world system in which they exist," since they "arise from production oriented toward meeting demands expressed in the system of exchanges embodied in that world system and contribute to the concentration in the core." This challenge to the Marxist view of distinct modes of production defined by the internal division of labor and ordered in lineal succession has caused the most controversy. Wallerstein flatly states that there is only one mode of production and that is the capitalist world system (180, p. 390).

Trimberger (173) contrasts the unitary view of the capitalist mode of production contained in the Wallerstein model with the uneven development thesis put forth by Mandel (115) and Amin (4, 5). Mandel considers the world capitalist system to be made up of a variety of modes of production found in diverse social formations united by capitalist modes of exchange. Thus: "The historical specificity of imperialism lies in the fact that, although it unites the world economy into a single market, it does not unify world society into a homogeneous capitalist milieu" (quoted in Trimberger (173, p. 129)). This view is supported by Amin (4, p. 147), who shows the persistence of several modes of production with strong resistance to absorption in the capitalist sector. This viewpoint is consistent with that of English social historians, Trimberger notes (173, p. 131), citing the work of John Foster (61), and E. P. Thompson (172), who found the most militant anticapitalist consciousness among those artisans who were not absorbed in capitalist production. Gutman (85) cites the frequent incidence of worker resistance to debasement of craft skills in New England's nascent industrial cities and the introduction of immigrant labor to break the solidarity of these craft workers in the mill towns of New England. Resistance to the penetration of the world capitalist system may pivot around women's resistance to the loss of their economic production and the values surrounding it. This can be seen in the contributions to the anthology on *Women and Colonization* (48), particularly those dealing with the Seneca, the Bari of Colombia, the Montaignais, the Luo, the Trobriand Islanders, and the Ivory Coast. The Ibo women's war (95) was a fight against a taxation system that threatened the subsistence agriculture managed by women, and it was interpreted by them as a threat on life itself.

The acceptance or rejection of the thesis concerning a single dominant mode of production may depend upon the timing and place of ethnographic inquiry. Sidney

Mintz (120) and Jane and Peter Schneider (153) find it compatible with the analysis of class formation in peripheral countries – the Caribbean islands and Sicily – particularly up to the nineteenth century. Mintz (120) shows how interdependent forms of labor with local initiative and local response made it possible for forced labor to exist in the periphery along with free labor in western European manufacturies up to the nineteenth century. This paradigm, Mintz states (120, p. 253), "calls into question attempts to analyze local economic subsystems in terms of their component modes of production, to the extent that such analyses ignore or circumvent the significance of the overarching world system within which such subsystems must function." In contrast, "To examine the capitalist system globally when looking at any one of its sectors means taking into account the accumulation of capital through wage-labor at the core, while seeing other sectors as satisfying the systemic requirements of that core" (120, p. 259). Thus the coexistence of different modes of labor control, slave and free labor, within the capitalist mode of production, is not a paradox but a stimulus to the operation of the world exchange system. Similarly, this global perspective enables Jane and Peter Schneider (153) to view the Mafia of Sicily as businessmen acting in defense of their interests as pastoralists and wheat growers in the developing world market rather than as politicians frustrated with the weakness of central political authority.

I shall not try to resolve the differences between those who stress the unity of the world system against those who emphasize the variety of coexisting modes of production since I am convinced that the concept of mode of production and its application to particular historical formations can only be clarified by further discussion in relation to field data, some of which I assess later on. As others (91, 120) have noted, the advantage of the Wallerstein model, and that of dependency theorists (23, 24, 41, 64, 65), is that one avoids the false opposition of "feudal" vs. "capitalist" in attending to the overarching framework. We can see how, for example, the interests of nascent capitalizing interests join with those of foreign capitalists when a Brazilian coffee producer employing labor in various forms of contract and sharecropping labor invests in a branch of a multinational corporation operating in Sao Paulo. If his activities were consigned to separate modes of production, we would miss the special dynamic of Brazilian politics.

The problem of the passive periphery

Anthropologists will probably have greater difficulty with the treatment of the periphery (or dependent country in Frank's (64) model) as a passive recipient of the dynamic penetration of the modernizing capitalist system. Root (145) rejects this assumption in Chirot's *Social Change in a Peripheral Society: The Creation of a Balkan Colony* (27) on the basis that the state's priorities were not strong enough to undermine social relations based on land tenure until the late seventeenth century. Hence internal class relations could not be defined adequately by a worldwide division of labor organized under the Ottoman empire since social relations based on land tenure were still in effect. Hechter's (86) analysis of Celtic resistance to British domination is a case in point.

Similarly, Sella (156) criticizes the tendency of the Wallerstein model to "exaggerate the influence of the newly emerging pattern of relationships on the internal life of the areas involved." He argues that one cannot explain all forms of labor control in core and periphery in terms of the capitalist imperative since sixteenth-century capitalism made use of preexisting forms of labor review. Skocpol (158) criticizes the overemphasis on market processes to the neglect of technological invention. Since everything is treated as though it reinforced the system, the stability of the system is overstated. This treatment ignores other than economic variables such as historically preexisting institutional patterns that result in the threat of rebellion or other geopolitical pressures which ultimately determine what class will be in the best position to take advantage of available trade opportunities.

These arguments countering the priority Wallerstein gives to the global system are most concisely stated in Sella's (156) statement:

> To go back to Wallerstein's contention that the combination of free and coerced labor was the "essence of capitalism," it would seem preferable and more accurate to say that, insofar as the new world-system involved the clash and the blend of widely different cultures, its vitality if not its essence resulted from its ability to adapt to its own ends whatever forms of labor control came its way in different parts of the world, not because they were the most economical, but simply because they happened to be available. The failure of the Spanish monarchy to transform the American Indians into wage earners after the European model illustrates this point.

Historians of Spanish America might well question whether it was the policy of the Spanish monarchy to transform American Indians into wage earners, since the crown often countered the measures of colonists to mobilize labor by any means. However, the thesis concerning the importance of local modes of labor control feeding into the productive relations established after colonization is worth emphasizing.

Jane Schneider (152) also criticizes a world's systems approach that ignores the dynamic of precapitalist empires of Asia. Because Wallerstein views trade in preciosities as nonsystemic, Schneider (152, p. 20) maintains, he cannot explain the expansion of countries such as Portugal which was only minimally interested in basic commodities. A similar criticism might be made of Smith's (160) emphasis on the structure imposed by the world system.

The implicit treatment of periphery as a "passive victim" universally giving way to the capitalist invasion is a corollary of the unitary perspective on mode of production in Wallerstein, according to Trimberger (173). This reinforces her favoring uneven development approaches which recognize "specific combinations of precapitalist, semi-capitalist and capitalist relations of production." She argues that

> this model opens the way for understanding between distinct social formations in the world system and a dynamic which is not unidirectional. Precapitalist relations of production are subordinated and distorted by the impact of capitalism, but they too have their own dynamic which has an impact on capitalist development and may serve as the material base of the genesis of resistance to capitalism.

An example of such a dynamic is the variation in economic position among peasantry, often assumed to be a homogeneous, subordinated group. The historic significance of such variation can best be envisioned by the microanalytic anthropological perspective (146).

Time and space in the emergence of the world capitalist system

Another problem brought up in connection with the first volume of Wallerstein's projected series is the spatial boundary and chronology for the world system. Dodgshon (40) draws upon Polanyi (138) and Dalton (37) in questioning the emergence of an integrated system in the sixteenth century. Citing Dalton's (37) statement that "only when the market is self-regulating can we talk of a capitalist system," he accuses Wallerstein of confusing a world-based economy with the world system which took its place. This transformation occurs when there is a move from penetration through distribution to penetration through production, a change that Polanyi believes did not exist until 1750. Since there are no political institutions marking the transition (122), it is more difficult to set the time. Other problems on the timing of the emergence of the world system rise when one considers the significance of luxury trade (152) and long-distance trade (171) prior to European developments.

One can also expect disagreement with the allocation of countries according to core, semiperiphery, and periphery as specific regions are taken into account. The growing integration of production processes on a world scale may break down all geographical boundaries. With the present trend toward accumulation by a few transnational corporations which are not subject to redistribution by any political entity, there may be no core population benefiting from the system. But before that level of integration is reached, the system will indeed be in demise (180, 187).

Development, Dependency, and Unequal Exchange

The difficulty for anthropologists concerned with problems of development and underdevelopment is in the shift from general statements about the world system to microfieldwork (62). Proponents of the world systems model are specific about what is forbidden; the "ethnographic present" is negated, as is the reification of structures in polarities contrasting subsistence cropping and cash cropping or folk-urban (91). However, Hopkins (91) is less definite on what should be done. What will be done may well depend on the current polemic concerning: (i) the focus on exchange relations or productive relations as the central dynamic; (ii) the question of the articulation of the mode(s) of production; and (iii) explanations for the growing inequality between sectors of the international economy. . . .

The problem of the widening gap

The widening gap between core and peripheral regions, and between rich and poor classes, was becoming increasingly apparent in the decade of the 1960s (1). A decade of development focusing on import substitution industrialization (43) and green revolution agriculture (78) not only had failed to improve the position of Third World populations but had contributed to trade imbalances, increasing debt and impoverishment revealed in indices of infant mortality and life expectancy. Schneider (151) and C. T. Smith (159) summarize some of the case studies by anthropologists (11, 22, 54–6, 82, 149) showing how a small number of entrepreneurs benefited from development programs. Smith (159, p. 815) concludes that, "Economic development, left unconstrained with mechanisms to assure equitable distribution at all levels, produces benefits most effectively for the upper levels in the hierarchy." While he would search for equality "rooted in planning," the world systems proponents would discount that possibility since they see inequality as endemic to the system. Amin (3) argues that the value of the work force is maintained at a level of subsistence in the dependent countries while wages may multiply 20 or 30 times that in "imperialist centers." It is precisely from this abyss that unequal exchange arises. In a later article, Amin (4) spells out the consequences of monopolistic competition: (i) the growth of selling costs through advertising to create special needs reduces the profitability of producing goods; (ii) the state bears an increasing share of infrastructural costs for roads and communication; and (iii) the difference between the rewards to labor in the periphery is greater than the difference in productivity between the two because of the higher rate of profit for investments in the periphery. The survival and reproduction of the labor force depends upon the extreme exploitation of the rural economy, and particularly of women who produce subsistence crops (126, 185). Burawoy (21) and Gudeman (83) review the literature showing the impact of uneven development on labor throughout the world. The uneven character of development by monopoly capital is viewed by *dependistas* as intrinsic to the system. Sunkel (167, p. 519) concludes that:

> The concept of "dependency" links the postwar evolution of capitalism internationally to the discriminatory nature of the local process of development, as we know it. Access to the means and benefits of development is selective; rather than spreading them, the process tends to ensure a self-reinforcing accumulation of privilege for special groups as well as the continued existence of a marginal class.

Cultural Diversity in World Perspective

The pitfall of a world systems approach is twofold: (i) the outcome seems predictable in the model, and (ii) the mobilization of counterforces is doomed to failure (173). It is precisely for that reason that the anthropological quest for cultural diversity should be pursued. Foster (60, p. 321) points out that ethnographic materials provide "valuable information on the full range of possibilities for human social and cultural behavior...[which] have implications for developers interested in assessing the desirability of certain transformations." He urges that the field not lose attention to the local dimension, but see it enhanced in theory derived from a world perspective.

If we take a world perspective, what are the special contributions we can make as ethnographers? What descriptive techniques and methods can we draw upon as we carry out our "methodological speciality" – in Foster's words, that of "reconcile[ing] general formulations with observations from diverse cultural settings" (60, p. 321). I shall consider two such approaches here: the intensive case studies, and the emic and etic distinctions as a tool for arriving at universally valid terms of description.

Intensive case studies

The advances made in our understanding of how countryside is linked to the city, urban centers and industries related to the nation, and sometimes directly to the world market, have come about as a result of decades of intensive case studies. We should not lose sight of these nor underestimate their value in the enthusiasm for a world systems approach. Fortes (59) set forth the objectives of the intensive case study approach in his presidential address in 1954. His own work (57, 58) and that of his contemporaries (49, 54–6) inspired by Malinowski (114) demonstrated the interconnectedness of the internal operations of the society. Those who followed them to the field in the later 1950s and 1960s looked beyond the "tribal" boundaries that were constructed in the colonial encounter itself to the interaction of indigenous and capitalist systems (30, 46, 88, 121). But their central interest, and that of the many American anthropologists working in field research outside of the United States after World War II, retained that sense of the value of intensive analysis of the local, particular case, ignored, for the most part, by analysts of other disciplines. If at times, in reacting to the disdain of scholars in other disciplines to the local particularism of their approach, anthropologists developed a defensive blindness to the macrostructures that shaped the societies they studied, this has to be evaluated in terms of those times. One of the hazards in ethnographic work is that the field experience cultivates the emic view of one's informants that treats the overarching dominant structure as irrelevant. The tendency for informants to explain all cause and effect relationships as resulting from conditions contained within the boundaries of their community is contagious and often influences the ethnographic conclusions.

The danger of a world systems approach, to add to what Sella (156) pointed to, is that we might lose sight of these internal "logico-integrative" (69) schema that provide the motivation and apprehension of what is happening in the world. In our reappraisal of case studies, we should try to show the advances they made, as Frankenberg (66) does in his discussion of Gluckman's studies of the Barotse.

The emic and etic distinctions

Even – or especially – when ethnologists begin a study of their own society, they cannot take any terms for granted, since the particular segment of the society may contain variations from the subcultural variant they know. The process of discovery, as Goodenough points out, relies on discerning contrasts (76, p. 37):

> We start armed with the concepts our own culture has given us. We discover that other people make conceptual distinctions that we don't make and that we make distinctions that they don't make. To describe theirs and compare them with ours we have to find a set of concepts capable of describing their distinctions as well as our own. To do this, we have to analyze the phenomena more finely than we had to before, discovering and sorting out variables of which we were previously unaware.

This process is analogous to that of linguists when they try to describe the speech sounds of other languages. Etics provide the basic data for comparison, and here, in

Goodenough's words (76, p. 129), is the importance of our etic concepts for understanding the world system:

> As a kind of typology, a systematic set of etic concepts is a tool for describing and comparing cultural forms. Its adequacy is judged by its ability satisfactorily to describe all the emic distinctions people actually make in all the world's cultures in relation to the subject matter (whether functionally or otherwise defined) for which the etic concepts were designed... Such etic concepts satisfy the criteria for a comparative study of cultural forms free of ethnographic or specific cultural bias... If they succeed in embracing all of the distinctive features needed to describe the elementary emic units of any culture, they constitute the minimum number of concepts needed to determine the universal attributes of culture and by inference from them, the universal attributes of men as creators and users of culture – the nature of the human species which is the principal scientific aim of anthropology.

If we take this approach, which has been most developed in kinship analysis, and apply it to problems in the organization of work, distribution, and economic values, we would advance the old substantivist/formalist debate. Clammer (28, p. 213) warns us that, "Anthropologists, while correctly recognizing that much can be learned from other disciplines, have undoubtedly leaned far too heavily on the concepts that those subjects have developed for themselves. Economic anthropology perhaps more than most other specialized subbranches of the activity, must develop its own concepts appropriate to its own peculiar needs." Weeks (186, p. 27) picks up this warning and applies it to neoclassical models:

> in fastening a fiction that they abstract from institutional forms and therefore allegedly encompass a wide variety of institutional possibilities, do more than implicitly and explicitly justify development through capitalist exchange relationships. Implicitly they view poverty as arising from *internal* causes – the relationship of underdeveloped countries to the industrialised capitalist countries is ignored, or viewed as potentially beneficial if correct policies are pursued.

The concepts of economists, derived from neoclassical precepts, are, in Weeks' terms, a *prescription* for social relations for capitalist underdevelopment. These reevaluations of theory and method in economic anthropology are further explored in Clammer's (29) anthology. Godelier's (73) criticism of the concept of rationality as the key concept in the ideological justification for capitalist exchange is a fine example of what can be gained from such an analysis.

As we extend our understanding about economic systems, questioning the applicability of neoclassical terms to capitalist institutions as well as to nonmarket societies, we might overcome some of the ethnocentric projections as to what is universal in economic behavior. The "capitalist", "precapitalist" contrast inspired by the French Marxist school obscures emic contrasts existing within advanced capitalist economies just as it has obscured the interface between different modes of labor and exchange.

Just as the analysis of the many varieties of family structure enabled anthropologists to overcome the assumptions based on a Western model (123), so might we overcome the spell of economic rationality, technological determination, or profitability as the measure of progress. Appleby (6) has traced the process by which "The capacity to objectify human relations, to demythologize them and turn them into natural phenomenon [enabled] men . . . [to] manipulate their social and material environment." This is an ongoing process, since the terms the neoclassical economists developed to objectify production and exchange relations have become an ideology justifying the status quo. The debate between "formalists" and "substantivists" might shift from the question whether neoclassical terms can be extended from "market" economies to "primitive" exchange systems, to the question whether these terms apply to capitalist economies given the monopolistic practices. . . .

Colonialism, Imperialism, and Transnational Corporations

The anthropological view of the world system has been concerned with the impact of global institutions in peripheral or semiperipheral zones more than with the system itself. In the process of "reinventing" anthropology, some anthropologists have tried to study the global institutions themselves. Hymes (94, p. 35) asks us "to employ our ethnographic tradition of work, and such ethnological insight as informs it, in the study of the emergence of cultural form in concrete settings and in relation to a world society." In the first flush of interest in development studies, social scientists in other disciplines came to anthropologists in search of concepts and understandings of exotic cultures; now we are required either to adopt some of the findings and methods of the other social sciences or to accept a division of labor in which we share in the study of emergent forms. But, as Hymes suggests, we should not forget the unique sensibilities that ethnographers have developed in field situations that clearly presented distinct phenomenal categories.

Transnational corporations

As anthropologists, we are best trained to study the impact of transnational corporations throughout the world and, as a result, less likely to view the organization of production and distribution on a worldwide scale directly. By opening our minds to the manifold possibilities of reinterpretation by the societies undergoing the transition into industrialization, we have shown some unique features in the sociocultural integration that develops (or fails to develop) in the wake of global transfers of technology, management, and labor (129, 193).

A far more difficult task is the study of multinational corporations. A pioneer in this study is Alvin Wolfe (192), who as early as 1963 discussed the implications of integration of industry on a supranational level. While the study of multinationals – industries based in an industrial center with branches established in one or more foreign countries – and transnationals – industries whose international operations take priority over the claim of any home base – is dominated by economists, political scientists, and sociologists, anthropologists can make a contribution by maintaining an holistic approach and evolutionary perspective.

Wolfe (193) emphasizes the integrative evolution as firms established overseas branches and then proceeded to integrate the manufacturing process itself. This has already happened in electronics, garment manufacturing, and to a lesser extent, automobile production (162). However, the integration of corporate management through transnational organizations has resulted in the disintegration of national states (168) and of labor organizations (67, 72, 93, 96, 97). We can mark three stages in the integrative evolution. The initial thrust overseas was an attempt to get behind tariff barriers, particularly after World War I in Canada and Latin America. The greatest surge of overseas expansion came after World War II and the establishment of the European Economic Community when US firms tried to maintain a share in that market by establishing a branch firm. Starting about 1964, when changes in the tariff laws permitted reshipment of components with tariffs only on the value added, or labor of assembling parts that were then incorporated in final products at the home base and sold in a domestic market, a new phase of integration took place. This evolving international division of labor (72) is bringing about an integration of manufacturing processes that is beginning to erase the boundaries of "core," "periphery," and "semiperiphery" as transnational firms move production sites to whatever areas contain reserves of cheap, available labor and where they will expect the least resistance from government or labor unions. The integration of the productive system is occurring simultaneously with a breakdown in social organization. The resulting crisis (187) is exploding before us in our field research, often inhibiting the entry and participant observations essential to good fieldwork.

Changes brought about by these dramatic shifts in the locus and volume of production are only beginning to be analyzed. Change in the employment rates of women and men is affecting the household and gender relations in ways that are now being assessed (53, 81, 99, 107, 112, 148). The variations in employment practices of multinational corporations in branches at home and abroad are another significant problem area anthropologists could follow up on analyses by economists (96, 131, 135). The effect on class consciousness created by the changing structure of employment in transnational organizations has hardly been touched. This is an area in which traditional ethnographic methods, including oral histories and symbolic analyses, can get us beyond the ideological facade which masks sentiment and behavior (176, 177).

Anthropologists can play a distinctive role in analyzing the changes brought about in the international organization of production by investigating the "logico-meaningful integration" which Geertz (69) defines as the unity of style, meaning, and value, distinct from the "causal-functional integration" where each part is an element that keeps the system going (129). We might also pursue comparative studies of the work process within branches of the same plant in different countries in order to test assumptions about the limits of variability posed by a shared technology and management. Just as our studies of household organization of production where there is a merging of economic base and political and ideological superstructure contributed to the understanding of mode of production, so might our study of transnational organizations, where economic base seems divorced from logico-integrative structures, go beyond the questions raised by economists or other social scientists. Our holistic approach will enable us to investigate the impact of development and change on populations and environment, as Davis (39) does in his study of Amazonian forest people, within a structural historical framework. It can also encompass the logico-meaningful integration in the encounter with capitalist institutions, as Taussig (169) attempts....

Summary

Wallerstein's paradigm of a world capitalist system challenges social scientists to view all societies and cultures of the world as integrated in a worldwide division of labor. Drawing on analyses of dependency and uneven exchange, the paradigm promotes systemic analyses of the interrelationships between "core" industrial states, "semiperipheral" regions, and "periphery." Anthropology, as a discipline oriented toward worldwide descriptions and comparisons of society, has developed ethnographic methods and a vocabulary for talking about particular features in relation to universal characteristics of the human condition. The respect for internal variation and resistance to ethnocentric judgments imposed on other cultures which has been cultivated by ethnologists can overcome some of the difficulties critics have raised with the world systems approach. The tendency to take the emergence and dominance of the capitalist system as a foregone conclusion, to assume passive acceptance by peripheral and semiperipheral regions to the imposed will of core nations can be corrected by methods and findings of ethnographers past and present.

I have considered some of the ethnographic concepts and methods developed in the search for universally valid cross-cultural categories. This includes a reassessment of intensive case study approaches, emic and etic distinctions in ethnographic description, and cross-cultural comparisons. Noting the loss of cultural variability in subsistence systems as the world's population becomes dependent on employment and income generated in capitalist enterprises, I have summarized some of the dangers inherent in the vulnerability to contraction in the world system.

BIBLIOGRAPHY

1 Adelman, I. and Morris, C. T. (1973) *Economic Growth and Social Equity in Developing Countries.* Stanford University Press.
2 Amin, S. (1972) Underdevelopment and Dependence in Black Africa: Historical Origin. *Journal of Peace Research* 2: 105–19.
3 Amin, S. (1972) Underdevelopment and Dependence in Black Africa: Origins and Contemporary Forms. *Journal of Modern African Studies* 4: 503–24.
4 Amin, S. (1976) *Unequal Development: An Essay on the Social Formations of Peripheral Capitalism.* New York: Monthly Review Press.
5 Amin, S. (1977) *Imperialism and Unequal Development, Essays by Samir Amin.* New York: Monthly Review Press.
6 Appleby, J. (1978) Modernization Theory and the Formation of Modern Social Theories in England and America. *Comparative Studies in Society and History* 20: 259–85.
7 Asad, T., ed. (1973) *Anthropology and the Colonial Encounter.* New York: Humanities.
8 Barth, F. (1963) *The Role of Entrepreneurship in Social Change in Northern Norway.* Oslo: Universitetsforlaget.
9 Bartra, R. (1974) *Estructura Agraria y Clases Sociales en México.* Mexico City: Era.
10 Bartra, R. (1975) Sobre la articulación de modes de producción en América Latina: Algunos problemas teoricas, *History and Society* 5: 5–19.
11 Belshaw, C. (1965) *Traditional Exchange and Modern Markets.* Englewood Cliffs, NJ: Prentice Hall.
12 Bienefeld, M. A. (1972–3) Planning People. *Development and Change* 4: 51–77.

13 Bloch, M. (1975) Property and the End of Affinity. In *Marxist Analyses and Social Anthropology*, pp. 203–28. London: Malaby.

14 Bohannon, P. (1979) You Can't Do Nothing. Presidential Address presented at Annual Meeting of the American Anthropological Association 78th. *American Anthropology* 82: 508–24.

15 Bourguignon, E. and Greenbaum, L. S. (1973) *Diversity and Homogeneity in World Societies*. New Haven: Human Relations Area File.

16 Bradby, B. (1975) The Destruction of Natural Economy. *Economy and Society* 4: 127–61.

17 Braudel, F. (1980) Will Capitalism Survive? *Wilson Quarterly* (Spring) 4: 102–17.

18 Brock, L. L. (1980) Marriage Exchange and Class Formation: Strategies of Production and Reproduction in a Tuareg Community 1860–1976. Presented at 79th Annual Meeting of the American Anthropological Association, Washington DC.

19 Bronfenbrenner, M. (1978) Review article: A World Class Economist from Underdeveloped Africa. *Economic Development and Culture Change* 27: 195–201.

20 Buechler, H., Buechler, J. and Hess, M. (1976) Something funny happened on the way to the Agora. A comparison of Bolivian and Spanish Galician female migrants. *Anthropological Quarterly* 49(1): 62–8.

21 Burawoy, M. (1979) The Anthropology of Industrial Work. *Annual Review of Anthropology* 8: 231–66.

22 Cancian, F. (1965) *Economics and Prestige in a Maya Community: The Religious Cargo System*. Stanford: Stanford University Press.

23 Cardoso, F. H. (1972) Dependency and Development in Latin America. *New Left Review* 74: 83–95.

24 Cardoso, F. H. (1972–3) Industrialization, Dependency and Power in Latin America. *Berkeley Journal of Sociology* 17: 79–95.

25 Cardoso, F. H. and Faletto, E. (1979) *Dependency and Development in Latin America*. Trans. M. M. Urquidi. Berkeley: University of California Press.

26 Chilcote, R. H. (1974) A Critical Synthesis of the Dependency Literature. *Latin American Perspectives* 1: 1–15.

27 Chirot, D. (1976) *Social Change in a Peripheral Society: The Creation of a Balkan Colony*. New York: Academic.

28 Clammer, J. (1975) Economic Anthropology and the Sociology of Development: "Liberal" Anthropology and its French Critics. See 133, pp. 208–28.

29 Clammer, J. (ed.). (1978) *The New Economic Anthropology*. New York: St. Martin's.

30 Cohen, A. (1969) *Custom and Politics in Urban Africa: A Study of Hausa Migrants in Yoruba Towns*. London: Routledge & Kegan Paul; Berkeley: University of California Press.

31 Cole, D. P. (1977) Bedouins of the Oilfields. In *Arab Society in Transition, A Reader*, ed. S. E. Ibrahim, N. S. Hopkins, pp. 632–8. Cairo: American University Press.

32 Coleman, R. G. (1980) Household Structure and Capitalist Incorporation on the Periphery in North Sumatra. Presented at 79th Annual Meeting of the American Anthropological Association, Washington DC.

33 Colson, E. (1976) Culture and Progress. Distinguished Lecture presented at 74th Annual Meeting of the American Anthropological Association. *American Anthropology* 78: 261–71.

34 Cook, S. (1976) Value, Price and Simple Commodity Production: Zapotec Stoneworkers. *Journal of Peasant Studies* 3: 395–427.

35 Copans, J. (1975) *Anthropologie et imperialismé*. Paris: Maspero.

36 Cotler, J. (1969) Actuales pautas de cambio en la sociedad rural del Perú. In *Dominación y cambios en el perú rural: la microorganización del Valle de Cancai*, ed. J. Matos Mar et al., pp. 60–79. Lima: Instituto de Estudios Peruanos.

37 Dalton, G. (1974) *Economic Systems and Society: Capitalism, Communism and the Third World*. Baltimore: Penguin.

38 Dandler, J. (1976) *Campesinado y reforma agraria en Cochabamba: dinamica de un movimiento campesino en Bolivia*. La Paz: Centro Investigaciones de Promoción de Campasino.

39 Davis, S. (1977) *Victims of the Miracle; Development and the Indians of Brazil*. Cambridge: Cambridge University Press.

40 Dodgshon, R. A. (1977) A Spatial Perspective. *Peasant Studies* 6: 8–19.

41 dos Santos, T. (1973) The Crisis of Development Theory and the Problem of Dependency in Latin America. In *Underdevelopment and Development*, ed. H. Bernstein, pp. 76–7. Hammondsworth: Penguin.

42 Dupré, G., Rey, P. P. (1973) Reflections on the Pertinence of a Theory of the History of Exchange. *Economy and Society* 2: 131–63.

43 Economic Commission on Latin America, United Nations. (1970), (1972) *Economic Survey of Latin America*. New York: United Nations.

44 Eggan, F. (1968) One Hundred Years of Ethnology and Social Anthropology. In *One Hundred Years of Anthropology*, ed. J. O. Brew, pp. 119–52. Cambridge, Mass.: Harvard University Press.

45 Emmanuel, A. (1972) *Unequal Exchange: A Study of the Imperialism of Trade*. New York/London: Monthly Review.

46 Epstein, A. L. (1958) *Politics in an Urban African Community*. Manchester: Manchester University Press.

47 Epstein, T. S. (1973) *South India: Yesterday, Today and Tomorrow; Mysore Village Revisited*. New York: Macmillan.

48 Etienne, M. and Leacock, E. (1980) *Women and Colonization*. Brooklyn: Bergin.

49 Evans-Pritchard, E. E. (1940) *The Nuer*. Oxford: Clarendon Press.

50 Fallers, T. (1959) *Bantu Bureaucracy; A Century of Political Evolution Among the Basoga of Uganda*. Chicago: University of Chicago Press.

51 Fallers, T. (1963) Equality, Modernity, and Democracy in the New State. In *Old Societies and New States. The Quest for Modernity in Asia and Africa*, ed. C. Geertz, pp. 158–219. New York: Free Press.

52 Fals Borda, O. (1979) Investigating Reality in Order to Transform it: The Colombian Experience. *Dialectical Anthropology* 4: 33–55.

53 Fernandez, M. P. (1980) Mexican Border Industries: Female Labor Force Participation and Migration. Ph.D. thesis. Rutgers University, New Brunswick, NJ.

54 Firth, R. (1929) *Primitive Economics of the New Zealand Maori*. Wellington, NZ: Owen.

55 Firth, R. (1936) *We the Tikopia*. London: Unwin.

56 Firth, R. (1966) *Malay Fishermen*. Hamden, Conn: Archon.

57 Fortes, M. (1945) *The Dynamics of Clanship among the Tallensi*. Oxford: Oxford University Press.

58 Fortes, M. (1949) *The Web of Kinship among the Tallensi*. London: Oxford University Press.

59 Fortes, M. (1953) Analyses and Description in Social Anthropology. Presidential Address, Sect. H., British Association for the Advancement of Science, 38th publication, 1970. *In Time and Social Structure and Other Essays*, pp. 127–46. London: Athlone.

60 Foster, B. L. (1978) Development, Modernization and Comparative Parochialism: A Review Article. *Comparative Studies in Society and History* 20: 319–28.

61 Foster, J. (1974) *Class Struggle and the Industrial Revolution: Early Industrial Radicalism in Three English Towns* London: Weidenfeld & Nicolson.

62 Foster-Carter, A. (1978) The Modes of Production Controversy. *New Left Review* 107: 47–78.

63 Frank, A. G. (1964) *Capitalism and Underdevelopment in Historical Studies of Chile and Brazil*. New York: Monthly Review.

64 Frank, A. G. (1967) *Capitalism and Underdevelopment in Latin America*. New York: Monthly Review.

65 Frank, A. G. (1975) *On Capitalist Underdevelopment*. New York: Oxford University Press.

66 Frankenberg, R. (1978) Economic Anthropology or Political Economy? The Barotse Social Formation: A Case Study. See no. 29, pp. 32–57.

67 Fröbel, F., Heinrichs, J., Krëye, O. (1978) The new international division of labour. *Social Sciences Information* 17: 123–42.

68 Geertz, C. (1960) "The Javanese Kijaji: The Changing Role of a Cultural Brother." *Comparative Studies in Society and History* 2: 228–49 *Comparative Studies in Society and History* 2: 28–49.

69 Geertz, C. (1973) Ritual and Social Change: A Javanese Example. In *The Interpretation of Cultures: Selected Essays of Clifford Geertz*, pp. 142–69. New York: Basic Books.

70 Geertz, C. (1963) *Peddlers and Princes: Social Change and Economic Modernization in Two Indonesian Towns*. Chicago: University of Chicago Press.

71 Geertz, C. (1963) The Dutch Colonial Period in Indonesia: Agrarian Involution. In *Agricultural Involution*, pp. 38–123.

72 Giersch, H., ed. (1974) *The International Division of Labor; Problems and Perspectives*. Tubingen: Möhr.

73 Godelier, M. (1973) *Rationality and Irrationality in Economics*. Trans. B. Pearce. New York: Monthly Review.

74 Godelier, M. (1978) Infrastructures, Society and History. *New Left Review* 112: 84–96.

75 Gonzalez, N. L. (1969) Patron–client Relationships at the International level. See no. 166, pp. 178–209.

76 Goodenough, W. H. (1970) *Description and Comparison in Cultural Anthropology*. Chicago: Aldine.

77 Gough, K. (1969) World Revolution and the Science of Man. In *The Dissenting Academy*, ed. T. Roszak, pp. 135–58. New York: Pantheon.

78 Gough, K. (1978) Changing Agrarian Relations in South Eastern India. *Current Anthropology* 19: 399.

79 Green, S. (1980) Silicon Valley's Women Workers: A Theoretical Analysis of Sex-Segregation in the Electronics Industry Labor Market. *Occasional Papers of the East West Center*, Honolulu.

80 Grondin, M. (1978) Peasant Cooperation and Dependency: The Case of the Electricity Enterprise of Muquiyauyo. See no. 111, pp. 99–127.

81 Grossman, R. (1978) Women's Place in the Integrated Circuits. *South East Asia Chronicle*, Pacific Research, RSC Issue 9: 5–6.

82 Gudeman, S. F. (1978) *The Demise of a Rural Economy: From Subsistence to Capitalism in a Latin American Village*. London: Paramis.

83 Gudeman, S. F. (1978) Anthropological Economics: The Question of Distribution. In *Annual Review of Anthropology* 7: 347–77.

84 Gulliver, P. H. (1973) Negotiations as a Model of Dispute Settlement: Towards a General Model. *Law Society Review* 7: 667–69.

85 Gutman, H. (1976) *Work, Culture, and Society in Industrializing America: Essays in American Working-Class and Social History*. New York: Knopf.

86 Hechter, M. (1975) *Internal Colonialism: The Celtic Fringe in British National Development 1536–1966*. Berkeley: University of California Press.

87 Hill, P. (1963) *The Migrant Cocoa Farmers of Southern Ghana: A Study in Rural Capitalism*. Cambridge: Cambridge University Press.

88 Hill, P. (1977) *Population, Prosperity, and Poverty*. Cambridge: Cambridge University Studies in Rural Capitalism in West Africa.

89 Holmberg, A. R. (1950) *Nomads of the Long Bow: The Siriono of Eastern Bolivia*. Washington: GPO.

90 Hopkins, N. S. (1977) The Impact of Technological Change on Political Centralization: The Case of Tunisia. In *Arab Society in Transition*, ed. S. E. Ibrahim, N. S. Hopkins, pp. 620–31. Cairo: American University.

91 Hopkins, T. (1978) World Systems Analysis: Methodological Issues. In *The Capitalist World Economy*, ed. B. H. Kaplan, pp. 100–217. Beverly Hills: Sage.

92 Huizer, G. and Mannheim, B., eds. (1979) *The Politics of Anthropology: from Colonialism and Sexism Toward a View from Below*. The Hague: Mouton.

93 Hymer, S. (1973) The Internationalization of Capital. In *International Business*, ed. D. S. Henley, pp. 278–98. East Lansing: Michigan State University Press.

94 Hymes, D., ed. (1972) *Reinventing Anthropology*. New York: Pantheon.

95 Ifeka-Moller, C. (1975) Female Militancy and Colonial Revolt: The Women's War of 1929, Eastern Nigeria. In *Perceiving Women*, ed. S. Ardner, pp. 127–58. New York: Wiley.

96 International Labor Office. (1977) *Social and Labour Practices of Some U.S. Based Multinationals in the Metal Trades*. Geneva: United Nations.

97 Jagor, E. R. (1975) U.S. labor and Multinationals. In *International Labor and the National Enterprises: Studies in International Economics and Development*, ed. D. Kujawa, pp. 22–46. New York: Prager.

98 Jorgensen, J. G. (1979) Cross-cultural comparisons. *Annual Review of Anthropology* 8: 309–31.

99 Katz, N. (1980) Women Electronic Workers in the Silicon Valley. Presented at the 79th Annual Meeting of the American Anthropological Association, Washington DC.

100 Laclau, E. (1979) Modos de producción, sistemas economicos y población exedente: approximación historica a los casos argentina y chileno. *Revista Latinoamericana Sociología* 5: 344–83.

101 Laclau, E. (1971) Feudalism and Capitalism in Latin America. *New Left Review* 67: 19–38.

102 Laite, J. (1978) Processes of Industrial and Social Change in Highland Peru. See no. 111, pp. 73–97.

103 Lane, F. C. (1976) Economic Growth in Wallerstein's Social Systems. A review article. *Comparative Studies in Society and History* 18: 517–32.

104 Leacock, E. B. and Lurie, N. O. (1971) *North American Indians in Historical Perspective*. New York: Random House.

105 Lennihan, L. (1980) *As the World Turns: Capital, Class, and the Household in Northern Nigeria*. Presented at the 79th Annual Meeting of the American Anthropological Association, Washington DC.

106 Leviatan, U. (1976) The Process of Industrialization in the Israel Kibbutzim. In *Popular Participation in Social Change*, ed. J. Nash, J. Dandler, N. Hopkins, pp. 549–58. The Hague: Mouton.

107 Lim, L. Y. C. (1978) Women Workers in Multinational Corporations: The Case of the Electronics Industry in Malaysia and Singapore. *Michigan Occasional Papers* 9.

108 Lomax, A. and Arensberg, C. M. (1977) A Worldwide Evolutionary Classification of Culture by Subsistence Systems. *Current Anthropology* 18: 659–79.

109 Long, N. (1975) Structural Dependency, Modes of Production, and Economic Brokerage in Rural Peru. See no. 133, pp. 253–82.

110 Long, N. and Richardson, P. (1978) Informal Sector, Petty Commodity Production and the Social Relations of Small-scale Enterprise. See no. 29, pp. 176–209.

111 Long, N. and Roberts, B. R., eds. (1978) *Peasant Cooperation and Capitalist Expansion in Central Peru*. Austin: University of Texas Press.

112   Long, N. and Roberts, B. R. (1978) Peasant Cooperation and Underdevelopment in Central Peru. See no. 111, pp. 297–328.

113   Magubane, B. (1979) *The Political Economy of Race and Class in South Africa* New York: Monthly Review.

114   Malinowski, B. (1932) *Argonauts of the Western Pacific*. London: Routledge.

115   Mandel, E. (1970) The Laws of Uneven Development. *New Left Review* 59: 19–38.

116   Maquet, J. (1964) Objectivity in Anthropology. *Current Anthropology* 5: 47–55.

117   Matos Mar, J. et al., eds. (1969) *Dominacion y Cambios en el Peru Rural*. Lima: Inst. Estudios Peruanos.

118   Mencher, J. (1970) Change Agents and Villagers, their Relationship and Role of Class Values. *Economic and Political Weekly* (Bombay) 5(9): 1187–97.

119   Mintz, S. (1974) *Caribbean Transformation*. Chicago: Aldine.

120   Mintz, S. (1977) The So-called World System: Local Initiative and Local Response. *Dialectical Anthropology* 2: 253–70.

121   Mitchell, J. C. (1956) *The Kalela Dance: Aspects of Social Relationships among Urban Africans in North Rhodesia*. Manchester: Manchester University Press.

122   Modelski, G. (1978) The Long Cycle of Global Politics and the Nation State. *Comparative Studies in Society and History* 20: 214–35.

123   Murdock, G. P. (1937) Correlations of Matrilineal and Patrilineal Institutions. In *Studies in the Science of Society presented to Albert Galloway Keller*, ed. G. P. Murdock, pp. 445–70. New Haven: Yale University Press.

124   Mwaria, C. B. (1980) Household Structure in a Changing Economy: The Case of Akimba. Presented at the 78th Annual Meeting of the American Anthropological Association Washington, DC.

125   Naroll, R. (1973) Holocultural Theory Tests. In *Main Currents in Cultural Anthropology*, ed. R. Naroll and F. Naroll, pp. 309–84. Englewood, NJ: Prentice-Hall.

126   Nash, J. (1977) Women in Development: Dependency and Exploitation. *Development and Change* 8: 161–82.

127   Nash, J. (1975) Nationalism and Fieldwork. *Annual Review of Anthropology* 4: 225–45.

128   Nash, J. (1975) Dependency and the Failure of Feedback. *Proceedings of the 40th International Congress of Americanists*, Rome, 1972, pp. 507–27. Rome: Tilgher.

129   Nash, J. (1979) Anthropology of the Multinational Corporations. In *New Directions in Political Anthropology*, ed. M. B. Leons and F. Rothstein, pp. 173–200. Westport, Conn: Greenfield.

130   Nash, J. (1979) *We Eat the Mines and the Mines Eat US: Dependency and Exploitation in Bolivian Tin Mines*. New York: Columbia University Press.

131   Nash, J. (1979) Women, Men, and the International Division of Labor. Presented at the Annual Meeting of the Latin American Studies Association, Pittsburgh.

132   O'Laughlin, B. (1975) Marxist Approaches in Anthropology. *Annual Review of Anthropology* 4: 341–70.

133   Oxaal, I., Barnet, T., and Booth, D., eds. (1975) *Beyond the Sociology of Development: Economy and Society in Latin America and Africa*. London/Boston: Routledge & Keegan Paul.

134   Padgug, R. A. (1976) Problems in the Theory of Slavery and Slave Society. *Science and Society* 40: 3–27.

135   Palloux, C. (1973) *Les Firms Multinationales et le proces d'Internationalisation*. Paris: Maspero.

136   Parry, J. H. (1963) *The Age of Reconnaissance*. London: Weidenfeld & Nicolson.

137   Pelto, P. J. (1963) *The Snowmobile Revolution; Technology and Social Change in the Arctic*. Menlo Park, Calif: Cummings.

138 Polanyi, K., Arensberg, C., and Pearson, N., eds. (1957) *Trade and Markets in the Early Empires: Economics in History and Theory.* New York: Praeger.

139 Powdermaker, H. (1962) *Coppertown: Changing Africa; The Human Situation on the Rhodesian Copperbelt.* New York: Harper & Row.

140 Radcliffe-Brown, A. R. (1940) On Social Structure. *Journal of the Royal Anthropological Institute of Great Britain and Ireland* 7: 1–12.

141 Rey, P. P. (1975) The Lineage Mode of Production. *Critical Anthropology* 3: 27–70.

142 Roberts, B. R. (1978) The Bases of Industrial Cooperation in Huancayo. See no. 111, pp. 129–62.

143 Roberts, B. R., Samaniego, C. (1978) The Evolution of Pastoral Villages and the Significance of Agrarian Reform in the Highlands of Central Peru. See no. 111, pp. 241–63.

144 Rollwagon, J. (1980) New Directions in Urban Anthropology: Building an Ethnography and an Ethnology of the World System. *Urban Life* 9, pp. 370–82.

145 Root, H. (1978) The Debate on the Origins of the 'Modern World System': The Ottoman Example. A review article. *Comparative Studies in Society and History* 20: 626–9.

146 Roseberry, W. (1976) Rent, Differentiation and the Development of Capitalism among Peasants. *American Anthropologist* 78: 45–58.

147 Rubbo, A. (1975) La extensión del capitalismo rural: sus efectos sobre las mujeres negras en la valle de Cauca, Colombia occidental. *Estudios Andinas* 5: 119–38.

148 Safa, H. I. (1979) Multinationals and the Employment of Women in Developing Areas. Presented at the Annual Meeting of the Latin American Studies Association, Pittsburgh.

149 Sahlins, M. D. (1958) *Social Stratification in Polynesia.* Seattle: University of Washington Press.

150 Salisbury, R. F. (1962) *From Stone to Steel: Economic Consequences of a Technological Change in New Guinea.* Victoria: Melbourne University Press.

151 Schneider, H. K. (1975) Economic Development and Anthropology. *Annual Review of Anthropology* 3: 271–92.

152 Schneider, J. (1977) Was There a Pre-capitalist World-system? *Journal of Peasant Studies* 6: 20–8.

153 Schneider, J. and Schneider, P. (1975) *Culture and Political Economy in Western Sicily.* New York: Academic.

154 Scott, C. (1976) Peasants, Proletarianization and the Articulation of Modes of Production: The Case of Sugar Cane Cutters in Northern Peru 1948–69. *Journal of Peasant Studies* 3: 321–47.

155 Seddon, D. (1978) Economic Anthropology or Political Economy? Two Approaches to the Analysis of Pre-Capitalist Formation in the Maghred. See no. 29, pp. 61–109.

156 Sella, D. (1977) The World System and its Dangers. *Journal of Peasant Studies* 6: 29–32.

157 Silverman, S. (1965) Patronage and Community–Nation Relationships in Central Italy. *Ethnology* 4: 172–89.

158 Skocpol, T. (1977) Wallerstein's World Capitalist System: A Theoretical and Historical Critique. *American Journal of Sociology* 82: 1075–90.

159 Smith, C. T. (1980) Community Wealth Concentration: Comparisons in General Evolution and Development. *Economic Development and Cultural Change* 28: 801–17.

160 Smith, D. (1978) Domination and Containment: An Approach to Modernization. *Comparative Studies in Society and History* 20: 177–213.

161 Smith, G. A. and Cano, P. (1978) Some Factors Contributing to Peasant Land Occupations in Peru: The Example of Huasicancha 1963–68. See no. 111, pp. 163–90.

162 Snow, R. T. (1980) The New International Division of Labor and the U.S. Workers: The Case of the Electronics Industry. *Occasional Paper of the East-West Center, Honolulu.*

163 Stavenhagen, R. (1965) Classes, colonialismo y acculturacion: Ensayo sobre un sistema de relaciones interetnicas en Mesoamerica. *America Latina* 6(4): 63–104.

164 Stavenhagen, R. (1966) Social Aspects of Agrarian Structure in Mexico. *Sociological Research* 33 (3-Autumn): 463–85.

165 Strauss, D. and Orans, M. (1976) "Reply" [to an article on z factors] *Current Anthropology* 17: 754–5.

166 Strickon, A. and Greenfield, S. M., eds. (1972) *Structure and Process in Latin America.* Albuquerque: University of New Mexico Press.

167 Sunkel, O. (1972) Big Business and *'dependencia'. Foreign Affairs* 50: 517–31.

168 Sunkel, O. (1973) Transnational Capitalism and National Disintegration. *Social and Economic Studies* 22: 132–76.

169 Taussig, M. T. (1980) *The Devil and Commodity Fetishism in South America.* Chapel Hill: University of North Carolina Press.

170 Terray, E. (1972) Historical Materialism and Segmentary Lineage-based Societies. In *Marxism and "Primitive" Societies. Two Studies*, pp. 93–186. Trans. M. Klopper. New York: Monthly Review.

171 Terray, E. (1974) Long Distance Exchange and the Formation of the State: The Case of the Abron Kingdom of Gyaman. *Economy and Society* 3: 314–45.

172 Thompson, E. P. (1963) *The Making of the English Working Class.* New York: Vintage.

173 Trimberger, K. E. (1979) World Systems Analysis: The Problem of Unequal Development. *Theory and Society* 8: 127–37.

174 Tylor, E. B. (1889) On a Method of Investigating the Development of Institutions: Applied to Laws of Marriage and Descent. *Journal of the Royal Anthropological Institute of Great Britain and Ireland* 18: 245–72.

175 Udy, S. H. Jr. (1973) Cross-cultural Analysis: Methods and Scope. *Annual Review of Anthropology* 2: 253–70.

176 Wachtel, H. M. (1975) Class Consciousness and Stratification in the Labor Process. In *Labor Market Segmentation*, ed. R. C. Edwards et al., pp. 95–122. Lexington: Heath.

177 Walker, P. (1979) *Between Labor and Capital.* Boston: South End.

178 Wallerstein, I. (1966) *Social Change: The Colonial Situation.* New York: Wiley.

179 Wallerstein, I. (1974) Dependence in an Interdependent World: The Limited Possibilities of Transformation within the Capitalist World Economy. *African Studies Review* 17: 1–26.

180 Wallerstein, I. (1974) The Rise and Future Demise of the World Capitalist System: Concepts for Comparative Analysis. *Comparative Studies in Society and History* 16: 387–415.

181 Wallerstein, I. (1975) The Present State of the Debate on World Inequality. In *World Inequality: Origins and Perspectives on the World System*, ed. I. Wallerstein, pp. 9–29. Montreal/Quebec: Black Rose Books.

182 Wallerstein, I. (1975) *The Modern World System: Capitalist Agriculture and the Origins of the European World Economy in the Sixteenth Century.* New York: Academic.

183 Wallerstein, I. (1976) Semi-peripheral Countries and the Contemporary World Crisis. *Theory and Society* 3: 461–83.

184 Wallerstein, I. (1980) *The Modern World System II: Mercantilism and the Consolidation of the European World Economy.* New York: Academic.

185 Watson, W. (1958) *Tribal Cohesion in a Money Economy.* Manchester: Manchester University Press.

186 Weeks, J. (1978) Fundamental Economic Concepts. See no. 29, pp. 21–30.

187 Weisskopf, T. (1979) Marxist Perspectives on Cyclical Crisis. In *U.S. Capitalism in Crisis*. New York: Union for Radical Political Economy.

188 Williams, E. (1944) *Capitalism and Slavery*. Chapel Hill: University of North Carolina Press.

189 Wolf, E. (1959) *Sons of the Shaking Earth*. Chicago: University of Chicago Press.

190 Wolf, E. (1964) *Anthropology*. Englewood Cliffs, NJ: Prentice-Hall.

191 Wolf, E. (1969) *Peasant Wars of the Twentieth Century*. New York: Harper & Row.

192 Wolfe, A. W. (1963) The African Mineral Industry. Evolution of a Supranational Level of Integration. *Social Problems* 10: 153–64.

193 Wolfe, A. W. (1977) The Supranational Organization of Production: An Evolutionary Perspective. *Current Anthropology* 18: 615–36.

194 Wolpe, H. (1972) Capitalism and Cheap Labour-power in South Africa: From Segregation to Apartheid. *Economy and Society* 1: 425–56.

195 Wolpe, H. (1975) The Theory of Internal Colonialism: The South African Case. See no. 133, pp. 229–52.

196 Worsley, P. (1964) *The Third World*. Chicago: University of Chicago Press.

197 Zenner, W. P. and Jarvenpa, R. (1980) Scots in the Northern Fur Trade: A Middleman Minority Perspective. *Ethnic Groups* 2: 189–219.

198 Zucher, H. G. (1977) More Solutions to Galton's Problem. *Current Anthropology* 18: 117–91.

Part IV

Cosmopolitics: Confronting a New Millennium

- define globalization & liberalization
- globalization is important to relationships w/ int
  because g. has the potential to create a
  world w/o borders
- why is G affecting relationships?
  (273)
- view of areas (275)

Introduction

In this final section the anthropology of politics is brought up to date, as it observes and analyses the twenty-first century world. The authors represented here are divided in their understanding of the processes that have led to the present. The first three chapters are theoretical explorations of disorder and globalization. Anderson (chapter 2) suggests that to understand what is happening in the world today we need go no further back in history than to the break-up of European empires after the Second World War and the resultant great power struggle between the United States and the Soviet Union. Appadurai (chapter 22) focuses specifically on globalization, viewing it as a feature of postmodernity, and thus calls for new research programs. Friedman (chapter 23), on the other hand, explains today's global insecurities in terms of a global model of expansion and contraction. A list of the concepts he introduces provides something of a preface to the concerns explored in the remaining readings in Part IV. These concepts include: the transhistorical; neo-traditionalism; modernity, modernism, postmodernism; developmentalism; alterity; ethnicity, ethnification, ethnic hierarchies, multi-ethnification; individualization; tribalism, *Gemeinschaft*, communitarianism; nation-state, national identity, trans-nationalization; modern world system, cosmopolitanism and globalization.

The Cold War arose over the fate of Central Europe, but it was fought almost everywhere else. And here, with political anthropology still primarily concerned with Third-World countries – now polarized (imprecisely) as North and South – chapters 24–6 address the question of civil wars and civil insurrection that meet with "policing" by outside forces. Independent African nations appear to have been particularly vulnerable to what are being called "failing state" processes. Drawing on five African case studies, Reyna's "Deadly Developments" (chapter 24) asks why. Another essay that might well have been included here is Sharon Hutchinson's ethnography of militarization and civil war among the Nuer of the Sudan that was placed in Part II (chapter 2). This might well be read again in the light of Reyna's findings.

Nugent's ethnography of a peripheral situation in Peru (chapter 25) presents a contrasting instance of state-building in Peru. In Chachapoyas, a mountain region bordering the modern nation state of Peru, subaltern groups appealed to the state to take over the region in order that they might maintain their customary rights. Nugent explores their embrace of the enlightenment values in modernity. Tsing (chapter 26), on the other hand, writes about a peripheral region in Indonesia that has been marginalized politically and culturally by the state but whose people are able, through protesting and reinterpreting marginality, to take advantage of their exclusion. In her highly original ethnography, *In the Realm of the Diamond Queen* (1993), Tsing interleaves her own analysis with a fieldwork narrative of her encounter with Uma Adang, a potent spiritual leader who listens to voices from a legendary past so that she may teach others the traditions of her community. Here, in chapter 26, space permits only the beginning and end of this unique narrative.

Throughout the Reader, a number of chapters invoke distinct notions of the state and, as we have seen (in the Introduction), state theory has a very long pedigree in political anthropology. Here, what is striking is the recognition and delineation of alternatives to classical Enlightenment models. Ong and Glick Schiller (chapters 27 and 28) pursue the thorny question of sovereignty and the modern nation state by expanding on the idea of "flexible citizenship" and "long distance nationalisms." Glick Schiller suggests that a new form of nation state has come into being with globalization – the transnational nation state – and with it new forms of citizenship – trans-border citizenship. Ong finds the mobility of Chinese cosmopolitans, and the accommodation to it made by several nations' citizenship legislation, pushes to the utmost the parameters of flexible capitalism and flexible citizenship. Biographically and autobiographically nuanced, these chapters exemplify what in an age of globalization might be called "grounded cosmopolitanism." Ong's ethnographic essay (surrounded, as it is in P. Cheah, and B. Robbins, *Cosmopolitics: Thinking and Feeling Beyond the Nation* (1998) by critics anguished over Kant) is a breath of fresh air in the hothouse intellectual atmosphere of global warming.

The ethnographies of chapters 25–8 carry us beyond classic western models of society and nation state. The next two chapters are concerned with the problematic break-up of the Soviet Union, which, after the Second World War, was made up of Russia and its immediate neighbors. Socialism has, of course, long been recognized as an other-than-capitalist route to modernity but one that had been neglected by political anthropologists, as Kathleen Gough reminded them in 1968 (see chapter 10). With the fall of the Berlin Wall in 1989, both the need and the opportunity came for a reassessment of the relation of ideology to actuality in Russia and the newly independent eastern European nation states. The two readings here (chapters 29 and 30) reflect the work of two anthropologists who have conducted field research in eastern bloc countries behind what was called in Cold War days the "Iron Curtain." To understand the uncertain, even disordered status of former Soviet territories now it is necessary to understand where they have been. Hence Verdery's analysis (in chapter 29) of "real Socialism," the workings of the socialist system prior to the collapse of communism throughout the eastern bloc in 1989. Very different is Humphrey's account of her return to two collective farms in a remote region in eastern Russia where she had first carried out field research as a graduate student in the 1960s. What had actually changed? "Marx went away but Karl stayed behind" is Caroline Humphrey's enigmatic answer (see chapter 30).

The classic route to modernization in the eyes of eighteenth-century political economists lay in "improvement," whether in education or agriculture. June Nash (chapter 20) reviewed the 1970s argument that Europe *under*developed the Third World, and that development *per se* led to increased local, national, and global inequalities. Edelman (chapter 32) reviews a current debate on "development" that pits Foucauldian scholars, who believe that "underdevelopment" is a fiction propagated by international agencies with their own agendas, against those who say that this analysis deflects from recognition of profound inequalities between First- and Third-World countries. Ferguson (chapter 31) provides a pioneering analysis of the first position based on field research in Lesotho in South Africa; Edelman's critique (chapter 32) of the argument is extracted from his ethnography, *Peasants against Globalization: Rural Social Movements in Costa Rica* (1999).

What one finds constantly referred to as the banality of evil in the world today is addressed by Farmer in an essay "On Suffering and Structural Violence" (chapter 33). An anthropologist who is also a doctor in the nation state of Haiti, he writes of those who have suffered "from below." Through a series of biographical cameos, he conveys something of the despair of poverty and AIDS, and the terror of police brutality and military aggrandizement.

Finally, two very different papers take us back full circle to where we began with Enlightenment principles and research imagination (chapters 34 and 35). A critical discussion of commitment and responsibility in the academy (by Gledhill) is followed by, as it were, the sting in the scorpion's tail: a speech Gayatri Chakravorty Spivak delivered at Cape Town University in South Africa. The subject was academic freedom. As a "native informant" (Spivak's self-selected term for herself) she turns the tables on the academy in her prescient observations on where academic freedom truly lies.

SUGGESTIONS FOR FURTHER READING

For a suggestion that anthropological knowledge plays a crucial role in defining what any cosmopolitan project might be about, see D. Harvey "Cosmopolitanism and the Banality of Geographical Evils," *Public Culture* 12(2) (2000): 529–64. A useful reference tool is: E. Hobsbawm, *The Age of Extremes: A History of the World, 1914–1991* (New York: Pantheon Books, 1994). For key programmatic analyses of the literature on civil society, see J. L. J. Comaroff. Introduction, in *Civil Society and the Political Imagination: Critical Perspectives* (Chicago: University of Chicago Press, 1999) and on millennial capitalism: "First Thoughts on a Second Coming," *Public Culture* 12(2) (2000): 291–343.

On the philosophical turn in present day anthropology: C. Geertz, *Available Light: Anthropological Reflections on Philosophical Topics*, ch. XI, "The World in Pieces: Culture and Politics at the End of the Century" (Princeton: Princeton University Press, 2000). On the contested concepts of the Enlightenment and the neo-Kantians: E. Wolf, *Envisioning Power: Ideologies of Dominance and Crisis*, ch. 2 (Berkeley: University of California Press, 1999). For a reading of Kant, Hegel, and Marx as remote discursive precursors, rather than as repositories of "ideas": G. C. Spivak, *A Critique of Postcolonial Reason: Toward a History of the Vanishing Present* (Cambridge, Mass.: Harvard University Press, 1999). For the decentering of capitalism from its Eurocentrism: A. Dirlik, *After the Revolution: Working to Global Capitalism*, (Hanover, NH: Wesleyan University Press, 1994).

For the inequalities of global change: D. Massey, "Power Geometry and a Progressive Sense of Place," in *Mapping the Futures: Local Cultures, Global Change* ed. J. Bird, et al. (London: Routledge, 1993). For a critique of models of global capitalism that fail to consider cultural commitments: L. Rofel, *Other Modernities: Gendered Yearnings in China after Socialism*

(Berkeley: University of California Press, 1999). For refutation of her theme: A. Ong, *Flexible Citizenship: The Cultural Logics of Transnationality* (Durham, NC: Duke University Press, 1999) and L. Lowe, and D. Lloyd, *The Politics of Culture in the Shadow of Capitalism* (Durham, NC: Duke University Press, 1997).

For ethnography that underpins theorizing on the modern state, modernity and marginality, see D. Nugent, *Modernity at the Edge of Empire: State, Individuals and Nation in the Northern Peruvian Andes, 1885–1935* (Stanford: Stanford University Press, 1997) and A. Tsing, *In the Realm of the Diamond Queen: Marginality in an Out-of-the-Way Place* (Princeton: Princeton University Press, 1993). On representation and subaltern groups, see G. Bond, Introduction, in G. Bond, and A. Gilliam, (eds.) *The Social Construction of the Past: Representation as Power* (New York: Routledge, 1997). For thoughts on the interplay of ethnography, theory, and critique in European post-socialist studies (with a conclusion on Foucault's "governmentality") see T. Wolf, "Cultures and Communities in the Anthropology of Eastern Europe and the Former Soviet Union," *Annual Review of Anthropology* 29 (2000): 195–216. For an ethnography of political terror in Western Europe: A. Feldman, *Formations of Violence: The Narrative of the Body and Political Terror in Northern Ireland* (Chicago: University of Chicago Press, 1991).

The postmodernist discussion of "development" is, perhaps, best represented by A. Escobar, *Encountering Development: The Making and Unmaking of the Third World* (Princeton: Princeton University Press, 1995). For an ethnographic testing of "new-movement" theories in an unusual setting – the city of Palermo in Sicily – see J. Schneider and P. Schneider, "From Peasant Wars to Urban Wars: The Anti-Mafia Movement in Palermo," in G. Sider, and G. Smith, (eds.) *Between History and Histories: The Making of Silences and Commenmorations*, pp. 230–62 (Toronto: Toronto University Press, 1997).

21

The New World Disorder

Benedict Anderson

It is quite possible that historians of the 2050s, looking back into our now closing century, will pick out, as one deep tectonic movement stretching across more than two centuries, the disintegration of the great polyethnic, polyglot, and often poly-religious monarchical empires built up so painfully in mediaeval and early modern times. In most cases the disintegration was accompanied by great violence, and was often followed by decades of civil and interstate wars. In the 1770s the first nation-state was born in North America out of armed resistance to imperial Britain, but it was inwardly so divided that it subsequently endured the bloodiest civil war of the nineteenth century. Out of the prolonged collapse of the Spanish empire between 1810 and 1830 came the brutal despotisms, rebellions and civil strife that have plagued Latin America until our own time. As a result of the Great War of 1914–1918 the Hohenzollern, Habsburg, Romanov and Ottoman empires blew up, leaving in their wake a congeries of small, weak, and generally unstable nation-states in Central and Eastern Europe and in the Near East. The fall of the Ch'ing empire in 1911 opened two generations of civil wars in China. Partition in British India, massive interethnic violence in Sri Lanka, the Thirty Years War in Vietnam, the continuing civil strife in Northern Ireland, the bloody collapse of the Ethiopian Empire, the horrors in Uganda and Zaire – all in differing ways can be seen as outcomes of the same long process.

Seeming to counteract this tectonic movement – which involved, of course, liberation as much as disintegration – was Communism in its early internationalist form. The success of the Bolshevik Revolution in the very heart of the evaporated Romanov empire permitted Lenin and his associates to reassemble many of the pieces of that empire during the early 1920s. But the Soviet Union did not regard itself as a huge new nation-state, rather as a sort of model for a future in which nationalism as a political principle would be finally superseded. Indeed, for a time, under the centralized control of a multiethnic and militant Communist Party, nationalism was reduced generally to a politically insignificant 'cultural' ethnicity.

From *New Left Review* 193 (1992), pp. 3–13.

This phase, however, did not last very long. Reeling under the ferocious onslaught of Hitler's armies, Stalin and his associates discovered that encouraging nationalism was crucial to the war effort. In a famous speech delivered on 7 November 1941, the CPSU's general secretary urged his listeners thus: 'Let the manly images of our great ancestors Aleksandr Nevsky, Dmitri Donskoi, Kuzma Minin, Dmitri Pozharsky, Aleksandr Suvorov and Mikhail Kutusov inspire you in this war.' Prosperous Europe has today forgotten how much it owes both to Stalin and to Russian nationalism for the destruction of the Nazi empire. But in the war's aftermath, it proved implausible to add the communized states of Eastern Europe to the USSR, and thus began a pluralization of Communist states bearing national names. After Eastern Europe came Yugoslavia, North Korea, China, Cuba, and Vietnam, Laos and Cambodia. In 1979 the first, and, it may well be, the last, wars between Communist states broke out, as Vietnam invaded Cambodia and China invaded Vietnam. A historical logic was already visible, if then generally unnoticed. Nationalism could be halted, but not permanently restrained or superseded. So that, during the 1980s, Stalin's empire was just as surely imploding as Churchill's had done.

Meanwhile, also in the aftermath of World War II, the bourgeois colonial empires of France, Britain, Holland, Belgium, and even Portugal collapsed, creating by the end of the 1970s a United Nations with four times the membership that had made up the pioneering League of Nations half a century earlier.

The last reincarnation of a pre-modern empire is China, where Mao Tse-tung, taking leaves out of the books of both Stalin and the Sons of Heaven, attempted heroically to create a socialist state on imperial foundations. But it was named The People's Republic of China, and thus represented from the start a forlorn attempt to stretch the short, tight skin of nationalism over a vast multiethnic, multireligious, multilinguistic imperium. One is reminded of France in the 1950s, which still included Algeria as a part of the metropole, and which fought a horrifically brutal – and futile – war to keep things that way. It is thus quite possible that Mao's empire too will crumble, at least at the edges. Taiwan is already effectively independent. Tibet may well follow, and perhaps China's Turkic and Mongol zones in due course. There is no reason to think that late empires die more peacefully than their predecessors, or that the aftermaths of their dying are any less tormented.

Dangerous Fancies

In what perspective does it make sense to reflect on all of this? There are, I believe, four misconceptions which ought to be discarded from the outset. The first is that what is going on is 'fragmentation' and 'disintegration' – with all the menacing, pathological connotations these words bring with them. For this language makes us forget the decades or centuries of violence out of which Frankensteinian 'integrated states' such as the United Kingdom of 1800, which included all of Ireland, were constructed. Should we not really regard such 'integrations' as pathological when we see how calmly the Irish Republic and the United Kingdom have coexisted since the former was established in 1921 – after decades of often violent repression and resistance? Or when we observe the brutal warfare still continuing in 'integrated' Northern Ireland? Behind the language of 'fragmentation' lies always a Panglossian conservatism that likes to imagine that every status quo is nicely normal.

The second prejudice, which is related to, and grows partly out of the first, has to do with the relationship between capitalism, markets, and state size. Unreflecting commentators – on the Left and on the Right – frequently assume that 'small' countries, with limited resources in raw materials and labour, are somehow not 'real' countries or are 'barely' viable in the face of the industrial giants and the exigencies of the world capitalist economy. This kind of thinking goes back to early modern mercantilism, and was given additional force in the late eighteenth century by the American nationalist Alexander Hamilton, and in the mid-nineteenth century by the German nationalist Friedrich List, who argued for 'big' nation-states on the grounds that only these had sufficiently large internal markets to permit 'economic sovereignty' and a seriously competitive place in an industrializing world.

But revisionist students of political economy have for some time been arguing that in a highly interconnected world economy it is quite often small, ethnically and religiously homogeneous countries that do best. In Europe they point to The Nether-lands and Finland, Norway and Austria by comparison with Italy, France and the United Kingdom. In Asia they refer us to South Korea and Thailand, Singapore and Japan, by comparison with India, Indonesia, Sri Lanka or Pakistan. The argument is quite simple at bottom. It is that in such small, homogeneous countries the sense of national solidarity is especially strong, making it easier for political and economic leaders to ask for sacrifices without expensive coercion, to develop smoother indus-trial relations, and effectively to seek specialized niches in the international division of labour. Conversely, domestically troubled giants like the United States or India face enormous political difficulties in bending and renovating the national economy in the contemporary environment.

The third fancy is that 'transnational corporations' have somehow made nation-alism obsolete. After all, people say, we see General Electric abandoning high-wage America to locate its new plants in labour-cheap Venezuela and Zambia, as well as hiring Venezuelans and Zambians as local managers. This view, however, overlooks the obvious facts that the effective controllers of General Electric are overwhelm-ingly American citizens, live in America, are active politically in America, and can be quite antagonistic to Japanese, or German, or French 'transnationals'. Their indiffer-ence to the plight of American workers is not at all new, and is in fact easier to get away with because of the vast size of the United States.

The fourth prejudice is that there is some inscrutable connection between capital-ism and 'peace', such that the 'free market' is instinctively juxtaposed not merely to the command economy but to war. This idea flies flatly in the face of all the historical evidence. No country fought more wars in the nineteenth century than 'free trade' Britain. No country has fought more wars in the second half of the twentieth century than would-be free-market America. Both World Wars were instigated by capitalist giants.

All four fancies are not merely profoundly conservative. To the extent that powerful leaders in big countries actually believe them, they are dangerous, for they have the cumulative effect of encouraging such people to imagine that they stand for progress and peace, while their adversaries stand for 'narrow' nationalism, sectionalism, and often 'terrorism'. In turn, this view encourages them to unleash the preponderant military power at their disposal to make their wishes prevail. A simple example is Indonesia's bloody 'integration' of the old Portuguese colony of East Timor, which between 1975 and 1980 took the lives of one third of the local population. Today, in the face of ever bolder resistance to this 'integration', the regime in Jakarta prepares for more repression against 'disintegrationists', 'separatists' and 'anti-Indonesian elements'. Everyone sensible knows that all significant violence would cease the minute Jakarta agreed to quit East Timor and leave its wretched and heroic people alone.

Modern Imaginings

What, then, accounts for the driving power of nationalism and its much less respectable younger relation 'ethnicity'? And how are the two related? Two common types of explanation quite clearly can not stand serious investigation. One is that they are the natural creatures of economic discontent and relative deprivation. It is true that many nationalist and ethnic movements build on, or exploit, such discontents. Yet these same discontents have also fired a wide variety of other, often competing, social movements – socialist, communist, religious, millenarian, and so forth. Nonetheless, many of these competitors, for a variety of reasons, seem today to have lost their ideological power for the time being. Hence nationalism and ethnicity are very likely to move in to take their place. We are seeing a good deal of this 'moving-in' in today's Eastern Europe, where once-staunch Stalinists are turning themselves into strident nationalists. The other explanation, typically propounded by the political leaders of nationalist and ethnic movements, is that they represent deep historical memories and traditional communities. In fact, however, such movements are distinctly modern imaginings, and none go back further than the last quarter of the eighteenth century. The truth is that it is precisely their modernity which gives nationalism and ethnicity such contemporary power.

The two most significant factors generating nationalism and ethnicity are both linked closely to the rise of capitalism. They can be described summarily as mass communications and mass migrations. Up until the nineteenth century the vast majority of the people in even the most advanced states could neither read nor write, and for the most part lived and died near where their ancestors had lived and died before them. But capitalism, and especially industrial capitalism, changed all this, first in Europe and the Americas, later, and with increasing speed, around the rest of the world.

Capitalism linked to the technology of printing had already created in early modern times an impressive production of books in vernacular languages. In the nineteenth century appeared the mass-oriented newspaper, consumed not merely by the book-reading middle classes but by the growing working classes, who, unlike their peasant forebears, had to be made literate to function effectively in factories and their new urban environments. Governments, intensely aware of the educated-manpower needs of capitalism and of their own conscript-based, industrialized military machines, began developing modern school systems, with standardized textbooks, standardized curricula, and standardized examinations – in the politically dominant vernaculars. (Imperialism quickly spread these structures and habits to the colonized territories.) In conjunction with the spread of the political doctrines of republicanism, liberalism and popular democracy, print capitalism brought into being mass publics who began to imagine, through the media, a new type of community: the nation. In the twentieth century, with the development of radio and television, these impulses have been enormously reinforced, and stretch still further, in that their messages are accessible to people who do not have to be very literate in the dominant vernacular – messages, furthermore, which have a colloquial, auditory and visual immediacy that print can scarcely match.

Mass Migration and the World Market

Mass migration also took on a new character in early modern times in that it was stimulated less by disaster and war than by commerce and capitalism's development of increasingly rapid and safe long-distance transportation. Over the seventeenth, eighteenth and nineteenth centuries millions of minimally free Europeans and millions of enslaved Africans moved across the Atlantic to the Americas. In the nineteenth century there came an extraordinary market- and state-induced flow of non-Europeans from continent to continent. Chinese to California, Southeast Asia and Australia; Indians to South America, Africa, Southeast Asia and Oceania, followed by Armenians, Lebanese, Arabs, and so many others. In our own time the pace is fast, and likely to increase in speed, thanks to the train, the bus and the aeroplane: Koreans in Canada, Filipinos in Italy, Thais in Japan, Turks in Germany, West Indians in England, Algerians in France – in their tens, if not hundreds of thousands. To be sure, many are 'pushed' by political repression in their homelands, but the great majority are 'pulled' by exactly that force – the market – which George Bush imagines as a force for peace and order, but all modern history shows to be the most deeply subversive institution that we know.

Human bodies, though caught up in the vortex of the market, are not merely another form of commodity. As they follow in the wake of grain and gold, rubber and textiles, petrochemicals and silicon chips, they carry with them memories and customs, beliefs and eating habits, musics and sexual desires. And these human characteristics, which, in their places of origin, are usually borne lightly and unselfconsciously, assume quickly a drastically different salience in the diasporas of modern life. It is no accident that nationalism's historical debut occurred in the Americas among the descendants of Scots and Castilians who shared language and religion with Scots and Spaniards in Europe, but who had rarely seen Scotland or Castile. The metropoles thought of them scornfully as 'creoles' or 'colonials' – as it were, non-European Europeans – and this imposed, placeless, identity eventually fused with attachment to their non-European homes, to create the possibility of becoming Mexicans, Venezuelans and 'Americans'. Such people, however, were peculiarly fortunate compared to their successors elsewhere. 'Debased' they might be in the eyes of the imperial metropole, but they were still more or less 'white', still spoke European languages, and still followed European religions. They could not be treated with the full brutality inflicted on Indians, Africans and Asians. Furthermore, they were following the market out of the metropole, not back into it. In the Americas they quickly made themselves masters of the indigenous populations. (Following independence from the metropoles, they encouraged huge new immigrations from non-British and non-Spanish Europe to consolidate this domination and to promote accumulation in a labour-scarce environment). Afterwards, only in Australia, New Zealand, Canada and South Africa could their example be followed. In all later market migrations, people moved away from the periphery towards more inward centres, they had no choice but to be subordinated, and they were never regarded even as 'debased Europeans'.

The scale and speed of these modern market-driven migrations made any traditional form of gradual assimilation to the new environments very difficult. In the face of bewilderingly alien environments it was only to be expected that the migrants would turn to each other for moral and economic support – and so they clustered in ghettoes small or large – in Detroit, Berlin, Huddersfield, São Paolo, or Marseilles. More serious still, capitalism paradoxically also held them, in strange ways, in their homelands' grip. For one thing, they could, in principle, easily go home, by the same ships, trains, buses and aeroplanes that had vacuumed them out of those homes in the first place. The telex, the telephone and the post office encouraged them to keep 'in touch', in a way unimaginable in earlier centuries. Hence many of them dreamed of circulatory migration rather than of finding a new permanent home, even if that was what, finally, they found themselves stuck with. But it was not only local and familial memories that they brought with them. Capitalism had its own way of helping them imagine a more mediated identity. We may recall the famous photograph of a Peloponnesian *Gastarbeiter* sitting mournfully in his tiny room in some anonymous German industrial town – Stuttgart perhaps? The pitiful little room is bare of any decoration except a travel poster of the Parthenon, produced en masse by Lufthansa, with a subscription, in German, encouraging the gazer to take a Holiday in Sunny Greece. This Lufthansa Parthenon is transparently not a real memory for the melancholy worker. He has put it on his wall because he can read it as sign for 'Greece', and – in his Stuttgart misery – for an 'ethnicity' that only Stuttgart has encouraged him to imagine.

On the other side, the mass appearance, in settled communities, of thousands of immigrants, did not, and will not, fail to produce its own ethnicizations. Le Pen's neofascist movement in France finds its strongest support among two once visibly antagonistic groups: workers who used to be faithful supporters of the French Communist Party but whose rundown neighbourhoods are exactly where the poor immigrants are compelled to cluster; and former *pied-noir* (putatively 'white' colonial) elements who fled free Algeria in 1962, and who despite their Maltese, Italian, Spanish and Levantine ancestries, feel themselves more than ever French. Neo-Nazis and skinheads behind the recent outrages in United Germany, the National Front in the United Kingdom, 'White Power' extremists in the United States – who advertize themselves 'ethnically' as the *real* Germans, English or Americans – are also in part responses to the labour flows created on a mass scale by contemporary world capitalism.

Dangerous Convergences

There is still another way in which the market is making a special contribution to the new world disorder, and it intersects frequently with the upheavals sketched out above. In the early days of industrialism, the munitions industries in the advanced Western states operated largely outside the market. They typically had but a single customer, the state, produced commodities to customer specifications, charged administered prices, and were, because of imperial rivalries, usually surrounded with a wall of secrecy. But by the 1880s, some of these munitions giants, for example

Armstrong in Britain and Krupp in Germany, had broken out of the state's mono-psonistic grip, and were building an infant world arms market. Characteristically, these conglomerates' free-market customers were weak, peripheral and agrarian states which were incapable of constructing the high-tech metallurgical and chemical plants necessary for making modern weapons of their own on a mass scale. Thus British and American arms flowed to the recently independent states of South America, German weapons primarily to Eastern Europe and the Ottoman Empire. For two basic reasons, this process picked up increasing speed after World War I. The first was the collapse of the Romanov, Habsburg, Ottoman, Hohenzollern and Ch'ing empires, and the proliferation in the debris of a host of new, weak, agrarian nation-states, also completely incapable of self-armament. The second was the new speed with which weapons systems were becoming obsolete as the pace of invention accelerated: in one generation, aeroplanes, submarines, aircraft carriers, tanks and poison gas were all born. The great munitions industries were now in the business of supplying their core customers with the most advanced and expensive war machinery possible, but also selling off obsolescent, cheaper lines of goods on the world market.

The logic behind these developments only deepened its thrust after World War II, as technological innovation picked up further speed, and as the number of weak, agrarian states proliferated. But two new conditions substantially aggravated the situation. On the one hand, as a result of the oil crisis of 1973, the world saw for the first time immensely *rich* weak, agrarian states, such as Saudi Arabia, Iran and Iraq, which had the purchasing power to acquire 'first-class' arms from the industrial cores. On the other hand, the onset of the Cold War pitted two superpowers in a global struggle fought largely through proxies in the periphery, precisely because the two powers were terrified by the prospect of a nuclear war between themselves. As a matter of state policy, military-assistance programmes on a vast scale developed, largely outside the international market, in that their beneficiaries' bills were often paid for by the superpowers themselves. Hence the massive arms races of the 1960s, 1970s and 1980s in the Near East, South, Southeast, and East Asia, Latin America, and even Africa. The character of superpower competition in the periphery also encouraged both sides to sell or grant quite sophisticated weapons to customer-clients who were not the leaderships of nation-states: guerrillas, rebels, terrorists and counter-terrorists, above all in zones where the rival superpower was hegemonic. We recall American operations against Soviet-influenced Afghanistan, Angola and Cuba, and Soviet operations against American-influenced South Africa and various parts of Latin America. In a substantial number of such cases, superpower military support was provided to subgroups which, to a greater or lesser degree, defined themselves in nationalist, ethnic or racial terms. (The temptations were particularly great in Asia and Africa. There, nineteenth- and early-twentieth-century imperialisms had forcibly 'integrated', within iron colonial cages, a huge variety of older polities, ethnolinguistic groups and religious communities. The independent successor-states born after World War II were thus peculiarly vulnerable to external manipulation of ethnic sentiments.)

The example of the superpowers was quickly followed by intermediary powers: small industrial countries such as France and Britain; and barely industrial states which enjoyed special relations with a superpower, such as Israel, or surplus wealth, such as Iran. Some at least of these states have been attempting to go nuclear despite the efforts of the existing nuclear club to maintain its exclusive membership. Finally, a substantial number of Third World states, incapable of producing sophisticated armaments themselves, have proved quite ready to divert arms received or bought from the cores to friendly opposition groups in neighbouring states with which they have serious bones to pick (for example, Tanzania's military support of the opponents of Idi Amin, or India's arming of the early Bengali rebellion against Old Pakistan).

Up to a point, it is plausible to argue that the end of the Cold War and the implosion of the Soviet Union may to some extent reduce the flow of munitions around the world. But Moscow's contribution to the flow was always substantially smaller than that of Washington, let alone of the West as a whole. Furthermore, it was largely state-directed and outside the market. At the same time, half a century of Cold War has created huge military-industrial complexes in the West, which will powerfully resist attempts to curb their reach, and for which the world arms market – with its substantial new customers in Eastern Europe – remains an irresistible magnet. Arms production itself has spread quite rapidly outside the old cores – to Brazil and Argentina, Israel, India, China, even places like Thailand and Indonesia. It may even be that the decline in world fears of a major nuclear war will further stimulate the working of the market, in that the drive to sell may be less inhibited by large strategic and/or moral considerations.

From the beginnings of nationalism, based as this culture was on an idea of popular sovereignty, it was accepted a priori that one central guarantor of the reality of that sovereignty was a national army. Even in such core industrial polities as Germany, France and Japan, however, these national armies soon played a central role in domestic politics. In the weak peripheral states, militaries largely armed and trained from the outside were even more likely to turn inwards, as the nineteenth-century experience of Latin America shows. The world today is full of national armies that have never fought an external enemy, but continue to torment their own fellow-citizens.

Among the many reasons for this introversion have been, especially in the ex-colonial periphery, the processes of decolonization itself, as well as the temptations posed by the general absence of countervailing domestic powers in poor, weak, and still heavily agrarian nations. In the first place, when the imperial powers began creating local militaries in the colonies, they trained them for purposes of domestic control. The Burma Rifles, for example, were destined to be deployed only in British Burma and against domestic Burmese resistance to British rule. In the second place, for obvious political reasons, they recruited on a heavily ethnicized basis, characteristically favouring backward and/or Christian minorities: 'Martial Races' in India, Ambonese in the Dutch Indies, Karens in Burma, Berbers in Algeria, Ibos in Nigeria, and so forth. The transfer of sovereignty therefore often created a fundamental and dangerous antagonism between an ethnic minority in control of the most powerful domestic organization, and majorities or pluralities that claimed state power on the basis of popular elections and representative government. Even where coups did not rapidly ensue, militaries were too important for the new national governments not to attempt to seize control of recruitment into the officer corps. Under the best of conditions – that is, where some genuine conception of national representation in the military was adhered to – majoritarianism usually threatened the hitherto powerful minorities inside the military with the long-term erosion of their ascendancy, and, perhaps, their ability to help their fellow ethnics in time of trouble. In other cases, such as in Latin America, recruitment to the officer corps was heavily biased on class and ethnic-racial lines, generally excluding 'Indians', and favouring creoles and mestizos from the middle and upper classes. Small wonder then that militaries have been extensively used in the periphery to maintain power structures which, despite nationalist rhetoric, have been profoundly ethnicized. Still less wonder that discontent and rebellion against such status quos should have also disposed themselves along ethnic, quasi-ethnic, or racial lines.

Hence, despite the end of the Cold War, dangerous convergences that were already born in the nineteenth century show every sign of continuing to develop: market-led proliferation of weapons-systems, mythologization of militaries as *sine qua non* symbols and guarantors of national sovereignty, and ethnicization of officer corps.

The Emergence of the Long-distance Nationalist?

There are profoundly deep economic, social and cultural forces at work here, over which political leaderships even in advanced, 'democratic' states have only tangential control. To sense these forces one does not need to go outside Old Europe itself. As the crow flies, Belfast is less than 500 kilometres from London, but has been an armed camp for the past twenty-five years [since the late 1960s], despite British use of the most sophisticated urban counter-insurgency methods against the IRA, and despite British leaders as aggressive as Margaret Thatcher. The IRA survives not only because of its local nationalist appeal and its ruthless methods, but because it has gained political and financial support in the United States and inside England, weapons on the international arms market, and training and intelligence from Libya and in the Near East. Belgrade is less than 1,000 kilometres from Berlin, capital of the most powerful state in Europe and hub of the European Community. But Berlin, the Community and the United States seem largely impotent in the face of the civil war destroying Old Yugoslavia. Belgrade is the headquarters of a putatively 'national' army which was and is disproportionately Serbian and is now being used for Serbian rather than Yugoslavian ends. Croat politicians, on the other hand, have been highly active on the world arms market, and draw substantial resources from emigrant Croat communities in various countries around the world.

What these instances show is not at all that nationalism is obsolete. Rather, the vast migrations produced over the past 150 years by the market, as well as war and political oppression, have profoundly disrupted a once seemingly 'natural' coincidence of national sentiment with lifelong residence in fatherland or motherland. In this process 'ethnicities' have been engendered which follow nationalisms in historical order, but which are today also linked to such nationalisms in complex and often explosive ways. This is why some of the most strongly 'Irish nationalist' supporters of the IRA live out their lives as 'ethnic Irish' in the United States. The same goes for many Ukrainians settled in Toronto, Tamils in Melbourne, Jamaicans in London, Croats in Sydney, Jews in New York, Vietnamese in Los Angeles, and Turks in Berlin. It may well be that we are faced here with a new type of nationalist: the 'long-distance nationalist' one might perhaps call him. For while technically a citizen of the state in which he comfortably lives, but to which he may feel little attachment, he finds it tempting to play identity politics by participating (via propaganda, money, weapons, any way but voting) in the conflicts of his imagined *Heimat* – now only fax-time away. But this citizenshipless participation is inevitably non-responsible – our hero will not have to answer for, or pay the price of, the long-distance politics he undertakes. He is also easy prey for shrewd political manipulators in his *Heimat*.

22

Grassroots Globalization and the Research Imagination

Arjun Appadurai

Anxieties of the Global

Globalization is certainly a source of anxiety in the US academic world. And the sources of this anxiety are many: social scientists (especially economists) worry about whether markets and deregulation produce greater wealth at the price of increased inequality. Political scientists worry that their field might vanish along with their favorite object, the nation-state, if globalization truly creates a "world without borders." Cultural theorists, especially cultural Marxists, worry that in spite of its conformity with everything they already knew about capital, there may be some embarrassing new possibilities for equity hidden in its workings. Historians, ever worried about the problem of the new, realize that globalization may not be a member of the familiar archive of large-scale historical shifts. And everyone in the academy is anxious to avoid seeming to be a mere publicist of the gigantic corporate machineries that celebrate globalization. Product differentiation is as important for (and within) the academy as it is for the corporations academics love to hate.

Outside the academy there are quite different worries about globalization that include such questions as: What does globalization mean for labor markets and fair wages? How will it affect chances for real jobs and reliable rewards? What does it mean for the ability of nations to determine the economic futures of their populations? What is the hidden dowry of globalization? Christianity? Cyber-proletarianization? New forms of structural adjustment? Americanization disguised as human rights or as MTV? Such anxieties are to be found in many national public spheres (including that of the United States) and also in the academic debates of scholars in the poorer countries.

Among the poor and their advocates the anxieties are even more specific: What are the great global agencies of aid and development up to? Is the World Bank really committed to incorporating social and cultural values into its developmental agenda? Does Northern aid really allow local communities to set their own agendas?

From *Public Culture* 12(1) (2000), pp. 1–19.

Can large banking interests be trusted to support microcredit? Which parts of the national state are protectors of stakeholding communities and which parts are direct affiliates of global capital? Can the media ever be turned to the interests of the poor?

In the public spheres of many societies there is concern that policy debates occurring around world trade, copyright, environment, science, and technology set the stage for life-and-death decisions for ordinary farmers, vendors, slum-dwellers, merchants, and urban populations. And running through these debates is the sense that social exclusion is ever more tied to epistemological exclusion and concern that the discourses of expertise that are setting the rules for global transactions, even in the progressive parts of the international system, have left ordinary people outside and behind. The discourse of globalization is itself growing dangerously dispersed, with the language of epistemic communities, the discourse of states and inter-state fora, and the everyday understanding of global forces by the poor growing steadily apart.

There is thus a double apartheid evolving. The academy (especially in the United States) has found in globalization an object around which to conduct its special internal quarrels about such issues as representation, recognition, the "end" of history, the spectres of capital (and of comparison), and a host of others. These debates, which still set the standard of value for the global professoriate, nevertheless have an increasingly parochial quality.

Thus the first form of this apartheid is the growing divorce between these debates and those that characterize vernacular discourses about the global, worldwide, that are typically concerned with how to plausibly protect cultural autonomy and economic survival in some local, national, or regional sphere in the era of "reform" and "openness." The second form of apartheid is that the poor and their advocates find themselves as far from the anxieties of their own national discourses about globalization as they do from the intricacies of the debates in global fora and policy discourses surrounding trade, labor, environment, disease, and warfare.

But a series of social forms has emerged to contest, interrogate, and reverse these developments and to create forms of knowledge transfer and social mobilization that proceed independently of the actions of corporate capital and the nation-state system (and its international affiliates and guarantors). These social forms rely on strategies, visions, and horizons for globalization on behalf of the poor that can be characterized as "grassroots globalization" or, put in a slightly different way, as "globalization from below." This essay is an argument for the significance of this kind of globalization, which strives for a democratic and autonomous standing in respect to the various forms by which global power further seeks to extend its dominion. The idea of an international civil society will have no future outside of the success of these efforts to globalize from below. And in the study of these forms lies an obligation for academic research that, if honored, might make its deliberations more consequential for the poorer 80 per cent of the population of the world (now totalling 6 billion) who are socially and fiscally at risk.

To take up this challenge to American academic thought about globalization, this essay moves through three arguments. The first is about the peculiar optical challenges posed by the global. The second is about area studies – the largest institutional epistemology through which the academy in the United States has apprehended much of the world in the last fifty years. The third concerns the very ground from which academics typically and unwittingly speak – the category of "research" itself.

These three steps bring me to a conclusion about the relations between pedagogy, activism, and research in the era of globalization.

The Optics of Globalization

Globalization is inextricably linked to the current workings of capital on a global basis; in this regard it extends the earlier logics of empire, trade, and political dominion in many parts of the world. Its most striking feature is the runaway quality of global finance, which appears remarkably independent of traditional constraints of information transfer, national regulation, industrial productivity, or "real" wealth in any particular society, country, or region. The worrisome implications of this chaotic, high velocity, promiscuous movement of financial (especially speculative) capital have been noted by several astute critics (Greider 1997; Rodrik 1997; Soros 1998, among others) so I will not dwell on them here. I am among those analysts who are inclined to see globalization as a definite marker of a new crisis for the sovereignty of nation-states, even if there is no consensus on the core of this crisis or its generality and finality (Appadurai 1996; Rosenau 1997; Ruggie 1993; Sassen 1996).

My concern here is with the conditions of possibility for the democratization of research about globalization in the context of certain dominant forms of critical knowledge, especially as these forms have come to be organized by the social sciences in the West. Here we need to observe some optical peculiarities. The first is that there is a growing disjuncture between the globalization of knowledge and the knowledge of globalization. The second is that there is an inherent temporal lag between the processes of globalization and our efforts to contain them conceptually. The third is that globalization as an uneven economic process creates a fragmented and uneven distribution of just those resources for learning, teaching, and cultural criticism that are most vital for the formation of democratic research communities that could produce a global view of globalization. That is, globalization resists the possibility of just those forms of collaboration that might make it easier to understand or criticize.

In an earlier, more confident epoch in the history of social science – notably in the 1950s and 1960s during the zenith of modernization theory – such epistemological diffidence would have been quickly dismissed, since that was a period when there was a more secure sense of the social in the relationship between theory, method, and scholarly location. Theory and method were seen as naturally metropolitan, modern, and Western. The rest of the world was seen in the idiom of cases, events, examples, and test sites in relation to this stable location for the production or revision of theory. Most varieties of Marxist theory, though sharply critical of the capitalist project behind modernization theory, nevertheless were equally "realist," both in their picture of the architecture of the world system and in their understanding of the relationship between theory and cases. Thus much excellent work in the Marxist tradition had no special interest in problems of voice, perspective, or location in the study of global capitalism. In short, a muscular objectivism united much social science in the three decades after World War II, whatever the politics of the practitioners.

Today, one does not have to be a postmodernist, relativist, or deconstructionist (key words in the culture wars of the Western academic world) to admit that political subjects are not mechanical products of their objective circumstances, that the link between events significantly separated in space and proximate in time is often hard to explain, that the kinds of comparison of social units that relied on their empirical separability cannot be secure, and that the more marginal regions of the world are not simply producers of data for the theory mills of the North.

Flows and Disjunctures

It has now become something of a truism that we are functioning in a world fundamentally characterized by objects in motion. These objects include ideas and ideologies, people and goods, images and messages, technologies and techniques. This is a world of flows (Appadurai 1996). It is also, of course, a world of structures, organizations, and other stable social forms. But the apparent stabilities that we see are, under close examination, usually our devices for handling objects characterized by motion. The greatest of these apparently stable objects is the nation-state, which is today frequently characterized by floating populations, transnational politics within national borders, and mobile configurations of technology and expertise.

But to say that globalization is about a world of things in motion somewhat understates the point. The various flows we see – of objects, persons, images, and discourses – are not coeval, convergent, isomorphic, or spatially consistent. They are in what I have elsewhere called relations of disjuncture. By this I mean that the paths or vectors taken by these kinds of things have different speeds, axes, points of origin and termination, and varied relationships to institutional structures in different regions, nations, or societies. Further, these disjunctures themselves precipitate various kinds of problems and frictions in different local situations. Indeed, it is the disjunctures between the various vectors characterizing this world-in-motion that produce fundamental problems of livelihood, equity, suffering, justice, and governance.

Examples of such disjunctures are phenomena such as the following: media flows across national boundaries that produce images of well-being that cannot be satisfied by national standards of living and consumer capabilities; flows of discourses of human rights that generate demands from workforces that are repressed by state violence which is itself backed by global arms flows; ideas about gender and modernity that circulate to create large female workforces at the same time that cross-national ideologies of "culture," "authenticity," and national honor put increasing pressure on various communities to morally discipline just these working women who are vital to emerging markets and manufacturing sites. Such examples could be multiplied. What they have in common is the fact that globalization – in this perspective a cover term for a world of disjunctive flows – produces problems that manifest themselves in intensely local forms but have contexts that are anything but local.

If globalization is characterized by disjunctive flows that generate acute problems of social well-being, one positive force that encourages an emancipatory politics of globalization is the role of the imagination in social life (Appadurai 1996). The imagination is no longer a matter of individual genius, escapism from ordinary life, or just a dimension of aesthetics. It is a faculty that informs the daily lives of ordinary people in myriad ways: it allows people to consider migration, resist state violence, seek social redress, and design new forms of civic association and collaboration, often across national boundaries. This view of the role of the imagination as a popular, social, collective fact in the era of globalization recognizes its split character. On the one hand, it is in and through the imagination that modern citizens are disciplined and controlled – by states, markets, and other powerful interests. But it is also the faculty through which collective patterns of dissent and new designs for collective life emerge. As the imagination as a social force itself works across national lines to produce locality as a spatial fact and as a sensibility (Appadurai 1996), we see the beginnings of social forms without either the predatory mobility of unregulated capital or the predatory stability of many states. Such social forms have barely been named by current social science, and even when named their dynamic qualities are frequently lost. Thus terms like "international civil society" do not entirely capture the mobility and malleability of those creative forms of social life that are localized transit points for mobile global forms of civic and civil life.

One task of a newly alert social science is to name and analyse these mobile civil forms and to rethink the meaning of research styles and networks appropriate to this mobility. In this effort, it is important to recall that one variety of the imagination as a force in social life – the academic imagination – is part of a wider geography of knowledge created in the dialogue between social science and area studies, particularly as it developed in the United States after World War II. This geography of knowledge invites us to rethink our picture of what "regions" are and to reflect on how research itself is a special practice of the academic imagination. These two tasks are taken up below.

Regional Worlds and Area Studies

As scholars concerned with localities, circulation, and comparison, we need to make a decisive shift away from what we may call "trait" geographies to what we could call "process" geographies. Much traditional thinking about "areas" has been driven by conceptions of geographical, civilizational, and cultural coherence that rely on some sort of trait list – of values, languages, material practices, ecological adaptations, marriage patterns, and the like. However sophisticated these approaches, they all tend to see "areas" as relatively immobile aggregates of traits, with more or less durable historical boundaries and with a unity composed of more or less enduring properties. These assumptions have often been further telescoped backward through the lens of contemporary US security-driven images of the world and, to a lesser extent, through colonial and postcolonial conceptions of national and regional identity.

In contrast, we need an architecture for area studies that is based on process geographies and sees significant areas of human organization as precipitates of various kinds of action, interaction, and motion – trade, travel, pilgrimage, warfare, proselytization, colonization, exile, and the like. These geographies are necessarily large scale and shifting, and their changes highlight variable congeries of language, history, and material life. Put more simply, the large regions that dominate our current maps for area studies are not permanent geographical facts. They are problematic heuristic devices for the study of global geographic and cultural processes. Regions are best viewed as initial contexts for themes that generate variable geographies, rather than as fixed geographies marked by pre-given themes. These themes are equally "real," equally coherent, but are results of our interests and not their causes.

The trouble with much of the paradigm of area studies as it now exists is that it has tended to mistake a particular configuration of apparent stabilities for permanent associations between space, territory, and cultural organization. These apparent stabilities are themselves largely artifacts of the specific trait-based idea of "culture" areas, a recent Western cartography of large civilizational land-masses associated with different relationships to "Europe" (itself a complex historical and cultural emergent), and a Cold-War-based geography of fear and competition in which the study of world languages and regions in the United States was legislatively configured for security purposes into a reified map of geographical regions. As happens so often in academic inquiry, the heuristic impulse behind many of these cartographies and the contingent form of many of these spatial configurations was soon forgotten and the current maps of "areas" in "area studies" were enshrined as permanent.

One key to a new architecture for area studies is to recognize that the capability to imagine regions and worlds is now itself a globalized phenomenon. That is, owing to the activities of migrants, media, capital, tourism, and so forth the means for imagining areas is now itself globally widely distributed. So, as far as possible, we need to find out how others, in what we still take to be certain areas as we define them, see the rest of the world in regional terms. In short, how does the world look – as a congeries of areas – from other locations (social, cultural, national)?

For example, the Pacific Rim is certainly a better way of thinking about a certain region today, rather than splitting up East Asia and the Western coast of North America. But a further question is: How do people in Taiwan, Korea, or Japan think about the Pacific Rim, if they think in those terms at all? What is their topology of Pacific traffic?

To seriously build an architecture for area studies around the idea that all "areas" also conceive or produce their own "areas," we need to recognize the centrality of this sort of recursive refraction. In fact this perspective could be infinitely regressive. But we do not have to follow it out indefinitely: one or two moves of this type would lead us a long way from the US Cold War architecture with which we substantially still operate.

Following this principle has a major entailment for understanding the apparatus through which areal worlds are globally produced. This production happens substantially in the public spheres of many societies, and includes many kinds of intellectuals and "symbolic analysts" (including artists, journalists, diplomats, businessmen, and others) as well as academics. In some cases, academics may be only a small part of this world-generating optic. We need to attend to this varied set of public spheres, and the intellectuals who constitute them, to create partnerships in teaching and research so that our picture of areas does not stay confined to our own first-order, necessarily parochial, world pictures. The potential payoff is a critical dialogue between world pictures, a sort of dialectic of areas and regions, built on the axiom that areas are not facts but artifacts of our interests and our fantasies as well as of our needs to know, to remember, and to forget.

But this critical dialogue between world pictures cannot emerge without one more critical act of optical reversal. We need to ask ourselves what it means to internationalize any sort of research before we can apply our understandings to the geography of areas and regions. In essence, this requires a closer look at research as a practice of the imagination.

The Idea of Research

In much recent discussion about the internationalization of research, the problem term is taken to be "internationalization." I propose that we focus first on research, before we worry about its global portability, its funding, and about training people to do it better. The questions I wish to raise here are: What do we mean when we speak today of research? Is the research ethic, whatever it may be, essentially the same thing in the natural sciences, the social sciences, and the humanities? By whatever definition, is there a sufficiently clear understanding of the research ethic in the academic world of North America and Western Europe to justify its central role in current discussions of the internationalization of academic practices?

Such a deliberately naive, anthropological reflection upon the idea of research is difficult. Like other cultural keywords, it is so much part of the ground on which we stand and the air we breathe that it resists conscious scrutiny. In the case of the idea of research, there are two additional problems. First, research is virtually synonymous with our sense of what it means to be scholars and members of the academy, and thus it has the invisibility of the obvious. Second, since research is the optic through which we typically find out about something as scholars today, it is especially hard to use research to understand research.

Partly because of this ubiquitous, taken-for-granted, and axiomatic quality of research, it may be useful to look at it not only historically – as we might be inclined to do – but anthropologically, as a strange and wonderful practice that transformed Western intellectual life perhaps more completely than any other single procedural idea since the Renaissance. What are the cultural presumptions of this idea and thus of its ethic? What does it seem to assume and imply? What special demands does it make upon those who buy into it?

Today, every branch of the university system in the West, but also many branches of government, law, medicine, journalism, marketing, and even the writing of some kinds of fiction and the work of the armed forces must demonstrate their foundation in research in order to command serious public attention or funds. To write the history of this huge transformation of our fundamental protocols about the production of reliable new knowledge is a massive undertaking, better suited to another occasion. For now, let us ask simply what this transformation in our understanding of new knowledge seems to assume and imply.

Consider a naive definition. Research may be defined as the systematic pursuit of the not-yet-known. It is usually taken for granted that the machine that produces new knowledge is research. But the research ethic is obviously not about just any kind of new knowledge. It is about new knowledge that meets certain criteria. It has to plausibly emerge from some reasonably clear grasp of relevant prior knowledge. The question of whether someone has produced new knowledge, in this sense, requires a community of assessment, usually pre-existent, vocational, and specialized. This community is held to be competent to assess not just whether a piece of knowledge is actually new but whether its producer has complied with the protocols of pedigree: the review of the literature, the strategic citation, the delineation of the appropriate universe – neither shapelessly large nor myopically small – of prior, usually disciplinary, knowledge. In addition, legitimate new knowledge must somehow strike its primary audience as interesting. That is, it has to strike them not only as adding something recognizably new to some predefined stock of knowledge but, ideally, as adding something interesting. Of course, boring new knowledge is widely acknowledged to be a legitimate product of research, but the search for the new-and-interesting is always present in professional systems of assessment.

Reliable new knowledge, in this dispensation, cannot come directly out of intu-ition, revelation, rumor, or mimicry. It has to be a product of some sort of systematic procedure. This is the nub of the strangeness of the research ethic. In the history of many world traditions (including the Western one) of reflection, speculation, argu-mentation, and ratiocination, there has always been a place for new ideas. In several world traditions (although this is a matter of continuing debate) there has always been a place for discovery, and even for discovery grounded in empirical observa-tions of the world. Even in those classical traditions of intellectual work, such as those of ancient India, where there is some question about whether empirical observation of the natural world was much valued, it is recognized that a high value was placed on careful observation and recording of human activity. Thus, the great grammatical works of Panini (the father of Sanskrit grammar) are filled with observations about good and bad usage that are clearly drawn from the empirical life of speech communities. Still, it would be odd to say that Panini was conducting research on Sanskrit grammar, any more than that Augustine was conducting research on the workings of the will, or Plato on tyranny, or even Aristotle on biological structures or politics. Yet these great thinkers certainly changed the way their readers thought, and their works continue to change the way we think about these important issues. They certainly produced new knowledge and they were even systematic in the way they did it. What makes it seem anachron-istic to call them researchers?

The answer lies partly in the link between new knowledge, systematicity, and an organized professional community of criticism. What these great thinkers did not do was to produce new knowledge in relation to a prior citational world and an imagined world of specialized professional readers and researchers. But there is another important difference. The great thinkers, observers, discoverers, inventors, and innovators of the pre-research era invariably had moral, religious, political, or social projects, and their exercises in the production of new knowledge were there-fore, by definition, virtuoso exercises. Their protocols could not be replicated, not only for technical reasons but because their questions and frameworks were shot through with their political projects and their moral signatures. Once the age of research (and its specific modern ethic) arrives, these thinkers become necessarily confined to the protohistory of the main disciplines that now claim them or to the footnotes of the histories of the fields into which they are seen as having trespassed. But in no case are they seen as part of the history of research, as such. This is another way to view the much discussed growth of specialized fields of inquiry in the modern research university in the course of the nineteenth and twentieth centuries.

These considerations bring us close to the core of the modern research ethic, to something that underpins the concern with systematicity, prior citational contexts, and specialized modes of inquiry. This is the issue of replicability, or, in the aphoris-tic comment of my colleague George Stocking, the fact that what is involved here is *not search but re-search*. There is of course a vast technical literature in the history and philosophy of science about verifiability, replicability, falsifiability, and the transparency of research protocols. All of these criteria are intended to eliminate the virtuoso technique, the random flash, the generalist's epiphany, and other private sources of confidence. All confidence in this more restricted ethic of new knowledge reposes (at least in principle) in the idea that results can be repeated, sources can be checked, citations can be verified, calculations can be confirmed by one or many other researchers. Given the vested interest in showing their peers wrong, these other researchers are a sure check against bad protocols or lazy inferences. The fact that such direct cross-checking is relatively rare in the social sciences and the humanities is testimony to the abstract moral sanctions associated with the idea of replicability.

This norm of replicability gives hidden moral force to the idea, famously associated with Max Weber, of the importance of value-free research, especially in the social sciences. Once the norm of value-free research successfully moves from the natural sciences into the social and human sciences (no earlier than the late nineteenth century), we have a sharp line not just between such "ancients" as Aristotle, Plato, and Augustine on the one hand and modern researchers on the other, but also a line between researchers in the strict academic sense and such modern thinkers as Goethe, Kant, and Locke. The importance of value-free research in the modern research ethic assumes its full force with the subtraction of the idea of moral voice or vision and the addition of the idea of replicability. It is not difficult to see the link of these developments to the steady secularization of academic life after the seventeenth century.

Given these characteristics, it follows that there can be no such thing as individual research, in the strict sense, in the modern research ethic, though of course individuals may and do conduct research. Research in the modern, Western sense, is through and through a collective activity, in which new knowledge emerges from a professionally defined field of prior knowledge and is directed toward evaluation by a specialized, usually technical, body of readers and judges who are the first sieve through which any claim to new knowledge must ideally pass. This fact has important implications for the work of "public" intellectuals, especially outside the West, who routinely address nonprofessional publics. I will address this question below. Being first and last defined by specific communities of reference (both prior and prospective), new knowledge in the modern research ethic has one other crucial characteristic that has rarely been explicitly discussed.

For most researchers, the trick is how to choose theories, define frameworks, ask questions, and design methods that are most likely to produce research with a plausible shelf life. Too grand a framework or too large a set of questions and the research is likely not be funded, much less to produce the ideal shelf life. Too myopic a framework, too detailed a set of questions, and the research is likely to be dismissed by funders as trivial, and even when it is funded, to sink without a bubble in the ocean of professional citations. The most elusive characteristic of the research ethos is this peculiar shelf life of any piece of reliable new knowledge. How is it to be produced? More important, how can we produce institutions that can produce this sort of new knowledge predictably, even routinely? How do you train scholars in developing this faculty for the lifelong production of pieces of new knowledge that function briskly but not for too long? Can such training be internationalized?

I have already suggested that there are few walks of modern life, both in the West and in some other advanced industrial societies, in which research is not a more or less explicit requirement of plausible policy or credible argumentation, whether the matter is child abuse or global warming, punctuated equilibrium or consumer debt, lung cancer or affirmative action. Research-produced knowledge is everywhere, doing battle with other kinds of knowledge (produced by personal testimony, opinion, revelation, or rumor) and with other pieces of research-produced knowledge.

Though there are numerous debates and differences about research style among natural scientists, policy makers, social scientists, and humanists, there is also a discernible area of consensus. This consensus is built around the view that the most serious problems are not those to be found at the level of theories or models but those involving method: data gathering, sampling bias, reliability of large numerical data sets, comparability of categories across national data archives, survey design, problems of testimony and recall, and the like. To some extent, this emphasis on method is a reaction to widespread unease about the multiplication of theoretical paradigms and normative visions, especially in the social sciences. Furthermore, in this perspective, method, translated into research design, is taken to be a reliable machine for producing ideas with the appropriate shelf life. This implicit consensus and the differences it seeks to manage take on special importance for any effort to internationalize social science research.

Democracy, Globalization, and Pedagogy

We can return now to a deeper consideration of the relationship between the knowledge of globalization and the globalization of knowledge. I have proposed that globalization is not simply the name for a new epoch in the history of capital or in the biography of the nation-state. It is marked by a new role for the imagination in social life. This role has many contexts: I have focused here on the sphere of knowledge production, especially knowledge associated with systematic academic inquiry. I have suggested that the principal challenge that faces the study of regions and areas is that actors in different regions now have elaborate interests and capabilities in constructing world pictures whose very interaction affects global processes. Thus the world may consist of regions (seen processually), but regions also imagine their own worlds. Area studies must deliberate upon this aspect of the relationship between regions, as must any discipline that takes subjectivity and ideology as something more than ephemera in the saga of capital and empire. Such deliberation is a vital prerequisite for internationalizing academic research, especially when the objects of research themselves have acquired international, transnational, or global dimensions of vital interest to the human sciences.

One aspect of such deliberation involves a recognition of the constitutive peculiarities of the idea of research, which itself has a rather unusual set of cultural diacritics. This ethic, as I have suggested, assumes a commitment to the routinised production of certain kinds of new knowledge, a special sense of the systematics for the production of such knowledge, a quite particular idea of the shelf life of good research results, a definite sense of the specialized community of experts who precede and follow any specific piece of research, and a distinct positive valuation of the need to detach morality and political interest from properly scholarly research.

Such a deparochialization of the research ethic – of the idea of research itself – will require asking the following sorts of questions. Is there a principled way to close the gap between many US scholars, who are suspicious of any form of applied or policy-driven research, and scholars from many other parts of the world who see themselves as profoundly involved in the social transformations sweeping their own societies? Can we retain the methodological rigor of modern social science while restoring some of the prestige and energy of earlier visions of scholarship in which moral and political concerns were central? Can we find ways to legitimately engage scholarship by public intellectuals here and overseas whose work is not primarily conditioned by professional criteria of criticism and dissemination? What are the implications of the growing gap, in many societies, between institutions for technical training in the social sciences and broader traditions of social criticism and debate? Are we prepared to move beyond a model of internationalizing academic research that is mainly concerned with improving how others practice our precepts? Is there something for us to learn from colleagues in other national and cultural settings whose work is not characterized by a sharp line between social scientific and humanistic styles of inquiry? Asking such questions with an open mind is not just a matter of ecumenism or goodwill. It is a way of enriching the answers to questions that increasingly affect the relationship between academic research and its various constituencies here in the United States as well.

If we are serious about building a genuinely international and democratic community of researchers – especially on matters that involve cross-cultural variation and intersocietal comparison – then we have two choices. One is to take the elements that constitute the hidden armature of our research ethic as given and unquestionable and proceed to look around for those who wish to join us. This is what may be called "weak internationalization." The other is to imagine and invite a conversation about research in which, by asking the sorts of questions I have just described, the very elements of this ethic could be subjects of debate. Scholars from other societies and traditions of inquiry could bring to this debate their own ideas about what counts as new knowledge and what communities of judgement and accountability they might judge to be central in the pursuit of such knowledge. This latter option – which might be called strong internationalization – might be more laborious, even contentious. But it is the surer way to create communities and conventions of research in which membership does not require unquestioned prior adherence to a quite specific research ethic. In the end, the elements I have identified as belonging to our research ethic may well emerge from this dialogue all the more robust for having been exposed to a critical internationalism. In this sense, Western scholarship has nothing to fear and much to gain from principled internationalization.

It may be objected that this line of reasoning fails to recognize that all research occurs in a wider world of relations characterized by growing disparities between rich and poor countries, by increased violence and terror, by domino economic crises, and by runaway traffic in drugs, arms, and toxins. In a world of such overwhelming material dependencies and distortions, can any new way of envisioning research collaboration make a difference?

Globalization from Below

While global capital and the system of nation-states negotiate the terms of the emergent world order, a worldwide order of institutions has emerged that bears witness to what we may call "grassroots globalization," or "globalization from below." The most easily recognizable of these institutions are NGOs (nongovernmental organizations) concerned with mobilizing highly specific local, national, and regional groups on matters of equity, access, justice, and redistribution. These organizations have complex relations with the state, with the official public sphere, with international civil society initiatives, and with local communities. Sometimes they are uncomfortably complicit with the policies of the nation-state and sometimes they are violently opposed to these policies. Sometimes they have grown wealthy and powerful enough to constitute major political forces in their own right and sometimes they are weak in everything except their transparency and local legitimacy. NGOs have their roots in the progressive movements of the last two centuries in the areas of labor, suffrage, and civil rights. They sometimes have historical links to the socialist internationalism of an earlier era. Some of these NGOs are self-consciously global in their concerns and their strategies, and this subgroup has recently been labelled transnational advocacy networks (hereafter, TANs), whose role in transnational politics has only recently become the object of serious study (Keck and Sikkink 1998). Although the sociology of these emergent social forms – part movements, part networks, part organizations – has yet to be developed, there is a considerable progressive consensus that these forms are the crucibles and institutional instruments of most serious efforts to globalize from below.

There is also a growing consensus on what such grassroots efforts to globalize are up against. Globalization (understood as a particular, contemporary configuration in the relationship between capital and the nation-state) is demonstrably creating increased inequalities both within and across societies, spiraling processes of ecological degradation and crisis, and unviable relations between finance and manufacturing capital, as well as between goods and the wealth required to purchase them. The single most forceful account of this process is to be found in the work of William Greider (1997), though his alarming prognostications have not gone unchallenged (Krugman 1998; Rodrik 1997). Nevertheless, in implying that economic globalization is today a runaway horse without a rider, Greider has many distinguished allies (Garten 1997; Soros 1998). This view opens the prospect that successful TANs might offset the most volatile effects of runaway capital.

Global capital in its contemporary form is characterized by strategies of predatory mobility (across both time and space) that have vastly compromised the capacities of actors in single locations even to understand, much less to anticipate or resist, these strategies. Though states (and what we may call "state fractions") vary in how and whether they are mere instruments of global capital, they have certainly eroded as sites of political, economic, and cultural sovereignty. This sense of compromised sovereignty – to which I referred earlier – is the subject of intense debate among political theorists and analysts, but a significant number of these theorists concede that momentous changes in the meaning of state sovereignty are underway (Keohane 1995; Rosenau 1997; Ruggie 1993; Sassen 1998). These changes suggest that successful transnational advocacy networks might be useful players in any new architecture of global governance.

But – and here is the challenge to the academy – most TANs suffer from their inability to counter global capital precisely in its global dimensions. They often lack the assets, the vision, the planning, and the brute energy of capital to globalize through the capture of markets, the hijacking of public resources, the erosion of state sovereignties, and the control of media. The current geographical mobility of capital is unique in its own history and unmatched by other political projects or interests. Again, there is some debate about whether globalization (as measured by the ratio of international trade to GDP) has really increased over the last century...but a significant number of observers agree that the scale, penetration, and velocity of global capital have all grown significantly in the last few decades of this century (Castells 1996; Giddens 1996; Held 1995), especially when new information technologies are factored in as measures of integration and interconnectivity.

Thus it is no surprise that most transnational advocacy networks have thus far had only limited success in self-globalization, since there is a tendency for stakeholder organizations concerned with bread-and-butter issues to oppose local interests against global alliances. Thus, their greatest comparative advantage with respect to corporations – that they do not need to compete with each other – is underutilized. There are many reasons for this underutilization, ranging from political obstacles and state concerns about sovereignty to lack of information and resources for networking. While the number of nonstate actors has grown monumentally in the last three decades, especially in the areas of human rights and environmental activism (Keck and Sikkink 1998), there is much more confusion about their relative successes in competing with the organized global strategies of states and corporate interests (Matthews 1997).

But one problem stands out. One of the biggest disadvantages faced by activists working for the poor in fora such as the World Bank, the UN system, the WTO, NAFTA, and GATT is their alienation from the vocabulary used by the university-policy nexus (and, in a different way, by corporate ideologues and strategists) to describe global problems, projects, and policies. A strong effort to compare, describe and theorize "globalization from below" could help to close this gap. The single greatest obstacle to grassroots globalization – in relation to the global power of capital – is the lack of a clear picture among their key actors of the political, economic, and pedagogic advantages of counterglobalization. Grassroots organizations that seek to create transnational networks to advance their interests have not yet seen that such counterglobalization might generate the sorts of locational, informational, and political flexibility currently monopolized by global corporations and their national-civic allies.

By providing a complex picture of the relationship between globalization from above (as defined by corporations, major multilateral agencies, policy experts, and national governments) and below, collaborative research on globalization could contribute to new forms of pedagogy (in the sense of Freire 1987) that could level the theoretical playing field for grassroots activists in international fora.

Such an account would belong to a broader effort to understand the variety of projects that fall under the rubric of globalization, and it would also recognize that the world *globalization*, and words like *freedom, choice,* and *justice,* are not inevitably the property of the state-capital nexus. To take up this sort of study involves, for the social sciences, a serious commitment to the study of globalization from below, its institutions, its horizons, and its vocabularies. For those more concerned with the work of culture, it means stepping back from those obsessions and abstractions that constitute our own professional practice to seriously consider the problems of the global everyday. In this exercise, the many existing forms of Marxist critique are a valuable starting point, but they too must be willing to suspend their inner certainty about understanding world histories in advance. In all these instances, academics from the privileged institutions of the West (and the North) must be prepared to reconsider, in the manner I have pointed to, their conventions about world knowledge and about the protocols of inquiry ("research") that they too often take for granted.

There are two grounds for supposing that this sort of exercise is neither idle nor frivolous. The first is that all forms of critique, including the most arcane and abstract, have the potential for changing the world: surely Marx must have believed this during his many hours in the British Museum doing "research." The second argument concerns collaboration. I have already argued that those critical voices who speak for the poor, the vulnerable, the dispossessed, and the marginalized in the international fora in which global policies are made lack the means to produce a systematic grasp of the complexities of globalization. A new architecture for producing and sharing knowledge about globalization could provide the foundations of a pedagogy that closes this gap and helps to democratize the flow of knowledge about globalization itself. Such a pedagogy would create new forms of dialogue between academics, public intellectuals, activists, and policy-makers in different societies. The principles of this pedagogy will require significant innovations. This vision of global collaborative teaching and learning about globalization may not resolve the great antinomies of power that characterize this world, but it might help to even the playing field.

REFERENCES

Appadurai, Arjun. (1996) *Modernity at Large: Cultural Dimensions of Globalization*. Minneapolis: University of Minnesota Press.

Castells, Manuel. (1996) *The Rise of Network Society*. Cambridge, Mass.: Blackwell Publishers.

Freire, Paolo. (1987) *Pedagogy of the Oppressed*. New York: Continuum.

Garten, Jeffrey E. (1997) Can the World Survive the Triumph of Capitalism? *Harvard Business Review* 75: 144.

Giddens, A. (1996) Globalization – A Keynote Address. *UNRISD News* 15: 4–5.

Greider, William. (1997) *One World, Ready or Not: The Manic Logic of Global Capitalism*. New York: Simon Schuster.

Held, David. (1995) *Democracy and the Global Order*. London: Polity Press.

Keck, Margaret E., and Kathryn Sikkink. (1998) *Activists Beyond Borders: Advocacy Networks in International Politics*. Ithaca: Cornell University Press.

Keohane, Robert O. (1995) Hobbes's Dilemma and Institutional Change in World Politics: Sovereignty in International Society. In *Whose World Order?* ed. H. Holm and G. Sorensen. Boulder: Westview Press.

Krugman, Paul R. (1998) *The Accidental Theorist and Other Dispatches from the Dismal Science*. New York: Norton Publishers.

Matthews, Jessica T. (1997) Power Shift. *Foreign Affairs*, January/February: 50–66.

Rodrik, D. (1997) *Has Globalization Gone Too Far?* Washington, DC: Institute for International Economics.

Rosenau, James. (1997) *Along the Domestic-foreign Frontier: Exploring Governance in a Turbulent World*. Cambridge: Cambridge University Press.

Ruggie, John Gerard. (1993) Territoriality and Beyond: Problematizing Modernity in International Relations. *International Organization* 47: 139–74.

Sassen, Saskia. (1996) *Losing Control? Sovereignty in an Age of Globalization*. New York: Columbia University Press.

——. (1998) *Globalization and its Discontents*. New York: The New Press.

Soros, George. (1998) Toward a Global Open Society. *Atlantic Monthly*, January: 20–4, 32.

23

Transnationalization, Socio-political Disorder, and Ethnification as Expressions of Declining Global Hegemony

Jonathan Friedman

The title of this article may appear somewhat misleading insofar as it uses terms such as ethnification and transnationalization which would imply, from my standpoint, that it was a question of the modern world system. However, the research perspective for which I shall be arguing would maintain a transhistorical global framework while modifying the terms that are related to what have been argued to be essentially modern phenomena. There are good reasons for attempting to maintain such a framework. The most important of these is that many of the problems, conflicts, and tragedies of the contemporary world, or the world that is usually referred to in terms of modernity, in the classical sense of the post-Enlightenment world, are issues that have a long history of repetition. I would go further and suggest, as many others have done, that a full understanding of what is happening in today's insecure existence, in which "culture wars" and clashes of civilization abound, can only be understood as a phenomenon that has occurred before and whose mechanisms are not part of some recent "evolution."

The analytical frame for this discussion is a global process model of hegemonic expansion and contraction (Friedman 1994). In periods of expansion a center establishes a dominant position in a larger established realm of control and becomes a focus of identification for the larger arena. The establishment of a global hegemony is thus the establishment of cultural dominance as well, either via homogenization or the ranking of differences.... Contraction of a hegemonic center which is accompanied by the tangential rise of centers in new geographical areas in the midst of a period of political and economic fragmentation (increasing competition) is also a period of combined cultural renewal and disintegration of the larger cultural whole. The current emergence of postmodernism and neo-traditionalism are expressions of

From *International Political Science Review* 19(3) (1998), pp. 233–46, 248–50. Reprinted by permission of Sage Publications Ltd.

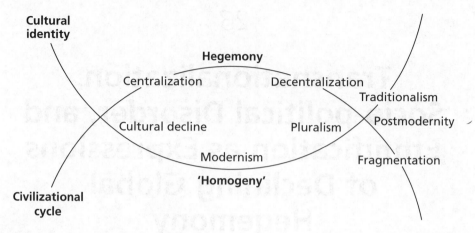

Figure 1 Cultural and Civilization Cycles
Source: Friedman 1994: 39

precisely this kind of breakdown of a formerly hegemonic cultural space. It is accompanied by instability and cultural politics, a competition of identities in an arena in which dominance is no longer exercised. This kind of process can be exemplified as in Figure 1.

The figure is meant to show, as simply as possible, the inverse relation between cycles of hegemony and cycles of cultural identity. In reality, these relations can be very much more complex since such cycles can be distributed within smaller regions of a larger hegemonic order that is in transformation. Thus, while fragmentation is common in the declining imperial structures of Eastern Europe, homogenization, often violent, seems to be occurring in Eastern Indonesia and China. In other words, hegemonic cycles can be relatively local and embedded in larger cycles. A few words about some of the terms is in order here since several different approaches and research traditions are involved in this endeavor.... [T]he terms *modernity, modernism, postmodernity*, and *postmodernism* ... are, in my usage, structural rather than historical. That is, they are meant to be useful in transhistorical analysis. This assumes that modernity emerges in the right kind of social conditions that have been replicated several times and in several places in world history. I do not like the use of definitions, since words such as "modernity" are meant to open exploration rather than closing it. Modernity is a kind of identity space or field of alternative identities that is structured by certain parameters such as individualization and developmentalism, which are themselves generated by the rise of a hegemonic power or zone in a system based on commercial reproduction. The disintegration of larger kinship or other "holistic" social categories (Dumont 1983) leads to a number of new cultural tendencies, a particular distinction between public and private, the separations of state from cosmos, of role from individual, of achieved from ascribed, and of notions of personal and social development (like achievement in the larger world).

Foundational for modernity as an identity space is precisely its alterity, what Campbell (1987) has called the Walter Mitty principle. This implies everything from voluntaristic life-style politics to increasingly collectivist identifications as

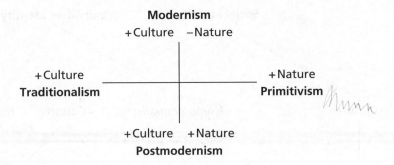

Figure 2 Modernity as an identity space
Source: Friedman 1994: 228

expressed in communitarianism, ethnic and religious movements, and the like. In my discussion of this phenomenon (Friedman 1994) I have used a space defined by four polarities (Figure 2).

Here modernism, traditionalism, primitivism, and postmodernism are four poles of potential identification that define a space of identity variation. Modernism, which dominates in periods of hegemony, is based on rationalist developmentalism where both the cultural and the natural are regarded as problems to be overcome. In periods of decline there is increasing polarization in which neo-traditional investment in cultural roots and religious identity may tend to dominate tendencies toward a more naturalistic primitivism (as in youth cultures) and a more cynical postmodernism. This presentation stresses that traditionalism, primitivism, postmodernism as well as modernism are part and parcel of the culture of modernity rather than external to it. So, when I use the term postmodernity (Figure 1), I am referring to the decline or transformation of the entire space, that is, the establishment of new "non-modern" conditions of identification.

Intersection of Social and Individual Identification

The question of ethnicity and of forms of socio-cultural integration such as empire or nation-state have rarely been explored in a systematic world historical and comparative perspective and I do not propose to do more than offer some suggestions in what follows. In an earlier work (Friedman 1994) I suggested a division of forms of cultural identification into a continuum bounded by a holistic/segmentary identity at one end and individualist/citizenship at the other. In Figure 3 the relation between individual and social identity is traced through the continuum from holistic to commercial capitalist civilizations.

Here the nation-state can vary from the more formal citizenship model of individualist modernism in which voluntary identification and an instrumental view of the state is dominant, to an ethnified version in which the nation is dominant, where the nation-state is converted from a contractual to a familistic-ascriptive model. The question of national solidarity and the experience of "organic" belonging are central to this phenomenon. European nations, with the possible exception of Great Britain, are ethnic states, in which a particular "rooted" population or peoplehood is

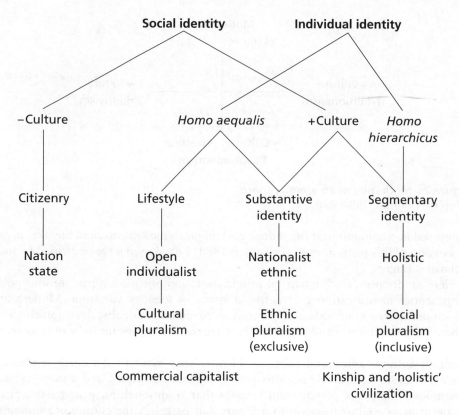

Figure 3   Social and individual identity
Source: Friedman 1994: 34

associated with statehood. I have suggested that the degree of ethnification of such states is dependent on globally determined conditions of existence (Friedman 1994). The United States and other nation-states based on mass immigration are quite different insofar as they lack the clear association of an ethnic identity with the state. In the United States, ethnicity as opposed to "race" is commonly an individual identity arena in which subjects identify themselves in terms of several generations of ancestors from X, Y, and Z (Waters 1990). Mixed ancestry is, logically, an individual issue in such societies, and it is at odds with ethnic group formation. In periods of ethnification even such groups seek collective identities, as in the recent middle-class hybrid and mixed race movement in the United States. This seeking does not imply that national societies such as the United States, Australia, and Canada are entirely different from the societies of Europe, but that the forms of identification are at variance with one another. Cycles of assimilation and multiethnification occur in both cases, but the consequences have been somewhat different; and the immigrant societies have been much weaker in their cultural assimilation than the ethnically based nation-states. National identity in the United States is very much about the state itself, the flag, international success, democracy, and opportunity, while in continental Europe it is more often a question of nature, community, and national roots or history.

In more general and ideal-typical terms there are certain general and common characteristics of commercial civilizations. These are a function, also variable, of the degree of individualization, the degree to which the internal capitalization of society disintegrates local kin, community, and local-regional sodalities (see above). The "liberation" process creates a vacuum with respect to collective identification. This vacuum is filled both with individualist modernism and national identity. The nation-state, in this sense is a product of the Western sector of the modern world system, but it has, I shall argue, its forerunners in the ancient world. Modernism is an identity that, paradoxically, denies all fixed and rooted identities in the sense of culturally defined and essentialist, that is, ethnic. It may be national but in a political-territorial sense rather than an ethnic one. Modernism (which is not identical with "modern" (Friedman 1994) ... is based on the notion of supersession, of growth and development as a general process for individuals and societies (see Figure 2). Fixed identity in such terms is a kind of neurotic paralysis, and tradition is translated into the "repetition compulsion." Modernism reigns supreme in the hegemonic realms of the modern world system, but when hegemony declines, it is a difficult project to maintain. The concomitant of declining modernist identity is an increase in narcissistic tendencies that became the focus of works like that of Lasch (1979), where collective identities become a solution to the threat of ego disintegration. It is in such conditions that roots, ethnicity, religion, and postmodernism become increasingly dominant and that individualism is replaced increasingly by what is referred to as tribalism (Maffésoli 1988), not only in its ethnic form, but as a form of social organization in which a fragmented public sphere becomes increasingly divided into clientelistic hierarchies. This is the "new Middle Ages" referred to by political scientists (Minc 1993). These variations are predicated on a well-developed individualization in which community and tradition or *gemeinschaft*, become essential aspects of the modern fantasy of the world we have lost. Real communitarianism is in this sense a phenomenon of modernity rather than a leftover from the past.

At the other end of the scale are holistic identity formations. These are based on very different and historically more common constructions of the individual subject, in which abrupt weaning and a strong socialization to a cosmologically organized structure of authority located outside of the individual body generates a different kind of ethnic belonging. A segmentary structure of encompassment leads from local kin groups to increasingly inclusive structures up to the State. These are not simply categories of membership, but dynamic principles that constitute the subject in powerful ways. Bruce Kapferer's milestone comparison of Sinhalese and Australian forms of nationalism [1988] demonstrates clearly how the Buddhist State in Sri Lanka is internally organized into individual selfhood in ways that account for the particular nature of ethnic violence.

Comparative Integration

By comparing processes of integration one can gain some insight into the differences that I am trying to elucidate. In much of the work on Southeast Asian societies there is an understanding that individuals and groups can change their identity. Thus highland Kachin of Burma may become Buddhists as they settle among the valley-dwelling Shan, with whom they identify and take up irrigation agriculture instead of their former swiddening (Leach 1954). At a lower segmentary level, in-marrying men in patrilineal societies, who cannot afford bridewealth payments, are often integrated into their new lineages by a process of adoption which may require powerful rituals and a great deal of transformative activity. In both cases, the integrative process is one that turns X into Y. Ethnicity here is situational. It is about the practice of social relations with particular people in a particular place. It is not a question of "life-style" – "today I think I'll be Balinese." Nor is it a question of "blood" or any other traits that are inherited from generation to generation. The subject is not the bearer of several different essential identities because ethnicity is not located in the body, but in the social context. This does not mean that it is instrumental or weak, as can be seen by the Sinhalese example, but that it is the context itself, rather than the body, which is the site of the investment of the self.

In larger imperial organizations the segmentary nature of incorporation becomes salient. It can take a variety of forms of what has usually been referred to as pluralism. Such states and empires have been characterized by hierarchy among constituent groups. In South Asia this hierarchy is most elaborate in the caste system, in which a similar set of principles organizes the hierarchical incorporation of a great variety of social and ethnic groups, all of which are ranked in a homogeneous scale of purity/impurity. Studies of the expansion of the caste system into marginal areas provide evidence of the way this assimilation to a hierarchical order via Hinduiza-tion may have occurred historically. Other more loosely organized models are typical for the great East Asian and Middle Eastern empires, most recently exempli-fied in the Ottoman millet system. In the last-named system there is no need for assimilation in the modern sense, because the society is founded upon difference. In large parts of the world, this was not merely a cultural difference, but relative social autonomy. Many multi-ethnic empires were effectively multi-societal empires linked only by centralized taxation and/or economic specialization. Note, however, that this differentiation is extremely hierarchical in terms of power and privilege. The state is, in such systems, not a representative of the people, but an ethnic or multi-ethnic class whose primary characteristic is that of authoritarian rule over a great multiplicity of peoples.

It is in commercial city-states and in nation-states that one finds a strong tendency to both individualization and homogenization. In such states, there is a tendency of the state itself to be transformed from a ruling class to a governmental body. It becomes representative of the people and there are clear democratic proclivities as well. Questions of loyalty, legal equality, and solidarity become central. These are issues of social homogeneity, that is, the establishment of criteria of trust among citizens. These issues also imply a practice of boundedness, the notion that "This is our society, our state. It is a function of our will. It does not belong to everyone, that is, to outsiders," who could include foreign traders and a large slave population. While authors like McNeill have discussed this continuity between nation-state and city-state, they seem to argue that the city-state develops out of a real commu-nity of farmers, so that the city-state itself is no more than an outgrowth of an original homogeneous society. But the history of ancient city-states does not corroborate this scenario. Rather, they seem to emerge out of protracted struggles in which state–class elites are gradually transformed into something closer to "gov-ernments."

Multi-ethnicity in History

The argument that multi-ethnic societies have been the rule rather than the exception in history is, of course, true, but this is because the history of the world has been the history of empires and segmentary states, and such social organizations, however multi-ethnic, were also ethnic hierarchies. It is, perhaps, the latter aspect of such societies that is the secret of their relative ethnic peace. Significant, from our point of view, is that multi-ethnicity is a phenomenon that emerges and disappears, and is not merely a type of organization. Thus, the emergence of the Hellenistic empires was a movement from a city-state national ideology to a cosmopolitan and multi-ethnic ideology. The same transformation characterizes the movement from the Roman Republic to the Empire and it is clearly reflected in a whole series of changes. The Cynic school of philosophy provided an entire discourse, interestingly postmodern in character, for this shift, disavowing all social institutions, including marriage and property. They recognized only the natural world as a socially relevant fact. And in the world all men were equal – whether rich or poor, Greek or barbarian, citizen or foreigner. However, since the Cynics surmised that most men were also fools, and therefore incapable of using their freedom and equality to full individual advantage, they had to conclude that only the wise could actually be cosmopolites and make the world their city (Bozeman 1994: 103).

The Ciceronian system of education based on the cultivation of Roman virtues was transformed by the time of Augustus to one more accommodating of the Empire, in which all were to be citizens of Rome and where there was even a growing fear of foreigners, to which I shall return below. As communities that practice homogeneity expand into empires they also move toward a hierarchical heterogeneity. But as the latter begin to decline, the heterogeneity begins to assert itself as a political force. This takes us to the central theme of this discussion, the relation between cycles of expansion and contraction in global hegemonies and the forms of transnational or trans-state relations.

Global Process and Equifinality

All of these variations, and even discontinuities, in the way in which populations can be integrated and in the way cultural differences are maintained, do not necessarily help in accounting for the issues outlined in the title of this article. Part of the reason is that they pertain primarily to the global systemic and as such are products of a dominant commercial and urban organized central zone. There is no transnationalization without nation-states, or at least without some comparatively interesting type of organization, such as the city-states and empires which date back to antiquity. Ethnification is a more serious issue, for while it may be organized in different terms, that is, segmentary and inclusive vs. essentialist and exclusive, the practice of identification and differentiation can lead to similarly violent outcomes. In fact it is logical for essentialization to accompany ethnification no matter what the social and cultural conditions.

The claim that ethnicity is a product of modernity is true only if by ethnicity we mean a form of cultural identity that is essentialist, homogenizing and exclusive in conditions of peace. The idea that the individual is an X because he contains the substance (blood) of X may well be typically modern, but it is also the case that stereotypification in conditions of conflict is practically universal (Lévi-Strauss 1952). Disorder is, of course, a universal, along with many of the forms that it takes such as social fragmentation, individual crises, new collective identifications, and what I have referred to as ethnification. When a social arena becomes disordered by crisis, its particular reactions vary as a result of its variable constitution. Among the tribal and chiefly societies of highland Burma and Assam a series of phenomena are unleashed by crisis (often endogenously generated), including head-hunting, witchcraft, the appearance of were-tigers, anti-fertility and anti-chiefly movements and revolts. Such phenomena may invert the entire workings of former expansive societies in astonishing ways (Friedman 1997). Phenomena such as "cargo cults," witchcraft epidemics and cannibalism (Ekholm-Friedman 1993) are widespread reactions to crises in societies organized primarily by kinship. Now while these are surely quite specific local forms of action, there is plenty of evidence to suggest that they are not as specific as has usually been assumed. Societies in crisis are often societies in which people "cannibalize" one another in various ways, in which hate and fear rampage through the arenas of daily life and sow the ground for violent conflict. So rather than argue for the existence of entirely different phenomena I would suggest that there are interesting family resemblances at work.

Exploring the Model of Hegemonic Decline in Global Systems

I do not intend to present a model of global systems here, as that would take too much space (see Friedman 1994). Rather, I would like to suggest a series of inter-linked phenomena that seem to occur in periods of hegemonic decline. To begin with, I do not assume that decline in hegemony is anything like a general decline in the larger global system. On the contrary, periods of hegemonic decline are periods of commercial expansion, due to the process of decentralization itself. In fact it is the decentralization of capital (abstract wealth) accumulation in hegemonic organizations that is the basis of hegemonic decline. And it is the hegemons themselves that are the source of such decentralization because of the gradient of profitability or economic advantage that emerges in periods of strong centrality. The movement of wealth out of the hegemonic center is expressed in the processes of relocation of industrial production, not least of what are called modern mass production industries. Old centers become more oriented to consumption, to high levels of welfare spending, and to postindustrial and postmodern forms of wealth (so-called culture and information "industries," land and other forms of speculation) while new emergent areas in the system take over larger percentages of the former basic industrial activities, such as heavy industry and the production of mass consumption goods. Historically, the movements of textile, pottery, and other production have been important indicators of centrality and decentralization. Today textiles/clothing are still major indicators of such movements, but the entire gamut of mass consumption goods in the world market follows suit to a large degree. Even so-called high tech industries tend to globalize in today's world.

This is not, in distinction to the common view of globalization, an evolution to a higher stage of economic development: "Before we were local, now we are global," but primarily a phase that has occurred throughout the history of global systems (Ekholm-Friedman and Friedman 1987; Friedman 1994). Globalization is in such terms simply the phase of decentralization itself, in which a hegemony is replaced by a period of increased competition, political decentralization, and a shift of accumulation to a new region of the world system. The only factor that might alter this tendency to shift is the rapidity of the cycle itself. For largely technological reasons, not only in transportation rates and costs, but also in the speed of financial transactions and the ability of capital to move quickly from one location to another, one can argue that the hegemonic periodicities of the system have become so short as to preclude the establishment of new hegemons. In such cases we have a new ball game in which a generalized global competition might become normalized.

In any case the tendencies at present are still somewhat old-fashioned. The globalization of capital has led to the formation of a powerful Pacific Rim zone having the fastest growth rates in the world rather than a more even distribution of capital investment. Thus, an increasing degree of multinationalization should not detract us from understanding the differential flows of capital in the world system. In 1956 the United States had 42 of the top 50 corporations, a clear sign of hegemony over world production. In 1989 that number had dropped to 17. Europe as a whole has a larger number (21) of the 50 top firms today than the United States. While production and export have increased unabated since the 1960s, the developed market economies have seen a decrease in their share of total world production from 72 to 64 percent while in the developing countries it has more than doubled. Between 1963 and 1987 the US share of world manufacturing has decreased from 40.3 to 24 percent. Japan has increased its portion from 5.5 to 19 percent in the same period. West Germany is stable at around 9–10 percent, but the UK has declined from 6.5 to 3.3 percent. France, Italy, and Canada also have declined somewhat in this period. "It is especially notable that in the East and Southeast Asian NICs manufacturing growth rates remained at a high level throughout the 1970s and 1980s whereas those of the leading developed market economies fell to half or less of their 1960s levels" (Dicken 1992: 27). This is reflected in the changing rankings in the world arena, while at the same time the world leaders lost shares in the total world export of manufacturing (see Table 1).

Table 1 World Arena Rankings (1978, 1989) and Percentage of World Export Manufacturing (1963, 1989), after Dicken 1992

	World Arena Rankings		World Export of Manufacturing (%)		
Country	1978	1989	Country	1963	1989
Hongkong	27	11	Japan	6	9
Taiwan	21	12	W. Germany	15	11
Korea	20	13	UK	11	5
China	33	14	USA	17	12
Mexico	40	20			

The Question of Transnationalization

There are several uses of the term "transnational" in the various literatures on globalization. Most common and interesting is the political economy literature itself. Here some history is also worthwhile. The literature begins as late as the 1960s and 1970s, concentrating on the phenomenon of the internationalization of enterprise. The term "multinational corporation" is the most common and this refers to what appears to be a new kind of power structure in which firms establish themselves increasingly in international arenas where advantages are greater than in the home market. The reasons for the internationalization of firms and its consequences for local labor and other economic factors were debated for quite some time. It seems to have been assumed in this period that such corporations had central headquarters that were nationally rooted. I criticized this concept on the grounds that it implied that profits were repatriated, which seemed contradicted by the fact of increasing capital investment in the global arena. The concept of multinational corporation was replaced by that of the transnational corporation, a more evolutionary concept in which it seems that the corporation is no longer linked to a particular place, but in some versions, hovers above the world in a transnational ether. The problem with this concept is that it often implies that there is a space equivalent to the global, something more than the relations between localities.

The other notion of the transnational refers to the movement of people, information, and goods in the global arena. It is sometimes characterized as a movement of culture, a globalization of meaning, via the media, via diaspora formation (mass migration), and via the movement of commodities. This literature is clearly an expression of a certain consciousness of what appears to be a changing world order. The time–space compression to which Harvey (1990) refers is the background for such consciousness, but it is most explicit among intellectuals and academics whose professions require a certain awareness (however minimal) of such expanding horizons. In Harvey's terms, this is a quantitative rather than a qualitative change. It does not mean that somehow the world has, quite recently, become "a single place," an ecumene of interconnectedness as opposed to the former mosaic of separate cultures and societies. Another understanding of transnationalization would place it in a cyclical historical framework. In the latter, globalization is a ubiquitous quality of global systems. What changes is the forms which it takes as well the modes of consciousness that accompany those forms.

Social, Political, and Cultural Parameters of Decline

The decline of hegemonic zones is accompanied by a general process of regional economic decline, increasing stratification, socio-cultural fragmentation, mass migration, and a general increase in social disorder. It should be stressed here that disorder is not limited to the central zones themselves, but may be especially severe in those dependent peripheries that are not the targets of outward moving capital. Thus, most of Africa and parts of western and central Asia are among the most unstable. The collapse of the Soviet empire has produced the same king of extreme and violent disorder. It is also accompanied, as I said above, by increasing

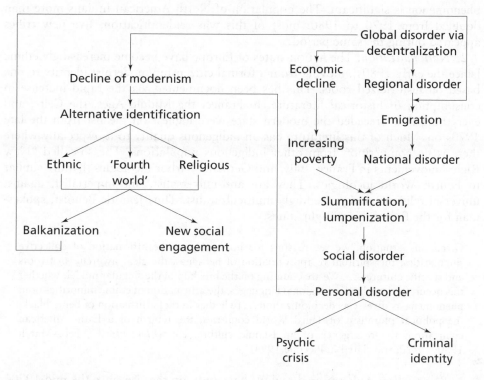

Figure 4   Global order/disorder in the center of the system
Source: Friedman 1994: 251

globalization, not just in economic terms but also in terms of the formation of global elites and elite global consciousness. I have suggested how these factors are connected in a systematic way (Figure 4).

Disorder and Fragmentation

The decentralization of capital accumulation creates disorder in areas abandoned by capital. This in turn leads to downward mobility and the economic crisis generates serious identity problems. The decline of modernism is closely related to the impossibility of maintaining a future orientation based on liberation from the past, from tradition with investment in the new, and in change in both personal and social development. In this decline, there is a turn to roots, to ethnicity and other collective identities, whether ethnic or religious, that replace the vacuum left by a receding modernist identity. This rerooting is the resonating base of cultural politics and political fragmentation that spreads throughout the hegemonic center. It takes the following forms:

1. *Indigenization*. Indigenous populations within state territories begin to reinstate their traditions and to claim their indigenous rights. The Fourth World movements have become a global phenomenon, institutionalized via United Nations organs such as the World Council of Indigenous Peoples. The demography of this

phenomenon is significant. The population of North American Indians more than doubled from 1970 to 1980; most of this was reidentification; five new tribes appeared during the same period.

2. *Nationalization.* The nation-states of Europe have become increasingly ethnic [since the early 1980s], moving from a formal citizenship/modernist identity to one based on historicized roots. This has been documented via the rapid increase in consumption of historical literature. In France, the Middle Ages, the Celts, and everything that preceded the modern state were highest on the list from the late 1970s on. Much of this literature has an indigenous quality to it, especially where there is no competition from other indigenous populations. The so-called "New Right" movements in France, Italy, and Germany harbor ideologies that are similar to Fourth World ideologies. They are anti-universalist, anti-imperialist, against universal religions and exceedingly multiculturalist. Thus Jean de Benoist, spokesman for the French New Right states:

> Given this situation, we see reasons for hope only in the affirmation of collective singularities, the spiritual re-appropriation of heritages, the clear awareness of roots and specific cultures.... We are counting on the breakup of the singular model, whether this occurs in the rebirth of regional languages, the affirmation of ethnic minorities or in phenomena as diverse as decolonization... [whether in the] affirmation of being black, the political pluralism of Third World countries, the rebirth of a Latin American civilization, the resurgence of an Islamic culture, etc. (*Eléments* 33, Feb.–March 1980: 19–20; translated in Piccone 1994).

3. *Regionalism.* Sub-national regions have been on the rise since the mid-1970s. After several decades during which it was assumed that assimilation was the general solution to ethnic problems, when social scientists calculated how many generations it would take for ethnic minority groups to disappear into larger national populations, the 1970s came as a surprise to many (Esman 1977). The weakening of the national projects of Europe became increasingly evident: Scotland, Cornwall, Brittany, Occitania, and Catalonia, today being supplemented by the Lega Nord and a Europe-wide lobby organization for the advancement of the interests of a Europe of Regions rather than nation-states. In the former Soviet empire to the east, the break-up of larger units is rampant and violent in Central Asia and Southern Europe.

4. *Immigrant ethnification.* Optimism with respect to regional identities in Europe was identical to assimilationist/intergrationist predictions with regard to immigrant minorities, especially in the United States. What seemed to be a trend toward integration was broken and reversed in the late 1960s when multiethnicity of Black and then Red power movements was supported at both grass roots and elite levels (the Ford Foundation was heavily involved in ethnic community local control projects). Today this has become a major state interventionist project in many Western countries at the same time as identity politics has led to what some have called "culture wars," in which the very unity of the nation-state, its very existence, is questioned. The question of the diasporization process is simply the ethnification of transnational connections, so that communications, social relations, and economics become organized and even institutionalized across boundaries rather than immigrant groups becoming transformed into separate minorities. Diasporization

is simply the ethnification of the immigration process. It is unlike other processes of fragmentation because it structures itself in global terms, being both subnational and transnational.

The process of fragmentation has not been a peaceful one. In 1993, for example, there were 52 major violent conflicts in the world in 42 countries, the most severe conflicts being in Eastern Europe, Central Asia, and Africa. Half of these conflicts had been under way for more than a decade (UNRISD 1995: 15). This is very different from the previous decades of the Cold War when there was a simpler division and a much stronger degree of control in the world system. "All but five of the twenty-three wars being fought in 1994 are based on communal rivalries and ethnic challenges to states. About three-quarters of the world's refugees, estimated at nearly 27 million people, are in flight from or have been displaced by these and other ethnic conflicts" (Gurr 1994: 350).

Globalization, Class and Elite Formation

Globalization in institutional terms entails the formation of international "communities," however loosely knit, that share common interests. There is an interesting and, I think, still to be researched, connection between the larger transformation of the global system and the emergence of new cosmopolitan elites. The aspect of that transformation that seems most interesting is the increasing proportion of the world economy that is collected in the form of public and private funds, primarily based on tax monies from Western countries. UN organizations, especially Unesco, the European Union, and other similar organizations (primarily nationally based) form what might be called global pork barrels that finance institutions, consultancies, etc., that pay enormous tax-free salaries to globalized bureaucrats and consultants and which join in the ranks of other elites, such as those of the international media and culture industries (to which we might add international sports, for example, the Olympic Committee and the entire organization of Olympic and world sports events). These elites are very different from former industrial capitalist elites, not least because many of them are not owners of production but are what might be called "pork barrel" elites. Robert Reich's characterization of this new class (Reich 1992) is "symbolic analysts" who in Lasch's words "live in a world of abstract concepts and symbols, ranging from stock market quotations to the images produced by Hollywood and Madison Avenue" (Lasch 1995: 35). In Lasch's terms, "They have more in common with their counterparts in Brussels or Hong Kong than with the masses of Americans not yet plugged into the network of global communications."

This is still an emergent phenomenon and is understudied. In economic terms it might be part of a general shift of capital from productive to unproductive investment, to the general increase in fictitious accumulation in the old cores of the world system. What is interesting is that a relatively coherent identity seems to have emerged in these elites. It combines a rather self-assured and superior cosmopolitanism with a model of hybridity, border-crossing, and multiculturalism (even if there is much inconsistency). The cosmopolitanism of the elite is not modernistic, nor is it devoid of cultural identification, but, on the contrary, is postmodernist in its attempt to encompass the world's cultures in its own self-definition. This elitism distances itself from "the people" who represent "the national," the unsophisticated, the "racist," and expresses loyalty to humanity rather than to its own fellow citizens, or if to its own citizens, to immigrants above nationals. The urban upper middle class has become one of the principal focal points of this development. Sennett's *The Uses of Disorder* (1970) is a virtual handbook in global cosmopolitan multiculturality. The enemy is the fixed, boring *gemeinschaft* and the believed-in future is something like the singles bar where people without strong social bonds can meet to have their mutually edifying communication, and have fun without personal responsibility, except the responsibility to maintain plurality and the supposed creativity that ensues from this plurality. The urbane, cosmopolitan, and multicultural are well expressed in CNN's advertising for itself. One well-known advertisement shows a series of images: an Australian Aborigine, a Tuareg nomad, several Northern Europeans, and Asians all to a nostalgic theme which ends with a statement of CNN's globally encompassing network. All are part of the larger humanity of the CNN family. What is interesting about Sennett, as about CNN, is the normative aspect of their representations. The cosmopolitan multicultural world is a model of how things ought to be and is part of a concerted struggle against the red-necked rural essentialist-nationalist "people." Similarly, the wave of discourses on cultural hybridity (Canclini 1992; Gilroy 1993; Hall 1996) consists of the analysis of cultural elites and their discourses. World music may be taken up as an example of hybridization, but in spite of the name of this popular genre, a closer examination reveals that it is a metropolitan product and a media industry creation rather than a street phenomenon. In other words, it can be argued that the ideology of hybridity is primarily an elitist discourse in a world that is otherwise engaged in the opposite; the drawing of boundaries to be defended, not just from land or region to land and region but from street to street. Hybridization and balkanization are two simultaneous processes of the global shift in hegemony....

Conclusion

The argument of this article has been that ethnification and social and political disorder are expressions of declining hegemony in global systems and that this relation occurs in spite of the fact that the societies involved might practice different forms of ethnicity. Whether ethnification occurs on the basis of an essentialist or non-essentialist structure of identity, it has similar effects on the outcome of ethnic conflicts. However, global systems insofar as they are based on commercial economies tend to be characterized by hegemonic centers in which individualism is developed to such an extent that ethnicity takes on essentialist characteristics. The world of hegemonic growth is one in which hegemonic classes tend to form as the elites of culturally homogenizing states and where the multicultural is spatially differentiated and hierarchical. The world of decline is a complex world, one that combines balkanization and globalization of cultural and social identities, in which the multicultural invades the center and the global and central state hierarchy disintegrates at the same time as new cosmopolitan elites identify with the larger world instead of with the hegemon itself. New rising centers (such as East Asia) become new zones of nationalization and homogenization where a former cultural and political diversity is less tolerated.[1]

NOTE

1 In the data base constructed by Ted Gurr (homepage: http://www.bsos.umd.edu), the distribution of minority conflicts seems, on the surface, to reflect this distribution of forces in the current shifting world system. The great majority of conflicts in East and Southeast Asia appear to relate to problems of incorporation in which minorities are clearly at a disadvantage. In those areas of the West and in Central Europe and Asia with declining hegemonies, minorities have either become nations or are struggling to liberate themselves from larger units. In Africa, in which the larger political units were always rather weak and based on alliances and clientships, the major conflicts seem to be about control of the state, which is the entry point for international funds or for control over natural resources, the major source of wealth and power in this region. In other words, in rising areas, integration of minorities would seem to be the major trend, while in declining areas, fragmentation is the rule. This does not mean that there is a difference in the degree of conflict, but that the outcomes are very different.

REFERENCES

Bozeman, A. (1991) *Politics and Culture in International History*. New Brunswick, NJ: Transaction.

Campbell, C. (1987) *The Romantic Ethic and the Spirit of Modern Consumerism*. Oxford: Blackwell Publishers.

Canclini, N. (1992) *Hybrid Cultures*. Minneapolis: University of Minnesota Press.

Dicken, P. (1992) *Global Shift: The Internationalization of Economic Activity*. London: Chapman.

Dumont, L. (1983) *Essais sur l'individualisme*. Paris: Le Seuil.

Ekholm-Friedman, K., (1993) *Catastrophe and Creation: The Transformation of an African Culture*. London: Harwood.

Ekholm-Friedman, K., and J. Friedman. (1987) "Towards an Anthropology." In *History and Underdevelopment*, ed. L. Blussé, J. W. Wesseling and E. D. Winius. Leiden: Center for the History of European Expansion.

Esman, M. (ed.) (1977) *Ethnic Conflict in the Western World*. Ithaca, NY: Cornell University Press.

Friedman, J. (1994) *Cultural Identity and Global Process*. London: Sage.

——. (1997) *System, Structure and Contradiction in the Evolution of "Asiatic" Social Formations*. Walnut Creek, CA: Altamira-Sage (originally published in 1979 by the National Museum of Denmark, Copenhagen).

Gilroy, P. (1993) *The Black Atlantic*. Cambridge, MA: Harvard University Press.

Gurr, T. R. (1994) "Peoples Against States: Ethnopolitical Conflict and the Changing World System." *International Studies Quarterly* 38: 347–77.

——. (1997) "Minorities at Risk Project." homepage: http://www.bsos.umd.edu

Hall, S. (1996) "When Was the Postcolonial?" In *The Post-Colonial in Question*, ed. L. Curti and I. Chambers. London: Routledge.

Harvey, D. (1990) *The Conditions of Postmodernity*. Oxford: Blackwell Publishers.

Kapferer, B. (1988) *Legends of People, Myths of State: Violence, Intolerance, and Political Culture in Sri Lanka and Australia*. Washington, DC: Smithsonian Institute Press.

Lasch, C. (1979) *The Culture of Narcissism*. New York: Norton.

——. (1995) *The Revolt of the Elites*. New York: Norton.

Leach, E. (1954) *Political Systems of Highland Burma*. London: Athlone.

Lévi-Strauss, C. (1952) *Race et histoire*. Paris: Unesco.

Maffésoli, M. (1988) *Le Temps des tribus*. Paris: Le Seuil.

Minc, A. (1993) *Le Nouveau Moyen Âge*. Paris: Gallimard.

Piccone, P. (1994) "Confronting the French New Right: Old Prejudices or a New Political Paradigm." *Telos: A Quarterly Journal of Critical Thought* 98–9 (winter 1993 – fall 1994): 3–22.

Reich, R. (1992) *The Work of Nations: Preparing Ourselves for the 21st Century*. New York: Vintage.

Sennett, R. (1970) *The Uses of Disorder: Personal Identity and City Life*. New York: Knopf.

UNRISD. (1995) *States of Disarray: The Social Effects of Globalization*. Geneva: Unesco.

Waters, M. (1990) *Ethnic Options: Choosing Identities in America*. Berkeley: University of California Press.

24

Deadly Developments and Phantasmagoric Representations

S. P. Reyna

phantasmagoria: ...a constantly shifting, complex succession of things seen or imagined as in a dream or fever state.

(Webster's 1966: 1693)

Classical nineteenth-century social theory arose as an attempt to understand the emergence of modernity. Theorists thought that modern society was "civilized," and that this quality was related to economic developments. So thinkers proceeded by formulating economic dichotomies that distinguished the uncivilized from the civilized. Saint-Simon made the main dichotomy one between feudal and industrial economies; Comte and Spencer distinguished military and industrial societies; Marx emphasized the transition from pre-capitalist to capitalist modes of production; and Durkheim believed that segmental societies, integrated by mechanical solidarity, evolved into industrial ones, integrated by organic solidarity. Not only Comte and Spencer, but Marx and Durkheim as well believed that war dominated the earlier societies and that it would become infrequent, or die out entirely, in states with industrial capitalism.[1] Classic social theory, then, to a considerable degree, represented modern social order to be one of pacific, capitalist states developing out of some warring uncivilized Other.

[My] goals are to introduce readers to the rich variety in anthropological analyses of modern war and, in so doing, to give them some understanding of the intimacies between capitalist states and war.[2] The present introduction contributes to the realization of these goals by providing some analytic tools helpful when studying wars and states, by offering previews of the articles' arguments, and by raising the alarm that certain scholarly traditions peddle phantasmagoric representations that darken comprehension of modern war. The volume [Reyna and Downs 1997] includes nine articles by ten anthropologists who investigate warfare in different times and places during the evolution of modern governments and capitalism.

From S. P. Reyna and R. E. Downs (eds.) *Deadly Developments: Capitalism, States and War* (Amsterdam: Gordon and Breach, 1997), pp. 1–5, 7–21.

Included are studies from what came to be the crucible of modern society, Atlantic Europe, to what came to be its peripheries in the Third World. Certain findings of these articles provide a basis for evaluating different representations of capitalism, states, and wars. It turns out that classic social theory's insistence that capitalist states were pacific is a phantasm, a chimera that hides deadly developments.

I

The articles that compose this book [Reyna and Downs 1997] analyze warfare in societies with states. So it is important to begin by specifying an understanding of this social form. The "state" is a territory within which there are two sets of institutions, those of government and those of civil society. "Government" is understood to be a roughly hierarchical organization of offices with different amounts of power and authority in executive, legislative, and judicial domains. Modern governments are distinguished from their premodern counterparts, among other things, by the enormous variety and amounts of resources at their disposal as well as by the prodigious differentiation of their offices that allows them to utilize these resources. Both of these differences contribute to the vastly superior powers of modern *vis-à-vis* pre modern governments. "Civil society" includes the economic, kin, religious, and other non-governmental institutions found in states.

"Capitalism" refers to the nature of institutions that have increasingly come to dominate the civil society of modern states. Capitalist institutions exhibit five attributes: (1) ownership of the factors of production by private persons (who are the capitalists); (2) provision of labor by workers who are politically free to dispose of their labor as they wish; (3) the orientation of workers' and capitalists' activity to the objective of the maximization of profit; (4) the realization of profit through the operation of the market; and (5) the appropriation of profit by the capitalists. Capitalism, because it exhibits these five attributes, is a process of capital accumulation. Two forms of capitalism have been important. Most capital accumulation in the early modern period (c.1415–c.1760) resulted from the maximization of profits of mercantile enterprises. After this time, capital accumulation increasingly resulted from the maximization of the profits of manufacturing enterprises that utilized machine technologies. These two varieties of capitalism have been respectively called "commercial" and "industrial." A "capitalist state" is one in which either of the two forms of capitalist enterprise dominate the civil society's economic life. The essays constituting this book [Reyna and Downs 1997] analyze different forms of warfare in capitalist states or in populations influenced by such states. A brief précis of these articles is in order. . . .

The . . . volume . . . [contains] . . . five articles analyzing warfare in [contemporary] Africa. Three articles consider the eastern portion of the continent. Joan Vincent analyzes Ugandan government attacks upon various elements of its civil society, warring that has plagued Uganda almost since Independence. David Turton contemplates an instance of "tribal" war, one involving the Mursi and their neighbors in Ethiopia. Carolyn Nordstrom seeks to understand war in Mozambique between the government and a guerilla movement whose brutality has seemed to epitomize "savagery." Two articles are set in West Africa. Although wars between states have been rare in postcolonial Africa, John Magistro seeks to explain one such case that erupted between Mauritania and Senegal in the late 1980s and early 1990s. A comparative piece by Pierre Bonte looks at the relationship between land and ethnic conflict in the Sahel, the arid savanna immediately south of the Sahara....

Elsewhere (Reyna 1994) I have suggested that the term war is applied properly only to societies with states. Specifically, war involves practices of organized violence performed by institutions within states. The articles [in Reyna and Downs 1997] explore two types of war: international and internal. "International" war is that waged between the military institutions of the governments of different states. ... "Internal" war is that conducted within a state. There are two major sorts of internal war. First there is "civil" war, which happens when the military institutions of a state's government wage war against different institutions in that state's civil society. Then there is "civil society" war that arises when different institutions in a civil society fight each other in the absence of government intervention.

A further distinction might be made between "ethnic" and "non-ethnic" internal wars. Civil or civil society wars between religious groups or gangs are non-ethnic internal wars.... Turton concentrates his analysis upon ethnic civil society war. Magistro and Bonte investigate instances of ethnic civil war. Nordstrom... explores cases of non-ethnic civil war.

The articles tend to identify determinants or accelerants of the different types of wars. By "determinant" is not meant the sole cause of a conflict. Rather, a determinant is understood ... to be a phenomenon that played a role in bringing about, in the sense of "making occur," organized violence. "Accelerants" are like gasoline on a fire, for they are phenomena that, in the presence of existing conflict, make the violence occur more frequently and/or intensely.

Further, the articles generally explore structural and subjective categories of determinants or accelerants. "Structural" phenomena are those involving the actions of organizations that, in the cases analyzed, are largely those of the governments and civil societies of capitalist states. "Subjective" phenomena are those having to do with peoples' thoughts and emotions. People are born with neuro-physiologies that allow them to experience an enormous variety of cognitions and sentiments. Their subjectivities are what they actually think and feel in different contexts. Subjectivities, however, are "constructed." Construction involves the activities of organizations that embody – i.e., literally put-in-the-body, in the sense of placing within neuro-physiologies – systems of cultural meaning, so that people will experience different cognitions and affects as they have been constructed to experience them. It is time to look a bit more closely at what the articles identify as structurally and subjectively important in the determination and acceleration of modern warfare....

II

...Kay Warren has recently argued for the "'centrality of cultural issues' in the study of organized violence" (1993: 1). Joan Vincent's contribution [in Reyna and Downs 1997] shows readers how such issues can be central in an analysis that links cultural to political and economic factors. She seeks to understand the civil war that has plagued Uganda almost since Independence. Specifically, she is interested in accounting for differences in the ferocity of the conflict, for she finds that the fighting conducted in more southerly areas was in a number of instances less brutal than that in the north. In an analysis blending Foucauldian and Gramscian insights with her own rich ethnography, Vincent shows how colonialism resulted in a cultural hegemony, one of whose properties was what might be termed a geographic consciousness, a consciousness that helped legitimate different levels of violence.

The concept of cultural hegemony, with a genealogy deriving from Antonio Gramsci via Raymond Williams and John and Jean Comaroff, is a useful tool for the analysis of the role of subjectivities in domination. Hegemony in Williams's influential definition is a "system of meanings and values – constitutive and constituting – which as they are experienced as practices appear as reciprocally confirming" (1977: 118).[3] Specifically, hegemonic meanings, which tend "to be taken for granted as the natural and received shape of the world" (J. and J. Comaroff 1991: 23), construct peoples' subjectivities so that they will be more likely to consent to their domination. Colonial officials, according to Vincent, were interested in introducing agro-capitalist enterprises into Uganda to satisfy the needs of British industrial capitalism at home. These officials and their minions introduced a cultural hegemony in which things associated with capitalism were valued, while those not associated with it were devalued. Agro-enterprises introduced by the British were largely located in more southerly areas and included such export cash crops as coffee. More northerly areas were less touched, except as reservoirs of cheap labor.

Given the prevailing hegemony, people living in these two areas came to be conceptualized differently. Those in the south were seen as more modern and civilized, while those in the north were understood to be less modern and rather uncivilized. Here is the crucial point. This constitution of values, a veritable hegemonic geography of where the British had introduced capitalism, persisted into the postcolonial times. So when southern Ugandan commanders and soldiers campaigned against northerners in the north, they fought with greater fury, a ferocity in some measure determined by their consciousness of what awaited them in the heartland of the uncivilized. Vincent, thus, shows how a certain type of subjective phenomena, the cultural hegemonic geography, introduced to facilitate the introduction of capitalism into Uganda, acted to accelerate violence in certain regions of that country.

Turton takes readers to the isolated Omo River valley in Ethiopia, to a people called the Mursi. His analysis explores the effect of the acquisition of automatic weapons upon Mursi "traditional" warfare. A key question, however, is why do the Mursi, who live in an outback beyond the outback, suddenly find themselves massacring clan rivals with AK 47s and the like?

An answer to this question has to do with threats to industrial capitalism due to Communist expansion. Many people came to resist the domination they experienced under capitalism. One way they did so was to develop Communist ideologies, which helped to construct the subjectivities of those opposing capitalism. Such opposition was effective. Russia fell in 1917, much of eastern Europe went after 1945, and China was lost in 1949. Such events closed off enormous areas of the globe to capitalism and threatened to deny still more. This meant that by 1950 *the* primary threat to continued capitalist accumulation was Communist expansion. Such a threat had to be addressed on many levels, one of which was to call upon the assistance of governments to harass Communism politically.

One way this was done throughout the Third World was to arm opponents of the Communists, which, of course, motivated Communists to arm their supporters. One area where such an arms race was prosecuted vigorously was in the Horn of Africa. As a result, Ethiopia in the 1970s and 1980s became awash in weapons, some of which eventually trickled down to the Mursi.

Turton notes that when the Mursi finally got their guns, "tribal" warfare in the Omo River valley was part of a regional, inter-ethnic system of reciprocity involving the exchange of violence as well as goods. In such fighting an act of violence by a group must be reciprocated by those attacked. Once this reciprocation has occurred, it becomes the basis for restoring peace. Turton is especially insightful in showing how the introduction of automatic weapons acted as an accelerant to this system, one that, as was the case among the New Irelanders, unbalanced it. When the Mursi's opponents got machine guns, the Mursi had to get them or be annihilated. When all groups get these weapons the killing may be so inflated that they all will be threatened with extermination. However, should the Mursi be exterminated, it will not be because they were acting upon primordial antagonisms. Rather, it would be an unintended consequence of political decisions taken by officials of capitalist Great Powers to defend capitalism.

Mozambique became independent in 1975 as a result of a decade of war against Portuguese colonial rule. This anti-colonial revolt was conducted by a Marxist oriented Frelimo (*Frente de Libertação de Moçambique*). In the years immediately after independence, Frelimo instituted a Marxist-Leninist government dedicated to assisting liberation movements in Rhodesia and South Africa. Southern Africa, in general, is an area that has enormous quantities of natural resources. Moreover, the regional hegemon, South Africa, then operating under a racist Apartheid regime, was a country that both supplied a wide range of raw materials to US and European capitalist enterprise and benefited from their substantial investments in its developing industrial sector. So capitalism stood to suffer big losses if southern Africa fell. Mozambique, then, in the late 1970s directly threatened capitalism in a region where losses would be great. Mozambique had to be neutralized, which was, of course, a task for governments in the region that favored capitalism.

Rhodesia formed and controlled a terrorist movement called Renamo (*Resistência Nacional de Moçambique*) with the covert, but strong, support of Great Britain and Portugal. After the white regime fell and Rhodesia became Zimbabwe with a left-leaning government, the prospects for capitalism in southern Africa seemed even more threatened. As a consequence, South Africa, encouraged by the Reagan administration, began an anti-Communist war throughout the region. Mozambique, of course, became one theater in this war. The South African military greatly strengthened Renamo around 1980, using it as their weapon in Mozambique.

Renamo's strategy was one of "dirty war," i.e., the use of terrorism against civilian populations. Nordstrom provides a phenomenology of such violence. She seeks to understand the experience of unimaginable butchery. For example, Renamo forced children to watch, or on occasion to perpetrate, the murder and cannibalism of family and friends. It commonly asked husbands and children to watch their wives and mothers being gang raped and murdered.

Nordstrom interprets such cultures of terror as rituals that are destructive of life-world viability. "Life-world" is a central subjective notion of the philosopher Husserl and is his concept of the everyday, unreflected-upon experience of the way things are.[4] It is that part of a person's psyche that is like a computer's operating system. Without an operating system a computer cannot connect with its external environment. Without a life-world a person cannot connect with, in the sense of having experience of, reality. Nordstrom shows how eating one's mother, a horrific perversion of normal experience, tends to obliterate one's life-world; as one of her informants says, "Who am I? I am nothing." Such persons, with their subjectivities literally "deconstructed," and wandering in a world chaotic experience, simply can not fight and hence could not oppose Renamo and their South African patrons.

Nordstrom suggests that Renamo's dirty war was waged more by "habit" than by "rational" strategy. This may well be true in certain instances. However, South African security forces took Renamo over in 1980 to suppress Communist threats to South African dominance and a whole way of life that had a capitalistic bias. Renamo made life so miserable in Mozambique that Frelimo backed off the business of exporting Marxist-Leninism to other countries and, for that matter, it pretty much curtailed anything that smacked of Communism in Mozambique. Dirty wars are cheap wars. So it seems that for relatively little money South Africa got Renamo to help contain the spread of Communism in a big region. This seems perfectly rational if one's goal is the maintenance of capitalism. It is, however, the rationale of savagery.

Mobs of one ethnicity have butchered those of other ethnicities in the Senegal River Valley since 1980. This fighting has pitted Maures from Mauritania against sub-Saharan ethnicities, especially Toucouleurs, who reside on both sides of the river in Senegal and Mauritania. Magistro explores the causes of this violence, which, however, appear to have little to do with ethnicity *per se*.

Since the 1970s there have been massive donor lending and foreign capital investment in the Senegal River valley. These funds have been used largely to construct an irrigation infrastructure. Once, while on a development mission to this region in 1980, a natty European Community official confided to me that such lending would give a "nice little boost" to European and other core nations' agro-industries. It turns out that he was right. The lending has stimulated sales for these firms. Such donor lending might be seen as a mechanism that allowed core governments to lend money, derived to a considerable extent from the taxes of their middle classes, to Mauritania and Senegal, which then spent it largely upon the products of European industry owned by wealthy capitalists. This is a public subsidy of private, capitalist enterprise. Ultimately such structural action helped provoke ethnic war.

Certain Maures are called *bidan* (white). Wealthy *bidan* control the Mauritanian government. They have lived in the recent past in the Sahara. However, they have come to realize that the enormous irrigation investments have conferred great value on the southern riverine areas. Consequently, *bidan* have used their government connections to expropriate lands from those who formerly exploited it. The latter are often Toucouleur, and the loss of their lands is a fighting matter to them. It is this expropriation that is at the heart of the ethnic conflict.

No person, or persons, consciously planned for Maure and non-Maure ethnicities to butcher each other. However, some officials did consciously plan river basin development, which they expected would provide, among other things, a "boost" to EC business. Unfortunately it was the unintended consequences of this rational planning that produced the irrational mob butcheries that have characterized the ethnic violence in the Senegal River valley.

Bonte extends Magistro's analysis of the Senegal River Valley to include other areas of the Sahel. His article reminds readers of the crucial roles of the postcolonial state and land tenure in the construction of ethnic identities and conflict; especially between herders and farmers. Specifically, he investigates countries – Mauritania, Niger, and Mali – whose governments are dominated by officials from either pastoral or agricultural ethnic groups.

In the Séno Mango region of Mali he shows that, as the commercialization of food production has occurred, it has for the most part benefited the agricultural Dogons at the expense of pastoral Fulani. This has allowed wealthier Dogon to purchase Fulani lands. Mali's government is dominated by people from farming ethnicities, and their national development projects in the Séno Mango have added to the expropriation of Fulani lands. The result has been an increased potential for Dogon/Fulani conflict as the latter have been increasingly marginalized.

Bonte reports on a somewhat similar situation in the interior delta of the Niger River. This is an area that has been a major source of dry-season pasture for herders throughout the central Sahel. Here the Malian government has again favored development programs that privilege farming. This has resulted in a situation where former pastoral areas are being given over to different forms of commercial farming, tending to marginalize people from herding ethnicities.

Bonte's third case comes from Tuareg areas of Mali and Niger. The Tuareg, of course, are the most famous of the saharan camel pastoralists. However, both Niger's and Mali's governments are dominated by farmers and have followed policies that have tended to expropriate Tuareg pastures. This ethnic marginalization has created a situation of conflict, one that has evolved to the stage of armed revolt.

The final region Bonte investigates is that of the Senegal River Valley. Mauritania is the only sahelian state whose officials derive predominantly from a herder ethnicity, that of the Maures. The Mauritanian government has used its powers to help wealthy *bidan* Maures expropriate the land of riverain farmers, especially the Toucouleurs, which they then use to set up commercial farming operations. This ethnic marginalization of riverain folk, as we already know from Magistro's piece, has produced inter-ethnic fighting.

A crucial point to grasp is that ethnic conflict does not result from deeply embedded, "traditional" pastoralist/farmer rancor. Rather, in the particular instances discussed it is derived from structural changes in the access to productive land that come about as governments seek to aid their supporters to get into the business of capitalist agriculture. . . .

. . . It is time to move out of this realm of hell and into that of phantasmagoric representation and then, perhaps, out of the phantasmic into a clearer apprehension of modern war.

III

Remember, from the beginning of the introduction, that a phantasmagoria is "a . . . succession of things . . . imagined (as in a dream)." The articles just discussed provide grounds for separating dreaming from fact and suggest that three commonly held approaches to understanding modern war do strain towards the phantasmagoric.

Let us begin with the oldest, most persistent, at least in the Western intellectual tradition, approach to the explanation of war, which was first articulated in ancient Greece by Thucydides in his *The Peloponnesian War* (1949) to account for wars between Athens and Sparta in the fifth century BC. It was introduced into modern discourse by Thomas Hobbes in *Leviathan* (1968) during the seventeenth century. Thinkers hewing to the Thucydides–Hobbes line believe that warfare – any warfare, modern or otherwise – is an expression of natural human impulses, with "natural" here understood to mean pertaining to biology. War occurs, according to this view, as Hobbes pungently put it, because the natural state of people is "warre of every man against every man" (1968: 188). This approach might be called "naturalist," and it is so tenacious because for many people it is hegemonic. Of course, there will always be war: "It is human to hate" (Huntington 1996: 130)....

The evolutionary biological versions of the naturalist approach to war have been roundly criticized within sociocultural anthropology (see Alland 1973 and Montagu 1973 and 1976). There have been a number of lines of criticism. The most fundamental is that evidence supporting evolutionary biological accounts tends to be weak....

How do the findings of our essays bear upon the naturalist position in general? *None* of the articles supports it. In each case institutions of the capitalist state, institutions influenced by the capitalist state, or subjectivities constructed by these institutions, do the job of provoking war. The determinant or accelerant of violence is never biological.... Let us consider a second popular approach to explaining contemporary wars.

Officials, journalists, and scholars, as they contemplate the Northern Irelands and Bosnias of this world, often blame contemporary war upon "essentialist" tribal or ethnic antagonisms. Essentialist views of social groups are those that specify that groups have primordial, in the sense of immanent, attributes that are their fixed and unchanging essence.[5] Many believe that the current spate of ethnic or, more journalistically, "tribal" wars have resulted because these groups, today's savage Other, are essentially antagonistic towards each other. This is a second "ethnic essentialist" approach to the explanation of modern war.

However, the . . . Mursi did not start killing ethnic enemies at higher rates because of essentialist antipathies. Rather, more prosaically, they got guns, which allowed them to kill more.... Similarly the ethnic groups described by Magistro and Bonte that are at each other's throats in the Sahel have been made competitors over land. The case of Mozambique is the most striking. Its utter bestiality has nothing to do with tribal antagonisms, and everything to do with the governments of capitalist states fighting threats to capitalism, and doing this fighting through dirty wars devised by agents of these states.

Additionally, there is a considerable literature arguing that the spate of "ethnic" wars since the 1980s in Bosnia, India, Sri Lanka, Central Asia, Sudan, Rwanda, and Somalia are the result of the deliberate construction of antagonistic ethnic identities by political leaders seeking to control these states, often with the connivance of agents of advanced industrial capitalist states.[6] This suggests that those marketing ethnic essentialism – dreaming that all ethnic groups hate each other as the savage Other – peddle a phantasmagoria.

Let us end by considering a particular contention of a third approach, that of classic social theory's insistence upon the pacific nature of capitalist states.... Turton's data suggest that the acceleration of Mursi fighting was, in part, a consequence of the operation of government institutions protecting capitalist interests during the Cold War.

Magistro's argument may be interpreted as suggesting that Senegal River valley ethnic fighting has been partially determined by European Community government operations in support of the profits of their agro-enterprises. Bonte accounted for heightened ethnic tension throughout the Sahel as a result of African governments' taking sides between ethnic groups, helping some at the expense of others, especially with access to land that could then be utilized for capitalist farming. . . . Vincent and Nordstrom deal with the realm of subjectivities. They show how colonial government (in the case of Uganda) and postcolonial government (in that of Mozambique) took actions that constructed their peoples' subjectivities by creating cultural hegemonies or life-worlds. These subjectivities, then, disposed peoples to greater violence.

Thus, the conclusions of the different articles support the following generalization. Structural and subjective factors found in, or associated with, capitalist states help determine or accelerate the types of war found in the modern world. This means that any representation of capitalist states as pacific is delusional. Additionally, I have shown how naturalist and ethnic essentialist accounts tend to induce the sweet dreams of phantasmagoria.

IV

Let us place these generalizations within a broader context, that of the history of modern war since the emergence of industrial capitalism, in order to draw a broader conclusion. The capitalist states that had developed in Atlantic Europe by the eighteenth century were killing machines. Roughly 70 to 80 percent of their budgets were spent to pay the expenses of ongoing wars and the debts of past wars (Mann 1986). Industrial capitalist states began to emerge outside of their original crucible in Atlantic Europe during the nineteenth century. One of these, Germany, developed a different version of the military-capitalist complex, based in part on a vastly more lethal industrial weaponry, and fought its way to territorial conquest throughout central and western continental Europe. Two other newcomers, the US and Japan, joined Great Britain and France toward the end of the century in the use of the new weaponry to butcher non-capitalist peoples in North America, Africa, the Middle East, East Asia, and the Pacific. The term "butcher" in the previous sentence is appropriate. Enormous numbers of peoples fighting with spears and swords were slaughtered by those with automatic weapons and heavy artillery. Some of these wars, especially those against native Americans, were genocidal because they led to the extermination of whole peoples (see Stannard 1992 and Todorov 1984). They made it possible, however, for capitalist states first to free lands for capitalist development and then to supply raw materials and markets needed for this development.

The first half of the twentieth century was dominated by the most cataclysmic war the world has seen. World Wars I and II were a second Thirty Year War that ran from 1914 to 1945. In it, younger capitalist states, Japan and Germany, fought older capitalist states, Great Britain and France. Perhaps as many as 90 million people were killed as a result of the conflict (Mandel 1986: 169). The US emerged from it with by far the most powerful military-capitalist complex. It, not Germany or Japan, became the greatest of the Great Leviathans, and ever since there have been wars for the US to fight and people to kill. Between 1946 and 1976 there were 120 wars. The US intervened, overtly or covertly, in roughly 42 percent of these (Kende 1978).

It is time to step back and smell the daisies. First remember that many works in popular culture strive to convince folk that war is thrilling, while, at the same time, many contributors to scholarly culture labor to persuade us that it is natural, a natural high, or a product of the unchangeable reflexes of ethnic, alien Others. Such popular, naturalist, and ethnic essentialist representations construct subjectivities that take a kindly view of war as a natural thing, a good thrill, or a regretable necessity in a world of antagonistic, ethnic Aliens. Such representations make notions of war hegemonic, because, though they quibble over the nature and causes of war, they are based upon an unreflected upon, taken-for-granted, premise that people should be disposed towards war. Of course, such hegemonic notions help furnish capitalist states with a supply of culturally constructed killers.

Remember, however, that popular, naturalist, and ethnic essentialist depictions of war are phantasmagoric representations that hide an actuality. The reality is that there have been deadly developments along the highways and byways of capitalist states. These states – sometimes intentionally, often unintentionally, through intricate webs of causation involving government and capitalist institutions and the subjectivities they have constructed – have been instruments of internal and international war. The savage Other is (capitalist) us. The grossest delusion may be to ignore this reality, for if one does, one may not be around to smell the daisies.

NOTES

1 Comte said, "no enlightened mind disputes the continual decline of the military spirit, and the gradual ascendency of the industrial" (1975: 166). Spencer made Comte's observation a central part of his theories (1896). Engels believed that war would negate itself when capitalism evolved into socialism (1955: 239–40). Durkheim stated that war became "more intermittent and less common" (1957: 53) in industrial societies. Giddens has noted classic social theory's faith in the pacificity of capitalist states (1985).

2 Ferguson and Farragher (1988) have written a useful guide to the literature of the anthropology of war. Nagengast (1994) has reviewed studies concerned with violence as it pertains to the state.

3 There is a considerable literature concerning Gramscian hegemony, to which an especially useful introduction is Lears (1985). A distinction should be made between cultural and other forms of hegemony. "Cultural hegemony" is about cognition that reproduces domination *within* a state. Other forms of hegemony refer to situations where one state has the power to influence other states. This latter notion is about domination *between* states.

4 Husserl's life-world is, perhaps, best first approached in *The Crisis of European Sciences and Transcendental Phenomenology* (1970). It was introduced into social thought by Schutz (1972). Life-worlds are, in part, a product of past cultural traditions. Absent in the notion of life-world, as opposed to that of cultural hegemony, is any sense that a life-world might help to reproduce the domination of certain groups within a society.

5 The view of essentialism offered in the text is that of Aristotle (Fetzer and Almeder 1993: 47). Essentialist views of ethnic violence are expressed more often than not by those in governmental and journalistic communities. . . .

6 For alternatives to ethnic essentialist accounts readers might consult Denich (1993) and Kidieckel and Halpern (1993) on Bosnia; Lessinger (1994) on India; Schoeberlein-Engel (1994) on central Asia; Tambiah (1986) on Sri Lanka; Erny (1994) on Rwanda; Deng (1995) on Sudan; and Ahmed (1995) on Somalia.

REFERENCES

Ahmed, A. J. (1995) *The Invention of Somalia*. Lawrenceville, NJ: Red Sea Press.

Alland, A. (1973) *The Human Imperative*. New York: Columbia University Press.

Comaroff, J., and J. Comaroff. (1991) *Of Revelation and Revolution*. Chicago: University of Chicago Press.

Comte, A. (1975) *The Foundations of Sociology*. New York: Wiley.

Denich, B. (1993) Dismembering Yugoslavia: Nationalist Ideologies and the Symbolic Revival of Genocide. The State Under Siege Conference. New York: New York Academy of Sciences.

Deng, F. (1995) *War of Visions: Conflicts of Identities in the Sudan*. Washington, DC: Brookings Institute.

Durkheim, E. (1957) *Professional Ethics and Civic Morals*. London: Routledge.

Engels, F. (1955) *Anti-Dühring*. London: Lawrence and Wishart.

Erny, P. (1994) *Rwanda, 1994*. Paris: Harmattan.

Ferguson, R. B., and L. Farragher. (1988) *The Anthropology of War: An Annotated Bibliography*. New York: Harry Frank Guggenheim Foundation.

Fetzer, J. A., and R. F. Almeder. (1993) *Glossary of Epistemology / Philosophy of Science*. New York: Paragon House.

Giddens, A. (1985) *The Nation-State and Violence*. Los Angeles: University of California Press.

Hobbes, T. (1968) *Leviathan* [1651]. Harmondsworth: Penguin Books.

Huntington, S. M. (1996) *The Clash of Civilizations*. New York: Simon and Schuster.

Husserl, E. (1970) *The Crisis of European Sciences and Transcendental Phenomenology*. Evanston, IL: Northwestern University Press.

Kende, I. (1978) Wars of Ten Years (1967–76). *Journal of Peace Research* 3: 227–41.

Kideckel, D. A., and J. M. Halpern (eds.) (1993) War Among the Yugoslavs. Special Issue, *Anthropology of East Europe Review* 11.

Lears, T. J. J. (1985) The Concept of Cultural Hegemony: Problems and Possibilities. *American Historical Review* 9: 567–93.

Lessinger, H. (1994) Hindu Nationalism, Fascism, and Anti-Muslim Violence in India. The State Under Siege Conference. New York: New York Academy of Sciences.

Mandel, E. (1986) *The Meaning of the Second World War*. London: Verso.

Mann, M. (1986) *The Sources of Social Power*, vol. 1. Cambridge: Cambridge University Press.

Montagu, A. (ed.) (1973) *Man and Aggression*. Oxford: Oxford University Press.

——. (1976) *The Nature of Human Aggression*. Oxford: Oxford University Press.

Nagengast, C. (1994) Violence, Terror, and the Crisis of the State. *Annual Review of Anthropology* 23: 109–36.

Reyna, S. P. (1994) A Mode of Domination Approach to Organized Violence. In *Studying War, Anthropological Perspectives*, ed. S. P. Reyna and R. E. Downs. Newark, NJ: Gordon and Breach.

Reyna, S. P., and R. E. Downs (eds.) (1997) *Deadly Developments: Capitalism, States and War*. Amsterdam: Gordon and Breach.

Schoeberlein-Engel. (1994) Toppling the Balance: The Creation of "Interethnic" War in Tajikistan. The State Under Seige Conference. New York: New York Academy of Sciences.

Schutz, A. (1972) *The Phenomenology of the Social World*. London: Heineman.

Spencer, H. (1896) *The Principles of Sociology*. New York: Appleton and Co.

Stannard, D. (1992) *American Holocaust: Columbus and the Conquest of the New World*. New York: Oxford University Press.

Tambiah, S. (1986) *Sri Lanka: Ethnic Fratricide and the Dismantling of Democracy*. Chicago: University of Chicago Press.

Thucydides. (1949) *The Peloponnesian War*. Oxford: Oxford University Press.

Todorov, T. (1984) *The Conquest of America: The Question of the Other*. New York: Harper & Row.

Warren, K. B. (1993) Introduction. In *The Violence Within: Cultural and Political Opposition in Divided Nations*, ed. K. B. Warren. Boulder, CO: Westview.

Webster's International Dictionary. (1966) Springfield, MA: Merriams.

Williams, R. (1977) *Marxism and Literature*. Oxford: Oxford University Press.

25

Modernity at the Edge of Empire

David Nugent

This book [Nugent 1997] has grown out of efforts to understand why the process of building states and making national cultures described in much of the literature does not apply to the process by which the modern Peruvian nation-state took on a real presence in the Chachapoyas region.

In the case under consideration, state-building and nation-making were initiated from the *fringes* of the territorial state, by subaltern groups who had formerly been excluded from participation in the national community. Two key factors contributed to this development. First, although the social order was organized according to principles of aristocratic sovereignty, the ideological apparatus nonetheless espoused the legitimacy of popular sovereignty. Second, subaltern groups perceived popular sovereignty and modern nationhood (which were associated with equality, individual rights, private property, progress, and consensus) as representing powerful forces of liberation. The contradiction between aristocratic and popular sovereignty was rooted in the history of state-making in postcolonial Latin America. The perception that popular sovereignty and modern nationhood were emancipatory forces can only be understood in relation to the organization of everyday life during the period of aristocratic sovereignty.

... [C]ertain generalizations can be made concerning the countervailing forces – material and ideological – that characterized the operation of the aristocratic order and the state as a whole. At the turn of the twentieth century, the emerging Peruvian nation-state was rent by contradictions. Although founded as an independent state in the 1820s on liberal principles of democracy, citizenship, private property, and individual rights, the central government was not remotely able to make good on these arrangements even 100 years later. Although such principles were routinely invoked in political ritual and discourse, many parts of the country were organized according to principles diametrically opposed to these precepts of popular sovereignty.

From *Modernity at the Edge of Empire: State, Individual and Nation in the Northern Peruvian Andes, 1885–1935* (Stanford: Stanford University Press, 1997), pp. 308–23.

Chachapoyas was one such region. Here, society was divided into highly unequal socioeconomic categories based on race, gender, property, and ancestry. The small handful of families that made up the "noble," landed elite claimed descent from Spanish forebears, and saw it as their exclusive, inherited right to rule the region free from the interference of the Indios [poor cultivators of pre-Columbian descent] and cholos [urban dwellers (derogatory)], whose labor and product provided the elite with much of its wealth. Even social interaction with such people was kept to a minimum, and was structured in such a way as to require public deference and subservience from the subaltern.

The landed class, however, was far from internally unified. Rather, members of the elite saw themselves as having the inherited right to rule that *no one* – not even other members of the elite – could legitimately deny them. Furthermore, in order to exercise these rights, the elite did not hesitate to use violence. Those who interfered with the exercise of elite privilege therefore did so at their peril.

Because of peculiarities of the Peruvian political order, however, it was inevitable that each faction of the elite continually interfered with the others' ability to exercise positions of power. During this period, Peru was an internally fragmented polity. Unable to control its national territory directly, the central regime chose select elite groups in each region to act in its name, in the process denying the remainder of the elite access to political power. The result was endemic conflict, as elite-led factions struggled to control the local apparatus of state.

Competition for political office – with which came control over a variety of tribute-taking mechanisms – was especially intense in the Chachapoyas region. For landed families could not rely on their estates to provide them with wealth. Because of the poverty of agrarian pursuits, it was as if influential families were being thrust out of the agrarian world and into the public, political world, where all threatened to collide in their efforts to become the single privileged client of the state. Once in such a position, the ruling faction removed members of the opposition from public office, prosecuted them for supposed crimes, seized their goods, and did harm to their person and property. Because no one faction could control the political apparatus for any sustained period of time, however, members of *all* social classes and *all* elite-led factions suffered continual insecurity of person and property. For as each new faction rose to power, it persecuted its enemies in whatever way it could.

The ruling casta [elite coalition], then, used its powers of appointment and its control over armed force to persecute and harass members of the opposition in as systematic and comprehensive a manner as possible. Continuous persecution of the opposition was necessary because opposing castas refused to accept the position of the ruling group as legitimate. Rather, opposing castas saw their own aspirations as inherently more valid than the pretensions of those who controlled the prefecture, and thus constantly sought to take the place of the coalition in power. Only by engaging in consistent and coordinated persecution of opposing castas could the ruling casta fragment this hostile opposition sufficiently to make united action on the part of its enemies difficult or impossible. Only in this way could the ruling casta reproduce its position of regional dominance.

The ruling faction was also the official representative of the independent republic of Peru within the department of Amazonas – a republic founded on liberal Enlightenment principles of individual rights and protections, the sanctity of person and property, and equality under the law. As a result, although committed to making constant attacks upon the life and property of the opposition, the ruling faction was equally compelled to present itself in all political ritual, and in all political discourse, as the sole and true defender of state-endorsed principles of popular sovereignty. In these rhetorical and ritual spaces, the ruling elite elaborated a mythical social order that was the antithesis of factional politics and aristocratic hierarchy. In place of violence, insecurity, and privilege, everyday life was depicted as consensual and orderly, and individuals were portrayed as universally enjoying the protections of life, liberty, and property granted them by the Constitution. In ritual and discourse, unity and harmony prevailed, and distinctions of race, gender, and class – upon which the entire aristocratic order was based – ceased to exist. In place of such distinctions, the ruling faction asserted the existence of a mass of identical "citizens," all of whom were united behind the cause of promoting "progress" and "advancement."

The particular elite faction that controlled the apparatus of state was thus forced to offer public accounts of its deeds by invoking notions of equality, individual rights and protections, progress, and the "common good" that were in direct contradiction with its own actions – and that also provided a critical commentary on the cultural and material logic of aristocratic privilege itself. Aristocratic "sovereignty" could not be celebrated, or even acknowledged, in formal political spheres. Popular sovereignty had to be celebrated, on an ongoing basis, despite the fact that it had virtually no relation to any existing social reality. Indeed, there was a conspicuous silence about the very existence of the aristocratic order in all political ritual and discourse.

The ruling casta's ability to persecute the opposition in a systematic manner could not be sustained, however. Indeed, the period of strength and solidarity that characterized its initial phase of control was followed by a period of growing weakness, during which ruling casta members suffered many of the same violations of person and property as did members of the opposition. As contradictions inherent in casta rule made themselves manifest, political appointees from Lima who were not beholden to ruling casta leaders took on roles of growing importance in local affairs. Their presence made systematic and coordinated persecution of casta enemies increasingly difficult, as the Lima appointees broke the monopoly on political positions formerly enjoyed by the ruling casta and weakened its control over armed force. At the same time, members of the ruling casta began to struggle among themselves for access to key political positions and for control of tributary revenue, further undermining the effectiveness with which the ruling casta could persecute its enemies. In these transformed conditions, members of the opposition were able to unite against the ruling casta, and eventually to drive it from power. Just as the ruling casta was forced to demonstrate its ability to violate the "rights" of others in public in order to reproduce its position of dominance, the only means by which opposing castas could rise to power was by publicly violating the "rights" of members of the ruling casta. These conflictual dynamics of shame and countershame, violence and counterviolence, characterized the particular form of aristocratic sovereignty encountered in the Chachapoyas region.

Even as ruling faction and opposition alike were involved in a series of violent encounters with one another that served as public spectacles and statements about the ability of each to rule, rulers and ruled employed the central regime's discourse of popular sovereignty, progress, equal protection under the law, and the common good to represent their actions and those of their adverseries – if for different purposes (the ruling casta to legitimate, the opposition to delegitimate). The use of this discourse by *both* groups, however, blatantly contradicted the violent, persona-listic, and competitive actions that characterized casta behavior in general. Despite this contradiction, however, neither group made any effort to conceal its violent behavior. To the contrary: the principles of aristocratic sovereignty required those who wished to occupy positions of rule to demonstrate their ability to dominate, shame, and impose their will on their adverseries.

Although casta groups routinely invoked the rhetoric of popular sovereignty in political ritual and discourse, it was clear to all that aristocratic sovereignty was the reigning social reality of the time. Conformity with the precepts of popular sover-eignty never went beyond the limited domains of ritual and discourse, never had any concrete impact on the daily lives of the people of the region. Rather, these principles openly contradicted the aristocratic order throughout the period. Repeating such principles mechanically in ritual and discourse was thus in one sense a concession that the aristocratic elite made in order to maintain a relationship of mutual non-interference with the central government. Indeed, whenever the central regime attempted to go beyond these realms and impinge on elite privilege directly, it encountered outrage and fierce resistance.

In another sense, then, invoking the principles of popular sovereignty in ritual and discourse was anything but a concession to the central state. For what was important about ritual performances and discursive statements was not the egalitarian, con-sensual, selfless principles that figured so prominently within them, but rather which casta group was able to articulate these principles – which group was able to make ritual pronouncements that were in such blatant contradiction with the reality of the time.

The ruling casta's ability to represent its particular interest as the general interest, and to depict its abuse of power as rule by consensus, did much to transform the potentially subversive nature of the principles of popular sovereignty into a legitim-ating mechanism for the structure of aristocratic sovereignty. It did so not because the ruling casta hid its abuse of power from view, but because it did not. That is, the principles of aristocratic sovereignty required that rulers show their ability to dominate, shame, and impose their will upon those who would challenge their position. Making use of egalitarian rhetoric in political ritual and discourse to justify the persecution of their local enemies, and to ridicule their patrons in the national capital, accomplished precisely this for those in power.

The elite's active celebration of the principles of equality, citizenship, and individual rights in all political ritual and discourse, even as it ridiculed and violated these principles in everyday life, was ultimately its undoing. The vision of a world in which the material, behavioral, and symbolic distinctions of aristocratic sovereignty were made to disappear, in which violence and insecurity were eliminated, and in which individual rights and protections truly obtained for all, proved very powerful for people of all social classes. For it provided everyone with a vision of social justice and social order that could act as a radical alternative to the insecurities to which all were subject under casta rule. Only in the context of the massive dislocations in culture and economy experienced throughout Peru as a by-product of the late nineteenth-century crisis in global capitalism, however, did this vision of social justice become a powerful motivating force in local affairs. In the midst of the chaotic conditions that prevailed during this period, marginalized middle sectors of the local population coalesced into a "movement of democratization," and declared themselves the defenders of popular rule and the enemies of aristocratic privilege. In 1930, at a moment of crisis in the national political order, these marginalized groups rose up to challenge the elite in an armed confrontation and managed to seize control of regional affairs. Thereafter, these middle sectors made good on their earlier vows. They were instrumental in forming a new public culture in Chachapoyas based on the principles of popular sovereignty.

The success of the "revolution of 1930" was contingent upon a prior period of intense political mobilization among the mestizo [mixed race] artisans of the towns and the Indian peasants of the countryside. In the years leading up to the revolution, the democratización movement had attracted much of the local population to its cause. The movement's widespread appeal was (in part) a function of the new cultural order and moral universe to which it gave expression in public discourse – one that offered the subaltern a radical alternative to the demeaning and oppressive structure of casta rule.

Chachapoyas's marginalized middle sectors began to construct a new identity for themselves predominantly in the pages of a local newspaper – *Amazonas*. *Amazonas* asserted that the region *did* have a general interest, that its people *did* have common enemies, and that they *could* build an effective future. They could do so by rising up against the aristocratic families, whose incessant struggles for power had consistently undermined the common good. The paper asserted that Chachapoyas's ruling elite was anything but a noble caste descended from aristocratic forebears. Filling its pages with the litany of elite abuses with which the subaltern was intimately familiar, *Amazonas* argued that the elite was brutal and rapacious. Its members' ancestors had come to power centuries before (during the Conquest) through deception and murder, and thereafter had divided, victimized, and abused the defenseless population in whatever way possible – all in order to satisfy its insatiable hunger for power, privilege, and wealth.

Nor, the paper argued, were the region's mestizos and Indios the uncouth, semi-civilized group they were depicted to be. Rather, they were the local embodiment of *el pueblo Peruano* (the Peruvian people). As such, they represented the region's only hope for salvation. It was el pueblo that was committed to the ideals of democracy, equality, and justice. It was *el pueblo Chachapoyano* who sought to end the abuses of its own aristocratic elite. In the absence of adequate protections by the state, however, el pueblo had been left to be mistreated by the elite families. Indeed, because these elite families had hung on so tenaciously to their positions of privilege, democracy and justice had yet to be established in Chachapoyas – and thus el pueblo Chachapoyano continued to be victimized by abuses from which other peoples had been liberated long before. Once rid of such coercive influences, el pueblo Chachapoyano would be free to realize its true potential, to make its unique contribution to the Peruvian nation. In the meantime, however, Chachapoyas was best understood as a remote backwater where prenational sentiments and archaic forms of behavior lingered that had long since disappeared from the rest of the civilized world.

The new cultural order imagined discursively within the movement of democratización thus directly contradicted the cultural logic of the aristocratic order – in particular, elite assertions of fundamental, inherent differences among distinct racial groups. The democratización movement undermined elite assertions of hereditary distinction by making common cause among those identified as belonging to inferior races (Indios, cholos, runa [rural Indian cultivators (derogatory)]), and by combining them into a single, inclusive, nonracial category – el pueblo. El pueblo, taught the movement, was the region's only hope for salvation, for el pueblo represented the region's only progressive force for change.

In this way, the movement of democratización sought to place the region and its people in a historical imaginary independent of and more powerful than the aristocratic families' parochial claims to nobility. The explicitly *national* dimension to these efforts was crucial. El pueblo was a category derived in large part from the discourse of the nation-state, and thus the democratización movement invoked a national form of authority and a national system of social classification in challenging the aristocratic order. The authority and legitimacy of el pueblo, however, was not strictly national in character. By taking on the mantle of "the people," the marginalized middle sectors of Chachapoyas associated themselves with a movement that transcended national boundaries. They claimed to be a part of the rise of modernity – the movement of global proportions that had catapulted western Europe to preeminence worldwide, that had everywhere vanquished "backward," feudal elites, that had liberated the individual from *his* oppressors, and had ushered in an era of justice and prosperity.

The movement of democratización that swept through Chachapoyas in the 1920s and ultimately led to the overthrow of the landed elite exhibits several features worthy of comment. First, contrary to what is described in much of the literature on state-building and nation-making, modern, national culture did not come to Chachapoyas in the shape of an externally imposed set of cultural forms whose arbitrariness had to be naturalized by the institutions of the state. Rather, those involved in the movement embraced modern notions of time, space, and personhood without having been coerced or coopted, prior to the establishment of state institutions and their normalizing gaze. Indeed, the entire mobilization of the middle sectors occurred in the context of a broad cultural movement that opposed tradition to modernity – that branded the former as a backward, oppressive structure based on artificial and imposed distinctions that were used to justify brutality and greed. Modernity and nationhood were welcomed as powerful moral forces of emancipation – forces that would liberate the region from its oppressors, and would allow the true potential of the people at last to be realized.

In challenging the aristocratic order, then, the movement of democratización openly embraced "things modern" and "things national." In addition to doing away with exclusionary racial divisions, reconfiguring history, and reconceptualizing space, this challenge included accepting modern notions of discipline, order, hygiene, and morality. For these "personal" characteristics were seen as the antithesis of the violent and abusive behavior of the decadent aristocratic elite. In short, as an outgrowth of the movements of democratización, time and space were nationalized, and individuality was modernized.

Second, the new cultural identity and alternative moral universe authored from within the movement of democratización appeared to movement participants as anything but imposed, external, or arbitrary. Rather, these were to a significant degree created by the people themselves, and emerged in the form of a *recognition* on their part of the region's most essential and enduring characteristics. Indeed, these features were regarded as being eternal. Reflected in phenomena as diverse as the ancient architecture of the Inca and the personal proclivities of el pueblo, they were seen as integral to the region and its people.

National culture thus first emerged from within local society as something natural, eternal, and true – and as sufficiently motivating to the subaltern that, in order to make it a reality, they risked their lives in order to overthrow the elite in an armed confrontation. Thereafter, the formerly marginalized middle sectors took it upon themselves to actualize a new form of public culture based on popular sovereignty. It was only at this point that the modern nation-state began to take on a real presence in the Chachapoyas region – and that the state was able even to begin to implement the individualizing, homogenizing, naturalizing institutional practices discussed at length in the literature on making national cultures.

The process by which the nation-state took on a tangible presence in the Chachapoyas region thus inverts the scenario described in much of the literature on the formation of modern nation-states. Most recent literature on the subject has emerged out of the study of western Europe, or out of areas that were colonies (or near-colonies) of western European nation-states in the nineteenth and twentieth centuries. Relatively few recent works have focused on the study of Latin America. The history of state formation, the class structures, the relationship of dominant classes to the state, and the attitude toward popular sovereignty of those who controlled the state apparatus were all profoundly different in western European countries (and their colonies) than in Latin America in general, and in Chachapoyas in particular. These differences, I believe, do much to explain why oppositional models of state-building and coercive understandings of making modern, national cultures are of limited use in understanding the history of state- and nation-building in postcolonial Latin America.

European nation-states of the nineteenth and early twentieth centuries and their colonial domains existed in an imperial context that differed in fundamental ways from the position of Chachapoyas within the Peruvian polity. In the context of western Europe, the 1900s are commonly cited as the century of the nation-state – as the period during which centralized, bureaucratic states that had been hundreds of years in the making came under the control of solidary national communities based on the principles of popular sovereignty. The rise of capitalism is clearly fundamental to this process (Gellner 1983; Hobsbawm 1962, 1975; Nairn 1977; Tilly 1975). It was the triumphant bourgeoisie that, from its vantage point of state control, and on the basis of its identification with the principles of modernity and nationhood, employed the classificatory, regulatory capacities of the state apparatus to monitor and oversee the gradual incorporation of select subaltern groups into the political community (Frader and Rose 1996; McClelland 1993; Rose 1992, 1993). Ironically, the universalistic and inclusive discourse of the Enlightenment was used toward exclusionary ends in this process (Mehta 1990). This occurred because the bourgeoisie equated its own culture with human nature, and made full participation in the political community contingent (in part) upon the subaltern adopting "proper" and "respectable" attitudes, practices, and forms of behavior. The result of this process was to shape subjectivity in "modern" directions – and to produce a national citizenry and a more pliable labor force. In the process, differences of race and gender became essentialized and naturalized, and were used to reproduce bourgeois values as well as to exclude from the political community those who exhibited a nature that deviated from the culture of the bourgeoisie.

These developments in the metropole had significant repercussions in the more distant parts of empire. As Cooper and Stoler (1989) point out, the rise of the nation-state, citizenship, and the centrality of post-Enlightenment thought in general in defining legitimate forms of political association in western Europe created unique tensions in the colonies. For the coercive and exclusionary mechanisms and relationships upon which colonial rule was largely based blatantly contradicted the universalistic and voluntaristic discourses that defined legitimate political rule. Just as in the metropole, exclusionary practices were justified in the colonies by equating the culture of the metropolitan ruling elite with human nature, and by finding little of this human nature among "indigenous races and peoples" (thus the "civilizing mission" of the colonizers). Exclusionary practices in the colonies were in many ways more rigid than within the metropole (Cohn 1987; Kaplan 1995), and were organized more explicitly on the basis of race (Kelly 1995; Stoler 1989, 1992). In the colonies, the threat to metropolitan rule – and to bourgeois respectability – represented by the possible blurring of boundaries between colonized and colonizers (via social relationships and sexual liaisons) led to an extraordinary interest in the sexual and family lives of the colonized. This perceived threat also led to elaborate attempts on the part of colonizers to regulate these domains – to police racial divides, and at times to prohibit sexual unions. Indeed, the sexual morality and virtue of the colonized (and the colonizers) often became matters of "public" concern. Similar developments occurred within western European nation-states, if on a somewhat reduced scale.

Peru and Chachapoyas could not represent more of a contrast with conditions in western Europe and its colonies. Chachapoyas was not colonized and controlled by a centralized European nation-state during the nineteenth and twentieth centuries. Nor did it lie within such a nation-state. For most of the nineteenth and early twentieth centuries, no centralized state existed in Peru whatsoever. Opinions as to precisely when Peru can be regarded as truly having become a territorial state differ from specialist to specialist. Regardless of the specific date chosen, however, it is clear from the analysis presented in the chapters above that the state had very limited capacity to implement its central decisions, or to regulate/monitor the activities of its populace.

Not only was the Peruvian state poorly developed during the period in question, but no self-consciously modern bourgeois class committed to the principles of popular sovereignty arose to seize control of the apparatus of state. Rather, the "pseudo-state" that was Peru remained in the hands of shifting groups of regional elites who were strongly wedded to notions of aristocratic sovereignty. As a result, popular sovereignty did not become an ideological tool manipulated by elites. Nor did it become harnessed to the machinery of state as a means of molding a national citizenry and managing discontent among working classes (via limited extension of membership in the political community) – as it did in western Europe. Nor was modernity used as a boundary marker between primitive (subaltern) and civilized (elite) – or as a rationale for the domination of "inferior peoples and races" by a bourgeois, metropolitan elite (as it was in the European colonies).

To the contrary: in Chachapoyas, popular sovereignty was used as an explicitly anti-elite ideology – one that was seized upon by marginalized middle sectors to confront aristocratic privilege. It tended toward inclusion, not exclusion, of marginalized categories. In the hands of the subaltern, popular sovereignty was used to reconfigure racial boundaries from below. It did away with several derogatory racial categories completely (cholo, Indio, runa) by aggregating them into a single, nonracial category derived from the discourse of popular sovereignty – el pueblo. Furthermore, to the extent that formerly denigrated racial categories (Indio) continued to be recognized, the attitude toward them was one of inclusion. Only the racial category of the oppressors – blanco [white] – became the object of hostility. By exorcizing the category "blanco" from the local scene, el pueblo did away with superordinate and subordinate racial categories altogether, defined itself in explicitly nonracial, national terms, and thus eliminated race as a means of social classification.

Unlike the situation that prevailed in western Europe and its colonies, then, in Chachapoyas race was not used in an exclusionary manner – for purposes of boundary maintenance, in order to mark clear and unequivocal lines between those who ruled and those who did not. Rather, because el pueblo was constituted by erasing/collapsing the boundaries between several formerly distinct subaltern racial categories, there was no interest in carefully policing racial divides, nor in prohibiting sexual liaisons. Nor did the sexual morality and virtue of the subaltern become matters of "public" concern, as they did in many European nation-states and their colonies.

In direct contrast with the behavior of European bourgeois classes, in Chachapoyas members of the aristocratic elite played no positive role in the implementation of popular sovereignty. Indeed, they were completely opposed to it. They did everything in their power to retain their traditional aristocratic privileges, to limit expressions of popular sovereignty to the domains of ritual and discourse, and to prevent popular sovereignty from moving directly into social life. Indeed, the elite went so far as to insist on the right to ridicule popular sovereignty – to counter all rhetorical and discursive expressions of equality and inclusion with public demonstrations of hierarchy and exclusion.

El pueblo's embrace of modernity and popular sovereignty must be understood in this light. El pueblo did indeed adopt modern notions of time, space, and personhood, did indeed adopt much of the discourse of self-discipline and control found among the European bourgeoisie – and reproduced (albeit in changed form and for different purposes) in the colonies under the institutional gaze of the colonial state apparatus. In so doing, however, el pueblo was not aping its own bourgeoisie. Nor was it being offered entrance into a political community on terms dictated by such a bourgeoisie. Rather, its members were opposing themselves to an indigenous aristocracy. And they embraced the principles of popular sovereignty voluntarily, as a way of differentiating themselves from this aristocracy in moral and ethical terms, in their efforts to divest this aristocratic elite of control of the state apparatus.

The Chachapoyan aristocratic elite therefore did not employ the classificatory, regulatory mechanisms of the state in order to monitor the gradual incorporation of the subaltern into the political community. Nor did this aristocratic elite employ the institutional gaze of state institutions to mold and shape subjectivity in "modern" directions – and thus produce a national citizenry and a malleable labor force. The elite did not do so because, first, its members did not themselves identify with notions of modern nationhood or personhood; and second, the government apparatus was poorly formed, and lacked the enforcement mechanisms in the absence of which the institutional gaze of the state has little effect (see Biolsi 1995; Corrigan and Sayer 1985; Verdery 1991).

The subaltern in Chachapoyas confronted an aristocratic elite that used its control over a weak state apparatus to reproduce traditional privilege. This meant that subaltern groups could realistically seize upon both modernity and a strong state as liberating forces. For modernity condemned traditional privilege and provided the subaltern with the vision of an alternative moral/ethnical universe. And a strong state promised to safeguard and defend this alternative social order. The interest of the subaltern in implementing the institutions, values, practices, and other accouterments of modernity after it had seized control of state institutions must be understood in the same terms.

In other words, unlike the situation that prevailed in western Europe, an existing bourgeoisie already in control of state institutions did not use popular sovereignty as a way of managing the rise of subaltern groups. Rather, rising subaltern groups used popular sovereignty as a way of challenging an aristocratic elite, and in the process helped bring the modern state into being. Modernity and nation-state thus represented powerful forces of liberation that were spontaneously adopted from below rather than imposed from above.

This is not to say, of course, that the image of society and personhood contained within the discourse of popular sovereignty corresponded to actual social conditions. As has been emphasized . . . what people involved in the movement of democratización called "democracy" was anything but a process involving open and equal participation of all. Exclusion was an integral part of the movement. Democratización meant not only the empowerment of the urban, male middle class, but also the systematic exclusion of women and peasants from the more "open" society envisaged within the movement. Even though the transformations in local life effected by the movement were consistently cast in the universalistic language of the Enlightenment, these changes represented the interest and motivations of particular groups depicted as the interests and motivations of all groups. These and related processes of exclusion – built into the very process of state-building and nation-making – were to come to the fore in subsequent decades (see Nugent 1996).

The analysis presented above points to the dangers of attempting to generalize about processes of state-building and nation-making on the basis of the experiences of western European nation-states and their colonies. National cultures are not always constructed from above, by the imposition of a unitary and homogeneous national essence on (what are assumed to be) subject populations with their own distinct, local cultures. Rather, in the making of national cultures, the "periphery" may reach toward the center to embrace the nation as much as (if not more than) the center reaches out to the periphery. Furthermore, in embracing the center, those in the peripheral locale do not necessarily abandon what is distinctively local (Hobsbawm 1990: 11; Sahlins 1989: 8–9). Local and national identifications may be interdependent and co-constitutive. The local and the national may call one another into being. Indeed, I would argue that state and nation are most solidary precisely when these conditions obtain.

The material from Chachapoyas shows that it is a mistake to assume that national cultures are best understood as elite projects at cultural homogenization. They do not necessarily imply an exclusive set of dominant meanings and essences that compete jealously with alternative subaltern meanings. They are not necessarily "totalizing" phenomena. Despite the apparent uniformity and homogeneity of national identifications, a single national identity may be embraced in quite distinct ways by different groups, for reasons that are regionally specific, historically variable, and grounded in local-level conflicts (cf. Hobsbawm 1990: 11).

It follows that the making of a national culture does not necessarily involve effecting a mystifying transformation on the artifical, arbitrary, and temporary, making it seem real, natural, and eternal. Rather, national cultures can emerge from within local/regional populations, as the result of being perceived as natural, true, and real. Thus state institutions and technologies of power that reorder space, rewrite history, and reconstruct subjectivity are not necessarily prior to the formation of a national culture. Instead, local populations' receptivity to state and nation may be important preconditions to such institutions and technologies ever becoming established in any given locale.

The widespread use of notions such as ideology, hegemony, habitus, and so on, in making sense of the rise of national cultures – conceived of as invented and arbitrary traditions – clearly indicates that analysts who employ these concepts regard those who hold national identities to be in bad faith – to be confused, mystified, the victims of a kind of hoax. As Benedict Anderson (1983: 6) has shown, however, what is important about communities in general is not that some are real and others are false, but the style in which they are imagined. I would add that it is equally important regarding national communities to ask who does and does not imagine the community to be national, in which forms, in which times and places, and why.

The foregoing suggests that the boundary between "nation-state" and "society" is most easily drawn when the mission of the nation-state has failed, when its power has been forced into coercive form by those with whom it seeks interrelationship. To conceive of the nation-state as *only* coercive, however – to view its relations with society as strictly oppositional – is to privilege above all else one limited and contingent dimension of a relationship that is in reality much more dense and complex. This is reflected in the voluntary embrace by many people throughout the world of the reformulations of time, space, and personhood effected within nationalist imaginings, precisely because of their emancipatory appeal. It would be foolish to assert that these imaginings were *exclusively* liberating, even for those who embraced them so willingly. To ignore the empowering dimension of nationalist yearnings completely, however, is to disregard a long and distinguished genealogy in theoretical understandings of power – a genealogy that insists on understanding power as simultaneously enabling and disabling. Moreover, it is to reify the nation, and to deny people any active, productive role in making and remaking their own lives.

REFERENCES

Anderson, B. (1983) *Imagined Communities: Reflections on the Origin and Spread of Nationalism*. London: Verso.

Biolsi, T. (1995) The Birth of the Reservation: Making the Modern Individual among the Lakota. *American Ethnologist* 22(2): 28–53.

Cohn, B. (1987) The Census, Social Structure, and Objectification in South Asia. In B. Cohn, *An Anthropologist among the Historians and other Essays*, pp. 224–54. Delhi: Oxford University Press.

Cooper, F. and Stoler, L. (1989) Tensions of Empire: Colonial Control and Visions of Rule. *American Ethnologist* 16(4): 609–21.

Corrigan, P. and Sayer, D. (1981) How the Law Rules. In B. Fryer et al. (eds.) *Law, State, and Society*. Beckenham: Croom Helm.

—— and ——. (1985) *The Great Arch: English State Formation as Cultural Practice*. Oxford: Blackwell Publishers.

Frader, L. and Rose, S. (eds.) (1996) *Gender and the Reconstruction of European Working Class History*. Ithaca, NY: Cornell University Press.

Gellner, E. (1983) *Nations and Nationalism*. Ithaca, NY: Cornell University Press.

Hobsbawm, E. (1962) *The Age of Revolution, 1848–75*. New York: Scribner.

——. (1975) *The Age of Capital, 1848–1875*. New York: Scribner.

——. (1990) *Nations and Nationalism since 1780: Programme, Myth, Reality*. Cambridge: Cambridge University Press.

Kaplan, M. (1995) Panopticon in Poona: An Essay on Foucault and Colonialism. *Cultural Anthropology* 10(1): 85–98.

Kelly, J. (1995) Threats to Difference in Colonial Fiji. *Cultural Anthropology* 10(1): 64–84.

McClelland, K. (1993) Rational and Responsible Men: Gender, the Working Class, and Citizenship in Britain, 1850–1867. Paper presented at the Annual Meeting of the Social Science History Association, Baltimore, Nov. 4–7.

Mehta, U. (1990) Liberal Strategies of Exclusion. *Politics and Society* 18: 427–54.

Nairn, T. (1977) *The Break-up of Britain: Crisis and Neo-Functionalism*. London: New Left Books.

Nugent, D. (1996) From Devil Pact to Drug Deals: Commerce, Unnatural Accumulation and Moral Economy in Modern Peru. *American Ethnologist* 23(2): 382–97.

——. (1997) *Modernity at the Edge of Empire: State, Individual and Nation in the Northern Peruvian Andes, 1885–1935*. Stanford: Stanford University Press.

Rose, S. D. (1992) *Limited Livelihoods: Gender and Class in Nineteenth Century England*. Berkeley: University of California Press.

——. (1993) Respectable Men, Disorderly Others: The Language of Gender and the Lancashire Weavers' Strike of 1878 in Britain. *Gender and History* 5(3): 382–97.

Sahlins, P. (1989) *Boundaries: The Making of France and Spain in the Pyrenees*. Berkeley: University of California Press.

Stoler, A. (1989) Making Empire Respectable: The Politics of Race and Sexual Morality in Twentieth Century Colonial Cultures. *American Ethnologist* 16(4): 634–60.

——. (1992) Sexual Affronts and Racial Frontiers: European Identities and the Cultural Politics of Exclusion in Colonial Southeast Asia. *Comparative Studies in Society and History* 34(3): 514–51.

Tilly, C. (1975) *The Formation of National States in Western Europe*. Princeton: Princeton University Press.

Verdery, K. (1991) Theorizing Socialism: A Prologue to the "Transition". *American Ethnologist* 18(3): 419–39.

26

Politics on the Periphery

Anna Lowenhaupt Tsing

This book [Tsing 1993] is about the cultural and political construction of marginality. It is about the process in which people are marginalized as their perspectives are cast to the side or excluded. It is also about the ways in which people actively engage their marginality by protesting, reinterpreting, and embellishing their exclusion. Marginality has been an important concern in recent discussions of colonial discourse, race, class, and gender. I hope to contribute to these discussions; yet my account stresses the specificity of marginalizing discourses, institutions, and experiences. In this spirit, my book is an ethnographic account. It describes how, in the early 1980s, Dayak shifting cultivators of the rainforested Meratus Mountains of South Kalimantan, Indonesia, worked to define and redefine their situation on the periphery of state power. I explore the intersection of three processes within which Meratus marginality is shaped: state rule, the formation of regional and ethnic identities, and gender differentiation....

Hiking down from the forests and scattered swiddens of the Meratus Mountains toward the markets, offices, and mosques of the Banjar plains, I came to pass through the Meratus border settlement of Kalawan. Meratus friends in the mountains had told me of a Kalawan woman, Uma Adang, whom they thought I would enjoy meeting. But when I pressed for details, they had merely nodded knowingly....

As powerful demands for resources, land, and military control have guided state expansion to the most remote corners of the earth, the autonomy and mobility of the marginal cultural groups of once inaccessible places – rainforests, rugged mountains, deserts, tundra – have increasingly been threatened. The dominant frameworks for understanding recent encroachments, however, ignore long histories of marginality to posit conditions of "before" versus "after" – of pristine isolation, on the one hand, and rapid cultural destruction or modernization, on the other. In such frameworks,

From *In the Realm of the Diamond Queen* (Princeton: Princeton University Press, 1993), pp. 5, 7–10, 13–18, 22–6. Copyright © 1993 by Princeton University Press. Reprinted by permission of Princeton University Press.

marginal people become archaic survivors who, for better or worse, are forced to "catch up with the twentieth century." These frameworks create "primitives" within a medley of interlinked narratives about progress and civilization. Whether as objects of romantic fascination or of missionizing zeal, these imagined primitives are a provocative reminder of all that civilized humanity has lost....

[Here] I explore the making of an Indonesian marginal culture. Meratus Dayaks could easily be described as primitives; they are probably as isolated as any Indonesian minority about whom I have read. They are subsistence cultivators and forest foragers of thick rainforests. They live in rough terrain, often a hike of several days from the nearest market. They hunt with dogs and spears and bring their sick to shamans for healing rites. These are ways of life that invite a conventional set of questions about strange and different forms of knowledge and society. My focus on marginality involves a choice to formulate a perspective on culture and community that stands in contrast to those perspectives most commonly found in both popular imagery and classic ethnography.

I begin with an awareness that "the Meratus" are not just a site of endogenous, localized knowledge but are also, and always, a *displacement* within powerful discourses on civilization and progress. As untamed hill people, Meratus are formed in the imagination of the Indonesian state, the "civilized" regional majority, and the visiting anthropologists and travellers who learn to "know" them. Indeed, the name *Meratus* itself is my own awkward imposition, offered to avoid the derogatory ethnic term *Bukit*.

Yet these powerful names and discourses do not have an unquestioned hegemony: Meratus respond, reinterpret, and challenge even as they accept and are shaped by these forms of knowledge. My analysis locates itself primarily at a "Meratus" level, in order to emphasize local negotiations – and, in the process, to reformulate anthropological ideas of the local. I feature stories, narratives of people and events, because these stories show sites of discursive contestation.[1]

It is in this genre-stretching sense that [my] book is an ethnography. I am concerned particularly with the way in which the women and men I knew explained and commented upon local cultural politics in the context of regional dilemmas. For example, Meratus relations to state power were rarely absent from local discussions of culture and community. In contrast to the self-generating solidarity basic to most ethnographic accounts of community, I heard Meratus describe community formation as a state project that they could fulfill or frustrate. Local leaders constructed their authority not by reiterating community hierarchy but by emphasizing their ties to state rule. Yet this enthusiasm forms the crux of a contradiction: rather than integrating Meratus into Indonesian politics as citizens, national political discourse has demarcated Meratus as savages outside its reaches. It is this kind of contradiction that I explore under the rubric of *marginality*.

I argue, too, that gender-differentiated responses to peripheral political status are central to understanding the distinctive debates of Meratus culture. Most Meratus leaders are men; in a number of ways, women are disadvantaged political actors. Many women I met considered themselves politically uninformed. Yet they were not silent; even the least ambitious offered complaints and sarcastic remarks, and a few challenged local standards to become leaders themselves and publicize their views. Their comments reminded me not to assume that "community" inspires a homogeneous form of consciousness; instead, I began to listen for shifting, multistranded conversations in which there never was full agreement. Precisely because of their unlikely authority, unusually ambitious women pointed me toward the creative possibilities as well as the constraints inherent in Meratus marginalities. The commentaries of exceptional women play an important role in my project because they guide my analysis to linked asymmetries of gender, ethnicity, and state rule – yet they destabilize these asymmetries.

My project involves the study of intersecting discursive fields in which social identities, such as those I call "Meratus," are created and maintained. Such an analysis departs from more conventional cultural anthropology to the extent that it does not focus on underlying principles and structures that unite contextually and historically changing commitments and actions. Critics of the latter approach have suggested that the depth and coherence of culture are artifacts of a particular gaze from abroad, a gaze that focuses on the differences between a Western-trained "us" and a non-Western "them." These critics point to the way in which this gaze obscures local debates and historicities (for example, Clifford and Marcus 1986; Said 1978; Wolf 1982). I argue that an alternative lies in situating local commentaries – such as those of the Meratus women and men I knew – within wider negotiations of meaning and power at the same time as recognizing local stakes and specificities.

By putting gender at the center of my analysis, I create a continually oppositional dialogue with more familiar ethnographic genres which segregate an endogenous cultural logic from regional-to-global influences. Generally, studies of gender and wider political relations hardly overlap. Histories of local–global interconnections still ignore gender; and gender tends to be studied as an "internal" cultural issue. "External" influences are portrayed as influencing gender – as in much of the literature on women, colonialism, and development – only as foreign impositions upon once stable and self-regulating traditions.[2] These conventions obscure the regionally ramifying debates and practices that produce both gender and politics. By transgressing conventions of segregated "internal" and "external" cultural analysis, this book shows the connections between intercommunity divisions, including gender difference, and Meratus regional and national marginality. Attention to gender, as both an imaginative construct and a point of divergent positionings, brings wider cultural negotiations to the center of local affairs.

In this project I join many other contemporary scholars who are interested in cultural heterogeneity and the trans-communal links through which "communities" are forged.[3] Unlike much of this work, however, [my] book describes the kind of out-of-the-way terrain familiar from classic ethnographies, rather than focusing on urban centers, mass media, and the latest technological developments. Too often, generalizations about modern and postmodern cultural processes rest on surprisingly unrefurbished stereotypes of primitive, traditional enclaves. (I think, for example, of Pierre Bourdieu's analysis of "archaic" Algerian culture as a foil to "modern" France (1990), or, in a rather different vein, of Frederic Jameson's attempt (1991) to show a unilinear evolution to postmodernism.) In my analysis I refuse divisions of dynamic core and culturally stagnant periphery by showing the importance of analyzing heterogeneity and transcultural dialogue in even the most out-of-the-way places. In such contexts, perhaps even more than in the urban centers where researchers expect contest and debate, cultural analysts are challenged to reexamine theory and create new forms of description....

My interest in Meratus marginality began during my fieldwork as I found that it was difficult to have a discussion about almost any topic I might want to explore – gender, forest use, ritual, etc. – without paying attention to the context of ethnic asymmetry and political status *vis-à-vis* the state. It was this context that made local culture worth discussing for the Meratus I knew; it gave shape to what was imaginable as well as interesting to talk about. At first, I thought of marginality as an ethnographic *feature*, which made the Meratus different from other groups. However, theoretical developments in cultural studies and anthropology have opened new ways to think about marginality. Scholars have developed an active discussion of the political processes of cultural production – inside and outside academe – in which "cultures" are no longer separate worlds. Rather than characterizing any given culture, marginality becomes key to reformulating cultural theory.

The critique of anthropology as a form of Western colonial discourse has become well known within the field, and it has stimulated a number of important responses. Anthropologists have criticized unself-conscious caricatures of tribal peoples, initiated careful textual analyses of past and present ethnographic writing, and turned toward the long-neglected study of dominant culture in Europe and the United States.[4] Yet many of these admittedly rich responses retain one of the most problematic features of colonial discourse: the fantasized gulf between the West and its Other. The responses turn from the study of the Other to the study of the West, but they continue to ignore the complexity of cultural production within the interactions of colonizers and colonized. Thus, anthropological writing is most commonly studied in relation to Western formats of representation – but not in its engagement with local (Western and non-Western) struggles over power and meaning. And the cultures of white people are still studied in isolation from Third World and minority dialogues. This retreat to an imaginary segregation does not improve anthropology's analytic tools.

In contrast, a number of self-consciously "postcolonial" and "minority" scholars, working from and across a variety of academic disciplines, have opened a theoretical discussion about the cultural engagements of people in politically asymmetrical positions. The most vigorous wing of this discussion asks about these engagements from the position of the excluded and the insubordinate: those at the "margins" of cultural domination. It is, of course, possible to differentiate scholars here – this one a Derridean, that one a Marxist – but it is precisely against the grain of these European genealogies that I introduce their focus on the marginal. Literary critic Homi Bhabha articulates the challenge of this emerging field in a question he draws from Frantz Fanon: "How can a human being live Other-wise?" (Bhabha 1989: 147). This is a field that considers the negotiation of cultural differences that have emerged both because of and despite Western imperial power, as well as the ensuing nationalisms and ethnicities this power has bred. It is a theoretical discussion that anthropologists, as well as anyone else interested in global cultural interactions, can no longer afford to neglect. The promise of a postcolonial anthropology that goes beyond the re-analysis of its own problematic past depends upon engagement with the questions and challenges raised by those concerned with cultural heterogeneity, power, and "marginality."

The "marginal" began as a point from which theoretical criticism in academe could be launched. Literary critics crafted the marginal as intervention into Western humanism; margins are the sites of exclusion from this tradition from which its categories and assumptions can be seen more clearly. A number of critics have shown how asymmetries of race, gender, and colonial status have been produced *within* rather than *in spite of* humanist standards (for example, Irigaray 1985; Spillers 1987; Spivak 1987). Similarly, the marginal has been a rejoinder to Marxist class-oriented approaches that do not adequately address colonialism and racism. Unlike class, the latter power relations cannot be understood within a homogeneous, taken-for-granted cultural regime; they construct and bind systems of cultural difference. Thus, attention to the marginal has opened discussion of linked cultural constructions of domination and difference (Hall 1990; hooks 1990; Taussig 1987). From this criticism, then, marginality began to signal a discussion that moves beyond rereading dominant theories to formulate new objects of study. Yet, in contrast to conventional anthropology, this trajectory refuses a theoretical separation of analysts and objects of study as two distinct classes; marginalities created both inside and outside the academy are interconnected. The knowledge of an author, like that of the people about whom he or she writes, is always partial, situated, and perspectivistic (Clifford 1986; Haraway 1988; Lewis 1973).

A caution seems in order: although self-positioning can be an opening move for crafting new forms of cultural analysis (Rosaldo 1989), this is not a literature of authentic or representative "voices" of excluded minorities. It would be easy and unfortunate to deintellectualize this literature as the recording of the essential experiences of Others. ("Let's hear," they say, "from the X perspective.") Instead, the goal is to open new possibilities for thinking and writing; anyone can participate.

Yet the way in which writers imagine their own marginality is perhaps one way to understand a central tension that divides current scholars analyzing the marginal. Because it raises key questions for all cultural analysis, including the present study, it is worth some attention here. I refer to a tension around the political implications of notions of cultural difference. Edward Said (1978) has led the way among those self-identified as diasporic postcolonials (Third World scholars working in Europe or the United States) in emphasizing how colonial discourse constructs "other cultures" to separate colonizer and colonized. He and others show how the notion of cultural difference has been used to debase and control Third World peoples (Mani 1987; Trinh 1989). As Gayatri Spivak puts it, the "pluralist aesthetes of the First World are, willy-nilly, participants in the production of an exploitative society" (1987: 179). This analysis self-consciously draws from the experience of having to struggle for an academic voice – against classifications as an alien – despite the best Western education and talent (for example, Spivak 1989).[5]

In contrast, minority scholars in the United States have had more to say about empowering aspects of self-involvement with cultural difference. The discourse of domination that seems most constraining is not that of encrusted difference, but that of white privilege falsely universalized to erase the struggles, accomplishments, and dilemmas of people of color. Thus, Cornel West writes of the "modern Black diaspora problematic of invisibility and namelessness" and the importance of building "subcultures and networks of people of color who cultivate critical sensibilities and personal accountability" (1990: 27, 34). Breaking out of the cultural homogenizations of the United States involves the creativity of making difference matter (for example, hooks 1989; Lorde 1984).

Both groups thus locate their critiques as border skirmishes that open up the carefully patrolled closures of dominant modes of thought. Yet the cultural construction of domination looks different from each per spective. Postcolonial critics worry about "essentialist" political moves (see, for example, Najmabadi 1991; Spivak 1989b), as US minorities argue against the elitist assumptions and obfuscations of poststructuralist (sometimes postcolonial) writing (for example, Christian 1988)[6]

A closer look at the work of individual scholars reveals many whose approaches cut across this dichotomization and call its terms into question. I introduce the contrast not in order to predetermine scholarly positions but to open a discussion that is easily neglected in throwing together "Other" perspectives. The tension is an intellectually invigorating one for my project, and it needs to be seen in relation to varied political and intellectual challenges.

An example can illuminate both the contrast and the complexity of scholarly positions. A number of postcolonial scholars theorizing the marginal have revived the work of anticolonial psychoanalyst Frantz Fanon. Homi Bhabha, for example, turns to Fanon to help focus discussion on the subjectivity of the colonized, at the margins of colonial discourse. Bhabha uses Fanon to move beyond theorists who overemphasize the hegemony of colonial discourse, such as, in his view, Edward Said: "There is always, in Said, the suggestion that colonial power and discourse [are] possessed entirely by the colonizer" (1990: 77). Bhabha, instead, emphasizes the limits of colonial authority in its ambivalences, incongruities, misreadings, and vulnerability to parodic mimicry on the part of the colonized. Bhabha thus comes much closer to a notion of oppositional cultural practices than I have stereotyped above as the "postcolonial" position.

Yet the limits of Bhabha's interest in cultural negotiation are nicely pointed out in "Critical Fanonism," an essay by African-American literary critic Henry Louis Gates, Jr. (1991). Gates criticizes Bhabha – and other postcolonial readers of Fanon – for making Fanon a "global theorist" with an "imperial agenda" that ignores the cultural and political specificity of its own interventions. In Bhabha's scheme, the colonized can parody but can never remake culture. All cultural negoti- ation thus reproduces the dichotomy between a globally homogeneous Colonizer and Colonized. Gates also criticizes Gayatri Spivak, who, he argues, can see "noth- ing outside (the discourse) of colonialism": "Spivak's argument, put in its strongest form, entails the corollary that all discourse is colonial discourse" (1991: 466). In contrast, Gates suggests that Fanon be historicized as a West Indian in Algeria whose background and training helped shape a particular utopian vision of a race-free Third World. Yet, of course, Gates's move toward cultural and historical specificity embroils his analysis in the logics of "cultural difference" and "historical narrative," which postcolonial critics such as Spivak have worked hard to show as colonial discourses that divide and conquer the empire's subjects. It may be useful to think of Bhabha and Spivak as speaking from the space *between* asymmetrically ranked nations; this space depends on unsettling the cultural and historical logics that support (ranked) nations. In contrast, Gates argues from a disadvantaged space *within* a nation in which unmarked "universal" status establishes privilege; this space inspires challenges to minority-silencing global agendas.

The way in which I have organized my exposition of these issues should by now reveal a good deal about my own stake in this matter. By pointing to the divergence of strategies between groups of scholars, I, like Gates, argue for recognition and respect for a variety of different political and intellectual agendas. This is not the same as a naive endorsement of cultural diversity; instead, the point is to specify the political challenges at hand.

The question of the marginality of Meratus Dayaks of South Kalimantan, Indonesia, poses challenges that tap and criticize both sides of the intellectual tension I have described. This project brings the issue of minority status out of the metropolitan context in which it has most commonly been discussed, and in which the political conditions of domination and debate are too often taken for granted. In contrast to much writing about minorities in the United States, my study forces analysis of the national ideologies and institutions that create minority status and shape minorities' attempts to be heard. The project also refuses global dichotomies of colonizer and colonized, as it requires a finer, more contradictory specification of national and regional discourses of exclusion and struggle. Yet the history of colonialism is never entirely absent in informing transnational projects such as this one; Meratus marginality in the Indonesian nation cannot be divorced from Indonesian marginality in international rankings. Raising the question of Meratus marginality thus calls attention to the complexity and specificity of cultural intersections.

The analyses of the marginal that have had the most to say about specificity and different kinds of marginality are those which have emerged within feminist theory. Yet, ironically, feminist theory is also the source of perhaps the most "global" and unspecified of all theories of the marginal. Feminists using and criticizing Lacanian psychoanalytic frameworks have explored female marginality in relation to phallogocentric subject formation; these theories formulate only one globally and historically homogeneous kind of "woman." The fact that she is disadvantaged in the ways best known to privileged white women goes unremarked. According to these theories, female marginalization is *parallel* in its form to the marginalization of the colonized, the nonwhite, or the poor. This is a formulation in which the intersection of gender with class, race, or national status necessarily remains invisible. At best, these factors are added on as additional layers of exclusion.

In contrast, and in response, many feminists have taken on the project of specification in which particular forms of "female" marginality must be studied in relation to the conditions of women's lives – as immigrants, minorities, wealthy, poor, black, white, sex workers, maids, or academics (for example, Bookman and Morgen 1988; Mohanty et al. 1991). This work rejects the notion that gender asymmetries are parallel to those of race, class, and nationality, for race, class, and national hierarchies are themselves everywhere constructed in gendered ways, and gender divisions are established with "communal" materials. The work I find most promising does not set up exemplar marginal women but, rather, opens up the defensive boundaries of cultural nationalisms by attention to gender (for example, Ebron 1991; Moraga 1983; White 1990). Yet a tension remains as feminists argue for specificity and refuse dominant, constraining readings of "difference." As feminist theorist Trinh Minh-ha (1989) explains, attention to "difference" both traps and empowers marginalized women as artists and political actors.

The analytic space created by this tension – in which ethnic and national marginalities are gendered (rather than parallel to gender), and in which marginality is a source of both constraint and creativity – is that which is explored in [my] book. . . .

In writing about Meratus marginality, I am fortunate to be able to draw from a rich literature on political culture in Indonesia. Scholars have long been fascinated by Indonesia's Indic (and Islamic) heritage and by the self-consciously concentric models of power of the kingdoms of Java, Bali, Sumatra, Sulawesi, and Kalimantan which preceded and overlapped with Dutch control of these areas (for example, Errington 1989; Geertz 1980; Moertono 1968). Furthermore, a number of scholars have shown how the postcolonial Indonesian state has structured Javanese notions of stratification and potency into its program of rule (for example, Anderson 1972; Dove 1985). Political formulas familiar to international analysts become transformed in the Indonesian context. For example, Shelly Errington (1992) has argued that European temporal notions of progress and development have, in current Indonesian state policy, been transformed into an Indic spatial framework of exemplary centers (as showcases of "development") and disorganized peripheries (as the not-yet-developed). In this framework, the once-and-future glory of "Java" is the center of a national potency that extends outward to rule what, since colonial times, have been called the "Outer Islands."

Much of the literature on political culture in Indonesia stresses the contrast between Indonesian notions of power and political models from the "West." Read in only a slightly against-the-grain way, this literature on cultural contrasts also shows the emergence of "Indonesia" at the margins of the postcolonial world system. Internationally mandated "national" standards are reinterpreted as Indonesia struggles for a national identity both within and against the neocolonial logics that have allowed Third World nations to exist.

This framework makes it possible to think about the ways in which the nation-state has simultaneously endorsed both colonial and precolonial models of government. For example, under President Suharto's New Order, the state has adopted the authoritarian style of the Dutch administration of the late colonial period (McVey 1982). In the 1920s and 1930s, the Dutch colonial admininstration worked for "peace and order" as they quelled strikes and protests and silenced unions, communists, reformists, and nationalists. Since the 1965 military crackdown that brought President Suharto to power, the postcolonial state has used similar tactics to promote political stability and order. Indeed, the state has argued their necessity on the grounds of international sponsorship of economic growth. It makes sense that New Order officials would use familiar colonial logics to address what they see as a problem within transnational administrative standards. At the same time, however, the New Order is associated with a revival of Javanese culture that has helped shape the bureaucracy from village administration to the highest political levels.

The research of John Pemberton (1989) is especially illuminating in understanding this conjunction. Pemberton shows how New Order notions of Javanese culture also derive from the logics of colonial rule – but those of indirect, rather than direct, rule. He argues that New Order cultural models draw from the life-styles of the politically restricted but wealthy Javanese elites of the colonial era. Javanese rulers whose "rule" was paralyzed within colonial constraints turned their attention to ritualistic formality; this formality is the "culture" that has been revived and reinterpreted in the New Order. Indeed, New Order reenactments replay an earlier Dutch colonial revival. Although, in the first decade of the twentieth century, the Dutch discouraged the Javanese elite from "feudal" displays of status, in the late 1920s – following years of nationalist organizing, union strikes, and rural protest – they told officials to resume their old (but now outdated) signs of power, to create a nostalgically recalled stability. By the 1930s, Javanese began to speak of *upacara* "rituals" as stable, traditional ceremonies of power (1989: 273–6). Drawing from this history, the New Order has promoted a nostalgic "Javanese culture," to promote stability and dispel the disarray of pre-1965 nationalist politics. "Culture" is endorsed as an alternative to "politics," as *order* is to *disorder*.

It is through cultural politics, then, that the New Order has established its focus on order itself as a ritualized stability in which, as Pemberton suggests, the greatest political success occurs when nothing happens. He describes how Indonesian elections have become a well-orchestrated "national ritual" (*upacara nasional*) in which the government party always wins by the same margin. Development programs are best expressed as floats in a parade; they present models for popular emulation. Although the New Order makes ethnic diversity an emblem of national unity, ethnic diversity is tamed within these Javanese cultural notions. Pemberton offers a striking example of state views of ethnicity: an exhibition at Mrs Suharto's Indonesia Museum shows the nation as an elite Javanese wedding with ethnic minorities represented as differentially dressed guests. The image suggests that minority groups are "invited" into the nation as long as they bow to Javanese standards.

State programs conflate acceptance of this nostalgic and stabilizing cultural tradition with appropriate citizenship. Yet this program has relied heavily on the pervasive presence of the army in rural and urban life to guarantee local quietude and cooperation with top-down development plans.

In turning to coercive but only partially successful government intervention in Javanese village ceremonies, Pemberton's work also draws attention to another challenge in studying Indonesian political culture: specifying the relationship between state and village. Study of the Indonesian state has long had the advantage over state-oriented scholarship in many other areas of the world. Moving beyond classic Marxist or Weberian frameworks, in which the state is an instrument of class interests or bureaucratic rationalization, Indonesianists have pointed to the symbolic fields in which power and politics are constituted. Such analyses take scholarly understanding of the state beyond the apparatus of government to show how the magic and power of the state are formed in everyday discursive practice. Continuities in political discourse between rulers and ruled become evident. Yet it is also important not to lose sight of disjunctions and discontinuities. Political discourse is not spread evenly across lines of class, region, ethnicity, gender, and urban – rural difference. Some scholars, such as Robert Hefner (1990), have usefully reintegrated political economy with symbolic analysis to show regional and class diversity in Indonesian national development. An alternative approach, which I pursue here, is to begin with the disjunctions created within national political discourse as they themselves shape – but never fully control – forms of unevenness.

In the Indonesian political system, a gap has been constructed between "the government" (*pemerintah*) and "the people" (*masyarakat*). In part, this gap is a heritage of colonial rule, which may account for some of its resemblance to European folk notions of the split between state and society. The Dutch, for example, instituted the codes that now differentiate "national" and "customary" law; those rural people associated with "custom" are conceptually segregated from national administrators. Even in this example of reformulated colonial policy, however, the split between rulers and ruled has its own contemporary specificity. In most areas of the country, governing officials are appointed from above at the provincial (*pro-pinsi*), regency (*kabupaten*), and district (*kecamatan*) levels of government. In contrast, village (*kampung*) and neighborhood (*runkun tetangga*) officials are expected to be community representatives. Villages look up to the governing apparatus, which looks down at them. The job of the village head (*kepala kampung*) is to mediate between "the government" and "the people." The split created by this bidirectional governing system is particularly evident under the current regime, as government policies stress that the village is the site of popular (i.e., nonstate) forms which must forcefully be brought into line with top-down development policy.

Other political dichotomies are overlaid on this split between "government" and "community." Center – periphery political distinctions distinguish Java from the other, "Outer" islands; people in Kalimantan tend to view government as a Jakarta project. Similarly, within the status-ranked areas, low-status people may see government as a high-status project. Finally, groups which in official discourse are marginalized as tribal minorities, outside "civilization," are further peripheralized from the projects of governance. From the perspective of the people in the Meratus Mountains, the gap between government and local politics looks wide.

It is important to recognize that attention to this gap does not tell the whole story. Village politics contribute to making the state; the categories of state rule are actualized in local politics. Yet an analysis of the formation of local communities properly begins with the subjective experience of being both outside and subject to state power.... I use the term *state* to refer to those aspects of the governing, administrative, and coercive apparatus that are experienced as external yet hegemonic. In discussing perspectives from the periphery, I stress the coherent, imposed quality of state authority. I also work to expand analyses of the workings of the state to include the political negotiations of out-of-the-way people. My approach moves back and forth between these two perspectives on the state, to avoid two tempting but oversimplifying poles on a continuum of political analysis. First, I do not want to imply that official state categories have an "always already" quality wherever they are found. Second, I do not argue that the state is a recent, external intrusion into the domain of an independent "primitive society."

Can one be simultaneously inside and outside the state? This is the dilemma of marginality. Uma Adang introduced me to the paradox: Marginals stand outside the state by tying themselves to it; they constitute the state locally by fleeing from it. As culturally "different" subjects they can never be citizens; as culturally different "subjects," they can never escape citizenship.

NOTES

1   Of the many vocabularies for understanding culture and power currently circulating, I have already introduced two in the last two paragraphs: the first ("discourse") associated with Foucault and the second ("hegemony") with Gramsci. The former vocabulary is particularly useful for bringing together issues of meaning and practice in examining the construction of power; the latter calls attention to divergent political stakes in processes of social transformation. Used together eclectically, they make it possible to ask how people reshape the very ideas and institutions that make it possible for them to act as subjects.

2   See, for example, Boserup 1970; Etienne and Leacock 1980; and, for Southeast Asia, Chandler et al. 1988.
3   See, for example, Appadurai 1990; Dominguez 1989; Ferguson and Gupta 1992.
4   Clifford and Marcus 1986; Fabian 1983; and Geertz 1988 have been influential in urging anthropological self-consciousness about textual construction.
5   Spivak carefully marks the contradictions of her own postcoloniality, writing, for example, of the need for "a persistent unlearning of the privilege of the postcolonial elite in a neocolonial world" (1989b: 289). Since all intellectual positions involve complicity with power, she argues, every scholar must engage in such "persistent critique" (1989a: 126).
6   In her interview with Afsaneh Najmabadi (1991: 128), Spivak is adamant: "I'm not an essentialist." Yet Spivak (1989a) warns against "anti-essentialist" ire as well as against essentialism. Essentialism is a tool, she suggests, that we may not be able to do without, even as we know its limitations. Nevertheless, her caution here is in striking contrast to Barbara Christian's concerns: Spivak's "persistent critique" brings her political concerns into dialogue with discussions of difference in Western philosophy; Christian stretches academic conceptions of philosophy to forge a dialogue about difference with a nonacademic community.

REFERENCES

Appadurai, A. (1990) Disjuncture and Difference in the Global Cultural Economy. *Public Culture* 2(2): 1–24.

Bhabha, H. K. (1989) Remembering Fanon: Self, Psyche, and the Colonial Condition. In B. Kriger and P. Mariani (eds.) *Remaking History*, pp. 131–48. Seattle: Bay Press.

——. (1990) The Other Question: Difference, Discrimination and the Discourse of Colonialism. In R. Ferguson, M. Gever, Trinh T. Minha, and Comel West (eds.) *Out There: Marginalization and the Discourse of Colonialism*. Cambridge, MA: MIT Press.

Bookman, A. and Morgen, S. (1988) *Women and the Politics of Empowerment*. Philadelphia: Temple University Press.

Boserup, E. (1970) *Women's Role in Economic Development*. London: Allen and Unwin.

Bourdieu, P. (1990) *The Logic of Practice*. Stanford: Stanford University Press.

Chandler, G., Sullivan, N., and Branson, J. (eds.) (1988) *Development and Displacement: Women in Southeast Asia*. Clayton, Australia: Monash University Centre of Southeast Asian Studies.

Christian, B. The Race for Theory. *Feminist Studies* 14(2): 13.

Clifford, J. (1986) Introduction: Partial Truths. In *Writing Culture: The Poetics and Politics of Ethnography*: Berkeley: University of California Press.

Clifford, J. and Marcus, G. (eds.) (1986) *Writing Culture: The Poetics and Politics of Ethnography*. Berkeley: University of California Press.

Dominguez, V. (1989) *People as Subject, People as Object: Selfhood and Peoplehood in Contemporary Israel*. Madison: University of Wisconsin Press.

Ebron, P. (1991) Rapping between Men: Performing Gender. *Radical America* 23(4): 23–7.

Etienne, M. and Leacock, E. (1980) *Women and Colonization: Anthropological Perspectives*. New York: Praeger.

Fabian, J. (1983) *Time and the Other: How Anthropology Makes Its Object*. New York: Columbia University Press.

Ferguson, J. and Gupta, A. (eds.) (1992) Space, Identity, and the Politics of Difference. *Cultural Anthropology*, Theme Issue 7(1).

Gates, H. L. (1991) Critical Fanonism. *Critical Inquiry* 17(3): 457–71.

Geertz, C. (1988) *Works and Lives: The Anthropologist as Author*. Stanford: Stanford University Press.

Hall, S. (1990) Cultural Identity and Diaspora. In J. Rutherford (ed.) *Identity: Community, Culture, Difference*, pp. 222–37. London: Lawrence and Wishart.

Haraway, D. (1988) Situated Knowledges: The Science Question in Feminism and the Privilege of Partial Perspective. *Feminist Studies* 14(3): 575–99.

hooks, b. (1989) *Talking Back: Thinking Feminist, Thinking Black*. Boston: South End Press.

——. (1990) *Yearning, Race, Gender, and Cultural Politics*. Boston: South End Press.

Irigaray, L. (1985) *Speculum of the Other Woman*. Ithaca: Cornell University Press.

Jameson, F. (1991) *Postmodernism, or the Cultural Logic of Late Capitalism*. Durham, NC: Duke University Press.

Lewis, D. (1973) Anthropology and Colonialism. *Current Anthropology* 14: 581–602.

Lorde, A. (1984) The Master's Tools Will Never Dismantle the Master's House. In *Sister Outsider: Essays and Speeches*, pp. 110–13. Trumansburg, NY: Crossing Press.

Mani, L. (1987) Contentious Traditions: The Debate on SATI in Colonial India. *Cultural Critique* 7(Fall): 119–56.

Mohanty, C., Russo, A., and Torres, L. (1991) *Third World Women and the Politics of Feminism*. Bloomington: Indiana University Press.

Moraga, C. (1983) A Long Line of Vendidas. In *Loving in the War Years: lo que nunca pasó por sus labios*, pp. 90–114. Boston: South End Press.

Najmabadi, A. (1991) Interview with Gayatri Spivak. *Social Text* 28: 122–34.

Rosaldo, R. (1989) *Culture and Truth: The Remaking of Social Analysis*. Boston: Beacon Press.

Said, E. (1978) *Orientalism*. New York: Pantheon Books.

Spillers, H. (1987) Mama's Baby, Papa's Maybe: An African American Grammar Book. *Diacritics* 17(2): 65–81.

Spivak, G. C. (1987) Draupadi (pp. 179–96) and Subaltern Studies: Deconstructing Historiography (pp. 197–221). In *Other Worlds: Essays in Cultural Politics*, New York: Routledge.

——. (1989a) In a Word. Interview with Ellen Rooney. *differences* 2: 124–54.

——. (1989b) Who Claims Alterity? In B. Kruger and P. Mariani (eds.) *Remaking History*, pp. 269–92. Seattle: Bay Press.

Taussig, M. (1987) *Shamanism, Colonialism and the Wild Man: A Study in Terror and Healing*. Chicago: Chicago University Press.

Trinh T. Minha. (1989) *Woman, Native, Other: Writing Postcoloniality and Feminism*. Bloomington: Indiana University Press.

Tsing, A. L. (1993) *In the Realm of the Diamond Queen*. Princeton: Princeton University Press.

West, C. (1990) The New Cultural Politics of Difference. In R. Ferguson, M. Gever, Trinh T. Minh-ha, and C. West (eds.) *Out There: Marginalization and Contemporary Cultures*, pp. 19–36. Cambridge MA: MIT Press.

White, E. F. (1990) Africa on My Mind: Gender, Counter-Discourse and African-American Nationalism. *Journal of Women's History* 2(1): 73–97.

Wolf, E. (1982) *Europe and the People without History*. Berkeley: University of California Press.

On Political Culture in Indonesia

Anderson, B. (1972) The Idea of Power in Javanese Culture. In C. Holt (ed.) *Culture and Politics in Indonesia*. Ithaca: Cornell University Press.

Dove, M. (1985) The Agroecological Mythology of the Javanese and the Political Economy of Indonesia. *Indonesia* 39 (April): 1–36.

Errington, S. (1989) *Meaning and Power in a Southeast Asian Realm*. Princeton: Princeton University Press.

——. (1992) Making Progress on Borobudu: An Old Monument in New Order. Paper presented at the Conference on Ruins, University of California, Santa Cruz.

Geertz, C. (1980) *Negara: The Theatre State in Nineteenth-Century Bali*. Princeton: Princeton University Press.

Hefner, R. (1990) *The Political Economy of Mountain Java: An Interpretive History*. Berkeley: University of California Press.

McVey, R. (1982) The Beamtenstaat in Indonesia. In B. Anderson and A. Kahin (eds.) *Interpreting Indonesian Politics: Thirteen Contributions to the Debate*. Ithaca: Cornell University Press.

Moertono, S. (1968) *State and State Craft in Old Java*. Monograph Series, Southeast Asia Program, Cornell University, Ithaca.

Pemberton, J. (1989) The Appearance of Order: A Politics of Culture in Colonial and Postcolonial Java. Ph.D. dissertation, Cornell University.

27

Flexible Citizenship among Chinese Cosmopolitans

Aihwa Ong

Destablizing Chineseness

Stories cribbed from the business pages:

> A recent late summer in the Ukraine. An angry mob dragging down a statue of Lenin enacted the political collapse, while vendors selling Bolshevik trinkets reinvented the economy. David Chang, representing The Asia Bank in New York, was in town to snap up apartment houses and real estate before the dust settles. "Governments come and go," he says, "but business stays."[1]

> In California, "the Silicon Valley way of divorce" among new Chinese immigrants results in one failure out of five marriages. A "typical" Chinese couple – he is an engineer, she an accountant – used to live in a half-a-million-dollar house with two well-schooled children. They invested in a second home and vacationed in Lake Tahoe. When the wife asked for a divorce, it was not because her husband had an affair, or at least not with another woman. "My husband works on his computer in the office during the day, comes home at 8 p.m., and continues to sit in front of his computer after dinner.... I am a 'computer widow' who is never asked how she was doing, nor what has happened to the family lately."[2]

Postmodern elements jostle for attention: *displacement* – Asians in Western worlds; *fragmentation* – families broken up by emigration and divorce; *difference* – male and female subjectivities; *impermanence* – in everyday arrangements. Were these reports about people other than the Chinese, they would attract no more than a passing glance. But to me, such postmodern snapshots are a jarring reproach to academic descriptions of Chinese identity, family, and cultural practices.

Much scholarship on Chinese subjects has been shaped by Orientalist concerns with presenting the Other as timeless, unchanging culture. Recent attempts to revise the static images of Chineseness nevertheless still confine the analysis of ways of

From P. Cheah and B. Robbins (eds.) *Cosmopolitics: Thinking and Feeling Beyond the Nation* (Minneapolis: University of Minnesota Press, 1998), pp. 134–42, 146–62.

"being Chinese" within clearly defined Chinese contexts of the nation-state or of culture. An essentializing notion of Chineseness continues to dog the scholarship, because the Chinese past, nation, singular history, or some "cultural core" is taken to be the main and unchanging determinant of Chinese identity. Sometimes we forget that we are talking about one-quarter of the world's population. What is conveyed is the sense that people identifiable as "Chinese" exist in their own worlds, and even when they participate in global processes, they continue to remain culturally distinct. I suspect the grand Orientalist legacy continues to lurk in a field, dominated by historians, convinced of the singularity of this great inscrutable Other. Younger scholars and feminists who seek to provide more complex historically and geopolitically contingent accounts of Chinese cultural practices are often merely tolerated, if not marginalized for threatening to disrupt the stable tropes of high Sinology. Perhaps not so ironically, as I have mentioned above, ambitious Asian politicians have made much political capital by borrowing academic representations of Chineseness for their own self-orientializing projects. Grand Orientalist statements are dialectically linked to the petty orientalisms generated by transnational corporate and advertising media that make pronouncements about Oriental labor, skills, values, families, and mystery. The legend for Singapore Airlines used to be "Singapore Girl, what a great way to fly."

But stories about capital, displacements, hybridity explode reigning notions about being Chinese. How do discrepant images reflect changing social, economic, and political relations in which Chinese subjects are important participants? Today, overseas Chinese are key players in the booming economies of the Asia-Pacific. In what ways have their border-crossing activities and mobility within the circuits of global capitalism altered their cultural values and class strategies? In this essay, I explore how the flexible positioning of diasporic Chinese subjects on the edge of political and capitalist empires affects their family relations, their self-representation, and the ways they negotiate the political and cultural rules of different countries on their itineraries. In contrast to Edward Said's unilateral construction of the objects of orientalisms as silent participants in Western hegemonic projects,[3] I trace the agency of Asian subjects as they selectively participate in orientalist discourses encountered on travels through the shifting discursive terrains of the global economy. Yet their countercultural productions should not be interpreted as a self-reproduction of "the ways we are situated by the West," but as complex maneuvers that subvert reigning notions of national self and the Other in transnational relations.

Perhaps more than other travelers and migrants, international managers and professionals have the material and symbolic resources to manipulate global schemes of cultural difference, racial hierarchy, and citizenship to their own advantage. Today, flexibility reigns in business, industry, labor, and financial markets, all technologically enhanced innovations that have effects on the way people are differently imagined and regulated, and on the way people represent and conduct themselves transnationally.[4] But whereas international managers and professionals may be adept at strategies of economic accumulation, positioning, and maneuver, they do not operate in free-flowing circumstances, but in environments controlled and shaped by nation-states and capital markets.

For instance, the form and meaning of citizenship have been transformed by global markets and floods of skilled and unskilled workers crossing borders. Although citizenship is conventionally thought of as membership based on the political rights and participation within a sovereign state, globalization has made economic calculation a major element of diasporic subjects' choice of citizenship, as well as in the ways nation-states redefine immigration laws. I use the term *flexible citizenship* to refer especially to the strategies and effects of mobile managers, technocrats, and professionals who seek to both circumvent *and* benefit from different nation-state regimes by selecting different sites for investments, work, and family relocation. Such repositioning in relation to global markets, however, should not lead one to assume that the nation-state is losing control of its borders. State regimes are constantly adjusting to the influx of different kinds of immigrants, and to ways of engaging global capitalism that will benefit the country while minimizing the costs. For instance, nation-states are reworking immigration law to attract capital-bearing subjects while limiting the entry of unskilled labor. From the perspective of such immigrants as well-heeled Hong Kongers, however, citizenship becomes an issue of handling the diverse rules or "governmentality" of host societies where they may be economically correct in terms of human capital, but culturally incorrect in terms of ethnicity.[5]

In order to understand the tactical practices of this diasporic managerial class, we must locate them within and one step ahead of the various regimes of truth and power to which they, as traveling persons, are subject. Michel Foucault uses *regime* to refer to power/knowledge schemes that seek to normalize power relations.[6] By appealing to particular "truths" developed about science, culture, and social life, these systems of power/knowledge define and regulate subjects, normalizing their attitudes and behavior. The regimes that will be considered here are the regime of Chinese kinship and family, the regime of the nation-state, and the regime of the marketplace, all providing the institutional contexts and webs of power within which Chinese subjects (re)locate and (re)align themselves as they traverse global space.

As Don M. Nonini has argued, each kind of regime requires for its effect "the localization of disciplinary subjects" – that persons be locatable and confinable to specific spaces and relations defined by the various regimes: the kinship network, the "nation," the marketplace.[7] In this sense, "flexible citizenship" also denotes the localizing strategies of subjects who, through a variety of familial and economic practices, seek to evade, deflect, and take advantage of political and economic conditions in different parts of the world. Thus we cannot analytically delink the operations of family regimes from the regulations of the state and of capital. One can say, for example, that Chinese family discipline is in part shaped by the regulation of the state and by the rules of the global marketplace, but the convergence of Chinese family forms with flexible strategies of capital accumulation enables them to bypass or exploit citizenship rules, as the case may be, as they relocate capital and/ or family members overseas. So while I talk about flexible citizenship, I am also talking about the different modalities of governmentality – as practiced by the nation-state, the family, capital – that are interconnected and have effects on each other, variously encoding and constraining flexibility in global (re)positioning. By analyzing different modalities of flexibility *and* governmentality under globalization, I identify contemporary forms that shape culture making and its products. I will first discuss the regime of diasporic Chinese kinship and how it structures, deploys, and limits flexible practices.

Middling Modernity: *Guanxi* and Family Regimes in Diaspora

One form of elite Chinese sensibility developed in the context of the late nineteenth century, when interregional commerce flourished under European colonialism in East and Southeast Asia. This entry of Chinese into mercantile capitalism ruptured the traditional links of filiation among Chinese subjects, Chinese families, and the Chinese nation. Alienated from the colonial powers, commercial classes redirected Confucian filiation away from the political system, and paternalism collapsed into an ethos narrowly focused on family well-being and interests, and firmly under male control. Outmigration and the dispersal of family firms outside China exposed emigrants to different possibilities of being Chinese in the world.

A diasporic Chinese modernity – in the "middling" sense of pragmatic everyday practices – developed among emigrant Chinese in the colonial worlds of East and Southeast Asia. In city ports and colonial enclaves, Chinese subjects facing political mistreatment and intense competition for survival evolved an instrumentality in norms concerning labor organization, family practice, links between family and the wider economy, and dealings with political authorities. For instance, in nineteenth-century China, the Confucian ideology of filial piety (*xiao*) governed the relations of superior and subordinate (father-son, husband-wife, older-younger brothers). Because the family was considered a microcosm of the moral order, *xiao* relations also figured relations to rules. But European imperial domination in treaty ports like Canton and Shanghai soon undermined Confucian hegemony. One outcome was early modern anti-imperialist, antipatriarchy movements, especially among university students in Beijing. However, the commercial legacy of European rule, which resulted in a family-centered notion of Confucianism, developed among overseas Chinese communities existing under colonial rule in Southeast Asia. Among the new commercial classes, loyalty to the modern state (founded in 1911) was barely formed, and the detested colonial powers were tolerated so long as money could be made. The Chinese comprador class became notorious for the systematic ways its members amassed personal power and wealth at the expense of the new republic. By forming profitable links overseas, merchant and industrial families repositioned themselves as subjects of global trade rather than loyal subjects of the Chinese motherland. The age-old notion of filial piety to the social order collapsed, freeing diasporic kinship systems to adjust to overseas colonial empires.

Modern Chinese transnationalism thus has roots in these historical circumstances of diaspora and European colonial capitalism, and in the post-colonial era, Chinese family enterprises became fully integrated within the larger global economy. Chinese traders recruited labor gangs, organized construction and mining crews, and ran brothels, gambling houses, and opium dens – all activities that transgressed the localizing regimes of colonial powers – while becoming more firmly integrated within the colonial economies. Their regional networks for labor and capital accumulation enabled Chinese traders to be the "wild men" who continually challenged political regimes and eluded their regulation.[8] Many Chinese sojourners did express a residual political loyalty to the Chinese motherland by contributing funds to the leaders of the struggling republic. But in the colonies, paternal bonds and interpersonal relations (*guanxi*) structured networks for interregional trade and provided the institutional basis for a sense of a larger, diffused "imagined community" of overseas Chinese (*huaqiao*).

In the postcolonial era, most Southeast Asian states have remained suspicious of the political loyalty of their Chinese citizens, partly because of the economic domination and extensive overseas connections of these citizens. Only Singapore and Taiwan, both possessing a Chinese majority, have promoted Confucian education to inculcate state loyalty as continuous with filial piety in the family. But in most countries, especially in Islam-dominated Malaysia and Indonesia, the discourse of nationalism draws on colonial models of race-based multiethnic nationhood.[9] Thus there are different cultural politics of being Chinese in different countries, but for many overseas Chinese, there is no obvious continuity between family interests and political loyalty (especially given their rather common experience of anti-Chinese discrimination in the host countries). Outside of Taiwan and Singapore, there is a disengagement between Chinese cultural interests and national belonging in host countries identified with dominant ethnicities, such as Vietnamese or Malay. For instance, in Malaysia, lower-class Chinese subjects often seek to evade the localizing mechanisms of the state that stigmatize them as "more Chinese" (i.e., less assimilated than upper-class Chinese) and hence subject to regulation as second-class citizens. This diffused sense of being diasporic Chinese has also been shaped by their flexible, mobile relations across political borders, and by the kinship regime of truth and control.

Launching family businesses on the edges of empires, Chinese subjects depend on a careful cultivation of *guanxi* (interpersonal) relations and instrumentalist family practices. These habits, attitudes, and norms are not a simple continuation or residual of some essentialized bundle of "traditional Chinese" traits. *Guanxi* networks in Southeast Asia are historically contingent, a kind of (post) colonial "habitus"[10] – that is, the dispositions and practices that emphasize pragmatism, interpersonal dependence, bodily discipline, gender and age hierarchies, and other ethnic-specific modes of social production and reproduction in diaspora and under foreign rule. Such overseas Chinese habitus has ensured that the emigrant family survives for generations while evading the discipline of the colonial, and later the postcolonial, state, with its special regimes of othering Chineseness.

Produced and shaped under such conditions, the familial regimes of diasporic Chinese based on *guanxi* are not without their own violence and exploitation of workers, family members, kinsmen, and so on. In the early days of colonial capitalism, *guanxi* networks deployed Chinese emigrants in the "pig trade," supplying coolies to labor camps throughout Asia, thus subjecting many to brutal control, lifelong indebtedness, poverty, and crime while enriching their patrons. *Guanxi*, as a historically evolved regime of kinship and ethnic power, controls and often entraps women and the poor while benefiting fraternal business associations and the accumulation of wealth for Chinese families in diaspora.

In everyday life, however, there is widespread misrecognition of *guanxi*'s violence, while its humanism is widely extolled by ordinary folk, businessmen, and cultural chauvinists alike. Such symbolic violence[11] – or the erasure of collective complicity over relations of domination and exploitation – is also present in academic writings that unduly celebrate *guanxi* as the basis of recent overseas Chinese affluence.[12] Misrecognition of business *guanxi* as basically a structure of limits and inequality for many and enabling of flexibility and mobility for the few to accumulate wealth is part of the ritual euphemization of "Chinese values," especially among transnational Chinese and their spokesmen.

Indeed, *guanxi* regimes and networks have proliferated within the institution of subcontracting industries, the paradigmatic form of flexible industrialization throughout the Asia-Pacific. Many Chinese firms enter light manufacturing by subcontracting for global companies, producing consumer items such as jewelry, garments, and toys in "living-room factories."[13] In recent years, *guanxi* networks have been the channels for subcontracting arrangements between overseas Chinese capital and enterprises in mainland China. A Sino-Thai tycoon who is the largest investor in China invokes *guanxi* to explain the growth of his conglomerate on the mainland compared to what he sees as the inflexibility of Western firms: "American and European companies have adapted themselves to a very sophisticated legal-based society.... In China there is no law. There is no system. It is a government by individuals, by people."[14] As such, the *guanxi* institution, as invoked and practiced, is a mix of instrumentalism – fostering flexibility and the mobility of capital and personnel across political borders – and humanism – "helping out" relatives and hometown folk on the mainland. Although patriotic sentiments may be be inter-mixed with *guanxi* connections, overseas Chinese investors are also moved by opportunities for mobilizing cheap labor in China's vast capitalist frontier.[15] It is probably not possible to disentangle nostalgic sentiments toward the homeland from the irresistible pulls of flexible accumulation, but the logic of *guanxi* points to sending capital to China while shipping the family overseas.

It may sound contradictory, but flexible citizenship is a result of familial strategies of regulation. Michel Foucault suggests that we think of modern power, in its "gov-ernment" of population and its welfare (biopolitics), as productive of relations, rituals, and truths. I consider the rational, normative practices that regulate healthy, productive, and successful bodies within the family and their deployment in economic activities for economic well-being as family governmentality. The biopolitics of families, however, are always conditioned by wider political economic circumstances.

The rise of Hong Kong as a global manufacturing center was secured after British colonial rule put down and domesticated trade unions and student activitists during the 1960s, a state strategy that was common throughout Asia. In subsequent decades, refugee families in all classes have adapted through hard work, fierce competitiveness, and tight control over the family in order to improve overall family livelihood and wealth. Local social scientists use the term *utilitarian familialism* to describe the everyday norms and practices whereby Hong Kong families place family interests above all other individual and social concerns. One scholar observes that economic interdependency is the basic structuring principle, expressed as "all in the family," a principle that mobilizes the immediate family and other relatives in common interests.[16] An individual's sense of moral worth is based on endurance and diligence in income-making activities, compliance with parental wishes, and the making of sacrifices and deferral of gratification, especially on the part of women and children. In her study of factory women, Janet Salaff found that daughters are instilled with a sense of debt to their parents, which they "repay" by shortening their schooling and earning wages that often go toward their brothers' higher educa-tion.[17] The writers cited above seem to identify such family practices as something inherent in "Chinese culture," ignoring the effects of state discipline and a highly competitive marketplace on refugee families. Such family regimes among the working classes have been responsible for the phenomenal growth of Hong Kong into a manufacturing giant. Among the upwardly mobile, biopolitical considerations inform family discipline in production and consumption. Besides acquiring the habitus of continual striving, children, especially sons, are expected to collect symbolic capital in the form of educational certificates and well-paying jobs that help raise the family class position and prestige. In imperial and republican China, the accumulation of degrees was an established way to rise from peasant to mandarin status, or a way for merchants to rise socially in the eyes of officials. In Hong Kong, the entrepreneur's rise to the highest status is determined solely by his wealth, regardless of how it has been accumulated, although he too may take on the trappings of mandarin learning.

Such familial regimes, which regulate the roles of sons and daughters for the family well-being, can also become discontinuous with or subvert the biopolitical agenda of the state. The British government's laissez-faire policy encourages the population to pursue wealth with "flexibility and vigor" and, until the eve of the return of Hong Kong to China rule, to express political freedom as a market phenomenon. This market-driven sense of citizenship was until recently viewed as the right not to demand full democratic representation, but to promote familial interests apart from the well-being of society. Middling modernity thus places a premium on material goods and an instrumental approach to social life, indexed by the ownership of Mercedes Benzes and market shares. There is a joke that professors spend more time playing the stock market than teaching. Risk taking and flexibility in the entrepreneurial sense induce an attenuated sense of citizenship. A young, single civil servant posted to San Francisco confided to me:

> I don't think I need to associate myself with a particular country. I would rather not confine myself to a nationality defined by China or by the U.K. I am a Hong Kong person, I grew up there, my family and friends are there, it's where I belong.... I lack a sense of political belonging due to the British colonial system, but we have thrived on the system – in terms of the quality of life, roughly fair competition, in terms of moving up through the educational system, even though Hong Kong is not a democracy.

This young man plans to get a British passport and try his luck wherever he can practice his talents. Like many savvy Hong Kongers, he is outwardly mobile, aligned more by world market conditions than the moral meaning of citizenship in a particular nation. Such middling, disaffected modernism has been shaped within the politics of colonialism and the nation-states over a refugee and diasporic population, and yet these strategies are adept at subverting the political regimes of localization and control.

[A section headed "National Character and the Biopolitics of Citizenship" is omitted.]

Plotting Family Itineraries

Big business families provide the clearest examples of a careful blending of discipline in familial practice and flexibilization in business and citizenship. The likes of Li

Ka-Shing and the late Sir Y. K. Pao, who rose from refugee poverty to immense wealth, are considered the most brilliant realization of such innovative entrepreneurial border running in the Chinese diaspora. Many tycoon families emerged in the 1960s, when businessmen amassed fortunes in real estate, just as its manufacturing industries helped make Hong Kong a household word for inexpensive consumer products. In interviews with the sons of some of these wealthy families, I found the familial regime of control to be very firm, even as the family business takes off overseas. Fame and business power relations are inseparable, and the company founding father is a patriarch who regulates the activities of sons who must be trained and groomed to eventually take over the family business. *Xiao* relations are instilled through the force of family wealth. From the top floor of his San Francisco high-rise, Alex Leong,[18] a mild-mannered middle-aged investor, tells me:

> I remember, even when I was in junior high [in Hong Kong], my objective was to follow my father's footsteps and be in business . . . to take over the family business rather than to try to work for someone else or to do my own thing. Because I think it is very important for sons to carry on the family business, something that has been built up by your father. To me, that's the number-one obligation. . . . If your family has a business, why would you go work for somebody else, and leave a hired man to look after your family business? To me, that doesn't make any sense.

Alex comes from a prominent family that traces back to a granduncle who was once the governor of Guangdong province. Alex's father went to school in Germany, but after the Communist victory in 1949, he took his family to Australia. His father then explored business opportunities in Brazil, where the family lived for a few years. They finally returned to Hong Kong, where his father went into real estate and set up a firm called Universal Enterprises. *Xiao* dictates that Alex and his brothers take on the roles mapped out by their father. Alex explains that it is a common practice for big business families to distribute their sons across different geographic sites:

> The fathers make a very clear subdivision whereby one brother doesn't infringe on the others, fearing that there would be too much fighting among them. For instance, my oldest brother works in Hong Kong. I take care of everything in North America. We always talk, but we know whose responsibility it is here and over there.

In another wealthy family, the eldest son (who obtained a Tonga passport) remains in Hong Kong to run the family hotel chain in the Pacific region, while the second brother, based in San Francisco, takes care of the North American and European hotels. The youngest brother, who came on board later, is managing family business in Southern California. Daughters, no matter how qualified, are never put into management positions in the family business, which is considered their brothers' patrimony. Three Hong Kong-born women are working as investors in the San Francisco Bay Area, but they are running their own firms using seed money from their fathers. Their businesses are not part of the family enterprises founded by their fathers. Alex refers to one of these women as "one of the men," because she has been highly successful in what is still considered a male vocation.

Although Alex cannot imagine doing anything else, he confesses that he sometimes feels "stifled" by the fact that the reins of control are in his father's hands:

> When you have a father as a boss, to me that's a double boss, right? You can't just say, "I don't agree, I quit, and resign." . . . You can't just walk away from your father. And then a father who has been in business for so long, he'll never recognize you as an equal, so you are always in a subordinate position.

The familial regime is so powerful that even sons who try to slip its nets are sometimes pulled right back into conformity. Alex's youngest brother graduated from college a few years ago, but having observed his older brothers' predicament, has resisted working in the family business. The young man expressed his rebellion by working in a bank, but under the paternalistic eye of one of his father's wealthy friends. Alex expects that "eventually, when my youngest brother joins in, it is our objective to continue to expand here in the U.S. and to wind down in Hong Kong." Scholars of rural China maintain that a man who has inherited family property rather than acquired his own fortune enjoys more power over his sons,[19] but here in the tumult of the global economy, it is the self-made tycoon who appears to exert strong control over his family throughout his lifetime and who directs and regulates the behavior of his sons, who are sent out across the world to carve out new niches for the family business empire. Alex's father has been retired for some years now, but the sons continue to consult him on major selling and buying decisions. A political analogue to this system of boss rule is the continuing power of the former prime minister of Singapore, Lee Kuan Yew, who still appears to exert tremendous *towkay* (boss) power over his state enterprise.

Thus the masculine subjectivity of this elite diaspora community is defined primarily in terms of the individual's role as a father or a son, the role of maintaining the paternalistic filial structure that both nurtures and expands family wealth. Unlike daughters, who will inherit a small share of the family fortune (about 30 percent of what the sons get in Alex's family) and then have nothing to do with the male estate, sons must remain active, integral parts of the family business throughout their lives. To be merely passive, as in drawing an income without involvement in the daily operation of the business, is to play a feminine role, like sisters, who marry out, or wives, who may manage the finances but rarely take on management roles. However, as uncertainties increase in Hong Kong, and more sons can break away and emigrate on their own, a few young women have taken over running their family businesses. But the familial system has been to rely on men, and in families without sons, even "foreign devil" sons-in-law who have proved their loyalty to the family business can take the place of sons. For instance, the business empire of Sir Y. K. Pao, the late shipping and hotel magnate, is now run by his two Caucasian sons-in-law. One can say that *xiao* has been bent and channeled to serve the governmentality not only of the family, but of global capitalism as well.

Families in America, Fathers in Midair

The modernist norms and practices of diaspora Chinese anticipate their relocation, along with capital infusions, into the Western hemisphere. Earlier Chinese immigrants to the United States were largely laborers, with a sprinkling of merchants. Today, Chinese investors and professionals arrive as cosmopolitans already wise in the ways of Western business and economic liberalism. With new modes of travel and communication, familial regimes have become more flexible in both dispersing and localizing members in different parts of the world. Hong Kong papers talk about the business traveler as an "astronaut" who is continually in the air, while his wife and children are located in Australia, Canada, or the United States, earning rights of residence.

The turn toward the United States began in the 1960s, when teenagers from middle- and upper-middle-class families applied to American schools and colleges. Alex's father often told him, "Your future is really going to be outside Hong Kong. So you should be educated outside, as long as you maintain some Chinese customs and speak Chinese." The well-off used their children's overseas education as entrée into a Western democracy, buying homes for the children and setting up bank accounts and exploring the local real estate. Upon graduation, sons are expected to help expand the family business in the country. After graduating from Berkeley and the University of Wisconsin business school, Alex set up a local branch of his father's company in San Francisco. Because he is not yet a citizen, his parents plan to retire in Vancouver, Canada, where residential rights can be had for an investment of C$300,000. They expect to join him eventually in the Bay Area, while the sons take over greater control in running the family empire. This mix of family and business strategies allows them to weave in and out of political borders as they accumulate wealth and security.

Many entrepreneurs, however, continue to shuttle between both coasts of the Pacific (because it is still more profitable to do business in Hong Kong) while their wives and children are localized in North America. The astronaut as a trope of Chinese postmodern displacement also expresses the costs of the flexible accumulation logic and the toil it takes on an overly flexible family system. The astronaut wife in the United States is euphemistically referred to as "inner beauty" (*neizaimei*), a term that suggests two other meanings for "inner person," that is, "wife" (*neiren*) as well as "my wife in the Beautiful Country (i.e., America)" (*neiren zai Meiguo*). Wives thus localized to manage suburban homes and take care of the children – lessons in ballet, classical music, Chinese language – sarcastically refer to themselves as "widows" (and computer widows), expressing their feeling that family life is now thoroughly mediated and fragmented by the technology of travel and business.

In a Canadian suburb, some widows have formed a group called Ten Brothers in order to share domestic problems and chores in the absence of their husbands. "We have to start doing men's work like cutting grass in the summer and shoveling snow in the winter. So we call ourselves 'brothers' instead of 'sisters.'" This sense of role reversal induced by flexible citizenship has also upset other prior arrangements. In the Bay Area, wives bored by being "imprisoned" in America parlay their well-honed sense of real estate property into a business sideline. Down the peninsula, the majority of real estate agents are immigrant Chinese women selling expensive homes to other newly arrived widows. Here also, flexibility reigns as wives keep trading up their own homes in the hot residential market. A Hong Kong industrialist tells me that he has moved five times over the past sixteen years as a result.

In some cases, the flexible logic deprives children of both parents. The teenagers dropped off in Southern California suburbs by their Hong Kong and Taiwan parents are referred to as "parachute kids." One such child left to fend for herself and her brother refers to her father as the "ATM machine," because he issues money but little else from some extraterrestrial space. Familial regimes of dispersal and localization then discipline family members to make do with very little emotional support; disrupting parental responsibility, straining marital relations, and abandoning children are such common practices that they have special terms. They thus challenge claims that the "Confucian affective model" is at the heart of Chinese economic success[20] when the flexible imperative in family life and citizenship requires a form of isolation and disciplining of women and children that is both critiqued and resisted. The logic of flexibilization expresses the governmentality of transnational capitalism within which many elite families are caught up, and their complex maneuvers around state regulations reveal the limits and pathos of such strategies.

American Liberalism, Citizenship, and Pacific Rim Capital

I have argued elsewhere that in the United States, neoliberalism plays a role in shaping our notion of the deserving citizen. The history of racial conflict also tends to produce a perception that different kinds of ethnic and racial groups embody different forms of economic and political risks.[21] Following Foucault, I consider liberalism not merely an ethos but a regime of normalizing whereby *Homo economicus* is the standard against whom all other citizens are measured and ranked.

At the turn of the twentieth century, the Chinese had the dubious distinction of being the first "racial" group to be excluded as undesirable and unsuitable immigrants to the United States. Earlier, Chinese immigrants had been welcomed by capitalists and missionaries as cheap, diligent, and docile laborers, but they were eventually attacked as unfair competitors by white workers in the railroad and mining industries. During the Cold War, the public image of Chinese oscillated between that of the good Chinese, as represented by America's Guomindang allies, and the bad Chinese associated with "Red China." In the 1960s, the emergence of a middle-class Chinese population provided contrast with the growth of a nonwhite "underclass," a term used mainly for inner-city blacks. The media popularized the term *model minority* to refer to Asian Americans, who were perceived as a minority group that collectively raised itself up by its bootstraps, thus fitting the criteria for the good or at least deserving citizen. Images of Oriental docility, diligence, self-sufficiency, and productivity underpin contemporary notions that the Asian minority embodies the human capital desirable in good citizens, in contrast to those who make claims on the welfare program.

Through the next decade, the influx of immigrants from Hong Kong and Taiwan, many of them students bound for college, swelled the middle-class ranks of Asian Americans. The rise of a Chinese immigrant elite – many suburb-living professionals – coincided with the restructuring of the American economy and its increasing reliance on skilled immigrant labor and overseas capital. In the public's mind, the Asian newcomers seemed to embody the desired disciplinary traits of an increasingly passé model of American character. For instance, in the aftermath of the Tiananmen crackdown, a letter to the *San Francisco Chronicle* defended the admission of Chinese (student) refugees:

> The opportunity to welcome the best and the brightest of China and Hong Kong into our area is fantastic. These are motivated, energetic, courageous people, with strong

cultural traditions of taking care of their families, working hard, and succeeding in business. We need more of these values in our midst, not less.[22]

It appears that "traditional" American values are to be found in these newcomers, who are coming with different kinds of capital, but perhaps not so strong "cultural traditions." Earlier images of the Chinese railroad worker, laundryman, houseboy, and garment worker have been replaced by the masculine executive, a *Homo economicus* model inspired in part by the so-called neo-Confucian challenge from across the Pacific.

Increasingly, the reception of skilled and capital-bearing Chinese new comers represents the triumph of corporate discourses and practices that invoke the "Pacific Rim" and its Oriental productivity and new wealth. For instance, under pressure from corporate and Asian lobbies, US immigration laws were modified in 1990 to attract some of the Pacific Rim capital flowing toward Australia and Canada, where the laws are less stringent. A new "investor category" allows would-be immigrants to obtain a green card in return for a million-dollar investment that results in the creation of at least ten jobs. On Wall Street, seminars directed at Asian Americans offer suggestions on how to "get U.S. citizenship through real estate investment and acquisition." A consultant urges, "Think of your relatives in Asia. If they invest in you, they get a green card and you get a new business."[23] As in other Western countries with finance-based immigration, citizenship has become an instrument of flexible accumulation for the nation-state, as a way to subvert its own regulatory mechanisms in order to compete more effectively in the global economy.

Narrating Cosmopolitan Citizenship

In what ways has the arrival of the diaspora Chinese reworked the cultural meanings of *Asian American* and produced a new discourse of Pacific Rim romanticism, and even symbolic violence? Whereas Said has described Orientalism as a one-sided and self-reifying process, I have tried throughout this essay to represent the discursive objects themselves as cocreators in Orientalism. This has been, after all, part of their flexibility in negotiating the multicultural worlds of European imperialism. For centuries, Asians and other peoples have been shaped by a perception and experience of themselves as the Other of the Western world.[24] The new prominence of Asians in the world markets has enabled Chinese subjects to play a bigger role in identifying what counts as "Chinese" in the West. Diaspora Chinese academics now use Orientalist codes to (re)frame diaspora Chinese as enlightened cosmopolitans who possess both economic capital and humanistic values. Wang Gungwu, formerly chancellor of Hong Kong University, hails overseas Chinese living "among non-Chinese" as "a modern kind of cosmopolitan literati" who have embraced Enlightenment ideals of rationality, individual freedom, and democracy.[25] Perhaps. US-based scholars claim that "Confucian humanism" will create "an Oriental alternative" to the destructive instrumental rationality and individualism of the West – in other words, a kinder and gentler capitalism for the twenty-first century. One wonders whether these scholars have bothered to visit factories run by Chinese "humanists" and observed whether their practices are really that "humanistic" and uninformed by the logic of capital accumulation.

These grand claims circle around and occlude the complex, wide-ranging realities of East Asian capitalism, or at least its Chinese variant. For instance, Hong Kongers hail from a colonial territory where there has been little nurturing of Confucian humanism and democratic values. Until Tiananmen, many had developed a radically apolitical stance toward the state. Just as Hong Kong is viewed as a place to maximize wealth, so the Western democracies to which many are bound are considered "gold mountains" of opportunity. The subcontracting system of production used in Hong Kong and Taiwan, and now in China, is among the most exploitative of women and children in the world. In Hong Kong, "democracy" for many entrepreneurs often means freedom from political constraints on making money, and the state and wider society are of concern only when they can be made relevant to family interests. In the view of the business elite, the modern social order is built upon the domination of those who possess intellectual and economic power, and wealthy people are the models of envy and emulation, rather than enemies of the poor. Like investors all over the world, Chinese businessmen who engage in philanthropy are seeking to escape property taxes and to gain social status as prominent members of society; it is a stretch to construct these as acts of Confucian benevolence. As billionaire Li Ka-shing says, "There is no other criterion of excellence [except money]."[26] But such prideful discourses on diaspora Chinese elites as humanistic citizens persist, and they are intervening in narratives about the role of Asian Americans in the United States.

From across the Pacific, corporate America answers the call to reconsider Chinese immigrants as exceptional citizens of the New World Order imaginary. Of course, the reception is not unambivalent, for global trade is viewed as war.[27] This contradictory attitude was expressed by David Murdock, chairman and CEO of Dole Foods Company, at a conference on Asian Americans in Los Angeles. Murdock personifies corporate America: his company has operations in more than fifty countries and employs thousands of employees in the Asia-Pacific. He warned that in a world of many big economic powers, technological edge has shifted East. There are, however, more than seven million Asian Americans. He continued:

> We need to be more competitive. We need people who understand the languages, cultures, the markets, the politics of this spectacular region. Many Asian Americans have language ability, cultural understanding, direct family ties, and knowledge of economic conditions and government practices throughout Asia. This knowledge and ability can help Americans achieve political and business success in the region.... much of their insight and ability can [help] in opening doors for the U.S., building a new structure for peace in the Pacific.[28]

By defining a role for Asian Americans as good citizen and trade ambassadors, Murdock's speech situated them in the wider narrative of the Oriental as trade enemy.

At the same conference, Los Angeles City Councilman Michael Woo, who was then seeking to be the first Asian mayor of Los Angeles, picked up the narrative by reframing the question, "What then is this new person, this Asian American? In the new era of the Pacific?"[29] The question, reminiscent of European queries about Anglos earlier in the century, subverts the view that whites are the undisputed key players on the West Coast. Woo, whose family has close ties with Asian capital, went on to propose "a new hybrid role" whereby new Asian immigrants (rather than long-resident Asian Americans, he seemed to suggest) can act as "translators, go-betweens [between] one culture and another, using skills that have brought us to such prominence and success in the business world and in the professions, and entering into the public arena" to become mediators in community relations.

Asians are "bridge builders," Woo claimed. In his view, the Asian American "middleman minority" is not the besieged ethnic group of academic theorizing.[30] He was using the term in the larger global sense, coming dangerously close to the meaning that evokes compradors, the Chinese elites who acted as middlemen between colonial governments and the masses in Asia. Indeed, such *muchachos*, as Fred Chiu (following Mike Taussing) has pointed out, are "the ideal-typical mediating and (inter)mediating category/force in the reproduction of a world of – out-going as well as in-coming – nationalism and colonialism."[31] And of course the term *bridge* has gained new resonance for overseas Chinese in their new prominence as transnational capitalists. In Chinese, the word for bridge (*qiao*) puns with the term for overseas Chinese (the *qiao* in *huaqiao*), and as I have argued elsewhere, diaspora Chinese have been quick to play on the metaphor of bridging political boundaries in their role as agents of flexible accumulation and flexible citizenship.[32] The bridge-building metaphor appeals to an Asian elite that sets great store in being engineers, doctors, managers, businessmen, and bankers, and who see themselves as self-made men who are now building the infrastructures of modern affluence on both sides of the Pacific. Woo saw a continuity between Asian economic and cultural middleman roles. He noted that trading skills developed in the diaspora, "in the midst of cultures very different from their own," included not just those of use in "the handling of money, but also skills in sizing up people, negotiating a deal, and long-term planning." He suggested that these "survival skills" could be "transferred" to non-Asians. Woo thus echoed the *Homo economicus* construction of Chinese immigrants and elevated their role in the American social order.

Such narrativization is never simply complicit with hegemonic constructions, but seeks to reposition Asian immigrants and Asian Americans as new authority figures, while suggesting declining human capital and leadership qualities among Anglos. By calling Asian Americans the new Westerners, Woo implied that Anglos have been surpassed in diligence, discipline, moral capital, and even knowledge of the changing multicultural world that is critical to America's success. His narrative carves out a space of Asian Americans as mediators in American race and class relations. The bridge-building citizen evokes the tradition of American communities, the ideal of a civil society where neighbors look out for each other.[33] Asian American leaders, Woo seemed to suggest, could build bridges between racial minorities and the government. By identifying Pacific Rim bodies with Pacific Rim capital, the concept of bridge builders gentrifies Asian American identity in both its local and its global aspects, in moral contrast to less privileged minorities and their dependence on the welfare state. When Woo's talked ended, the largely Asian audience rose up and clapped enthusiastically, and voted to replace the *model minority* label with the *bridge-building* minority, a term that apparently enables Asian Americans to share the transnational role of diaspora Chinese building the Pacific century.

Conclusion

The emigration of Chinese corporate elites out of Asia has entailed the cultural work of image management as they seek wider acceptance in Western democracies and in different zones of late capitalism. By revising the academic images of Chinese as money handlers, trading minorities, and middlemen, corporate spokesmen paint a picture that mixes humanistic values with ultrarationalism, values that suggest the ideal-type *Homo economicus* of the twenty-first century. Such self-representations are not so much devised to collaborate in the biopolitical agenda of any nation-state, but to convert political constraints in one field into economic opportunities in another, to turn displacement into advantageous placement in different sites, and to elude state disciplining in order to reproduce the family in tandem with the propulsion of capitalism.

Of course, whereas for bankers boundaries are always flexible, for migrant workers, boat people, persecuted intellectuals and artists, and other kinds of less well-heeled refugees, this apparent mix of humanistic concerns and capitalist rationality is a harder act to follow. For instance, Don Nonini has identified the tensions and pathos experienced by middle-class Malaysian Chinese whose familial strategies of emigration are intended to escape second-class citizenship as much as to accumulate wealth overseas. Although small-business-owning Chinese consider themselves locals in their Malaysian hometowns (e.g., as "natives of Bukit Mertajam"), many are vulnerable to anti-Chinese policies and feel that they have no choice but to send their children overseas, where they may feel less discrimination. These businessmen postpone joining their children in places like New Zealand, which do not feel like "home." Their loyalty to home places in Malaysia is ironically disregarded by state policies that discriminate against them as lower-class ethnics in a way that does not affect wealthy Chinese who are viewed as more "cosmopolitan" and open-minded about Malay rule. As Jim Clifford has reminded us, there are "discrepant cosmopolitanisms," and the cosmopolitanism of lower-class Chinese from Malaysia is fraught with tensions between sentiments of home and pressures to emigrate. This is not to say that the Hong Kong Chinese elites do not have patriotic feelings for the Chinese motherland, but rather that the investor emigrants are well positioned to engage in a self-interested search for citizenship and profits abroad, a strategy that will enhance their economic mobility and yet sidestep the disciplining of particular nation-states.

Among this elite group, though not limited to them, such a mix of ultra-instrumentalism and familial moralism reveals a postnationalist ethos. They readily submit to the governmentality of capital, while plotting all the while to escape state discipline. In the most extreme expressions, their loyalty appears to be limited to the family business; it does not extend to any particular country. A Chinese banker in San Francisco explains that he can live in Asia, Canada, or Europe: "I can live anywhere in the world, but it must be near an airport." Such bravado constructs a bearable lightness of being that capital buoyancy can bring. Yet the politics of imagining a transnational identity dependent on global market mobility should not disabuse us of the fact that there are structural limits, and personal costs, to such flexible citizenship.

This essay should not be interpreted as an argument for a simple opposition between cosmopolitanism and patriotism (taken to an extreme, either is an undesirable or dangerous phenomenon). I have noted elsewhere that a Confucian cultural triumphalism has arisen alongside modern Chinese transnationalism in Southeast Asia.[34] Some scholars have been tempted to compare the role of modern Chinese economic elites to that of medieval Jewish bankers, whose activities protected free trade along with liberalism and other Enlightenment values in the Dark Ages. We should resist such comparison. Although contemporary Chinese merchants, bankers, and managers have burst through closed borders and freed up spaces for economic activities, they have also revived premodern forms of child, gender, and class oppression, as well as strengthened authoritarian regimes in Asia. A different kind of cosmopolitical right is at play. The point is not that all Chinese are thus painted with the same broad brush of elite narratives, but that the image of the border-running Chinese executive with no state loyalty has become an important figure in the era of Pacific Rim capital. What is it about flexible accumulation – the endless capacity to dodge state regulations, spin human relations across space, find ever new niches to exploit – that allows a mix of humanistic relations and ultra-instrumentality to flourish? Indeed, there may not be anything uniquely "Chinese" about flexible personal discipline, disposition, and orientation; they are rather the expressions of a habitus that is finely tuned to the turbulence of late capitalism.

NOTES

1 Summary of a story in the *New York Times*, 31 August 1991, A1.
2 Summary of "The Silicon Valley Way of Divorce," *Overseas Scholars' Monthly* (Taipei), January 1991, 71.
3 Edward Said, *Orientalism* (New York: Pantheon, 1978).
4 David Harvey identifies our era as one of "flexible accumulation," but he underestimates the ways culture shapes material forces and the effects of political economy on culture. David Harvey, *The Conditions of Postmodernity* (Oxford: Blackwell Publishers, 1989).
5 Foucault uses *governmentality* to mean the deployment of modern forms of (nonrepressive) disciplining power – especially in the bureaucratic realm – and other kinds of institutions that produce rules based on knowledge/power about populations. See Michel Foucault, "Governmentality," in *The Foucault Effect: Studies in Governmentality*, ed. G. Burchell, C. Gordon, and P. Miller (Chicago: University of Chicago Press, 1991), pp. 87–104.
6 Michel Foucault, *Discipline and Punish: The Birth of the Prison*, trans. A. Sheridan (New York: Random House, 1977); Michel Foucault, *The History of Sexuality*, vol. 1, trans. M. Hurley (New York: Pantheon, 1978).
7 Don M. Nonini, "Shifting Identities, Positioned Imaginaries: Transnational Traversals and Reversals by Malaysian Chinese," in *Ungrounded Empires: The Cultural Politics of Modern Chinese Transnationalism*, ed. Aihwa Ong and Don M. Nonini (New York: Routledge, 1997), 203–27.
8 See Don M. Nonini and Aihwa Ong, "Introduction: Transnationalism as an Alternative Modernity," in *Ungrounded Empires*, ed. Ong and Nonini, pp. 3–36.
9 See Benedict Anderson, *Imagined Communities: Reflections on the Origins and Spread of Nationalism*, 2nd ed. (London: Verso, 1991). Anderson underplays the centrality of race in colonial-inspired notions of nationalism in Southeast Asia, seeking instead to focus on the "good" kind of anti-imperialist, civic nationalism.
10 Pierre Bourdieu, *Outline of a Theory of Practice* (Cambridge: Cambridge University Press, 1977), pp. 90–5.

11 Bourdieu, *Outline of a Theory of Practice*, pp. 190–7.

12 See Peter Berger and Hsia Hsin Huang, eds., *In Search of an East Asian Development Model* (New Brunswick, NJ: Transaction, 1988); Hung-chao Tai, ed., *Confucianism and Economic Development: An Oriental Alternative?* (Washington, DC: Washington Institute Press, 1989).

13 Ping-Chun Hsiung, *Living Rooms as Factories: Class, Gender, and the Satellite Factory System in Taiwan* (Philadelphia: Temple University Press, 1995).

14 Quoted in Edward A. Gargan, "An Asian Giant Spreads Roots," *New York Times*, November 14, 1995, C3.

15 Aihwa Ong, "Anthropology, China, and Modernities: The Geopolitics of Cultural Knowledge," in *The Future of Anthropological Knowledge*, ed. Henrietta Moore (London: Routledge, 1996), pp. 60–92.

16 Emily Siu-kai Lau, *Society and Politics in Hong Kong* (New York: St. Martin's, 1983), pp. 72–4.

17 Janet W. Salaff, *Working Daughters of Hong Kong: Filial Piety or Power in the Family?* (Cambridge: Cambridge University Press, 1981).

18 To protect the privacy of all my subjects, I have given them pseudonyms.

19 See, for example, Sung Lung-sheng, "Property and Family Division," in *The Anthropology of Taiwanese Society*, ed. Emily Martin and Hill Gates (Stanford, Calif.: Stanford University Press, 1981).

20 See Tai, *Confucianism and Economic Development*, pp. 18–19.

21 Aihwa Ong, "Cultural Citizenship as Subject-Making: Immigrants Negotiate Racial and Cultural Boundaries in the United States," *Current Anthropology* 37(5) (1996): 737–62.

22 Letter to the editor, *San Francisco Chronicle*, June 16, 1989, op-ed.

23 Through this opening, the US government hoped to attracted 4 billion dollars a year and to create as many as forty thousand jobs annually. Lourdes Lee Valeriano, "Green-Card Law Means Business to Immigrants," *Wall Street Journal*, February 21, 1992, B1. The actual gains so far have fallen short of both goals. Hong Kong investors I spoke to said that the investment figure is too steep, given that they can obtain a Canadian passport for less than $300,000. Furthermore, since the law was passed, great investment opportunities in China have sucked most of the overseas Chinese capital back to Asia. See Ong, "Anthropology, China, and Modernities."

24 Stuart Hall, "Cultural Identity and Diaspora," in *Identity, Community, Difference*, ed. J. Rutherford (London: Verso, 1990), pp. 225–6.

25 See Wang Gungwu, "Among Non-Chinese," *Daedalus* 12(2) (1991): 148–52. It is interesting that the term *non-Chinese* has emerged as a category in such self-Orientalizing discourses as displayed in the *Daedalus* special issue "The Living Tree." This term seems to herald the elevation of Chineseness to the global status enjoyed by Westerns *vis-à-vis* less developed parts of the world, commonly referred to as the conceptual and geographic South. By taking the East out of the underdeveloped category, this discursive move reinforces the model of global binarism.

26 Quoted in Lynn Pan, *Sons of the Yellow Emperor: A History of the Chinese Diaspora* (Boston: Little, Brown, 1990), pp. 366–7.

27 This view is promoted by the bestseller *Rising Sun*, by Michael Crichton (New York: Ballantine, 1992), and suggested by James Fallows's *Looking at the Sun*.

28 Murdock's speech is one of two taped by the Asia Society, "The Asian American Experience: Looking Ahead. Speeches by Keynote Speakers David Murdock and Michael Woo," Los Angeles, October 1991.

29 Asia Society, "The Asian American Experience."

30 See Edna Bonacich, "A Theory of Middleman Minorities," *American Sociological Review* 38 (1973): 583–94.

31   Fred Chiu, "Non-mediating Forces versus Mediating Forces: New 'Subjecthood' in Local/Regional Resistance against Nation/Global Systemic Drives," paper presented at the workshop "Nation-States, Transnational Publics, and Civil Society in the Asia-Pacific," University of California, Berkeley, June 28–30, 1996.

32   Ong, "Anthropology, China, and Modernities."

33   As a politician with a tiny Asian support base, Woo depended primarily on votes from multiethnic constituencies, especially Anglos and African Americans. There is something about his bridge-building metaphor that suggests the Confucian norm of relations between older and younger brothers, which he seems to suggest as a model for city politics. This representation apparently found some acceptance among Los Angeles citizens, because, despite the failure of interethnic coalitions during the 1992 class and racial rioting, Michael Woo remained for a time the most popular candidate in the mayoral race.

34   Ong, "A Momentary Glow of Fraternity" *Identities* (Winter 1996): 331–66.

28

Long-distance Nationalism Defined

Nina Glick Schiller and Georges Fouron

Why am I so hung up on Haiti? In my house, in every room I have a radio tuned to a Haitian station. I can't shake it. And yet I know better. Isn't that strange? I always say that people shouldn't have a blind allegiance to a country. But my love for Haiti is for Haiti. It is not for conquest; it is not against anyone else. In my case I am looking for a place where I feel I belong, a place to retire later in life in peace. Haiti is my universe, the place I should have been all the time. I have a strong feeling and commitment to Haiti. I would love to see the country and the people having a decent way of life and receive respect in the world of nations....

... Georges is a long-distance nationalist and long-distance nationalism is a potent contemporary political ideology. In order to explore the constructive energy Georges finds within long-distance nationalism, we must from the onset define the terms nationalism, long-distance nationalism, nation-state, transnational nation-state and trans-border citizenship. We do so remembering that Georges' wife, Rolande, and Nina's mother, Evelyn, have requested a book without jargon that they can read and enjoy, so while we build our definitions on the scholarly literature, we will not review its intricacies.

Nationalism can be defined as a set of beliefs and practices that link together the people of a nation and its territory. The nation is understood to be people who share common origins and history as indicated by their shared culture, language, and identity.[1] Central to nationalism is the belief that a nation has the right to control the territory that is its homeland by having its own state, whose territorial boundaries stretch to the borders of the homeland. Therefore, it is difficult to speak of nations without also discussing states.

The "state" is generally understood to be a sovereign system of government within a particular territory. The apparatus of the modern state includes a head of state, a legislative body, a court system, and armed forces. Increasingly, theorists of the state have begun to realize that the power of states resides not in the government

From *Georges Woke Up Laughing: Long-distance Nationalism and the Search for Home* (Durham, NC: Duke University Press, forthcoming).

institutions themselves but in the processes, routines, and everyday activities that operate together to create and legitimate social order and discipline.[2] People may promote ideas about the state as much through critique as through unquestioning acceptance. When a person denounces a corrupt or venal public official, avoids taxes, decries the state of the public schools, roads, or order, s/he circulates and endorses certain ideas about "the state." When we put together the terms "nation" and "state" and designate a particular polity as a nation-state, we make the assumption that people who share an identity as a nation also contribute to the quotidian routines, ritual, and discourse that form the state within a particular territory. When people contest a particular set of leaders, they often do so in the name of the nation which claims a particular state and its territory. The government of each such state represents the nation that lives within its borders.

People around the world settled into a pattern of thinking about the world as divided into territorially based nation-states only after two world wars were fought in the name of nation-states, and colonial states in Africa, Asia, the Pacific, and the Caribbean were granted independence. This dominant, but still not totally hegemonic, model of the world is exemplified and made concrete by the United Nations. This organization projects a view of the world in which each nation is located exclusively within its own separate national territory, which is demarcated by internationally recognized borders.[3] Inherent to the logic of this model is the assumption that each individual can be a citizen of only one state and identify with only one nation.[4] Yet the world has never been completely organized this way and now, in a new age of migration and in a renewed and intensified period of globalization, long-distance nationalism is reconfiguring the way many people understand the relationship between populations and the states that claim to represent them. Currently, an increasing number of states are developing legal ways of reclaiming emigrants and their descendants, and those who have emigrated are publically declaring their full-fledged incorporation into two or more states.

A new form of state has emerged that extends its reach across borders, claiming that its emigrants and their descendants remain an integral and intimate part of their ancestral homeland, even if they are legal citizens of another state. In some ways this trans-border state represents a resurgence of a form of nationalism and political practice that existed in the nineteenth and first half of twentieth century. In that period national leaders saw their emigrants more as colonists than as permanent settlers abroad. Mussolini's efforts to mobilize Italians settled in the United States was one of the most visible efforts of the long-distance political projects of a number of political leaders from states that included Greece, Hungary, Ireland, Korea, China, Mexico, and Japan. However, in earlier cases transmigrants were expected to eventually return home and long-distance nationalism contained a call to come and rebuild the land. To accept permanent settlement elsewhere was generally defined as national betrayal. The current political moment is very different. Political leaders and the emigrants themselves are increasingly ready to see emigrants as permanently settled abroad but also continuing to be part of the body politic of their homeland.

In the course of the past decade, as we have mapped the emergence of this project to reconstitute nation-states so as to encompass populations well incorporated into the social, economic, and political life of other states, we have searched for the best term to describe these states. In 1994, Nina and her colleagues, Linda Basch and Cristina Szanton Blanc, employed the term "deterritorialized nation-state" for nation-states which define their population as extending beyond the state's territorial borders.[5] However, the adjective "deterritorialized" evokes an image of a nation without borders or territory, and the states in question maintain a territorial base. Others have built on Arjun Appardurai's term "transnation" but this descriptor, although more felicitous, also often projects images of a world of nations without territorial based states. Consequently, we have decided to use the term "transnational nation-state." The dictionary defines transnational as "extending or going beyond national borders." When combined with the word nation-state, we believe this word represents the particular politics we examine . . . : the reconstitution of the concept of the state so that both the nation and the authority of the government it represents extend beyond the state's territorial boundaries and incorporate dispersed populations. This is not the only form of transnational politics. It is the one that concerns us . . . as we extend the scholarship of everyday forms of nation-state formation so that it can encompass long distance nationalism.

An Approach to Long-distance Nationalism

Our understanding of long-distance nationalism includes all five of the following specifications. First of all, long-distance nationalism resembles conventional localized nationalism as an ideology which links people to territory. As in other versions of nationalism, the concept of a territorial homeland governed by a state that represents the nation remains salient, but national borders are not thought to delimit membership in the nation. Long-distance nationalists differ from local nationalists in their assertion that people living in various disparate geographic locations within different states share a common identification with an ancestral territory and its government. Consequently, long-distance nationalism provides a justification for such a government to reconfigure itself as a *transnational nation-state*. Long distance nationalism binds together immigrants, their descendants, and people who have remained in their homeland into a single *trans-border citizenry*. Citizens residing within the territorial homeland view emigrants and their descendants as part of the nation, whatever legal citizenship the emigrés may have.

To legitimize the connection between the people who can claim membership in the transnational nation-state, long-distance nationalism highlights ideas about common descent and shared racialized identities that have long been a part of concepts of national belonging. For example, although Georges is an US citizen living in the United States, he continues to see Haiti as his homeland; many people in Haiti agree and see him as Haitian, despite the fact that he is not legally a Haitian citizen. They argue that "his blood remains Haitian."

Second, long-distance nationalism does not exist only in the domain of the imagination and sentiment. It leads to specific action. These actions link a dispersed population to a specific homeland and its political system. Long-distance nationalists may vote, demonstrate, contribute money, create works of art, give birth, fight, kill, and die for a "homeland" in which they may never have lived. Meanwhile, those who live in this land will recognize these actions as patriotic contributions to the well-being of their homeland.[6]

Georges is a long-distance nationalist not only because he dreams about Haiti but also because he takes actions on behalf of Haiti while continuing to live in New

York. He believes that when he assists family members in Haiti, speaks out about problems in Haiti, or counsels young people of Haitian descent born in the United States, he is working to reconstruct Haiti. People living in Haiti are also long-distance nationalists if they continue to claim Georges as their own and maintain that he continues to be responsible for Haiti and that his actions abroad reflect on the reputation and future of Haiti.

Third, long-distance nationalists have as their political objective the constitution of a transnational nation-state. Long-distance nationalists challenge established theories of states as well as nations. They endorse and in fact help to sustain the image of the world divided into separate, sovereign, territorially based states, each representing a nation, but they challenge the notion that relationships between citizens and their state are confined within that territory. Instead they envision transnational nation-states. While the concept of transnational nation-states contra-dicts conventional political theory, when we look at the way in which past and present generations of immigrants have actually experienced their ancestral states, transnational nation-states become not just thinkable but political realities that merit investigation.

Emigrants living outside of the territory controlled by the state not only continue to see themselves as part of an ancestral nation, but also take political action in relation-ship to those states. And they take these actions as representatives of the nation from which they are descended. Meanwhile, on their part, government officials of these states often claim to continue to represent their dispersed populations, no matter where such persons live and no matter what legal citizenship they may hold. In effect, they declare that not only their national population but also their government is trans-national. For example, a number of emigrant-sending states such as Mexico, Colom-bia, the Dominican Republic, Ecuador, and Brazil have adopted policies that turned them into transnational nation-states. Many have changed their laws and created government agencies to ensure that transmigrants remain incorporated in their native land. Some governments have granted dual nationality so that emigrants can carry two passports; others have extended voting to emigrants who have become US citizens. Through these changes, as well as the establishments of special ministries responsible for the diasporic population, the political leaders of these countries signal that trans-migrants, as well as their children, remain members of the nation of their birth.

Whether localized or long distance, nationalism brings together those who share a sense of "peoplehood" based on shared culture and history and the political project of building or defending a territorially-based state which speaks for its people. However long-distance nationalism differs from localized nationalism because long-distance nationalism situates people in an ancestral homeland and persons settled in other lands within a single political project. Although in many instances government officials embrace or reshape this political project, long-distance nationalism cannot be seen as a "top-down" fostering of elite beliefs. In many cases, the vision of the nation, as extending beyond the territorial boundaries of the state, springs from the life experiences of migrants of different classes, whose lives extend across borders and connect homeland and new land.[7] It is also rooted in the day-to day efforts of people in the homeland to live lives of dignity and self-respect that compel them to include those who have migrated in their definition of their national community.

Fourth, conditions in the homeland or in the new land may encourage or subvert the beliefs and practices that contribute to long-distance nationalism. Certain political circumstances make it difficult for persons abroad and persons at home to engage in transnational projects which contribute to building homeland. For example, under dictatorships such as that of the Duvalier regime in Haiti or the Salazar government in Portugal, or when revolutionary governments such as Cuba see themselves under siege by foreign powers, transnational political projects may be discouraged or forbidden. Those who left were labeled traitors, defectors, or betrayers of the nation. Similarly, states which receive immigrants may be suspicious of their transnational ties, especially if they wish to remain connected to a country perceived to be an enemy nation. After World War I, the United States not only closed its borders to most immigration but also launched an assimilationist policy which demanded that home-land identities and loyalties be abandoned. During World War II, Japanese and German long-distance nationalists in the United States were forced to renounce their homelands. On the other hand, if after even several generations it has been difficult for immigrants to obtain legal citizenship in their new land, which has been the experience of Turkish immigrants in Germany, or if immigrants and their des-cendants find that access to their legal citizenship does not guarantee them the full protection of the law, as has been the case with immigrants of color in the United States, long-distance nationalism as a set of both beliefs and practices may flourish.

Fifth and finally, long-distance nationalism must be distinguished from other forms of collective belonging. There is now a plethora of scholarly writing which use the term "diaspora" to describe trans-border belonging and identification, past and present.[8] We find this approach confusing because it confounds very different historical experiences and forms of consciousness. Instead, we differentiate between identification with a particular, existing state or the desire to construct a new state, which we call long-distance nationalism, and other forms of trans-border ideas about membership, such as those based on religion or a notion of shared history and dispersal. Dispersed populations who share an ideology of common descent and a history of dispersal, racialization, and oppression but who make no claim to nation-state building are probably best categorized as diasporas. Accordingly, we would speak about an African diaspora. The Jews in ancient times or in the Middle Ages praying for the Messianic Age in which the Temple in Jerusalem would be restored can best be understood as a diaspora.

It is only when a diasporic population begins to organize to obtain its own state, as Jews did in the twentieth century, that we would designate them as long-distance nationalists. In the case of Israel, this linkage between a concept of the Jewish people and a specific state has been written into Israeli law which extends citizenship rights to the Jewish diaspora. Individuals who have never even set foot on Israeli territory but whose genealogies establish Jewish identity have citizenship rights in Israel. When Serbs in Chicago and those in Belgrade work together to oust Muslims from Bosnia and build a greater Christian Serbia, they express long-distance nationalism by their actions as well as their words. The German law which made it possible for persons of German descent, who have lived for generations outside of Germany, to return as citizens because they were "ethnic Germans" was an expression of long-distance nationalism. Portugal's efforts to redesign itself as a "global nation" and reclaim persons of Portuguese descent settled around the world are efforts of a transnational nation-state to encourage long-distance nationalism.[9] Long-distance nationalism is the motivation that stands behind headlines about American citizens of Chinese, Israeli, Kosovar, Irish, or Korean descent who lobby, spy, fight, and even die for a homeland they may never have seen or in which they may no longer feel "at home."[10] Haitians who live in the United States as citizens or as permanent residents but contribute to development projects that they deem crucial to improving Haiti are long-distance nationalists.

Despite the intensity of the passion engendered by long-distance nationalism and the prevalence of this ideology in the world today, we know relatively little about it. Apart from Anderson,[11] most theorists of nationalism have not addressed the question of long-distance nationalism. This is because it is a political ideology that falls outside of what has become the standard-issue model of how the world currently is supposed to be organized. Long-distance nationalism calls into question our understanding of the current structure of political and economic relationships in the world. It allows us to address current debates about the relationship between globalization processes that are knitting the world into a single economic system and the significance of state structures. It helps us to understand better the roles that various nation-states are playing within the changing structure of the global economy.

The Question of Citizenship

All of us relate to states, the political units into which the world is divided, by means of both law and emotion. The government of each state creates laws which define who has rights to citizenship in that state and what those citizenship rights entail. The word citizen is now generally understood as a person who is a full member of a modern state and as such has legal rights in that state, including the right to vote, hold political office, and claim public benefits. Citizens of states also have certain responsibilities, which vary from country to country.[12] But this clear-cut textbook-style definition gets very muddy in practice and in different states people actually conceive of citizenship somewhat differently.

Moreover, as scholars of citizenship have noted, not all people who are legal citizens receive the same treatment from the state or are able to claim the same rights.[13] There are often categories of people who are legal citizens according to the laws of a state, yet who face various forms of exclusions and denials of civil rights because they are not considered to be truly part of the nation. For example, for long periods of US history, people of color and women, even when they were acknowledged to be citizens, were not granted equal rights and questions of equal treatment by state agencies are still points of contention. In Haiti until recently, people who lived in the countryside had the word "paysan" (peasant) written on their birth-certificates and peasants were called people outside (*moun andeyò*) to indicate that they were not considered to be part of the political classes. Participation in politics was reserved, in essence, for the elite and highly educated in Port-au-Prince.[14]

Because of the contradictions between the legal status of citizen and the actuality of state practices, some scholars, when discussing citizenship, focus on the "substantive" rather than the legal status of citizenship. When people make claims to belong to a state through collectively organizing to protect themselves against discrimination, gain rights, or make contributions to the development of that state and the life of people within it, they are said to be substantively acting as citizens, whether or not they have the legal documents that recognize their status of "citizen." This substantive approach to citizenship gives us a way to describe the behavior of long-distance nationalists who participate politically in states and make claims upon more than one state, even when they are not living within the territory of a state or are not legal citizens of a state. Building upon the concept of substantive citizenship which acknowledges the political participation in and claiming of rights and privileges from a state by persons who are not legally citizens of that state, we designate long-distance nationalists as "trans-border citizens." The term trans-border citizenship gives us a way to describe the relationship that people who live within transnational social fields have with more than one government. We use the term "transborder" rather than "transnational" citizenship to highlight the fact that while these "citizens" cross territorial borders, they do so in the name of only one nation.

Trans-border citizens may act as substantive citizens in more than one state but they do so as long-distance nationalists who are engaged in claiming a single national identity.[15] ... [Yet] because trans-border citizens participate in the political processes and political cultures of more than one state, they may draw on concepts of the state and ideas of civil and political rights of more than one polity. In the Haitian case, this has led many poor people to become a new politically-engaged citizenry, with political repercussions in both the United States and Haiti. While we speak of a "trans-border citizenry," we do not assume that these citizens speak with a single political voice. As with any other citizenry, a trans-border citizenry will have political divisions based on differences in political party or ideology. At the same time such a citizenry is united by a shared identity.[16]

However, while the term "trans-border citizen" proves useful in describing the political behavior of persons who live their lives across the borders of two or more nation-states, this use of the term citizen suffers from the same drawbacks as all approaches to citizenship that are not based on legal definitions. Whatever their claims to membership, people who are substantive but not legal citizens face legal restrictions and lack legal protections. Haitian transmigrants living in the United States may participate as members in the societal and political processes of both the United States and Haiti. However, if such people remain Haitian citizens, making their presence known publicly may have repercussions, especially if they are undocumented. At the same time, if Haitian transmigrants become US citizens but still participate in the Haitian political system without Haitian citizenship, their commitment to Haiti or their right to hold office in Haiti may be challenged.

... Many Haitian emigrants claim membership in their ancestral land and also engage in politics designed to shape the future of their homeland. Haiti does not allow dual citizenship but dual nationality is assumed by most Haitians... The Haitian government has found ways to recognize these claims without changing its citizenship laws.

Sometimes the political actions of trans-border citizens living outside of the territorial boundaries of the state can affect its political direction. In the Israeli election of 1999, it was generally assumed that if the election for Prime Minister was close, the votes of Israelis living in the US who were US citizens would prove to be crucial. Plane-loads of persons of Israeli origin, many of whom were US citizens, returned to Israel to vote in the Israeli elections. The long-distance nationalism of the returning Israeli/American voters was translated into much more than an emotional tie. These long-distance nationalists were trans-border citizens, asserting their political rights in two different states, and participating in both with political understandings shaped by both political systems.

. . . [E]ven though transmigrants challenge the concept of the bounded nation-state through their long-distance nationalism, they paradoxically reconstitute a concept of national sovereignty. When they make certain demands on the government of their homeland, they reinforce the older vision of a nation-state as a sovereign power. For example, Haitian transmigrants living in the United States join with people in Haiti in a critique of Haitian political officials based on their failure to lead Haiti into a period of economic development which can provide for the common welfare. However, these leaders, confronted by the pressures on them from "donors" of foreign aid and from transnational corporations whose capital far exceeds the worth of many states, are unable to respond to the demands of their people. To speak about this confusing situation of independent nation-states with little actual national sovereignty, we have developed the concept of the "apparent state." Apparent states are structures of government which have a distinctive set of institutions and political procedures but have little or no actual power to meet the needs of the population.

The concepts of long-distance nationalism, transnational nation-state, trans-border citizenship, and the apparent state allow us to explore the ways in which the life experiences, family values, self-esteem, and political identity of someone like Georges are intimately linked to conditions in both the homeland and the country of settlement. Our approach, which is ethnographic and autobiographical, demonstrates the ways in which the desires, ambitions, and mundane needs of women and men to give a brighter future to their children may still be intertwined with nationalism and states. . . .

NOTES

1 These definitions are based on approaches to nationalism found in Calhoun 1997; Gellner 1983; Hobsbawm 1990; Kedourie 1960; and McCrone 1998. These approaches to nationalism all link the concept of nationalism to territory. They differ from uses of the nationalism in the concepts such as black nationalism, Arab nationalism, or Hindu nationalism. Logically, it makes sense to differentiate identities based on common historical origins and shared racialization or religion – the substance of "black nationalism" – from political ideologies linked to efforts to form, claim, or defend territorially-based polities. However, political usage is often not logical. As will be seen, we define long-distance nationalism as a political ideology of a population linked to a particular territory and state, although all those who maintain this set of beliefs and related political practices do not reside within the borders of that particular state.

2 Abrams argued that the concept of the state obscures the class structure and the myriad of institutional arrangements through which power is held. He challenged the literature that saw the "the state" as object rather than an ongoing myth that obscures relationships of subordination (1988).

3 Political scientists often refer to this model of the political organization of the globe as the "Westphalian system" and tell us that it began in Europe in 1648 (Krasner 1999: 20–5).

4 The political theory that envisions each person as able to have only one nation is rooted in racialized views of the nation and the legal system of states and citizenship. This system was formalized after World War I.

5 Basch, Glick Schiller, and Szanton Blanc 1994.

6 In approaching long-distance nationalism as both words and action we build on Calhoun's work.

> [T]here is nationalism as discourse: the production of cultural understandings and rhetoric which leads people around the world to think and frame their aspirations in terms of the idea of nation and national identity.... [T]here is (also) nationalism as project: social movements and state policies by which people attempt to advance the interests of collectivities they understand as nation. (1997: 6)

7   Grahm (1996) provides a description of the role of migrants in the complex political dynamics that preceded the decision on the part of the Dominican government to grant citizenship rights to Dominican emigrants and their children who are US citizens.

8   In this usage we differ from those who have created a scholarship of diaspora studies which groups all examples of dispersal of populations through all periods of history under the term "diaspora" (Cohen: 1997). We find such an approach fuels the assumption that, in a world of global connections, states are increasingly irrelevant. We believe that this assumption cannot be substantiated.

9   Feldman-Bianco 1992.

10 In past years US citizens have been accused of spying or lobbying for Korea and of spying for Israel, with a similar uproar. For the long-distance nationalism of Kosovar immigrants see Sullivan 1998 and Stewart 1999. Some kinds of transnational military activity by US citizens has come to be taken for granted or endorsed by the US government, such as that by the Cuban militias in Florida or the efforts throughout the twentieth century to raise money and arms for the liberation of Ireland.

11 Anderson 1993; 1994.

12 For a review of the variations in the concepts of citizenship see Shafir 1998. For the contradictory legal and social statuses of immigrants see Bauböck 1994.

13 A classic delineation of the ways in which legal citizens of lower social classes may not have access to all rights is found in Marshall 1964. More recent scholarship links the exclusion of legal citizens from full access to rights to racialized and gendered concepts of who belongs to the nation. See for example, Haney-Lopez 1996; Hamilton and Hamilton 1997; Lister 1997; Lowe 1996; Yuval-Davis 1997.

14 Trouillot 1990.

15 We want to make it clear that not all persons embedded in transnational social fields who claim citizenship privileges or rights in more than one state act as trans-border citizens motivated by long-distance nationalism. Ong has identified a very different and pragmatic stance to states that has been historically practiced by elite sectors of "overseas" Chinese. She terms their citizenship practices "flexible citizenship" (1993).

16 Our concept builds on Laguerre's concept of diasporic citizens (1998) and Bauböck's discussion of transnational citizens (1994). We have chosen the term "transborder citizens" rather than transnational citizens because we found that long-distance nationalists tend to identify with one nation but act as members of more than one state. We found the term diasporic citizenship problematic for two reasons. While Haitians do use the term diaspora for emigrants who still make claims on the government of their ancestral land, the term "diaspora" has historically encompassed dispersed populations who may have a historic homeland but do not have a homeland government. In addition, we wish to be able to encompass in our terminology people within an emigrant-sending country who make claims on the states in which their emigrants have settled.

REFERENCES

Abrams, P. (1988) "Notes on the Difficulty of Studying the State." *Journal of Historical Sociology* 1: 58–89.

Anderson, Benedict. (1993) "The New World Disorder." *New Left Review* 193 (May/June): 2–13.

——. (1994) "Exodus." *Critical Inquiry* 20 (Winter): 314–327.

Basch, Linda, Nina Glick Schiller, and Cristina Szanton Blanc. (1994) *Nations Unbound: Transnational Projects, Postcolonial Predicaments, and Deterritorialized Nation-States.* Amsterdam: Gordon and Breach.

Bauböck, Rainer. (1994) *Transnational Citizenship: Membership and Rights in International Migration.* Aldershot, England: Edward Elgar Publishing.

Calhoun, Craig. (1997) *Nationalism.* Minneapolis: University of Minnesota Press.

Cohen, Robin. (1997) *Global Diasporas: An Introduction.* Seattle: University of Washington Press.

Feldman-Bianco, Bela. (1992) "Multiple Layers of Time and Space: The Construction of Class, Race, Ethnicity, and Nationalism among Portuguese Immigrants." In *Towards a Transnational Perspective on Migration,* ed. Nina Glick Schiller, Linda Basch, and Cristina Szanton Blanc, pp. 145–74. New York: New York Academy of Sciences.

Gellner, Ernest. (1983) *Nation and Nationalism.* Oxford: Blackwell Publishers.

Grahm, Pamela. (1996) "Nationality and Political Participation in the Transnational Context of Dominican Migration." In *Caribbean Circuits: Transnational Approaches to Migration,* ed. Patricia Pessar, pp. 91–126. Staten Island, NY: Center for Migration Studies.

Hamilton, Dona Cooper, and Charles V. Hamilton. (1997) *The Dual Agenda: The African-American Struggle for Civil and Economic Equality.* New York: Columbia University Press.

Haney-Lopez, Ian. (1996) *White by Law: The Legal Construction of Race (Critical America).* New York: New York University Press.

Hobsbawm, Eric J. (1990) *Nations and Nationalism Since 1780: Programme, Myth and Reality.* New York: Cambridge University Press.

Kedourie, Eli. (1960) *Nationalism.* New York: Praeger.

Krasner, Stephen. (1999) *Sovereignty: Organized Hypocrisy.* Princeton: Princeton University Press.

Laguerre, Michel S. 1998 *Diasporic Citizenship: Haitian Americans in Transnational America.* St. Martin's Press, New York.

Lister, Ruth. (1997) "Citizenship: Towards a Feminist Synthesis." *Feminist Review* 57 (Autumn): 28–47.

Lowe, Lisa. (1996) *Immigrant Acts: On Asian American Cultural Politics.* London: Duke University Press.

Marshall, T. H. (1964) *Class, Citizenship, and Social Development: Essays by T. H. Marshall.* Garden City, NY: Doubleday.

McCrone, David. (1998) *The Sociology of Nationalism.* London: Routledge.

Ong, Aihwa. (1993) "On the Edge of Empires: Flexible Citizenship Among the Chinese in Diaspora." *Positions* 1(3): 745–78.

Shafir, Gershon (ed.) (1998) *The Citizenship Debates: A Reader.* Minneapolis: University of Minnesota Press.

Stewart, Barbara. (1999) "Crisis in the Balkans: Volunteers Signing Up in Yonkers to Fight for Kosovo." April 12, *New York Times* online archives.

Sullivan, Stacy. (1998) "From Brooklyn to Kosovo, With Love and AK-47's." November 22, *New York Times* online archives.

Trouillot, Michel-Rolph. (1990) *Haiti: State Against Nation.* New York: Monthly Review Press.

Yuval-Davis, Nira. (1997) "Women, Citizenship and Difference." *Feminist Review* 57 (Autumn): 4–27.

29

Theorizing Socialism:
A Prologue to the "Transition"

Katherine Verdery

Although the embers still glow beneath the ashes of what was so lately (in Rudolf Bahro's phrase) "actually existing socialism" in eastern Europe, it is not too soon to take analytic stock of that system. Even before the final months of 1989, eastern Europeans anticipated the system's end with the joke that socialism was the longest and most painful road from capitalism to capitalism. The collapse of Communist Party rule there brought suddenly into being a new phenomenon for social scientists to flock to: the transition from socialism, or at least from its hitherto institutionalized Marxist-Leninist variant, to the diverse societal forms that will succeed it. In the study of this process, anthropologists will have a major part to play.

The unprecedented opportunity that the transition from socialism offers social scientists will bear more fruit, I believe, if our research is informed by conceptualizations of the social order that went before. In this essay, I hope to contribute to research on the transition by setting forth the theoretical model of socialism used in my own work on socialist Romania and in that of others (notably Stark 1990 and Burawoy 1985, 1991 on Hungary). By no means do all area specialists accept the analysis I offer below. The majority of political scientists, for example, have worked with a variety of models rather different from this one. What distinguishes those models from the one presented here is that the former are largely of US or western European provenance and emerge from the values underlying western polities – "rational choice" theories, "interest group" pluralist theories, modifications of the earlier "totalitarian" model, general political-process models in which one-party systems constitute merely a different set of values on a familiar set of variables, and so on. The conceptualization I present, by contrast, is a composite of ideas developed by several eastern European social theorists, most of whom work not from the models of liberal western political theory but from

From *American Ethnologist* 18(1) (1991), pp. 419–34, 437–9. Reprinted by permission of the American Anthropological Association.

modifications of a Marxist analysis, adapted to the realities of eastern European socialism.

The Hungarian and Romanian scholars whose work I describe developed their theories on the basis of long-term immersion in socialist societies. They had data vastly superior to those of western researchers, whose access to the social processes of socialism was at best intermittent and of necessity highly selective. These eastern European economists, sociologists, and philosophers were actively criticizing or seeking to modify the societies in which they lived at the time of their writing. Although their ideas were for the most part not published in their own countries at that time, these people were central participants in a larger movement of critique that at length undermined eastern European socialism by exposing its mechanisms and increasing resistance to it. In a very important way, the theories discussed below are part of the transition itself, not prior or external to it. Whether this fact fortifies or impedes their analytic utility is for the reader to decide.

The framework I set out can be used to analyze – henceforth, as historical questions – many aspects of life in socialist societies: processes of economic production, politicking within the bureaucracy, the parameters of daily experience and social relations, or intellectual politics in the production of culture (Verdery 1991). This kind of model can also illuminate already published ethnographies of socialism, such as Caroline Humphrey's extraordinary monograph on collective farm life in Buryatiya (Humphrey 1983). The framework I offer is useful for more than simply retrospective analysis, however. First, in purporting to characterize what eastern European societies are "transiting" *from*, it illuminates certain areas as critical for research in the coming decade. I will briefly mention some of these in my closing pages. Second, because the nature of a system often appears most clearly with its decomposition, we can expect to learn more about socialism during the transition than we have to date. Rendering explicit what we think we now know about it is essential to testing and perfecting our theories as fuller knowledge emerges henceforth.

Like all ideal-type models, this one describes no real socialist society perfectly. Moreover, it emphasizes tendencies of the societies as formally constituted rather more than the forms of resistance they engendered. It is also silent about the many forms of improvisation and spontaneity... to which people were driven by the center's expropriation of all capacity to plan. At best, the model indicates certain social processes as fundamental, while acknowledging that these were not the only processes at work and that they were more evident in some cases than in others. The model is especially suitable for the highly centralized, "command" form of socialism, best exemplified by the Soviet Union under Stalin and Brezhnev and by Romania during most of the 42 years of Communist Party rule there; it is least applicable to Yugoslavia after 1948 and to Hungary after 1968.... Scholars concerned with the Asian socialisms are better qualified than I am to judge its applicability to those societies; the events of 1989 suggest that those may have become the only cases, if any remain, that approximate the terms of the theory. Notwithstanding the theory's seeming obsolescence, in discussing it I use the present tense, as is common in the presentation of abstract models. I illustrate with examples from Romania, the country of my fieldwork.

The Dynamics of "Real Socialism"

Socialism's basic "laws of motion"

I dispense with a thorough review of literature on the nature of socialism and move directly to works analyzing the fundamental mechanisms of socialist systems...The most fruitful beginning on the question of socialism's "laws of motion" was Konrád and Szelényi's *The Intellectuals on the Road to Class Power*...Seeing the significance of private property ownership in capitalism as a matter of ideological legitimation and, hence, of system integration (cf. Polanyi et al. 1957), the authors explored the integration typical of socialism. What, they asked, legitimated socialism's appropriation of the surplus (Konrád and Szelényi 1979: 48)? They answered that the central legitimating principle was "rational redistribution," the ideology through which the bureaucratic apparatus justifies appropriating the social product and allocating it by priorities the party has set. From this they defined the "motor" of socialism as the drive to maximize redistributive power (in contrast to capitalism, whose "motor" is the drive to maximize surplus value) (Szelényi 1982: 318). I rephrase this as "allocative power" and speak of bureaucratic allocation rather than redistribution, so as to avoid confusing socialist redistribution with forms more familiar from economic anthropology.

Fehér, Heller, and Márkus...emphasize that maximizing allocative power does not necessarily mean maximizing the *resources available for allocation*, that is, the social surplus itself. To the contrary: these scholars argue that the "rationality" specific to socialist economies includes their often *sacrificing* an expanded total output, thereby diminishing the potential pool of resources to allocate. What is more important, systemically, than increasing the pool of resources is having the most important ones – especially the resources that generate *more* resources – *under the apparatus's control*; as a result, resources generated within the society will remain, insofar as possible, within the bureaucratic apparatus rather than falling out of it into consumption (Fehér et al. 1983: 67–8). When these systems appear to us to behave "irrationally," they are in fact piling up resources that enhance the bureaucracy's capacity to allocate. The best example is the "irrational" emphasis of socialist economies on building up heavy industry (which produces numerous resources that can be centrally controlled), at the expense of consumer industry (whose products fall out of central control into the hands of consumers). This systemic "preference" is, of course, one cause of the long queues for consumer goods, so characteristic of most socialist societies, and of the widespread cultivation of personal ties (which westerners usually call "corruption") through which people strive to procure consumption items made "scarce" by the reference for heavy industry.

Campeanu's phrasing of essentially the same point is the leanest: socialism's fundamental dynamic is to accumulate means of production (1988: 117–118). His way of approaching the question helps to explain why goods produced in socialist economies are so often of low quality and have difficulty competing on world markets. For a system accumulating means of production rather than profits from sales, he suggests, considerations of salability (that is, of consumption) are more an obstacle to accumulation than, as in capitalism, a condition of it: "Stalinist monopoly...produces the means of production precisely in order *not* to sell them.

Transmitting their non-value to all the salable objects they produce, these unsellable means of production veritably constitute the extra-economic base of the Stalinist economy" (Campeanu 1988: 132; emphasis added). That is, because power in this system is tied to social ownership of the means of production, enhancing the means of production so owned enhances the dominance of the political apparatus that controls them.

Although other theorists rationalize it somewhat differently, most share the crucial emphasis: socialism's central imperative is to increase the bureaucracy's *capacity* to allocate, and this is not necessarily the same as increasing the amounts to be allocated.

The capacity to allocate is buttressed by its obverse, which is the destruction of resources *outside* the apparatus. Because a social actor's capacity to allocate resources is relative to the resources held by other actors, power at the center will be enhanced to the extent that the resources of other actors are incapacitated and other foci of production prevented from posing an alternative to the central monopoly on goods. I draw this idea from Gross's analysis of the Soviet incorporation of the Polish Ukraine in 1939 (Gross 1988). Calling the Soviet state a "spoiler state," Gross argues that its power came from disabling actual or potential loci of organization, thus ensuring that no one else could get things done or associate for purposes other than those of the center. This conception helps to explain, among other things, why the central power in socialist states often persecutes small-scale production, even though this production might increase the resources available to society as a whole: such production constitutes a threat to the central monopoly on allocation. Therefore, research into political processes in socialist states should always look not only for the accumulation of resources at the bureaucracy's disposal but for the destruction or incapacitation of those external to it. (In Nicolae Ceauşescu's Romania, for instance, the sphere of "private" production was stringently contained. Peasants caught selling above the fixed price or found with more than a month's food supply on hand might be punished with as much as five years' imprisonment.) The need to disable all organizations of resources outside the center is apparent from the catastrophic consequences that have followed from the emergence of alternative organizations, such as Poland's Solidarity.

Shortage and bureaucratic allocation

Two observations should be made about this analysis. First, it should not be seen as a version of earlier western theories of "totalitarianism" or confused with such theories. It addresses socialist systems from a completely different theoretical angle and has very different implications for the analysis of nearly all social processes within them. The second observation concerns conscious intent. Although some party leaders may indeed consciously intend to increase control over means of production, the analysis is concerned less with the conscious intentions of socialist bureaucrats than with the systemic effects of their behavior. On the whole, bureaucrats are not consciously striving to increase allocative power (Márkus 1981: 246); most are preoccupied with fulfilling planned output targets. It is the cumulative effects of bureaucrats fulfilling plans that generates the system's central tendency – the accumulation of allocative power – something not consciously strategized as such by any actor.

To see why this is so requires understanding two basic elements of behavior within these systems: bargaining and shortage, on the one hand, and the logic of allocative bureaucracies, on the other. The Hungarian economists Bauer (1978) and Kornai (1980, 1986) have contributed brilliantly to revealing the mechanisms of bargaining and shortage within centrally planned economies. Fundamental to their arguments is that socialism's producing units operate within *soft budget constraints* – that is, firms that do poorly will be bailed out, and financial penalties for what capitalists would see as "irrational" and "inefficient" behavior (excess inventory, overemployment, overinvestment) are minimal. In consequence, socialist firms do not develop the internal disciplinary mechanisms generally characteristic of firms under capitalism. Because of this, and because central plans usually overstate productive capacities and raise output targets higher and higher each year, firms learn to hoard materials and labor. They overstate their material requirements for production, and they overstate their investment needs, in hopes of having enough to meet or even surpass their assigned production targets (thereby increasing their incomes). Whenever a manager encounters bottlenecks in production or fails to meet targets, he can always claim that he will be successful if he receives more investment. Processes of this sort go on at every level of the system, from small firms up to the largest steel combines and on through progressively more inclusive segments of the economic bureaucracy. At each level, manager-bureaucrats are padding their budgets. Thus, these systems have expansionist tendencies that are not just inherent in growth-oriented central plans but are also generated from below.

Soft budget constraints and access to bureaucratic favor are not distributed uniformly throughout the economy. Planners view some sectors (heavy industry, armaments) as more strategic and will therefore protect them more extensively. Knowing this, managers of strategic enterprises often argue for and obtain higher investment so as to preempt bottlenecks. Claims like theirs set up a gradient of more and less privileged access to investment. In consequence, smaller, less central firms or bureaucratic segments strive to increase their budgets so as to become more strategic and strengthen their claim on investments in the future. Moreover, in times of crisis or in the early phases of certain reforms, less strategic sectors may be released from central subsidy into quasi-market conditions, where they have to fend for themselves under "harder" budgets. In the 1980s, such variability in the hardness of budget constraints was felt even within the sphere of cultural production, in both "command" Romania and the "reforming" Soviet Union . . .

The result of bargaining and hoarding by enterprises is an "economy of shortage" (Kornai 1980). Hoarding at all levels freezes in place resources that are needed for production somewhere else; all producing units want more inputs than they can get. Shortages are sometimes relative, as when sufficient quantities of materials and labor for a given level of output actually exist, but not when and where they are needed. Sometimes shortages are absolute, owing to the nonproduction that results from relative shortage (or the export of items needed locally, as in 1980s Romania). Because what is scarce and problematic in socialist systems is *supplies*, rather than *demand*, as in capitalist ones, Kornai calls socialist systems supply- or resource-constrained (as opposed to demand-constrained capitalism). The cause of supply constraints is not some planning error but the investment hunger inherent in socialist planning. The combination of expansionist tendencies and insatiable investment demand is the main reason why the productive forces grew so incessantly during socialism's early phases (Kornai 1980: 201–2) – feeding, in this way, the central drive of the system as described above, which is to accumulate means of production and allocative capacity.

The systematic shortage that results from these expansionist tendencies and from accumulations of means of production has an additional consequence, so pervasive in socialist societies that it achieves the status of a central tension within them. Shortages, of consumer goods above all, provoke a variety of strategies by which people seek to acquire needed goods or income from *outside* the official system of production and distribution. The state in fact permits some of these responses; others are more or less illegal; together, they are generally termed the "second" (or "informal") economy. The second economy is analytically subdivided into several distinct categories – illegal "black market" exchanges and sales, the "private plots" legally allotted (within formal constraints) to collective-farm members, moonlighting for extra pay, personalism and corruption in distributive networks (the clerk who hides goods under the counter for friends and relatives or for a bribe, for instance), and the like ... These various forms have in common the parasitic use of the official economy as a source of the goods, materials, tools, status, and so forth that are essential to secondary economic activity. That is, the two economies are integrally tied to each other, the organization of the formal economy both necessitating and enabling the informal sphere.

These petty efforts to obtain goods operate at odds with the center's accumulation of resources and with its efforts to fortify its allocative capacity by *disabling* resources. As a result, the center in each socialist country normally persecuted such second economies (more so in some countries and periods than in others). To suppress them completely, however, was not wholly advisable, since consumers who could not acquire what they needed for livelihood were difficult to motivate and to control; not all party leaderships considered it wise to alienate the public by cutting off all access to secondary economies. In each socialist context, therefore, there remained a constant tension between suppressing and permitting a certain amount of secondary economic activity, which meant a constant threat to the allocative monopoly of the center. The social space of the second economy – even though it was in some sense the *result* of how the formal sector was organized – came to represent a space of opposition to that sector, a space which developed parallels in other spheres, such as the sphere of culture.

Allocative bureaucracy versus party center

The two previous paragraphs illuminate one contradiction of socialist systems, rooted in the production and distribution of goods and services. A second is to be found in the workings of bureaucratic allocation. Allocation is the business of what nearly all theorists of socialism call the "apparatus" and/or the "bureaucracy" (without always being very explicit about what they mean by this). The apparatus is not, however, a unitary organism. Most theorists make a distinction that I think is crucial for understanding some of the contradictory tendencies in these systems. Fehér et al. speak, on the one hand, of the bureaucratic apparatus, an all-embracing mono-organizational entity, and, on the other, of its "pinnacle," a "small circle of the political elite, the Party leadership, where all the basic-orientative decisions concerning the overall distribution of social surplus are made" (1983: 51, 70)....

Campeanu theorizes the distinction between what I will call "bureaucracy" and "apex" more explicitly than others. He attributes it to the division characteristic of monopolies of all kinds, including capitalist ones, between ownership and management. Most *ownership* functions, he argues, are monopolized by the apex; the role of the bureaucracy is to *manage*. This division suggests ways of discussing a source of the conflicting tendencies within socialism, based in the different interests of the body that owns/controls and the body that manages. The contradictory tendencies have something to do, I think, with "reform" – ideas about decentralization, market socialism, and so forth, which, before they changed the system definitively (and unexpectedly) in the 1980s, had appeared a number of times before. Whereas the apical "owners" of socialized means of production can persist in policies whose effect is to accumulate means of production without concern for things like productivity and output, the bureaucratic managers of the allocative process *must* be concerned with such things. There are two sets of reasons for this: processes involving bureaucrats' prestige, and the realities of their role as "allocators."

Behind the bureaucratic expansionism-within-shortage described above are competitive processes perhaps analogous to the dilemmas faced by the entrepreneurs in capitalism. Constrained by demand, capitalists strive for ever-greater domestication (predictability) of the demand structure, through such devices as advertising and through softening the budget constraints of consumers via credit and consumer debt. In a supply-constrained system, by contrast, what must be domesticated is supplies: everyone scrambles for access to the pot. At all points in the system, jobs or bureaucratic positions are used as platforms for amassing resources. Personal influence, "corruption," and reciprocal exchanges are some of the major mechanisms. This sort of behavior goes on throughout the society but is especially important for bureaucrats, whose entire reputation and prestige rest upon their capacity to amass resources. Any bureaucrat, any bureaucratic segment, tends to expand its own domain, increasing its capacity to give – whether the "gift" be education, apartments, medical care, permission and funds for publication, social welfare, wages, building permits, or funds for investments in factory infrastructure. Throughout the bureaucracy, then, there is rampant competition to increase one's budget at the expense of those roughly equivalent to one on a horizontal scale, so as to have potentially more to disburse to claimants below. That is, what counts most in the competition among social actors within allocative bureaucracies is *inputs to one's segment*, rather than outputs of production (Stark 1990: 17).

In the redistributive systems commonly described by anthropologists, chiefs redistribute goods to their followers, just as socialist bureaucrats allocate social rewards. The limits on a chief's power, as on a socialist bureaucrat's, come from the power of other chiefs to siphon followers away by giving – or creating the impression that they *can* give – bigger and better feasts or more generous loans. Like chiefs in such redistributive systems, bureaucrats are constantly under pressure not to be outdone by other bureaucrats: they must continue to strive for influence, amass more resources, and raise the standing of their segment of the bureaucracy. The form of competition specific to socialism consists of always trying to get more allocable inputs than others at one's level, so that one can move up closer to the privileged circle that always get what it asks for (the Soviet military, for example, until the mid-1980s).

This discussion of inputs suggests a problem, however. As I argued earlier, maximizing allocative *capacity* is not the same as maximizing the actual surplus – the concrete disposable resources over which a bureaucrat makes allocative decisions. But at some point, real resources do have to be delivered, and for this a bureaucrat's allocative reputation is not always enough. This is especially true in the domain of economic production, heavy industry above all. Without actual investments and hard material resources, lower-level units cannot produce the means of production upon which both bureaucracy and apex rely. Productive activity cannot be so stifled that nothing gets produced, or the prestige of those who supposedly allocate will enter a crisis. We might call it a crisis of "overadministration," as distinct from the crises of "overproduction" more common in capitalism.

Thus, I suggest that when central accumulation of means of production begins to threaten the capacity of lower-level units to produce; when persistent imbalances between investment in heavy industry and investment in light industry, between allocations for investment and allocations for consumption, and so on cause a decline in the accumulation of actual allocable goods; and when attempts by the apex to keep enterprises from appropriating surplus on their own actually obstruct the process of production itself: then pressure arises for a shift of emphasis. The pressure is partly from those in the wider society to whom not enough is being allocated and partly from bureaucrats themselves whose prestige and, increasingly, prospects of retaining power depend on having more goods. One then hears of decentralization, of the rate of growth, of productivity – in a word, of matters of *output* rather than of the inputs that lie at the core of bureaucratic performance. Bureaucratic calls for market reform sometimes enter an overt or de facto alliance with the independent activity in the second economy. The problem is, of course, that concern with output introduces mechanisms inimical to the logic of bureaucratic allocation; these include, above all, freer markets, which socialism suppresses precisely because they move goods *laterally* rather than vertically toward the center, as all redistributive systems require.

Inherent in the demands that management – as opposed to "ownership" – of social resources places on an allocative bureaucracy, then, is the necessity to see to it that resources are actually generated, and not merely by more coercive extraction: that the centralization of means of production does not stifle production altogether. Thus, quite aside from the second economies that flourish at the edges of the command economy, one finds within the apparatus of management itself an interest in mechanisms that subvert the system's central logic. As in capitalism, where, in Marx's view, the goal-function of the economy is to maximize surplus value but the subjective aim of capitalists is to maximize profit (not the same thing) – that is, subjective intention feeds something different from what accumulation objectively requires – so in socialist systems the goal-function of the economy is to maximize allocative capacity and control over means of production, but the subjective aim of at least some bureaucrats and enterprise managers some of the time is to maximize production of a disposable surplus.

This introduces into the system a subordinate rationality not wholly consonant with the overriding logic, a rationality based in recognition that the center cannot dictate values out of thin air, as if there were no such thing as production costs. Sometimes this subordinate rationality becomes amplified, such as when international credits and indebtedness to western banks bind socialism's dynamic with that of capitalism, requiring hard-currency exports premised on *salability* (which socialist economies generally ignore, as argued above). The tension between the central logic of command and the subordinate "counterrationalities" will then increase, sharpening the conflict between command and market, centralization and decentralization, investment and consumption (Fehér et al. 1983: 270–1). Campeanu summarizes the resulting tensions between apex ("supreme entity") and bureaucracy as follows:

> Thus a potential for revolt against the supreme entity is inscribed in the genetic code of Stalinist bureaucracy. Actualized in the hidden form of imperceptible but formidable daily pressures, this potential has drawn the bureaucracy into all the major conflicts which, from 1956 to the present, have shaken Stalinist societies. On each of these occasions, its inherent ambiguity has regularly divided its ranks into one segment which defended the supreme entity and another which contested it.... This potential for revolt nourishes the organic mistrust the supreme entity has of its bureaucracy, which in turn nourishes their historical tendency to transform their separation into conflict. (1988: 148)

From these tensions, I believe, emerged Mikhail Gorbachev's attempt to reform the Soviet system and the eastern European socialisms along with it. The unintended effect of his backing potentially reformist bureaucratic segments in the other socialist states was ultimately, of course, to fracture monolithic Communist parties, exposing their actual or potential fragility to restive publics and destroying party rule. The series of progressively more dramatic confrontations through which this came about culminated in the violent overthrow of Ceauşescu's Communist dictatorship in Romania, its violence fed precisely by the relentlessness with which this party apparatus, above all others in the bloc, had gathered social resources into its own hands, devastated productive capacity, and left the public destitute.

Weak states and the mode of control

In the preceding sections I have treated socialism's "laws of motion" and some of its bureaucratic politics. In this section I discuss some features of socialist states, particularly their inherent weakness and their principal modes of controlling their populations. Prior to 1989, a few scholars were suggesting what at the time was far less patently obvious than it soon became: that contrary to the original "totalitarian" image, socialist states were weak. Arguments to this effect had been emerging not only for eastern Europe but for China as well. Although it is now less necessary to justify this view, I might nonetheless suggest why these states proved as weak as they did.

We can conceptualize socialism's weak states from three different angles, each employing a different definition of power. Gross makes one kind of argument, based on a notion of power as the capacity to get things done. Gross contends that "[t]o gain a fresh insight into the essence of the political process under communism we must revise our notions about the monopolization of power by communist parties" (1989: 208). Because socialism's "spoiler" states insisted on monopolizing power by devastating the capacity of all *other* organizations to get things done, he argues, these states undermined *their own* capacity to get things done and, therefore, their power. "The image of Stalin's Russia as a gigantic, all-powerful, centralized terror machine is wrong": a state that denies power to any other social actor may gain *absolute* power, but it is not an *all-powerful* state, and it crumbles the instant an effective social challenge arises (Gross 1988: 232–3). To the extent that Stalin's state appeared all-powerful, in Gross's view, the reason was a pervasive "privatization" of the instruments of coercion, which – far from being concentrated somewhere at the top – were made available to everyone, through the mechanism of the *denunciation*. "The real power of a totalitarian state results from its being at the disposal of every inhabitant, available for hire at a moment's notice" (Gross 1988: 120). This is a dispersed kind of power, and the kind that remains at the center is purely the vacuum left after all foci of organization around the center have been destroyed – "[h]ence the perplexing 'weakness' of these all-powerful regimes" (Gross 1989: 209).

A second argument for the weakness of socialist states defines power as a relationship of dependency: if a social actor depends heavily upon another for a crucial resource or performance, it is not powerful, no matter how many means of coercion lie at its disposal (Emerson 1962). Bauer (1978) and Rév (1987) argue, for example, that the supposedly plan-forming political center in socialism is too weak to plan: the reason is that for the production figures necessary to planning, the center is utterly dependent upon reports from the point of production, where central control is minimal. But lower-level units *never* deliver reliable figures, either because they fear the consequences of failed targets or because they wish to continue inflating their investment requests . . . Because central agencies have inadequate information, they cannot easily detect excessive investment claims, which makes it impossible for them both to plan and to resist the expansionist drive from below. Moreover, bargaining and hoarding by firms in the "economy of shortage" make labor a scarce item within socialist economies; structurally speaking, that is, labor has considerable implicit leverage, as Solidarity and the Soviet miners' strikes made very clear. This source of leverage, even when it is not overtly manifest, is structurally debilitating to the state.

These two definitions of power are sometimes mixed together, as when power is seen as a capacity (to enact policies) mitigated by the center's dependency (on intermediate and lower-level cadres). Policies may be *made* at the center, but they are *implemented* in local settings, where those entrusted with them may ignore, corrupt, overexecute, or otherwise adulterate them. This sort of argument is especially common in the work of anthropologists, who have observed at close range some of the many ways in which local executors of central policy bend and redefine it in accord with their own styles of leadership, their capabilities for enforcement, and so on (see, for example, Kideckel 1982; Sampson 1984).

A third argument focuses less on power *per se* than on its cultural definition or legitimation. A state may be seen as strong to the extent that it effectively creates itself *as a cultural relation* with its citizen-subjects . . . to the extent that the terms through which it legitimates itself enter into daily practice more or less unproblematically, and to the extent that its symbolization is not widely challenged. By this definition, there is no doubt that eastern European socialist states were weak. Marxism-Leninism remained for most people an alien ideology unintegrated into consciousness and practice except in a wholly superficial manner, and challenges to official symbolization were rife.

Whatever argument one prefers, each brings to the fore a basic question about socialism's mode of domination: how can a relatively weak state control its subordinates – particularly the populace, who, unlike bureaucrats, are poorly served by the system and might therefore threaten its continuity? Control over the means of production and power to limit consumption give socialist leaderships extensive command over labor in the aggregate and do much to keep subordinates passive, but these are not sufficient. Because leaders cannot use labor markets, firings, lockouts, unemployment, bankruptcies, and so forth, the means for disciplining labor under socialism are much less subtle and varied than those available to capitalists. Even (perhaps especially) in regimes of maximum coercion, such as Romania in the late 1980s, workers do not necessarily perform as the center might wish. Numerous empirical studies show the problematic nature of incentives and coordination in the workplace . . . This invites us, then, to problematize the notion of "control" and to inquire into the various forms through which socialist regimes have sought to achieve it.

Several scholars have approached this problem by looking specifically at the mechanisms for controlling labor power and the labor process. To the extent that many different groupings in society (households, firms, the bureaucracy) compete for the "scarce" labor power that generates their resources or wealth, control over the labor of others is a crucial component of social power (see, for example, Böröcz 1989; Humphrey 1983: 124, 300–16, 370). Sociologists Böröcz and Burawoy point to two main modes of exercising social control over labor in socialism: the market and "political means" (Böröcz 1989: 289). Burawoy (1985: 12) nuances these "political means" by talking of production regimes that produce varying degrees of consent or coercion. . . . I find this typology of strategies which I will call "modes of control," useful for analyzing domination in socialism's weak states. I modify the argument only by calling the third control strategy "symbolic-ideological" rather than normative, to underscore the normative instability of "real" socialist societies.

Within the bureaucratic mode of domination characteristic of socialism, then, we can look for these three modes of control, the prevalence of any one of them within any given society reflecting the balance of forces within the party and the bureaucracy. Remunerative strategies entail giving markets a role in allocating goods and labor; such strategies have formed the heart of most efforts by Communist Party leaderships to reform the system. Coercive strategies entail not just systematic use of police and security forces but attempts to minimize nonofficial or market-derived sources of income, for these reduce people's vulnerability to coercion. Symbolic-ideological strategies entail value-laden exhortations, as well as attempts to saturate consciousness with certain symbols and ideological premises to which subsequent exhortations may be addressed. We can further subdivide symbolic-ideological strategies by the values to which they appeal: norms of kinship and friendship, important in organizing informal networks and local solidarities; various tenets of Marxism-Leninism, such as the emancipation of the proletariat or the values of science and knowledge in creating a just society; standards of living and material comfort; or patriotism and sacrifice for the nation. The third of these, sometimes referred to as "the new social contract," was an important auxiliary to the remunerative mode of control used in Hungary during much of the 1970s and early 1980s, as well as at various times in East Germany, Czechoslovakia, and Poland under Gierek. Appeals to patriotism and national values (alongside ineffective appeals to Marxist-Leninist norms), by contrast, were the foundation of party rule in Romania of the 1970s and 1980s.

Coercive strategies are inordinately expensive over the long run. Not only do they alienate the populace more than other strategies, generating sabotage and other forms of resistance that reduce production (and, therefore, state revenues), but they necessitate paying a far larger personnel corps than the other modes require. The corps of this repressive apparatus generally receives very high pay as well. In Romania of the 1980s, for example, the ratio of Secret Police operatives to population is thought to have been around 1 to 15, and the salary of a Secret Police colonel could be as high as 16,000 lei per month (compared with approximately 3500 lei for a skilled worker or 5000 for a university department chair). Remunerative modes of control, with their invitation to independent economic activity, avoid this costly apparatus and its alienating effects but have the drawback of undermining the center's monopoly on allocation and, thus, its control. Symbolic-ideological strategies have therefore played a very important, if varying, role in all socialist societies to date even where reliance on coercion was also high. This impels the sphere of symbolization and cultural production – a sphere in which anthropology claims preeminence – to the center of any analysis of socialism. In the following section I will briefly show why "culture" became the site of so much contestation, in eastern European socialist societies, and gave the intellectuals who produce culture such prominence that they achieved the very presidencies of two eastern European countries, during the "revolutions" of 1989.

Socialism and "Culture"

While the theorists discussed above have much to say about political, economic, and social life under socialism, they tend decidedly toward the inarticulate on the subject of culture and its production. They rarely pursue the implications of their new-class theory, ownership theory, or goal-function theory for how *meaning* is produced and controlled in socialist systems. Literature on cultural production in other social orders is not much help, for such thinkers as Bourdieu (1984, 1988) and Williams (1982) frame their analyses explicitly in terms of capitalist markets; yet the suppression of the market in socialist systems means that except when reforms reintroduce market mechanisms into its sphere, culture ceases to be a commodity.

The following arguments concerning the role of meaning and its official producers – intellectuals – must therefore be seen as exploratory. They aim to suggest what the properties of socialist systems might imply for the production of culture – here, specifically "high" culture – as well as for the relation of intellectuals to power within socialist society. Since adequate treatment of this subject would exceed the space available, I restrict definitions to a minimum. In brief, I follow such scholars as Bauman (1987b), Bourdieu (1988), and Foucault (1980) in defining intellectuals, first, by the kinds of claims and resources they employ in social struggles (invocations of knowledge, truth, or expertise as a form of social superiority; or position resting on symbolic/cultural capital as against political or economic capital) and, second, by their role in societal legitimation...The terrain they occupy is not exclusive but overlaps with that of persons we might call party bureaucrats and apparatchiks; during the course of social contests, given persons may cross the fuzzy boundary between these statuses, according to the kinds of claims they are making in a wider field of claims or the values upon which they stake their position.

"Intellectual" as I use it refers more to a social *space* than to a category of people (cf. Bauman 1987b: 19), a space whose relation to the political is illuminated by the discussion above.

We might begin with a 1988 observation from a Romanian émigré: "Of all the social strata of today's Romania, the only one whose aspirations bring it into touch with that domain which power considers inalienable is the intellectuals" (Solacolu 1988: 28). How is this so? One answer comes from Konrád and Szelényi: the legitimating myth of the system, "rational redistribution," gives the party a monopoly on "teleological knowledge," the knowledge necessary to setting and implementing goals for society, knowledge of the laws of social development and of the path to progress (cf. Szelényi 1982: 306). Yet at the same time, the party creates educated persons – a larger pool than it requires, so as to permit selection. Some of them specialize precisely in knowledge of society and social values, and not all of these people become (or want to become) apparatchiks. These two theorists see the intellectuals as a class-in-formation for this very reason: that is, that the form of intellectuals' work makes them basic to reproducing the inequality on which the allocative bureaucracy rests. By sharing with intellectuals a legitimation resting on claims to knowledge and by creating a stratum of knowledge-empowered persons, the party reinforces a privileged situation for intellectuals, even as it reinforces its own. As Zygmunt Bauman puts it, "The communist revolution explicitly proclaimed and ostensibly practiced the unity of power and knowledge, the innermost core of the intellectual idiom" (1987a: 177). One need scarcely look further than the slogans "The party knows best" and "The party is always right" to see, in their most blatant form, knowledge claims that intellectuals can easily contest, having the means to posit alternative values that might influence how resources are allocated and goals set.

Socialism's intellectuals are therefore both necessary and dangerous: necessary because their skills are implied in setting social values, and dangerous because they and the political center have potentially divergent notions of what intellectual practice should consist of. When – as often happens – these notions do not agree, a conflict emerges over who has the authority to define intellectual work: those who *do* it, or those who *order* it. For those who order it, matters are clear. From the heyday of Stalin's culture-czar Zhdanov onward, party bureaucrats have seen cultural production as a minor category of ideological activism, with art serving to indoctrinate. Writers report endless exchanges with censors, who call into question everything from words used to the artist's judgment in framing a story: "Why does the hero die at the end? What do you mean, he's killed? A crime? But crimes are not representative of our socialist spirit. . . . Hey, you can't hang the fellow, he's the driver for the collective farm!!" (Solacolu 1988: 28). In this we see the tangled relation between a party that thinks of itself as directing all aspects of society according to specialized knowledge and the potential revolt of those whom it has created to help with that task.

These examples merely underscore a more abstract point concerning the nature of intellectuals: their work necessarily involves them in processes of legitimation, which are of vital concern to a bureaucracy needing performances and compliance from its subjects. All intellectuals operate with subjectivity-forming symbolic means. Their talents are essential to power, and above all to any leadership or any period in which a symbolic-ideological mode of control predominates. The nature of intellectual work is such that all new regimes must seek to capture its producers and its products; socialist regimes are no exception. To the question of whether socialist systems show a special form of this general truth, I have suggested that the double legitimation of party and intellectuals via knowledge constitutes one peculiarity in the party's relation to intellectual work. Another comes from socialism's "laws of motion."

I have proposed as socialism's "motor" the systemic drive to accumulate allocative power, rooted in accumulating means of production. Is there some way in which *culture's* means of production are also susceptible to this tendency? If one asks what constitute the means of cultural production, one immediately thinks of (besides such things as printing presses, paper, paints, and the other material means) certain forms of accumulated knowledge that serve as bases of further cultural production: dictionaries, encyclopedias and other compendia, published documentary sources, treatises and works of synthesis – such as the official four-volume history of Romania (Constantinescu-Iaşi et al. 1960–4) published in the 1960s and intended as the point of departure for all subsequent writing in that discipline. In socialist eastern Europe, all such repositories of knowledge have been produced by large collectives, in public institutions, benefiting from huge allocations of funds for culture. The importance of these cultural equivalents of heavy industry requires that they be produced by "reliable" institutions under the guidance of the party; cultural bureaucracies in all socialist countries have made certain to maintain control over them.

There is another means of cultural production, more basic even than the ones just mentioned: language. For a party bent on transforming consciousness, control over language is vital. Gross captures an aspect of this when he writes that communist rule changes language so that it no longer reflects or represents reality; metaphor becomes more important than prosaic discourse, and magical words replace descriptive and logical ones (Gross 1988: 236–8). But whereas Gross sees in this the destruction of language, I see in it the retooling of language as a means of ideological production. I would develop this thought further with Bakhtin's discussion of authoritative discourse – any religious, moral, political, or parental discourse that demands we acknowledge it and make it our own. "We encounter it with its authority already fused to it" (Bakhtin 1981: 342). This discourse is not one to be selected from a range of equivalent possibilities: it imposes itself and demands unconditional allegiance. The semantic structure of such discourse is static, and its terms have been cleansed of all but one meaning; it is often marked by a special language or a different script (Bakhtin 1981: 343). This description fits very well the special "wooden language" of socialist officialdom, so well captured by Thom (1989), with its repetitive adjective-noun clusters and its impoverished lexicon. Gross might have said, then, that communist rule seeks to make all language authoritative discourse, to reduce the meanings of words, to straitjacket them into singular intentions, and to preclude any use of language that permits multiple meanings.

While one could argue that all regimes are concerned with language to some extent, I would hold that socialist ones lie at an extreme on this dimension. For, unlike the western European societies that benefited from several centuries of slow evolution in which consciousness came to be formed more through practice than through discourse (Bourdieu 1977; Foucault 1978), eastern European communists came to power with the intention of rapidly revolutionizing consciousness and with precious few means of doing so. Popular resistance to many imposed practices made language the principal arena for achieving this end. The social power deriving from control of the representations of reality became truly vital for rulers who disposed of relatively few such means. Language, and the cultural production that takes place through it, thus became crucial vehicles through which socialist leaders hoped to form consciousness and subjectivity and to produce ideological effects.

Indeed, one might say that in these societies, language and discourse are among the *ultimate* means of production. Through discourse even more than through practice, their rulers may hope to constitute consciousness, social objects, social life itself. We see here another reason, then, for the special place of intellectuals in socialist countries: any political regime as fragile as these, where discourse has a disproportionately productive role – and especially any regime whose self-proclaimed task is to change society – *must* incorporate the producers of discourse into itself. Indeed, the argument about socialism's "weak state" suggests that it is often only through discourse that the power and unity of such a fragile regime can be achieved . . .

For these reasons, one finds an extraordinary politicization of language in socialism, as the state's attempt to create an "authorized" language brings all speech under contest from those who resist the centralization of meanings. One hears constantly of writers and censors haggling over the specific words to be allowed in a text. The words that are prohibited vary from one time period to another, reflecting changes in the issues that are delicate or troublesome from the party's point of view, and they concern far more than what we might think of as the obviously "political." For example, Romanian writer Norman Manea (1990) reports that in the 1970s, relatively few of the words that the censor repeatedly struck from his manuscripts pertained to the overtly political sphere; they tended, rather, to be about unpleasant states of mind – sadness, discouragement, desperation, despondency. These words were, nonetheless, highly political for a party that had claimed to usher in a utopian world. By the 1980s, the ax was falling on words of a different kind: those relating to the unpleasant specifics of life under Ceauşescu's austerity policies of that decade. Censors now found deliberate provocation in such words as "coffee" and "meat" (impossible to find), "cold" and "dark" (the state of people's apartments), "informer" (what many around one were likely to be), "dictator" or "tyrant" (what everyone saw in Ceauşescu). Also interdicted were "nazism," "fascism," and "anti-Semitism" (the party leadership and its associated intellectuals having come to resemble all too closely the interwar Right). Certain things remained constant, however: during both periods, words offending the party's puritanical morality and atheism were excluded – sex, breasts, homosexuality, God. Evident in this, as in the Polish censorship rules extensively documented by Curry (1984), is the effort to control reality by circumscribing the ways it can be discussed. "Pollution," for instance, is not a social problem if it is not named. (The disastrous legacy of this prohibition has now become all too clear.)

Language and meanings are contested not merely between agents of party rule and intellectuals as a group but also among intellectuals themselves, competing for access to the bureaucratic favor essential to securing the resources for cultural production. Since the educational system of socialism produces more intellectuals than its "ideological apparatus" can absorb and more than its resources for culture can sustain, this struggle can become exceedingly fierce. Its stakes are one's access to meaningful livelihood and to outlets for one's talents. In Romanian historiography during 1984, for example, a heated argument arose as to whether a particular historical event was best termed an "uprising" or a "revolution." Each position argued that different values should be central to historiography and promoted different institutions of history writing (see Simmonds-Duke 1987; Verdery 1991). Similarly, in the 1970s and 1980s Romanian literary criticism was riven by competing views as to what values Romanian literature ought to implement. One set of views, which echoed certain emphases of the party leadership, gradually gained its advocates greater control over key publications and greater access to resources such as paper, press runs, and permission to publish (Verdery 1991). In both cases, the conflict was not chiefly between "dissident intellectuals" and "party" but *among* more-or-less professional historians and literati, whose field of production had been wholly politicized by the party's obsession with culture.

Another consequence of this pervasive politicization of culture is the emergence of a cultural equivalent of the second economy: the creation of unauthorized foci of cultural production, in the form of *samizdat* literature circulated in typescript or even, as in Poland during the 1980s, whole underground publishing operations that produced upward of a thousand books a year in press runs of respectable size. As with many forms of second economy, socialist leaderships have generally attempted to fortify their monopoly on the production of meaning by disabling these independent foci of cultural activity, persecuting those who engage in it. The epitome of such persecution was to be found in Romania, where all typewriters had to be registered with the police, who could then readily trace any underground text to its hapless author.

Such persecution of unauthorized symbolizing created dissidents of intellectuals who, in many cases, wanted only to be allowed to write their books. Instead of disabling them and enhancing its own power, the party made of them heroes and future postcommunist leaders. Even those it expelled, such as the writers of some texts discussed earlier in this essay, contributed to its downfall (thus proving the aptness of their analyses of socialism's "laws of motion" not only to politics and the economy but also to the cultural sphere). The party's inability either to disable these intellectuals as independent foci or to secure its control over them shows the fundamental and problematic link between socialism and culture.

Researching the Transition

As of 1989, the societies whose workings I have described above made a radical break with the model presented here. The most important changes have been the Communist Party's loss of monopoly control over both the bureaucratic apparatus and the political sphere; the rise of competing political parties and nonstate organizations; the actual or projected divestiture of much public property into a newly emerging "private" sector; and the intention to decentralize economic and political decision-making, as well as to allow a much increased integrative role to the market. If even a fraction of these projected changes are realized, societies fitting the image provided in this essay will cease to exist. Whether their successors will be best described through amendments to this model or through models of a wholly different kind will become clear with time.

Numerous fascinating research questions suggest themselves. Phrased at their simplest, they include the following. How will viable political parties be formed? More important, how will people long taught to be incapable of holding informed political opinions learn to hold such opinions? How will the process of "privatization" proceed, and what will be the role of foreign capital in that process? Will the growth of the market and more "efficient" production erode habits of personalism in daily life? How will collective farms be broken up (rather like latifundia after the abolition of serfdom and slavery)? Who will be judged suitable recipients of the land and with what will they cultivate it? By what mechanisms will rural differentiation reemerge in the wake of egalitarian propertylessness? How will persons privileged under the socialist order fare under the new circumstances, and how will the older forms of inequity continue to constrict people's chances? To what extent have socialist ideas about classlessness and equality entered into people's thinking, despite their categorical rejection of socialism overall, and what effects will this have?

One could string out such questions indefinitely. Most of them emerge from a seat-of-the-pants understanding of how socialism was organized, not from any complicated theories about it. To conclude, I will briefly suggest five research problems that follow directly from the model presented in this essay, so as to illustrate the directions in which it points.

One of the most vital processes to take place in eastern Europe will involve building up what many refer to as "civil society," something on which an extensive literature is already emerging, with eastern Europeans and émigrés among its contributors. I take the creation of civil society to mean the populating of an intermediate social space – between the level of households and that of the state itself – with organizations and institutions not directly controlled from above, such as (in western contexts) political parties, voluntary associations, independent trade unions, educational institutions more or less free of state control, and all manner of neighborhood, professional, charitable, special-purpose, and other groupings. The near-emptiness of this space in most socialist societies was the direct consequence of the absorption of resources into the political apparatus and of the disablement of all organizations external to it. A party bureaucracy that coexisted with universities, trade unions, or other parties independent of it would have been a party bureaucracy that did not monopolize social allocation – and that, according to the argument of this article, was antithetical to the operation of socialist systems. It was their nature to swell their own funds of resources and to incapacitate all others. In consequence, the social space of most socialist societies consisted of a mass of atomized households at the bottom and a massive bureaucratic and repressive apparatus at the top, with a near-vacuum in between. State-oriented institutions made it *appear* that this intermediate space was filled – with state-controlled trade unions, state-directed religious activity, state-created organizations for national minorities, state-sponsored folk festivals, and so on – but in fact it was virtually empty, devastated by the actions of socialism's "spoiler" states.

The task that various dissident and oppositional groups in these societies took on was to build organizations, however tenuously rooted, that were not controlled by the state and the party. These included, beginning in the 1970s, Czechoslovakia's Charter 77; Poland's Committee for the Defense of Workers (KOR) and, later, the Solidarity trade union; transient echoes of the same in Romania . . . , and Hungary's independent ecology and peace movements and the voluntary organization in support of needy families (SZETA). While such organizations were often fragile, they gave their members a taste of the experience that will be necessary to filling that intermediate space in society and to increasing social pluralism thereby.

This experience was not, however, widely distributed. The more common experience of eastern Europeans was one of atomization, of alienation from one another and from the sphere of meaningful political or collective activity, and of the expropriation of initiative and a capacity to make plans. Under these circumstances, the restoration of politics as a meaningful sphere and the building of new institutions and organizations – which must take over some of the redistributive functions of the socialist bureaucracy and restrain its resurrection – will be a lengthy and arduous process. To observe it should be a research objective of the highest priority.

Similar arguments pertain to a second area whose significance the western media have already confirmed: ethnic and national conflicts. Eastern Europe is a region long characterized by tense ethnonational relations. Contrary to the view widespread in America, the resuscitation of those ethnic conflicts is not simply a revival of "traditional" enmities from the interwar years – as if the intervening half-century were inconsequential. To begin with, ethnic ideologies were reinforced rather than diminished by socialism's "shortage economies," which favored any social device that reduced competition for unavailable goods. Ethnic ideas, with their drawing of clear boundaries between "in" and "out," are (alongside the more often noted "corruption") one such device. Second, with the end of government repression, ethnonational resentments flare up in an environment extremely unpropitious to managing them: an environment devoid of any intermediate institutions for settling disagreements peaceably. The Romanian case, in which the former Secret Police apparatus seems to have taken over some of the articulation of Romanian ethnic concerns while Romania's Hungarians have formed a strong, united new party, suggests both the danger of the situation and the importance of monitoring the efforts to contain ethnic conflict institutionally.

A third significant area involves the decentralization of decision-making, which most of the postsocialist governments have expressed as their aim. This process will run up against long-standing bureaucratic practices rooted in the system of centralized command, with its tendency to concentrate resources within the bureaucratic apparatus precisely because bureaucrats have learned to compete by amassing such resources. It is not simply that top bureaucrats will resist the devolution of decision-making from their domains; one could easily predict this without the aid of models such as the one presented here. At least as important is that *lower*-level bureaucrats – and even those citizens the bureaucracy once served, however poorly – will resist the dismantling of a structure within which they had become adept competitors or occasional beneficiaries. For example, in Romania it seemed for a time in the spring of 1990 that the Ministry of Religion was to be disbanded, on the grounds that it was no longer necessary in a society having a normal separation of church and state and having no official atheism that required surveillance over institutions of faith. A delegation of prelates to the Romanian President and Prime Minister, however, requested the reinstatement of such a Ministry and the naming of a Minister; without it (though this was not the reason given), they would have no outlet for their well-honed talents at influencing the Minister in their favor and at securing support for their projects. Otherwise, they would have to learn an entire new repertoire of behaviors requisite to the prospering of their enterprise, and this was not necessarily an appealing prospect.

The concentration of resources within the political apparatus produced a multitude of practices for influencing their allocation. These practices may prove difficult to eradicate, as we know from anthropological studies in which "market penetration" encounters determined resistance from those it threatens. One might expect to see not merely the former top elite but all manner of others – writers, doctors, publishers, clerks, teachers, even perhaps would-be entrepreneurs – calling upon the postsocialist state to take more responsibility for providing resources. In this way they will help to perpetuate a centralized power. The process positively invites its participant observers.

A fourth set of processes worth watching will emerge from the labor shortage endemic to socialism's shortage economies. Like other resources, labor was hoarded within socialist firms, giving rise to the lax labor discipline and overmanning so often remarked by outside observers. This labor shortage was one factor contributing to the potential strength of the working classes under socialism, epitomized in Poland's Solidarity. Now, however, the introduction of market forces is expected to produce massive unemployment, as newly profit-conscious firms release their labor reserves. Workers who learned from socialism of their right to work will have to be persuaded to relinquish that right, and we might imagine they will be hard to convince. Anthropologists could be crucial witnesses of both the efforts to persuade and the resistance to persuasion. The problem will be particularly acute, however, for women, who made considerable strides in the workplace under socialism (even if less spectacularly than was claimed, and often at great cost to them). They too were taught to expect certain rights, which they now stand to lose disproportionately, relative to men. Angry objections by East German women concerning the restrictive abortion and childcare policies of West Germany show one small facet of a much larger reconfiguration that gender economies will undergo during the transition.

Finally, I argued above that "symbolic-ideological control" and, therefore, "culture" had special significance in socialist systems. Let us assume that increased marketization of the economy will erode this special political significance of culture, as remunerative incentives increase; let us further assume that because Marxism-Leninism will no longer be enforcing transformations of consciousness, consciousness will come to be formed less through discourse and more through practices (now *not* seen as imposed by power). It follows, then, that intellectuals and the cultural production they oversee will enter a new time of crisis. They will discover themselves increasingly irrelevant to politics, rather like their American counterparts, and will find their public prestige in decline. Just as many intellectuals derived real benefit from the socialist state's subsidy of their work, so will they now resist the commodification of their creativity and knowledge...The response of intellectuals to this erosion of their place, in the various eastern European countries, will merit close scrutiny – particularly inasmuch as increased nationalism in the culture they produce is one certain consequence.

These suggestions merely scratch the surface of what researchers might expect to find henceforth in the formerly socialist countries of eastern Europe, now forging a new "articulation" with the world of the capitalist west. Fortified by oppositional theories that emerged from within the socialist order, we can perhaps better comprehend the directions this new articulation may take.

REFERENCES

Bakhtin, Mikhail. (1981) *The Dialogical Imagination.* Austin: University of Texas Press.

Bauer, Tamás. (1978) Investment Cycles in Planned Economies. *Acta Oeconomica* 21: 243–60.

Bauman, Zygmunt. (1987a) Intellectuals in East-Central Europe: Continuity and Change. *Eastern European Politics and Societies* 1: 162–86.

——. (1987b) *Legislators and Interpreters: On Modernity, Post-Modernity and Intellectuals.* Ithaca, NY: Cornell University Press.

Böröcz, József. (1989) Mapping the Class Structures of State Socialism in East-Central Europe. *Research in Social Stratification and Mobility* 8: 279–309.

Bourdieu, Pierre. (1977) *Outline of a Theory of Practice.* Cambridge: Cambridge University Press.

——. (1984) *Distinction: A Social Critique of the Judgement of Taste.* Cambridge, MA: Harvard University Press.

——. (1988) *Homo Academicus.* London: Polity Press.

Burawoy, Michael. (1985) *The Politics of Production.* London: Verso.

——. (1991) Painting Socialism. In *The Radiant Past: Ideology and Reality in Hungary's Road to Capitalism*, ch. 5. Michael Burawoy and János Lukács. Chicago: University of Chicago Press.

Campeanu, Pavel. (1988) *The Genesis of the Stalinist Social Order.* Armonk, NY: M. E. Sharpe.

Constantinescu-Iaşi, P., et al. (1960–4) *Istoria Rominiei*, vols. 1–4. Bucharest: Editura Academiei RPR.

Curry, Jane. (1984) *The Black Book of Polish Censorship.* New York: Vintage.

Emerson, Rupert. (1962) Power-Dependence Relations. *American Sociological Review* 27: 31–41.

Fehér, Ferenc, Agnes Heller, and György Márkus. (1983) *Dictatorship over Needs: An Analysis of Soviet Societies.* New York: Basil Blackwell.

Foucault, Michel. (1978) *Discipline and Punish: The Birth of the Prison.* New York: Pantheon.

——. (1980) *Power/Knowledge: Selected Interviews and Other Writings 1972–77.* New York: Pantheon.

Gross, Jan T. (1988) *Revolution from Abroad: The Soviet Conquest of Poland's Western Ukraine and Western Byelorussia.* Princeton, NJ: Princeton University Press.

——. (1989) Social Consequences of War: Preliminaries to the Study of Imposition of Communist Regimes in East Central Europe. *Eastern European Politics and Societies* 3: 198–214.

Humphrey, Caroline. (1983) *Karl Marx Collective: Economy, Society and Religion in a Siberian Collective Farm.* Cambridge: Cambridge University Press.

Kideckel, David. (1982) The Socialist Transformation of Agriculture in a Romanian Commune, 1945–62. *American Ethnologist* 9: 320–340.

Konrád, George, and Ivan Szelérryi. (1979) *The Intellectuals on the Road to Class Power: A Sociological Study of the Role of the Intelligentsia in Socialism.* New York: Harcourt Brace Jovanovich.

Kornai, János. (1980) *Economics of Shortage.* Amsterdam: North Holland Publishing Co.

——. (1986) *Contradictions and Dilemmas: Studies on the Socialist Economy and Society.* Cambridge, MA: MIT Press.

Manea, Norman. (1990) Censor's Report, with Explanatory Notes by the Censored Author. *Formations* 5: 90–107.

Márkus, György. (1981) Planning the Crisis: Remarks on the Economic System of Soviet-Type Societies. *Praxis International* 1(3): 240–57.

Polanyi, Karl, Conrad M. Arensberg, and Harry W. Pearson. (1957) *Trade and Market in the Early Empires*. Glencoe, IL: Free Press.

Rév, István. (1987) The Advantages of Being Atomized. *Dissent* 34(3): 335–50.

Sampson, Steven. (1984) *National Integration through Socialist Planning: An Anthropological Study of a Romanian New Town*. Boulder, CO: East European Monographs (distributed by Columbia University Press).

Simmonds-Duke, E. M. (1987) Was the Peasant Uprising a Revolution? The Meanings of a Struggle over the Past. *Eastern European Politics and Societies* 1: 187–224.

Solacolu, Ion. (1988) Conştiinţa pericolului ce vine din noi. *Dialog (Dietzenbach)* 85: 25–8.

Stark, David. (1990) La valeur du travail et sa rétribution en Hongrie. *Actes de la Recherche en Sciences Sociales* 85: 3–19.

Szelényi, Ivan. (1982) The Intelligentsia in the Class Structure of State-Socialist Societies. In *Marxist Inquiries*, ed. M. Burawoy and Theda Skocpol, pp. 287–327. *American Journal of Sociology Special Supplement*, vol. 88. Chicago: University of Chicago Press.

Thom, Françoise. (1989) *Newspeak: The Language of Soviet Communism*. London: Claridge Press.

Verdery, Katherine. (1991) *National Ideology under Socialism: Identity and Cultural Politics in Ceauşescu's Romania*. Berkeley and Los Angeles: University of California Press.

Williams, Raymond. (1982) *The Sociology of Culture*. New York: Schocken Books.

30

Marx Went Away but Karl Stayed Behind

Caroline Humphrey

When I returned to Bayangol in summer 1996 the monument to Marx was standing at the entrance as before. The great thinker's massive concrete head was flanked by the name of the farm – but someone had hacked off the word "MARX." The farm's name had become "COLLECTIVE FARM OF KARL." The villagers' cows grazed peaceably around. Seeing my curious glance, a local driver joked, "So Marx has gone away, but Karl has stayed behind." His quip provides me with an entrance to [my] subject. In the agricultural hinterlands of Russia the Marxist ideology has indeed disappeared. But its shadow remains, indeed perhaps something personal and non-dogmatic like a first name, something people have not been able to give up.[1]

[I] will paint a portrait of rural life in one of those seemingly conservative parts of Russia where the most violent consequences of the end of Communism are absent. It is not just that in Buryatiya there has been no war, no rabid nationalism, and relatively little aggressive commercialisation or mafiaisation, but even the tenor of everyday life seems continuous with that of the past. Elsewhere the very mechanisms for determining society's winners and losers have undergone rapid change (Ruble 1995: 2), but in Buryatiya despite the demise of the Party, political leadership remains largely in the hands of the old *nomenklatura* [elite holders of official posts]. To some extent this can be explained by the continued reproduction of the economic dependency of Buryatiya on Moscow and of the rural areas on the capital and by the fact that the few successful commercial firms work in tandem with the government rather than challenging it. Buryatiya's "quietness," however, belies a cultural ferment which is not at all separate from economic turmoil. The flow of credits from Moscow is in fact erratic and has to be constantly renegotiated. Increasingly, "wild" commercial sponsors are feverishly sought to save collapsed state services. The maintenance of the tenor of daily life, most crucially electricity supplies, winter heating, and fuel for the most basic travel, is at the edge of disaster. Within this fragile balance indigenous notions of polity are stirring and surfacing.

From *Marx Went Away – But Karl Stayed Behind* (Ann Arbor: University of Michigan Press, 1998), pp. vii–xix.

These are post-Soviet ideas (or they could be termed "ex-Soviet" to indicate a certain quality of continuity with the past), and yet in some ways they are also deeply historical, a refiguring of culture in the *longue durée* of Asia. In the chapters that follow I show how rural people, and not just the urban intellectuals, are generating indigenous projects for the future of their communities. It is a neglected aspect of the Soviet heritage that even villagers, perhaps particularly in Buryatiya, are well educated and until recently had a small proportion of people actually engaged in directly agricultural work. Similarly, little attention has been paid to people who see themselves as loyal to the Federal state, not as oppositional or marginal, and yet who maintain profound ties to specific district homelands and use kinship as the crux of their identity. The extraordinarily globalised and yet locality-producing worlds that Buryat *kolkhozniki* [members of a collective farm] are attempting to create around them as the Soviet structures slowly disintegrate are [my] subject.

What has happened in the Buryat countryside with the demise of Communism? The collectives remain in one form or another. Basically, they created a way of life that was not sustainable, and yet for most rural Buryats this is felt to have been a legitimate order with mistakes in policy, not a system "contrary to human nature" as was the case among Hungarian peasants (Lampland 1995: 339). True, Buryats say they resented the restrictions on individual smallholdings, and they remember the arbitrary campaigns and the fear. I met no one who really wanted to return to those conditions. But still a constant refrain in 1996 was, "We Buryats have no grudge against Soviet power." Unlike Russians, whose sense of their own responsibility for the Revolution gives rise to immense and contradictory outpourings of pride, despair, and anger, the Buryats talk of the Soviet regime as something that happened to them. Its massive impact, its totalising interpretation of society and history, seems disjunct from their own inner, domestic, knowledge of what really happened, and they do not care to (maybe do not dare to) confront the two. With some exceptions mostly among intellectuals, rural Buryats tend to speak like people who were absorbed into, and absorbed, the Soviet ideology, and their stance is to be grateful. Indeed, by 1996 there was a wall of silence about who could have sawn off the word "MARX." It was children playing, people said, averting their eyes.

Yet the two collective farms named after Karl Marx have had rather different fates. Today the farm in Selenga retains its Soviet-type organisation and still calls itself the Kolkhoz imeni Karla Marksa. Its monument to the great bearded German is intact, and a separate monument for the farm itself has become a ritual site for marking its troubled existence with a libation of vodka when people make a journey in or out. As during Soviet times, the other collective at Bayangol in Barguzin district was more "progressive" in following government policy. Its members decided to take the path toward individual farming which was promoted in the early 1990s. In 1992 it became a Union of Peasant Holdings (OKKh) and it is now known as the OKKh Bayangol. Constant reorganisations have destabilised this farm, whose rump nevertheless continues to function like a collective of old. This is the farm with the broken monument, and it is here that the farm's history museum, so devotedly set up in 1987 with an invitation to Marx's great-granddaughter to travel from Paris to attend the opening, is closed and boarded up.

Thus, the historical resonance of being "named after Karl Marx" has been construed differently in the two farms. In the auditorium of the Selenga farm's club at Tashir, a line of portraits of the chairmen hang in chronological order on the wall, and no one mentions any breaks or scandals of the past. I was told with some pride that farms named after lesser dignitaries like Stalin had been amalgamated with the Karl Marx in the 1940s, rather than the other way around, "because Karl Marx was the senior" in the revolutionary genealogy. Now the people of this farm are engaged in continuous, active generation of local sociality, going their own sweet way under the unquestioned sign of Marx. In Barguzin, on the other hand, the farm's fiftieth anniversary in 1987 was the occasion for taking Marx seriously. The new museum featured an interpretation of his life and works, thus inadvertently disclosing the historicity of Marxism-Sovietism as a tradition and the tangentiality of the farm's link with the great man. If such *lieux de mémoire* (sites of memory) are established when "natural memory" is lost (Nora 1989: 7), we can see the museum as an attempt to shore up and perpetuate a tradition that was already questioned. Now even that late 1980s interpretation of history is out-of-date, and the museum may never reopen, since not only has no agreed-on interpretation of the past emerged, but the collective farm itself as a unity for local identities is under threat and may soon split up into constituent villages.

I decided to reissue *Karl Marx Collective: Economy, Society and Religion in a Siberian Collective Farm* (1983) because it is still one of the few detailed studies of the great Soviet experiment of collectivised farming. Of course, the book is now historic, both in the sense that had I been writing it now I would have done it differently and in the sense that the phenomena it described have irrevocably changed. Many would argue, both inside and outside Russia, that the collective farm as a type of economic organisation is doomed. This may well be right, yet it will be argued here that collective enterprises of one kind or another are still highly relevant to our times. Why so? First, and very simply, large numbers of collectives still exist in Russia, and in many regions they and other forms of joint agricultural enterprise are indispensible to the way farming is now organised and the way people imagine their lives. In Buryatiya even those committed to reform acknowledge that the attempt to replace collectives with private commercial farms has failed. In Russia as a whole only 3 percent of agricultural workers are "private farmers," and their number is falling, though much larger numbers live off tiny subsidiary plots in an economy which is neither collective nor fully privatised. Second, there is the far broader globalised context in which we may consider collective action in economic practice. It is not just in Russia that people see that the problems facing them cannot be resolved simply by a choice between the State and the Market (Gregory 1997). In the hinterlands of Buryatiya both are regarded with despair. Indeed the two are seen as inextricably intertwined in political corruption and mysterious monopolistic deals. Yet battling it out as a lone household – though many people actually have to do this – is not regarded as a solution either. Not only is the household farm weak and incapable of feeding the populace at large; it is morally suspect, seen as a potential incubus of selfishness and exploitation of others. The only solution, people say, is local, community-based collectives. They are not referring here to a theoretical concept like civil society, with collectives appearing as intermediate institutions (Anderson 1996: 112–14), but to a real intervention in postsocialist life.

I should go no further before saying that agriculture in Buryatiya is now in a state of economic collapse. The Republic as a whole is one of the poorest in Russia, with 52 percent of the population having incomes below the minimum living standard (in Russia as a whole in 1995 the proportion was 24.7 percent). Birthrates have gone down, death rates risen health problems increased, and there are reported cases of near starvation. The crisis of the Buryat economy caused the President, L. V. Potapov, to announce an "extraordinary regime" in 1996, and this enabled him to negotiate a large one-off credit from Moscow to pay state wages and pensions. In agriculture, with the exception of grain, the prices received do not cover the costs of production. Agricultural subsidies create large regular debts with Moscow. Collective herds have been decimated, ploughed areas reduced, and production and productivity are down to around a half of late Soviet figures. Of the six "collectives" in the Barguzin district in 1995, only one made a small profit, while the Bayangol farm made a massive loss of 1,667,000,000 rubles. Webs of indebtedness trap farms and reduce their options. Wages in rural areas have not been paid for years, so money is virtually absent. As a result, private village shops set up hopefully in the early 1990s have mostly closed.

Just as the Buryat state budget depends on annual transfers of money from Moscow, most of the districts of Buryatiya are also in debt. Their leaders go to the capital, Ulan-Ude, personally to negotiate annual transfers to cover their budgets, and this procedure is one reason for the perpetuation of "people with good contacts" in leadership roles. These transfers much exceed the amounts raised locally by taxes. Of course, in Soviet times Buryatiya also depended on the state, but then this was generally regarded as normal, as it was part of the intricately complex planned economy of the USSR in which goods and credits flowed across the whole country...Now, however, the credits go only to government organisations, and even then they are usually paid months late and often in smaller amounts than promised. Farmers are suddenly aware of being economically on their own. Collectives, which are supposed to be independent, find it almost impossible to negotiate money loans. The idea of becoming a self-supporting unit has become a desperate goal for each administrative level and each enterprise. The impossibility of attaining this goal results in a schizophrenic anxiety. Reform-minded officials denounce the "dependency culture," and yet, when the President of Buryatiya made a state visit to the Barguzin region in 1996, the local newspaper ran a great pleading headline: "Please help the district, Leonid Vasil'ye-vich! We need a new flour mill. We produce enough grain to feed ourselves, but we have to import flour for bread because we have only one mill."

Villagers feel they are living in an extraordinary, incomprehensible epoch. The accustomed parameters of "progress" have melted away. Many collectives have abandoned their most technologically advanced methods, while villagers have to hone the arts of domestic production to survive. Newspapers are full of advice about when to plant onions or how to store carrots. Yet there is no post-industrial concept of "small is beautiful." Rather, villagers feel they are in the grip of de-modernisation (Platz 1996), a shameful turn "backwards into the past," as herders lamented to me, showing me their car lying unused (no petrol, no spare parts) and the horse they now rely on. At the same time, the other worlds of TV soaps – "Santa Barbara" especially – fascinate almost everyone; work stops, people watch together, blotting out the hardship outside, even when the cows are bellowing to be milked in the frosty evening. Turning back to everyday life is to confront endless difficulties: how to eke out hay for the sheep, how to get shoes for the children, how to cure the sick cow that has stopped giving milk, where to exchange a piglet for a video. These are the practical circumstances in which people will not let go of the collectives...

...[I] focus on the two farms in their district contexts rather than on issues concerning Buryatiya as a whole. Contemporary rural attitudes can only be explained, however, if we understand Buryat people in relation to their imagined vistas as well as their lived practice, and here there have been immense changes since the 1960s–70s. Global dimensions and historical perspectives have shifted and in some ways opened out, as I briefly discuss in the remainder of this preface.

Recent anthropology has destabilised the notion of culture as a taken-for-granted local entity, but, as Hastrup and Olwig suggest (1997: 3), rather than discarding the idea of culture, "it should be reinvented, as it were, through an exploration of the 'place' of culture in both the experiential and discursive spaces that people inhabit or invent." I understand this statement to suggest an exploration of the spaces and places made by culture, with the implication not only that histories may intertwine and overlap and thus engender conflicts but also that such narratives may be disjunct from practices which crosscut discursively created borders. In the case of the Buryats [I] argued . . . that even a remote Siberian collective farm could not be understood except in the wider context of the Soviet state, but I did not pay sufficient attention to the imaginative dimensions of this observation (using the word *imaginative* not in the sense of "untrue" but as pertaining to the conceptual). Today there are important differences from Soviet times: not only has the imagined domain of the USSR been replaced by the ethnicised and hence more ambiguous one of Russia, but the encompassing capitalist world has changed from being a straightforwardly enemy terrain to a space which the Buryats themselves must now engage with and enter. Accompanying this bouleversement is the re-evaluation of Buryat history in its Asian context. At the same time, the 1990s have seen a remarkable intensification of the production of locality, i.e., a distinctive, self-differentiating, and yet self-regenerating life-world constituted by shared histories and understandings. As Appadurai (1995: 215) points out, the production of neighbourhoods in this sense is often at odds with the projects of the nation-state, because the latter designate localities as mere instances of a generalised mode of belonging to the wider imaginary of the polity. And alongside these irreconcilable discourses there is yet another layer, that of everyday practice, which may be hardly narrativised at all and yet which may in different ways counteract rationalising accounts.

Today, as *de-collectivisation* is being promoted by the reformists in Buryatiya, it might seem that the history of collectivisation (1929–33) would be the subject of intense local scrutiny, especially since the opening of archives has revealed new facts about those times. This is an extremely complex subject, however, which fore-grounds both conflicting views and silences among Buryat people. Not only does collectivisation tragically highlight the conflict over modernisation or the struggle between European ("Russian") as opposed to Asian ("Mongolian") ways of life which had engaged Buryats since the beginning of the century, but it lays open the ghastly and irreconcilable two-sidedness of Stalinism itself. On the one hand, Stalin's policies caused the unjust deaths of thousands of people, destroyed Buryat Buddhist culture, and split the Buryat nation into separate administrative units amid hyster-ical accusations of "Pan-Mongolism." On the other hand, people lived their lives through Stalinism. That is, their everyday practices and rewards, the rules they observed, the careers they planned for themselves and their children, or the "sym-bolic capital" they struggled for, were all found in the structures set up first by the Stalinist state. Even now there is a kind of gut loyalty to this former everyday life, which older people especially cannot abandon. For some people there is simple continuity, while for others there is a sudden new consciousness that the old ways are indeed "historic" (cf. the situation in the former East Germany, where objects from the old *alltag* (everyday life) have suddenly become museum material (Ten Dyke 2000). All this means that it is impossible to delineate "a Buryat view" on collectivisation, as irreconcilable and bitterly opposed views surface in various contexts. A historical topic can be like an anti-focus, from which centrifugal rationalisations fly in different directions, and collectivisation is one of these.

There is now evidence of widespread armed risings against collectivisation in 1929–32 in the south, east, and west of Buryat lands. In the 1960s and 1970s, when I made my first studies, such topics were unmentionable and systematically excluded not only from books but also from conversations. One of the uprisings was based at Noyokhon, a settlement neighbouring the Selenga Karl Marx Collective, in 1930. At its height this rebellion encompassed several settlements of Russian and Buryat Cossacks, Old Believers, other Buryat and Russian villages, and virtually all of the nearby Zakamensk district; it had organised links with resistance elsewhere in the region and had raised around 300 men to leave their lands and take up arms. The slogans were: "For a Democratic Republic!" "Down with the Dictatorship of the Proletariat!" and "For the inviolability of property and free trade!"; and, in the village of Khonkholoi: "Collectivisation is a straight path to slavery!" "Hail the liberation of all those arrested!" and "Hail the freedom of worship!" (Dorzhiyev 1993: 65, 72). This was not an anti-Russian nor a class-based uprising. It seems to have been initiated mostly by Old Believers, and it included not only *kulaks*, so-called rich peasants, but also people of middling and poor economic status. The large number of such uprisings, although they were small, separate, and quickly put down by troops of the OGPU (NKVD), indicate that there was in most areas a widespread resistance to collectivisation in Buryatiya. The slogans show that this was not just a matter of "peasant" resentment of the expropriations and forced egalitarianism of the collectives. People were taking up arms for principled ideological and political concerns in opposition to Communism. The defeat of the peasant uprisings left only the Buddhist monasteries as centres of resistance during the 1930s. Their legitimacy was weakened by the accusations of obscurantism and corruption made earlier by the Buddhist reformists and by the socialist education campaigns, which had grabbed the high ground of modernisation for the Bolsheviks, taking it from the hands of Buryat educationalists, and which succeeded in turning many young people against the lamas.

By 1938 virtually all the early Buryat leaders, of whatever political hue, had been killed or purged (Naidakov 1993: 63–8) and the monasteries annihilated. A whole generation of eminent Buddhist lamas as well as writers, historians, artists, and social activists perished. Only recently has it been revealed that the entire Party and governmental leadership of Buryatiya was purged in 1938, including, on one terrible night of June, the shooting of nine ministers and senior managers of the economy. The accusations, of "Pan-Mongolism" or collaboration with the Japanese, were designed to cut the Buryats from Asiatic ties, separate them from one another, and enforce loyalty to Russia.

While this history is not hidden, being available in newspaper articles and books, it is significantly not a public preoccupation of ordinary rural people today. There are other parts of Buryat history which are also curiously obscured and very difficult to talk about in public, notably any events which cast Buryats and Russians against one another, particularly when Buryats suffered disproportionately. These include:

the "voluntary entry" of Buryats into the Russian state in the seventeenth century, in fact a time of fierce fighting in some areas (Forsyth 1992); the mass mobilization of Buryats for war work during World War I, in which many lives were lost; the takeover by Russians of Buryat lands at many points in history but especially the land revisions of 1917; and the very high loss of Buryat lives in World War II. In a republic numerically dominated by Russians and with a Russian President, these topics, which were opened in the early 1990s, are now rarely broached in public.

Dorzhiyev comments (1993: 82) that the peasant rebellions over collectivisation constitute the largest of the "blank spots" in the history of Buryatiya. He notes that, while the subject is relatively well covered in Russia in general,

> In Buryatiya there is so far not a single historical work specially devoted to the given theme. Furthermore, in the opinion of the author, the social consciousness of the republic is still in fact under the influence of a simplistic and negative attitude to the peasant risings of the 1920s and 30s....According to such stereotypes, the peasants who took part in the risings are still seen as ordinary bandits "brutalized by the kulaks."

It is true that there may be some (nonaccidental) misinformation about history among young people, but Dorzhiyev's remarks point more to a characteristic layering and hierarchisation, as well as diversification, of views, a point I explain with the example which follows.

In summer 1997 the leaders of Ust'-Orda Okrug, the Buryat region cast off into the Russian Irkutsk Province in 1937, celebrated the sixtieth anniversary of the founding of the Okrug by holding a magnificent *suur-kharbaan* [summer archery] festival. The Soviet official co-option of this Buryat festival was a regular matter... but the irony of the event in 1997 aroused furious comment in the newspapers. How could Buryats participate in the celebration of the splitting up of their nation? A farmer explained, "We all know very well about 1937, when our unified people (*narod*) was divided up by Stalin. It's the leadership of the Okrug who are busy with the sixtieth anniversary, but the people know their tragedy. We are just celebrating *suur-kharbaan*." Even though the Buryat leaders of the Okrug had just been removed in favour of Russians, it would be naive to see the farmer's statement just in terms of dominant (official, pro-Russian) as opposed to oppositional (people's, Buryat) discourse. There is plenty of economic realism among "the people" too, which acknowledges advantages in being a separate financial unit from Buryatiya in the long-standing structural competition between administrative units vying for resources. This strategic layering of responses is not unlike the reactions to the issue of collectivisation, in which evolutionist teachings – that the collectives were the instruments of the modernisation process in the twentieth century and Buryats are modern people – overlie painful historical knowledge.

Understandings of history and identity inevitably involve self-definition in relation to the discourse of the Soviet, now the Russian, state. It is important to understand that this discursive space does not "just exist" but is drawn forth by specific inter-locutionary situations, such as political arguments, public statements, and indeed discussions with foreigners such as myself. There is a public genre in which many rural people are prepared bitterly to criticise current government policies and personalities, but they draw back from anything that might cause them to reconsider *gosudarstvennost*, the abstract notion of the powerful State itself. The very existence of rebellions against collectivisation or the labour camps in Buryatiya would impugn the moral legitimacy of such a state, and therefore knowledge of such matters is thrust inward and hidden. The Soviet state is said to have performed its duty, i.e., positive advances for Buryats in education, medicine, technology, hygiene, and housing. Crucial to Buryat self-definition in this particular imagery is the rejection of ethnic identification with the Mongols, who are often said to be "backward," "Asiatic," and a different nation. People may even identify themselves not as Buryats but as *Rossiyan'ye*, citizens of Russia. They celebrate the idea of the strong state and their place as patriotic citizens in it. Now, discordantly with this line, there are voices which call on the Buryat government officially to register the Buryats as a "repressed people" of the Russian Federation. This would entitle the Buryats to apply for compensation for the sufferings of the 1930s and support for their culture, but, at the same time, it would place them in a "complainant" position *vis-à-vis* the state and undoubtedly rile the Russian majority in Buryatiya. We are dealing here not just with discourse but with effective decisions with long-term implications. The Buryat government has steadfastly refused all such calls to register the Buryats as "repressed"; instead, the stance is to be "loyal."

The ethnicisation of the notion of Russia, however, imposes a hierarchisation of different views. Looking not across the frontier to Mongolia but toward the wars and uncertainties in the west and south of Russia itself, Buryats' identification with Russia is more equivocal. In this perspective it is they who are Asiatic, and the buried memories of 1937 colour a justified fear of a Russian nationalist backlash against even small public encouragement of Buryat distinctiveness. Buryat enthusiasm for actually joining up with Mongolia in the early 1990s was limited and short-lived. Nevertheless, alternative theories inspired by diverse Mongolian and Asian themes have recently surged to the surface in intellectual circles. Energised by constant new interpretations of history, religion, and literature and sustained by a thoughtful press, some of these ideas not only create extended perspectives for discussion but are also put into action. For example, the Buryat National Congress is a forum for all ethnic Buryats, cross-cutting the divisions of the Russian nation-state, the Festival of Geser is a celebration of mythic Asian heroism, and in places environmental projects have been started to reintroduce "traditional pastoralism" with native breeds from Mongolia and China. The revival of Buddhism has created another significant space, linking Buryatiya with Mongolia, Inner Mongolia, Tyva, Kalmykiya, Tibet, and India. This is again a highly differentiated realm, impossible to discuss adequately here. In Buryatiya alone there are government-sponsored rituals, fierce conflicts over precedence among lay Buddhists and lamas, new initiatives such as a monastery for women in the capital city, and widespread renovation of old temples. Shamanic practice is just as active. An Association of Shamans has been established in Ulan-Ude. Famous Buryat shamans not only travel to the villages to conduct rituals, but many of them also recognise the power and seniority of shamans living in Mongolia, while others have links with new religions and are invited all over the world. All of this cultural ferment is not just a one-way movement from the centre to the periphery. The cult of Soodei Lama of Barguzin, for example, was a matter of local oral transmission until spreading rivulets of interest brought grand lamas to the remote valley to take part in the revival of his memory in 1996. Just because people live in distant areas does not mean they cannot imagine vast space or are debarred from pontificating discourse. There is nothing new about this for

Buryats: Soodei Lama in the late nineteenth century corresponded with Turgeniyev and with people in France, Germany, Tibet, and India. Thus, there are rural as well as city projections about the grand subject of "What is to be done?"

Oral genealogies are like bridges between private remembrance and more shared forms of discourse. *Karl Marx Collective* discussed genealogies as shaping the historical imagination and kinship strategies such as exogamy and adoption as part of the accumulation of political capital. The new chapters outline different ways in which the genealogical imagination has changed in post-Soviet times. But I must emphasize here that genealogies are also practices of remembrance. Thus, the *individual people* who died in the fight against collectivisation (and in the numerous wars fought by Soviet troops) are not at all forgotten. They are remembered in their families, as personalities, and they are never categorised in terms such as "resistance fighters" or "bandits." This is why, when I discussed *Karl Marx Collective* with the villagers, they pored over the kinship diagrams and were taken aback and disappointed that I had changed most of the names of people in recent generations. They wanted all of the real names to be there.

To illustrate some of these points and show how the shifts of the last few years have affected individual lives, I end with the stories of two people whose photographs appeared in the first edition. Oyuna Lubsanova Ukhanayeva is the real name of the little girl who appears sitting on her shepherd father's knee. I have a vivid memory of taking this photograph in 1967 in the dusty sunshine at the remote pastures of Selenga, of the shepherd tired and motionless leaning on the veranda of his hut. I remember being so impressed that Lubsan and his wife, Medegma, with just one other helper, were herding nearly 700 sheep with over 600 lambs. I recall how Lubsan explained that when they were successful as shepherds, which meant raising 100 lambs from 100 ewes, they were rewarded with all-expenses paid holidays at the Black Sea. In 1996 I heard the rest of the story of this family. When they reached school age Oyuna and her siblings were sent from the pastures to the family's village house, where they were brought up by Lubsan's mother. After Lubsan died, Medegma continued for a time as a shepherd. Now Medegma says, "I could hardly read or write, but my daughter is a scientist." Oyuna grew up to take a *kandidat* degree in anatomical morphology. She lives in the city of Ulan-Ude, and shortly is to do a doctorate if she gets a grant. In August 1996 Oyuna had come back home on a visit to take part in the hay cutting. Charming and well dressed, she brought the aura of the town to the village, speaking about the competition for places at the Institute, the new reading she had to do on zoology to prepare for a temporary teaching job, the comparison of Moscow and provincial academies. But recent circumstances have given her admirable career a new twist and seem to have altered the mother–daughter relationship.

After she retired as a shepherd, Medegma had returned to the village, bringing her few privately owned cattle, sheep, and pigs and no doubt expecting a quiet old age. As times grew hard in the 1990s and wages from her children stopped coming in, however, Medegma taught herself vegetable and fruit production. Her plot is a model of proficiency: there are glasshouses and raised beds, which are fertilised and ingeniously irrigated. Rows of salads and vegetables are sown to ripen at regular intervals. In her light, clean, spacious house Medegma's eyes gleamed as she joked with her daughter and piled on the jams, conserves, creams and yoghurts, meat patties, and baked goods for me to consume. All of these were the produce of her own hands. Overwhelmed by her hospitality, I remarked what hard work must be involved these days. "No," replied Medegma, "It was hard work *then*, in the collective." I could see that she found great fulfillment in her present life, and I sensed the unique value of the things entirely made and given by the person sitting before me.

Here then are the altered vistas in the life of one ordinary family. Soviet organisation outlined a space constituting the pastures and the weekly visit by horse cart to the village, in which the holidays at the Black Sea were like the wonderful promises of socialism come true. The drudgery of the Soviet era always held a channel of hope for young people who could move upward by study. Today education and TV have given the family a more globalised space in imagination, but everyday practice has contracted their options. They are limited to the run between the village and the capital city (where Oyuna's brother also works, on a building site), education now costs money, which they do not have, and Black Sea holidays are altogether impossible. Oyuna achieved the Soviet dream, but now she does not know if she will get her grant; she has put off marrying, and I had the impression that her mother's marvellous self-sufficiency was a great comfort to her. Thus, the town turns to the village, the younger to the older generation.

Viktor Dabayevich Chimidtsyrenov... was at that time (1975) Chief Engineer of the Karl Marx Collective in the Barguzin Valley. Now in 1996 he is retired, but he has become the head of a "private farm" within the OKKh Bayangol. Viktor decided to call his new farm Arbijil, on the precedent of the famous commune of that name of the 1920s. It might seem curious to use a name so redolent of communist traditions for a new commercial enterprise, but... this is not strange when we see how Buryats are frequently turning to history as inspiration for the future. Viktor is someone who was always attracted to history and literature. His house in the collective has shelves of well-thumbed Pushkin, Gogol, Lermontov, Stendhal, and so forth, and he told me how in Soviet times, when there was no TV, he used to read aloud to his family in the evenings. Being one of a tiny group of local administrators who moved from post to post between the collective, the Soviet and the Party, Viktor can only be seen as a stalwart of the Soviet system. Yet it is he who was one of the first to set up a commercial farm, in fact a fairly common situation, and, more unusually, it is he who is the main genealogist of Bayangol.

Viktor studied the genealogies I published in *Karl Marx Collective* and said he could do "better than that." Just before I left he provided me with several handwritten scrolls containing hundreds of names and mapping all the major clan groupings. What was most interesting to me was that neatly written around the names were extensive notes on certain ancestors. Viktor had interviewed old people to verify oral narratives so the information would be "correct," but at the same time the tone of the stories was not quite matter-of-fact. In fact, the same means of mythicisation were used to elevate these narratives as in classical legends of inner Asia, namely the *fixing* of story themes to particular places in such a way as to render them both experimental-believable and at the same time make them archetypal and supramundane. Lack of space precludes me from proving this point, which would require analysing many examples, but at least I can cite one of Viktor's stories to show how the era of *Karl Marx Collective* is a source of heroic images for today. The Karalik irrigation system was mentioned earlier as a perennial technical and financial problem for the collective farm, but in what Viktor wrote it appears as an authored creation, inseparable from the people who built it, and thus given the hue of the genealogical imagination. Attached to the Butama Shono genealogy is the following:

> When collectives were first organised, on the initiative of Sangadin, the first chairman of the Arbizhil commune, the Karalik system was begun. First, using the plans of an Austrian prisoner-engineer, they laid foundations for the magistral canal at the place called Khügshööl, but because it required a huge amount of digging and concrete they could not finish the head work, and to this day this canal has no water in it and stands as a monument to the people's effort and engineers' mistakes. But a simple blacksmith, the illiterate Lobkhaarov Nanzan, crafted a home-made level from a gun-barrel and used it to construct another Karalik system, and to this day the main canal runs along the stream which was defined by this local hero-smith of the Butama Shono clan. Later, the system was supplied with engineering equipment and recently it has been in the hands of Garmayev Dashi Zabitorovich of the Butama Shono clan. It gives enough water to irrigate 5,000 hectares of land.

In 1996 there was a lightening of the atmosphere as compared to Soviet times, a new openness and realism, and my presence itself was as good a sounding-board for this as any. In the 1960s I was evidently suspected of being a spy, it being only puzzling who could have sent such a young and inexperienced person. But in 1996 I was able to travel to the Bayangol farm with Buryat friends to stay with their relatives, and to visit the Selenga farm quite unannounced. An elderly woman said, "We are not afraid of you now." Afraid or not, I shall never forget the extraordinary generosity of Buryat people on all of my visits. Whatever 'reasons' anthropologists might provide to explain generosity, or dissolve it in 'discourse', it is in the end simply very moving to be surrounded with the warmth of people to whom one can give so little in return.

This is a time of uncertainty in Russian history in which it would be inappropriate to attempt the delineation of a clear temporal succession of epochs and transitions. In this book I do not aim to sum up 'the lesson' of collectivisation, because the process is not finished. My more modest goal is to describe the fate of the farms and their people with the demise of Communism and the ways they are engaging with the present critical situation. Some general arguments will be made, but I do not claim for what I depict that it is the embodiment of any abstract principle. More valuable at this point is an attempt to unite the material and the interpretation of the material in such a way as to achieve an understandable representation, embracing the plasticity of the here and now.

NOTE

1   *Editorial note*: A student of Edmund Leach, Caroline Humphrey first carried out field research in Siberia as an exchange student in 1966–7. Further research between 1968 and 1975 led to her first monograph, *Karl Marx Collective: Economy, Society and Religion in a Siberian Collective Farm* (Cambridge: Cambridge University Press, and Paris: Editions de la Maison des Sciences de l'Homme) in 1983. *Marx Went Away – but Karl Stayed Behind* (Ann Arbor: University of Michigan Press, 1998) is an updated edition with a new preface (from which chapter 30 is extracted) and updates on the Siberian collective farms she re-visited.

REFERENCES

Anderson, D. (1996) Bringing civil society to an uncivilized place: citizenship regimes in Russia's Arctic frontier. In C. Hann and E. Dunn (eds.) *Surviving Post Socialism: Local Strategies and Regional Responses in Eastern Europe and the Former Soviet Union*. London: Routledge.

Appadurai, A. (1995) The production of locality. In R. Fardon (ed.) *Counterworks: Managing the Diversity of Knowledge*, pp. 204–5. London: Routledge.

Dorzhiyev, D. (1993) *Krest' yanskiye myatezhi i vosstaniya v Buryatii v 20–30 gody* (Peasant uprisings in Buryatiya in the 1920s–1930s). Ulan-Ude: Obshchestvenno-nauchnyi tsentr 'Sibir'.

Forsyth, J. (1992) *A History of the Peoples of Siberia: Russia's North Asian Colony 1581–1900*. Cambridge: Cambridge University Press.

Gregory, C. (1997) The Second Economy of the USSR. *Problems of Communism* 26 (Sept.–Oct.).

Hastrup, K. and Olwig, K. (1997) Introduction in K. Hastrup and K. Olwig (eds.) *Siting Culture: The Shifting Anthropological Subject*, pp. 1–6. London and New York: Routledge.

Lampland, M. (1995) *The Object of Labour: Commodification in Socialist Hungary*. Chicago: University of Chicago Press.

Naidakov, V. (ed.). (1993) *Istoriya Buryatii XX vek, chast' I*. (History of Twentieth Century Buryatiya, pt. I). Ulan-Ude: Obshchestvenno-nauchnyi tsentr 'Sibir'.

Nora, P. (1989) Between memory and history: les lieux de mémoire. *Representations* (Spring): 7–25.

Platz, S. (1996) Pasts and futures: space, history and Armenian identity, 1988–94. Ph.D. dissertation, University of Chicago.

Ruble, B. (1995) *Money Sings: The Changing Politics of Urban Space in Post-Soviet Yaroslavi*. Washington: Woodrow Wilson Press.

Ten Dyke, E. (2000) Memory, history and remembrance work in Dresden. In D. Berdahl, M. Bunzl, and M. Lampland (eds.) *Altering States: Ethnographies of Transition in Eastern Europe and the Former Soviet Union*. Ann Arbor: University of Michigan Press.

31

The Anti-politics Machine

James Ferguson

Introduction

The first issue to be raised, perhaps, is that the present study is an anthropological one. Unlike many anthropological works on "development," this one takes as its primary object not the people to be "developed," but the apparatus that is to do the "developing." This is not principally a book about the Basotho people, or even about Lesotho; it is principally a book about the operation of the international "development" apparatus in a particular setting.

To take on the task of looking at the "development" apparatus anthropologically is to insist on a particular sort of approach to the material. As an anthropologist, one cannot assume, for instance, as many political economists do, that a structure simply and rationally "represents" or "expresses" a set of "objective interests"; one knows that structures are multi-layered, polyvalent, and often contradictory, and that economic functions and "objective interests" are always located within other, encompassing structures that may be invisible even to those who inhabit them. The interests may be clear, and the intentions as well; but the anthropologist cannot take "planning" at its word. Instead of ascribing events and institutions to the projects of various actors, an anthropological approach must demote the plans and intentions of even the most powerful interests to the status of an interesting problem, one level among many others, for the anthropologist knows well how easily structures can take on lives of their own that soon enough overtake intentional practices. Whatever interests may be at work, and whatever they may think they are doing, they can only operate through a complex set of social and cultural structures so deeply embedded and so ill-perceived that the outcome may be only a baroque and unrecognizable transformation of the original intention. The approach adopted here treats such an outcome as neither an inexplicable mistake, nor the trace of a yet-undiscovered intention, but as a riddle, a problem to be solved, an anthropological puzzle.

From *The Anti-politics Machine: "Development," Depoliticization and Bureaucratic Power in Lesotho* (Cambridge: Cambridge University Press, 1990), pp. 17–21, 71–3, 252–6.

It is at this point that the issue of discourse becomes important. For writers such as Heyer et al. (1981) and Galli (1981), official discourse on "development" either expresses "true intentions" or, more often, provides an ideological screen for other, concealed intentions: "mere rhetoric." The bulk of "development" discourse, with all its professions of concern for the rural poor and so on, is for these writers simply a misrepresentation of what the "development" apparatus is "really" up to. The World Bank may talk a lot about helping poor farmers, for instance, but in fact their funds continue to be targeted at the large, highly capitalized farmers, at the expense of the poor. The much publicized "new strategy," then, is "largely rhetoric," serving only a mystifying function (Williams 1981).

In the anthropological approach adopted below, the discourse of the "development" establishment is considered much more important than this. It may be that much of this discourse is untrue, but that is no excuse for dismissing it. As Foucault (1971, 1973) has shown, discourse is a practice, it is structured, and it has real effects which are much more profound than simply "mystification." The thoughts and actions of "development" bureaucrats are powerfully shaped by the world of acceptable statements and utterances within which they live; and what they do and do not do is a product not only of the interests of various nations, classes, or international agencies, but also, and at the same time, of a working out of this complex structure of knowledge. Instead of ignoring the orderly field of statements produced by the "development" apparatus on the grounds that the statements are ideological, the study below takes this field as its point of departure for an exploration of the way in which "development" initiatives are produced and put into practice.

It should be clear from the above that the approach to be taken to the problem of the "development" industry in Lesotho will be, in keeping with the anthropological approach, "decentered" – that is, it will locate the intelligibility of a series of events and transformations not in the intentions guiding the actions of one or more animating subjects, but in the systematic nature of the social reality which results from those actions. Seeing a "development" project as the simple projection of the "interest" of a subject (the World Bank, Canada, Capital, Imperialism) ignores the non- and counter-intentionality of structural production, and is in this way profoundly non-anthropological. As in the case of Willis's treatment of the schooling apparatus (1981), one must entertain the possibility that the "development" apparatus in Lesotho may do what it does, not at the bidding of some knowing and powerful subject who is making it all happen, but behind the backs of or against the wills of even the most powerful actors. But this is not to say that such institutions do not represent an exercise of power; only that power is not to be embodied in the person of a "powerful" subject. A "development" project may very well serve power, but in a different way than any of the "powerful" actors imagined; it may only wind up, in the end, "turning out" to serve power.

At this point, the theoretical approach of the present work links up with another important body of literature, closely associated with the work of Foucault (1979, 1980a, 1980b). Using a decentered conception of power, a number of recent studies (e.g. Donzelot 1979; Foucault 1979, 1980a; Jones and Williamson 1979; Pasquino 1978; Procacci 1978) have shown how the outcomes of planned social interventions can end up coming together into powerful constellations of control that were never intended and in some cases never even recognized, but are all the more effective for being "subjectless." This theoretical innovation makes possible a different way of connecting outcomes with power, one that avoids giving a central place to any actor or entity conceived as a "powerful" subject.

Perhaps the best example of this kind of analysis is Foucault's "genealogy" of the prison (1979). The prison, Foucault shows, was created as a "correctional" institution. It was intended to imprint on the inmates the qualities of good citizenship: to make criminals into honest, hard working, law abiding individuals, who could return to a "normal" place in society. This idea of "rehabilitation" was behind the establishment of modern prisons throughout the world, and it continues to be offered as the chief justification for maintaining them and, from time to time, reforming them. But it is obvious upon inspection, according to Foucault, that prisons do not in fact "reform" criminals; that, on the contrary, they make nearly impossible that return to "normality" that they have always claimed to produce, and that, instead of eliminating criminality, they seem rather to produce and intensify it within a well-defined strata of "delinquents." While such a result must be conceived as a "failure" from the point of view of the planners' intentions, the result has quite a different character when apprehended as part of a different "strategy." For the constitution of a class of "delinquents," Foucault argues, turned out to be very useful in taming "popular illegalities" and transforming the political fact of illegality into the quasi-medical one of pathological "delinquency." By differentiating illegalities, and by turning one uniquely well-supervised and controlled class of violators against the others, the prison did end up serving as part of a system of social control, but in a very different way than its planners had envisioned. "If this is the case," Foucault writes:

> the prison, apparently "failing", does not miss its target; on the contrary, it reaches it, in so far as it gives rise to one particular form of illegality in the midst of others, which it is able to isolate, to place in full light and to organize as a relatively enclosed, but penetrable, milieu . . .
>
> For the observation that prison fails to eliminate crime, one should perhaps substitute the hypothesis that prison has succeeded extremely well in producing delinquency, a specific type, a politically or economically less dangerous – and, on occasion, usable – form of illegality; in producing delinquents, in an apparently marginal, but in fact centrally supervised milieu; in producing the delinquent as a pathologized subject . . . So successful has the prison been that, after a century and a half of 'failures', the prison still exists, producing the same results, and there is the greatest reluctance to dispense with it. (Foucault 1979: 276–7)

The point to be taken from the above argument is only that planned interventions may produce unintended outcomes that end up, all the same, incorporated into anonymous constellations of control – authorless "strategies," in Foucault's sense (1979, 1980b) – that turn out in the end to have a kind of political intelligibility. This is only another way of approaching the problem noted by Willis (1981) in his discussion of the school cited above: the most important political effects of a planned intervention may occur unconsciously, behind the backs or against the wills of the "planners" who may seem to be running the show.

This will turn out to be one of the key problems raised by the operation of the "development" apparatus in Lesotho, and the approach that is adopted owes much to the literature so briefly discussed above. The complex relation between the intentionality of planning and the strategic intelligibility of outcomes is perhaps the single most important theme winding through the pages that follow. As this theme appears and reappears ... one cardinal principle will be illustrated again and again: intentional plans are always important, but never in quite the way the planners imagined. In the pages that follow, I will try to show how, in the case of a development project in Lesotho, intentional plans interacted with unacknowledged structures and chance events to produce unintended outcomes which turn out to be intelligible not only as the unforeseen effects of an intended intervention, but also as the unlikely instruments of an unplotted strategy. Specifically, [I] will show how outcomes that at first appear as mere "side effects" of an unsuccessful attempt to engineer an economic transformation become legible in another perspective as unintended yet instrumental elements in a resultant constellation that has the effect of expanding the exercise of a particular sort of state power while simultaneously exerting a powerful depoliticizing effect. It is this unauthored resultant constellation that I call "the anti-politics machine" ...

The "Development" Apparatus

... [T]he techniques used in the World Bank Report do not represent the only possible solution to the puzzle of how to represent Lesotho in such a way as to maximize the potential role of "development" agencies. They are, however, in fact characteristic of the methods most commonly used in "development" discourse on Lesotho in the period under review.

To sum up: the most important theoretical premises in the construction of the "development" representation of Lesotho, together with their institutional rationales, are the following:

First, it must be *aboriginal*, not yet incorporated into the modern world, so that it can be transformed by roads and infrastructure, education, the introduction and strengthening of the cash economy (as against the "traditional subsistence sector"), and so on. A representation which failed to mask the extent of Lesotho's penetration by the "modern" capitalist regional economy of Southern Africa would be unable to provide a convincing justification for the "introduction" of roads, markets, and credit, as it would provide no grounds for believing that such innovations could bring about the "great transformation" to a "developed," "modern" economy. Indeed, such a representation would tend to suggest that such measures for "opening up" the country and exposing it to "the cash economy" would have little impact at all, since isolation from the world economy has never been Lesotho's problem.

Secondly, it must be *agricultural*, so that it can be "developed" through agricultural improvements, rural development projects, extension, and technical inputs. A representation in which Lesotho appeared as a labor reserve for South African mining and industry, and in which migrant wage labor was recognized as the basis of Basotho livelihood would leave the "development" agencies with almost no role to play. The World Bank mission to Lesotho is in no position to formulate programs for changing or controlling the South African mining industry, and it has no disposition to involve itself in the political challenges to the South African system of labor control known as *apartheid*. It is in an excellent position, however, to devise agricultural improvement projects, for the agricultural resources of Lesotho lie neatly within its jurisdiction and always present themselves as waiting to be "developed." For this reason, they tend to move to center stage in "development" accounts, and Lesotho thus becomes a nation of farmers.

Thirdly, it must constitute a *national economy*, in order to support the idea of national economic planning and nation- and sector-based economic programs. In a representation in which this notion of national economy is absent, the economic center of gravity is seen as lying squarely within South Africa, and thus as inaccessible to a "development" planner in Lesotho. Without the idea that Lesotho's boundaries define a national economy, no great claims can be made for the ability of programs based in Lesotho to bring about the sort of transformation "development" agencies claim to be able to bring about. The "development" apparatus unconsciously selects for representations in which it appears possible for "development" agencies to deliver the goods they are set up to promise.

Fourthly, it must be subject to the principle of *governmentality*. That is, the main features of economy and society must be within the control of a neutral, unitary, and effective national government, and thus responsive to planners' blueprints. If a representation for any reason tends to suggest that the "problems" of a country lie beyond the reach of national government policy, then it at the same time tends to deny a role to "development" agencies in addressing those problems. Because "development" agencies operate on a national basis, and because they work through existing governments and not against them, they prize representations which exaggerate the power of national policy instruments, and have little use for representations which emphasize the role of extra-national or extra-governmental determinations. Because government is the tool for planning and implementing economic and social policy, representations which ignore the political character of the state and the bureaucracy and downplay political conflicts within the nation-state are the most useful. Representations which present the state in such a way as to bring into question its role as a neutral tool of enlightened policy must force upon the "development" agencies a political stance they are ill-equipped to take on, and for this reason must fall by the wayside.

It must be evident by now that in a country like Lesotho, where capitalism and the labor reserve economy were well established more than a century ago, where farming contributes only 6 percent of rural household income, where concepts such as national economy and governmentality are more than usually absurd, and where nearly all the major determinants of economic life lie outside of the national borders, the task of drawing up governmentalist plans for transforming a "national economy" through technical, apolitical intervention requires preliminary theoretical rearrangements of a more than usually violent or imaginative kind. Lesotho is for this reason a privileged case in which the nature of this theoretical rearrangement is particularly visible, and in which the schism with academic discourse is unusually pronounced. It is to be expected that in other countries, where the economic situation is less far removed from that of the mythical generic LDC (countries possessing greater national autonomy, greater economic cohesion, and greater governmental control over the economy), the discontinuity between "development" discourse and academic discourse will be less sharp, and less easily observed, although the same processes may be at work.

Instrument-effects of a "development" project

... [W]hen the project's inability to effect the promised transformations in agriculture – particularly in the area of livestock – was compounded by the collapse of the "decentralization" scheme in 1980–1, CIDA [Canadian International Development Agency] elected to pull out. By 1982, CIDA's chief interest was in getting out as quickly and gracefully as possible. The 1982 revision to the Plan of Operations was tailored to do just that. Funding was gradually phased out and, by March 1984, the CIDA involvement in Thaba-Tseka was over. Moreover, I was told explicitly by officials at CIDA headquarters in Ottawa that the pullout had not been a matter of lack of funds, but that the project had been discontinued on its merits. At last report, neither CIDA nor any other donor has sought to continue the project.

But even if the project was in some sense a "failure" as an agricultural development project, it is indisputable that many of its "side effects" had a powerful and far-reaching impact on the Thaba-Tseka region. The project did not transform crop farming or livestock keeping, but it did build a road to link Thaba-Tseka more strongly with the capital; it did not bring about "decentralization" or "popular participation," but it was instrumental in establishing a new district administration and giving the Government of Lesotho a much stronger presence in the area than it had ever had before. The construction of the road and the "administrative center" may have had little effect on agricultural production, but they were powerful effects in themselves.

The general drift of things was clear to some of the project staff themselves, even as they fought it. "It is the same story over again," said one "development" worker. "When the Americans and the Danes and the Canadians leave, the villagers will continue their marginal farming practices and wait for the mine wages, knowing only that now the taxman lives down the valley rather than in Maseru."

But it was not only a matter of the taxman. A host of government services became available at Thaba-Tseka as a direct result of the construction of the project center and the decision to make that center the capital of a new district. There was a new Post Office, a police station, and an immigration control office; there were agricultural services such as extension, seed supply, and livestock marketing; there were health officials to observe and lecture on child care, and nutrition officers to promote approved methods of cooking. There was the "food for work" administration run by the Ministry of Rural Development, and the Ministry of the Interior, with its function of regulating the powers of chiefs. A vast number of minor services and functions that once would have operated, if at all, only out of one of the other distant district capitals had come to Thaba-Tseka.

But, although "development" discourse tends to see the provision of "services" as the purpose of government, it is clear that the question of power cannot be written off quite so easily. "Government services" are never simply "services"; instead of conceiving this phrase as a reference simply to a "government" whose purpose is to serve, it may be at least as appropriate to think of "services" which serve to govern.... [O]ne of the central issues of the deployment of the Thaba-Tseka Project was the desire of the government to gain political control over the opposition strongholds in the mountains [and] many of the project's own resources and structures were turned to this purpose. But, while this was going on, a much more direct political policing function was being exercised by other sections of the district administration the project had helped to establish. The Ministries of Rural Development and of the Interior, for instance, were quite directly concerned with questions of political control, largely through their control over "food for work" and chieftainship, respectively; then, too, there were the police. Another innovation that came with the "development" center in Thaba-Tseka was the new prison. In every case, state power was expanded and strengthened by the establishment of the local governing machinery at Thaba-Tseka.

In the increasingly militarized climate of the early 1980s . . . the administrative center constructed by the project in Thaba-Tseka quickly took on a significance that was not only political, but military as well. The district capital that the project had helped establish was not only useful for extending the governing apparatus of government services/government controls; it also facilitated direct military control. The project-initiated district center was home not only to the various "civilian" ministries, but also to the "Para-Military Unit," Lesotho's army. The road had made access much easier; now the new town provided a good central base. Near the project's end in 1983, substantial numbers of armed troops began to be garrisoned at Thaba-Tseka, and the brown uniforms of the PMU were to be seen in numbers throughout the district. Indeed, it may be that in a place like Mashai, the most visible of all the project's effects was the indirect one of increased government military presence in the region. The project of course did not cause the militarization of Thaba-Tseka, any more than it caused the founding of the new district and the creation of a new local administration. In both cases, however, it may be said to have unintentionally played what can only be called an instrumental role.

The Anti-politics Machine

It would be a mistake to make too much of the "failure" of the Thaba-Tseka Project. It has certainly been often enough described in such terms, but the same can be said for nearly all of the other rural development projects Lesotho has seen. One of the original planners of the project, while admitting that the project had its share of frustrations, and declaring that as a result of his experience with Thaba-Tseka, he would never again become involved in a range management project, told me that in fact of all the rural development projects that have been launched in Lesotho, only Thaba-Tseka has had any positive effects. Indeed, as the project came to an end, there seemed to be a general move in "development" circles both in Ottawa and Maseru toward a rehabilitation of the project's reputation. It may have been a failure, but not any worse than many other similar projects, I was told. Given the "constraints," the Project Coordinator declared in 1983, "I think we've got a success story here." As one CIDA official pointed out, with what appeared to be a certain amount of pride, the project "was not an unmitigated disaster."

In a situation in which "failure" is the norm, there is no reason to think that Thaba-Tseka was an especially badly run or poorly thought out project. Since, as we have seen, Lesotho is not the "traditional," isolated, "peasant" society the "development" problematic makes it out to be, it is not surprising that all the various attempts to "transform" it and "bring it into the twentieth century" characteristically "fail," and end up as more or less mitigated "disasters." But it may be that what is most important about a "development" project is not so much what it fails to do but what it does do; it may be that its real importance in the end lies in the "side effects" such as those reviewed in the last section. Foucault, speaking of the prison, suggests that dwelling on the "failure" of the prison may be asking the wrong question. Perhaps, he suggests,

> one should reverse the problem and ask oneself what is served by the failure of the prison; what is the use of these different phenomena that are continually being criticized; the maintenance of delinquency, the encouragement of recidivism, the transformation of the occasional offender into a habitual delinquent, the organization of a closed milieu of delinquency. (Foucault 1979: 272)

If it is true that "failure" is the norm for development projects in Lesotho, and that important political effects may be realized almost invisibly alongside with that "failure," then there may be some justification for beginning to speak of a kind of logic or intelligibility to what happens when the "development" apparatus is deployed – a logic that transcends the question of planners' intentions. In terms of this larger unspoken logic, "side effects" may be better seen as "instrument-effects" (Foucault 1979); effects that are at one and the same time instruments of what "turns out" to be an exercise of power.

For the planners, the question was quite clear: the primary task of the project was to boost agricultural production; the expansion of government could only be secondary to that overriding aim. In 1980, the Programme Director expressed concern about the project's failure to make headway in "what is really the only economic basis for the existence of the Thaba-Tseka District, the rangeland production of livestock." He went on to declare:

> If this economic base, now as shaky as it appears to be, is not put on a much firmer footing, it is inevitable that the Thaba-Tseka District will eventually become an agricultural wasteland where there will be no justification whatsoever for developing and maintaining a social infrastructure with its supporting services of health, education, roads, rural technology development, etc. (TTDP Quarterly Report, October–December 1980, p. 5)

If one takes the "development" problematic at its word, such an analysis makes perfect sense; in the absence of growth in agricultural output, the diversion of project energies and resources to "social infrastructure" can only be considered an unfortunate mistake. But another interpretation is possible. If one considers the expansion and entrenchment of state power to be the principal effect – indeed, what "development" projects in Lesotho are chiefly about – then the promise of agricultural transformation appears simply as a point of entry for an intervention of a very different character.

In this perspective, the "development" apparatus in Lesotho is not a machine for eliminating poverty that is incidentally involved with the state bureaucracy; it is a machine for reinforcing and expanding the exercise of bureaucratic state power, which incidentally takes "poverty" as its point of entry – launching an intervention that may have no effect on the poverty but does in fact have other concrete effects. Such a result may be no part of the planners' intentions – indeed, it almost never is – but resultant systems have an intelligibility of their own.

But the picture is even more complicated than this. For while we have seen that "development" projects in Lesotho may end up working to expand the power of the state, and while they claim to address the problems of poverty and deprivation, in neither guise does the "development" industry allow its role to be formulated as a political one. By uncompromisingly reducing poverty to a technical problem, and by promising technical solutions to the sufferings of powerless and oppressed people, the hegemonic problematic of "development" is the principal means through which the question of poverty is de-politicized in the world today. At the same time, by making the intentional blueprints for "development" so highly visible, a "development" project can end up performing extremely sensitive political operations involving the entrenchment and expansion of institutional state power almost invisibly, under cover of a neutral, technical mission to which no one can object. The "instrument-effect," then, is two-fold: alongside the institutional effect of expanding bureaucratic state power is the conceptual or ideological effect of depoliticizing both poverty and the state. The way it all works out suggests an analogy with the wondrous machine made famous in Science Fiction stories – the "anti-gravity machine," that at the flick of a switch suspends the effects of gravity. In Lesotho, at least, the "development" apparatus sometimes seems almost capable of pulling nearly as good a trick: the suspension of politics from even the most sensitive political operations. If the "instrument-effects" of a "development" project end up forming any kind of strategically coherent or intelligible whole, this is it: the anti-politics machine.

If unintended effects of a project end up having political uses, even seeming to be "instruments" of some larger political deployment, this is not any kind of conspiracy; it really does just happen to be the way things work out. But because things do work out this way, and because "failed" development projects can so successfully help to accomplish important strategic tasks behind the backs of the most sincere participants, it does become less mysterious why "failed" development projects should end up being replicated again and again. It is perhaps reasonable to suggest that it may even be because development projects turn out to have such uses, even if they are in some sense unforeseen, that they continue to attract so much interest and support.

REFERENCES

Donzelot, J. (1979) *The Policing of Families*. New York: Pantheon.
Foucault, M. (1971) *Archaeology of Knowledge*. New York: Harper and Row.
——. (1973) *The Order of Things*. New York: Vintage.
——. (1979) *Discipline and Punish: The Birth of the Prison*. New York: Vintage.
——. (1980a) *The History of Sexuality, Volume 1: An Introduction*. New York: Vintage.
——. (1980b) *Power/Knowledge: Selected Interviews and Other Writings, 1972–1977*. C. Gordon (ed.) New York: Pantheon.
Galli, R. (1981) *The Political Economy of Rural Development: Peasants, International Capital, and the State*. Albany: State University of New York Press.

Heyer, J., Roberts, P., and Williams, G. (eds.) (1981) *Rural Development in Tropical Africa*. New York: St. Martin's Press.

Jones, K. and Williamson, K. (1979) Birth of the Schoolroom. *Ideology and Consciousness* 6.

Pasquino, P. (1978) The Genealogy of Capital – Police and the State of Prosperity. *Ideology and Consciousness* 4.

Procacci, G. (1978) Social Economy and the Government of Poverty. *Ideology and Consciousness* 4.

Williams, G. (1981) The World Bank and the Peasant Problem. In J. Heyer, P. Roberts and G. Williams (eds.) *Rural Development in Tropical Africa*. New York: St. Martin's Press.

Willis, P. (1981) *Learning to Labour: How Working Class Kids Get Working Class Jobs*. New York: Columbia University Press.

32

Peasants against Globalization

Marc Edelman

Underdevelopment in Quotation Marks?

Since the mid-1980s, a growing coterie of scholars has attempted to apply one or another variant of Foucauldian discourse analysis to the study of Third World development (see Apfell et al. 1990; DuBois 1991; Esteva 1988; Ferguson 1990; Mitchell 1991; Prakash 1990; I. Sachs 1976; W. Sachs 1992). Echoing a favorite maxim of postmodernist critics of ethnographic writing (Clifford 1983: 6; 1988: 80), several even assert that "underdevelopment" is a "fictitious construct" (Escobar 1988: 429; 1984: 389; see also DuBois 1991: 25; Esteva 1988: 667). In so doing, they seek both to shock readers and to call attention to the historically conditioned nature of some unquestioned and perhaps cherished assumptions. Insofar as this kind of iconoclasm achieves these objectives it may represent a salutary antidote to much overly complacent mainstream thought and practice. But to the extent that such pronouncements divert attention from the profound inequalities that separate what are conventionally known as First World and Third World societies (or regions and classes within each) they cannot help but be deeply troubling.

The claim that "underdevelopment" and – by extension, one assumes – "development" are "fictions" is intended to emphasize that a particular set of "discourses" and associated "strategies" propagated by powerful international agencies (such as the World Bank) and their local allies contribute to altering not only social and economic relations in the targeted countries but also "cultural meanings and practices" (Escobar 1988: 438). This is hardly controversial (though it does tend to make something of a mockery of the semantic conventions and shared subjectivity necessary for scholarly or other interchange). "Discourses" do categorize people, and sometimes the labels are denatured caricatures of what those people are or believe themselves to be. It does not follow, however, that researchers must eschew all sociological categories simply because some social scientists or social engineers

From *Peasants against Globalization: Rural Social Movements in Costa Rica* (Stanford: Stanford University Press, 1999), pp. 7–21.

employ pejorative terms or labels that implicitly blame the labeled rather than the labelers. Indeed, it is curious that the same scholars (Escobar 1988: 435–6; 1991: 667–8) who are highly critical of designations such as "small farmers," "beneficiaries," and "pregnant and lactating women," use other such highly problematical categories – "peasant," for example – without the least acknowledgment of the hand-wringing and debate that they have caused among pre-postmodernist scholars (Leeds 1977; Shanin 1982). It is surprising too that, in discussing the power of labeling discourses, they downplay or ignore altogether another, contradictory tendency that is also a key postmodernist concern – the capacity of subalterns to appropriate labels (and more complex discourses) and infuse them with new and often positive meanings (but see Escobar 1995: 48–52). In an example close to the case at hand, I discuss...how in Costa Rica the term "small farmer" (*pequeño agricultor*) changed from a relatively bland category favored by government officials and agricultural-sector lobbyists to a highly charged, politicized badge of pride. Some agriculturalists, in the heat of struggle, not only adopted it as a new form of self-definition, but employed it – at times ironically and at other times unconsciously – as a virtual synonym for outlaw status.

Nor is it always true that in the "development encounter" – successor, of course, to the ignoble "colonial encounter" (Asad 1973) – "states, dominant institutions, and mainstream ways are strengthened and the domain of their action is inexorably expanded" (Escobar 1991: 667; cf. 1984: 388). This assertion – central to James Ferguson's study of the World Bank in Lesotho (1990: 253; cf. DuBois 1991: 11 and Mitchell 1991: 30) – completely misses the point about the main theory and practice of contemporary neoliberal development policy (as well as denying to subordinate groups, through its emphasis on the inexorableness of the "development" process, any possibility of political efficacy). The basic premises of neoliberalism – the reigning "development" model today – include the need to *drastically reduce* the reach of the state and, more broadly, that of the public sector. Somehow, postmodernist students of "development" have missed – have, in fact, inverted – this fundamental postulate of neoliberalism.

The deficiencies of the postmodernist anthropology of development are most obvious in its silences (or its "not-saids," to borrow an apt expression from Foucault (1972: 25). Flesh-and-blood human beings – the victims of development gone awry – might be, one supposes, the obvious subjects of an engaged and outraged anthropological investigation (as, for example, in Scheper-Hughes's 1992 tour-de-force, *Death Without Weeping*). But they are conspicuously absent in most of the writings of postmodernist critics of "development," such as those of Escobar and DuBois, which are generally pitched at such a high level of abstraction as to preclude analysis (or, at times, even mention) of historical examples or illustrative cases. Similarly missing is any serious attention to (or frequently any reference to) the relative differences in levels of living or the highly skewed distributions of wealth and income that distinguish Third World from First World societies. It is not necessary to favor the conventional indicators employed by the major aid and lending institutions (per capita GDP, etc.) or even to adopt the increasingly problematical "Third" and "First World" categories at all to recognize that hundreds of millions of people are not meeting their basic needs for food, clothing, and shelter (or that alternative measures of this fundamental problem exist – such as the effort to adjust per capita GDP figures to reflect purchasing power in different countries (Summers and Heston 1988); the Overseas Development Council's physical quality of life index (Morris 1979); the United Nations Development Program's human development index (UNDP 1995); or Amartya Sen's (1987) appealing notion that a measure of living standards should include a level of happiness, satisfaction of desires (i.e., "utility"), and choice). Recognition of this vast human tragedy need not imply uncritical acceptance of the accuracy or validity of much of the quantitative data that become "naturalized" and serve to justify the existence of the entire "development industry." But what is striking about the post modernist critics of "development" is how frequently they exclude from view *both* the affected people *and* the relevant macroeconomic and social indicators. They thus end up trivializing the day-to-day experience and aspirations of those who suffer by either ignoring their grinding poverty, by carping about the bureaucrats and social scientists who attempt to measure it, or by locating it and all efforts to reverse it at the level of an elite discourse. Despite these scholars' frequent exaltation of "civil society" as a panacea for the ills wrought by "development," a discourse-centered approach to power can lead to blanket cynicism about even innovative efforts for change. Marc DuBois, for example, a self-described follower of Foucault, charges that

> those small development organizations that operate on a grass-roots level, those often considered to be the most effective and certainly the most sensitive to local populations, appear to be potentially the most dangerous if a Foucauldian sense of power is used to examine development anew. (1991: 19)

Discourse certainly figures in the reproduction of the wretched poverty afflicting so much of the world's population. But so do other phenomena, such as forms of accumulation and distribution and the other, nondiscursive, largely material aspects of the physical and social reproduction of the classes, sectors, corporations, and family groups that make up any contemporary economy, but that pass largely unexamined in the postmodernist critiques of "development." Apart from frequent condemnation of the theoretical mainstream's association of "development" with industrialization, and of the institutionalization and expansion of the "development industry" itself, the postmodernist critics rarely mention any specific economic sector or even social reproduction in general except as a problem of competing discourses.

The rhetorical undermining of semantic conventions that pervades the postmodernist anthropology of "development" also gives rise to dubious syllogistic reasoning about the aspirations of the world's poor. Escobar (1991: 670), for example, questions Thayer Scudder's (1988: 366) assertion that "the large majority of the world's population want development for themselves and their families." "How can Scudder demonstrate this point?" Escobar asks. "It is not difficult to show...that there is widespread resistance to development projects in many parts of the Third World."

But do Scudder and Escobar intend the same thing when they say "development"? Certainly not. Scudder clearly means something like "improved well-being" or "rising living standards." For Escobar, on the other hand, "development" signifies a destructive discourse and its associated institutional manifestations. Having assigned this negative meaning to the term, he rightly questions whether people want it. But it hardly follows that "the large majority of the world's population" does not desire improved well-being. Indeed, poor people's opposition to development projects is usually rooted in their perception, too frequently well founded, that such schemes threaten their living standards (whether economically or culturally defined). Escobar would likely agree. But is this evidence of opposition to development, as he claims? Only in a world in which idiosyncratic understandings of everyday words and rhetorical sleight-of-hand substitute for empirical investigation and reasoned argument. In the Costa Rican context . . . to provide just one counter-example, militant peasant groups, following the common Latin American practice of appending aspirations or martyrs' names to the titles of popular organizations, proudly added the words "Justice and Development" to the name of the national-level coalition they founded in 1989 (Consejo Nacional de Pequeños y Medianos Productores Justicia y Desarrollo 1991). "Development," like "small agricultural-ist," could be appropriated and infused with new meanings.

The postmodernist critique of "development" constitutes a useful corrective to mainstream theory in several respects. James Ferguson (1990), for example, brilli-antly deconstructs the image of Lesotho presented in reports of the World Bank and other lending and aid agencies and shows how self-defeating, counterproductive "development" projects flow from an erroneous, ahistorical vision of this small, south African country as a nation of subsistence peasants (rather than of migrant laborers). Similarly, Tim Mitchell (1991) analyzes how development agency studies of Egypt employ a common leitmotif, the image of a dense, rapidly growing popula-tion crammed into the narrow Nile Valley, in order to elide questions of resource and income distribution. But it says a lot about the usefulness of the paradigm in question that in Ferguson's and Mitchell's work the Foucauldian framework is quite understated. Indeed, similar critiques of neo-Malthusianism's refusal to ac-knowledge inequality and of the ahistorical social science that saw "natural econ-omy" and "isolation" at every turn but ignored conspicuous evidence of capitalist exploitation had attracted wide attention in anthropology at least since the early 1970s (Hewitt de Alcantara 1984; Mamdani 1973; Vincent 1990), well before Foucault became part of the disciplinary canon.

A common thread in the postmodernist anthropology of development literature is the insistence that "development" arose full-blown in the post-World War II era as an ideology and practice with few significant historical or intellectual antecedents (e.g., Escobar 1988; 1995: ch. 1; Kearney 1996: 34; Sachs 1976). The most engaging and specific articulation of this position is from Mexican scholar-activist Gustavo Esteva:

> Until well into the nineteenth century, the world *development* [*desarrollo*] in Spanish was employed to describe the operation of unrolling a parchment: it signified to return an object to its original form. During the last century [the term] migrated through at least three scientific disciplines, where it was employed as a metaphor for opening new fields of knowledge. It remained for a long time confined to technical usage. In economics, neither Marx nor Schumpeter succeeded in gaining it general acceptance, except for very specific uses. But in 1949 something very strange occurred with *development*. Never before had a word achieved universal acceptance the very day of its political coining. On January 10, 1949, when Truman employed it in a speech, it immediately acquired a specific, distinguished meaning as Point Four of the Truman Doctrine. In a few days, two billion people became underdeveloped. (Esteva 1988: 665, italics in original)

Esteva goes on to note – correctly – that "today development is an amoeba word, without precise meaning, but full of connotations" (p. 665). Unfortunately, however, this semiotic sensitivity is not accompanied by a similar appreciation of the concept's complicated trajectory. "Development" and "underdevelopment" were not, as the postmodernists claim, simply invented in a post-World War II effort to "remake" the Third World. These "constructs" have instead varied and complex roots in at least three historical-ideological watersheds: nineteenth-century Liberalism (and evolutionism), turn-of-the-century US neocolonialism, and the debates between Latin American Marxists and populists that date to the 1920s.

It is beyond the scope of this [essay] to elaborate the argument in much detail. A bare outline should suffice, however, to make the point, at least as regards Latin America. Most Latin American countries attained independence burdened with weak notions of nationhood, property controlled by religious and community corporations, and economies which, despite a century of Bourbon reforms, were still shaped largely by metropolitan-oriented trade in a few primary products. Liberalism took root in post-independence Latin America as a *modernizing, developmentalist* ideology and practice aimed at overcoming this colonial heritage (C. A. Hale 1989; Katz 1991). Whether articulated as a struggle for "civilization" against "barbarism" (as in Argentina) or in more explicitly racist and social Darwinist terms (as in Mesoamerica and the Andes), Liberal ideology contained definite notions of development (or "modernity") and underdevelopment (or "backwardness"). While the periodization and the specific practice of Liberalism varied in different settings, the Liberals' adoption of free-market, secular policies usually involved, among other things, increased foreign indebtedness to finance construction of transport infrastructure, especially railways; the creation in government executive branches of "Development Ministries" (Ministerios de Fomento); the privatization of church, community, and state lands; and major giveaways to foreign capital which, it was hoped, would facilitate the transition to "modernity." In Costa Rica, during the Liberals' late-nineteenth-century apogee, virtually the entire "national project," as articulated by intellectuals and politicians, "was precisely to come to be *equal* to the developed countries of Europe" (Palmer 1992: 182, italics in original). Both Liberal ideology and the measures that accelerated market penetration of the most remote spaces remaining outside of the economy are clear precursors of the "development" that postmodernists such as Esteva claim emerged from a virtual *tabula rasa* on a single day in January 1949.

"Any aggressive North American," California traveler George Miller declared in his 1919 memoir, *Prowling About Panama*,

> looks upon the splendid areas of land, the fine rivers, the dense forests, and the other untouched resources of this rich country with amazement, and begins to plan *development projects* and dream of organizing syndicates, but the native loses no sleep over such vain imaginings. If he dreams at all, it is of his food if he be poor, and of politics if he be rich. (p. 135, emphasis added)

Miller's comment, brimming with the imperial arrogance of the nineteenth-century US doctrine of Manifest Destiny, was a concrete expression of economic theories that view regions, peoples, and entire nations as bundles of resources waiting to be exploited in optimal fashion. Its notions of "development" and "backwardness" resemble those of Latin American Liberal modernizers. His mention of "development projects" (while undoubtedly understood differently from the way the term is used today) also highlights the key role that developmentalist ideology and practice played in legitimizing and solidifying the early stages of US neocolonial expansion. Particularly after the Spanish-American War, the US interventions in Cuba, Puerto Rico, Haiti, and the Dominican Republic, and the US-engineered secession of Panama from Colombia, North American construction of roads, sewers, water systems, and public-health facilities (and, of course, the Panama Canal) became an essential justification for the neocolonial project. In Central America and Colombia, as well as in the Caribbean, US banana companies dredged harbors, drained swamps, combated tropical diseases, built railways, and erected entire towns of "sanitary" workers' barracks on stilts in the middle of what had often been impenetrable jungle. This vast, early-twentieth-century effort to transform the tropics – at once a rationale and a strategy for securing US domination – was, as the quotation from Miller indicates, permeated by a discourse about "development" and "underdevelopment" that resonates loudly in later discussions (Berger 1993; Black 1988). Aided and abetted by a bevy of diplomats and policy experts drawn from the leading universities, this developmentalist practice existed in a powerful synergetic relation with academic discourses that either echoed the racist social Darwinism of late-nineteenth-century Liberalism or propounded early versions of modernization or stage theory, maintaining that Latin America would eventually "progress" economically and politically along the lines of North American "civilization." As Mark Berger concludes, in an astute study of early-twentieth-century Latin Americanist academics in the United States, "between 1898 and 1945 the connection between the practice of U.S. foreign policy in Latin America and the dominant professional discourses on Latin America was *even closer than in later years*" (1993: 1, emphasis added).

These precursors of contemporary "development" theory and practice were linked to emerging systems of domination, domestic (in the case of the Liberals) and foreign (in the case of the US occupation forces and banana transnationals). In contrast, the debates between Latin American populists and Marxists in the 1920s and after were part of a growing counterhegemonic discourse that nonetheless considered development the fundamental social and political problem of the period. In a reflection on the Latin American contribution to development theory, Cristóbal Kay (1991: 32–5) points to the polemics between Peruvians José Carlos Mariátegui, a heterodox Marxist, and Víctor Raúl Haya de la Torre, a populist nationalist, as foreshadowing, respectively, the radical dependency and the reformist structuralist paradigms that shaped so many discussions of Third World development after 1950 (cf. Slater 1992: 291). I would add that the clash between Mariátegui and Haya de la Torre was emblematic of a broader Marxist-versus-populist struggle over development theory and practice which was played out with varying consequences in different Latin American countries after the 1920s.

The important point here is not to outline the 1920s and 1930s controversies between Marxists and populists, but rather to stress the centrality of notions of development and underdevelopment, both in their substantive theories and policies and in the passions that fueled their arguments and political movements (see Caballero 1987; Mariátegui 1979; Vanden 1986). Haya de la Torre and Mariátegui shared a view of Peru as a semi-feudal society and of the Peruvian capitalist class as so weak or so tied to foreign interests that it was incapable of assuming the progressive role historically played by European bourgeoisies. Both attributed Latin America's underdevelopment to the reactionary landlord class and to imperialism, and both advocated industrialization. Significantly, they emphasized that the dynamics of capitalist development were different at the center and at the periphery of the world economy (Kay 1991; Vanden 1986).

Haya and Mariátegui differed, however, in their opinions about what both saw as an inevitable, impending revolution. Haya maintained that the revolution had to be anti-feudal and anti-imperialist and that it was necessary to fully develop capitalism, albeit within a framework of national independence. Since the peasantry was too backward and the proletariat too small, the revolution was essentially a struggle for national liberation and had to be directed by members of the middle class. Mariátegui, in contrast, insisted that feudal and capitalist relations were elements of a single system of exploitation responsible for Peru's low level of development. He argued that the revolution had to skip the capitalist stage and be socialist right from the beginning. The peasantry was not only a revolutionary force but, with its community institutions rooted in pre-Columbian tradition, it contained as well the germ of the new socialist society (Godio 1983: 220–4; Kay 1991: 33–4; Mariátegui 1979: 76–9).

. . . I shall have more to say about some of the discussions over the peasantry's role as a political force in Latin America. Here, I wish merely to note that the populist regimes that came to power in Latin America in the early to mid-twentieth century – whether based on mass movements, charismatic leaders, or both – spoke a language of social reform and economic development, fused in some cases with anti-imperialism. Haya de la Torre in Peru, José Batlle y Ordóñez in Uruguay, Getulio Vargas in Brazil, Juan Domingo Perón in Argentina, and Rómulo Betancourt in Venezuela (to mention only the most important) all saw economic progress as their main challenge and geared their discourse to poor, multiclass constituencies that hoped to benefit from development. The early-twentieth-century industrialization of the larger countries in Latin America, particularly Brazil and Argentina, owed much to import substitution and other incentive measures implemented under populist regimes. This populist trend in Latin American politics, social thought, and economic policy eventually had a profound impact on such influential individuals and institutions as Raúl Prebisch and the United Nations Economic Commission for Latin America, both central to the "development" debate after 1949 (Kay 1991; Sikkink 1988). In describing the post-World War II concern with "development" as a full-blown genesis (rather than as a discursive shift based significantly on much older ideas), the postmodernists' Foucauldian "archeology" appears to have barely scraped the surface.

Material Objectives and Identity Politics

This facile reinvention of "development" as a post-World War II phenomenon is important not just as an illustration of the shortcomings of the post modernists' writing of intellectual history. It is basic to their understandings of collective action and social change in the Third World and their visions of what constitutes an emancipatory politics. Escobar, for example, hails the growing number of social movements that reject the economistic character of development, are deeply aware of other concerns (ecological, and those of peace and of women and indigenous peoples), and seek to use local knowledge to shift the existing architecture of power. It is in the vitality of these new movements that the dissolution of a 40-year-old development apparatus, already beginning to crumble but still in place, and the coming of new era, more pluralistic and less oppressive, can be visualized. (1988: 439)

One of [my] central themes is that Third World social movements of recent decades, and the Costa Rican peasant movements in particular, have often been neither prototypically "old" nor "new," at least in the sense in which this opposition is used in the "new social movements" (NSMs) literature. Concern with NSMs dates to the late 1960s when a tide of discontent swept over young people in diverse parts of the world – New York, Berkeley, Paris, Tokyo, Prague, Mexico City, and elsewhere (including Costa Rica [see González 1985: 267–8]). This worldwide political and cultural tumult – which some subsequently interpreted as a common howl of protest against "bureaucratic organization . . . in the post-industrial age of computerized identities and cold remote institutions" (Murphy 1991: 78) – impacted social scientific thinking with the usual long lag time between historical events and published analyses. Functionalist frameworks (Smelser 1962) that saw "collective behavior" as an irrational mass response to societal breakdown were clearly not up to the task of explaining major upheavals in democratic polities during an age of unprecedented affluence. Rational actor approaches (Olson 1965) that viewed social movements as the sum of participants' strategic, individually oriented choices could scarcely make sense of why student protesters, in the pursuit of seemingly abstract common goals, would risk ruining promising careers or having their heads split open by riot police. And traditional Marxists, who saw the bourgeoisie and proletariat as the main antagonists in capitalist societies, did not usually know what to make of movements that often had largely middle-class leadership and multiclass constituencies (see Cohen 1985: 667–73; Eyerman and Jamison 1991: 19–23; Gamson 1992: 58; Zald 1992: 330–2).

Alain Touraine (1974; 1981) was probably the first to articulate the outlines of what many came to consider the "new social movements" paradigm. In Europe, growing numbers of social scientists began to study the environmentalist, peace and anti-nuclear, women's, gay liberation, minority rights, and student and youth movements (Melucci 1989). Eventually, the approach caught on in Latin America, which it entered first through Buenos Aires, that most Europhile of Latin American cities. There, the list of "new" movements grew to include those struggling for human rights and democratization, the rights of indigenous peoples, regional autonomy, the needs of urban slum dwellers, and the creation of liberation theology-oriented Christian base communities (Jelin 1989; Slater 1985). As more social scientists began to focus on these movements, and as the list of "causes" grew, it became clear that a veritable "social movements 'industry'" was emerging in academia (Gledhill 1988: 257), though it was also increasingly difficult to speak of the NSMs framework as a coherent model.

Synthesizing what has become a rich area of discussion and debate entails obvious risks. Nevertheless, I think it is fair to say that proponents of new social movements approaches share several broad assumptions. First, they juxtapose the "classlessness" (Olofsson 1988) of the NSMs with the "old" labor or working-class movement for which class was the main social cleavage, category of analysis, principle of organization, and political issue. The "new" movements' rejection of class accompanies an aversion to seeking amelioration through existing institutional channels and a distancing from party politics and especially from the "verticality and sectarianism" of the traditional Left (Fals Borda 1992: 304). Social conflicts, rather than revolving primarily around a class dimension, proliferate in more and more areas of life, resulting in the politicization of more and more kinds of relations and in a blurring of public and private spheres (Laclau and Mouffe 1985). NSMs supersede parties and unions and become "the organic expression of civil society" (Vilas 1993: 42). Second, NSMs "emerge out of the crisis of modernity" and are engaged in "cultural struggles" over meanings, symbols, collective identities, and rights to "specificity and difference." Generally, these concerns are accorded more weight by both activists and scholars than those involving socioeconomic or political conditions (Escobar 1992: 396, 412; Jelin 1990: 206; Melucci 1989: 20; Touraine 1985: 784). Movement participants, often termed "new social subjects," have multiple social "locations" or "positions" and their political activity cannot, therefore, be derived a priori from a single principle of identity or a particular structurally defined "interest," especially a material one (Laclau 1985: 27). Third, NSMs, while at times contesting state efforts to dominate the construction of cultural meanings (Touraine 1988), usually engage instead "in creating bits of social practice in which power is not central" (Evers 1985: 48), and these are "below the threshold where the systemic imperatives of power and money become so dominant" (White 1991: 107). Finally – and especially germane in the light of the discussion below – advocates of NSMs approaches have, with few exceptions (Calderón et al. 1992; Esteva 1988; León 1990; Starn 1992), devoted scant attention to rural politics or peasant struggles (Fox 1990).

Despite postmodernists' adoption of "new social movements" as a political rallying cry and as both evidence of and explanation for the fragmented, contingent identities of "postindustrial" – or, contradictorily, "hyper industrial" – society (Touraine 1988: 25), the term appears rather like a new "meta-category," subsuming many disparate phenomena under a single overarching rubric (Calhoun 1993: 391; Gamson 1992: 58–9). The movements in question often tend to be highly critical of capitalism, and their activists, in many cases, are drawn from earlier anti-capitalist opposition movements. But the NSMs' versions of identity politics and postmodern scholarship nonetheless resonate with some of the more dehumanizing aspects of contemporary neoliberal economics. First, NSMs have "helped reproduce the fragmentation of the popular classes sought by the state and the market" (Vilas 1993: 42). The accentuation of difference and otherness that both their theory and practice imply is, in large measure, a reaction to rising inequality, economic insecurity, and competition (Burbach et al. 1997). It is also an adaptation to the "flexible accumulation" that characterizes contemporary capitalism – with its restless, profit-hungry investors roaming the world, electronic flows of information and money, and accelerated processes of technological and organizational innovation (Castells 1996). As David Harvey points out:

> The more unified the space, the more important the qualities of the fragmentations become for social identity and action. The free flow of capital across the surface of the

globe...places strong emphasis upon the particular qualities of the spaces to which
capital might be attracted. The shrinkage of space that brings diverse communities
across the globe into competition with each other implies localized competitive strategies and a heightened sense of awareness of what makes a place special and gives it a
competitive advantage. This kind of reaction looks much more strongly to the identification of place, the building and signaling of its unique qualities in an increasingly
homogeneous but fragmented world. (1989: 271)

Second, as Carlos Vilas indicates, the category "new social movements" implies
a view of politics common to both postmodernism and neoliberalism in which
civil society is "the result of an always circumstantial combination of...multiple
identities, among which class is just one – and never determinant" (1993: 39). In
other words, identities become potential resources in a resource-driven system, a
part of human capital, rather like university degrees, skilled hands, or fetching looks.
If it is true that what energizes "new" social movements is a sense of victimization,
rather than the "old" movements' search for equality (Apter 1992: 142), then the
pursuit of identity politics as an end in itself may contribute not to the alliance-
building that might temper the most oppressive aspects of the market (and
ultimately weaken the identities themselves), but to perpetuating the divisive processes that gave rise to those identities in the first place (Castells 1997; Harvey 1993:
64).

Critics of NSMs theory have questioned the assertions of "newness" that underlie
the paradigm, as well as postmodernists' view of the "old" labor movement (and,
more broadly, of "modernity" itself) as a coherent, unified entity with a single
"master narrative" (Foweraker 1995: 40–5; Gamson 1992: 59; Gledhill 1988:
258–9; C. R. Hale 1997: 569; Hellman 1995: 171–4; Nash 1992: 292). Like the
notion that two billion people suddenly became underdeveloped in a couple of days
in January 1949, the "newness" claim rests on a kind of historical amnesia. This, as
Barry Adam points out, arises

> from two sources: (a) the current crisis in Marxism which has allowed leftist social
> theory to "see" movement activity around it which it had long refused to recognize, and
> (b) the upswing of many of these movements in their "second wave" after having
> declined in the 1940s and 1950s due either to Nazi extermination, Stalinism, or
> McCarthyism. (1993: 323)

In a similar vein, Craig Calhoun argues that early workers' movements were, like
the NSMs, "engaged in a politics of identity" and that, before the late nineteenth
century, "class was seldom the self-applied label or the basis even of workers'
mobilization" (1993: 398, 401). Indeed,

> there was mobilization over wages, to be sure, but also over women and children
> working, community life, the status of immigrants, education, access to public services,
> and so forth. Movement activity constantly overflowed the bounds of the label *labor*.
> Similarly, the categories of class and class struggle have been used far from the Marxian
> ideal type of wage laborers in industrial capitalist factories. Artisans and agricultural
> workers, white collar and service employees, and even small proprietors (not to mention
> spouses and children of all these) have joined in the struggles or been grouped in the
> category of the working class. Throughout the history of labor and class movements,
> there has been contention over who should be included in them and how both common

and different identities should be established. Indeed, ironically, by leading to research on the protests of women, people of color, and other marginalized people, the recent growth of NSMs has helped to explode the myth that the narrowly white, male labor movement, against which NSMs were defined, was completely pre dominant. (p. 391)

Nor are contemporary NSMs as "classless" or as loath to confront state power and address material concerns as some theorists suggest; nor is the practice of the "old" labor movement as distant from that of the NSMs. Just as unions' demands for occupational health and safety are profoundly environmentalist, calls for equality, affirmative action, and nondiscrimination clauses in union contracts are profoundly economic, as are those for converting war industries to peaceful uses, moving toxic dump sites, or closing nuclear power plants (Adam 1993: 323–7). Many of the most significant recent struggles, especially in poorer countries, have occurred "precisely at the point of intersection between" class- and identity-based movements (Hellman 1995: 167). And for the impoverished inhabitants of today's crisis-ridden Third World (or the scholars who work with them), the "postmaterialist," "classless" arguments of NSMs theorists ring particularly hollow.

This critical appraisal of NSMs theory should not blind us, however, to its very positive contribution in highlighting aspects of popular movements that narrow, class-based interpretations often downplayed or missed. The NSMs theorists' views of social actors as bearers of multiple identities and of culture and politics as loci of contested claims constitute useful correctives to traditional understandings, as well as clues about where to look in understanding particular patterns of quiescence or processes of mobilization... But the replacement of "class reductionism with class rejectionism" (Vilas 1993: 40) often obscures more than it reveals and is part of a more general inattention to political economy and the workings of the state that often places social movements outside of history (Adam 1993: 317; Fox 1990: 2–3; Harvey 1993: 54–5; Williams 1983: 172–3). The triumphalism that marked the early NSMs literature had largely faded by the late 1980s along with some of the original NSMs themselves (Escobar and Alvarez 1992: 3; Foweraker 1995: 25). The sterility of the debate over "newness" becomes especially clear when researchers dig in the archives, trace organizational genealogies, or probe movement protagonists' political biographies and historical memories... Although some of these movements occasionally made alliances with wealthy groups... they drew their constituencies overwhelmingly from the poor and the powerless – not just the proletariat, of course, but from a wide range of social actors bearing various visions of a better, more just society.

The Costa Rican peasant movements... coalesced in response to the eminently material forces of economic collapse that were then followed by stabilization and structural adjustment, but they appealed nonetheless to deeply held notions of *campesino* identity and to fears that the cherished "culture of maize" – and, by extension, *maiceros*, or maize producers – had no place in the new development model. In some regions a long-dormant indigenous identity even surfaced sporadically among the exclusively mestizo peasantry as a metaphorical reference point and a justification for militant struggle... The movements' roots are diverse and often go way back in time: from local-level struggles for land decades ago to Catholic liberation theology in the 1970s, from participation in banana workers unions to residence in urban squatter camps, from disappointed expectations raised by thirty years of social democracy to a leftist vanguardism that once inspired them but which they came to reject. The influence of environmentalism, one of the prototypical NSMs, also figured significantly in the peasant movement (Blanco 1991; Blanco and Campos 1988; Brenes Castillo 1988). To some extent this reflected a transparent "greening of the discourse," as cooperatives and other groups curried favor with international donors. But environmentalism also trickled down to and arose from grass-roots practice, as agriculturalists who had no hope of ever securing foreign grants but who had seen drought wither their crops went, on their own initiative, into the few remaining primary forests to gather seeds to reforest their small plots with native tree species, which they preferred to the exotics touted by the state extension service. The Costa Rican movements are also characterized by debates over peasant identities, and inclusion and exclusion, that would be familiar to students of NSMs. Yet their participants and leaders are also acutely aware that the survival and reproduction of *the bearers* of these identities require struggles around economic policy issues. In an era of crisis, abstract and distant forces – a World Bank structural adjustment program, for example – can become distressingly concrete even in the most remote rural areas, as interest rates soar, producer price subsidies vanish, and banks restrict credit. As peasant leaders came to grips with these complexities, they had to learn the language of bankers and politicians (and to master the latest computer and communications technologies), challenging in the process timeless images of rural people as unsophisticated rustics.

REFERENCES

Adam, B. (1993) Post-Marxism and the New Social Movements. *Canadian Review of Sociology and Anthropology* 30(3): 316–36.

Apfell Marglin, F. and Marglin, S. (eds.). (1990) *Dominating Knowledge: Development, Culture, and Resistance*. Oxford: Clarendon Press.

Apter, D. (1992) Democracy and Emancipatory Movements: Notes for a Theory of Inversionary Discourse. *Development and Change* 23(3): 139–73.

Asad, T. (1973) *Anthropology and the Colonial Encounter*. London: Ithaca Press.

Berger, M. (1993) Civilising the South: The U.S. Rise to Hegemony in the Americas and the Roots of "Latin American Studies," 1898–1945. *Bulletin of Latin American Research* 12(1): 1–48.

Black, G. (1998) *The Good Neighbor: How the United States Wrote the History of Central America and the Caribbean*. New York: Pantheon.

Blanco, M. (1991) Lamento . . . o encuentro. *Evidencia* 1(2): 10–11.

Blanco, M. and Campos, C. (1988) Declaración de organizaciones campesinas de Costa Rica, ante la XVII Asamblea General de la Unión Internacional para la Conservación de la Naturaleza y los Recursos Naturales (UICN). In I. Hedstrom (ed.) *La situación ambiental en Centroamérica y el Caribe*. San José: Departamento Ecumenico de Investigaciones.

Brenes Castillo, C. (1988) Desarrollo forestal campesino? In I. Hedstrom (ed.) *La Situación ambiental en Centroamérica y el caribe*. San José: Departamento Ecuménico de Investigaciones.

Burbach, R., Nunez, O. and Kagarlitsky, B. (1997) *Globalization and its Discontents: The Rise of Postmodern Socialisms*. London: Pluto Press.

Caballero, M. (1987) *Latin America and the Comintern, 1919–1943*. Cambridge: Cambridge University Press.

Calderon, F., Piscitelli, A., and Reyna, J. (1992) Social Movements: Actors, Theories, Expectations. In A. Escobar and S. Alvarez (eds.) *New Social Movements in Latin America: Identity, Strategy, and Democracy*. Boulder, CO.: Westview.

Calhoun, C. (1993) New Social Movements of the Early Nineteenth Century. *Social Science History*. 17(3): 385–427.

Castells, M. (1996) *The Rise of the Network Society*. Oxford: Blackwell Publishers.

——. (1997) *The Power of Identity*. Oxford: Blackwell Publishers.

Clifford, J. 1983. Introduction: Partial Truths. In J. Clifford and G. Marcus (eds.) *Writing Culture: The Poetics and Politics of Ethnography*. Berkeley: University of California Press, pp. 1–26.

——. (1988) On Ethnographic Authority. In *The Predicament of Culture: Twentieth Century Ethnography, Literature and Art*. Cambridge, MA: Harvard University Press, pp. 21–54.

Cohen, J. (1985) Strategy of Identity: New Theoretical Paradigms and Contemporary Social Movements. *Social Research* 52(4): 663–716.

DuBois, M. (1991) The Governance of the Third World: A Foucauldian Perspective of Power Relations in Development. *Alternatives* 16(1): 1–30.

Escobar, A. (1984) Discourse and Power in Development: Michel Foucault and the Relevance of his Work to the Third World. *Alternatives* 10 (winter): 377–400.

——. (1988) Power and Visibility: Development and the Invention and Management of the Third World. *Cultural Anthropology* 3(4): 428–43.

——. (1991) Anthropology and the Development Encounter: The Making and Marketing of Development Anthropology. *American Ethnologist* 18(4): 658–82.

——. (1992) Culture, Practice and Politics: Anthropology and the Study of Social Movements. *Critique of Anthropology* 12(4): 395–432.

——. (1995) *Encountering Development: The Making and Unmaking of the Third World*. Princeton: Princeton University Press.

Escobar, A. and Alvarez, S. (1992) *The Making of Social Movements in Latin America: Identity, Strategy. and Democracy*. Boulder, CO; Westview.

Esteva, G. (1988) El desastre agrícola: Adios al México imaginario. *Comercio Exterior* (Mexico) 38(8): 662–72.

Evers, T. (1985) Identity: The Hidden Side of New Social Movements in Latin America. In D. Slater (ed.) *New Social Movements and the State in Latin America*. Amsterdam: CEDLA.

Eyerman, R. and Jamison, A. (1991) *Social Movements: A Cognitive Approach*. London: Polity Press.

Fals Borda, O. (1992) Social Movements and Political Power in Latin America. In A. Escobar and S. Alvarez (eds.) *The Making of Social Movements in Latin America: Identity, Strategy and Democracy*. Boulder, CO: Westview.

Ferguson, J. (1990) *The Anti-Politics Machine: "Development," Depoliticization and Bureaucratic Power in Lesotho*. Cambridge: Cambridge University Press.

Foucault, M. (1972) *The Archeology of Knowledge and the Discourse on Language*. New York: Pantheon Books.

Foweraker, J. (1995) *Theorizing Social Movements*. London: Pluto Press.

Fox, J. (1990) Editor's Introduction. *Journal of Development Studies* 26(4): 1–18.

Gamson, W. (1992) The Social Psychology of Collective Action. In A. Morris and C. Mueller (eds.) *Frontiers in Social Movement Theory*. New Haven: Yale University Press.

Gledhill, J. (1988) Agrarian Social Movements and Forms of Consciousness. *Bulletin of Latin American Research* 7(2): 257–76.

Godio, J. (1983) *Historia del movimiento obrero latinoamericano*, vol. 2. Mexico City: Nueva Sociedad-Editorial Nueva Imagen.

Gonzalez, P. (1985) Las luchas estudiantiles en Centroamérica 1970–1983. In D. Camacho and R. Menjívar (eds.) *Movimientos populares en Centroamérica*. San José: EDUCA.

Hale, C. A. (1989) Political and Social Ideas. In L. Bethell (ed.) *Latin America: Economy and Society, 1870–1930*. Cambridge: Cambridge University Press.

Hale, C. R. (1997) Cultural Politics of Identity in Latin America. *Annual Review of Anthropology* 26: 567–90.

Harvey, D. (1989) *The Condition of Postmodernity: An Enquiry into the Origins of Cultural Change*. Oxford: Blackwell Publishers.

——. (1993) Class Relations, Social Justice, and the Politics of Difference. In J. Squires (ed.) *Principled Positions: Postmodernism and the Rediscovery of Value*. London: Lawrence and Wishart.

Hellman, J. (1995) The Riddle of New Social Movements: Who They Are and What They Do. In S. Halebsky and R. Harris (eds.) *Capital, Power, and Inequality in Latin America*. Boulder, CO: Westview.

Hewitt de Alcantara, C. (1984) *Anthropological Perspectives on Rural Mexico*. London: Routledge and Kegan Paul.

Jelin, E. (ed.). (1989) *Los nuevos movimientos sociales: Mujeres, rock nacional, derechos humanos, obreros, barrios*. Buenos Aires: Centro Editor de America Latina.

——. (1990) Citizenship and Identity: Final Reflections. In E. Jelin (ed.) *Women and Social Change in Latin America*. London: Zed Books.

Katz, F. (1991) The Liberal Republic and the Porfiriato, 1867–1910. In L. Bethell (ed.) *Mexico since Independence*. Cambridge: Cambridge University Press.

Kay, C. (1991) Reflections on the Latin American Contribution to Development Theory. *Development and Change* 22(1): 31–68.

Kearney, M. (1996) *Reconceptualizing the Peasantry: Anthropology in Global Perspective*. Boulder, CO: Westview.

Laclau, E. (1985) New Social Movements and the Plurality of the Social. In D. Slater (ed.) *New Social Movements and the State in Latin America*. Amsterdam: CEDLA.

Laclau, E. and Mouffe, C. (1985) *Hegemony and Socialist Struggle: Towards a Radical Democratic Politics*. London: Verso.

Leeds, A. (1977) Mythos and Pathos: Some Unpleasantries on Peasantries. In R. Halperin and J. Dow (eds.) *Peasant Livelihood: Studies in Economic Anthropology and Cultural Ecology*. New York: St. Martin's Press.

León, R. (1990) Bartolina Sisa: The Peasant Women's Organization in Bolivia. In E. Jelin (ed.) *Women and Social Change in Latin America*. London: Zed Books.

Mamdani, M. (1973) *The Myth of Population Control: Family, Caste, and Class in an Indian Village*. New York: Monthly Review Press.

Mariátegui, J. (1979) Siete ensayos de interpretación de la realidad peruana [1928]. Mexico City: Serie Popular Era.

Melucci, A. (1989) *Nomads of the Present: Social Movements and Individual Needs in Contemporary Society*. Philadelphia: Temple University Press.

Mitchell, T. (1991) America's Egypt: Discourse of the Development Industry. *Middle East Report* 21(2): 18–36.

Miller, G. (1919) *Prowling about Panama*. New York: Abingdon Press.

Morris, D. (1979) *Measuring the Condition of the World's Poor: The Physical Quality of Life Index*. New York: Pergamon Press.

Murphy, R. (1991) Anthropology at Columbia: A Reminiscence. *Dialectical Anthropology* 16: 65–81.

Nash, J. (1992) Interpreting Social Movements: Bolivian Resistance to Economic Conditions Imposed by the International Monetary Fund. *American Ethnologist* 19(2): 275–93.

Olofsson, G. (1988) After the Working Class Movement? An Essay on What's "New" and What's "Social" in the New Social Movements. *Acta Sociologica* 31(1): 15–34.

Olson, M. (1965) *The Logic of Collective Action.* Cambridge: Harvard University Press.

Palmer, S. (1992) El consumo de heroina entre los artesanos de San José y el Pánico moral de 1929. *Revista de Historia* 25 (Jan.–Jun.): 29–63.

Prakash, G. (1990) Writing Post-Orientalist Histories of the Third World: Perspectives from Indian Historiography. *Comparative Studies in Society and History* 32(Apr.): 383–408.

Sachs, I. (1976) *The Discovery of the Third World.* Cambridge: MIT Press.

Sachs, W. (ed.) (1992) *The Development Dictionary: A Guide to Knowledge as Power.* London: Zed Books.

Scheper-Hughes, N. (1992) *Death Without Weeping: The Violence of Everyday Life in Brazil.* Berkeley: University of California Press.

Scudder, T. (1988) The Institute for Development Anthropology: The Case for Anthropological Participation in the Development Process. In J. Bennet and J. Bowen (eds.) *Production and Autonomy: Anthropological Studies and Critiques of Development.* Lanham, MD: University Press of America.

Sen, A. (1987) *The Standard of Living.* Cambridge: Cambridge University Press.

Shanin, T. (1982) Defining Peasants: Conceptualisations and Deconceptualisations: Old and New in a Marxist Debate. *Sociological Review* 30(3): 407–32.

Sikkink, K. (1988) The Influence of Raúl Prebisch on Economic Policy Making in Argentina, 1950–1962. *Latin American Research Review* 23(2): 91–114.

Slater, D. (ed.) (1985) *New Social Movements and the State in Latin America.* Amsterdam: CEDLA.

——. (1992) Theories of Development and Politics of the Post-modern – Exploring a Border Zone. *Development and Change* 23(3): 283–319.

Smelser, N. (1962) *The Theory of Collective Behavior.* New York: Free Press.

Starn, O. (1992) "I Dreamed of Foxes and Hawks": Reflections on Peasant Protest, New Social Movements, and the Rondas Campesinas of Northern Peru. In A. Escobar and S. Alvarez (eds.) *The Making of Social Movements in Latin America: Identity, Strategy, and Democracy.* Boulder, CO: Westview.

Summers, R. and Heston, A. (1988) A New Set of International Comparisons of Real Product and Price Levels Estimates for 130 Countries, 1950–1985. *Review of Income and Wealth* 34(1): 1–25.

Touraine, A. (1974) Les clases sociales. In R. Zenteno (ed.) *Las clases sociales en América Latina.* Mexico City: Siglo XXI.

——. (1981) *The Voice and the Eye: An Analysis of Social Movements.* Cambridge: Cambridge University Press.

——. (1985) An Introduction to the Study of Social Movements. *Social Research* 52(4): 749–87.

——. (1988) *Return of the Actor: Social Theory in Postindustrial Society.* Minneapolis: University of Minnesota Press.

UNDP. (1995) *Human Development Report.* New York: Oxford University Press.

Vanden, H. (1986) *National Marxism in Latin America: Jose Carlos Mariategui's Thought and Politics.* Boulder, CO: Lynne Rienner Publishers.

Vilas, C. (1993) The Hour of Civil Society. *NACLA Report on the Americas* 27(2): 38–42, 44.

Vincent, J. (1990) *Anthropology and Politics: Visions, Traditions and Trends.* Tucson: University of Arizona Press.

White, S. (1991) *Political Theory and Postmodernism.* Cambridge: Cambridge University Press.

Williams, R. (1983) *Towards 2000.* London: Chatto and Windus/Hogarth Press.

Zald, M. (1992) Looking Backward to Look Forward: Reflections on the Past and Future of the Resource Mobilization Research Program. In A. Morris and C. Mueller (eds.) *Frontiers in Social Movement Theory.* New Haven: Yale University Press.

33

On Suffering and Structural Violence: A View from Below

Paul Farmer

Everyone knows that suffering exists. The question is how to define it. Given that each person's pain has a degree of reality for him or her that the pain of others can surely never approach, is widespread agreement on the subject possible? Almost all of us would agree that premature and painful illness, torture, and rape constitute extreme suffering. Most would also agree that insidious assaults on dignity, such as institutionalized racism and sexism, also cause great and unjust injury.

Given our consensus on some of the more conspicuous forms of suffering, a number of corollary questions come to the fore. Can we identify those most at risk of great suffering? Among those whose suffering is not mortal, is it possible to identify those most likely to sustain permanent and disabling damage? Are certain "event" assaults, such as torture or rape, more likely to lead to late sequelae than are sustained and insidious suffering, such as the pain born of deep poverty or of racism? Under this latter rubric, are certain forms of discrimination demonstrably more noxious than others?

Anthropologists who take these as research questions study both individual experience and the larger social matrix in which it is embedded in order to see how various large-scale social forces come to be translated into personal distress and disease. By what mechanisms do social forces ranging from poverty to racism become *embodied* as individual experience? This has been the focus of most of my own research in Haiti, where political and economic forces have structured risk for AIDS, tuberculosis, and, indeed, most other infectious and parasitic diseases. Social forces at work there have also structured risk for most forms of extreme suffering, from hunger to torture and rape.

Working in contemporary Haiti, where in recent years political violence has been added to the worst poverty in the hemisphere, one learns a great deal about suffering. In fact, the country has long constituted a sort of living laboratory for the study of affliction, no matter how it is defined. "Life for the Haitian peasant of

From A. Kleinman, V. Das, and M. Lock (eds.) *Issues on Social Suffering*, reprinted by permission of *Daedalus, Journal of American Academy of Arts and Sciences* 125(1) (winter 1996), pp. 261–76, 278–83.

today," observed anthropologist Jean Weise some twenty-five years ago, "is abject misery and a rank familiarity with death."[1] The situation has since worsened. When in 1991 international health and population experts devised a "human suffering index" by examining measures of human welfare ranging from life expectancy to political freedom, 27 of 141 countries were characterized by "extreme human suffering." Only one of them, Haiti, was located in the Western hemisphere. In only three countries in the world was suffering judged to be more extreme than that endured in Haiti; each of these three countries is currently in the midst of an internationally recognized civil war.

Suffering is certainly a recurrent and expected condition in Haiti's Central Plateau, where everyday life has felt like war. "You get up in the morning," observed one young widow with four children, "and it's the fight for food and wood and water." If initially struck by the austere beauty of the region's steep mountains and clement weather, long-term visitors come to see the Central Plateau in much the same manner as its inhabitants: a chalky and arid land hostile to the best efforts of the peasant farmers who live here. Landlessness is widespread and so, consequently, is hunger. All the standard measures reveal how tenuous the peasantry's hold on survival is. Life expectancy at birth is less than fifty years, in large part because as many as two of every ten infants die before their first birthday. Tuberculosis is the leading cause of death among adults; among children, diarrheal disease, measles, and tetanus ravage the undernourished.

But the experience of suffering, it is often noted, is not effectively conveyed by statistics or graphs. The "texture" of dire affliction is perhaps best felt in the gritty details of biography, and so I introduce the stories of Acéphie Joseph and Chouchou Louis.[2] The stories of Acéphie and Chouchou are anything but "anecdotal." For the epidemiologist as well as the political analyst, they suffered and died in exemplary fashion. Millions of people living in similar circumstances can expect to meet similar fates. What these victims, past and present, share are not personal or psychological attributes – they do not share culture, language, or race. Rather, what they share is the experience of occupying the bottom rung of the social ladder in inegalitarian societies.[3]

Acéphie Joseph's and Chouchou Louis's stories illustrate some of the mechanisms through which large-scale social forces crystallize into the sharp, hard surfaces of individual suffering. Such suffering is structured by historically given (and often economically driven) processes and forces that conspire – whether through routine, ritual, or, as is more commonly the case, these hard surfaces – to constrain agency.[4] For many, including most of my patients and informants, life choices are structured by racism, sexism, political violence, *and* grinding poverty.

Acéphie's Story

For the wound of the daughter of my people is my heart wounded, I mourn, and dismay has taken hold of me.
Is there no balm in Gilead? Is there no physician there?
Why then has the health of the daughter of my people not been restored?
O that my head were waters, and my eyes a fountain of tears, that I might weep day and night for the slain of the daughter of my people!

(Jeremiah 8: 22–9.1)

Kay, a community of fewer than fifteen hundred people, stretches along an unpaved road that cuts north and east into Haiti's Central Plateau. Striking out from Port-au-Prince, the capital, it can take several hours to reach Kay. The journey gives one an impression of isolation, insularity. The impression is misleading, as the village owes its existence to a project conceived in the Haitian capital and drafted in Washington, DC: Kay is a settlement of refugees, substantially composed of peasant farmers displaced more than thirty years ago by Haiti's largest dam.

Before 1956, the village of Kay was situated in a fertile valley, and through it ran the Rivière Artibonite. For generations, thousands of families had farmed the broad and gently sloping banks of the river, selling rice, bananas, millet, corn, and sugar-cane in regional markets. Harvests were, by all reports, bountiful; life there is now recalled as idyllic. When the valley was flooded with the building of the dam, the majority of the local population was forced up into the stony hills on either side of the new reservoir. By all the standard measures, the "water refugees" became exceedingly poor; the older people often blame their poverty on the massive buttress dam a few miles away, and bitterly note that it brought them neither electricity nor water.

In 1983, when I began working in the Central Plateau, AIDS, although already afflicting an increasing number of city dwellers, was unknown in most areas as rural as Kay. Acéphie Joseph was one of the first villagers to die of the new syndrome. But her illness, which ended in 1991, was merely the latest in a string of tragedies that she and her parents readily linked together in a long lamentation, by now familiar to those who tend the region's sick.

The litany begins, usually, down in the valley hidden under the still surface of the lake. Acéphie's parents came from families making a decent living by farming fertile tracts of land – their "ancestors' gardens" – and selling much of their produce. M. Joseph tilled the soil, and his wife, a tall and wearily elegant woman not nearly as old as she looked, was a "Madame Sarah," a market woman. "If it weren't for the dam," M. Joseph assured me, "we'd be just fine now. Acéphie, too." The Josephs' home was drowned along with most of their belongings, their crops, and the graves of their ancestors.

Refugees from the rising water, the Josephs built a miserable lean-to on a knoll of high land jutting into the new reservoir. They remained poised on their knoll for some years; Acéphie and her twin brother were born there. I asked them what induced them to move up to Kay, to build a house on the hard stone embankment of a dusty road. "Our hut was too near the water," replied M. Joseph. "I was afraid one of the children would fall into the lake and drown. Their mother had to be away selling; I was trying to make a garden in this terrible soil. There was no one to keep an eye on them."

Acéphie attended primary school – a banana-thatched and open shelter in which children and young adults received the rudiments of literacy – in Kay. "She was the nicest of the Joseph sisters," recalled one of her classmates. "And she was as pretty as she was nice." Acéphie's beauty and her vulnerability may have sealed her fate as early as 1984. Though still in primary school, she was already nineteen years old; it was time for her to help generate income for her family, which was sinking deeper and deeper into poverty. Acéphie began to help her mother by carrying produce to a local market on Friday mornings. On foot or with a donkey it takes over an hour and a half to reach the market, and the road leads right through Péligre, the site of the dam and, until recently, a military barracks. The soldiers liked to watch the parade of women on Friday mornings. Sometimes they taxed them with haphazardly imposed fines; sometimes they taxed them with flirtatious banter.

Such flirtation is seldom unwelcome, at least to all appearances. In rural Haiti, entrenched poverty made the soldiers – the region's only salaried men – ever so much more attractive. Hunger was again a near-daily occurrence for the Joseph family; the times were as bad as those right after the flooding of the valley. And so when Acéphie's good looks caught the eye of Captain Jacques Honorat, a native of Belladère formerly stationed in Port-au-Prince, she returned his gaze.

Acéphie knew, as did everyone in the area, that Honorat had a wife and children. He was known, in fact, to have more than one regular partner. But Acéphie was taken in by his persistence, and when he went to speak to her parents, a long-term liaison was, from the outset, seriously considered:

> What would you have me do? I could tell that the old people were uncomfortable, worried; but they didn't say no. They didn't tell me to stay away from him. I wish they had, but how could they have known? . . . I knew it was a bad idea then, but I just didn't know why. I never dreamed he would give me a bad illness, never! I looked around and saw how poor we all were, how the old people were finished. . . . What would you have me do? It was a way out, that's how I saw it.

Acéphie and Honorat were sexual partners only briefly – for less than a month, according to Acéphie. Shortly thereafter, Honorat fell ill with unexplained fevers and kept to the company of his wife in Péligre. As Acéphie was looking for a *moun prensipal* – a "main man" – she tried to forget about the soldier. Still, it was shocking to hear, a few months after they parted, that he was dead.

Acéphie was at a crucial juncture in her life. Returning to school was out of the question. After some casting about, she went to Mirebalais, the nearest town, and began a course in what she euphemistically termed "cooking school." The school – really just an ambitious woman's courtyard – prepared poor girls like Acéphie for their inevitable turn as servants in the city. Indeed, domestic service was one of the rare growth industries in Haiti, and as much as Acéphie's proud mother hated to think of her daughter reduced to servitude, she could offer no viable alternative.

And so Acéphie, at age twenty-two, went off to Port-au-Prince, where she found a job as a housekeeper for a middle-class Haitian woman working for the US embassy. Acéphie's looks and manners kept her out of the backyard, the traditional milieu of Haitian servants: she was designated as the maid who, in addition to cleaning, answered the door and the telephone. Although Acéphie was not paid well – she received $30 each month – she tried to save a bit of money for her parents and siblings, recalling the hunger gnawing at her home village.

Still looking for a *moun prensipal*, Acéphie began seeing Blanco Nerette, a young man with origins identical to her own: Blanco's parents were also "water refugees" and Acéphie had known him when they were both attending the parochial school in Kay. Blanco had done well for himself, by Kay standards: he chauffeured a small bus between the Central Plateau and the capital. In a setting characterized by an unemployment rate of greater than 60 percent, his job commanded considerable respect. He easily won the attention of Acéphie. They planned to marry, and started pooling their resources.

Acéphie had worked as a maid for over three years when she discovered that she was pregnant. When she told Blanco, he became skittish. Nor was her employer pleased: it is considered unsightly to have a pregnant servant. So Acéphie returned to Kay, where she had a difficult pregnancy. Blanco came to see her once or twice; they had a disagreement, and then she heard nothing from him. Following the birth of her daughter, Acéphie was sapped by repeated infections. She was shortly thereafter diagnosed with AIDS.

Soon Acéphie's life was consumed with managing drenching night sweats and debilitating diarrhea, while attempting to care for her first child. "We both need diapers now," she remarked bitterly towards the end of her life, faced each day not only with diarrhea, but also with a persistent lassitude. As she became more and more gaunt, some villagers suggested that Acéphie was the victim of sorcery. Others recalled her liaison with the soldier and her work as a servant in the city, both locally considered risk factors for AIDS. Acéphie herself knew that she had AIDS, although she was more apt to refer to herself as suffering from a disorder brought on by her work as a servant: "All that ironing and then opening a refrigerator."

But this is not simply the story of Acéphie and her daughter. There is Jacques Honorat's first wife, who each year grows thinner. After Honorat's death, she found herself desperate, with no means of feeding her five hungry children, two of whom were also ill. Her subsequent union was again with a soldier. Honorat had at least two other partners, both of them poor peasant women, in the Central Plateau. One is HIV positive and has two sickly children. Blanco is still a handsome young man, apparently in good health and plying the roads from Mirebalais to Port-au-Prince. Who knows if he carries the virus? As an attractive man with a paying job, he has plenty of girlfriends.

Nor is this simply the story of those infected with the virus. The pain of Mme. Joseph and Acéphie's twin brother was manifestly intense, but few understood the anguish of her father. Shortly after Acéphie's death, M. Joseph hanged himself.

Chouchou's Story

History shudders, pierced by events of massive public suffering. Memory is haunted, stalked by the ghosts of history's victims, capriciously severed from life in genocides, holocausts, and extermination camps. The cries of the hungry, the shrieks of political prisoners, and the silent voices of the oppressed echo slowly, painfully through daily existence.

(Rebecca Chopp, *The Praxis of Suffering*)

Chouchou Louis grew up not far from Kay in another small village in the steep and infertile highlands of Haiti's Central Plateau. He attended primary school for a couple of years but was obliged to drop out when his mother died. Then in his early teens, Chouchou joined his father and an older sister in tending their hillside gardens. In short, there was nothing remarkable about Chouchou's childhood; it was brief and harsh, like most in rural Haiti.

Throughout the 1980s, church activities formed Chouchou's sole distraction. These were hard years for the Haitian poor, beaten down by a family dictatorship well into its third decade. The Duvaliers, father and son, ruled through violence, largely directed at people whose conditions of existence were similar to that of Chouchou Louis. Although many of them tried to flee, often by boat, US policy maintained that Haitian asylum-seekers were "economic refugees." As part of a 1981 agreement between the administrations of Ronald Reagan and Jean-Claude Duvalier, refugees seized on the high seas were summarily returned to Haiti. During the first ten years of the accord, 24,559 Haitians applied for political asylum in the United States; eight applications were approved.

A growing Haitian pro-democracy movement led, in February 1986, to the flight of Duvalier. Chouchou Louis must have been about twenty years old when "Baby Doc" fell, and he shortly thereafter acquired a small radio. "All he did," recalled his wife years later, "was work the land, listen to the radio, and go to church." It was on the radio that Chouchou heard about the people who took over after Duvalier fled. Like many in rural Haiti, Chouchou was distressed to hear that power had been handed to the military, led by hardened *duvaliéristes*. It was this army that the US government, which in 1916 had created the modern Haitian army, termed "Haiti's best bet for democracy." In the eighteen months following Duvalier's departure, over $200 million in US aid passed through the hands of the junta.

In early 1989, Chouchou moved in with Chantal Brisé, who was pregnant. They were living together when Father Jean-Bertrand Aristide – by then considered the leader of the pro-democracy movement – declared his candidacy for the presidency in the internationally monitored elections of 1990. In December of that year almost 70 percent of the voters chose Father Aristide from a field of ten presidential candidates.

Like most rural Haitians, Chouchou and Chantal welcomed Aristide's election with great joy. For the first time, the poor – Haiti's overwhelming majority, formerly silent – felt they had someone representing their interests in the presidential palace. These are the reasons why the military coup d'état of September 1991 stirred great anger in the countryside, where the majority of Haitians live. Anger was soon followed by sadness, then fear, as the country's repressive machinery, dismantled during the seven months of Aristide's tenure, was hastily reassembled under the patronage of the army.

In the month after the coup, Chouchou was sitting in a truck en route to the town of Hinche. Chouchou offered for the consideration of his fellow passengers what Haitians call a *pwen*, a pointed remark intended to say something other than what it literally means. As they bounced along, he began complaining about the conditions of the roads, observing that, "if things were as they should be, these roads would have been repaired already." One eyewitness later told me that at no point in the commentary was Aristide's name invoked. But Chouchou's complaints were recognized by his fellow passengers as veiled language deploring the coup. Unfortunately for Chouchou, one of the passengers was an out-of-uniform solider. At the next checkpoint, the solider had him seized and dragged from the truck. There, a group of soliders and their lackeys – their *attachés*, to use the epithet then in favor – immediately began beating Chouchou, in front of the other passengers; they continued to beat him as they brought him to the military barracks in Hinche. A scar on his right temple was a souvenir of his stay in Hinche, which lasted several days.

Perhaps the worst aftereffect of such episodes of brutality was that, in general, they marked the beginning of persecution, not the end. In rural Haiti, during this time, any scrape with the law (i.e., the military) led to blacklisting. For men like Chouchou, staying out of jail involved keeping the local attachés happy, and he did this by avoiding his home village. But Chouchou lived in fear of a second arrest, his wife later told me, and his fears proved to be well-founded.

On January 22, 1992, Chouchou was visiting his sister when he was arrested by two attachés. No reason was given for the arrest, and Chouchou's sister regarded as ominous the seizure of the young man's watch and radio. He was roughly marched to the nearest military checkpoint, where he was tortured by soldiers and the attachés. One area resident later told us that the prisoner's screams made her children weep with terror.

On January 25, Chouchou was dumped in a ditch to die. The army scarcely took the trouble to circulate the canard that he had stolen some bananas. (The Haitian press, by then thoroughly muzzled, did not even broadcast this false version of events.) Relatives carried Chouchou back to Chantal and their daughter under the cover of night. By early on the morning of January 26, when I arrived, Chouchou was scarcely recognizable. His face, and especially his left temple, was misshapen, swollen, and lacerated; his right temple was also scarred. His mouth was a pool of dark, coagulated blood. His neck was peculiarly swollen, his throat collared with bruises, the traces of a gun butt. His chest and sides were badly bruised, and he had several fractured ribs. His genitals had been mutilated.

That was his front side; presumably, the brunt of the beatings came from behind. Chouchou's back and thighs were striped with deep lash marks. His buttocks were macerated, the skin flayed down to the exposed gluteal muscles. Some of these stigmata appeared to be infected.

Chouchou coughed up more than a liter of blood in his agonal moments. Given his respiratory difficulties and the amount of blood he coughed up, it is likely that the beatings caused him to bleed, slowly at first, then catastrophically, into his lungs. His head injuries had not robbed him of his faculties, although it might have been better for him had they done so. It took Chouchou three days to die.

Explaining Versus Making Sense of Suffering

> *The pain in our shoulder comes*
> *You say, from the damp; and this is also the reason*
> *For the stain on the wall of our flat.*
> *So tell us:*
> *Where does the damp come from?*
> (Bertholt Brecht)

Are these stories of suffering emblematic of something other than two tragic and premature deaths? If so, how representative is each of these experiences? Little about Acéphie's story is unique; I have told it in detail because it brings into relief many of the forces constraining not only her options, but those of most Haitian women. Such, in any case, is my opinion after caring for dozens of poor women with AIDS. There is a deadly monotony in their stories: young women – or teenaged girls – who were driven to Port-au-Prince by the lure of an escape from the harshest poverty; once in the city, each worked as a domestic; none managed to find financial security.

The women interviewed were straightforward about the nonvoluntary aspect of their sexual activity: in their opinions, they had been driven into unfavorable unions by poverty.[5] Indeed, such testimony should call into question facile notions of "consensual sex."

What about the murder of Chouchou Louis? International human rights groups estimate that more than three thousand Haitians were killed in the year after the September 1991 coup that overthrew Haiti's first democratically elected government. Nearly all of those killed were civilians who, like Chouchou, fell into the hands of military or paramilitary forces. The vast majority of victims were poor peasants, like Chouchou, or urban slum dwellers. (The figures cited here are conservative estimates; I am quite sure that no journalist or observer ever came to count the body of Chouchou Louis.[6])

Thus, the agony of Acéphie and Chouchou was, in a sense, "modal" suffering. In Haiti, AIDS and political violence are two leading causes of death among young adults. These afflictions were not the result of accident or of force majeure; they were the consequence, direct or indirect, of human agency. When the Artibonite Valley was flooded, depriving families like the Josephs of their land, a human decision was behind it; when the Haitian army was endowed with money and unfettered power, human decisions were behind that, too. In fact, some of the same decision-makers may have been involved in both cases.

If bureaucrats and soldiers seemed to have unconstrained sway over the lives of the rural poor, the agency of Acéphie and Chouchou was, correspondingly, curbed at every turn. These grim biographies suggest that the social and economic forces that have helped to shape the AIDS epidemic are, in every sense, the same forces that led to Chouchou's death and to the larger repression in which it was eclipsed. What is more, both were "at risk" of such a fate long before they met the soldiers who altered their destinies. They were both, from the outset, victims of structural violence.

While certain kinds of suffering are readily observable – and the subject of countless films, novels, and poems – structural violence all too often defeats those who would describe it. There are at least three reasons why this is so. First, there is the "exoticization" of suffering as lurid as that endured by Acéphie and Chouchou. The suffering of individuals whose lives and struggles recall our own tends to move us; the suffering of those who are distanced, whether by geography, gender, "race," or culture, is sometimes less affecting.

Second, there is the sheer weight of the suffering, which makes it all the more difficult to render: "Knowledge of suffering cannot be conveyed in pure facts and figures, reportings that objectify the suffering of countless persons. The horror of suffering is not only its immensity but the faces of the anonymous victims who have little voice, let alone rights, in history."[7]

Third, the dynamics and distribution of suffering are still poorly understood. Physicians, when fortunate, can alleviate the suffering of the sick. But explaining its distribution requires more minds, more resources. Case studies of individuals reveal suffering, they tell us what happens to one or many people; but to explain suffering, one must embed individual biography in the larger matrix of culture, history, and political economy.

In short, it is one thing to make sense of extreme suffering – a universal activity, surely – and quite another to explain it. Life experiences such as those of Acéphie and Chouchou – who as Haitians living in poverty shared similar social conditions –

must be embedded in ethnography if their representativeness is to be understood. These local understandings are to be embedded, in turn, in the larger-scale historical system of which the fieldwork site is a part.[8] The social and economic forces that dictate life choices in Haiti's Central Plateau affect many millions of individuals, and it is in the context of these global forces that the suffering of individuals receives its appropriate context of interpretation.

Similar insights are central to liberation theology, which takes the suffering of the poor as its central problematic. In *The Praxis of Suffering*, Rebecca Chopp notes that, "In a variety of forms, liberation theology speaks with those who, through their suffering, call into question the meaning and truth of human history."[9] Unlike most previous theologies, and unlike much modern philosophy, liberation theology has attempted to use social analysis to both explain and deplore human suffering. Its key texts bring into relief not merely the suffering of the wretched of the earth, but also the forces that promote that suffering. The theologian Leonardo Boff, in commenting on one of these texts, notes that it "moves immediately to the structural analysis of these forces and denounces the systems, structures, and mechanisms that 'create a situation where the rich get richer at the expense of the poor, who get even poorer.'"[10]

In short, few liberation theologians engage in reflection on suffering without attempting to understand its mechanisms. Theirs is a theology that underlines connections. Robert McAfee Brown has these connections and also the poor in mind when, paraphrasing the Uruguayan Jesuit Juan Luis Segundo, he observes that "the world that is satisfying to us is the same world that is utterly devastating to them."[11]

Multiaxial Models of Suffering

Events of massive, public suffering defy quantitative analysis. How can one really understand statistics citing the death of six million Jews or graphs of third-world starvation? Do numbers really reveal the agony, the interruption, the questions that these victims put to the meaning and nature of our individual lives and life as a whole?
(Rebecca Chopp, *The Praxis of Suffering*)

How might we discern the nature of structural violence and explore its contribution to human suffering? Can we devise an analytic model, one with explanatory and predictive power, for understanding suffering in a global context? Some would argue that this task, though daunting, is both urgent and feasible. Our cursory examination of AIDS and political violence in Haiti suggests that analysis must, first, be *geographically broad*. As noted, the world as we know it is becoming increasingly interconnected. A corollary of this belief is that extreme suffering – especially when on a grand scale, as in genocide – is seldom divorced from the actions of the powerful.[12] The analysis must also be *historically deep* – not merely deep enough to remind us of events and decisions such as those which deprived Acéphie of her land and founded the Haitian military, but deep enough to remember that modern-day Haitians are the descendants of a people kidnapped from Africa in order to provide us with sugar, coffee, and cotton and to enrich a few in a mercantilist economy.

Factors including gender, ethnicity ("race"), and socioeconomic status may each be shown to play a role in rendering individuals and groups vulnerable to extreme human suffering. But in most settings these factors have limited explanatory power. *Simultaneous* consideration of various social "axes" is imperative in efforts to discern a political economy of brutality. Furthermore, such social factors are differentially weighted in different settings and at different times, as even brief consideration of their contributions to extreme suffering suggests.

The axis of gender

Acéphie Joseph and Chouchou Louis shared, as noted, a similar social status, and each died after contact with the Haitian military. But gender helps to explain why Acéphie died of AIDS whereas Chouchou died from torture. Gender inequality also helps to explain why the suffering of Acéphie is much more commonplace than that of Chouchou. Throughout the world, women are confronted with sexism, an ideology that designates them as inferior to men. When, in 1974, a group of feminist anthropologists surveyed the status of women living in several disparate settings, they found that, in every society studied, men dominated political, legal, and economic institutions to varying degrees; in no culture was the status of women genuinely coordinate, much less superior, to that of men.[13] This power differential has meant that women's rights may be violated in innumerable ways. Although male victims are clearly preponderant in studies of torture, the much more common crimes of domestic violence and rape are almost exclusively endured by females. . . .

It is *poor* women who bear the brunt of these assaults. This is true not only of domestic violence and rape, but also of AIDS and its distribution, as anthropologist Martha Ward points out:

> The collection of statistics by ethnicity rather than by socio-economic status obscures the fact that the majority of women with AIDS in the United States are poor. Women are at risk for HIV not because they are African-American or speak Spanish; women are at risk because poverty is the primary and determining condition of their lives.[14]

Similarly, only women can experience maternal mortality, a cause of anguish around the world. More than half a million women die each year in childbirth, but not all women are at increased risk of adverse outcomes in pregnancy. In 1985, the World Health Organization estimated that maternal mortality is, on average, approximately 150 times higher in developing countries than in developed nations. In Haiti, where maternal mortality is as high as fourteen hundred deaths per one hundred thousand live births – almost five hundred times higher than in the wealthy countries – these deaths are almost all registered among the poor.[15]

The axis of "race" or ethnicity

The idea of race, which is considered to be a biologically insignificant term, has enormous social currency. Racial classifications have been used to deprive certain groups of basic rights, and therefore have an important place in considerations of human suffering. In South Africa, for years a living laboratory for the study of the long-term effects of racism, epidemiologists report that the infant mortality rate among blacks may be as much as ten times higher than among whites. For South African blacks, the proximate cause of increased rates of morbidity and mortality is lack of access to resources: "*Poverty* remains the primary cause of the prevalence of many diseases and widespread hunger and malnutrition among black South Africans."[16] And social inequality is seen in the uneven distribution of poverty.

Significant mortality differentials between blacks and whites are also registered in the United States, which shares with South Africa the distinction of being the only two industrialized countries failing to record mortality data by socioeconomic status. In the United States, in 1988, life expectancy at birth was 75.5 years for whites and 69.5 years for blacks. Accordingly, there has been a certain amount of discussion about race differentials in mortality, but public health expert Vicente Navarro recently complained about the "deafening silence" on the topic of class differentials in mortality in the United States, where "race is used as a *substitute* for class." But in 1986, on "one of the few occasions that the US government collected information on mortality rates (for heart and cerebrovascular disease) by class, the results showed that, by whatever indicators of class one might choose (level of education, income, or occupation), mortality rates are related to social class."[17] Indeed, for the major causes of death (heart disease and cerebrovascular disease), class differentials were significantly larger than race differentials. "The growing mortality differentials between whites and blacks," Navarro concludes, "cannot be understood by looking only at race; they are part and parcel of larger mortality differentials – class differentials."[18] The sociologist William Julius Wilson made a similar point in his landmark study, *The Declining Significance of Race*. He argues that "trained and educated blacks, like trained and educated whites, will continue to enjoy the advantages and privileges of their class status."[19] It is the black poor – and an analysis of the mechanisms of their impoverishment – that are being left out....

Structural Violence and Extreme Suffering

At night I listen to their phantoms
shouting in my ear
shaking me out of lethargy
issuing me commands
I think of their tattered lives
of their feverish hands
reaching out to seize ours.
It's not that they're begging
they're demanding
they've earned the right to order us
to break up our sleep
to come awake
to shake off once and for all
this lassitude.

Claribel Alegría, "Visitas Nocturnas"

Any distinguishing characteristic, whether social or biological, can serve as pretext for discrimination, and thus as a cause of suffering. In discussing each of the above factors, however, it is clear that no single axis can fully define increased risk for extreme human suffering. Efforts to attribute explanatory efficacy to one variable lead to immodest claims of causality, for wealth and power have often protected individual women, gays, and ethnic minorities from the suffering and adverse outcomes associated with assaults on dignity. Similarly, poverty can often efface the "protective" effects of status based on gender, race, or sexual orientation. Leonardo Boff and Clodovis Boff, writing from Brazil, insist on the primacy of the economic:

> We have to observe that the socioeconomically oppressed (the poor) do not simply exist *alongside* other oppressed groups, such as blacks, indigenous peoples, women – to take the three major categories in the Third World. No, the "class-oppressed" – the socio-economically poor – are the infrastructural expression of the process of oppression. The other groups represent "superstructural" expressions of oppression and because of this are deeply conditioned by the infrastructural. It is one thing to be a black taxi-driver, quite another to be a black football idol; it is one thing to be a woman working as a domestic servant, quite another to be the first lady of the land; it is one thing to be an Amerindian thrown off your land, quite another to be an Amerindian owning your own farm.[20]

None of this is to deny the ill effects of sexism or racism, even in the wealthy countries of North America and Europe. The point is merely to call for more fine-grained and systemic analyses of power and privilege in discussions of who is likely to suffer and in what ways.

The capacity to suffer is, clearly, part of being human. But not all suffering is equal, in spite of pernicious and often self-serving identity politics that suggest otherwise. One of the unfortunate sequelae of identity politics has been the obscuring of structural violence, which metes out injuries of vastly different severity. Careful assessment of severity is important, at least to physicians, who must practice triage and referral daily. What suffering needs to be taken care of first and with what resources? It *is* possible to speak of extreme human suffering, and an inordinate share of this sort of pain is currently endured by those living in poverty. Take, for example, illness and premature death, in many places in the world the leading cause of extreme suffering. In a striking departure from previous, staid reports, the World Health Organization now acknowledges that poverty is the world's greatest killer: "Poverty wields its destructive influence at every stage of human life, from the moment of conception to the grave. It conspires with the most deadly and painful diseases to bring a wretched existence to all those who suffer from it."[21]

As the twentieth century draws to a close, the world's poor are the chief victims of structural violence – a violence which has thus far defied the analysis of many seeking to understand the nature and distribution of extreme suffering. Why might this be so? One answer is that the poor are not only more likely to suffer, they are also more likely to have their suffering silenced. As Chilean theologian Pablo Richard, noting the fall of the Berlin Wall, has warned, "We are aware that another gigantic wall is being constructed in the Third World, to hide the reality of the poor majorities. A wall between the rich and poor is being built, so that poverty does not annoy the powerful and the poor are obliged to die in the silence of history."[22]

The task at hand, if this silence is to be broken, is to identify the forces conspiring to promote suffering, with the understanding that these will be differentially weighted in different settings. In so doing, we stand a chance to discern the *forces motrices* of extreme suffering. A sound analytic purchase on the dynamics and distribution of such affliction is, perhaps, a prerequisite to preventing or, at least, assuaging it. Then, at last, there may be hope of finding a balm in Gilead.

NOTES

1 Jean Weise, "The Interaction of Western and Indigenous Medicine in Haiti in Regard to Tuberculosis," Ph.D. Dissertation, Department of Anthropology, University of North Carolina at Chapel Hill, 1971.

2 The names of the Haitians cited here have been changed, as have the names of their home villages.

3 For a recent review of the effects of inegalitarian social structures on the health of wealthier populations, see Michael Marmot, "Social Differentials in Health Within and Between Populations," *Dædalus* 123(4) (Fall 1994): 197–216.

4 Some would argue that the relationship between individual agency and supraindividual structures forms the central problematic of contemporary social theory.... For a concise statement of his (often revised) views on this subject, see Pierre Bourdieu, *In Other Words: Essays Towards a Reflexive Sociology* (Cambridge: Polity, 1990). That a supple and fundamentally non-deterministic model of agency would have such a deterministic – and pessimistic – "feel" is largely a reflection of my topic, suffering, and my fieldwork site.

5 Paul Farmer, "Culture, Poverty, and the Dynamics of HIV Transmission in Rural Haiti," in Han ten Brummelhuis and Gilbert Herdt (eds.) *Culture and Sexual Risk: Anthropological Perspectives on AIDS* (New York: Gordon and Breach, 1995), pp. 3–28.

6 For an overview of the human rights situation during the recent coup, see Americas Watch and the National Coalition for Haitian Refugees, *Silencing a People: The Destruction of Civil Society in Haiti* (New York: Human Rights Watch, 1993) and William O'Neill, "The Roots of Human Rights Violations in Haiti," *Georgetown Immigration Law Journal* 7(1) (1993): 87–117. I have reviewed these and other reports in Paul Farmer, *The Uses of Haiti* (Monroe, Me: Common Courage, 1994).

7 Rebecca Chopp, *The Praxis of Suffering* (Maryknoll, NY: Orbis, 1986), p. 2.

8 This argument is made at greater length in "AIDS and the Anthropology of Suffering," in Paul Farmer, *AIDS and Accusation: Haiti and the Geography of Blame* (Berkeley, Calif.: University of California Press, 1992). The term "historical system" is used following Immanuel Wallerstein,... *The Modern World-System: Capitalist Agriculture and the Origins of the European World-Economy in the Sixteenth Century* (San Diego, Calif.: Academic Press, 1974). The weakness of these analyses is, of course, their extreme divorce from personal experience.

9 Chopp, *The Praxis of Suffering*, p. 2....For anthropological studies of liberation theology in social context, see the ethnographies by John Burdick, *Looking for God in Brazil* (Berkeley, Calif.: University of California Press, 1993) and Roger Lancaster, *Thanks to God and the Revolution* (New York: Columbia University Press, 1988).

10 From the Puebla document, cited in Paul Farmer, "Medicine and Social Justice: Insights from Liberation Theology," *America* 173(2) (1995): 14.

11 Robert McAfee Brown, *Liberation Theology: An Introductory Guide* (Louisville, Ky.: Westminster, 1993), p. 44.

12 The political economy of genocide is explored by Christopher Simpson in *The Splendid Blond Beast: Money, Law, and Genocide in the Twentieth Century* (New York: Grove Press, 1993). . . . As regards the transnational political economy of human rights abuses, see the two-volume study by Noam Chomsky and Edward S. Herman, *The Washington Connection and Third World Fascism* and *After the Cataclysm* (Boston, Mass.: South End Press, 1979).

13 Michelle Rosaldo and Louise Lamphere (eds.), *Women, Culture, and Society* (Stanford, Calif.: Stanford University Press, 1974).

14 Martha Ward, "A Different Disease: HIV/AIDS and Health Care for Women in Poverty," *Culture, Medicine and Psychiatry* 17(4) (1993): 414.

15 World Health Organization, "Maternal Mortality: Helping Women Off the Road to Death," *WHO Chronicle* 40 (1985): 175–83.

16 Elena Nightingale, Kari Hannibal, Jack Geiger, Lawrence Hartmann, Robert Lawrence, and Jeanne Spurlock, "Apartheid Medicine: Health and Human Rights in South Africa," *Journal of the American Medical Association* 264(16) (1990): 2098. The italics are mine. . . .

17 Vicente Navarro, "Race or Class versus Race and Class: Mortality Differentials in the United States," *The Lancet* 336 (1990): 1238.

18 Ibid., p. 1240.

19 William Julius Wilson, *The Declining Significance of Race: Blacks and Changing American Institutions*, 2nd edn. (Chicago, Ill.: University of Chicago Press, 1980), p. 178.

20 Leonardo Boff and Clodovis Boff, *Introducing Liberation Theology* (Maryknoll, NY: Orbis Books, 1987), p. 29.

21 World Health Organization, *Bridging the Gaps* (Geneva: World Health Organization, 1995), p. 5.

22 Cited by Jack Nelson-Pallmeyer, *Brave New World Order: Must We Pledge Allegiance?* (Maryknoll, NY: Orbis, 1992), p. 14.

34

Anthropology and Politics: Commitment, Responsibility and the Academy

John Gledhill

At first sight, it seems self-evident that anthropology cannot avoid engagement with 'political' issues. Many anthropologists choose to work with indigenous peoples who are demanding that states and transnational capitalist enterprises recognize their rights and make restitution for past injustices. As 'experts' on 'non-Western cultures', anthropologists are drawn into legal proceedings concerned with such matters as indigenous land rights and act as expert witnesses in cases involving asylum-seekers and immigrants in the countries of the North. Nevertheless, the commitments of individual anthropologists vary, as do the positions they adopt with respect to the issues involved.

How, for example, do we balance the interests of an indigenous group in Amazonia with those of poor people from other sectors of national society who have migrated into their region in search of a livelihood? They may find themselves worse off than ever if the specific rights of indigenous people are recognized. How do we even decide who the 'authentic' indigenous people are? NGO aid in Guatemala has often been distributed on the basis of how 'Indian' people *look* by virtue of their clothing (Smith 1990). Anthropologists themselves do not necessarily reflect on the 'bigger picture' because of the personal commitments they form with the people amongst whom they do fieldwork. Their world-view often privileges the interests of 'indigenous' groups even if professional self-interest does not enter into their evaluation of the claims of different parties. As Nugent (1993) points out, 'peasants' in Amazonia are 'invisible' in many anthropological constructions of Amazonian society. Where they do appear, on the margins, they may be demonized.

Many anthropologists would not, in fact, want to see their role as a 'political' one, arguing that anthropologists should suppress personal sympathies, beliefs and commitments and participate solely as 'experts' whose testimony can be defended as academic knowledge. Participants in Manchester's 1995 GDAT (Group for Debates in Anthropological Theory) debate were unconvinced by the arguments put against

From *Power and its Disguises: Anthropological Perspectives on Politics* (London: Pluto Press, 2000), pp. 214–15, 221–34.

the motion that: 'Advocacy is personal commitment for anthropologists, not an institutional imperative for anthropology' (GDAT 1996). The same year saw *Current Anthropology* publish a debate centred on a paper by Roy D'Andrade, who argued that 'moral positions' get in the way of 'scientific' work, and a paper by Nancy Scheper-Hughes, who argued that anthropologists' 'ethical responsibilities' obliged them to 'take sides'. Scheper-Hughes's argument provoked some polemical responses, and I will return to this later, but let me begin with some general observations of my own.

The first is that it is not clear that any academic knowledge can legitimately claim 'objectivity' and 'detachment' or that academics can avoid 'taking a stance', even if they remain silent. What was problematic about colonial anthropology was precisely its silences, the reduction of questions of power to a neutral domain of 'administration' kept at arm's length in anthropological writing. We can still choose to be silent, by not dwelling on issues such as human rights violations and corruption in our ethnographies, even where they are part of the fabric of daily life. Yet, as we have seen, at least some modern anthropological research has attempted to engage the most challenging dimensions of contemporary local and global power relations in a non-euphemizing way. Today we must focus less on silence than on the greater dilemmas of speaking.

My focus...is on the relationship between academic knowledge and practical, political knowledge. The main form of dissemination of academic knowledge in Britain and the United States is through academic publications read by fellow academics. This is not, however, necessarily true of other countries in which anthropologists participate in an intellectual public culture which disseminates ideas through popular magazines and television programmes that reach a wider audience. Yet academic publishing is not the only form in which anthropological knowledge emerges from field-notes, even in Britain and the United States. Anthropologists who hold university jobs may produce reports for government agencies, NGOs or private companies, and a growing number of anthropology graduates are directly employed by such organizations. Whether we are writing a book or paper that enters the public domain, or compiling a report that is for the eyes of its sponsors alone, we need to ask ourselves for whom this knowledge is produced. Answers to that question are not necessarily straightforward....

Acting on the Basis of Knowledge

In November 1966, the annual business meeting of the American Anthropological Association (AAA) passed a resolution condemning 'the use of napalm, chemical defoliants, harmful gasses, bombing, the torture and killing of political prisoners and prisoners of war, and the intentional or deliberate policies of genocide or forced transportation of populations'. It asked 'all governments' to put an immediate end to their use and to 'proceed as rapidly as possible to a peaceful settlement of the war in Vietnam' (Gough 1968: 136).

As Kathleen Gough reveals in her account of the background to the resolution, what was finally passed was a watered down version of the motion originally tabled. The idea that any resolution be put forward at all had been opposed by the president-elect and a majority of the AAA executive board:

The chairman felt obliged to judge the resolution 'political' and hence out of order, since the Association's stated purpose is 'to advance the science of anthropology and to further the professional interests of American anthropologists.' A hubbub ensued at the conference in which the resolution was salvaged when one member suddenly proclaimed, 'Genocide is not in the professional interests of anthropologists!' This allowed the proponent to cite previous 'political' resolutions passed by the anthropologists on such subjects as racial equality, nuclear weapons, and the lives and welfare of aboriginal peoples. A motion to overrule the chair then passed by a narrow margin. Amendments were next introduced that removed an allegation that the United States was infringing international law by using forbidden weapons and transferred responsibility for the war from the United States government to 'all governments'...The proceedings showed that under pressure, most anthropologists were willing to put their profession on record as opposed to mass slaughter. But most are evidently unwilling to condemn their own government. (ibid.: 136–7)

The reluctance of US anthropologists to criticize their government was a reflection of their personal political positions and an anti-communism that Worsley (1992) shows was not restricted to Americans nor to the period when the Cold War was at its height. More than a question of attitudes was at stake here, however. Both Worsley and Gough are able to recount the more sinister underpinnings of anthropological conservativism through a history of their personal travails.

Worsley shows how research on aboriginal kinship systems in Australia was influenced by the anti-communist witch-hunting of not merely the state but the anthropological establishment itself. At the centre of his account is the persecution of Fred Rose, a committed communist who eventually moved to East Germany. Worsley points out that the stigmatization of Rose's academic work by the anthropological establishment was peculiarly inappropriate given that his rigorous and innovative methods for recording kinship data made it particularly easy for others to reinterpret his findings as they wished, in the confidence that the empirical material was sound. Nor would a dispassionate observer find it easy to demonstrate that Rose's political vision distorted his anthropological vision in some peculiarly pernicious way. Worsley himself was told by seniors of his profession that there was no future for a person with his political record in anthropology and thereafter pursued his distinguished career as a sociologist in Manchester. Yet 'Reds' were not the only victims. Other anthropologists who could hardly be accused of pro-Soviet sympathies, like David Turner, found themselves excluded from the field in Australia in the 1970s by more subtle forms of official obstruction. The reasons for their exclusion were never officially disclosed, in what Worsley describes as a 'terror of indeterminacy', but these events reflected the Australian state's reaction to growing public concern with Aboriginal rights and the Aborigines' own mobilization. Their backdrop was the increasingly devastating social and environmental impact of mining capitalism in the aboriginal reserves (Worsley 1992: 57).

In 1962, Kathleen Gough made a speech condemning the US blockade of Cuba at her university, which enjoyed a liberal reputation. She was instantly vilified and informed that her contract would not be renewed whatever the opinion of her colleagues on her academic merits. As an immigrant from Britain, she was then subject to investigation by the Immigration and Naturalization Service, who questioned colleagues on whether she should be considered a danger to national security.

A 1964 grant application to the National Science Foundation was turned down after State Department intervention on the grounds that the proposed research, on why villagers in south India had become Communist supporters, was not deemed in the national interest. This appeared somewhat paradoxical: 1964 was the year the United States Army allocated US$4–6 million to social science research on the factors which gave rise to social revolutionary movements in the Third World, the infamous 'Project Camelot' which was finally cancelled after an international outcry in 1965. Evidently those who might sympathize with revolutionary goals were not deemed suitable researchers into 'insurgency prophylaxis'. Gough eventually managed to fund her south Indian research, partly with her own money: the State Department proved interested enough in its results when she returned from the field (Gough 1968: 152).

Gough was, like Worsley, overtly left wing. She insisted that anthropology had to analyse the world order in terms of neo-imperialism and drew her students' attention to the way capitalist modernization was producing social polarization throughout the underdeveloped world. She saw armed revolution as the alternative to a creeping reimposition of Western domination and made no bones about her sympathies for what she saw as a swelling revolutionary tide. The world of the 1990s is clearly different from the one Gough anticipated in the 1960s, but it is a moot point how dated her writings have become, once we abstract from their over-optimistic assessment of the prospects for 'world revolution' in the ensuing decades.

There are few countries in the world at the end of the 1990s in which a widening gap between rich and poor is not apparent. Nor can Gough be accused of exaggerating the scope of the 'counter-revolutionary' strategies employed by the neo-imperialist powers. The controversial issue of US violation of international law, was, if anything, understated in the light of subsequent developments. Furthermore, most of the issues she posed about anthropology's role in relation to global problems seem to have lost none of their relevance.

Should anthropologists do applied work in the service of governments or other international agencies such as the World Bank? Should anthropologists work in parts of the world which are experiencing social and political ferment, and can they do so without taking sides? How can anthropologists do non-trivial work if we do not recognize the role of force, suffering and exploitation in the processes of social change and the way local situations are influenced by the global distribution of economic and politico-military power? How do we respond to the implications of the fact that anthropologists' salaries are paid by governments, their agencies or 'private segments of the power elite' (Gough 1968: 150), so that the rhetoric of democratic and academic freedoms is continually in danger of being compromised?

In confronting these issues, Gough was able to derive some comfort from the fact that in January 1967, Professor Ralph Beals and the AAA Committee on Research Problems and Ethics put forward a new association policy document. It advised scrupulous avoidance of entanglement with clandestine research activities and agencies, demanded the lifting of government restrictions on foreign research approved by academic institutions and the researcher's professional colleagues, advocated unrestricted dissemination of all aspects of the findings of research projects to people in the host countries, and defended the principle of freedom to publish without censorship and interference. Yet, echoed by other courageous whistle-blowers such as Eric Wolf and Joseph Jorgensen (1970), Gough also noted the way anthropologists had been recruited for work in military counter-insurgency projects as depressing evidence that such principles might not be respected in practice. Her principal hope lay in the next generation of students.

Intellectually and politically, much of what Gough stood for in the 1970s was to be developed in the anthropology of the 1970s and 1980s, but as Joan Vincent has pointed out, the politicization of 1970s anthropology did not lead to a simple paradigmatic renewal. The coexistence of contested paradigms made divisions within the academy more overt but also blurred some of the established boundaries between 'radicalism' and 'conservatism' as reflexive and postmodern approaches undermined the certainties implicit in Gough's perspective (Vincent 1990: 388). In practice, the next generation's susceptibility to radical intellectual paradigms was tempered by its susceptibility to unemployment.

It is important not to oversimplify the dilemmas the contemporary situation is provoking. Let us consider, for example, the issue of 'applied anthropology'. Applied anthropology might be considered a way of enhancing the discipline's commitment to putting its knowledge to work in addressing practical social problems. In areas such as social work and social medicine, an injection of 'knowledge about culture' can ameliorate some of the consequences of ethnocentrism and racism. What is achievable at this level is certainly constrained by larger fields of power relations. It might also be argued that the results of such work are always susceptible to manipulation by those seeking to improve strategies for implementing power/know-ledge systems in Foucault's sense, systems that may have a quite different agenda of 'containing' rather than solving people's problems. Yet theoretical and ideological purity is most easily asserted by academics enjoying the salaries necessary to sustain detachment, in publicly or privately funded universities of distinction. Such academics may even be willing to tolerate the casualization of academic labour to defend their own privileged positions, writing 'progressive' works on the suffering poor of the South whilst refusing to support struggles for improved pay and conditions by their own teaching assistants, junior colleagues and other university employees (DiGiacomo 1997).

Yet continuing debate on the ethics of applied anthropological work seems un-avoidable. Should anthropologists have participated, for example, in work related to transmigration programmes in Indonesia on the grounds that these things were going to happen anyway, even though they clearly formed part of the Indonesian state's strategy for consolidating its control over a territory expanded through annexation? Filer (1999) has tackled this issue in relation to the work many anthro-pologists do in supporting or advising indigenous groups fighting against the devel-opment of mining in their territories by transnational companies. He points out that mining companies are very powerful agencies, usually enjoying considerable support from the local state, which wants the mining revenue. Indigenous groups are seldom united in their opposition to mining development, and even if a majority wanted to hoist the red flag and create a social and political revolution, they would most likely *fail*. If our analysis of the situation does not encourage the view that 'radical' action *could* succeed, what kind of political stance would it be to advocate it? This line of argument seeks to justify anthropologists working for the mining companies them-selves, on the grounds that if we are genuinely committed to the best interests of 'the people' we study, it would be better *politics* to ensure that they get the best deal that they can.

Yet there are clear objections to anthropologists collaborating directly with the companies. The first is the arrogance of what is assumed – that the anthropologist, as a skilled professional, knows what is best for other people in the long run (as well as what is best for his or her personal good as a well-paid employee). This turns anthropologists into gatekeepers who define the 'authentic voice of the local people'. The Shell and Occidental oil companies in Colombia proved adept at finding a handful of urban migrants who could be presented as the voices of communities with which they retained little contact and in which they had no authority whatsoever. This should be a warning that anthropologists may be duped into believing company undertakings that they themselves then 'sell' to community representatives as 'honest brokers'. Even if companies do honour their undertakings to the letter, the community itself may remain divided on the issue, and the anthropologist may have to support the repression of minorities.

It may well be the case that the only thing that can often be done with powerful forces is to negotiate the terms of change. Yet it seems less problematic – though not *un*problematic – for anthropologists to participate in this process as adjuncts and helpers to community representatives than as paid employees of the more powerful party. Furthermore, it is quite clear that powerful forces are *not* always unstoppable, and that we need to ask o̶   e̶s whether the massive social dislocations caused by dams or n   ble. To argue that resistance is futile is not only to suspend   ent, but also to ignore the fact that   nd the world mobilizing against   etray fellow intellectuals from the   of their own states and placing   ents.

                        is also germane to the question of   national agencies such as the World   such as the Department for Inter-   werful critiques of the 'discourse of   s after the Second World War, many   support grassroots efforts to build   1995). Yet there have been clear   agencies involved in 'development', wit   World Bank. It could be argued that mos   t' has entered mainstream thinking, espec   UNICEF (Nederveen Pieterse 1998).

It w   that new rhetorics of 'empowerment' and 'participa-tion' reflect fundamental transformations in global power relations. It would be even more naive to imagine that such changes were brought about principally by academics rather than by the failure of old models, and the resistance and problems of governability that they provoked on the ground. Yet it is difficult to argue that the changes are completely inconsequential for people. It would be possible to write another book about the limitations of these formal policy shifts in terms of the de facto continuity of top-down practices of power and the measurement of 'success' in terms of the logics of development agencies' own 'audit cultures'. Nevertheless, it is not obvious that non-participation constitutes a more effective way of acting with respect to these issues and that participation has no impact on reality other than compromising a would-be critic. Arguments such as those advanced by Paul

Richards about what kind of aid would be 'smart' in terms of addressing Sierra Leone's real problems seem well worth making not only in print, but in the corridors of power (Richards 1996: 157–9).

There *are* continuing dangers in allowing organizations to appropriate the results of research work. Anthropologists who surrender raw data of a sensitive kind may not be able to control the uses to which it is put, particularly by government agencies. The results of work quoted out of context may be used to legitimate policies that the researcher actually opposes. There is also a basic problem of anthropological participation at the project level being used simply to provide an appearance of study and 'consultation' to legitimate a process of implementation that has already been decided. Last, but not least, the agency doing the hiring will usually dictate the terms of reference of the work performed, and it is often done so rapidly as to be unconvincing as a serious anthropological investigation, even if its aims are not controversial.

In the last analysis, it seems difficult to generalize about the desirability or undesirability of applied anthropological work. It will be clear that my personal view is that a blanket opposition is unsustainable. It is important that ethical and political considerations are kept firmly in view, that anthropologists continue to do the kind of research that offers a critical challenge to policy-makers, and that they actually press that challenge home. Yet a holier-than-thou attitude of scholarly detachment regarding the transcendental wisdom embodied in a discourse restricted to the academic arena hardly seems a more politically satisfactory position than selling one's conscience for a quick buck.

This brings us back to Gough's challenge to the conservatism and self-serving character of professional anthropology. Given the heat her commitment to socialism generated, it is easy to forget that the starting- and end-point of her critique was not Marx, Lenin or Fidel Castro but *Enlightenment* visions of 'the science of Man': 'How can the science of man help men to live more fully and creatively and to expand their dignity, self-direction, and freedom?' (Gough 1968: 148). Gough's view of the 'anthropologist as functionary' gives short shrift to claims of 'ethical neutrality' and pleads for a renewed consideration of fundamental goals. Anthropologists have, however, found it easier to agree on what is not ethical than establish common ethical goals. It may not be possible to achieve consensus simply because there are fundamental ideological cleavages within the profession at both the national and international levels which cannot be reconciled. Yet the question Gough's intervention still poses for the anthropology of the 1990s is how far we are continuing to evade even clarifying our differences, not out of commitment, but because of an absence of commitment based on the institutional realities of academic knowledge production.

Commitment at the Grassroots

At this point we should revisit Nancy Scheper-Hughes's argument for a more interventionist definition of an 'ethical stance'. Scheper-Hughes chose to make it by drawing on her own experience of a black township in the new South Africa. Her argument that anthropologists 'should be held accountable for what they see and what they fail to see, how they act or fail to act in critical situations' (Scheper-

Hughes 1995: 437) was not a philosophical generalization. It was directed without ambiguity at the White South African anthropological establishment. Nor did she content herself with the idea that anthropologists as 'witnesses' rather than 'spectators' were 'accountable to history' rather than to 'science' (ibid.: 419) for what they *wrote*. She insisted that taking an ethical stance should embrace *acting* and speaking *for* something in the situation of fieldwork, as she herself had done, first by taking a young recipient of 'popular justice' for hospital treatment and subsequently by addressing a township meeting. Although Scheper-Hughes was invited to speak (in order to explain her actions), she did so as a member of the African National Congress (ANC), in the expectation of reinforcing ANC efforts to replace 'neck-lacing' and whippings with less brutal forms of punishment.

In responding to her critics, Scheper-Hughes conceded that it might have been better to use others as exemplars of 'ethical anthropology' rather than assume the role of 'anthropologist as hero'. She also backtracked on the necessity for 'action', honouring scholars whose 'morally engaged and politically committed' anthropology expressed itself through the academic text (ibid.: 438). Yet some readers might have been left asking whether such concessions to academic civility did not, at the end of the day, weaken her argument. Did its power not lie in the risks that she had taken personally in the name of 'morality' and her demand for anthropologists to be held accountable for their silences and lack of engagement? In her Brazilian research (Scheper-Hughes 1992), she had been obliged to resume a career of militant partisanship, including campaigning for the Workers' Party candidate Lula in the 1989 elections, as the price of securing the cooperation of the women she wanted to study. Yet nothing had compelled her to put chronic hunger at the foreground of her account of Bom Jesús de Mata or to point her finger so insistently at the pharmacists and doctors who sought to efface its symptoms with tranquillizers and therefore failed in their ethical duty to heal. In her South African work, she made what might have been even more dangerous choices from the point of view of her personal safety, and used the outcome to make uncivil comments about academic colleagues. Perhaps this *is* the price that needs to be paid for taking an 'ethical stance'?

Scheper-Hughes recalls that her words and deeds in Brazil made it impossible for her to enjoy civil relations with elite (and some not so elite) members of the local society. Yet whatever academic consequences that might have had for her research, and however risky it might have been at the time, in the field, it seems to be a risk that can be transcended by career success and professional life. Many anthropologists never revisit the places that form the basis for their successful monograph after the fieldwork period is over. Assuming, however, that fieldwork is survived without physical harm, taking the politics on to the stage of denouncing academic colleagues may also be relatively costless for those whose careers are established. Anthropologist-activists who are 'barefoot' in terms of job security are in a less easy position, unless they encounter like-minded patrons. It is more difficult for them to join a community of 'negative workers' 'colluding with the powerless to identify their needs against the interests of the bourgeois institution: the university, the hospital, the factory' (ibid.: 420). As Scheper-Hughes notes, many academics would prefer not to have their days disrupted by even verbal references to sick people and dying babies. Yet even 'progressive' academics who do wish to hear about hunger and dying babies often have enough sense of self-interest and lifestyle maintenance to make their own contributions to the perpetuation of injustices closer to home, as I noted earlier. Faced with the evidence of our own narrow social worlds, we should be more questioning about the ease with which we can define 'an ethical stance' that is a guide to positive intervention or action.

Scheper-Hughes is quite clear about that in *Death without Weeping* (1992). The cruelty and everyday violence of our world is the result of dominant people and institutions abusing the kind of people anthropologists habitually study. We should 'speak truth to power' and do what we can to undermine the power of the powerful and support the resistance of the resistant. Scheper-Hughes argues that women practise a 'morality of triage' in the social circumstances imposed on them by elites in the Alto de Cruzeiro, which she compares with a hospital emergency room or the 'space of death' in a battlefield or concentration camp. We should not deny the 'disparate voices and sensibilities' of these women by embracing universalizing Western psychological theory but we should, at the end of the day, try to create a world in which women do not have to let babies die. In conducting research here, Scheper-Hughes had problems with maintaining the kind of cultural relativist position to which anthropologists supposedly subscribe. She felt obliged to act against the grain of local practices in trying to rescue a child from death. She also found that cultural relativism simply wasn't *good enough* from the point of view of enabling her to understand why people did what they did in a way that enabled her to empathize with them.

Yet defining an ethical stance to guide action remains difficult in many contexts, because those contexts are full of moral ambiguities. How do we *ground* our ethical judgements...? In an essay on human rights issues (Gledhill 1997), I discussed the efforts of the liberal political philosopher John Rawls to produce an account of how political institutions could realize 'justice and fairness' that did not rest on subscription to any particular 'comprehensive idea of the good'. What Rawls leaves us with is either a reliance on moral intuition or (as I suggested) a residual ethnocentrism based on an implicit theory of the inevitable historical transcendence of certain 'forms of life'. He 'solves' the problem of ethics by refusing to discuss ethics in any substantive way (beyond an appeal to history's onward march as a sociological fact). Scheper-Hughes, for her part, is forced to ground her own argument for 'the primacy of the ethical' in the idea that responsibility, accountability and answerability to 'the other' is pre-cultural, in the sense that morality enables us to judge culture. Since judgements about 'culture' are clearly made within specific cultural worlds (by people who challenge or defend dominant practices), a simple-minded relativism about morality – 'This is the way that people in culture X think, so their conduct is unproblematic by their standards' – clearly will not do. Yet it seems difficult to escape the conclusion that Scheper-Hughes invites us to share her moral intuitions as a transcendent and essential 'womanly ethic of care and responsibility' (Scheper-Hughes 1995: 419) without providing any very strong grounds for us to do so, from either anthropology or philosophy.

Why should 'we' care about 'others' whom we will never meet and whose sufferings may ultimately either be to our material benefit – as a factor in the world market price of sugar, for example – or be of total irrelevance to our own lives? Is it simply that anthropologists do meet some of these 'others' and feel guilty that their sufferings may be the stuff on which careers are built? For Scheper-Hughes the answer is clearly that this is a human experience that is unbearable for her and should not be borne by her 'others'. This does not, however, resolve the problem of what actions are best to end suffering, or the difficulty that there may be competing claims for justice between different groups of suffering, or at least disadvantaged, people, in the same setting.

Many situations are sufficiently complex and ambiguous to make a more generous approach to recognizing competing moral claims seem desirable. As a first illustration of this. I will recount an incident in my own fieldwork that involved the death of a very young child, who thus became an *angelito* or angel baby. The meaning of angel babies is a crucial issue in Scheper-Hughes's Brazilian ethnography. She argues that women in the Alto de Cruzeiro had to be taken at their word when they said that they did not grieve for the dead infants, contrary to the claims of Western pyschology about 'denial' and selves divided between public states and real 'inner states'. This was because their 'culture', shaped by their conditions of life, taught them 'how to feel' (Scheper-Hughes 1992: 431). The idea that small babies who die become angels is common to all Latin American Catholic cultures, but there are distinctive features in how such deaths are handled in Alto de Cruzeiro. There is only a perfunctory ritualization of the wake and burial, and children play an important role in burying the babies, making infant death a part of child socialization. Scheper-Hughes argues that normally this 'works', though her ethnography suggests that it works with tension, not only in the case of an occasional child who cries, but in the case of mature women who display 'inappropriate' emotions in recalling the dead and are scolded by other women for doing so.

Her argument here is that 'abstract' universal moral principles are something that these women cannot afford. The way the women are portrayed by more affluent local families, from a stance of moral superiority that appeals to such values, is essentially hypocrisy which not only fails to register the distinct voices and sensibilities of subalterns, but is complicit in maintaining their suffering. In this account, we are presented with evidence, reading between the lines, of subaltern sensibilities that are subject to stress and tension, but largely conditioned towards uniformity by circumstances. We are given less insight into the moral universe of the elites, because the ethnographer has made up her mind about them.

This may be a mistake, at least as a general recommendation. In 1983, I was asked to photograph an *angelito* in a village in Michoacán, Mexico, by his mother and an aunt. The child had toddled out behind a reversing truck and been crushed to death. In this region, people were less hungry than in Alto de Cruzeiro, but most women lost some children. The angel wake and burial are more elaborate and there is normally a muted display of grief, although it is tempered by the idea that the sinless child has gone straight to heaven. This, however, was an exceptional case. The mother was the youngest daughter of the man who had been the richest peasant in the community and a local boss (*cacique*). His widow, Cruz, had had twenty-one births, from which fourteen children survived to maturity. The daughter who was the mother of the dead child had married a landless fieldhand for love, against the advice of her family. He worked for one of her rich brothers. This was their first and only child.

The truck belonged to the rich brother but was being driven by his sister's husband's brother. The driver was hysterical with guilt as well as grief, but there was, of course, another element in the situation, because the instrument of the child's death was the truck, which symbolized the wealth of other members of the family. What everyone was thinking (but only said with their eyes) was that it was so unfair that the rich brother had taken away the one thing his poor sister had, the child of her love. Muted conversation did suggest that the fact that the father's brother had been behind the wheel added to the moral culpability of the better-off part of the family: they were held responsible for an event that would now haunt *him* for the rest of his life. The rich brother himself did, in fact, feel guilty and, unusually for him, later took to drinking.

In this tragically contingent event, a range of moral issues was unexpectedly exposed. They included issues of social inequality – how some peasants became richer than others. An 'objectivist' answer would consist in explaining the transformation of the political economy of the zone after land reform, which created a new agrarian bourgeoisie outside the land reform communities which needed to find 'insiders' able to mediate their difficult relations with discontented (and now armed) peasants. In terms of local values, however, the former *cacique* was a morally ambiguous figure. People told stereotypical stories about his finding gold under floorboards of a house rented from a poor widow, his cheating a previous *patrón* who was illiterate, and a repertoire of other tales that I heard told in many other places about many other people who had been able to pull their way out of poverty. Yet other stories about Chema, as he was called, suggested that what had made him so successful was his brilliance as a manager of personal clientship relations. He was able to foster the idea that he was, after all, a good *patrón* who looked after people and was, within the limits set by his private self-aggrandizement, caring and socially responsible. It was almost inevitable that none of the sons could match either the charisma or the authority of the father. The son who was best at business was, unfortunately, the least successful in terms of human relations (and the subsequent history of his children, a generation away from the social capital bequeathed by their grandfather, later proved tragic and violent).

Another issue raised by the child's death touched on family responsibilities and whether people had fulfilled them. The normal cultural process for dealing with infant death was of limited help in containing the whole scenario that made this an abnormal event. It simply failed to tell all the parties involved how and what to feel. Furthermore, although the trigger was a specific tragedy, its moral dimensions were observable across a gamut of tensions and conflicts in everyday life. Here, however, it is Scheper-Hughes's approach to inequality and the role of power relations in shaping the terrain of morality that seems of limited help.

Firstly, it is of immense importance for understanding the political and social history of this region to appreciate how people normally related to each other across class divisions within rural communities. Caught between an intensely conservative Catholicism and a disappointing experience of revolutionary land reform, driven to cross-border migration and socially and culturally transformed in the process, the local peasantry had considerable difficulty deciding who to blame for their problems. In the fullness of time they veered in a number of different political directions, yet have lived from 1940 to the present with morally ambivalent ideas about 'exploitation' and 'patronage'. The people themselves worry in a quite spontaneous and self-reflexive way about the apparent contradictions of their feelings.

Secondly, the assumption that the morality of elites is simply hypocrisy is somewhat dangerous. It would certainly be a mistake to assume that elites are homogeneous and that there is no moral contestation within them. I have noted...how lawyers from the upper echelons of Lima society have continued to contest the authoritarianism of Fujimori, for example. Mexico may have become an independent country to rescue the Church from secular reformers in Spain, but even the nineteenth century saw the emergence of a 'Social Catholicism' alongside the conservative forms dominant in western Mexico. This was not simply a pragmatic response to the rise of liberalism and socialism but grounded in a genuine difference of moral orientation, patronizing at one level, but sincere at another. It would also be unwise to ignore the strong sense of moral conviction that can accompany the defence of a religious order of things, at both the top and the bottom of a society in a region like this one, a hotbed of conflict between *cristeros* and agrarian rebels. For elites what is at stake is not simply material privilege, but a whole form of life. To see this simply as self-interested egotism is a barrier to understanding why elites sometimes do not embark on apparently sensible reforms that might, in the long term, have provided them with better guarantees of survival.

A more fundamental problem is, however, the fact that 'societies' of this kind are not simply layered into hierarchically ordered homogeneous strata. In the community where the infant was killed, families that were in equivalent socio-economic circumstances in the 1980s remained divided by legacies of history. These included the role that their forebears played in the days when the region was a vast landed estate, in a workforce which had its own systems of social distinction, still reproduced through marriage patterns long after the reform. Present divisions had also been shaped by the subsequent confrontations between secularizing land reformers and supporters of the Catholic *sinarquista* movement. The latter was...a mirror image of the agrarian reform movement itself and actually incorporated many disillusioned former agrarian fighters. The root of their disillusion was that the agrarian reform had not lived by its own moral claims. Leaders grabbed land at the expense of other peasants and turned into oppressive *caciques*, quite different in style from the new rich who dominated my study community.

In a local history in which identities had been further complicated by individually variable histories of international migration, micro-differences in socio-economic terms could carry enormous moral loads and impede everyday sociality in unpredictable ways. Furthermore, it would be difficult for anyone equipped with knowledge of the tangled history of land reform to make easy judgements about which actors occupied the moral high ground and how differences might best be reconciled. There would thus be a substantial gap between what might be done in terms of 'speaking truth to power' at a regional, national and international level and charting a course of justice and fairness as a concrete solution to the accumulated problems of decades.

For example, the official rules designed to ensure justice in the allocation of 'land to the tiller' had been widely perverted over a thirty-year period. Yet the outcomes were complex, and relatively poor as well as relatively rich people could be found in illegal possession of land. People who did not possess any land at all might remark on the injustice of this situation, but if they did not have the land themselves, they would prefer those who did have it to be more commercially successful farmers who could offer them work. Furthermore, it was quite difficult to see people who had actually succeeded in becoming small commercial farmers as an 'anomaly' in terms of the expressed goals of land reform, even if they had bought land titles illegally with migrant earnings or a public sector salary. Their semi-proletarianized poorer *compañeros* were neither making a living from the land nor producing the cheap food their urban resident children needed.

These kinds of issues are endemic to rural situations in many parts of the world. ... Yet the point I am making is not simply an academic one – that if we do not properly understand a situation, then we cannot hope to produce useful suggestions for changing it – but a moral and political one.

Some of the 'bad guys' are also victims of the power of others, and it would be much easier to improve a desperately bad situation if there was scope for negotiation between different factions. A small rancher whose land has been invaded feels as morally outraged as a landless peasant whose family is hungry: the rancher does not belong to the 'super-rich' and may be having economic difficulties of his own as global free-market economics bite. Neither peasant nor rancher economic strategies may be ideal for promoting 'sustainable development'. There might be other models of development that would make it possible to reconcile their claims to social justice in a way that the actors themselves would accept was fairer and better for all in the long run. On this point at least I find myself in agreement with Richard Rorty, when he argues that a rhetoric of 'no piecemeal solutions' is out of place in the contemporary world (Nystrom and Puckett 1998: 46). Dialogue and piecemeal solutions do not necessarily lead to utopias, but they are surely preferable to continuing violence, and the best guarantee that the ultimate victory will not go to the powers and interests with the weakest moral claims of all. By arguing that a 'good enough ethnography' will do to sustain an ethical stance, Scheper-Hughes (1995: 417–18) is risking failure in analysis of the subtleties and complexities of power relations and the micro-politics of difference. Understanding those complexities is central to thinking about ways of practising a politics that might help the oppressed to improve their position and win, if not everything, then at least something.

REFERENCES

DiGiacomo, S. (1997) The new internal colonialism. *Critique of Anthropology* 17(1): 91–7.

Escobar, A. (1995) *Encountering Development: The Making and Unmaking of the Third World*. Princeton: Princeton University Press.

Filer, C. (1999) The dialectics of negation and negotiation in the anthropology of mineral resource development in Papua New Guinea. In A. Cheater (ed.) *The Anthropology of Power: Empowerment and Disempowerment in Changing Structures*. London: Routledge.

GDAT. (1996) *Advocacy is a Personal Commitment for Anthropologists, not an Institutional Imperative for Anthropology*, ed. P. Wade. Manchester: Group for Debates in Anthropological Theory.

Gledhill, J. (1997) Liberalism, socio-economic rights and the politics of identity: from moral economy to indigenous rights. In R. Wilson (ed.) *Human Rights, Culture and Context: Anthropological Approaches*. London: Pluto Press.

Gough, K. (1968) World revolution and the science of man. In T. Roszak (ed.) *The Dissenting Academy*. New York: Pantheon Books.

Nederveen Pieterse, J. (1998) My paradigm or yours? Alternative development, post-development, reflexive development. *Development and Change* 29: 343–73.

Nugent, D. (1993) *Spent Cartridges of Revolution: An Anthropological History of Namiquipa, Chihuahua*. Chicago: University of Chicago Press.

Nystrom, D. and Puckett, K. (1998) *Against Bosses, Against Oligarchies: A Conversation with Richard Rorty*. Charlottesville, VA: Prickly Pear Press.

Richards, P. (1996) *Fighting for the Rain Forest: War, Youth and Resources in Sierra Leone*. Oxford: James Currey.

Scheper-Hughes, N. (1992) *Death Without Weeping: The Violence of Everyday Life in Brazil.* Berkeley: University of California Press.

——. (1995) The primacy of the ethical: propositions for a militant anthropology. *Current Anthropology* 36(3): 409–40.

Smith, C. (1990) The militarization of civil society in western Guatemala: economic reorganization as a continuation of war. *Latin American Perspectives* 17(4): 8–41.

Vincent, J. (1990) *Anthropology and Politics: Visions, Traditions and Trends.* Tucson: University of Arizona Press.

Wolf, E. and Jorgensen, J. (1970) Anthropologists on the warpath in Thailand. *New York Review of Books.* November 19: 27.

Worsley, P. (1992) The practice of politics and the study of Australian kinship. In C. Gailey (ed.) *The Politics of Culture and Creativity: A Critique of Civilization*, vol. II of *Dialectical Anthropology: Essays in Honor of Stanley Diamond.* Gainsville: University of Florida Press.

35

Thinking Academic Freedom in Gendered Post-coloniality

Gayatri Chakravorty Spivak

I am deeply honored to have been asked to deliver the T. B. Davie Memorial lecture that can at last celebrate the right to admit students on the grounds of academic merit alone. This right inaugurates a profound responsibility. I will attempt to describe the tasks that lie ahead.

In national liberation struggles, winning control over *structures* like constitutionality or academic freedom seems all that matters. In the new nation, the *textural* unevenness of the fabric that will stretch itself on those structures in times of domestic crisis matters much more. If the liberation struggle must continue to concentrate on race, now the concerns of subalternities, of class, culture, and gender must become equally important. (A subaltern is cut off from mobility within both foreign and domestic dominant structures.) Because the struggle cannot, perhaps does not, prepare for this change, the new nation cannot flourish internally and protect itself against the ravages of the international economic system, especially since the ruling paradigms for the now increasingly dominant discourse of "sustainable development" are biased in favor of the North and the elites of the South.[1] Support often comes from the academic echelons of the international development sector, and the international cultural private sector. In both these areas, certain internalized constraints are seen as freedom and determine what will be freely chosen.[2] International support, in other words, however well-meaning, can also bypass the inequalities within the new nation and stay on the high road of structural enablements. But who are these structures for? Who can or wants to use them? What must you know in order to (want to) use them? And even a further, more mysterious question, can we learn anything from those who seem not to know how to use the political structures we fought for? Or is that road closed?

The life and times of a post-colonial woman who is also a US academic are inscribed by these truisms and these questions. I want to share with you what I can read of this inscription.

From *Thinking Academic Freedom in Gendered Post-coloniality* (Cape Town: University of Cape Town Printing Department, 1992), pp. 1–5, 12–13, 16–20, 26–7. Copyright G. C. Spivak.

Academic freedom is part of the general Enlightenment project of the public use of reason. Let us recall those famous words: "if only freedom is granted, enlightenment is almost sure to follow...It is the freedom to make public use of one's reason at every point."[3] Yet in the Age of Reason itself, the author of these words was ready to concede that classroom lectures were too private a transaction for them not to be open to censorship. In *The Conflict of the Faculties*, Kant claimed freedom from censorship for teaching that was merely constative – stated a problem – but did not lead to action.[4] We would find both the concession and the claim singularly out of keeping with our notions of academic freedom. It is precisely in the so-called "privacy" of our classrooms that we want our academic freedom protected. And the question of academic freedom hardly ever arises unless our constatations seem dangerously close to improper action.

Historically, notions of public and private in the teaching of the humanities have changed as Kant's enlightened and exclusive idea of a *cosmo*polity has had to reckon with the ongoing operation of a *geo*-politics. Of course, Kant is not talking about the "Humanities" as we understand them at all, but the "Liberal Arts," where the idea of freedom or *libertas* lurks in the predication. He is also speaking of the "Moral Sciences." And, in spite of the intellectual-historical and political effort to empty the "moral" sciences of their civic responsibility by rewriting them as the *humanities* and separating them from the social sciences, it is precisely in the teaching of the human *sciences* (embracing both) that the public danger to the conservative state has repeatedly been located. (The imprisonment of Gramsci and Mandela are extreme extra-academic cases of this location that prove, yet once again, that the line between school and life is not as clear cut as Gorgias thought.) If academic freedom is a formal structure with a general and changeful history known to all institution-ally educated colonials and enslaved peoples through fantasmatic origins in a certain Greece, its contents are most strictly policed by the state when they seem to train for change in the history of the present and a future. This structure is by no means confined to the academy. If there is one item on our agenda it is to think of geo-political rather than cosmopolitical answers to the question "What is Enlighten-ment?"

The post-colonial academy must learn to use the Enlightenment from below; strictly speaking, ab-use it. If there is one academic lesson to learn from the revolu-tionary *political* experiment in South Africa, it is this one. Not to abuse it, except in the eyes of those who still think it can only be used from above, those who *must* ignore the hyphen in order to protect themselves. Let us even put a parenthesis around the pre-fix, make a neographism, since a gendered use of the Enlightenment is from the side, not, alas, *necessarily* from below. In Kant's essay, the unfree position of the bourgeois European woman found pride of place, after all.

I want to fill these typographic gestures – hyphen, parenthesis – with content. Marx was perhaps the first European to attempt an ab-use of the Enlightenment, the public use of reason where the public was proletarian. Let us consider a famous Marxian statement about the new social revolution: "Then the posturing words went beyond the content, now the content will go beyond the clichés." This sentence is better known in English as "Previously the phrase transcended the content; here the content transcends the phrase." *Phrase* in German carries an attitudinizing connotation which is missed in the conventional translation; and Marx does not mention transcendence. But whichever way we understand it, it remains a somewhat troubling and enigmatic sentence. One possible meaning is that all revolutions in Western Europe until the mid-nineteenth century made it possible for forms of political behavior to be gradually rationalized and that these rationalizations were accompanied by extravagant promises. (We must remember that this essay is driven by Marx's contempt for rejoicing over mere constitutional victories when the bottom layer of society was so ignorant of their real interests that they chose an enemy of the people as their representative.) The next revolution, the revolution of the future, will fill these forms, or perhaps this form – since reason can only ever have one form – with the appropriate content. What would that content be? A society where *all* adults (presumably male *and* female) would know that the abstract flow of average labor, properly employed in commodified exchange, can yield a surplus that can be redistributed for the benefit of all its members: to fill the forms of social institutions established by such redistribution with more and more enlightened content so that individuals could enhance the contents of their lives and minds.

All this, for Marx, lay in the future, but the immediate future. For now, only to educate the masses in the secret of the misappropriation of the abstract flow of average labor so that it could be set right.

It should be kept in mind that Marx thought of the formal access to an economic system that would tap the abstract flow of average labor, supported by rational political structures, as a potential "freeing." Real freedom was just around the corner: socialism would fulfill the extravagant promises of capitalist democracy by turning capitalism around so that it became unrecognizable as such.

The obvious criticisms of Marx's hope have been made many times:

Marx did not take national sentiment into account; the proper use of the abstract flow of average labor assumed inter-nationality.

Marx did not take race into account. The *im*proper use of the abstract average flow of labor, *also* required internationality. The white-skinned races established this inter-nationality by force upon black, brown, red, yellow. (The previous examples of empire were not so clean-cut down race lines.) Marx went so far as to see this as a sort of homeopathy. Curing poison with poison, forced internationality making way for true internationality: Imperialism making way for Development and the New World Order.

Marx did not take gender into account. It was possible for his new society to see unpaid female labor as no work, and sexuality as an instrument of heterosexual reproduction, augmented in bad times because of men's need for pleasure and comfort.

And, finally, Marx had no theory of the subject. His entire project rested on the confidence in the public use of reason produced by the European Enlightenment. . . .

In the Northwestern sandbanks of Bangladesh, villagers have opened night-schools for children.[5] They are selfless, poor rural people of all ages, receiving a token salary from an indigenous non-governmental organization. The main worker of the region, an MA in English from the local university, six hours by bus, train, and bicycle or horse-drawn platform from this particular rural area, has undoubtedly conscientized these organizers and teachers with metaphors of the Enlightenment. In their descriptive discourse of persuasion, they insist that learning dispelled the darkness of the mind. They undoubtedly believe that education (literacy and numeracy of the most rudimentary sort) is an unquestioned good. Everyone believes it for the boys, who would be able to reckon better and get a trade. And the rural women guard it ferociously, like a lifeline. The women probably credit the enlightenment metaphor with greater seriousness. Although rural Bangladesh is a far cry from Kant's Konigs-berg, the general fact of escape from the worst of patriarchy has probably allowed them to hold the reverse of Kant's proposition to be true: if only enlightenment is granted, freedom is almost sure to follow; where enlightenment is little more than three or four years of the three Rs, and freedom is freedom from poverty. There too the same dilemma that I am repeating today has to be kept alive, I think: Why should we trust the form alone, if we do not attend to content? (Their idea of right content is, of course, crude nationalism, treacherous merchandise; or, worse, religion.) Have they not seen that the best educated are the worst thieves or, if women, the least caring?

You will notice that I am now bringing the question of academic freedom into areas – primary education, literacy – where it is usually not extended. I believe that consider-ations of freedom in the post-colonial academy must be aware of these levels in some detail. Otherwise, the constitutive subject of the academy, the subject of academic freedom who is performed by the exercise of that freedom, remains the indigenous elite modelled on the noblest aspirations of the imperialists – the radical element at best cloned on it with imperfect success, at worst cowed, sullen, actively or passively destructive of our unexamined idea of a university. This is true even in situations of internal colonization. It was indeed such a discrepancy between the constitutive formality of academic freedom and the constitution of the subject of freedom in subalternity that allowed John Searle to docket the student movement of the mid-sixties at the University of California at Berkeley as a variety of McCarthyism.[6]

And, on the other side of the coin, an assimilated post-colonial like Jacques Derrida makes us feel the importance of early education when he writes of himself

> as someone who, not being completely European by birth, for I come from the southern shore of the Mediterranean, also takes himself, more and more with age, for a sort of European *metis* [half-breed] super-acculturated, super-colonized.... It is perhaps the sentiment...of someone who had, from his school days in French Algeria, to try to capitalize the old age of Europe while preserving a bit of that imperceptible and impassive youth of the other shore. In fact, all the marks of an ingenuousness still incapable of that other old age from which French culture separated him too soon.[7]

If we ignore signals of this sort, all messages from the Enlightenment and/or high imperialist culture will be make-up on a corpse's face....

I repeat this metaphor because I want to quote two writers who have staged the notion of the unburied dead in connection with post-colonial efforts to gain access to cultural responsibility. Farhad Mazhar, a Bangladeshi poet, contrasts the contem-porary Bengali archaeologists, more "British" than the Royal Asiatic Society, to the poet-persona forever guarding the unburied corpses of the Sepoy Mutiny:

> Lord, Dhaka's mosque is world-renowned
> Much varied work on pillar and cloister. In British days
> the Whites, right or wrong, put in place
> th' Asiatic Society and researched it all
> Here. In the white eyes
> Of whites the new Bengalis dig now

And look for things we see.
I wish them good luck. But doctor's degrees,
Make them twice
As wily as their White forebears.
Lord, I'm an unlettered fool,
Can't grasp the art of architecture, paint,
Yet my heart aches empty
As I stand by the old Ganga.
The Sepoys seem to hang still on hangman's ropes
Waiting for last rites, the ropes uncut,
Their bodies still aloft, no one to mourn,
To perform *zannat*.
Don't you mock me with minaret and arcade,
Me, the corpse-keeper of revolt.[8]

Assia Djebar complicates the metaphor with the double difficulty of regaining an active perspective for women in the unperformed burial rites for the dead old culture when the colonial culture seemingly gave access to the new. The men fighting, the women mourning, is all she can recover.[9] It is well-known that most sub-Saharan African cultures had a more active role for women. Yet, if we are reckoning with colonialism, and Enlightenment-model liberatory struggles, and the constitution of the subject of academic freedom, what percentage of female *subalternity* will be able to deploy this or a simulacrum of this, within the enclosure of the University? And can this be seamlessly sutured to the European tradition of academic freedom?

Here is the passage from Djebar: "the body, not embalmed by ritual lamentations, is found dressed in rags. As an echo the cries of our ancestors, unhorsed in forgotten battles, return; and the dirges of the women who watched them die, accompany them."[10]

These passages should make clear that I am not attempting to bring the dead to life. I am suggesting that the unlamented corpses of colonized cultures must be lamented anew as we attempt to (ab)-use their unaffiliated living after-runners (not their "proper inheritors"). I have never been at all interested in designating "proper" inheritors of anthropologized older cultures so that they can be distanced from the advantages of the unaffiliated after-running colonizing culture and its indigenous collaborators. I am, however, profoundly interested in the persistent performance of those funeral rites by bringing the question of academic freedom down, in post-colonial countries, to the constitution of the subject for academic freedom, in the primary education of the subaltern.[11] That is where the resources of the (ab)-use of the Enlightenment are located.

Sometimes the possibility of progress is infinitesimal. We are reminded of this when we attend lavish international conferences on *Decolonizing the Imagination* (for the world's best-educated people, of course) or "Global Civilization/Local Cultures" (from the European Universalist perspective, of course).

The night-schools in the remoter rural areas of Bangladesh meet out of doors. They cannot afford to have more than thirty students at each school, and not more than two hurricane lanterns. No blackboards. One teacher. At best five levels of students. Teachers with minimal basic training but considerable goodwill.

The schools meet at night because the boys must work by day. Field labor, any sort of hired work. As I said before, it is clear how they would gain through knowledge of reading and numbers. The girls do not often return after the third year. In support of the future-enlightenment-of-children argument, local men say that if the girls get more education, they would have to find matriculate husbands. Well-placed critics should appreciate that this creates a problem for poor parents.

This is not immediately unreasonable. Just as primary health care is not clinical support in case of disease, so also the constitution of the subject for academic freedom is not legal aid when patriarchy leads to visible violence.

The men's argument is an example of patriarchy assigning responsibility (as duty) from above, even in subalternity, and successful gendering convincing the woman to be inferior in public status to her husband. This bit of internalized gendering can be broken, and it is part of the task of the constitution of the subject for academic freedom. In this arena, the (ab)-use of the Enlightenment has led indigenous female activists to persist with rural mothers over months to win one female child to schooling, convincing them with obviously sincere expression of physical affection for the children. These activist women are, however, totally separated from that enclave of urban radicalism which can think academic freedom. In post-coloniality, especially in gendering, the issue of academic freedom begins with the gender-sensitive style of rural literacy.

If we are gender-sensitive, we must be able to imagine the very long haul, and think of constituting the future subject for academic freedom for a much-delayed opening of access to the University. What follows is an extended example:

Winning over rural girl-children one by one is obviously not an achievement commensurate with the large-scale systemic change necessary for people in general not to offer the need for matriculate husbands as a reason against women's education. . . . In the meantime, the devising of small survival techniques . . . can happen only if we expand the area of our concern.

In these remote night-schools, literacy is focussed on reading. Considerable importance is attached to memorizing – the alphabet, multiplication tables, poems and so on. It fits in with the rote learning emphasized in all but the best schools in the colonies because of the anterior richness of orality even within so-called "literate" cultures. As a result, the children will often "read" something different from the page they are following with finger and eye. To "correct" them from above is a total undermining of the entire delicate effort. Yet those interested in the eventual subject for academic freedom must devote some of their energies to these sorts of details because there are not enough resources at this ground-level for the kind of individual attention for which one might agitate under more favorable circumstances. Arrived here, it is the class-separated (though not necessarily race-separated) universitarian who must learn and change: the task is not to make the schoolchild terrified. We are, after all, speaking of the countryside after nightfall – not urban children who frequently have had to learn counter-warfare too soon. What one is testing is a teaching system compromised by dead tradition, not the child.

If the girl-child is asked to write her own message to someone, the emphasis on memory and reading does not come to her aid. And yet, when after three years she is confined to home, yard, and perhaps field and stream, soon to be married, she finds no books in her rural households. If in those three years, emphasis had been laid on writing a free-style sentence every day, it is at least remotely possible that, when deprived of her education and yoked to household labor and childbirth, she would have had a companion in writing. We have examples of slave narratives and women's secret writing to corroborate this. (To offer another example: organizing in Indian villages against wife-beating, agitating for a supply of teachers at the supposedly free State primary schools, it is still possible for the organizers to mark the time of survival by teaching "the practice of writing," even if for fifteen minutes a day.) Thus do we make provision for a continuity of the potential for freedom until the patriarchial or political system changes sufficiently, also through our efforts in other spheres. A poor provision at best. Yet something that can escape notice if academic freedom does not concern itself with gendered subalternity....

... [I]n the case of academic freedom we are not proposing to turn our backs on the Enlightenment but rather to learn how to revise and recycle it through lessons learned from below...

Academic "freedom," like all rational formal freedoms, can only be exercised by its own transgression, by being "bound" to content. Pure "freedom" is "guaranteed" by the exercise of the constitution of a possible subject, already the commitment to a content. We have experience of a society of largely unexercised guarantees, a society just by default. A robustly just society is where the members, when acting self-consciously within rational and privative norms – never adequately possible – see freedoms not as ends but absolute means to protect their transgression, which is also their exercise. No justification of the *exercise* of academic freedom can be drawn from within academic freedom. It comes into being in its own binding.

NOTES

1   Vandana Shive, *Ecology and the Politics of Survival: Conflict Over Natural Resources in India* (London: Sage, 1991), p. 12.
2   Howard Zinn mentioned this problem in his T. B. Davie Memorial Lecture.
3   Immanuel Kant, "What is Enlightenment?", in *On History*, trans. Lewis White Beck (New York: Macmillan, 1963), pp. 4–5.
4   Kant, The Conflict of the Faculties trans. Mary J. Gregor (New York: Liberal Arts, 1968)....
5   My source is extensive yearly travel and hands-on contact.
6   John Searle, *The Campus War* (New York: World Publishing Co., 1971).
7   Jacques Derrida, L'Autre cap (Paris: Minuit, 1991), pp. 13–14.
8   Farhad Mazhar, "The Corpse-Keeper of Revolt." in *Ebadatnama 2* (Dhaka: Prabartana, 1989), p. 36. Translation mine.
9   This theme is continued in the depiction of the Algerian War of 1957–62 in a film named after the prison Barberousse. The women active in the war were so vocal in their objection, that the director Bouabdallah invited them to participate in a documentary where they recount their participation and their critique: *Barberousse mes soeurs*. I am grateful to Dr. Nadia Ait-Sahalia for showing me a private video of this film.
10   Assia Djebar, Fantasia: an Algerian Cavalcade, trans. Dorothy S. Blair (New York: Quartet, 1985), p. 157; translation modified.
11   I borrow the construction "subject for" rather than "subject of" from Helene Cixous, "The Laugh of the Medusa," in *New French Feminisms: An Anthology*, ed. Elaine Marks and Isabelle de Courtivron (New York: Schocken, 1981), pp. 252–3. For a discussion of this see Spivak, "French Feminism Revisited: Ethics and Politics," in Judith Butler and Joan W. Scott (eds.), *Feminists Theorize the Political* (New York: Routledge, 1992), pp. 69–70. "Constitution of the subject for academic freedom" is not just a fancy way of talking about community involvement for the college teacher. It means investigating the

details of rural literacy in the post-colonial state. I am thinking not only of Paolo Freire's well-known *Pedagogy of the Oppressed*, trans. Myra Bergman Ramos (New York: Continuum, 1981), but also of the "Freedom Schools" in the American South, Gonopathshala in Bangladesh, and the schools run by the Shabar Kheriya Kalyan Samiti in Purulia District in West Bengal, India.

Index